John Knox, William Guthrie, Thomas Kitchin, James Ferguson

A New Geographical, Historical and Commercial Grammar

and present state of the several kingdoms of the world - Vol. 1, Second Edition

John Knox, William Guthrie, Thomas Kitchin, James Ferguson

A New Geographical, Historical and Commercial Grammar
and present state of the several kingdoms of the world - Vol. 1, Second Edition

ISBN/EAN: 9783337274061

Printed in Europe, USA, Canada, Australia, Japan

Cover: Foto ©Andreas Hilbeck / pixelio.de

More available books at **www.hansebooks.com**

A NEW Geographical, Historical, and Commercial GRAMMAR;

AND PRESENT STATE

OF THE SEVERAL

KINGDOMS OF THE WORLD.

CONTAINING

I. The Figures, Motions, and Distances of the Planets, according to the Newtonian System and the latest Observations.

II. A general View of the Earth considered as a Planet; with several useful Geographical Definitions and Problems.

III. The grand Divisions of the Globe into Land and Water, Continents and Islands.

IV. The Situation and Extent of Empires, Kingdoms, States, Provinces, and Colonies.

V. Their Climate, Air, Soil, vegetable Productions, Metals, Minerals, natural Curiosities, Seas, Rivers, Bays, Capes, Promontories, and Lakes.

VI. The Birds and Beasts peculiar to each Country.

VII. Observations on the Changes that have been any where observed upon the Face of Nature since the most early Periods of History.

VIII. The History and Origin of Nations: their Forms of Government, Religion, Laws, Revenues, Taxes, naval and military Strength.

IX. The Genius, Manners, Customs, and Habits of the People.

X. Their Language, Learning, Arts, Sciences, Manufactures, and Commerce.

XI. The chief Cities, Structures, Ruins, and artificial Curiosities.

XII. The Longitude, Latitude, Bearings, and Distances of principal Places from London.

XIII. A General Index.

With a TABLE of the COINS of all Nations, and their Value in ENGLISH MONEY.

By WILLIAM GUTHRIE, Esq.

ILLUSTRATED WITH
A NEW AND CORRECT SET OF LARGE MAPS,
Engraved by Mr. KITCHIN, Geographer.

THE SECOND EDITION.

IN TWO VOLUMES.

VOLUME I.

LONDON:
Printed for J. KNOX, at N°. 148, near Somerset-House, in the Strand. MDCCLXXI.

THE
PREFACE.

TO a man sincerely interested in the welfare of society and of his country, it must be particularly agreeable to reflect on the rapid progress, and general diffusion of learning and civility, which, within the present age, have taken place in Great-Britain. Whatever may be the case in some other kingdoms of Europe, we, in this island, may boast of our superiority to those illiberal prejudices, which not only cramp the genius, but sour the temper of man, and disturb all the agreeable intercourse of society. Among us, learning is no longer confined within the schools of the philosophers, or the courts of the great; but, like all the greatest advantages which heaven has bestowed on mankind, it is become as universal as it is useful.

This general diffusion of knowledge is one effect of that happy constitution of government, which, towards the close of the last century, was confirmed to us, and which constitutes the peculiar glory of this nation. In other countries, the great body of the people possess little wealth, have little power, and consequently meet with little respect; in Great-Britain the people are opulent, have great influence, and claim, of course, a proper share of attention. To their improvement, therefore, men of letters have lately directed their studies; as the great body of the people, no less than the dignified, the learned, or the wealthy few, have an acknowledged title to be amused and instructed. Books have been divested of the terms of the schools, reduced from that size which suited only the purses of the rich, and the avocations of the studious; and adapted to persons of more ordinary fortunes, whose attachment to other pursuits admitted of little leisure for those of knowledge. It is to books of this kind, more than to the works of our Bacons, our Lockes, and our Newtons, that the generality of our countrymen owe that superior improvement, which distinguishes them from the lower ranks of men in all other countries. To promote and advance this improvement, is the principal design of our present undertaking. No subject appears more interesting than that we have chosen, and none seems capable of being handled in a manner that may render it more generally useful.

The knowledge of the world, and of its inhabitants, though not the sublimest pursuit of mankind, it must be allowed, is that which most nearly interests them, and to which their abilities are best adapted. And Books of Geography, which describe the situation, extent, soil, and productions of kingdoms; the genius, manners, religion, government, commerce, sciences, and arts of all the inhabitants upon earth, promise the best assistance for attaining this knowledge.

The Compendium of Geography, we now offer to the public, differs in many particulars from other books on that subject. Besides exhibiting an easy, distinct, and systematic account of the theory and practice of what may be called Natural Geography, the Author has attempted to render the following performance, an instructive, though compendious detail of the general history of the world. The character of nations depends on a succession of a great many circumstances which reciprocally affect each other. There is a nearer connection between the learning, the commerce, the government, &c. of a state, than most people seem to apprehend. In a work of this kind, which pretends to include moral, or political, as well as natural geography, no one of those objects should pass unnoticed. The omission of any one of them would, in reality, deprive us of a branch of knowledge, not only interesting in itself, but which is absolutely necessary for enabling us to form an

adequate

PREFACE.

adequate and comprehensive notion of the subject in general. We have thought it necessary, therefore, to add a new article to this work, which comprehends the history and present state of learning, in the several countries we describe, with the characters of such persons as have been most eminent in the various departments of letters and philosophy. This subject will, on a little reflection, appear altogether requisite, when we consider the powerful influence of learning upon the manners, government, and general character of nations. These objects, indeed, till of late, seldom found a place in geographical performances; and, even where they have been introduced, are by no means handled in an entertaining or instructive manner. Neither is this to be altogether imputed to the fault of geographical writers. The greater part of travellers, acting solely under the influence of avarice, the passion which first induced them to quit their native land, were at little pains, and were indeed ill-qualified to collect such materials as are proper for gratifying our curiosity, with regard to these particulars. The geographer then, who could only employ the materials put into his hands, was not enabled to give us any important information upon such subjects. In the course of the present century, however, men have begun to travel from different motives. A thirst for knowledge, as well as for gold, has led many into distant lands. These they have explored with a philosophic attention; and by laying open the internal springs of action, by which the inhabitants of different regions are actuated, exhibit to us a natural and striking picture of human manners, under the various stages of barbarity and refinement. Without manifest impropriety, we could not but avail ourselves of their labours, by means of which, we have been enabled to give a more copious, and a more perfect detail of what is called Political Geography, than has hitherto appeared.

PREFACE

In considering the present state of nations, few circumstances are of more importance than their mutual intercourse. This is chiefly brought about by commerce, the prime mover in the œconomy of modern states, and of which therefore we have never lost sight in the present undertaking.

We are sensible that a reader could not examine the present state of nations with much entertainment or instruction, unless he was also made acquainted with their situation during the preceding ages, and of the various revolutions and events, by the operation of which they have assumed their present form and appearance. This constitutes the historical part of our Work; a department which we have endeavoured to execute in a manner entirely new. Instead of fatiguing the reader with a dry detail of news-paper occurrences, occurrences no way connected with one another, or with the general plan of the whole, we have mentioned only such facts as are interesting, either in themselves, or from their relation to objects of importance. Instead of a meagre index of incoherent incidents, we have drawn up a regular and connected epitome of the history of each country, such an epitome as may be read with equal pleasure and advantage, and which may be considered as a proper introduction to more copious accounts.

Having, through the whole of the work, mentioned the antient names of countries, and in treating of their particular history sometimes carried our researches beyond the limits of modern times, we have thought it necessary, for the satisfaction of such readers as are unacquainted with classical learning, to begin our historical Introduction with the remote ages of antiquity. By inserting an account of the antient world in a book of geography, we afford an opportunity to the reader, of comparing together not only the manners, government, and arts of different nations, as they now appear, but

as

as they subsisted in antient ages; which exhibiting a general map, as it were, of the history of mankind, renders our work more complete than any geographical treatise extant.

In the execution of our design, we have all along endeavoured to observe order and perspicuity. Elegance we have sacrificed to brevity. Happy to catch the leading features which distinguish the characters of nations, and by a few strokes to hit off, though not completely to finish, the picture of mankind in antient and modern times.

What has enabled us to comprise so many subjects within the narrow bounds of this work, is the omission of many immaterial circumstances, which are recorded in other performances of the same kind, and of all those fabulous accounts or descriptions which, to the disgrace of the human understanding, swell the works of geographers; though the falsity of them, both from their own nature and the concurring testimony of the most enlightened and best-informed travellers and historians, be long since detected.

As to particular parts of the work, we have been more or less diffuse, according to their importance to us as men, and as subjects of Great-Britain. Our own country, in both respects, deserved the greatest share of our attention. Great-Britain, though she cannot boast of a more luxuriant soil or happier climate than many other countries, has advantages of another and superior kind, which make her the delight, the envy, and the mistress of the world: these are, the equity of her laws, the freedom of her political constitution, and the moderation of her religious system. With regard to the British empire we have therefore been singularly copious.

Next to Great-Britain, we have been most particular upon the other states of Europe; and always in proportion as they present us with the largest field for useful reflection.

reflection. By comparing together our accounts of the European nations, an important system of practical knowledge is inculcated, and a thousand arguments will appear in favour of a mild religion, a free government, and an extended, unrestrained commerce.

Europe having occupied so large a part of our volume, Asia next claims our attention; which, however, tho' in some respects the most famous quarter of the world, offers, when compared to Europe, extremely little for our entertainment or instruction. In Asia, a strong attachment to antient customs, and the weight of tyrannical power, bears down the active genius of the inhabitants, and prevents that variety in manners and character, which distinguishes the European nations. The immense country of China alone, renowned for the wisdom of its laws and political constitution, equally famous for the singularity of its language, literature, and philosophy, deserves to be considered at some length.

In Africa, the human mind seems degraded below its natural state. To dwell long upon the manners of this country, a country immersed in rudeness and barbarity, besides that it could afford little instruction, would be disgusting to every lover of mankind. Add to this, that the inhabitants of Africa, deprived of all arts and sciences, without which the human mind remains torpid and inactive, discover no great variety in manners or character. A gloomy sameness almost every where prevails; and the trifling distinctions which are discovered among them, seem rather to arise from an excess of brutality on the one hand, than from any perceptible approaches towards refinement on the other. But tho' these quarters of the globe are treated less extensively than Europe, there is no district of them, however barren or savage, intirely omitted.

America, whether considered as an immense continent, inhabited by an endless variety of different people, or as a country intimately connected with Europe by the ties of commerce and government, deserves very particular attention. The bold discovery, and barbarous conquest of this new World, and the manners and prejudices of the original inhabitants, are objects, which, together with the description of the country, deservedly occupy no small share of this performance.

In treating of such a variety of subjects, some less obvious particulars, no doubt, must escape our notice. But if our general plan be good, and the outlines and chief figures sketched with truth and judgment, the candour of the learned, we hope, will excuse imperfections which are unavoidable in a work of this extensive kind.

We cannot, without exceeding the bounds of a Preface, insist upon the other parts of our plan. The Maps, which are new, and corrected with care, will, we hope, afford satisfaction. The science of natural geography, for want of proper encouragement from those who are alone capable of giving it, still remains in a very imperfect state; and the exact divisions and extent of countries, for want of geometrical surveys, are far from being well ascertained. This consideration has induced us to adopt the most unexceptionable of Templeman's Tables; which, if they give not the exactest account, afford at least a general idea of this subject; which is all indeed we can attain, until the geographical science arrives at greater perfection. They are, besides, recommended by their brevity; and the making use of them has enabled us to introduce some subjects more necessary in this undertaking than the minute divisions of countries, whose boundaries and situations we are yet little acquainted with.

Thus

PREFACE.

Thus far the original Preface, with respect to the design and general plan of the work, which a few months ago made its first appearance in one very large octavo volume, closely but distinctly printed.

Tho' the book was chiefly intended for schools, and the more uninformed part of mankind, we have the pleasure to find, by the rapidity of its sale, and the universal approbation it has met with, that it has attracted the notice of those who are best able to judge of the execution, and, contrary to the general fate of modern publications, has already found a place in the libraries of the learned.

One advantage it certainly possesses, which few historical productions can boast of—Throughout the whole, the Author seems to have divested himself of political, religious, and national prejudices; and where he discovers any biass, it is always in favour of civil and religious liberty.

The smallness of the type of the first edition, tho' extremely proper for schools, and young people, has however prevented many, who are more advanced in life, from becoming purchasers. It was therefore judged necessary to give the public an edition on a larger type, and consequently in two volumes, which enables us to accommodate every class of readers.

The present edition likewise appears with several other advantages. The scientific part of the work has been corrected and improved throughout by JAMES FERGUSON, F. R. S. The historical and miscellaneous parts have gone through the hands of some gentlemen of distinguished abilities, and the different articles, or heads, are more methodically arranged.

The same attention has been given to the maps, which are newly engraved at a very considerable expence by the first artist in this kingdom, who, being chiefly employed in executing the latest surveys, has availed himself of many new discoveries, and is thereby enabled to enrich this Work with the most correct Atlas hitherto published,

INTRODUCTION.

PART I.

Of Astronomical Geography.

SECT. I.

THE science of Geography cannot be compleatly understood without considering the earth as a planet, or as a body moving round another at a considerable distance from it. But the science which treats of the planets, and other heavenly bodies, is called Astronomy. Hence the necessity of beginning this work with an account of astronomy, or of the heavenly bodies. Of these, the most conspicuous is that glorious luminary the Sun, the fountain of light and heat to the several planets which move round it, and which, together with the sun, compose what astronomers have called the Solar System. The way, or path, in which the planets move round the sun, is called their Orbit; and it is now fully proved by astronomers, that there are six planets which move round the sun, each in its own orbit. The names of these, according to their nearness to the center, or middle point of the sun, are as follow: Mercury, Venus, the Earth, Mars, Jupiter, and Saturn. The two first, because they move within the orbit of the earth (being nearer the sun) are called inferior planets, or, perhaps more properly, interior or inner planets; the three last, moving without the orbit of the earth, are called superior, or, perhaps more properly, exterior or outer planets. If we can form a notion of the manner in which any one of these planets, suppose our earth, moves round the sun, we can easily conceive the manner in which all the rest do it. We shall only therefore particularly consider the motion of the earth, or planet on which we live, leaving that of the others to be collected from a table, which we shall set down with such explications as may render it intelligible to the meanest capacity.

The earth, upon which we live, was long considered as one large extensive plane. The heavens, above it, in which the sun, moon, and stars appeared to move daily from east to west, were conceived to be at no great distance from it, and to be only designed for the use or ornament of our earth: several reasons, however, occurred, which rendered this opinion improbable; it is needless to mention them, because we have
now

now a sufficient proof of the figure of the earth, from the voyages of many navigators who have actually sailed round it: as from that of Magellan's ship, which was the first that surrounded the globe, sailing east from a port in Europe in 1519, and returning to the same, after a voyage of 1124 days, without apparently altering his direction, any more than a fly would appear to do in moving around a ball of wax.

The roundness of the earth being thoroughly established, proves the way for the discovery of its motion. For while it was considered as a plane, mankind had an obscure notion of its being supported, like a scaffolding on pillars, though they could not tell what supported these. But the figure of a globe is much better adapted to motion. This is confirmed by considering, that if the earth did not move round the sun, not only the sun, but all the stars and planets must move round the earth. Now, as philosophers, by reckonings founded on the surest observations, have been able to guess pretty nearly at the distances of the heavenly bodies from the earth, and from each other, just as every body that knows the first elements of mathematics can measure the height of a steeple, or any object placed on it; it appeared, that if we conceived the heavenly bodies to move round the earth, we must suppose them endowed with a motion or velocity so immense as to exceed all conception: whereas all the appearances in nature may be as well explained by imagining the earth to move round the sun in the space of a year, and to turn on its own axis once in the 24 hours.

To form a conception of these two motions of the earth, we may imagine a ball moving on a billiard-table or bowling-green: the ball proceeds forwards upon the green or table, not by sliding along like a plane upon wood, or a slate upon ice, but by turning round its own axis, which is an imaginary line drawn through the centre or middle of the ball, and ending on its surface in two points called its poles. Conceiving the matter then in this way, and that the earth, in the space of 24 hours, moves from west to east, the inhabitants on the surface of it, like men on the deck of a ship, who are insensible of their own motion, and think that the banks move from them in a contrary direction, will conceive that the sun and stars move from east to west in the same time of 24 hours, in which they, along with the earth, move from west to east. This daily or diurnal motion of the earth being once clearly conceived, will enable us easily to form a notion of its annual or yearly motion round the sun. For as that luminary seems to have a daily motion round our earth, which is really occasioned by the daily motion of the earth round its

axis,

INTRODUCTION.

axis, so in the course of a year, he seems to have an annual motion in the heavens, and to rise and set in different points of them, which is really occasioned by the daily motion of the earth in its orbit or path round the sun, which it compleats in the time of a year. Now as to the first of these motions we owe the difference of day and night, so to the second we are indebted for the difference in the length of the days and nights, and in the seasons of the year.

This much being said with regard to the motion of the earth, which the smallest reflection may lead us to apply to the other planets, we must observe, before exhibiting our table, that beside the six planets already mentioned, which move round the sun, there are other ten bodies which move round three of these, in the same manner as they do round the sun; and of these our earth has one, called the moon; Jupiter has four, and Saturn has five: these are all called moons, from their agreeing with our moon, which was first attended to; and sometimes they are called secondary planets, because they seem to be attendants of the Earth, Jupiter and Saturn, about which they move, and which are called primary.

There are but two observations more necessary for understanding the following table. They are these: we have already said that the annual motion of the earth occasioned the diversity of seasons. But this would not happen, were the axis of the earth exactly parallel, or in a line with the axis of its orbit; because then the same parts of the earth would be turned towards the sun in every diurnal revolution; which would deprive mankind of the grateful vicissitude of the seasons, arising from the difference in length of the days and nights. This therefore is not the case—the axis of the earth is inclined to the plane of the earth's orbit, which we may conceive by supposing a spindle put through a ball, with one end of it touching the ground; if we move the ball directly forwards, while one end of the spindle continues to touch the ground, and the other points towards some quarter of the heavens, we may form a notion of the inclination of the earth's axis to its orbit, from the inclination of the spindle to the ground. The same observation applies to some of the other planets, as may be seen from the table. The only thing that now remains, is to consider what is meant by the mean distances of the planets from the sun. In order to understand which, we must learn that the orbit, or path which a planet describes, were it to be marked out, would not be quite round or circular, but in the shape of a figure called an ellipse, which, though resembling a circle, is longer than

broad.

INTRODUCTION.

broad. Hence the same planet is not always at the same distance from the sun, and the mean distance of it is that which is exactly betwixt its greatest and least distance. Here follows the table.

A TABLE of the Diameters, Periods, &c. of the several Planets in the Solar System.

Names of the planets.	Diameters in English miles.	Mean distance from the sun, as determined from observations of the transit of Venus in 1761.	Annual periods round the sun.	Diurnal rotation on its axis.	Hourly motion in its orbit.	Hourly motion of its equator.	Inclination of Axis to orbit.
			y. d. h.	d. h. m.			
Sun	890,000			25 6 0		3,818	8° 0'
Mercury	3,000	36,841,468	0 87 23	unknown.	109,699	unknown	unkn.
Venus	9,330	68,891,486	0 224 17	24 8 0	80,295	43	75° 0'
Earth	7,970	95,173,000	1 0 0	1 0 0	68,243	1,042	23° 29'
Moon	2,180	ditto.	1 0 0	29 12 44	22,290	9½	2° 10'
Mars	5,400	145,014,148	1 321 17	0 24 40	55,287	556	0° 0'
Jupiter	94,000	494,990,976	11 314 18	0 9 56	29,083	25,920	0° 0'
Saturn	78,000	907,956,130	22 167 6	unknown.	22,101	unknown	unkn.

The reader having obtained an idea of the solar system from this table, and the previous observations necessary for understanding it, must next turn his reflection to what are called the fixed stars, which comprehend the luminaries above our heads that have not been explained. The fixed stars are distinguished by the naked eye from the planets, by being less bright and luminous, and by continually exhibiting that appearance which we call the twinkling of the stars. This arises from their being so extremely small, that the interposition of the least body, of which there are many constantly floating in the air, deprives us of the sight of them; when the interposed body changes its place, we again see the star, and this succession being perpetual, occasions the twinkling. But a more remarkable property of the fixed stars, and that from which they have obtained their name, is their never changing their situation, with regard to each other, as the planets, from what we have already said, must evidently be always changing theirs. The stars which are nearest to us seem largest, and are therefore called of the first magnitude. Those of the second magnitude appear less, being at a greater distance; and so proceeding on to the sixth magnitude, which include all the fixed stars which are visible without a telescope. As to their number, though in a clear winter's night without moonshine they seem to be innumerable, which is owing to their strong sparkling, and our looking at them in a confused manner, yet when the whole firmament is divided, as it has been done by the antients, into signs and constellations, the number that can be seen at a time by the bare eye, is not above a thousand. Since the introduction of telescopes indeed, the number of the fixed stars has been justly considered as immense; because the greater perfection we arrive at in our glasses, the more stars always appear to us. Mr. Flamstead, royal astronomer at Greenwich, has given us a catalogue of about 3000 stars, which is the most compleat that has hitherto appeared. The immense distance of the fixed stars from our earth, and one another, is of all considerations the most proper for raising our ideas of the works of God. For notwithstanding the great extent of the earth's orbit or path (which is at least 162 millions of miles in diameter) round the sun, the distance of a fixed star is not sensibly affected by it; so that the star does not appear to be any nearer us when the earth is in that part of its orbit nearest the star, than it seemed to be when the earth was at the most distant part of its orbit, or 162 millions of miles further removed from the same star. The star nearest us, and consequently the biggest in appearance, is the dog-star, or Sirius. Modern discoveries make it probable that each of these fixed stars is a sun, having worlds revolving round it, as our sun has the earth and other planets revolving round him. Now the dog-star appears 27,000 times less than the sun, and as the distance of the stars must be greater in proportion as they seem less, mathematicians have computed the distance of Sirius from us to be two billions and two hundred thousand millions of miles. The motion of light therefore, which though so quick as to be commonly thought instantaneous, takes up more time in travelling from the stars to us, than we do in making a West-India voyage. A sound would not arrive to us from thence in 50,000 years; which, next to light, is considered as the quickest body we are acquainted with. And a cannon ball flying at the rate of 480 miles an hour, would not reach us in 700,000 years.

The stars, being at such immense distances from the sun, cannot possibly receive from him so strong a light as they seem to have; nor any brightness sufficient to make them visible to us. For the sun's rays must be so scattered and dissipated before they reach such remote objects, that they can never be transmitted back to our eyes, so as to render these objects visible by reflexion. The stars therefore shine with their own native and unborrowed lustre, as the sun does; and since each particular star, as well as the sun, is confined to a particular portion of space, it is plain that the stars are of the same nature with the sun.

It is no ways probable that the Almighty, who always acts with infinite wisdom and does nothing in vain, should create so many glorious suns, fit for so many important purposes, and place them at such distances from one another, without proper objects near enough to be benefited by their influences. Whoever imagines they were created only to give a faint glimmering light to the inhabitants of this globe, must have a very superficial knowledge of astronomy*, and a mean opinion of the Divine Wisdom: since, by an infinitely less exertion of creating power, the Deity could have given our earth much more light by one single additional moon.

Instead then of one sun and one world only in the universe, as the unskilful in astronomy imagine, *that* science discovers to us such an inconceivable number of suns, systems, and worlds, dispersed through boundless space, that if our sun, with all the planets, moons, and comets belonging to it, were annihilated, they would be no more missed, by an eye that could take in the whole creation, than a grain of sand from the sea-shore. The space they possess being comparatively so small, that it would scarce be a sensible blank in the universe, although Saturn, the outermost of our planets, revolves about the sun in an orbit of 4884 millions of miles in circumference, and some of our comets make excursions upwards of ten thousand millions of miles beyond Saturn's orbit; and yet, at that amazing distance, they are incomparably nearer to the sun than to any of the stars; as is evident from their keeping clear of the attracting power of all the stars, and returning periodically by virtue of the Sun's attraction.

From what we know of our own system, it may be reasonably concluded that all the rest are with equal wisdom contrived, situated, and provided with accommodations for rational inhabitants. For although there is almost an infinite variety in the parts of the creation which we have opportunities of examining, yet there is a general analogy running through and connecting all the parts into one scheme, one design, one whole!

Since the fixed stars are prodigious spheres of fire, like our sun, and at inconceivable distances from one another, as well as from us, it is reasonable to conclude they are made for the same purposes that the sun is; each to bestow light, heat, and

---

* Especially since many more stars require the assistance of a good telescope to find them out, than are visible without that instrument, and therefore instead of giving light to this world, they can only be seen by a few astronomers.

INTRODUCTION.

and vegetation on a certain number of inhabited planets, kept by gravitation within the sphere of its activity.

What an august! what an amazing conception, if human imagination can conceive it, does this give of the works of the Creator! Thousands of thousands of suns, multiplied without end, and ranged all around us, at immense distances from each other, attended by ten thousand times ten thousand worlds, all in rapid motion, yet calm, regular, and harmonious, invariably keeping the paths prescribed them; and these worlds peopled with myriads of intelligent beings, formed for endless progression in perfection and felicity.

If so much power, wisdom, goodness, and magnificence is displayed in the material creation, which is the least considerable part of the universe, how great, how wise, how good must HE be, who made and governs the whole!

The first people who paid much attention to the fixed stars, were the shepherds in the beautiful plains of Egypt and Babylon; who, partly from amusement, and partly with a view to direct them in their travelling during the night, observed the situation of these celestial bodies. Endowed with a lively fancy, they divided the stars into different companies or constellations, each of which they supposed to represent the image of some animal, or other terrestrial object. The peasants in our own country do the same thing, for they distinguish that great northern constellation which philosophers call the Ursa Major, by the name of the plough, the figure of which it certainly may represent with a very little help from the fancy. But the constellations in general have preserved the names which were given them by the antients; and they are reckoned 21 northern, and 12 southern: but the moderns have increased the number of the northern to 34, and of the southern to 31. Beside these there are the 12 signs or constellations in the Zodiac, as it is called from a Greek word signifying an animal, because each of these 12 represent some animal. This is a great circle which divides the heavens into two equal parts, of which we shall speak hereafter. In the mean time, we shall conclude this section with an account of the rise, progress, and revolutions in astronomy.

Mankind must have made a very considerable improvement in observing the motions of the heavenly bodies, before they could so far disengage themselves from the prejudices of sense and popular opinion, as to believe that the earth upon which we live was not fixed and immoveable. We find accordingly, that Thales, the Milesian, who, about 600 years before Christ, first taught astronomy in Europe, had gone so far in this subject as to calculate eclipses, or interpositions of the moon betwixt the earth and the sun, or of the earth between the sun and the moon (the nature of which may be easily understood, from what we have already observed.) Pythagoras, a Greek philosopher, flourished about 50 years after Thales, and was, no doubt, equally well acquainted with the motion of the heavenly bodies. This led Pythagoras to conceive an idea, which there is no reason to believe had ever been thought of before, namely, that the earth itself was in motion, and that the sun was at rest. He found that it was impossible, in any other way, to give a consistent account of the heavenly motions. This system, however, was so extremely opposite to all the prejudices of sense and opinion, that it never made great progress, or was widely diffused in the antient world. The philosophers of antiquity despairing of being able to overcome ignorance by reason, set themselves to adapt the one to the other, and to form a reconciliation between them. This was the case with Ptolemy, an Egyptian philosopher, who flourished 138 years before Christ. He supposed, with the vulgar, who measure every thing by themselves, that the earth was fixed immovably in the center of the universe, and that the seven planets, considering the moon as one of the primaries, were placed near to it; above them was the firmament of fixed stars, then the chrystalline orbs, then the primum mobile, and, last of all, the cœlum empyrium, or heaven of heavens. All these vast orbs he supposed to move round the earth once in 24 hours; and besides that, in certain stated or periodical times. To account for these motions, he was obliged to conceive a number of circles called excentrics and epicycles, crossing and interfering with one another. This system was universally maintained by the Peripatetic philosophers, who were the most considerable sect in Europe, from the time of Ptolemy to the revival of learning in the sixteenth century.

At length, Copernicus, a native of Poland, a bold and original genius, adopted the Pythagorean, or true system of the universe; and published it to the world in 1530. This doctrine had been so long in obscurity, that the restorer of it was considered as the inventor; and the system obtained the name of the Copernican philosophy, though only revived by that great man.

Europe, however, was still immersed in sense and ignorance; and the general ideas of the world were not able to keep pace with those of a refined philosophy. This occasioned Copernicus to have few abetters, but many opponents. Tycho Brache, in particular, a noble Dane, sensible of the defects of the Ptolemaic system, but unwilling to acknowledge the motion of the earth, endeavoured to establish a new system of his own, which was still more perplexed and embarrassed than that of Ptolemy. It allows a monthly motion to the moon round the earth, as the center of its orbit; and it makes the

sun

sun to be the center of the orbits of Mercury, Venus, Mars, Jupiter, and Saturn. The sun, however, with all the planets, is supposed to be whirled round the earth in a year, and even once in the twenty-four hours. This system however, absurd as it was, met with its advocates. Longomontanus and others, so far refined upon it, as to admit the diurnal motion of the earth, though they insisted that it had no annual motion.

About this time, after a darkness of a great many ages, the first dawn of learning and taste began to appear in Europe. Learned men in different countries began to cultivate astronomy. Galileo, a Florentine, about the year 1610, introduced the use of telescopes, which discovered new arguments in support of the motion of the earth, and confirmed the old ones. The fury and bigotry of the clergy indeed had almost checked this flourishing bud: Galileo was obliged to renounce the Copernican system, as a damnable heresy. The happy reformation in religion, however, placed the one half of Europe beyond the reach of the papal thunder. It taught mankind that the scriptures were not given for explaining systems of natural philosophy, but for a much nobler purpose, to make us just, virtuous, and humane: that instead of opposing the word of God, which in speaking of natural things suits itself to the prejudices of weak mortals, we employed our faculties in a manner highly agreeable to God himself, in tracing the nature of his works, which the more they are considered, afford us the greater reason to admire his glorious attributes of power, wisdom, and goodness. From this time, therefore, noble discoveries were made in all the branches of astronomy. The motions of the heavenly bodies were not only clearly explained, but the general law of nature, according to which they moved, was discovered and illustrated by the immortal Newton. This law is called Gravity, or Attraction, and is the same by which any body falls to the ground, when disengaged from what supported it. It has been demonstrated, that this same law which keeps the sea in its channel, and the various bodies which cover the surface of this earth from flying off into the air, operates throughout the universe, keeps the planets in their orbits, and preserves the whole fabric of nature from confusion and disorder.

SECT. II.
Of the Doctrine of the SPHERE.

HAVING, in the foregoing Section, treated of the universe in general, in which the earth has been considered as a planet, we now proceed to the Doctrine of the Sphere, which ought always to be premised before that of the globe or earth, as we shall see in the next Section. In handling this subject, we shall consider the earth as at rest, and the heavenly bodies, as performing their revolutions around it. This method cannot lead the reader into any mistake, since we have previously explained the true system of the universe, from which it appears that it is the *real* motion of the earth, which occasions the *apparent* motion of the heavenly bodies. It is besides attended with this advantage, that it perfectly agrees with the information of our senses, which always lead us to conceive the matter in this way. The imagination therefore is not put on the stretch; the idea is easy and familiar, and in delivering the elements of science, this object cannot be too much attended to. N. B. In order more clearly to comprehend what follows, the reader may occasionally turn his eye to the figure of the artificial sphere, on the opposite page.

The antients observed that all the stars turned (in appearance) round the earth, from east to west, in twenty-four hours: that the circles, which they described in those revolutions, were parallel to each other, but not of the same magnitude; those passing over the middle of the earth, being the largest of all, while the rest diminished in proportion to their distance from it. They also observed that there were two points in the heavens, which always preserved the same situation. These points they termed celestial poles, because the heavens seemed to turn round them. In order to imitate these motions, they invented what is called the Artificial Sphere, through the center of which they drew a wire or iron rod, called an Axis, whose extremities were fixed to the immoveable points called Poles. They farther observed, that on the 20th of March, and 23d of September, the circle described by the sun, was at an equal distance from both of the poles. This circle, therefore, must divide the earth into two equal parts, and on this account was called the Equator or Equaller. It was also called the Equinoctial Line, because the sun, when moving in it, makes the days and nights of equal length all over the world. Having also observed that from the 21st of June, to the 22d of December, the sun advanced every day towards a certain point, and having arrived there, returned towards that from whence he set out from 22d of December, to the 21st of June; they fixed these points which they called Solstices, because the direct motion of the sun was stopped at them; and represented the bounds of the sun's motion, by two circles, which they named Tropicks, because the sun no sooner arrived there than he turned back. Astronomers observing the motion of the sun, found its quantity, at a mean rate, to be nearly a degree (or the 360th part) of a great circle in the heavens, every 24 hours. This great circle is called the Ecliptic, and it

passes

passes through certain constellations, distinguished by the names of animals, in a zone called the Zodiac. It touches the tropic of Cancer on one side, and that of Capricorn on the other, and cuts the equator obliquely. To express this motion they supposed two points in the heavens, equally distant from, and parallel to this circle, which they called the Poles of the Zodiac, which, turning with the heavens, by means of their axis, describe the two polar circles. In the artificial sphere, the equinoctial, the two tropics, and two polar circles, are cut at right angles, by two other circles called Colures, which serve to mark the points of the solstices, equinoxes, and poles of the zodiac. The ancients also observed that, when the sun was in any point of his course, all the people inhabiting directly north and south, as far as the poles, have noon at the same time. This gave occasion to imagine a circle passing through the poles of the world, which they called a Meridian, and which is immoveable in the artificial sphere, as well as the horizon; which is another circle representing the bounds betwixt the two hemispheres, or half spheres, viz. that which is above it, and that which is below it.

SECT. III.

The Doctrine of the GLOBE naturally follows that of the SPHERE.

BY the Doctrine of the Globe is meant the representation of the different places and countries, on the face of the earth, upon an artificial globe or ball. Now the manner in which geographers have represented the situation of one place upon this earth with regard to another, or with regard to the earth in general, has been by transferring the circles of the sphere to the artificial globe; and this is the only method they could employ. This will be abundantly obvious from an example. After that circle in the heavens, which is called the equator, was known to astronomers, there was nothing more easy than to transfer it to the earth, by which the situation of places was determined, according as they lay on one side of the equator or another. The same may be observed of the other circles of the sphere above-mentioned. The reader having obtained an idea of the principle upon which the Doctrine of the Globe is founded, may proceed to consider this doctrine itself, or in other words, the description of our earth, as represented by the artificial globe.

FIGURE OF THE EARTH.] Though in speaking of the earth, along with the other planets, it was sufficient to consider it as a spherical or globular body: yet it has been discovered, that this is not its true figure, and that the earth, though nearly a sphere or ball, is not perfectly so. This matter occasioned great dispute between the philosophers of the last age, among whom Sir Isaac Newton and Cassini, a French astronomer, were the heads of two different parties. Sir Isaac demonstrated from mechanical principles, that the earth was an oblate sphere, or that it was flatted at the poles or north and south points, and jutted out towards the equator; so that a line drawn through the center of the earth, and passing thro' the poles, which is called a Diameter, would not be so long as a line drawn thro' the same center, and passing thro' the east and west points. The French philosopher asserted quite the contrary. But the matter was put to a trial by the French king in 1736, who sent out a company of philosophers towards the north pole, and likewise towards the equator, in order to measure a degree, or the three hundred and sixtieth part of a great circle in these different parts; and from their report, the opinion of Sir Isaac Newton was confirmed beyond dispute. Since that time, therefore, the earth has always been considered as more flat towards the poles, than towards the equator. The reason of this figure may be easily understood, if the reader fully comprehends what we formerly observed, with regard to the earth's motion. For if we fix a ball of clay on a spindle, and whirl it round, we shall find that it will jut out or project towards the middle, and flatten towards the poles. Now this is exactly the case, with regard to our earth, only that its axis, represented by the spindle, is imaginary. But though the earth be not perfectly spherical, the difference from that figure is so small, that it may be represented by a globe or ball, without any sensible error.

CIRCUMFERENCE AND DIAMETER OF THE EARTH.] In the general table we have exhibited, page 14, the diameter of the globe is given, according to the best observations: so that its circumference is 25,038 English miles. This circumference is conceived, for the conveniency of measuring, to be divided into three hundred and sixty parts or degrees, each degree containing sixty geographical miles, or sixty-nine English miles and an half. These degrees are in the same manner conceived to be divided each into sixty minutes.

AXIS AND POLES OF THE EARTH.] The Axis of the Earth is that imaginary line passing through its center, on which it is supposed to turn round once in twenty-four hours. The extreme points of this line are called the Poles of the Earth; one in the north, and the other in the south, which are exactly under the two points of the heavens called the North and South Poles. The knowledge of these poles is of great use to the geographer, in determining the distance and situation of places; for the poles mark, as it were, the ends of the earth, which is divided in the middle by the equator; so that the nearer one approaches to the poles, the farther he removes from the equator, and contrariwise, in removing from the poles you approach the equator.

CIRCLES OF THE GLOBE.] These are commonly divided into the greater and lesser. A great circle is that whose plane passes through the center of the earth, and divides it into two equal parts or hemispheres. A lesser circle is that which, being parallel to a greater, cannot pass through the center of the earth, nor divide it into two equal parts. The greater circles are six in number, the lesser only four.

EQUATOR.] The first great circle we shall speak of is the Equator, which we have had occasion to hint at already. It is called sometimes the Equinoctial, the reason of which we have explained; and by navigators it is also called the Line, because, according to their rude notions, they believed it to be a great Line drawn upon the sea from east to west, dividing the earth into the northern and southern hemispheres, and which they were actually to pass in sailing from the one into the other. The poles of this circle are the same with those of the world. It passes through the east and west points of the world, and, as has been already mentioned, divides it into the northern and southern hemispheres. It is divided into three hundred and sixty degrees, the use of which will soon appear.

HORIZON.] This great circle is represented by a broad circular piece of wood, encompassing the globe, and dividing it into the upper and lower hemispheres. Geographers very properly distinguish the horizon into the sensible and rational. The first may be conceived to be made by any great plane on the surface of the sea, which seems to divide the heavens into two hemispheres, the one above, the other below the level of the earth. This circle determines the rising or setting of the sun and stars, in any particular place; for when they begin to appear above the eastern edge, we say they rise, and when they go beneath the western, we say they are set. It appears then that each place has its own sensible horizon. The other horizon, called the rational, encompasses the globe, exactly in the middle. Its poles (that is two points in its axis, each ninety degrees distant from its plane, as those of all circles are) are called the Zenith and Nadir; the first exactly above our heads, and the other directly under our feet. The broad wooden circle, which represents it on the globe, has several circles drawn upon it: of these the innermost is that exhibiting the number of degrees of the twelve signs of the Zodiac (of which hereafter) viz. thirty to each sign. Next to this

B 4 you

you have the names of these signs. Next to this the days of the month according to the old stile, and then according to the new stile. Besides these there is a circle, representing the thirty-two rhumbs, or points of the mariner's compass. The use of all these will be explained afterwards.

MERIDIAN.] This circle is represented by the brass ring, on which the globe hangs and turns. It is divided into three hundred and sixty degrees, and cuts the equator at right angles; so that counting from the equator each way to the poles of the world, it contains four times ninety degrees, and divides the earth into the eastern and western hemispheres. This circle is called the meridian, because when the sun comes to the south part of it, it is then meridies or midday, and then the Sun has its greatest altitude for that day, which is therefore called its meridian altitude. Now as the sun is never in its meridian altitude, at two places east or west of one another, at the same time, each of these places must have its own meridian. There are commonly marked on the globe twenty-four meridians, one through every fifteen degrees of the equator.

ZODIAC.] The Zodiac is a broad circle, which cuts the equator obliquely; in which the twelve signs above-mentioned are represented. In the middle of this circle is supposed another called the Ecliptick, from which the sun never deviates in his annual course, and in which he advances thirty degrees every month. The twelve signs are,

1. Aries ♈	March	7. Libra ♎	September
2. Taurus ♉	April	8. Scorpio ♏	October
3. Gemini ♊	May	9. Sagittarius ♐	November
4. Cancer ♋	June	10. Capricorn ♑	December
5. Leo ♌	July	11. Aquarius ♒	January
6. Virgo ♍	August	12. Pisces ♓	February.

COLURES.] If you imagine two great circles passing both through the poles of the world, and one of them through the equinoctial points Aries and Libra, and the other through the solstitial points Cancer and Capricorn, these are called the Colures, the one the Equinoctial, the other the Solstitial Colure. These divide the ecliptic into four equal parts or quarters, which are denominated according to the points which these pass through, viz. the four cardinal points, and are the first points of Aries, Libra, Cancer and Capricorn; and these are all the great circles.

TROPICS.] If you suppose two circles drawn parallel to the equinoctial, at twenty-three degrees thirty minutes distance from it, measured on the brasen meridian, and one towards the north, the other towards the south, these are called Tropics, because the sun appears, when in them, to turn backwards from his former course. The one is called the Tropic of Cancer, the other of Capricorn, becaufe they pafs through thefe points.

POLAR CIRCLES.] If two other circles are fuppofed to be drawn at the like diftance of twenty-three degrees thirty minutes, reckoned on the meridian from the polar points, thefe are called the Polar Circles. The northern is called the Arctick, becaufe the north pole is near the conftellation of the Bear, the fouthern, the Antarctick, becaufe oppofite to the former. And thefe are the four leffer circles. Befide thefe ten circles now defcribed, which are always drawn on the globe, there are feveral others, which are only fuppofed to be drawn on it. Thefe will be explained as they become neceffary, left the reader fhould be difgufted with too many definitions at the fame time, without feeing the purpofe for which they ferve. The main defign then of all thefe circles being to exhibit the refpective fituation of places on the earth, we fhall proceed to confider more particularly how that is effected by them. It was found eafier to diftinguifh places by the quarters of the earth, in which they lay, than by their diftance from any one point. Thus after it was difcovered, that the equator divided the earth into two parts, called the Northern and Southern hemifpheres, it was eafy to fee that all places on the globe might be diftinguifhed according as they lay on the north, or fouth fide of the equator. Befides, after the four leffer circles we have mentioned came to be known, it was found that the earth, by means of them, might be divided into five portions, and confequently that the places on its furface might be diftinguifhed according as they lay in one or other of thefe portions, which are called Zones or Belts, from their partaking of breadth. That part of the earth between the Tropics, was called by the antients the Torrid or Burnt Zone, becaufe they conceived, that, being continually expofed to the perpendicular or direct rays of the fun, it was rendered uninhabitable, and contained nothing but parched and fandy defarts. This notion however has long fince been refuted. It is found that the long nights, great dews, regular rains and breezes, which prevail almoft throughout the torrid zone, render the earth not only habitable, but fo fruitful, that in many places they have two harvefts in a year; all forts of fpices and drugs are almoft folely produced there; and it furnifhes more perfect metals, precious ftones, and pearls, than all the reft of the earth together. In fhort, the countries of Africa, Afia, and America, which lie under this zone, are in all refpects the moft fertile and luxuriant upon earth.

The two temperate zones are comprifed between the tropics and polar circles. They are called temperate, becaufe meeting the rays of the fun obliquely, they enjoy a moderate degree of heat.

heat. The two frigid zones lie between the polar circles and the poles, or rather are inclofed within the polar circles. They are called the Frigid or Frozen, becaufe moft part of the year it is extremely cold there, and every thing is frozen fo long as the fun is under the horizon, or but a little above it. However thefe zones are not quite uninhabitable, though much lefs fit for living in than the torrid.

None of all thefe zones is thoroughly difcovered by the Europeans. Little is known to us of the fouthern temperate zone, and though fome iflands and fea coafts in the northern frigid zone have come to our knowledge, we have none at all of the fouthern frigid zone. The northern temperate, and torrid zones, are thofe we are beft acquainted with.

CLIMATES.] But the divifions of the earth into hemifpheres and zones, though it may be of advantage in letting us know in what quarter of the earth any place lies, is not fufficiently minute for giving us a notion of the diftances between one place and another. This however is ftill more neceffary; becaufe it is of more importance to mankind, to know the fituation of places, with regard to one another, than with regard to the earth itfelf. The firft ftep taken for determining this matter, was to divide the earth into what is called Climates. It was obferved that the day was always twelve hours long on the equator, and that the longeft day encreafed in proportion as we advanced north or fouth on either fide of it. The antients therefore determined how far any place was north or fouth of the equator, or what is called the Latitude of the place, from the greateft length of the day from that place. This made them conceive a number of circles parallel to the equator, which bounded the length of the day at different diftances from the equator. And as they called the fpace contained between thefe circles, Climates, becaufe they declined from the equator towards the pole, fo the circles themfelves may be called Climatical Parallels. This therefore was a new divifion of the earth, more minute than that of zones, and ftill continues in ufe, though, as we fhall fhew, the defign which firft introduced it, may be better anfwered in another way. There are 30 climates between the equator and either pole. In the firft 24, the days encreafe by half hours, but in the remaining fix, between the polar circle and the poles, the days encreafe by months. This the reader will be convinced of, when he becomes acquainted with the ufe of the globe; in the mean time we fhall infert a table, which will ferve to fhew in what climate any country lies, fuppofing the length of the day, and the diftance of the place from the equator to be known.

INTRODUCTION.

Climate	Latitude. D. M.	Breadth. D. M.	Long. Day. H. M.	Names of countries and remarkable places situated in every climate north of the Equator.
1	8 25	8 25	12 30	I. Within the first Climate lie the Gold and Silver Coast in Africa; Malacca, in the East-Indies; Cayenne and Surinam, in Terra Firma, S. Amer.
2	16 25	8	13	II. Here lie Abyssinia, in Africa; Siam, Madrass, and Pondicherry, in the East-Indies; Straits of Darien, between N. and S. America; Tobago, Granades, St. Vincent, and Barbadoes, in the W. Ind.
3	23 50	7 25	13 30	III. Contains Mecca, in Arabia; Bombay, part of Bengal, in the East-Indies; Canton, in China; México, Bay of Campeachy, in N. America; Jamaica, Hispaniola, St. Christophers, Antego, Martinico, and Guadalupe, in the West-Indies.
4	30 25	6 30	14	IV. Egypt, and the Canary Islands, in Africa; Delly, capital of the Mogul Empire, in Asia; Gulph of Mexico, and East Florida, in N. America; the Havanna, in the West-Indies.
5	36 28	6 8	14 30	V. Gibraltar, in Spain; part of the Mediterranean sea; the Barbary coast, in Africa; Jerusalem; Ispahan, capital of Persia; Nankin, in China; California, New Mexico, West Florida, Georgia, and the Carolinas, in N. America.
6	41 22	4 54	15	VI. Lisbon, in Portugal; Madrid in Spain; Minorca, Sardinia, and part of Greece, in the Mediterranean; Asia Minor; part of the Caspian Sea; Samarcand, in Great Tartary; Pekin, in China; Corea and Japan; Williamsburgh, in Virginia; Maryland, and Philadelphia, in N. America.
7	45 29	4 7	15 30	VII. Northern provinces of Spain; southern ditto of France; Turin, Genoa, and Rome, in Italy; Constantinople, and the Black Sea, in Turkey; the Caspian Sea, and part of Tartary; New York, Boston in New England, N. America.
8	49 01	3 32	16	VIII Paris, Vienna, cap. of Germany; New-Scotland, Newfoundland, and Canada, in N. Amer.
9	52 00	2 57	16 30	IX. London, Flanders, Prague, Dresden; Cracow, in Poland; southern provinces of Russia; part of Tartary; north part of Newfoundland.
10	54 27	2 29	17	X. Dublin, York, Holland, Hanover, and Tartary; Labrador, and New South-Wales, in N. Amer.
11	56 37	2 10	17 30	XI. Edinburgh, Copenhagen, Moscow, cap. of Russia.
12	58 29	1 52	18	XII. South part of Hudson's Bay, in N. America.
13	59 58	1 29	18 30	XIII. Orkney Isles, Stockholm, capital of Sweden.
14	61 18	1 20	19	XIV. Bergen, in Norway; Peterburg, in Russia.
15	62 25	1 7	19 30	XV. Hudson's straits, N. America.
16	63 22	57	20	XVI. Siberia, and the south part of W. Greenland.
17	64 06	44	20 30	XVII. Drontheim, in Norway.
18	64 49	43	21	XVIII. Part of Finland, in Russia.
19	65 21	32	21 30	XIX. Archangel, on the White Sea, Russia.
20	65 47	22	22	XX. Hecla, in Iceland.
21	66 06	19	22 30	XXI. Northern parts of Russia and Siberia.
22	66 20	14	23	XXII. New North Wales, in N. America.
23	66 28	8	23 30	XXIII. Davis's straits, in ditto.
24	66 31	3	24	XXIV. Samoieda.
25	67 21		1 Month	XXV. South part of Lapland.
26	69 48		2 Months	XXVI. West-Greenland.
27	73 37		3 Months	XXVII. Zembla Australis.
28	78 30		4 Months	XXVIII. Zembla Borealis.
29	84 05		5 Months	XXIX. Spitzbergen or East Greenland.
30	90		6 Months	XXX. Unknown.

INTRODUCTION.

The distance of places from the equator, or what is called their Latitude, is easily measured on the globe, by means of the meridian above described. For we have only to bring the place, whose latitude we would know, to the meridian, where the degree of latitude is marked, and will be exactly over the place. Now this is the manner alluded to, by which the distance of places from the equator, is most properly distinguished; but it could not be adopted, until the figure and circumference of the earth were known, after which it was easy to determine the number of miles in each 360th part or degree of this circumference, and consequently know the latitude of places. As latitude is reckoned from the equator towards the poles, it is either northern or southern, and the nearer the poles the greater the latitude; and no place can have more than 90 degrees of latitude, because the poles, where they terminate, are at that distance from the equator.

PARALLELS OF LATITUDE.] Through every degree of latitude, or more properly through every particular place on the earth, geographers suppose a circle to be drawn, which they call a parallel of latitude. The intersection of this circle, with the meridian of any place, shews the true situation of that place.

LONGITUDE.] The longitude of a place is its situation with regard to its meridian, and consequently reckoned towards the east or west; in reckoning the longitude there is no particular spot from which we ought to set out preferably to another, but for the advantage of a general rule, the meridian of Ferro, the most westerly of the Canary Islands, was considered as the first meridian in most of the globes and maps, and the longitude of places was reckoned to be so many degrees east or west of the meridian of Ferro. These degrees are marked on the equator. No place can have more than 180 degrees of longitude, because the circumference of the globe being 360 degrees, no place can be moved from another above half that distance; but many foreign geographers very improperly reckon the longitude quite round the globe. The degrees of longitude are not equal like those of latitude, but diminish in proportion as the meridians incline, or their distance contracts in approaching the pole. Hence in 60 degrees of latitude, a degree of longitude is but half the quantity of a degree on the equator, and so of the rest. The number of miles contained in a degree of longitude, in each parallel of latitude, are set down in the following table.

A TABLE

SHEWING

The Number of Miles contained in a Degree of Longitude, in each Parallel of Latitude from the Equator.

Degrees of Latitude.	Miles.	100th Parts of a Mile.	Degrees of Latitude.	Miles.	100th Parts of a Mile.	Degrees of Latitude.	Miles.	100th Parts of a Mile.
1	59	96	31	51	43	61	29	04
2	59	94	32	50	88	62	28	17
3	59	92	33	50	32	63	27	24
4	59	86	34	49	74	64	26	30
5	59	77	35	49	15	65	25	36
6	59	67	36	48	54	66	24	41
7	59	56	37	47	92	67	23	45
8	59	40	38	47	28	68	22	48
9	59	20	39	46	62	69	21	51
10	59	08	40	46	00	70	20	52
11	58	89	41	45	28	71	19	54
12	58	68	42	44	95	72	18	55
13	58	46	43	43	88	73	17	54
14	58	22	44	43	16	74	16	53
15	58	00	45	42	43	75	15	52
16	57	60	46	41	68	76	14	51
17	57	30	47	41	00	77	13	50
18	57	04	48	40	15	78	12	48
19	56	73	49	39	36	79	11	45
20	56	38	50	38	57	80	10	42
21	56	00	51	37	73	81	09	38
22	55	63	52	37	00	82	08	35
23	55	23	53	36	18	83	07	32
24	54	81	54	35	26	84	06	28
25	54	38	55	34	41	85	05	23
26	54	00	56	33	55	86	04	18
27	53	44	57	32	67	87	03	14
28	53	00	58	31	79	88	02	09
29	52	48	59	30	90	89	01	05
30	51	96	60	30	00	90	00	00

INTRODUCTION.

Longitude and Latitude found.] To find the Longitude and Latitude of any place, therefore, we need only bring that place to the brazen meridian, and we shall find the degree of longitude marked on the equator, and the degree of latitude on the meridian. So that to find the difference between the latitude or longitude of two places, we have only to compare the degrees of either, thus found, with one another, and the reduction of these degrees into miles, according to the table above given, and remembering that every degree of longitude at the equator, and every degree of latitude all over the globe, is equal to 60 geographic miles, or $69\frac{1}{2}$ English, we shall be able exactly to determine the distance between any places on the globe.

Distance of places measured.] The Distance of Places which lie in an oblique direction, i. e. neither directly south, north, east, or west, from one another, may be measured in a readier way, by extending the compasses from the one to the other, and then applying them to the equator. For instance, extend the compasses from Guinea in Africa, to Brazil in America, and then apply them to the equator, and you will find the distance to be 25 degrees, which at 60 miles to a degree, makes the distance 1500 miles.

Quadrant of altitude.] In order to supply the place of the compasses in this operation, there is commonly a pliant narrow plate of brass, screwed on the brazen meridian, which contains 90 degrees, or one quarter of the circumference of the globe, by means of which the distances and bearings of places are measured without the trouble of first extending the compasses between them, and then applying the same to the equator. This plate is called the Quadrant of Altitude.

Hour circle.] This is a small brass circle fixed on the brazen meridian, divided into 24 hours, and having an index moveable round the axis of the globe.

PROBLEMS PERFORMED BY THE GLOBE.

Prob. I.} *THE diameter of an artificial globe being given, to find its surface in square, and its solidity in cubic measure.*

Multiply the diameter by the circumference, which is a great circle dividing the globe into two equal parts, and the product will give the first: then multiply the said product by one sixth of the diameter, and the product of that will give the second. After the same manner we may find the surface and solidity of the natural globe, as also the whole body of the atmosphere surrounding the same, provided it be always and

every

every where of the same height; for having found the perpendicular height thereof, by that common experiment of the ascent of Mercury at the foot and top of a mountain, double the said height, and add the same to the diameter of the earth; then multiply the whole, as a new diameter by its proper circumference, and from the product subtract the solidity of the earth, it will leave that of the atmosphere.

PROB. 2. *To rectify the globe.*

The globe being set upon a true plane, raise the pole according to the given latitude; then fix the quadrant of altitude in the zenith, and if there be any mariner's compass upon the pedestal, let the globe be so situate, as that the brazen meridian may stand due south and north, according to the two extremities of the needle, allowing their variation.

PROB. 3. *To find the longitude and latitude of any place.*

For this, see the preceding page.

PROB. 4. *The longitude and latitude of any place being given, to find that place on the globe.*

Bring the degree of longitude to the brazen meridian; reckon upon the same meridian the degree of latitude, whether south or north, and make a mark with chalk where the reckoning ends; the point exactly under the chalk is the place desired.

PROB. 5. *The latitude of any place being given, to find all those places that have the same latitude.*

The globe being rectified (*a*) according to the latitude of the given place, and that place being brought to the brazen meridian, make a mark exactly above the same, and turning the globe round, all those places passing under the said mark have the same latitude with the given place.

(*a*) PROB. 2.

PROB. 6. *To find the Sun's place in the Ecliptic at any time.*

The month and day being given, look for the same upon the wooden horizon; and over-against the day you will find the particular sign and degree in which the Sun is at that time, which sign and degree being noted in the ecliptic, the same is the Sun's place, or nearly, at the time desired.

PROB. 7. *The month and day being given, as also the particular time of that day, to find those places of the globe to which the Sun is in the meridian at that particular time.*

The pole being elevated according to the latitude of the given place, bring the said place to the brazen meridian, and
setting

setting the index of the horary circle at the hour of the day, in the given place, turn the globe till the index points at the upper figure of XII. which done, fix the globe in that situation, and observe what places are exactly under the upper hemisphere of the brazen meridian, for those are the places desired.

PROB. 8. *To know the length of the day and night in any place of the earth at any time.*

(*a*) PROB. 2.
(*b*) PROB. 6.

Elevate the pole (*a*) according to the latitude of the given place; find the Sun's place in the ecliptic (*b*) at that time, which being brought to the east side of the horizon, set the index of the horary circle at noon, or the upper figure XII. and turning the globe about till the aforesaid place of the ecliptic touch the western side of the horizon, look upon the horary circle, and wheresoever the index pointeth, reckon the number of hours between the same and the upper figure of 12; for that is the length of the day, the complement whereof to 24 hours is the length of the night.

PROB. 9. *To know what a clock it is by the globe in any part of the world, and at any time, provided you know the hour of the day where you are at the same time.*

(*c*) PROB. 3.

Bring the place in which you are to the brazen meridian, the pole being raised (*c*) according to the latitude thereof, and set the index of the horary circle to the hour of the day at that time. Then bring the desired place to the brazen meridian, and the index will point out the present hour at that place wherever it is.

PROB. 10. *A place being given in the Torrid Zone, to find those two days of the year in which the Sun shall be vertical to the same.*

Bring the given place to the brazen meridian, and mark what degree of latitude is exactly above it. Move the globe round, and observe the two points of the ecliptic that pass through the said degree of latitude. Search upon the wooden horizon (or by proper tables of the Sun's annual motion) on what days he passeth through the aforesaid points of the ecliptic, for those are the days required in which the Sun is vertical to the given place.

PROB. 11. *The month and day being given, to find by the globe those places of the North Frigid Zone, where the Sun beginneth*

neth then to *shine constantly without setting*; as also those places of the *South Frigid Zone*, where he then begins to be totally absent.

The day given, (which must always be one of those either between the vernal equinox and the summer solstice, or between the autumnal equinox and winter solstice) find (*a*) the Sun's place in the ecliptic, and marking the same, bring it to the brazen meridian, and reckon the like number of degrees from the north pole towards the equator, as there is between the equator and the Sun's place in the ecliptic, setting a mark with chalk where the reckoning ends. This done, turn the globe round, and all the places passing under the said chalk are those in which the Sun begins to shine constantly without setting upon the given day. For solution of the latter part of the problem, set off the same distance from the south pole upon the brazen meridian towards the equator, as was formerly set off from the north; then marking with chalk, and turning the globe round, all places passing under the mark are those where the Sun begins his total disappearance from the given day.

(*a*) PROB. 6.

PROB. 12. *A place being given in the North Frigid Zone, to find by the globe what number of days the Sun doth constantly shine upon the said place, and what days he is absent, as also the first and last day of his appearance.*

Bring the given place to the brazen meridian, and observing its latitude (*b*) elevate the globe accordingly; count the same number of degrees upon the meridian from each side of the equator as the place is distant from the pole; and making marks where the reckonings end, turn the globe, and carefully observe what two degrees of the ecliptic pass exactly under the two points marked in the meridian; first for the northern arch of the circle, namely that comprehended between the two degrees remarked, being reduced to time, will give the number of days that the Sun doth constantly shine above the horizon of the given place; and the opposite arch of the said circle will in like manner give the number of days in which he is totally absent, and also will point out which days those are. And in the interval he will rise and set.

(*b*) PROB. 2.

PROB. 13. *The month and day being given, to find those places on the globe, to which the Sun, when on the meridian, shall be vertical on that day.*

VOL. I. C The

(a) Prob. 6.

The Sun's place in the ecliptic being (a) found, bring the same to the brazen meridian, in which make a small mark with chalk, exactly above the Sun's place. Which done, turn the globe, and those places which have the Sun vertical in the meridian, will successively pass under the said mark.

Prob. 14. *The month and day being given, to find upon what point of the compass the Sun then riseth and setteth in any place.*

Elevate the pole according to the latitude of the desired place, and finding the Sun's place in the ecliptic at the given time, bring the same to the eastern side of the horizon, and you may there clearly see the point of the compass upon which he then riseth. By turning the globe about till his place coincide with the western side of the horizon, you may also see upon the said circle the exact point of his setting.

Prob. 15. *To know by the globe the length of the longest and shortest days and nights in any part of the world.*

Elevate the pole according to the latitude of the given place, and bring the first degree of Cancer, if in the northern, or Capricorn if in the southern hemisphere, to the east side of the horizon; and setting the index of the horary circle at noon, turn the globe about till the sign of Cancer touch the western side of the horizon, and then observe upon the horary circle the number of hours between the index and the upper figure of XII. reckoning them according to the motion of the index, for that is the length of the longest day, the complement whereof is the extent of the shortest night. As for the shortest day and longest night, they are only the reverse of the former.

Prob. 16. *The hour of the day being given in any place, to find those places of the earth where it is either noon or midnight, or any other particular hour at the same time.*

Bring the given place to the brazen meridian, and set the index of the horary circle at the hour of the day in that place. Then turn about the globe till the index point at the upper figure of XII. and observe what places are exactly under the upper semicircle of the brazen meridian, for in them it is midday at the time given. Which done, turn the globe about till the index point at the lower figure of XII. and what places are then in the lower semicircle of the meridian, in them it is midnight at the given time. After the same manner we may find those places that have any other particular hour at the
time

time given, by moving the globe till the index point at the hour defired, and obferving the places that are then under the brazen meridian.

PROB. 17. *The day and hour being given, to find by the globe that particular place of the earth to which the Sun is vertical at that very time.*

The Sun's place in the ecliptic (*a*) being found and brought to the brazen meridian, make a mark above the fame with chalk; then (*b*) find thofe places of the earth in whofe meridian the Sun is at that inftant, and bring them to the brazen meridian; which done, obferve narrowly that individual part of the earth which falls exactly under the forefaid mark in the brazen meridian; for that is the particular place to which the Sun is vertical at that very time.

(*a*) PROB. 6.

(*b*) PROB. 16.

PROB. 18. *The day and hour at any place being given, to find all thofe places where the Sun is then rifing, or fetting, or on the meridian; confequently, all thofe places which are enlightened at that time, and thofe which are in the dark.*

This problem cannot be folved by any globe fitted up in the common way, with the hour circle fixed upon the brafs meridian; unlefs the Sun be on or near fome of the tropics on the given day. But by a globe fitted up according to Mr. Jofeph Harris's invention, where the hour-circle lies on the furface of the globe, below the meridian, it may be folved for any day in the year, according to his method; which is as follows.

Having found the place to which the Sun is vertical at the given hour, if the place be in the northern hemifphere, elevate the north pole as many degrees above the horizon, as are equal to the latitude of that place; if the place be in the fouthern hemifphere, elevate the fouth pole accordingly; and bring the faid place to the brazen meridian. Then, all thofe places which are in the weftern femicircle of the horizon, have the Sun rifing to them at that time; and thofe in the eaftern femicircle have it fetting: to thofe under the upper femicircle of the brafs meridian, it is noon; and to thofe under the lower femicircle, it is midnight. All thofe places which are above the horizon, are enlightened by the Sun, and have the Sun juft as many degrees above them, as they themfelves are above the horizon; and this height may be known, by fixing the quadrant of altitude on the brazen meridian over the place to which the Sun is vertical; and then, laying it over any other place,

place, obferve what number of degrees on the quadrant are intercepted between the faid place and the horizon. In all thofe places that are 18 degrees below the weftern femicircle of the horizon, the morning twilight is juft beginning; in all thofe places that are 18 degrees below the eaftern femicircle of the horizon, the evening twilight is ending; and all thofe places that are lower than 18 degrees, have dark night.

If any place be brought to the upper femicircle of the brazen meridian, and the hour index be fet to the upper XII or noon, and then the globe be turned round eaftward on its axis; when the place comes to the weftern femicircle of the horizon, the index will fhew the time of fun-rifing at that place; and when the fame place comes to the eaftern femicircle of the horizon, the index will fhew the time of fun-fet.

To thofe places which do not go under the horizon, the fun fets not on that day: and to thofe which do not come above it, the Sun does not rife.

PROB. 19. *The month and day being given, with the place of the Moon in the zodiac and her true latitude, to find thereby the exact hour when fhe fhall rife and fet, together with her fouthing, or coming to the meridian of the place.*

The Moon's place in the zodiac may be found readily enough at any time by an ordinary almanac; and her latitude, which is her diftance from the ecliptic, by applying the femicircle of pofition to her place in the zodiac. For

(*a*) PROB. 2. the folution of the problem (*a*), elevate the pole according to the latitude of the given place, and the Sun's place in the ecliptic at that time

(*b*) PROB. 6. being (*b*) found and marked with chalk, as alfo the Moon's place at the fame time, bring the Sun's place to the brazen meridian, and fet the index of the horary circle at noon, then turn the globe till the Moon's place fucceffively meet with the eaftern and weftern fide of the horizon, as alfo the brazen meridian, and the index will point at thofe various times the particular hours of her rifing, fetting and fouthing.

PROB. 20. *Two places being given on the globe, to find the true diftance between them.*

Lay the graduated edge of the quadrant of altitude over both the places, and the number of degrees intercepted between them will be their true diftance from each other, reckoning every degree to be $69\frac{1}{2}$ Englifh miles.

PROB. 21. *A place being given on the globe, and its true diftance from a fecond place, to find thereby all other places of the earth that are of the fame diftance from the given place.*

INTRODUCTION. 37

Bring the given place to the brazen meridian, and elevate the pole according to the latitude of the said place; then fix the quadrant of altitude in the zen'th, and reckon, upon the said quadrant, the given distance between the first and second place, provided the same be under 90 degrees, otherwise you must use the semicircle of position, and making a mark where the reckoning ends, and moving the said quadrant or semi-circle quite round upon the surface of the globe, all places passing under that mark, are those desired.

GEOGRAPHICAL OBSERVATIONS.

1. The latitude of any place is equal to the elevation of the pole above the horizon of that place, and the elevation of the equator is equal to the complement of the latitude, that is, to what the latitude wants of 90 degrees.

2. Those places which lie on the equator, have no latitude, it being there that the latitude begins; and those places which lie on the first meridian have no longitude, it being there that the longitude begins. Consequently, *that* particular place of the earth where the first meridian intersects the equator, has neither longitude nor latitude.

3. All places of the earth do equally enjoy the benefi the sun, in respect of time, and are equally deprived of^t ^{of}

4. All places upon the equator have their days and nig^{h}ts equally long, that is, 12 hours each, at all times of the y^{e}ar. For although the sun declines alternately, from the equator towards the north and towards the south, yet, as the horizon of the equator cuts all the parallels of latitude and declination in halves, the sun must always continue above the horizon for one half a diurnal revolution about the earth, and for the other half below it.

5. In all places of the earth between the equator and poles, the days and nights are equally long, viz. 12 hours each, when the sun is in the equinoctial: for, in all elevations of the pole, short of 90 degrees (which is the greatest) one half of the equator or equinoctial will be above the horizon, and the other half below it.

6. The days and nights are never of an equal length at any place between the equator and polar circles, but when the sun enters the signs ♈ Aries and ♎ Libra. For in every other part of the ecliptic, the circle of the sun's daily motion is divided into two unequal parts by the horizon.

7. The nearer that any place is to the equator, the less is the difference between the length of the days and nights in that place; and the more remote, the contrary. The circles which the sun describes in the heaven every 24 hours, being

being cut more nearly equal in the former case, and more unequally in the latter.

8. In all places lying upon any given parallel of latitude, however long or short the day and night be at any one of these places, at any time of the year, it is then of the same length at all the rest; for in turning the globe round its axis (when rectified according to the sun's declination) all these places will keep equally long above or below the horizon.

9. The sun is vertical twice a year to every place between the tropics; to those under the tropics, once a year, but never any where else. For, there can be no place between the tropics, but that there will be two points in the ecliptic, whose declination from the equator is equal to the latitude of that place; and but one point of the ecliptic which has a declination equal to the latitude of places on the tropic which that point of the ecliptic touches; and as the sun never goes without the tropics, he can never be vertical to any place that lies without them.

10. In all places lying exactly under the polar circles, the sun, when he is in the nearest tropic, continues 24 hours above the horizon without setting; because no part of that tropic is below their horizon. And when the sun is in the farthest tropic, he is for the same length of time without rising; because no part of that tropic is above their horizon. But, at all other times of the year, he rises and sets there, as in other places; because all the circles that can be drawn parallel to the equator, between the tropics, are more or less cut by the horizon, as they are farther from, or nearer to, that tropic which is all above the horizon: and when the sun is not in either of the tropics, his diurnal course must be in one or other of these circles.

11. To all places in the northern hemisphere, from the equator to the polar circle, the longest day and shortest night is when the sun is in the northern tropic; and the shortest day and longest night is when the sun is in the southern tropic; because no circle of the sun's daily motion is so much above the horizon, and so little below it, as the northern tropic; and none so little above it, and so much below it, as the southern. In the southern hemisphere, the contrary.

12. In all places between the polar circles and poles, the sun appears for some number of days (or rather diurnal revolutions) without setting; and at the opposite time of the year without rising; because some part of the ecliptic never sets in the former case, and as much of the opposite part never rises in the latter. And the nearer unto, or the more remote from the pole, these places are, the longer or shorter is the sun's continuing presence or absence.

13. If a ship sets out from any port, and sails round the earth eastward to the same port again, let her take what time she will to do it in, the people in that ship, in reckoning their time, will gain one compleat day at their return, or count one day more than those who reside at the same port; because, by going contrary to the sun's diurnal motion, and being forwarder every evening than they were in the morning, their horizon will get so much the sooner above the setting sun, than if they had kept for a whole day at any particular place. And thus, by cutting off a part proportionable to their own motion, from the length of every day, they will gain a compleat day of that sort at their return; without gaining one moment of absolute time more than is elapsed during their course, to the people at the port. If they sail westward they will reckon one day less than the people do who reside at the said port, because by gradually following the apparent diurnal motion of the sun, they will keep him each particular day so much longer above their horizon, as answers to that day's course; and by that means, they cut off a whole day in reckoning, at their return, without losing one moment of absolute time.

Hence, if two ships should set out at the same time from any port, and sail round the globe, one eastward and the other westward, so as to meet at the same port on any day whatever; they will differ two days in reckoning their time, at their return. If they sail twice round the earth, they will differ four days; if thrice, then six, &c.

OF THE NATURAL DIVISIONS OF THE EARTH.

THE constituent parts of the Earth are two, the land and water. The parts of the land are continents, islands, peninsulas, isthmus's, promontories, capes, coasts, mountains, &c. This land is divided into two great continents, (besides the islands) viz. the eastern and western continent. The eastern is subdivided into three parts, viz. Europe, on the north-west; Asia, on the north-east; and Africa, (which is joined to Asia by the isthmus of Suez, 60 miles over) on the south. The western continent consists of North and South America, joined by the isthmus of Darien, 60 or 70 miles broad.

A continent is a large portion of land, containing several countries or kingdoms, without any entire separation of its parts by water, as Europe. An island is a smaller part of land, quite surrounded by water, as Great-Britain. A peninsula is a tract of land every where surrounded by water, except at one narrow neck, by which it joins the neighbouring continent; as the Morea in Greece: and that neck of land which so joins

joins it, is called an isthmus; as the isthmus of Suez, which joins Africa to Asia; the isthmus of Darien, which joins North and South America. A promontory is a hill, or point of land, stretching itself into the sea, the end of which is called a cape; as the cape of Good-Hope. A coast or shore is that part of a country which borders on the sea-side. Mountains, vallies, woods, deserts, plains, &c. need no description. The most remarkable are taken notice of, and described in the body of this work.

The parts of the water are oceans, seas, lakes, straits, gulphs, bays, or creeks, rivers, &c. The waters are divided into three extensive oceans (besides lesser seas, which are only branches of these) viz. the Atlantic, the Pacific, and the Indian Ocean. The Atlantic or Western Ocean, divides the eastern and western continents, and is 3000 miles wide. The Pacific, divides America from Asia, and is 10,000 miles over. The Indian Ocean lies between the East Indies and Africa, being 3000 miles wide.

The ocean is a great and spacious collection of water, without any entire separation of its parts by land; as the Atlantic Ocean. The sea is a smaller collection of water, which communicates with the ocean, confined by the land; as the Mediterranean and the Red Sea. A lake is a large collection of water, entirely surrounded by land; as the lake of Geneva, and the lakes in Canada. A strait is a narrow part of the sea, restrained or lying between two shores, and opening a passage out of one sea into another; as the strait of Gibraltar, or that of Magellan. This is sometimes called a sound; as the strait into the Baltic. A gulph is a part of the sea running up into the land, and surrounded by it, except at the passage whereby it is communicated with the sea or ocean. If a gulph be very large, it is called an inland sea; as the Mediterranean: if it do not go far into the land, it is called a bay; as the Bay of Biscay: if it be very small, a creek, haven, station, or road for ships; as Milford Haven. Rivers, canals, brooks, &c. need no description, for these lesser divisions of water, like those of land, are to be met with in most countries, and every one has a clear idea of what is meant by them. But in order to strengthen the remembrance of the great parts of land and water we have described, it may be proper to observe, that there is a strong analogy or resemblance between them.

The description of a continent resembles that of an ocean, an island encompassed with water resembles a lake encompassed with land. A peninsula of land is like a gulph or inland sea. A promontory, or cape of land, is like a bay or creek of sea: and an isthmus, whereby two lands are joined,

resembles

resembles a strait, which unites one sea to another. To this description of the divisions of the earth, rather than add an enumeration of the various parts of land and water, which correspond to them, and which the reader will find in the body of the work, we shall subjoin a table, exhibiting the superficial content of the whole globe in square miles, sixty to a degree, and also of the seas and unknown parts, the habitable earth, the four quarters or continents; likewise of the great empires and principal islands, which shall be placed as they are subordinate to one another in magnitude.

	Square Miles.	Islands.	Square Miles.	Islands.	Squ. Mls.
The Globe	199,512,595	Hispaniola	36,000	Skye	900
Seas and unknown Parts	160,522,026	Newfoundland	35,500	Lewis	880
The Habitable World *	38,990,569	Ceylon	27,730	Funen	768
Europe	4,456,065	Ireland	27,457	Yvica	625
Asia	10,768,823	Formosa	17,000	Minorca	520
Africa	9,654,807	Anian	11,900	Rhodes	480
America	14,110,874	Gilolo	10,400	Cephalonia	420
Persian Empire under Darius	1,650,000	Sicily	9400	Amboyna	400
Roman Emp. in its utmost height	1,610,000	Timor	7800	Orkney Pomona	324
Russian	3,303,485	Sardinia	6600	Scio	300
Chinese	1,749,000	Cyprus	6300	Martinico	260
Great Mogul	1,116,000	Jamaica	6000	Lemnos	220
Turkish	960,057	Flores	6000	Corfu	194
Present Persian	806,000	Ceram	5400	Providence	168
		Briton	4000	Man	160
Borneo	228,000	Socatra	3600	Bornholm	160
Madagascar	163,000	Candia	3220	Wight	150
Sumatra	129,000	Porto Rico	3200	Malta	150
Japan	118,000	Corsica	2520	Barbadoes	140
Great Britain	72,926	Zeland	1935	Zant	120
Celebes	68,400	Majorca	1400	Antigua	100
Manila	58,500	St. Jago	1400	St. Christopher's	80
Iceland	46,000	Negropont	1300	St. Helena	80
Terra del Fuego	42,075	Teneriff	1272	Guernsey	50
Mindinao	39,200	Gotland	1000	Jersey	43
Cuba	38,400	Madeira	950	Bermudas	40
Java	38,250	St. Michael	920	Rhode	36

WINDS AND TIDES.] We cannot finish the doctrine of the earth, without considering Winds and Tides, from which the changes that happen on its surface principally arise.

WINDS.] The earth on which we live is every where surrounded by a fine invisible fluid, which extends to several miles above its surface, and is called Air. It is found by experiments,

* The number of inhabitants computed at present to be in the known world at a medium, taken from the best calculations, are about 953 millions.

Europe contains   153 Millions
Asia   —   —   500
Africa   —   —   150
America   —   150

Total   953 Millions

INTRODUCTION.

experiments, that a small quantity of air is capable of being expanded, so as to fill a very large space, or to be compressed into a much smaller compass than it occupied before. The general cause of the expansion of air is heat, the general cause of its compression is cold. Hence if any part of the air or atmosphere receive a greater degree of cold or heat than it had before, its parts will be put in motion, and expanded or compressed. But when air is put in motion, we call it wind in general; and a breeze, gale, or storm, according to the quickness or velocity of that motion. Winds therefore, which are commonly considered as things extremely variable and uncertain, depend on a general cause, and act with more or less uniformity in proportion as the action of this cause is more or less constant. It is found by observations made at sea, that from thirty degrees north latitude, to thirty degrees south, there is a constant east-wind throughout the year, blowing on the Atlantic and Pacific oceans, and called the Trade Wind. This is occasioned by the action of the sun, which in moving from east to west heats, and consequently expands the air immediately under him; by which means a stream, or tide of air, always accompanies him in his course, and occasions a perpetual east-wind within these limits. This general cause however is modified by a number of particulars, the explication of which would be too tedious and complicated for our present plan; which is to mention facts rather than theories.

It is likewise found, that in some parts of the Indian ocean, which are not more than two hundred leagues from land, there are periodical winds, called Monsoons, which blow half the year one way, and half the year another way. At the changing of these monsoons, which always happen at the equinoxes, there are terrible storms of thunder, lightning, wind and rain. It is discovered also, that in the same latitudes, there is another kind of periodical winds, which blows from the land in the night and good part of the morning, and from the sea about noon, till midnight; these however do not extend above two or three leagues from shore. Near the coast of Guinea in Africa, the wind blows always from the west, south-west, or south. On the coast of Peru in South America, the winds blow constantly from the south-west. Beyond the latitude of thirty north and south, the winds, as we daily perceive in Great-Britain, are more variable, though they blow oftener from the west than any other point. Between the fourth and tenth degrees of north latitude, and between the longitude of Cape Verd and the easternmost of the Cape Verd islands, there is a tract of sea condemned to perpetual calms,

calms, attended with terrible thunder and lightning, and such rains, that this sea has acquired the name of *the Rains*.

TIDES.] By the tides is meant that regular motion of the sea, according to which it ebbs and flows twice in twenty-four hours. The doctrine of the Tides remained in obscurity till the immortal Sir Isaac Newton explained it by his great principle of gravity or attraction. For having demonstrated that there is a principle in all bodies, within the solar system, by which they mutually draw or attract one another, in proportion to their distance, it follows, that those parts of the sea which are immediately below the moon, must be drawn towards it, and consequently wherever the moon is nearly vertical, the sea will be raised, which occasions the flowing of the tide there. A similar reason occasions the flowing of the tide likewise in those places where the moon is in the nadir, and which must be diametrically opposite to the former; for in the hemisphere farthest from the moon, the parts in the nadir being less attracted by her than the other parts which are nearer to her, gravitate less towards the earth's center, and consequently must be higher than the rest. Those parts of the earth, on the contrary, where the moon appears on the horizon, or ninety degrees distant from the zenith and nadir, will have low water; for as the waters in the zenith and nadir rise at the same time, the waters in their neighbourhood will press towards those places to maintain the equilibrium; to supply the places of these, others will move the same way, and so on to the places ninety degrees distant from the zenith and nadir, where the water will be lowest. By combining this doctrine with the diurnal motion of the earth, above explained, we shall be sensible of the reason why the tides ebb and flow, twice in twenty-four hours, in every place on this globe.

The tides are higher than ordinary, twice every month, that is about the times of new and full moon, and are called Spring Tides; for at these times the actions of both the sun and moon are united, and draw in the same straight line, and consequently the sea must be more elevated: at the conjunction, or when the sun and moon are on the same side of the earth, they both conspire to raise the waters in the Zenith, and consequently in the Nadir; and at the opposition, or when the earth is between the sun and moon, while one occasions high water in the Zenith and Nadir, the other does the same. The tides are less than ordinary twice every month, about the first and last quarters of the moon, and are called Neap Tides; for in the quarters the sun raises the waters where the moon depresses them, and depresses where the moon raises them; so that the tides are only occasioned by the difference by which the action of the moon, which is nearest us, prevails over that of the sun. These things would happen uniformly, were the whole surface of the earth covered with water; but since there are a multitude of islands, and continents, which interrupt the natural course of the water, a variety of appearances are to be met with in different places, which cannot be explained without regarding the situation of shores, straits, and other objects, which have a share in producing them.

There are frequently streams or currents in the Ocean, which set ships a great way beyond their intended course. There is a current between Florida and the Bahama Islands, which always runs from north to south. A current runs constantly from the Atlantic, through the straits of Gibraltar into the Mediterranean. A current sets out of the Baltic sea, through the Sound or strait between Sweden and Denmark, into the British channel, so that there are no tides in the Baltic. About small islands and head lands in the middle of the ocean, the tides rise very little, but in some bays, and about the mouths of rivers, they rise from 12 to 50 feet.

MAPS.] A map is the representation of the earth, or a part thereof, on a plane surface. Maps differ from the Globe in the same manner as a picture does from a statue. The Globe truly represents the earth, but a map no more than a plane surface can represent one that is spherical. But although the earth can never be exhibited exactly by one map, yet, by means of several of them, each containing about ten or twenty degrees of latitude, the representation will not fall very much short of the globe for exactness; because such maps, if joined together, would form a spherical convex nearly as round as the globe itself.

CARDINAL POINTS.] The north is considered as the upper part of the map; the south is at the bottom, opposite to the north; the east is on the right hand, the face being turned to the north; and the west on the left hand, opposite to the east. From the top to the bottom are drawn meridians, or lines of longitude; and from side to side, parallels of latitude. The outermost of the meridians and parallels are marked with degrees of latitude and longitude, by means of which, and the scale of miles commonly placed in the corner of the map, the situation, distances, &c. of places, may be found, as on the artificial globe. Thus to find the distance of two places, suppose London and Paris, by the map, we have only to measure the space between them with the compasses or a bit of thread, and to apply this distance to the scale of miles, which shews that London is 210 miles distant from Paris. If the places lie directly north or south, east or west from one another, we have only to observe the degrees on the meridians and parallels, and by turning these into miles, we obtain the distance without measuring.

INTRODUCTION.   45

measuring. Rivers are described in maps by black lines, and are wider towards the mouth than towards the head or spring. Mountains are sketched on maps as on a picture. Forests and woods are represented by a kind of shrub; bogs amd morasses, by shades; sands and shallows are described by small dots; and roads usually by double lines. Near harbours, the depth of the water is expressed by figures representing fathoms.

LENGTH OF MILES IN DIFFERENT COUNTRIES.] There is scarce a greater variety in any thing than this sort of measures; not only those of separate countries differ, as the French from the English, but those of the same country vary, in the different provinces, and all commonly from the standard. Thus the common English mile differs from the statute mile, and the French have three sorts of leagues. We shall here give the miles of several countries compared with the English by Dr. Halley.

The English statute mile consists of 5280 feet, 1760 yards, or 8 furlongs.

The Russian vorst is little more than ¾ English.

The Turkish, Italian, and old Roman leller mile is nearly 1 English.

The Arabian, antient and modern, is about 1¼ English.

The Scotch and Irish Mile is about 1½ English.

The Indian is almost 3 English.

The Dutch, Spanish, and Polish, is about 3½ English.

The German is more than 4 English.

The Swedish, Danish, and Hungarian, is from 5 to 6 English.

The French common League is near 3 English, and

The English marine League is 3 English miles.

PART II.
OF THE ORIGIN OF NATIONS, LAWS, GOVERNMENT, AND COMMERCE.

HAVING, in the following work, mentioned the antient names of countries, and even sometimes, in speaking of these countries, carried our historical researches beyond modern times; it was thought necessary, in order to prepare the reader for entering upon the particular history of each country we describe, to place before his eye a general view of the history of mankind, from the first ages of the world, to the reformation in religion during the 16th century. By a history of the world, we do not mean a mere list of dates, which, when taken by itself, is a thing extremely insignificant; but an account of the most interesting and important events

which

which have happened among mankind; with the causes which have produced, and the effects which have followed from them. This we judge to be a matter of high importance in itself, and indispensibly requisite to the understanding of the present state of commerce, government, arts, and manners, in any particular country; which may be called commercial and political geography, and which, undoubtedly, constitutes the most useful branch of that science.

It appears in general, from the first chapters of Genesis, that the world, before the flood, was extremely populous, that mankind had made considerable improvement in the arts, and were become highly licentious in their morals and behaviour. Their irregularity gave occasion to a memorable catastrophe, by which the whole human race, except Noah and his family, were swept from off the face of the earth.

<small>Before Ch. 3044.</small>

The deluge produced a very considerable change on the soil and atmosphere of this globe, and gave them a form less friendly to the frame and texture of the human body. Hence the abridgment of the life of man, and that formidable train of diseases which hath ever since made such havock in the world. A curious part of history follows that of the deluge, the repeopling of the world, and the rising of a new generation from the ruins of the former. The memory of the three sons of Noah, the first founders of nations, was long preserved among their several descendants. Japhet continued famous among the western nations under the celebrated name of Japetus; the Hebrews paid an equal veneration to Shem, who was the founder of their race; and among the Egyptians, Ham was long revered as a divinity, under the name of Jupiter-Hammon. It appears that hunting was the principal occupation some centuries after the deluge. The world teemed with wild beasts, and the great heroism of those times consisted in destroying them. Hence Nimrod acquired immortal renown; and by the admiration which his courage and dexterity universally excited, was enabled to acquire an authority over his fellow creatures, and to found at Babylon the first monarchy, whose origin is particularly mentioned in history.

<small>2640.</small>

Not long after the foundation of Nineveh was laid by Assur; and in Egypt, the four governments of Thebes, Theri, Memphis, and Tanis, began to assume some appearance of form and regularity. That these events should have happened so soon after the deluge, whatever surprize it may have occasioned to the learned some centuries ago, need not in the smallest degree excite the wonder of the present age. We have seen, from many instances, the powerful effects of the principles of population, and how speedily mankind en-

creafe

crease when the generative faculty lies under no restraint. The kingdoms of Mexico and Peru were incomparably more extensive than those of Babylon, Nineveh and Egypt, during this early age; and yet these kingdoms are not supposed to have existed four centuries before the discovery of America by Columbus. As mankind continued to multiply on the earth, and to separate from each other, the tradition concerning the true God, was obliterated or obscured. This occasioned the calling of Abraham to be the father of a chosen people. From this period the history of antient nations begins a little to expand itself; and we learn several particulars of very considerable importance. 2026.

Mankind had not long been united into societies before they set themselves to oppress and destroy one another. Chaderlaomer, king of the Elamites, or Persians, was already become a robber and a conqueror. His force, however, must not have been very considerable, since, in one of these expeditions, Abraham, assisted only by his houshold, set upon him in his retreat, and after a fierce engagement, recovered all the spoil that had been taken. Abraham was soon after obliged, by a famine, to leave Canaan, the country where God had commanded him to settle, and to go into Egypt. This journey gives occasion to Moses to mention some particulars with regard to the Egyptians, and every stroke discovers the characters of an improved and powerful nation. The court of the Egyptian monarch is described in the most brilliant colours. He is surrounded with a crowd of courtiers, solely occupied in gratifying his passions. The particular governments into which this country was divided, are now united under one powerful prince; and Ham, who led the colony into Egypt, is become the founder of a mighty empire. We are not, however, to imagine that all the laws which took place in Egypt, and which have been so justly admired for their wisdom, were the work of this early age. Diodorus Siculus, a Greek writer, mentions many successive princes, who laboured for their establishment and perfection. But in the time of Jacob, the first principles of civil order and regular governments seem to have been tolerably understood among the Egyptians. The country was divided into several districts or separate departments; councils, composed of experienced and select persons, were established for the management of public affairs; granaries for preserving corn were erected; and, in fine, the Egyptians in this age, enjoyed a commerce far from inconsiderable. These facts, though of an ancient date, deserve our particular attention. It is from the Egyptians, that many of the arts, both of elegance and utility, have been handed down 1833.

in

in an uninterrupted chain to the modern nations of Europe. The Egyptians communicated their arts to the Greeks; the Greeks taught the Romans many improvements both in the arts of peace and war; and to the Romans, the prefent inhabitants of Europe are indebted for their civility and refinement. The kingdoms of Babylon and Nineveh remained feparate for feveral centuries; but we know not even the names of the kings who governed them, till the time of Ninus, king of Nineveh, who, by the fplendour of his actions, reflects light on this dark hiftory. Fired by the fpirit of conqueft, he extends the bounds of his kingdom, adds Babylon to his dominion, and lays the foundation of that monarchy which, under the name of the Affyrian empire, kept Afia under the yoke for many ages.

The hiftory of Europe now begins to dawn. Javan, fon of Japhet, and grandfon of Noah, is the ftock from whom all the people known by the name of Greeks are defcended. Javan eftablifhed himfelf in the iflands in the weftern coaft of Afia Minor, from whence it was impoffible that fome wanderers fhould not pafs over into Europe. To thefe firft inhabitants fucceeded a colony from Egypt, who, about the time of Abraham, penetrated into Greece, and, under the name of Titans, endeavoured to eftablifh monarchy in this country, and to introduce into it the laws and civil policy of the Egyptians. But the empire of the Titans foon fell afunder; and the antient Greeks, who were at this time the moft rude and barbarous people in the world, again fell back into their lawlefs and favage manner of life. Several colonies, however, foon after paffed over from Afia into Greece, and by remaining in that country, produced a more confiderable alteration on the manners of its inhabitants. The moft antient of thefe were the colonies of Inachus and Ogyges; of whom the former fettled in Argos, and the latter in Attica. We know extremely little of Ogyges or his fucceffors. Thofe of Inachus endeavoured to unite the difperfed and wandering Greeks; and their endeavours for this purpofe were not altogether unfuccefsful.

[2025.]

But the hiftory of God's chofen people, is the only one with which we are much acquainted during thofe ages. The train of curious events which occafioned the fettling of Jacob and his family in that part of Egypt of which Tanis was the capital, are univerfally known. That patriarch died, according to the Septuagint verfion, 1794 years before Chrift. This is a pretty remarkable æra with refpect to the nations of heathen antiquity, and concludes that period of time which the Greeks confidered as altogether unknown, and which they

[1794.]

they have hardly disfigured by their fabulous narrations. Let us view this period then in another point of view, and confider what we can learn from the facred writings, with refpect to the arts, manners and laws of antient nations.

It is a common error among writers on this fubject, to confider all the nations of antiquity as being on the fame footing with regard to thofe matters. They find fome nations extremely rude and barbarous, and hence they conclude that all were in that fituation. They difcover others acquainted with many arts, and hence they infer the wifdom of the firft ages. There appears, however, to have been as much difference between the inhabitants of the antient world, in points of art and refinement, as between the civilifed kingdoms of modern Europe and the Indians in America or Negroes on the coaft of Africa. Noah was, undoubtedly, acquainted with all the arts of the antediluvian world; thefe he would communicate to his children, and they again would hand them down to their pofterity. Thofe nations therefore who fettled neareft the original feat of mankind, and who had the beft opportunities to avail themfelves of the knowledge which their great anceftor was poffeffed of, early formed themfelves into regular focieties, and made confiderable improvements in the arts which are moft fubfervient to human life. Agriculture appears to have been known in the firft ages of the world. Noah cultivated the vine; in the time of Jacob, the fig-tree and the almond were well known in the land of Canaan; and the inftruments of hufbandry, long before the difcovery of them in Greece, are often mentioned in the facred writings. It is hardly to be fuppofed that the antient cities, both in Afia and Egypt, whofe foundation as we have already mentioned, afcends to the remoteft antiquity, could have been built, unlefs the culture of the ground had been practifed at that time. Nations who live by hunting or pafturage only, lead a wandering life, and feldom fix their refidence in cities. Commerce naturally follows agriculture; and though we cannot trace the fteps by which it was introduced among the antient nations, we may, from detached paffages in facred writ, afcertain the progrefs which had been made in it during the patriarchal times. We know, from the hiftory of civil fociety, that the commercial intercourfe between men muft be pretty confiderable, before the metals come to be confidered as the medium of trade; and yet this was the cafe even in the days of Abraham. It appears, however, from the relations which eftablifh this fact, that the ufe of money had not been of an antient date; it had no mark to afcertain its weight or finenefs: and in a contract for a burying-place, in exchange for which Abram gave filver, the metal is weighed in presence of all the people. But as commerce improved, and bargains of this sort became more common, this practice went into disuse, and the quantity of silver was ascertained by a particular mark, which saved the trouble of weighing it. But this does not appear to have taken place till the time of Jacob, the second from Abram. The kesitah, of which we read in his time, was a piece of money, stamped with the figure of a lamb, and of a precise and stated value. It appears, from the history of Joseph, that the commerce between different nations was by this time regularly carried on. The Ismaelites and Medianites, who bought him of his brethren, were travelling merchants, resembling the modern caravans, who carried spices, perfumes, and other rich commodities, from their own country into Egypt. The same observations may be made from the book of Job, who, according to the best chronology, was a native of Arabia Felix, and cotemporary with Jacob. He speaks of the roads of Thema and Saba, i. e. of the caravans who set out from those cities of Arabia. If we reflect that the commodities of this country were rather the luxuries than the conveniences of life, we shall have reason to conclude, that the countries into which they were sent for sale, and particularly Egypt, were considerably improved in arts and refinement; for few people think of luxuries until the useful arts have made high advancements among them.

In speaking of commerce, we ought carefully to distinguish between the species of it which is carried on by land, or inland commerce, and that which is carried on by sea; which last kind of traffic is both later in its origin, and slower in its progress. Had the descendants of Noah been left to their own ingenuity, and received no tincture of the antediluvian knowledge from their wise ancestors, it is improbable they should have ventured on navigating the open seas so soon as we find they did. That branch of his posterity who settled on the coasts of Palestine, were the first people of the world among whom navigation was made subservient to commerce; they were distinguished by a word which in the Hebrew tongue signifies merchants, and are the same nation afterwards known to the Greeks by the name of Phenicians. Inhabiting a barren and ungrateful soil, they set themselves to better their situation by cultivating the arts. Commerce was their capital object; and with all the writers of pagan antiquity, they pass for the inventors of whatever is subservient to it. At the time of Abraham they were regarded as a powerful nation; their maritime commerce is mentioned by Jacob in his last words to his children: and if we may believe Herodotus in a matter of such remote antiquity, the Phenicians had by this time navigated

gated the coasts of Greece, and carried off the daughter of Inachus.

The arts of agriculture, commerce, and navigation, suppose the knowledge of several others ; astronomy, for instance, or a knowledge of the situation and revolutions of the heavenly bodies, is necessary both to agriculture and navigation ; that of working metals, to commerce ; and so of other arts. In fact, we find that before the death of Jacob, several nations were so well acquainted with the revolutions of the moon, as to measure by them the duration of their year. It had been an universal custom among all the nations of antiquity, as well as the Jews, to divide time into the portion of a week, or seven days : this undoubtedly arose from the tradition with regard to the origin of the world. It was natural for those nations who led a pastoral life, or who lived under a serene sky, to observe that the various appearances of the moon were compleated nearly in four weeks : hence the division of a month. Those people again who lived by agriculture, and who had got among them the division of the month, would naturally remark, that twelve of these brought back the same temperature of the air, or the same seasons : hence the origin of what is called the lunar year, which has every where taken place in the infancy of science. This, together with the observation of the fixed stars, which, as we learn from the book of Job, must have been very antient, naturally paved the way for the discovery of the solar year, which at that time would be thought an immense improvement in astronomy. But with regard to those branches of knowledge which we have mentioned, it is to be remembered that they were peculiar to the Egyptians and a few nations of Asia. Europe offers a frightful spectacle during this period. Who could believe that the Greeks, who in later ages became the patterns of politeness and every elegant art, were descended from a savage race of men, traversing the woods and wilds, inhabiting the rocks and caverns, a wretched prey to wild animals, and sometimes to one another. This, however, is no more than what was to be expected. The descendants of Noah, who removed at a great distance from the plains of Sennaar, lost all connection with the civilised part of mankind. Their posterity became still more ignorant; and the human mind was at length sunk into an abyss of misery and wretchedness.

We might naturally expect that, from the death of Jacob, and as we advance forward in time, the history of the great empires of Egypt and Assyria would emerge from their obscurity : this, however, is far from being the case ; we only get a glimpse of them, and they disappear intirely for many ages. After the reign of Ninius, who succeeded Ninus in the Assyrian throne, we find an astonishing blank in 2122.

the history of this empire for no less than eight hundred years. The silence of antient history on this subject is commonly attributed to the softness and effeminacy of the successors of Ninus, whose lives afforded no events worthy of narration. Wars and commotions are the great themes of the historian, while the gentle and happy reigns of a wise prince pass unobserved and unrecorded. Sesostris, a prince of wonderful abilities, is supposed about this time to have mounted the throne of Egypt. By his assiduity and attention, the civil and military establishments of the Egyptians received very considerable improvements. Egypt, in the time of Sesostris and his immediate successors, was in all probability the most powerful kingdom upon earth, and according to the best calculation is supposed to have contained twenty-seven millions of inhabitants. But antient history often excites, without gratifying our curiosity; for from the reign of Sesostris to that of Boccharis, we know not even the names of the intermediate princes. If we judge, however, from collateral circumstances, the country must still have continued in a very flourishing condition, for Egypt continued to pour forth her colonies into distant nations. Athens, that seat of learning and politeness, that school for all who aspire after wisdom, owes its foundation to Cecrops, who landed in Greece, with an Egyptian colony, and endeavoured to civilise the rough manners of the original inhabitants. From the institutions which Cecrops established among the Athenians, it is easy to infer in what situations they must have lived before his arrival. The laws of marriage, which few nations are so barbarous as to be altogether unacquainted with, were not known in Greece. Mankind, like the beasts of the field, were propagated by accidental rencounters, and without all knowledge of those to whom they owed their generation. Cranaus, who succeeded Cecrops in the kingdom of Attica, pursued the same beneficial plan, and endeavoured, by wise institutions, to bridle the keen passions of a rude people.

2341.

760.

1582.

1532.

Whilst these princes used their endeavours for civilising this corner of Greece, the other kingdoms, into which this country, by the natural boundaries of rocks, mountains, and rivers, is divided, and which had been already peopled by colonies from Egypt and the East, began to assume some appearance of form and regularity. This engaged Amphiction, one of those uncommon geniusses who appear in the world for the benefit of the age in which they live and the admiration of posterity, to think of some expedient by which he might unite in one plan of politicks the several independent kingdoms of Greece, and thereby deliver them from those intestine divisions which

1522.

which muſt render them a prey to one another, or to the firſt enemy who might think proper to invade them. Theſe reflections he communicated to the kings or leaders of the different territories, and by his eloquence and addreſs engaged twelve cities to unite together for their mutual preſervation. Two deputies from each of theſe cities aſſembled twice a year at Thermopylæ, and formed what, after the name of its founder, was called the Amphictionic Council. In this aſſembly, whatever related to the general intereſt of the confederacy was diſcuſſed and finally determined. Amphiction likewiſe, ſenſible that thoſe political connections are the moſt laſting which are ſtrengthened by religion, committed to the Amphictions the care of the temple at Delphi, and of the riches which, from the dedications of thoſe who conſulted the oracle, had been amaſſed in it. This aſſembly, conſtituted on ſuch ſolid foundations, was the great ſpring of action in Greece, while that country preſerved its independence; and by the union which it inſpired among the Greeks, enabled them to defend their liberties againſt all the force of the Perſian empire.

Conſidering the circumſtances of the age in which it was inſtituted, the Amphictionic council is perhaps the moſt remarkable political eſtabliſhment which ever took place among mankind. The Greek ſtates, who formerly had no connection with one another, except by mutual inroads and hoſtilities, ſoon began to act with concert, and to undertake diſtant expeditions for the general intereſt of the community. The firſt of theſe was the obſcure expedition of the Argonauts, in which all Greece appears to have been concerned. The 1292. object of the Argonauts was to open the commerce of the Euxine Sea, and to eſtabliſh colonies in the adjacent country of Colchis. The ſhip Argo, which was the admiral of the fleet, is the only one particularly taken notice of; though we learn from Homer, and other antient writers, that ſeveral ſail were employed in this expedition. The fleet of the Argonauts was, from the ignorance of thoſe who conducted it, long toſſed about upon different coaſts. The rocks, at ſome diſtance from the mouth of the Euxine ſea, occaſioned great labour: they ſent forward a light veſſel, which paſſed through, but returned with the loſs of her rudder. This is expreſſed in the fabulous language of antiquity, by their ſending out a bird which returned with the loſs of its tail, and may give us an idea of the allegorical obſcurity in which the other events of this expedition are involved. The fleet, however, at length arrived at Æon, the capital of Colchis, after performing a voyage, which, conſidering the mean condition of the naval art during this age, was not leſs conſiderable than the circumnavigation

navigation of the world by our modern discoverers. From this expedition, to that against Troy, which was undertaken to recover the fair Helena, a queen of Sparta, who had been carried off by Paris, son of the Trojan king, the Greeks must have made a wonderful progress in power and opulence: no less than twelve hundred vessels were employed in this voyage, each of which, at a medium, contained upwards of a hundred men. These vessels, however, were but half decked; and it does not appear that iron entered at all into their construction. If we add to these circumstances, that the Greeks had not the use of the saw, an instrument so necessary to the carpenter, a modern must form but a mean notion of the strength or elegance of this fleet.

1218.

Having thus considered the state of Greece as a whole, let us examine the circumstances of the particular countries into which it was divided. This is of great importance to our present undertaking, because it is in this country only that we can trace the origin and progress of government, arts, and manners, which compose so great a part of our present work. There appears originally to have been a very remarkable resemblance between the political situation of the different kingdoms of Greece. They were governed each by a king, or rather a chieftain, who was their leader in time of war, their judge in time of peace, and who presided in the administration of their religious ceremonies. This prince, however, was far from being absolute. In each society there were a number of other leaders, whose influence over their particular clans or tribes was not less considerable than that of the king over his immediate followers. These captains were often at war with one another, and sometimes with their sovereign. Such a situation was in all respects extremely unfavourable: each particular state was in miniature what the whole country had been before the time of Amphiction. They required the hand of another delicate painter to shade the opposite colours, and to enable them to produce one powerful effect. The history of Athens affords us an example of the manner in which these states, which, for want of union, were weak and insignificant, became, by being cemented together, important and powerful. Theseus, king of Attica, had acquired a flourishing reputation by his exploits of valour and ability. He saw the inconveniencies to which his country, from being divided into twelve districts, was exposed, and he conceived that by means of the influence which his personal character, united to the royal authority with which he was invested, had universally procured him, he might be able to remove them. For this purpose he endeavoured to maintain, and

1260.

1257.

even

INTRODUCTION.

even to encrease his popularity among the peasants and artisans: he detached, as much as possible, the different tribes from the leaders who commanded them: he abolished the courts which had been established in different parts of Attica, and appointed one council-hall common to all the Athenians. Theseus, however, did not trust solely to the force of political regulations. He called to his aid all the power of religious prejudices; by establishing common rites of religion to be performed in Athens, and by inviting thither strangers from all quarters, by the prospect of protection and privileges, he raised this city from an inconsiderable village to a powerful metropolis. The splendor of Athens and Theseus now totally eclipsed that of the other villages and their particular leaders. All the power of the state was united in one city, and under one sovereign. The petty chieftains, who had formerly occasioned so much confusion, by being divested of all influence and consideration, became humble and submissive; and Attica remained under the peaceable government of a monarch.

This is a rude sketch of the origin of the first monarchy, of which we have a distinct account, and may, without much variation, be applied to the other states of Greece. This country, however, was not destined to continue long under the government of kings. A new influence arose, which in a short time proved too powerful both for the king and the nobles. Theseus had divided the Athenians into three distinct classes; the nobles, the artisans, and the husbandmen. In order to abridge the exorbitant power of the nobles, he had bestowed many privileges on the two other ranks of persons. This plan of politicks was followed by his successors; and the lower ranks of the Athenians, partly from the countenance of their sovereign, and partly from the progress of arts and manufactures, which gave them an opportunity of acquiring property, became considerable and independent. These circumstances were attended with a remarkable effect. 1095.

Upon the death of Codrus, a prince of great merit, the Athenians, become weary of the regal authority, under pretence of finding no one worthy of filling the throne of that monarch, who had devoted himself to death for the safety of his people, abolished the regal power, and proclaimed that none but Jupiter should be king of Athens. This revolution in favour of liberty was so much the more remarkable, as it happened almost at the same time that the Jews became unwilling to remain under the government of the true God, and desired a mortal sovereign, that they might be like unto other nations. 1079.

The government of Thebes, another of the Grecian states, much about the same time, assumed the republican form.

INTRODUCTION.

Near a century before the Trojan war, Cadmus, with a colony from Phenicia, had founded this city, which from that time had been governed by kings. But the last sovereign being overcome in single combat, by a neighbouring prince, the Thebans abolished the regal power. Till the days, however, of Pelopidas and Epaminondas, a period of seven hundred years, the Thebans performed nothing worthy of the republican spirit. Other cities of Greece, after the examples of Thebes and Athens, erected themselves into republics. But the revolutions of Athens and Sparta, two rival states, which by means of the superiority they acquired, gave the tone to the manners, genius, and politicks of the Greeks, deserve our principal attention. We have seen a tender shoot of liberty spring up in the city of Athens, upon the decease of Codrus, its last sovereign. This shoot gradually improved into a vigorous plant; and it cannot but be pleasant to observe its progress. The Athenians, by abolishing the name of king, did not intirely subvert the legal authority: they established a perpetual magistrate, who, under the name of Archon, was invested with almost the same rights which their kings had enjoyed. The Athenians, however, in time, became sensible that the archonic office was too lively an image of royalty for a free state. After it had continued therefore three hundred and thirty-one years in the family of Codrus, they endeavoured to lessen its dignity, not by abridging its power, but by shortening its duration. The first period assigned for the continuance of the archonship in the same hands, was three years. But the desire of the Athenians for a more perfect system of freedom than had hitherto been established, increased in proportion to the liberty they enjoyed. They again called out for a fresh reduction of the power of their archons; and it was at length determined that nine annual magistrates should be appointed for this office. These magistrates were not only chosen by the people, but accountable to them for their conduct at the expiration of their office. These alterations were too violent not to be attended with some dangerous consequences. The Athenians, intoxicated with their freedom, broke out into the most unruly and licentious behaviour. No written laws had been as yet enacted in Athens, and it was impossible that the antient customs of the realm, which were naturally supposed to be in part abolished, by the successive changes in the government, should sufficiently restrain the tumultuary spirits of the Athenians, in the first flutter of their independance. This engaged the wiser part of the state, who began to prefer any system of government to their present anarchy and confusion, to cast their eyes on Draco, a man of

an

an austere but virtuous disposition, as the fittest person for composing a system of law, to bridle the furious and unruly manners of their countrymen. Draco undertook the office, but executed it with so much rigour, that in the words of an ancient historian, "His laws were written with blood, and not with ink." Death was the indiscriminate punishment of every offence, and the laws of Draco were found to be a remedy worse than the disease. Affairs again returned into confusion and disorder, and remained so till the time of Solon. The gentle manners, disinterested virtue, and wisdom more than human, by which this sage was distinguished, pointed him out as the only character adapted to the most important of all offices, the giving laws to a free people. Solon, though this employment was assigned him by the unanimous voice of his country, long deliberated whether he should undertake it. At length, however, the motives of public utility overcame all considerations of private ease, safety, and reputation, and determined him to enter on an ocean pregnant with a thousand dangers. The first step of his legislation was to abolish all the laws of Draco, except those relating to murder. The punishment of this crime could not be too great; but to consider other offences as equally criminal, was to confound all notions of right and wrong, and to render the law ineffectual, by means of its severity. Solon next proceeded to new model the political law; and his establishments on this head, remained among the Athenians, while they preserved their liberties. He seems to have set out with this principle, that a perfect republic, in which each citizen should have an equal political importance, was a system of government, beautiful indeed in theory, but not reducible into practice. He divided the citizens therefore into four classes, according to the wealth which they possessed, and the poorest class he rendered altogether uncapable of any public office. They had a voice however in the general council of the nation, in which all matters of principal concern were determined in the last resort. But lest this assembly, which was composed of all the citizens, should in the words of Plutarch, like a ship with too many sails, be exposed to the gust of folly, tumult, and disorder, he provided for its safety by the two anchors of the Senate and Areopagus. The first of these courts consisted of four hundred persons, a hundred out of each tribe of the Athenians, who prepared all important bills that came before the assembly of the people; the second, though but a court of justice, gained a prodigious ascendant in the republic, by the wisdom and gravity of its members, who were not chosen, but after the strictest scrutiny, and most serious deliberation.

594.

Such

Such was the fyftem of government eftablifhed by Solon, which, the nearer we examine it, will afford the more matter for our admiration. Upon the fame plan moft of the other antient republicks were eftablifhed. To infift on all of them, therefore, would neither be entertaining nor inftructive. But the government of Sparta, or Lacedemon, had fomething in it fo peculiar, that the great lines of it at leaft ought not to be omitted even in a delineation of this fort. Sparta, like the other ftates of Greece, was originally divided into a number of petty principalities, of which each was under the jurifdiction of its own immediate chieftain. At length, the two
1072. brothers Eurifthenes and Proiles, getting poffeffion of this country, became conjunct in the royalty; and what is extremely fingular, their pofterity, in the direct line, continued to rule conjunctly for nine hundred years. The Spartan government, however, did not take that fingular form
870. which renders it fo remarkable, until the time of Lycurgus, the celebrated legiflator. The plan of policy devifed by Lycurgus, agreed with that already defcribed, in comprehending a fenate and affembly of the people, and in general in all thofe eftablifhments which are deemed moft requifite for the fecurity of political independance. It differed from that of Athens, and indeed from all other governments, in having two kings, whofe office was hereditary, though their power was fufficiently circumfcribed by proper checks and reftraints. But the great characteriftic of the Spartan conftitution arofe from this, that in all his laws, Lycurgus had at leaft as much refpect to war, as to political liberty. With this view, all forts of luxury, all arts of elegance or entertainment, every thing, in fhort, which had the fmalleft tendency to foften the minds of the Spartans, was abfolutely profcribed. They were forbid the ufe of money, they lived at public tables on the coarfeft fare, the younger were taught to pay the utmoft reverence to the more advanced in years, and all ranks capable to bear arms, were daily accuftomed to the moft painful exercifes. To the Spartans alone war was a relaxation, rather than a hardfhip, and they behaved in it with a fpirit of which none but a Spartan could even form a conception. In order to fee the effect of thefe principles, and to connect under one point of view the hiftory of the different quarters of the globe, we muft caft our eye on Afia, and obferve the events which happened in thofe great empires, of which we have fo long loft fight. We have already mentioned in what obfcurity
762. the hiftory of Egypt is involved, until the reign of Bac-
528. charis. From this period, to the diffolution of their government, the Egyptians are more celebrated for the wifdom

INTRODUCTION.

dom of their laws, and political inftitutions, than for the power of their arms. Several of thefe feem to have been dictated by the true fpirit of civil wifdom, and were admirably calculated for preferving order and good government in an extenfive kingdom. The great empire of Affyria likewife, which had fo long difappeared, becomes again an object of attention, and affords the firft inftance we meet with in hiftory, of a kingdom which fell afunder by its own weight, and the effeminate weaknefs of its fovereigns. Sardanapulus, the laft emperor of Affyria, neglecting the adminiftration of affairs, and fhutting himfelf up in his palace with his women and eunuchs, fell into contempt with his fubjects. The governors of his provinces, to whom, like a weak and indolent prince, he had entirely committed the command of his armies, did not fail to lay hold of this opportunity of raifing their own fortune on the ruins of their mafter's power. Arbaces, governor of Media, and Belefis, governor of Babylon, confpire againft their fovereign, fet fire to his capital, and divide between them his extenfive dominions. Thefe two kingdoms, fometimes united under one prince, and fometimes governed each by a particular fovereign, maintained the chief fway in Afia, till Cyrus the Great reduced this quarter of the world under the Perfian yoke. The manners of this people as brave, hardy, and independent, as well as the government of Cyrus, in all its various departments, are elegantly defcribed by Xenophon, a Grecian philofopher and hiftorian. It is not neceffary, however, that we fhould enter on the fame detail upon this fubject, as with regard to the affairs of the Greeks. We have, in modern times, fufficient examples of monarchical government; but how few are our republics? But the æra of Cyrus is in one refpect extremely remarkable, becaufe with it the hiftory of the great nations of antiquity, which has hitherto engaged our attention, may be fuppofed to finifh. Let us confider then the genius of the Affyrians, Babylonians, and Egyptians, in arts and fciences, and if poffible difcover what progrefs they had made in thofe acquirements, which are moft fubfervient to the interefts of fociety.

767.

536.

The tafte for the great and magnificent, feems to have been the prevailing character of thefe nations; and they principally difplayed it in their works of architecture. There are no veftiges, however, now remaining, which confirm the teftimony of ancient writers, with regard to the great works, which adorned Babylon and Nineveh: neither is it clearly determined in what year they were begun or finifhed. There are three pyramids ftill remaining in Egypt, at fome leagues diftance

from

from Cairo, which are supposed to have been the burying places of the antient Egyptian kings. The largest is five hundred feet in height, and two thousand six hundred and forty broad each way at bottom. It was a superstition among this people, derived from the earliest times, that even after death, the soul continued in the body as long as it remained uncorrupted. Hence proceeded the custom of embalming, or of throwing into the dead body, such vegetables as experience had discovered to be the greatest preservatives against putrefaction. The pyramids were erected with the same view. In them the bodies of the Egyptian kings were concealed. This expedient, together with embalming, as these superstitious monarchs conceived, would inevitably secure a safe, and comfortable retreat for their souls after death. From what we read of the walls of Babylon, the temple of Belus, and other works of the east, and from what travellers have recorded of the pyramids, it appears that indeed they were superb and magnificent structures, but totally devoid of elegance. The orders of architecture were not yet known, nor even the constructing of vaults. The arts, in which these nations, next to architecture, principally excelled, were sculpture and embroidery. As to the sciences, they had all along continued to bestow their principal attention on astronomy. It does not appear, however, that they made great progress in explaining the causes of the phenomena of the universe, or indeed in any species of rational and sound philosophy. To demonstrate this to an intelligent reader, it is sufficient to observe, that according to the testimony of sacred and profane writers, the absurd reveries of magic and astrology, which always decrease in proportion to the advancement of true science, were in high esteem among them, during the latest periods of their government. The countries which they occupied, were extremely fruitful, and afforded without much labour all the necessaries, and even luxuries of life. They had long been accustomed to a civilized and polished life in great cities. These circumstances had tainted their manners with effeminacy and corruption, and rendered them an easy prey to the Persians, a nation just emerging from barbarity, and of consequence, brave and warlike. This was still more easy in the infancy of the military art: when strength and courage were the only circumstances which gave the advantage to one nation over another, when, properly speaking, there were no fortified places, which in modern times have been discovered to be so useful in stopping the progress of a victorious enemy, and when the event of a battle commonly decided the fate of an empire. But we must now turn our attention to other objects.

INTRODUCTION. 61

The history of Persia, after the reign of Cyrus, offers little, when considered in itself, that merits our regard: but when combined with that of Greece, it becomes particularly interesting. The monarchs who succeeded Cyrus, gave an opportunity to the Greeks to exercise those virtues, which the freedom of their government had created and confirmed. Sparta remained under the influence of Lycurgus's institutions: Athens had just recovered from the tyranny of the Pisistratidæ, a family who had trampled on the laws of Solon, and usurped the supreme power. Such was their situation, when the lust of universal empire, which never fails to torment the breast of tyrants, led Darius to send forth his numerous armies into Greece. But the Persians were no longer those invincible soldiers, who under Cyrus had conquered Asia. Their minds were enervated by luxury and servitude. Athens, on the contrary, teemed with great men, whose minds were nobly animated by the late recovery of their freedom. Miltiades, in the plains of Marathon, with ten thousand Athenians, overcame the Persian army of a hundred thousand foot, and ten thousand cavalry. His countrymen, Themistocles and Aristides, the first celebrated for his abilities, the second for his virtue, gained the next honours to the general. It does not, however, fall within our plan to mention the events of this war, which, as the noblest monuments of virtue over force, of courage over numbers, of liberty over servitude, deserve to be read at length in antient writers.

520.

Xerxes, the son of Darius, came in person into Greece, with two million one hundred thousand men, and being every where defeated by sea and land, escaped to Asia in a fishing boat. Such was the spirit of the Greeks, so well did they know that " wanting virtue, life is pain and " woe, that wanting liberty, even virtue mourns, and looks " around for happiness in vain." Though the Persian war concluded gloriously for the Greeks, it is, in a great measure, to this war, that the subsequent misfortunes of that nation are to be attributed. It was not the battles in which they suffered the loss of so many brave men, but those in which they acquired an immensity of Persian gold; it was not their enduring so many hardships in the course of the war, but their connection with the Persians, after the conclusion of it, which subverted the Grecian establishments, and ruined the most virtuous confederacy that ever existed upon earth. The Greeks became haughty after their victories: delivered from the common enemy, they began to quarrel with one another: their quarrels were fomented by Persian gold, of which they had acquired enough to make them desirous of more. Hence proceeded

484.

463.

ceeded the famous Peloponnesian war, in which the Athenians and Lacedemonians acted as principals, and drew after them the other states of Greece. They continued to weaken themselves by these intestine divisions, till Philip, king of Macedon, (a country till his time little known, but which, by the active and crafty genius of this prince, became important and powerful) rendered himself the absolute master of Greece, by the battle of Cheronæa. But this conquest is one of the first we meet in history, which did not depend on the event of a battle. Philip had laid his schemes so deep, and by bribery, promises and intrigues, gained over such a number of considerable persons in the several states of Greece to his interest, that another day would have put in his possession what Cheronæa had denied him. The Greeks had lost that virtue, which was the basis of their confederacy. Their popular governments served only to give a sanction to their licentiousness and corruption. The principal orators, in most of their states, were bribed into the service of Philip; and all the eloquence of a Demosthenes, assisted by truth and virtue, was unequal to the mean, but more seductive arts of his opponents, who, by flattering the people, used the surest method of winning their affections.

Philip had proposed to extend the boundaries of his empire beyond the narrow limits of Greece. But he did not long survive the battle of Cheronæa. Upon his decease, his son Alexander was chosen general against the Persians, by all the Grecian states, except the Athenians and Thebans. These made a feeble effort for expiring liberty. But they were obliged to yield to superior force. Secure on the side of Greece, Alexander set out on his Persian expedition, at the head of thirty thousand foot, and five thousand horse. The success of this army in conquering the whole force of Darius, in three pitched battles, in overrunning and subduing not only the countries then known to the Greeks, but many parts of India, the very names of which had never reached an European ear, has been described by many authors both antient and modern, and constitutes a singular part of the history of the world. Soon after this rapid career of victory and success, Alexander died at Babylon. His captains, after sacrificing all his family to their ambition, divided among them his dominions. This gives rise to a number of æras and events, too complicated for our present purpose, and even too uninteresting. After considering therefore the state of arts and sciences in Greece, we shall pass over to the Roman affairs, where the historical deduction is more simple, and also more important.

The bare names of illustrious men, who flourished in Greece, from the time of Cyrus to that of Alexander, would fill a large volume. During this period, all the arts were carried to the highest pitch of perfection; and the improvements we have hitherto mentioned, were but the dawnings of this glorious day. Though the eastern nations had raised magnificent and stupendous structures, the Greeks were the first people in the world, who in their works of architecture, added beauty to magnificence, and elegance to grandeur. The temples of Jupiter Olympus, and the Ephesian Diana, are the first monuments of good taste. They were erected by the Grecian colonies, who settled in Asia Minor, before the reign of Cyrus. Phidias, the Athenian, is the first sculptor whose works have been immortal. Zeuxis Parrhasius and Timantheus, during the same age, first discovered the power of the pencil, and all the magic of painting. Composition, in all its various branches, reached a degree of perfection in the Greek language, of which a modern reader can hardly form an idea. After Homer, the tragic poets Æschylus, Sophocles, and Euripides, were the first considerable improvers of poetry. Herodotus gave simplicity and elegance to prosaic writing. Isocrates gave it cadence and harmony, but it was left to Thucydides and Demosthenes, to discover the full force of the Greek tongue. It was not however in the finer arts alone that the Greeks excelled. Every species of philosophy was cultivated among them with the utmost success. Not to mention the divine Socrates, whose character has had the honour to be compared with that of the great founder of our religion; his three disciples, Plato, Aristotle, and Xenophon, may for strength of reasoning, justness of sentiment, and propriety of expression, be put on a footing with the writers of any age or country. Experience, indeed, in a long course of years, has taught us many secrets in nature, with which these philosophers were unacquainted, and which no strength of genius could divine. But whatever some vain empirics in learning may pretend, the most learned and ingenious men, both in France and in England, have acknowledged the superiority of the Greek philosophers, and have reckoned themselves happy in catching their turn of thinking, and manner of expression. But the Greeks were not less distinguished for their active than for their speculative talents. It would be endless to recount the names of their famous statesmen and warriors, and it is impossible to mention a few without doing injustice to a greater number. War was first reduced into a science by the Greeks. Their soldiers fought from an affection to their country, and an ardor for glory, and not from a

dread

dread of their superiors. We have seen the effect of this military virtue in their wars against the Persians: the cause of it was the wise laws which Amphiction, Solon, and Lycurgus, had established in Greece. But we must now leave this nation, whose history, both civil and philosophical, is as important, as their territory was inconsiderable, and turn our attention to the Roman affairs, which are still more interesting, both on their own account, and from the relation in which they stand to those of modern Europe.

753. The character of Romulus, the founder of the Roman state, when we view him as the leader of a few lawless and wandering banditti, is an object of extreme insignificance. But when we consider him as the founder of an empire as extensive as the world, and whose progress and decline have occasioned the two greatest revolutions, that ever happened in Europe, we cannot help being interested in his conduct. His disposition was extremely martial; and the political state of Italy, divided into a number of small, but independent districts, afforded a noble field for the display of military talents. Romulus was continually embroiled with one or other of his neighbours, and war was the only employment by which he and his companions expected not only to aggrandize themselves, but even to subsist. In the conduct of his wars with the neighbouring people, we may observe the same maxims by which the Romans afterwards became masters of the world. Instead of destroying the nations he had subjected, he united them to the Roman state, whereby Rome acquired a new accession of strength from every war she undertook, and became powerful and populous from that very circumstance which ruins and depopulates other kingdoms. If the enemies, with which he contended, had, by means of the art or arms they employed, any considerable advantage, Romulus immediately adopted that practice, or the use of that weapon, and improved the military system of the Romans, by the united experience of all their enemies. We have an example of both these maxims, by means of which the Roman state arrived at such a pitch of grandeur, in the war with the Sabines. Romulus having conquered that nation, not only united them to the Romans, but finding their buckler preferable to the Roman, instantly threw aside the latter, and made use of the Sabine buckler in fighting against other states. Romulus, though principally attached to war, did not altogether neglect the civil policy of his infant kingdom. He instituted what was called the Senate, a court originally composed of a hundred persons, distinguished for their wisdom and experience. He enacted laws for the administration of justice,

justice, and for bridling the fierce and unruly passions of his followers: and after a long reign spent in promoting the civil or military interests of his country, was, according to the best conjecture, treacherously put to death by the members of that senate, which he himself had instituted. 715.

The successors of Romulus were all very extraordinary personages. Numa, who came next to him, established the religious ceremonies of the Romans, and inspired them with that veneration for an oath, which was ever after the soul of their military discipline. Tullus Hostilius, Ancus Martius, Tarquinius Priscus, Servius Tullius, laboured each during his reign, for the grandeur of Rome. But Tarquinius Superbus, the seventh and last king, having obtained the crown by the execrable murder of his father-in-law Servius, continued to support it by the most cruel and infamous tyranny. This, together with the insolence of his son Sextus Tarquinius, who, by dishonouring Lucretia, a Roman lady, affronted the whole nation, occasioned the expulsion of the Tarquin family, and with it the dissolution of the regal government. As the Romans however were continually engaged in war, they found it necessary to have some officer invested with supreme authority, who might conduct them to the field, and regulate their military enterprizes. In the room of the kings therefore they appointed two annual magistrates called Consuls, who, without creating the same jealousy, succeeded to all the power of their sovereigns. This revolution was extremely favourable to the Roman grandeur. The consuls, who enjoyed but a temporary power, were desirous of signalizing their reign by some great action: each vied with those who had gone before him, and the Romans were daily led out against some new enemy. When we add to this, that the people, naturally warlike, were inspired to deeds of valour by every consideration which could excite them: that the citizens of Rome were all soldiers, and fought for their lands, their children, and their liberties, we need not be surprized, that they should, in the course of some centuries, extend their power all over Italy. 264.

The Romans, now secure at home, and finding no enemy to contend with, turn their eyes abroad, and meet with a powerful rival in the Carthaginians. This state had been founded on the coast of the Mediterranean in Africa, some time before Rome, by a colony of Phenicians, and, according to the practice of their mother country, they had cultivated commerce and naval greatness.

Carthage, in this design, had proved wonderfully successful. She now commanded both sides of the Mediterranean. Besides that

that of Africa, which she almost entirely possessed, she had extended herself on the Spanish side, through the streights. Thus mistress of the sea, and of commerce, she had seized on the islands of Corsica and Sardinia. Sicily had difficulty to defend itself; and the Romans were too nearly threatened not to take up arms. Hence a succession of hostilities between these rival states, known in history by the name of Punic wars, in which the Carthaginians, with all their wealth and power, were an unequal match for the Romans. Carthage was a powerful republic, when Rome was a truckling state; but she was now become corrupt and effeminate, while Rome was in the vigour of her political constitution. Carthage employed mercenaries to carry on her wars; Rome, as we have already mentioned, was composed of soldiers. The first war with Carthage taught the Romans the art of fighting on the sea, with which they had been hitherto unacquainted. A Carthaginian vessel was wrecked on their coast; they used it for a model, in three months fitted out a fleet, and the consul Duilius, who fought their first naval battle, was victorious. It is not to our purpose to mention all the transactions of these wars. The behaviour of Regulus, the Roman general, may give us an idea of the spirit which then animated this people. Being taken prisoner in Africa, he is sent back on his parole to negotiate a change of prisoners. He maintains in the senate, the propriety of that law, which cut off from those who suffered themselves to be taken, all hopes of being saved, and returns to a certain death.

264.

260.

255.

Neither was Carthage, though corrupted, deficient in great men. Of all the enemies the Romans ever had to contend with, Hannibal the Carthaginian, was the most inflexible and dangerous. His father Hamilcar had imbibed an extreme hatred against the Romans, and having settled the intestine troubles of his country, he took an early opportunity to inspire his son, though but nine years old, with his own sentiments. For this purpose he ordered a solemn sacrifice to be offered to Jupiter, and leading his son to the altar, asked him whether he was willing to attend him in his expedition against the Romans; the courageous boy, not only consented to go, but conjured his father by the gods present, to form him to victory, and teach him the art of conquering. That I will joyfully do, replied Hamilcar, and with all the care of a father who loves you, if you will swear upon the altars, to be an eternal enemy to the Romans. Hannibal readily complied, and the solemnity of the ceremony, and the sacredness of the oath, made such an impression upon his mind, as nothing

afterwards

afterwards could ever efface. Being appointed general at twenty-five years of age, he crosses the Ebro, the Pyrenees, and the Alps, and in a moment falls down upon Italy. The loss of four battles threatens the fall of Rome. Sicily sides with the conqueror. Hieronymus, king of Syracuse, declares against the Romans, and almost all Italy abandons them. In this extremity Rome owed its preservation to three great men. Fabius Maximus, despising popular clamour, and the military ardour of his countrymen, declines coming to an engagement. The strength of Rome has time to recover. Marcellus raises the siege of Nola, takes Syracuse, and revives the drooping spirits of his troops. The Romans admired the character of these great men, but saw something more divine in the young Scipio. The success of this young hero confirmed the popular opinion, that he was of divine extraction, and held converse with the gods. At the age of four and twenty, he flies into Spain, where both his father and uncle had lost their lives, attacks New Carthage, and carries it at the first assault. Upon his arrival in Africa, kings submit to him, Carthage trembles in her turn, and sees her armies defeated. Hannibal, sixteen years victorious, is in vain called home to defend his country. Carthage is rendered tributary, gives hostages, and engages never to enter upon a war, but with the consent of the Roman people. After the conquest of Carthage, Rome had inconsiderable wars but great victories; before this time its wars were great, and its victories inconsiderable. At this time the world was divided, as it were, into two parts; in the one fought the Romans and Carthaginians; the other was agitated by those quarrels which had lasted since the death of Alexander the Great. Their scene of action was Greece, Egypt, and the East. The states of Greece had once more disengaged themselves from a foreign yoke. They were divided into three confederacies, the Etolians, Acheans, and Beotians; each of these was an association of free cities, which had assemblies and magistrates in common. Of them all the Etolians were the most considerable. The kings of Macedon maintained that superiority, which, in ancient times, when the balance of power was little attended to, a great prince naturally possessed over his less powerful neighbours. Philip, the present monarch, had rendered himself odious to the Greeks, by some unpopular and tyrannical steps; the Etolians were most irritated; and hearing the fame of the Roman arms, called them into Greece, and overcame Philip by their assistance. The victory, however, chiefly redounded to the advantage of the Romans. The Macedonian garrisons were

220.

212.

210.

202.

obliged

obliged to evacuate Greece; the cities were all declared free; but Philip became a tributary to the Romans, and the states of Greece became their dependants. The Etolians, discovering their first error, endeavoured to remedy it by another still more dangerous to themselves, and more advantageous to the Romans. As they had called the Romans into Greece to defend them against Philip, they now called in Antiochus, king of Syria, to defend them against the Romans. The famous Hannibal too had recourse to the same prince, and who was at this time the most powerful monarch in the East, and the successor to the dominions of Alexander in Asia. But Antiochus did not follow his advice so much, as that of the Etolians; for instead of renewing the war in Italy, where Hannibal, from experience, judged the Romans to be most vulnerable, he landed in Greece with a small body of troops, and being overcome without difficulty, fled over into Asia. In this war the Romans made use of Philip, for conquering Antiochus, as they had before done of the Etolians for conquering Philip. They now pursue Antiochus, the last object of their resentment, into Asia, and having vanquished him by sea and land, compel him to submit to an infamous treaty.

182.

In these conquests the Romans still allowed the ancient inhabitants to possess their territory; they did not even change the form of government; the conquered nations became the allies of the Roman people, which however, under a specious name, concealed the most servile of all conditions, and inferred, that they should submit to whatever was required of them. When we reflect on these easy conquests, we have reason to be astonished at the resistance which the Romans met with from a barbarous prince, Mithridates king of Pontus. This monarch however had great resources. His kingdom, bordering on the inaccessible mountains of Caucasus, abounded in a race of men, whose minds were not enervated by pleasure, and whose bodies were firm and vigorous.

The different states of Greece and Asia, who now began to feel the weight of their yoke, but had not spirit to shake it off, were transported at finding a prince, who dared to shew himself an enemy to the Romans, and chearfully submitted to his protection. Mithridates, however, was compelled to yield to the superior star of the Romans. Vanquished successively by Sylla and Lucullus, he was at length subdued by Pompey, and stripped of his dominions and of his life. In Africa the Roman arms met with equal success. Marius, in conquering Jugurtha, made all secure in that quarter.

65.

105.

Even the barbarous nations beyond the Alps, began to feel the weight of the Roman arms. Gallia Narbonensis had
been

been reduced into a province. The Cimbri, Teutones, and other northern nations of Europe, broke into this part of the empire. The same Marius, whose name was so terrible in Africa, made the north of Europe to tremble. The Barbarians retired to their wilds and deserts, less formidable than the Roman legions. But while Rome conquered the world, there subsisted an internal war within her walls. This war had subsisted from the first periods of the government. Rome, after the expulsion of her kings, enjoyed but a nominal liberty. The descendents of the senators, who were distinguished by the name of Patricians, were invested with so many odious privileges, that the people felt their dependance, and became determined to shake it off. A thousand disputes on this subject arose betwixt them and the Patricians, which always terminated in favour of liberty.

121.

102.

These disputes, however, while the Romans preserved their virtue, were not attended with any dangerous consequences. The Patricians, who loved their country, chearfully parted with some of their privileges to satisfy the people; and the people, on the other hand, though they obtained laws, by which they might be admitted to enjoy the first offices of the state, and though they had the power of nomination, always named Patricians. But when the Romans, by the conquest of foreign nations, became acquainted with all their luxuries and refinements; when they became tainted with the effeminacy and corruption of the eastern courts, and sported with every thing just and honourable, in order to obtain them, the state, torn by the factions between its members, and without virtue on either side, to keep it together, became a prey to its own children. Hence the bloody seditions of the Gracchi, which paved the way for an inextinguishable hatred between the nobles and commons, and made it easy for any turbulent demagogue, to put them in action against each other. The love of their country was now no more than a specious name; the better sort were too wealthy and effeminate to submit to the rigours of military discipline, and the soldiers, composed of the dregs of the republic, were no longer citizens. They knew none but their commander; under his banner they fought and conquered and plundered, and for him they were ready to die. He might command them to embrue their hands in the blood of their country. They who knew no country but the camp, and no authority but that of their general, were ever ready to obey him. The multiplicity of the Roman conquests, however, which required their keeping on foot several armies at the same time, retarded the subversion of the republic. These armies were so many checks upon each other.

Had it not been for the soldiers of Sylla, Rome would have surrendered its liberty to the army of Marius.

 Julius Cæsar at length appears. By subduing the Gauls, he gained his country the most useful conquest it ever made.
58.
 Pompey, his only rival, is overcome in the plains of Pharsalia. Cæsar victorious appears in a moment all over
48.
the world, in Egypt, in Asia, in Mauritania, in Spain, in Gaul, and in Britain: conqueror on all sides, he is acknowledged master at Rome, and in the whole empire. Brutus and Cassius think to give Rome her liberty, by
43.
stabbing him in the senate house. But they only subject her to tyrants, who, without his clemency or abilities, were not inferior in ambition. The republic falls into the hands of Mark Anthony; young Cæsar Octavianus,
31.
nephew to Julius Cæsar, wrests it from him by the seafight at Actium; there is no Brutus nor Cassius, to put an end to his life. The friends of liberty have killed themselves in despair, and Octavius, under the name of Augustus, and title of emperor, remains the undisturbed master of the empire. During these civil commotions, the Romans still preserved the glory of their arms among distant nations, and while it was unknown who should be master at Rome, the Romans were without dispute the masters of the world; their military discipline and valour abolished all the remains of the Carthaginian, the Persian, the Greek, the Assyrian, and Macedonian glory, and they were now only a name. No sooner therefore was Octavius established on the throne, than embassadors from all quarters of the known world, crowd to make their submissions. Æthiopia sues for peace, the Parthians, who had been a most formidable enemy, court his friendship, the Indies seek his alliance, Pannonia acknowledges him, Germany dreads
24.
15.
him, and the Weser receives his laws. Victorious by
7.
sea and land, he shuts the temple of Janus. The whole earth lives in peace under his power, and Jesus Christ comes into the world.

 Having thus traced the progress of the Roman government, while it remained a republic, our plan obliges us to say a few words with regard to the arts, sciences, and manners of that people. During the first ages of the republic, the Romans lived in a total neglect, or rather contempt of all the elegant improvements of life. War, politicks, and agriculture were the only arts they studied, because they were the only arts they esteemed. But upon the downfal of Carthage, the Romans, having no enemy to dread from abroad, began to taste the sweets of security, and to cultivate the arts. Their progress however was not gradual as in the other countries we
have

have described. The conquest of Greece at once put them in possession of every thing most rare, curious or elegant. Asia, which was the next victim, offered all its stores, and the Romans, from the most simple people, speedily became acquainted with the arts, the luxuries, and refinements of the whole earth. Eloquence they had always cultivated as the high road to eminence and preferment. The orations of Cicero are only inferior to those of Demosthenes, which, according to all our ideas, are perfect productions. In poetry Virgil yields only to Homer, whose verse, like the prose of Demosthenes, is perfect and inimitable. Horace however, in his satires and epistles, had no model among the Greeks, and stands to this day unrivalled in that species of writing. In history the Romans can boast of Livy, who possesses all the natural ease of Herodotus, and is more descriptive, more eloquent, and sentimental. Tacitus indeed did not flourish in the Augustan age, but his works do himself the greatest honour, while they disgrace his country and human nature, whose corruption and vices he paints in the most striking colours. In philosophy, if we except the works of Cicero, and the system of the Greek philosopher Epicurus, described in the nervous poetry of Lucretius, the Romans, during the time of the republic, made not the least attempt. In tragedy, they never produced any thing excellent; and Terence, though remarkable for purity of style, wants that comica vis, or lively vein of humour, which distinguished the Greek comedians, and which distinguishes our Shakespeare.

We now return to our history, and are arrived at an æra, which presents us with a set of monsters, under the name of emperors, whose histories, a few excepted, disgrace human nature. They did not indeed abolish the forms of the Roman republic, though they extinguished its liberties, and while they were practising the most unwarrantable cruelties upon their subjects, they themselves were the slaves of their soldiers. They made the world tremble, while they in their turn trembled at the army. Rome, from the time of Augustus, became the most despotic empire that ever subsisted in Europe. To form an idea of their government, we need only recal to our mind the situation of Turkey at present. It is of no importance therefore to consider the character of the emperors, since they had no power but what arose from a mercenary standing army, nor to enter into a detail with regard to the transactions of the court, which were directed by that caprice, and cruelty and corruption, which universally prevail under a despotic government. When it is said that the Roman republic conquered the world, it is only meant of the civilized part of it, chiefly in Greece, Carthage, and Asia. A more difficult task still remained, for the emperors to subdue the barbarous nations of Europe; the Germans, the Gauls, the Britons, and even the remote corner of Scotland; for though these countries had been discovered, they were not effectually subdued by the Roman generals. These nations, though rude and ignorant, were brave and independent. It was rather from the superiority of their discipline than of their courage, that the Romans gained any advantage over them. The Roman wars, with the Germans, are describ'd by Tacitus, and from his accounts, though a Roman, it is easy to discover with what bravery they fought, and with what reluctance they submitted to a foreign yoke. From the obstinate resistance of the Germans, we may judge of the difficulties the Romans met with in subduing the other nations of Europe. The contests were on both sides bloody; the countries of Europe were successively laid waste, the inhabitants perished in the field, many were carried into slavery, and but a feeble remnant submitted to the Roman power. This situation of affairs was extremely unfavourable to the happiness of mankind. The barbarous nations, indeed, from their intercourse with the Romans, acquired some taste for the arts, sciences, language, and manners, of their new masters. These however were but miserable consolations for the loss of liberty, for being deprived of the use of their arms, for being over-awed by mercenary soldiers kept in pay to restrain them, and for being delivered over to rapacious governors, who plundered them without mercy. The only circumstance which could support them under these complicated calamities, was the hope of seeing better days.

The Roman empire, now stretched out to such an extent, had lost its spring and force. It contained within itself the seeds of dissolution; and the violent irruption of the Goths and Vandals, and other Barbarians, hastened its destruction. These fierce tribes, who came to take vengeance on the empire, either inhabited the various provinces of Germany, which had never been subdued by the Romans, or were scattered over the vast countries of the north of Europe, and north-west of Asia, which are now inhabited by the Danes, the Swedes, the Poles, the subjects of the Russian empire, and the Tartars. They were drawn from their native country, by that restlessness which actuates the minds of Barbarians, and makes them rove from home in quest of plunder, or new settlements. The first invaders met with a powerful resistance from the superior discipline of the Roman legions; but this, instead of daunting men of a strong and impetuous temper, only

INTRODUCTION. 73

only roused them to vengeance. They return to their companions, acquaint them with the unknown conveniencies and luxuries that abounded in countries better cultivated, or blessed with a milder climate than their own; they acquaint them with the battles they had fought, of the friends they had lost, and warm them with resentment against their opponents. Great bodies of armed men, (says an elegant historian, in describing this scene of desolation) with their wives and children, and slaves and flocks, issued forth, like regular colonies, in quest of new settlements. New adventurers followed them. The lands which they deserted were occupied by more remote tribes of Barbarians. These, in their turn, pushed forward into more fertile countries, and like a torrent continually increasing, rolled on, and swept every thing before them. Wherever the Barbarians marched, their rout was marked with blood. They ravaged or destroyed all around them. They made no distinction between what was sacred, and what was profane. They respected no age, or sex, or rank. If a man was called upon to fix upon the period, in the history of the world, during which, the condition of the human race was most calamitous and afflicted, he would, without hesitation, name that which elapsed from the death of Theodosius the Great, A. D. 395, to the establishment of the Lombards in Italy, A. D. 571. The contemporary authors, who beheld that scene of desolation, labour, and are at a loss for expressions to describe the horror of it. *The scourge of God, the destroyer of nations*, are the dreadful epithets by which they distinguish the most noted of the barbarous leaders.

Constantine, who was emperor about the beginning of the fourth century, and who had embraced Christianity, changed the seat of empire from Rome to Constantinople. This occasioned a prodigious alteration. The western and eastern provinces were separated from each other, and governed by different sovereigns. The withdrawing the Roman legions from the Rhine and the Danube to the east, threw down the western barriers of the empire, and laid it open to the invaders.

Rome (now known by the name of the Western Empire, in contradistinction to Constantinople, which, from its situation, was called the Eastern Empire) weakened by this division, becomes a prey to the barbarous nations. Its antient glory, vainly deemed immortal, is effaced, and Adoaces, a Barbarian chieftain, sits down on the throne of the Cæsars. These irruptions into the empire, were gradual and successive. The immense fabric of the Roman empire was the work of many ages, and several centuries were employed in demolishing it. The antient discipline of the Romans, in military affairs,

was

was so efficacious, that the remains of it descended to their successors, and must have proved an over-match for all their enemies, had it not been for the vices of their emperors, and the universal corruption of manners among the people. Satiated with the luxuries of the known world, the emperors were at a loss to find new provocatives. The most distant regions were explored, the ingenuity of mankind was exercised, and the tribute of provinces expended upon one favourite dish. The tyranny, and the universal depravation of manners that prevailed under the emperors, or as they are called Cæsars, could only be equalled by the barbarity of those nations, who overcame them.

Towards the close of the sixth century, the Saxons, a German nation, were masters of the southern, and more fertile provinces of Britain; the Franks, another tribe of Germans, of Gaul; the Goths, of Spain; the Goths and Lombards, of Italy, and the adjacent provinces. Scarce any vestige of the Roman policy, jurisprudence, arts or literature remained. New forms of government, new laws, new manners, new dresses, new languages, and new names of men and countries, were every where introduced.

From this period till the 16th century, Europe exhibited a picture of most melancholy Gothic barbarity. Literature, science, taste, were words scarce in use during these ages. Persons of the highest rank, and in the most eminent stations, could not read or write. Many of the clergy did not understand the breviary which they were obliged daily to recite; some of them could scarce read it. The human mind neglected, uncultivated, and depressed, sunk into the most profound ignorance. The superior genius of Charlemagne, who, about the beginning of the 9th century, governed France, Germany, with part of Italy; and Alfred the Great in England, endeavoured to dispel this darkness, and gave their subjects a short glimpse of light. But the ignorance of the age was too powerful for their efforts and institutions. The darkness returned, and settled over Europe more thick and heavy than formerly.

A new division of property gradually introduced a new species of government formerly unknown; which singular institution is now distinguished by the name of the Feudal System. The king or general, who led the Barbarians to conquest, parcelled out the lands of the vanquished among his chief officers, binding those on whom they were bestowed, to follow his standard with a number of men, and to bear arms in his defence. The chief officers imitated the example of the sovereign, and in distributing portions of their lands among their dependants,

INTRODUCTION.

dependants, annexed the same condition to the grant. But though this system seemed to be admirably calculated for defence against a foreign enemy, it degenerated into a system of oppression.

The usurpation of the nobles became unbounded and intolerable. They reduced the great body of the people into a state of actual servitude. They were deprived of the natural and most unalienable rights of humanity. They were slaves fixed to the soil, which they cultivated, and together with it were transferred from one proprietor to another, by sale, or by conveyance. Every offended baron, or chieftain, buckled on his armour, and sought redress at the head of his vassals. His adversaries met him in like hostile array. The kindred and dependants of the aggressor, as well as of the defender, were involved in the quarrel. They had not even the liberty of remaining neuter *.

The monarchs of Europe perceived the encroachments of their nobles with impatience. They declared, that as all men were by nature free born, they determined it should be so in reality as well as in name. In order to create some power, that might counterbalance those potent vassals, who, while they enslaved the people, controuled or gave law to the crown, a plan was adopted of conferring new privileges on towns. These privileges abolished all marks of servitude, and formed them into corporations, or bodies politic, to be governed by a council and magistrates of their own nomination.

The acquisition of liberty made such a happy change in the condition of mankind, as roused them from that stupidity and inaction into which they had been sunk by the wretchedness of their former state. A spirit of industry revived; commerce became an object of attention, and began to flourish.

Various causes contributed to revive this spirit of commerce, and to renew the intercourse between different nations. Constantinople, the capital of the eastern, or Greek empire, had escaped the ravages of the Goths and Vandals, who overthrew that of the west. In this city, some remains of literature and science were preserved: this too, for many ages, was the great emporium of trade, and where some relish for the precious commodities and curious manufactures of India was retained. They communicated some knowledge of these to their neighbours in Italy; and the crusades, which were begun by the

Christian

---

* This Gothic system still prevails in Poland: a remnant of it continued in the Highlands of Scotland so late as the year 1748. And even in England, a country renowned for civil and religious liberty, some relicks of these Gothic institutions are perceivable at this day.

Christian powers of Europe with a view to drive the Turks from Jerusalem, opened a communication between Europe and the East. Constantinople was the general place of rendezvous for the Christian armies, in their way to Palestine or on their return from thence. Though the object of these expeditions was conquest and not commerce, and though the issue of them proved unfortunate, their commercial effects were both beneficial and permanent.

Soon after the close of the holy war, the mariners compass was invented, which facilitated the communication between remote nations, and brought them nearer to each other. The Italian states, particularly those of Venice and Genoa, began to establish a regular commerce with the East, and the ports of Egypt, and drew from thence all the rich productions of India. These commodities they disposed of to great advantage among the other nations of Europe, who began to acquire some taste of elegance, unknown to their predecessors, or despised by them. During the 12th and 13th centuries, the commerce of Europe was almost in the hands of the Italians, more commonly known in those ages by the name of Lombards. Companies or societies of Lombard merchants settled in every different kingdom; they became the carriers, the manufacturers, and the bankers of Europe. One of these companies settled in London; hence the name of Lombard Street.

While the Italians in the south of Europe cultivated trade with such industry and success, the commercial spirit awakened in the North towards the middle of the thirteenth century. As the Danes, Swedes, and other nations around the Baltic, were at that time extremely barbarous, and infested that sea with their piracies, this obliged the cities of Lubec and Hamburgh, soon after they had began to open some trade with the Italians, to enter into a league of mutual defence. They derived such advantages from this union, that other towns acceded to their confederacy; and, in a short time, eighty of the most considerable cities, scattered through those vast countries of Germany and Flanders which stretch from the bottom of the Baltic to Cologne on the Rhine, joined in an alliance, called the Hanseatic League; which became so formidable, that its alliance was courted, and its enmity was dreaded by the greatest monarchs. The members of this powerful association formed the first systematic plan of commerce known in the middle ages, and conducted it by common laws enacted in their general assemblies. They supplied the rest of Europe with naval stores; and pitched on different towns, the most eminent of which was Bruges, in Flanders, where they established staples, in which their commerce was regularly carried on.

INTRODUCTION.

on. Thither the Lombards brought the productions of India, together with the manufactures of Italy, and exchanged them for the more bulky, but not less useful commodities of the North.

As Bruges became the center of communication between the Lombards and Hanseatic merchants, the Flemings traded with both in that city to such extent as well as advantage, as spirited among them a general habit of industry, which long rendered Flanders and the adjacent provinces the most opulent, the most populous, and best cultivated countries in Europe.

Struck with the flourishing state of these provinces, of which he discovered the true cause, Edward III. of England, endeavoured to excite a spirit of industry among his own subjects, who, blind to the advantages of their situation, and ignorant of the source from which opulence was destined to flow into their country, totally neglected commerce, and did not even attempt those manufactures, the materials of which they furnished to foreigners. By alluring Flemish artisans to settle in his dominions, as well as by many wise laws for the encouragement and regulation of trade, he gave a beginning to the woollen manufactures of England; and first turned the active and enterprizing genius of his people towards those arts which have raised the English to the first rank among commercial nations.

The Christian princes, after their great losses in the crusades, endeavoured to cultivate the friendship of the great khans of Tartary, whose fame in arms had reached the most remote corners of Europe and Asia, that they might be some check upon the Turks, who had been such enemies to the Christian name; and who, from a contemptible handful of wanderers, serving occasionally in the armies of contending princes, had begun to extend their ravages over the finest countries of Asia.

The Christian embassies were managed chiefly by monks, a wandering profession of men, who, impelled by zeal, and undaunted by difficulties and danger, found their way to the remote courts of these infidels. The English philosopher, Roger Bacon, was so industrious as to collect from their relations, or traditions, many particulars of the Tartars, which are to be found in Purchas's Pilgrims, and other books of travels. The first regular traveller of the monkish kind, who committed his discoveries to writing, was John du Plant Carpin, who, with some of his brethren, about the year 1246, carried a letter from pope Innocent to the great khan of Tartary, in favour of the Christian subjects in that prince's extensive dominions. Soon after this, a spirit of travelling into Tartary and India became general; and it would be no difficult

cult matter to prove that many Europeans, about the end of the fourteenth century, served in the armies of Tamerlane, one of the greatest princes of Tartary, whose conquests reached to the most remote corners of India; and that they introduced into Europe the use of gunpowder and artillery; the discovery made by a German chymist being only partial and accidental.

After the death of Tamerlane, who, jealous of the rising power of the Turks, had checked their progress, the Christian adventurers, upon their return, magnifying the vast riches of the East Indies, inspired their countrymen with a spirit of adventure and discovery, and were the first that rendered a passage thither by sea probable and practicable. The Portuguese had been always famous for their application to maritime affairs; and to their discovery of the Cape of Good-Hope, Great-Britain is at this day indebted for her Indian commerce.

At first they contented themselves with short voyages, creeping along the coast of Africa, discovering cape after cape; but by making a gradual progress southward, they, in the year 1497, were so fortunate as to sail beyond the cape, which opened a passage by sea to the eastern ocean, and all those countries known by the names of India, China and Japan.

While the Portuguese were intent upon a passage to India by the east, Columbus, a native of Genoa, conceived a project of sailing thither by the west. His proposal being condemned by his countrymen, as chimerical and absurd, he laid his scheme successively before the courts of France, England, and Portugal, where he had no better success. Such repeated disappointments would have broken the spirit of any man but Columbus. The expedition required expence, and he had nothing to defray it. Spain was now his only resource, and there, after eight years attendance, he succeeded, through the interest of queen Isabella, who raised money upon her jewels to defray the expences of his expedition, and to do honour to her sex.

Columbus now set sail, anno 1492, with a fleet of three ships, upon the most adventurous attempts ever undertaken by man, and in the fate of which the inhabitants of two worlds were interested.

In this voyage he had a thousand difficulties to contend with, and his sailors, always discontented, began to insist upon his return, threatening, in case of refusal, to throw him overboard; but the firmness of the commander, and the discovery of land, after a passage of 33 days, put an end to the commotion. From the appearance of the natives, he found to his surprize, that this could not be the Indies he was in quest of, and which he soon discovered to be a new world: of which the reader will find a more circumstantial account in that part of the following work which treats of America.

Europe now began to emerge out of that darkness into which she had been sunk since the subversion of the Roman empire. These discoveries, from which such wealth was destined to flow to the commercial nations of Europe, were succeeded by others of unspeakable benefit to mankind. The invention of printing, the revival of learning, arts, and sciences; and, lastly, the happy reformation in religion, all distinguish the 15th and 16th century as the first æra of modern history. "It was in these ages that the powers of Europe were formed into one great political system, in which each took a station, wherein it has since remained, with less variation than could have been expected, after the shocks occasioned by so many internal revolutions, and so many foreign wars, of which we have given some account in the history of each particular state in the following sheets. The great events which happened then have not hitherto spent their force. The political principles and maxims then established, still continue to operate; and the ideas concerning the balance of power then introduced, or rendered general, still influence the councils of European nations."

From all which it seems extremely certain, that the concurrence of so many rival princes will always prevent any one of them from gaining the empire over Europe. But it is no less certain, that in contending for it, they must weaken their own force, and may at length render themselves uncapable of defending even their just possessions. The partial conquests they may make are extremely illusive; instead of promoting, they rather oppose their designs; the more any kingdom is extended, it becomes the weaker, and great projects have not been so often executed by slow reiterated efforts, as in the course of a few years, and sometimes by a single expedition. A prince may form a deliberate plan of destroying the rights of his subjects; he may proceed by slow degrees in the execution of it, and if he die before it is compleated, his successor may pursue the same steps, and avail himself of what was done before him. But external conquests cannot be concealed; they generally occasion more fear than hurt, and are almost always less solid than brilliant. Hence the alarms they excite, the confederacies they give occasion to, by which the prince, who, by misfortune, has been a conqueror, is commonly reduced to the last extremities. This doctrine, however contrary to the prejudices of a powerful and victorious nation, is one of the best established in the science of politicks. It is confirmed by examples both ancient and modern. The states of Greece, in particular, delivered from the terror of

the

the Persian invasions, exhibit the same truth in a great variety of lights. There was not one of the most considerable of these little societies, but in its turn imbibed the frenzy of conquest, and in its turn too was reduced by this frenzy to the utmost misery and distress *. The modern examples are so well known, that it is almost unnecessary to mention them. Who does not know that the house of Austria excited the terror of all Europe, before it excited the pity of Great Britain! Had that family never been the object of fear, the empress queen would never have become the object of compassion. France affords an example no less striking. The nerves of that kingdom were strained so far beyond their strength, by an ambitious monarch, that it is impossible they should acquire their natural tone in the course of this century. The debility of their late efforts, prove the greatness of the evil, and the inefficacy of any remedy which is not slow and gradual.

GREAT BRITAIN is at present that kingdom in Europe which enjoys the greatest prosperity and glory. She ought to be the more attentive therefore to preserve so brilliant an existence. The spirit of conquest neither suits with her physical situation, nor with her political constitution. Every attempt to extend her dominion, must be attended with two infallible consequences. The first, to alarm her neighbours; the second, to augment her armies. We have said enough to shew the danger of the one; the other well deserves to be traced thro' all its effects. The encrease of taxes, the decay of manufactures, that species of commerce which alone is not precarious, are objects which need only to be hinted at.—But the augmentation of armies must, in some future period, be attended with a consequence of another kind, that is, the establishment of absolute monarchy in Great-Britain. The farther our conquests are removed from home, this danger becomes the greater. British subjects of consideration or property will, in time, grow weary of transporting themselves into climates scorched by heat, or frozen by cold. Our foreign armies must, of course, be composed of men, who, having no moral tie to attach them to their native country, will soon, by living in a distant clime, lose all natural affection for the land in which they were born. This consequence seems to escape some of our modern statesmen, guided more perhaps by sentiment than by reason, and who, by speeches extremely seductive to human pride or ambition, would inadvertently lead this country into a course of public measures that naturally tends to despotism.

---

* The reader who would see this subject fully illustrated, may look at Isocrates' Oration on the Peace; one of the most finished models of antient eloquence; and which contains a rich fund of political knowledge.

PART III.

OF THE ORIGIN AND PROGRESS OF RELIGION.

DEITY is an awful object, and has ever roused the attention of mankind. But incapable of elevating their ideas to all the sublimity of his perfections, they have too often brought down his perfections to the level of their own ideas. This is more particularly true with regard to those nations whose religion had no other foundation but the natural feelings, and more often the irregular passions of the human heart, and who had received no light from heaven respecting this important object. In deducing the history of religion, therefore, we must make the same distinction which we have hitherto observed in tracing the progress of arts, sciences, and of civilization among mankind. We must separate what is human from what is divine, what had its origin from particular revelations from what is the effect of general laws, and of the unassisted operations of the human mind.

Agreeably to this distinction we find that in the first ages of the world, the religion of the eastern nations was pure and luminous. It arose from a divine source, and was not then disfigured by human fancies or caprice. In time, however, these began to have their influence; the ray of tradition was obscured, and among those tribes which separated at the greatest distance, and in the smallest numbers, from the more improved societies of men, it was altogether obliterated.

In this situation a particular people were selected by God himself, to be the depositories of his laws and worship; but the rest of mankind were left to form hypotheses upon these subjects, which were more or less perfect according to an infinity of circumstances, which cannot properly be reduced under any general heads.

The most common religion of antiquity, that which prevailed the longest, and extended the widest, was Polytheism, or the doctrine of a plurality of Gods. The rage of system, the ambition of reducing all the phænomena of the moral world to a few general principles, has occasioned many imperfect accounts, both of the origin and nature of this species of worship. For without entering into a minute detail, it is impossible to give an adequate idea of the subject; and what is said upon it in general, must always be liable to a great many exceptions.

One thing however may be obferved, that the polytheifm of the antients feems neither to have been the fruit of philofophical fpeculations, nor of disfigured traditions, concerning the nature of the divinity. It feems to have arifen during the rudeft ages of fociety, while the rational powers were feeble, and while mankind were under the tyranny of imagination and paffion. It was built therefore folely upon fentiment; as each tribe of men had their heroes, fo likewife they had their gods. Thofe heroes who led them forth to the combat, who prefided in their councils, whofe image was engraved on their fancy, whofe exploits were imprinted on their memory, even after death enjoyed an exiftence in the imagination of their followers. The force of blood, of friendfhip, of affection, among rude nations, is what we cannot eafily conceive; but the power of imagination over the fenfes is what all men have in fome degree experienced. Combine thefe two caufes, and it will not appear ftrange, that the image of departed heroes fhould have been feen by their companions, animating the battle, taking vengeance on their enemies, and performing, in a word, the fame functions which they performed when alive. An appearance fo unnatural would not excite terror among men unacquainted with evil fpirits, and who had not learned to fear any thing but their enemies. On the contrary, it confirmed their courage, flattered their vanity, and the teftimony of thofe who had feen it, fupported by the extreme credulity and romantic caft of thofe who had not, gained an univerfal affent among all the members of their fociety. A fmall degree of reflection however would be fufficient to convince them, that as their own heroes exifted after death, it might likewife be the cafe of thofe of their enemies. Two orders of gods, therefore, would be eftablifhed, the propitious and the hoftile; the gods who were to be loved, and thofe who were to be feared. But time which wears off the impreffions of tradition, the frequent invafions by which the nations of antiquity were ravaged, defolated or tranfplanted, made them lofe the names, and confound the characters of thofe two orders of divinities, and form various fyftems of religion, which, tho' warped by a thoufand particular circumftances, give no fmall indications of their firft texture and original materials. For in general the gods of the antients gave abundant proof of human infirmity. They were fubject to all the paffions of men; they partook even of their partial affections, and in many inftances difcovered their preference of one race or nation to all others. They did not eat and drink the fame fubftances with men; they lived on nectar and ambrofia; they had a particular pleasure in smelling the steam of the sacrifices, and they made love with a ferocity unknown in northern climates. The rites by which they were worshipped, naturally resulted from their character.

It must be observed, however, that the religion of the ancients was not much connected either with their private behaviour, or with their political arrangements. If we except a few fanatical societies, whose principles do not fall within our plan, the greater part of mankind were extremely tolerant in their principles. They had their own gods who watched over them; their neighbours, they imagined, also had theirs; and there was room enough in the universe for both to live together in good fellowship, without interfering or jostling with one another.

The introduction of Christianity, by inculcating the unity of God, by announcing the purity of his character, by explaining the service he required of men, produced a total alteration on their religious sentiments and belief. But this is not the place for handling this sublime subject. It is sufficient to observe here, that a religion, which was founded on the unity of the Deity, which admitted of no association with false gods, must either be altogether destroyed, or become the prevailing belief of mankind. The latter was the case. Christianity made its way among the civilized part of mankind, by the sublimity of its doctrines and precepts; and before it was supported by the arm of power, sustained itself by the voice of wisdom.

The management of whatever related to the church, being naturally conferred on those who had established it, first occasioned the elevation of the clergy, and afterwards of the bishop of Rome, over all the members of the Christian world. It is impossible to describe within our narrow limits all the concomitant causes, some of which were extremely delicate, by which this species of universal monarchy was established. The bishops of Rome, by being removed from the controul of the Roman emperors, then residing in Constantinople; by borrowing, with little variation, the religious ceremonies and rites established among the heathen world, and otherwise working on the credulous minds of Barbarians, by whom that empire began to be dismembered; and by availing themselves of every circumstance which Fortune threw in their way, slowly erected the fabric of their power, at first an object of veneration, and afterwards of terror, to all temporal princes. The causes of its happy dissolution are more palpable, and operated with greater activity. The most efficacious was the rapid improvement of arts, government and commerce, which after

INTRODUCTION.

many ages of barbarity, made its way into Europe. The scandalous lives of those who called themselves the ministers of Jesus Christ, their ignorance and tyranny, the desire natural to sovereigns of delivering themselves from a foreign yoke, the opportunity of applying to national objects, the immense wealth which had been diverted to the service of the church in every kingdom of Europe, conspired with the ardour of the first reformers, and hastened the progress of reformation. The absurd mummeries established by the Romish clergy in order to elevate their power, and augment their riches, were happily turned into ridicule by men of letters, who, on that account, deserve to be held in everlasting esteem, as they contributed, in a very eminent degree, to that astonishing event, so favourable to the civil as well as to the religious liberties of mankind.

We shall now proceed to the main part of our work, beginning with Europe.

EUROPE.

EUROPE, though the least extensive quarter of the globe, is in many respects that which most deserves our attention. It is in Europe that the human mind has made the greatest progress towards its improvement; and where the arts, whether of utility or ornament, the sciences both military and civil, have been carried to the greatest height and perfection. If we except the earliest ages of the world, it is in Europe we find the greatest variety of character, government and manners, and from whence we draw the greatest number of facts and memorials either for our entertainment or instruction.

Geography discovers to us two circumstances with regard to Europe, which perhaps have had a considerable tendency in giving it the superiority over the rest of the world. First, the happy temperature of its climate, no part of it lying within the torrid zone; and secondly, the great variety of its surface. The effect of a moderate climate, both on plants and animals, is well known from experience. The immense number of mountains, rivers, seas, &c. which divide the different countries of Europe from one another, is likewise extremely commodious for its inhabitants. These natural boundaries check the progress of conquest or despotism, which has always been so rapid in the extensive plains of Africa and the East: the seas and rivers facilitate the intercourse and commerce between different nations; and even the barren rocks and mountains are more favourable for exciting human industry and invention, than the natural unsolicited luxuriancy of more fertile soils. There is no part of Europe so diversified in its surface, so interrupted by natural boundaries or divisions, as Greece; we have seen that it was in Greece the human mind began to know and to avail itself of its strength, and that many of the arts subservient to utility or pleasure, were invented, or at least greatly improved. What Greece therefore is with regard to Europe, Europe itself is with regard to the rest of the globe. The analogy may even be carried further, and it is worth while to attend to it. As antient Greece (for we do not speak of Greece, at present under the unnatural tyranny of Barbarians) was distinguished above all the rest of Europe, for the equity of its laws, and the freedom of its political constitution, so has Europe in general been remarkable for smaller deviations, at least from the laws of nature and equality, than have been admitted in other quarters of the world. Though most of the European governments are monarchical, we may discover, on due examination, that there are a thousand little springs, which check the force, and soften the rigour of monarchy in Europe, which do not exist any where else. In proportion to the number and force of these checks, the monarchies of Europe, such as Russia, France, Spain and Denmark, differ from one another. Besides monarchies, in which one man bears the chief sway, there are in Europe, aristocracies or governments of the nobles, and democracies or governments of the people. Venice is an example of the former; Holland, and some states of Italy and Switzerland, afford examples of the latter. There are likewise mixed governments, which cannot be assigned to any one class. Great Britain, which partakes of all the three, is the most singular instance of this kind we are acquainted with. The other mixed governments in Europe, are composed only of two of the simple forms, such as Poland, Sweden, several states of Italy, &c. all which shall be explained at length in their proper places.

The Christian religion is established throughout every part of Europe, except Turkey; but from the various capacities of the human mind, and the different lights in which speculative opinions are apt to appear, when viewed by persons of different educations and passions, that religion is divided into a number of different sects, but which may be comprehended under three general denominations; 1st, The Greek church; 2d, Popery; and 3d, Protestantism: which last is again divided into Lutheranism, and Calvinism, so called from Luther and Calvin, the two distinguished reformers of the 16th century.

The languages of Europe are derived from the six following. The Greek, Latin, Teutonic or old German, the Celtic, Sclavonic, and Gothic.

Grand Divisions of EUROPE.

THIS grand division of the earth is situated between the 10th degree west, and the 65th degree east long. from London; and between the 36th and 72d degree of north lat. It is bounded on the north, by the Frozen Ocean; on the east, by Asia; on the south, by the Mediterranean Sea, which divides it from Africa; and on the west, by the Atlantic Ocean, which separates it from America: being 3000 miles long, and 2500 broad. It contains the following kingdoms and states.

EUROPE.

ingdoms.	Length.	Breadth.	Chief City.	Dift. & Bearing from London.	Diff. of Time from London.	Religions.
				Miles.	H. M.	
gland	360	300	London	* * *	* * *	Lutherans
otland	300	150	Edinburgh	400 N.	0 12 aft.	Calvinifts
land	285	160	Dublin	270 N. W.	0 26 aft.	Luth. Cal. and Pap.
rway	1000	300	Bergen	540 N.	0 24 bef.	Lutherans
nmark	240	180	Copenhagen	500 N. E.	0 50 bef.	Lutherans
eden	800	500	Stockholm	750 N. E.	1 10 bef.	Lutherans
ffia	1500	1100	Peterfburg	1140 N. E.	2 4 bef.	Greek Church
land	700	680	Warfaw	760 E.	1 24 bef.	Pap. Luth. & Calv.
of Pru. omin.	uncertain		Berlin	540 E.	0 59 bef.	Luth. & Calv.
rmany	600	500	Vienna	600 E.	1 5 bef.	Pap. Luth. & Calv.
hemia	300	250	Prague	600 E.	1 4 bef.	Papifts
lland	150	100	Amfterdam	180 E.	0 18 bef.	Calvinifts
nders	200	200	Bruffels	180 S. E.	0 16 bef.	Papifts
ance	600	500	Paris	200 S. E.	0 9 bef.	Papifts
ain	700	500	Madrid	800 S.	0 17 aft.	Papifts
rtugal	300	100	Lifbon	850 S. W.	0 33 aft.	Papifts
itzerland	260	100	Bern	420 S. E.	0 28 bef.	Calvin. & Papifts.
everal all ftates	Piedmont, Montferrat, Milan, Parma, Modena, Mantua, Venice, Genoa, Tufcany, &c. Turin, Cafal, Milan, Parma, Modena, Mantua, Venice, Genoa, Florence.					
pedom	240	120	Rome	820 S. E.	0 52 bef.	Papifts
ples	280	120	Naples	870 S. E.	1 0 bef.	Papifts
ngary	300	200	Buda	780 S. E.	1 17 bef.	Papifts
nubian ovinces	600	420	Conftantinople	1320 S. E.	1 58 bef.	Mahometans, and Greek Church.
t. Tartary	380	240	Caffa	1500 E.	2 24 bef.	
eece	400	240	Athens	1360 S. E.	1 37 bef.	

Exclufive of the Britifh ifles, mentioned above, Europe contains the following principal iflands:

Iceland, in the Northern Seas, fubject to Denmark.

IN THE BALTIC SEA.

1. Zeeland, Funen, Alfen, Femeren, Laland, Falfter, Mona, Bornholm; } fubject to Denmark.
2. Gothland, Aland, Rugen, — — fubject to Sweden.
3. Ofel, Dagho, — — fubject to Ruffia.
4. Ufedom, Wollin, — — fubject to Pruffia.

IN THE MEDITERRANEAN SEA.

1. Ivica, fubject to Spain.
2. Majorca, ditto.
3. Minorca, fubject to Great Britain.
4. Corfica, formerly fubject to Genoa, now to France.
5. Sardinia, fubject to the king of Sardinia.
6. Sicily, fubject to the king of Naples.
7. Archipelago iflands, fubject to Turkey, with the ifland of Candia.

IN THE ADRIATIC AND IONIAN SEA.

1. Liefiena. 2. Corfu. 3. Cephalonia. 4. Zant, — — } fubject to Venice.
5. Leucadia, fubject to the Turks.

DENMARK.

I Shall, according to my plan, begin this account of his Danish majesty's dominions with the most northerly situations, and divide them into four parts: 1st. East and West Greenland, Iceland, and the islands in the Atlantic Ocean; 2d. Norway; 3d. Denmark proper; and 4th. his German territories.

The dimensions of these countries may be seen in the following table.

		Denmark.	Square miles.	Length.	Breadth.	Chief cities.
		Jutland,	9,600	155	98	Wyburg,
		Sleswick,	2,115	70	63	Sleswick,
Islands in the Baltic.		Zealand,	1,935	60	60	COPENHAGEN,
		Funen,	768	38	32	Odensee,
		Falster and Laland,	220	27	12	Nikoping, Naxkaw,
		Femeren,	50	13	8	Borge,
		Alsen,	54	15	6	Sonderborge,
		Mona,	39	14	5	Stege,
		Bornholm,	160	20	12	Rottomby,
In the Nor. seas,		Iceland,	46,000	435	185	Skalholt,
		Norway,	71,400	750	170	Bergen,
	Danish	Lapland,	28,400	285	172	Wardhuys,
Westphalia,		Oldenburg,	1260	62	32	Oldenburg,
Lower Saxony,		Stromar,	1000	52	32	Gluckstat.
		Total—	163,001			

The reader may perceive, that in the above table no calculation is made of the dimensions of East and West Greenland; because, in fact, they are not yet known, or known very imperfectly: we shall, however, proceed to give the latest accounts of them, and from the best authorities that have come to our hands.

EAST AND WEST GREENLAND, ICELAND, AND THE ISLANDS IN THE ATLANTIC OCEAN.

EAST GREENLAND.

THE most northerly part of his Danish majesty's dominions; or, as others call it, New Greenland, and the country of Spitzbergen, lies between 10 and 11 deg. E. long. and 76 and 80 deg. N. lat. Though it is now claimed by Denmark, it certainly was discovered by Sir Hugh Willoughby, in 1553; and is supposed to be a continuation of Old Greenland.

land. It obtained the name of Spitzbergen, from the height and raggedness of its rocks. There is a whale-fishery, chiefly prosecuted by the Dutch and some British vessels, on its coasts. It likewise contains two harbours; one called South Haven, and the other Maurice-Bay; but the inland parts are uninhabited.

WEST GREENLAND.

LIES between the meridian of London, and 50 deg. W. long. and between 60 and 73 deg. N. lat.

INHABITANTS.] By the latest accounts from the missionaries, employed for the conversion of the Greenlanders, their whole number does not amount to above 957 stated inhabitants: Mr. Crantz, however, thinks that the roving southlanders of Greenland may amount to about 7000. There is a great resemblance between the aspect, manners, and dress of those natives, and the Esquimaux Americans, from whom they naturally differ but little, even after all the pains which the Danish and German missionaries have taken to convert and civilize them. They live in huts during their winter, which is incredibly severe; but Mr. Crantz, who has given us the latest and best accounts of this country, says, that in their longest summer days it is so hot that the inhabitants are obliged to throw off their summer garments. They have no trade, tho' they have a most improveable fishery upon their coasts; but they employ all the year either in fishing or hunting, in which they are very dextrous.

CURIOSITIES.] The taking of Whales in the seas of Greenland, among the fields of ice that have been increasing for ages, is one of the greatest curiosities in nature. These fields, or pieces of ice, are, frequently, more than a mile in length, and upwards of 100 feet in thickness; and when they are put in motion by a storm, nothing can be more terrible; the Dutch had 13 ships crushed to pieces by them in one season.

There are several kinds of whales in Greenland; some white, and others black. The black sort, the grand bay whale, is in most esteem, on account of his bulk, and the great quantity of fat or blubber he affords, which turns to oil. His tongue is about 18 feet long, inclosed in long pieces of what we call whalebone, which are covered with a kind of hair like horse-hair; and on each side of his tongue are 250 pieces of this whalebone. As to the bones of his body, they are as hard as an ox's bones, and of no use. There are no teeth in his mouth; and he is usually between 60 and 80 feet long; very thick about the head, but grows less from thence to the tail.

When

When the seamen see a whale spout, the word is immediately given, *fall, fall,* when every one hastens from the ship to his boat; six or eight men being appointed to a boat, and four or five boats usually belong to one ship.

When they come near the whale, the harpooner strikes him with his harpoon (a barbed dart) and the monster finding himself wounded, runs swiftly down into the deep, and would carry the boat along with him, if they did not give him line fast enough; and to prevent the wood of the boat taking fire by the violent rubbing of the rope on the side of it, one wets it constantly with a mop. After the whale has run some 100 fathoms deep, he is forced to come up for air, when he makes such a terrible noise with his spouting, that some have compared it to the firing of cannon. So soon as he appears on the surface of the water, some of the harpooners fix another harpoon in him, whereupon he plunges again into the deep; and when he comes up a second time, they pierce him with spears in the vital parts, till he spouts out streams of blood instead of water, beating the waves with his tail and fins, till the sea is all in a foam, the boats continuing to follow him some leagues, till he has lost his strength; and when he is dying, he turns himself upon his back, and is drawn on shore, or to the ship, if they be at a distance from the land. There they cut him in pieces, and by boiling the blubber, extract the oil, if they have conveniencies on shore; otherwise they barrel up the pieces, and bring them home; but nothing can smell stronger than these ships do. Every fish is computed to yield between 60 and 100 barrels of oil, of the value of 3 l. or 4 l. a barrel. Though the Danes claim this country of East Greenland, where these whales are taken, the Dutch have in a manner monopolized this fishery.

ICELAND.

LIES between 63 and 68 deg. N. lat. and between 10 and 26 deg. W. long. from the meridian of London; extending from east to west about 720 miles.

INHABITANTS.] The inhabitants are supposed to be about 80,000; though it is thought that they were formerly far more numerous, till the country was depopulated by the small-pox, and pestilential diseases. They are subject to the crown of Denmark, and conform to the religion and laws of Norway. His Danish majesty names their governor, called Staffs-amptmaud; but he appoints a deputy-governor, called Amptmaud, who resides in Iceland, at the king's palace of Ressested, on a salary of 400 rixdollars; and he has magistrates under him, both in civil and spiritual cases. The people are naturally hardy,

NORWAY.

hardy, honest, and industrious. They amuse themselves with chess and singing. In some things they differ little from the Danes and Norwegians; though they have many customs peculiar to themselves.

TRADE.] The commerce of this island is monopolized by a Danish company. Its exports consist of dried fish, salted mutton and lamb, beef, butter, tallow, train-oil, coarse woollen cloth, stockings, gloves, raw wool, sheep-skins, lamb-skins, fox-furs of various colours, eider-down, and feathers. Their imports consist of timber, fishing-lines and hooks, tobacco, bread, horse-shoes, brandy, wine, salt, linen, and a little silk; exclusive of some necessaries and superfluities for the more wealthy.

STRENGTH AND REVENUE.] As Iceland affords no bait for avarice or ambition, the inhabitants depend entirely upon his Danish majesty's protection; and the revenue he draws from the country, amounts to about 30,000 crowns a year.

THE FARO ISLANDS.

SO called from their lying in a cluster, and the inhabitants ferrying from one island to another. They are about 24 in number, and lie between 61 and 63 deg. W. long. from London. The space of this cluster extends about 60 miles in length, and 40 in breadth, to the westward of Norway; having Shetland and the Orkneys on the south-east, and Greenland and Iceland upon the north and north-west. The trade and income of the inhabitants, who may be about 3000 or 4000, add little or nothing to the revenues of Denmark.

NORWAY.

NAME, BOUNDARIES, AND EXTENT.} THE natural signification of Norway is, the Northernway. It is bounded on the south by the entrance into the Baltic, called the Scaggerac, or Categate; on the west and north, by the northern ocean; and on the east, it is divided from Sweden by a long ridge of mountains, called at different parts by different names; as Fillefield, Dofrefield, Rundfield, and Dourfield. The reader may consult the table of dimensions in Denmark for its extent; but it is a country so little known to the rest of Europe, that it is difficult to fix its dimensions with precision.

CLIMATE.] The climate of Norway varies according to its extent, and its exposition towards the sea. At Bergen, the winter is moderate, and the sea is practicable. The eastern parts of Norway are commonly covered with snow; and the cold generally sets in about the middle of October, with intense

tense severity, to the middle of April; the waters being all that while frozen to a considerable thickness. In 1719, 7000 Swedes, who were on their march to attack Drontheim, perished in the snow, on the mountains which separate Sweden from Norway; and their bodies were found in different postures. But even frost and snow have their conveniencies, as they facilitate the conveyance of goods by land. As to the more northerly parts of this country, called Finmark, the cold is so intense, that they are but little known. At Bergen, the longest day consists of about 19 hours, and the shortest about six. In summer, the inhabitants can read and write at midnight, by the light of the sky; and in the most northerly parts, about midsummer, the sun is continually in view. In those parts, however, in the middle of winter, there is only a faint glimmering of light at noon, for about an hour and a half; owing to the reflection of the sun's rays on the mountains. Nature, notwithstanding, has been so kind to the Norwegians, that in the midst of their darkness, the sky is so serene, and the moon and the aurora borealis so bright, that they can carry on their fishery, and work at their several trades in open air.

The air is so pure in some of the inland parts, that the inhabitants live so long as to be tired of life; and cause themselves to be transported to a less salubrious air. Sudden thaws, and snow-falls, have, however, sometimes dreadful effects, and destroy whole villages.

MOUNTAINS.] Norway is reckoned one of the most mountainous countries in the world; for it contains a chain of unequal mountains running from south to north: to pass that of Hardanger, a man must travel about seventy English miles; and to pass others, upwards of fifty. Dofrefield is counted the highest mountain, perhaps, in Europe. The rivers and cataracts which intersect those dreadful precipices, and are passable only by flight tottering wooden bridges, render travelling in this country very terrible and dangerous; though the government is at the expence of providing, at different stages, houses accommodated with fire, light, and kitchen furniture. Detached from this vast chain, other immense mountains present themselves all over Norway; some of them with reservoirs of water on the top; and the whole forming a most surprizing landscape. The activity of the natives, in recovering their sheep and goats, when penned up, through a false step, in one of those rocks, is wonderful. The owner directs himself to be lowered down from the top of the mountain, sitting on a cross stick, tied to the end of a long rope; and when he arrives at the place where the creature stands, he fastens it to the same cord, and it is drawn up with himself.

The

The caverns that are to be met with in those mountains, are more wonderful than those, perhaps, in any other part of the world, though less liable to observation. One of them, called Dolsteen, was, in 1750, visited by two clergymen; who reported, that they proceeded in it till they heard the sea dashing over their heads; that the passage was as wide and high as an ordinary church, the sides perpendicular, and the roof vaulted: that they descended a flight of natural stairs; but when they arrived at another, they durst not venture to proceed, but returned; and that they consumed two candles going and returning.

FORESTS.] The chief wealth of Norway lies in its forests, which furnish foreigners with masts, beams, planks, and boards; and serve beside for all domestic uses; particularly the construction of houses, bridges, ships, and for charcoal to the founderies. The chief timber growing here are fir and pine, elm, ash, yew, benreed, (a very curious wood) birch, beech, oak, eel, or alder, juniper, the aspin-tree, the comel, or sloe-tree, hasel, elder, and even ebony; (under the mountains of Kolen) lyme and willows. The sums which Norway receives for timber, are very considerable; but the industry of the inhabitants is greatly assisted by the course of their rivers, and the situation of their lakes; which affords them not only the conveniency already mentioned, of floating down their timber, but that of erecting saw-mills, for dividing their large beams into planks and deals. A tenth of all sawed timber belongs to his Danish majesty, and forms no inconsiderable part of his revenue.

STONES, METALS, } Norway contains quarries of excel-
  AND MINERALS. } lent marble, as well as many other kinds of stones; and the magnet is found in the iron mines. The amianthus, or asbestos, which when its delicate fibres are wove into cloth, are cleaned by the fire, is likewise found here; as are crystals, granates, amethysts, agate, thunder-stones, and eagle-stones. Gold found in Norway, has been coined into ducats. His Danish majesty is now working, to great advantage, a silver mine at Koningsberg; other silver mines have been found in different parts of the country; and one of the many silver masses that have been discovered, weighing 560 pounds, is to be seen at the Royal Museum at Copenhagen. The lead, copper, and iron mines, are common in this country: one of the copper-mines at Roraas, is thought to be the richest in Europe. Norway likewise produces quicksilver, sulphur, salt, and coal mines; vitriol, allum, and various kinds of loam; the different manufactures of which bring in a large revenue to the crown.

RIVERS

RIVERS AND LAKES.] The rivers and fresh-water lakes in this country, are well stocked with fish; and navigable for vessels of considerable burden. The most extraordinary circumstance attending the lakes is, that some of them contain floating islands, formed by the cohesion of roots of trees and shrubs; and though torn from the main land, bear herbage and trees. So late as the year 1702, the noble family seat of Borge, near Fredericstadt, suddenly sunk, with all its towers and battlements, into an abyss a hundred fathom in depth; and its site was instantly filled with a piece of water, which formed a lake 300 ells in length, and about half as broad. This melancholy accident, by which 14 people and 200 head of cattle perished, was occasioned by the foundation being undermined by the waters of a river.

UNCOMMON ANIMALS, FOWLS AND FISHES.] All the animals that are natives of Denmark, are to be found in Norway, with an addition of many more. The wild beasts peculiar to Norway, are the elk, the rein-deer, the hares, the rabbit, the bear, the wolf, the lynx, the fox, the glutton, the leming, the ermine, the martin and the beaver. The elk is a tall ash-coloured animal, its shape partaking at once of the horse and the stag; it is harmless, and, in the winter, social; and their flesh tastes like venison. The rein-deer is a species of stag; but we shall have occasion to mention him more particularly afterwards. The hares are small; and are said to live upon mice in the winter time, and to change their colour from brown to white. The Norwegian bears are strong and sagacious: they are remarkable for not hurting children; but their other qualities are in common with the rest of their species in northern countries; nor can we much credit the very extraordinary specimens of their sagacity, recorded by the natives: they are hunted by little dogs; and some prefer bear hams to those of Westphalia. The Norwegian wolves, though fierce, are shy even of a cow or a goat, unless impelled by hunger: the natives are dextrous in digging traps for them, in which they are taken or killed. The lynx, by some called the goupes, is smaller than a wolf, but as dangerous: they are of the cat-kind, and have claws like tygers; they dig under ground, and often undermine sheepfolds, where they make dreadful havock. The skin of the lynx is beautiful and valuable; as is that of the black fox. White and red foxes are likewise found in Norway, and partake of the nature of that wily animal in other countries; they have a particular way of drawing crabs ashore, by dipping their tails in the water, which the crab lays hold of.

The

The glutton, otherwife called the erven, or vielfras, refembles a turn-fpit dog; with a long body, thick legs, fharp claws and teeth; his fur, which is variegated, is fo precious, that he is fhot with blunt arrows, to preferve the fkin unhurt: he is bold, and fo ravenous, that it is faid he will devour a carcafe larger than himfelf, and unburthens his ftomach by fqueezing himfelf between two clofe-ftanding trees: when taken, he has been even known to eat ftone and mortar. The ermine is a little creature, remarkable for its fhynefs and cleanlinefs; and few of our readers need to be told, that their fur forms a principal part even of royal magnificence. There is little difference between the martin and a large brown foreft cat, only its head and fnout are fharper; it is very fierce, and its bite dangerous. I fhall have occafion to mention the beaver in treating of North America.

No country produces a greater variety of birds than Norway. The alks build upon rocks; their numbers often darken the air, and the noife of their wings refembles a ftorm; their fize is the bignefs of a large duck: they are an aquatic fowl, and their flefh is much efteemed. No fewer than 30 different kinds of thrufhes refide in Norway; with various kinds of pigeons, and feveral forts of beautiful wild ducks. The Norwegian cock-of-the-wood, is of a black or dark-grey colour, his eye refembling that of a pheafant; and he is faid to be the largeft of all eatable birds. Norway produces two kinds of eagles, the land and the fea; the former is fo ftrong, that he has been known to carry off a child of two years old: the fea, or fifh-eagle, is larger than the other; he fubfifts on aquatic food; and fometimes darts on large fifhes with fuch force, that being unable to free his talons from their bodies, he is dragged into the water and drowned.

Nature feems to have adapted thefe aërial inhabitants for the coaft of Norway; and induftry has produced a fpecies of mankind peculiarly fitted for making them ferviceable to the human race: thefe are the birdmen, or climbers, who are amazingly dexterous in mounting the fteepeft rocks, and bringing away the birds and their eggs: the latter are nutritive food, and are fometimes parboiled in vinegar; the flefh is eaten by the peafants, who generally relifh it; while the feathers and down form a profitable commodity. Even the dogs of the farmers in the northern diftricts, are trained up to be affiftants to thofe bird-men in feizing their prey.

The Scandinavian lakes and feas are aftonifhingly fruitful in all fifh that are found on the fea-coafts of Europe, which need not here be enumerated. Some fifhes in thofe feas, however, have their peculiarities. The haac-mœren, is a fpecies of
fhark

shark ten fathoms in length, and its live-yields three casks of train-oil. The tuello-flynder is an excessive large turbot, which has been known to cover a man who had fallen overboard, to keep him from rising. The season for herring-fishing is announced to the fishermen by the spouting of water from the whales (of which seven different species are mentioned) in following the herring shoals. The large whale resembles a cod, with small eyes, a dark marbled skin, and white belly: they spout out the water, which they take in by inspiration, through two holes or openings in the head. They copulate like land-animals, standing upright in the sea. A young whale, when first produced, is about nine or ten feet long; and the female sometimes brings forth two at a birth. The whale devours such an incredible number of small fish, that his belly is often ready to burst; in which case he makes a most tremendous noise from pain. The smaller fish have their revenge; some of them fasten on his back, and incessantly beat him; others, with sharp horns, or rather bones, on their beaks, swim under his belly, and sometimes rip it up; some are provided with long sharp teeth, and tear his flesh. Even the aquatic birds of prey declare war against him when he comes near the surface of the water; and he has been known to be so tortured, that he has beat himself to death on the rocks. The coasts of Norway may be said to be the native country of herrings. Innumerable are the shoals that come from under the ice at the north-pole; and about the latitude of Iceland divide themselves into three bodies: one of these supply the Western Isles and coasts of Scotland, another directs its course round the eastern part of Great-Britain down the Channel, and the third enters the Baltic through the Sound. They form great part of the food of the common people; and the cod, ling, kabeliau, and torsk-fishes, follow them, and feed upon their spawn; and are taken in prodigious numbers in 50 or 60 fathoms water: these, especially their roes, and the oil extracted from their livers, are exported and sold to great advantage; and above 150,000 people are maintained by the herring and other fishing on the coast of Norway. The sea-devil is about six feet in length, and is so called from its monstrous appearance and voracity. The sea-scorpion is likewise of a hideous form, its head being larger than its whole body, which is about four feet in length; and its bite is said to be poisonous.

The most seemingly fabulous accounts of the ancients, concerning sea-monsters, are rendered credible by the productions of the Norwegian seas; and the sea-snake, or serpent of the ocean, is no longer counted a chimera. In 1756, one of them was shot by a master of a ship; its head resembled that of a horse; the mouth

mouth was large and black, as were the eyes, a white mane hanging from its neck: it floated on the furface of the water, and held its head at leaſt two feet out of the ſea: between the head and neck were ſeven or eight folds, which were very thick; and the length of this ſnake was more than a hundred yards, ſome ſay fathoms. They have a remarkable averſion to the ſmell of caſtor; for which reaſon, ſhip, boat, and bark maſters, provide themſelves with quantities of that drug, to prevent being overſet; the ſerpent's olfactory nerves being remarkably exquiſite. The particularities recounted of this animal would be incredible, were they not atteſted upon oath. Egede (a very creditable author) ſays, that on the 6th day of July, 1734, a large and frightful ſea-monſter raiſed itſelf ſo high out of the water, that its head reached above the main-top-maſt of the ſhip; that it had a long ſharp ſnout, broad paws, and ſpouted water like a whale; that the body ſeemed to be covered with ſcales; the ſkin was uneven and wrinkled, and the lower part was formed like a ſnake. The body of this monſter is ſaid to be as thick as a hogſhead; his ſkin is variegated like a tortoiſe-ſhell; and his excrement, which floats upon the ſurface of the water, is corroſive, and bliſters the hands of the ſeamen if they handle it.

I ſhould be under great difficulty in mentioning the kraken, or korven, were not its exiſtence proved ſo ſtrongly, as ſeem to put it out of all doubt. Its bulk is ſaid to be a mile and a half in circumference; and when part of it appears above the water, it reſembles a number of ſmall iſlands and ſand-banks, on which fiſhes diſport themſelves, and ſeaweeds grow: upon a farther emergement, a number of pellucid antennæ, each about the height, form, and ſize of a moderate maſt, appear; and by their action and re-action he gathers his food, conſiſting of ſmall fiſhes. When he ſinks, which he does gradually, a dangerous ſwell of the ſea ſucceeds, and a kind of whirlpool is naturally formed in the water. In 1680, a young kraken periſhed among the rocks and cliffs of the pariſh of Aliſtahong; and his death was attended by ſuch a ſtench, that the channel where it died was impaſſable. Without entering into any romantic theories, we may ſafely ſay, that the exiſtence of this fiſh being proved, accounts for many of thoſe phænomena of floating iſlands, and tranſitory appearances in the ſea, that have hitherto been held as fabulous by the learned, who could have no idea of ſuch an animal.

The mermen and mer-women, hold their reſidence in the Norwegian ſeas; but I cannot give credit to all that is related concerning them by the natives. The merman is about eight ſpans long, and, undoubtedly, has as much reſemblance as an ape

ape has to the human species; a high forehead, little eyes, a flat nose, and large mouth, without chin or ears, characterize its head; its arms are short, but without joints or elbows, and they terminate in members resembling a human hand, but of the paw kind, and the fingers connected by a membrane: the parts of generation indicate their sexes; though their under part, which remain in the water, terminate like those of fishes. The females have breasts, at which they suckle their young ones. It would far exceed the bounds allotted to this article, to follow the Norwegian adventurers through all the different descriptions which they have given us of their fishes; but they are so well authenticated, that I make no doubt, a new and very surprizing theory of aquatic animals may in time be formed.

CURIOSITIES.] Those of Norway are only natural. On the coast, latitude 67, is that dreadful vortex, or whirlpool, called by navigators, the navel of the sea, and by some Malestrom, or Moskoestrom. The island Moskoe, from whence this stream derives its name, lies between the mountain Hesseggen in Lofoden, and the island Ver, which are about one league distant; and between the island and coast on each side, the stream makes its way. Between Moskoe and Lofoden, it is near 400 fathoms deep; but between Moskoe and Ver, it is so shallow, as not to afford passage for a small ship. When it is flood, the stream runs up the country between Lofoden and Moskoe with a boisterous rapidity; and when it is ebb, returns to the sea with a violence and noise, unequalled by the loudest cataracts. It is heard at the distance of many leagues, and forms a vortex or whirlpool of great depth and extent; so violent, that if a ship comes near it, it is immediately drawn irresistibly into the whirl and there disappears; being absorbed and carried down to the bottom in a moment, where it is dashed to pieces against the rocks; and just at the turn of ebb and flood, when the water becomes still for about a quarter of an hour, it rises again in scattered fragments, scarcely to be known for the parts of a ship. When it is agitated by a storm, it has reached vessels at the distance of more than a Norway mile, where the crews have thought themselves in perfect security. Perhaps it is hardly in the power of fancy to conceive a situation of more horror, than of being thus driven forward by the sudden violence of an impetuous torrent, to the vortex of a whirlpool, of which the noise and turbulence still increasing as it is approached, are an earnest of quick and inevitable destruction; while the wretched victims, in an agony of despair and terror, cry out for that help which they know to be impossible; and see before them the dreadful abyss, in which they
are

are about to be plunged and dashed among the rocks at the bottom.

Even animals which have come too near the vortex, have expressed the utmost terror, when they find the stream irresistible. Whales are frequently carried away, and the moment they feel the force of the water, they struggle against it with all their might, howling and bellowing in a frightful manner. The like happens frequently to bears, who attempt to swim to the island to prey upon the sheep.

It is the opinion of Kircher, that the Malestrom is a sea vortex, which attracts the flood under the shore of Norway, and discharges it again in the gulph of Bothnia: but this opinion is now known to be erroneous, by the return of the shattered fragments of whatever happens to be sucked down by it. The large stems of firs and pines rise again so shivered and splintered, that the pieces look as if covered with bristles. The whole phænomena are the effects of the violence of the daily ebb and flood, occasioned by the contraction of the stream in its course between the rocks.

PEOPLE, LANGUAGE, RELIGION, AND CUSTOMS OF NORWAY. } The Norwegians are a middling kind of people, between the simplicity of the Greenlanders and Icelanders, and the more polished manners of the Danes. Their religion is Lutheran; and they have bishops, as those of Denmark, without temporal jurisdiction. Their viceroy, like his master, is absolute; but we may easily conceive that he makes no barbarous use of his power, because we know of few or no representations or insurrections of the people against it.

The Norwegians in general, are strong, robust, and brave; but quick in resenting real or supposed injuries. The women are handsome and courteous; and the Norwegian forms, both of living, and enjoying property, are mild, and greatly resembling the Saxon ancestors of the present English. Every inhabitant is an artizan, and supplies his family in all its necessaries with is own manufactures; so that in Norway, there are few, by profession, who are hatters, shoe-makers, taylors, tanners, weavers, carpenters, smiths, and joiners. The lowest Norwegian peasant is an artist and a gentleman, and even a poet. They often mix with oatmeal the bark of the fir, made into a kind of flower; and they are reduced to very extraordinary shifts for supplying the place of bread, or farinaceous food. The manners of the middling Norwegians, form a proper subject of contemplation even to a philosopher, as they lead that kind of life which we may say is furnished with plenty; but they are neither fond of luxury, nor dreading penury: this middle state prolongs their ages surprizingly. Though their dress is accommodated to their climate, yet, by custom, instead of guarding against the inclemency of the weather, they outbrave it; for they expose themselves to cold, without any coverture upon their breasts or necks. A Norwegian of a hundred years of age, is not accounted past his labour: and in 1733, four couples were married, and danced before his Danish majesty at Fredericshall, whose ages, when joined, exceeded 800 years.

The funeral ceremonies of the Norwegians contain vestiges of their former paganism: they play on the violin at the head of the coffin, and while the corpse is carried to the church, which is often done in a boat. In some places the mourners ask the dead person why he died; whether his wife and neighbours were kind to him, and other such questions; frequently kneeling down and asking forgiveness, if ever they had offended the deceased.

COMMERCE.] We have little to add to this head, different from what shall be observed in our account of Denmark. The duties on their exports, most of which have been already recounted, amount to about 100,000 rixdollars a year.

STRENGTH AND REVENUE.] By the best calculations, Norway can furnish out 14,000 excellent seamen, and above 30,000 brave soldiers, for the use of their king, without hurting either trade or agriculture. The royal annual revenue from Norway amounts to about 200,000 l. and till his present majesty's accession, the army, instead of being expensive, added considerably to his majesty's income, by the subsidies it brought him in from foreign princes.

HISTORY.] We must refer to Denmark likewise for this head. The antient Norwegians certainly were a very brave and powerful people, and the hardiest seamen in the world. If we are to believe their histories, they were no strangers to America long before it was discovered by Columbus. Many customs of their ancestors are yet discernible in Ireland and the north of Scotland, where they made frequent descents, and some settlements, which are generally confounded with those of the Danes. From their being the most turbulent, they are become now the most loyal subjects in Europe; which we can easily account for, from the barbarity and tyranny of their kings, when a separate people. Since the union of Calmar, which united Norway to Denmark, their history, as well as interests, are the same with that of Denmark.

DENMARK Proper.

Extent and Situation.

Length 240 } between { 8 and 13 East longitude.
Breadth 180 }   { 54 and 58 North latitude.

BOUNDARIES AND DIVISIONS.] IT is divided on the north from Norway by the Scaggerac sea, and from Sweden on the east by the Sound; on the south by Germany and the Baltic; and the German sea divides it from Great-Britain on the west.

Denmark Proper is divided into two parts; Jutland, and the islands at the entrance of the Baltic sea.

MOUNTAINS, FORESTS, LAKES, RIVERS, CLIMATE, AND SOIL.] Jutland consists chiefly of barren mountains, but some corn grows in the vallies. The face of the country presents a number of large forests; but there is scarcely in Denmark a river navigable to a ship of burden. Some lakes, which contain delicious fishes, are found in the inland parts of the country. The climate is more temperate here, on account of the vapours from the surrounding sea, than it is in many more southerly parts of Europe. Spring and autumn are seasons scarcely known in Denmark, where winter, and sultry heats during June, July, and August, possess the air. The soil is more recommendable for its pasturage, than for its common vegetable productions. The vallies are in general fruitful; but the soil is sandy in the islands, and requires plentiful showers to raise even a crop of hay.

ANIMALS.] Denmark produces an excellent breed of horses, both for the saddle and carriage; and numbers of black cattle, sheep, and hogs, besides game; and its sea-coasts are generally well supplied with fish.

POPULATION, MANNERS AND CUSTOMS.] By an actual numeration, made in 1759, of his Danish majesty's subjects, in his dominions of Denmark, Norway, Holstein, the islands in the Baltic, and the counties of Oldenburg and Delmenhorst, in Westphalia; they amounted to 2,444,000 souls, exclusive of the Icelanders and Greenlanders. However disproportioned this number may seem, to the extent of his Danish majesty's dominions, yet, every thing considered, it is far greater than could have been expected from the uncultivated state of his possessions; and it is more than sufficient for all the purposes of commerce. As population generally keeps pace with plenty, especially in northern countries, there can be no doubt that the number of his Danish majesty's subjects, in a few years, will be vastly encreased, by the improvements introduced among them in agriculture and other arts.

The noble difposition of his Danifh majefty for improving his country, renders it very difficult to fpeak with any certainty concerning the manners and cuftoms, the police and manufactures of his dominions. Commerce, undoubtedly, is on the reviving hand in Denmark; and fince the kings there have been rendered abfolute, particular titles of honour, fuch as thofe of count and baron, have been introduced into the kingdom; but the adventuring, warlike fpirit, feems to be loft among their nobility, whofe civil powers are indeed annihilated, but they are tyrants over their inferiors and tenants, who, as to property, are ftill in a ftate of vaffalage. It is more than probable, however, that his prefent Danifh majefty will, in that and all other refpects, give a new face to the police of his country; and he has already taken fome effectual meafures for that purpofe, by meliorating the ftate of the peafants; the only fpur to induftry.

The Danes, like other northern nations, are given to intemperance in drinking, and convivial entertainments; but their nobility, who now begin to vifit the other courts of Europe, are refining from their provincial habits and vices.

RELIGION.] The religion is Lutheran; and the kingdom is divided into fix diocefes; one in Zealand, one in Funen, and four in Jutland: thefe diocefes are governed by bifhops, whofe profeffion is entirely to fuperintend the other clergy; nor have they any other mark of pre-eminency than a diftinction of their ecclefiaftical drefs, for they have neither cathedrals nor ecclefiaftical courts, nor the fmalleft concern with civil affairs: their morals, however, are fo good, that they are revered by the people.

LANGUAGE AND LEARNING.] The language of Denmark is a dialect of the Teutonic; but High Dutch and French are fpoken at court; and the nobility have lately made great advances in the Englifh, which is now publickly taught at Copenhagen as a neceffary part of education. A company of Englifh comedians occafionally vifit that capital, where they find tolerable encouragement.

The univerfity of Copenhagen is faid now to be encouraged by the government; but the Danes in general make no great figure in literature; though aftronomy and medicine are highly indebted to Tycho Brahe, Borrichius, and the Bartholines; not to mention that the Danes begin now to make fome promifing attempts in hiftory, poetry, and the drama.

CITIES AND CHIEF BUILDINGS.] Copenhagen, which is fituated on the fine ifland of Zealand, makes a magnificent
appearance

appearance at a diſtance. It is very ſtrong, and defended by four royal caſtles or forts. It contains ten pariſh churches, beſides nine others, belonging to Calviniſts and other perſuaſions, and ſome hoſpitals. Copenhagen is adorned by ſome public and private palaces, as they are called. Its ſtreets are 186 in number; and its inhabitants amount to 100,000. The houſes in the principal ſtreets are built of brick, and thoſe in their lanes chiefly of timber. Its univerſity has been already mentioned. But the chief glory of Copenhagen is its harbour, which admits indeed of only one ſhip to enter at a time, but is capable of containing 500. Several of the ſtreets have canals, and quays for ſhips to lie cloſe to the houſes; and its naval arſenal is ſaid far to exceed that of Venice.

The fineſt palace belonging to his Daniſh majeſty, lies about 20 Engliſh miles from Copenhagen, and is called Fredericſburg. It is a moſt magnificent houſe, and built in the modern taſte; but ill contrived, and worſe ſituated; being in a moiſt unhealthy ſoil. While the kings of Denmark reſide, as they often do, at this palace, they lay aſide great part of their ſtate, and mingle with their ſubjects in their diverſions both of the court and the field.

Jagerſburg, is a park which contains a royal country ſeat, called the Hermitage; which is remarkable for the diſpoſition of its apartments, and the quaintneſs of its furniture; particularly a machine, which conveys the diſhes to and from the king's table in the ſecond ſtory. The chief eccleſiaſtical building in Denmark, is the cathedral of Roſchild, where the kings and queens of Denmark were formerly buried, and their monuments ſtill remain. Joining to this cathedral, by a covered paſſage, is a royal palace, built in 1733.

COMMERCE.] I ſhall, under this head, include the commodities and manufactures imported to and exported from the country. Fir, and other timber, black cattle, horſes, butter, ſtock-fiſh, tallow, hides, train-oil, tar, pitch, and iron, are the natural product of the Daniſh dominions; and conſequently are ranked under the head of exports. To theſe we may add furs; but the exportation of oats is forbid. The imports are, ſalt, wine, brandy and ſilk from France, Portugal, and Italy. Of late the Danes have had a great intercourſe with England, from whence they import broad-cloths, clocks, cabinet, lockwork, and all other manufactures carried on in the great trading towns of England. But nothing ſhews the commercial ſpirit of the Danes in a ſtronger light, than their eſtabliſhments in the Eaſt and Weſt-Indies.

In 1612, Chriſtiern IV. of Denmark, eſtabliſhed an Eaſt-India company at Copenhagen; and, ſoon after, four ſhips ſailed from thence to the E. ft-Indies. The hint of this trade was given to his Danifh majefty by James I. of England, who married a princefs of Denmark; and in 1617 they built and fortified a caftle and town at Tranquebar, on the coaft of Coromandel. The fecurity which many of the Indians found under the cannon of this fort, invited numbers of them to fettle here; fo that the Danifh Eaft-India company were foon rich enough to pay to their king a yearly tribute of 10,000 rix-dollars. The company, however, willing to become rich all of a fudden, in 1620, endeavoured to poffefs themfelves of the fpice-trade at Ceylon; but were defeated by the Portuguefe. The truth is, they foon embroiled themfelves with the native Indians on all hands; and had it not been for the generous affiftance given them by Mr. Pit, an Englifh Eaft-India governor, the fettlement at Tranquebar muft have been taken by the rajah of Tanjour. Upon the clofe of the wars of Europe, after the death of Charles XII. of Sweden, the Danifh Eaft-India company found themfelves fo much in debt, that they publifhed propofals for a new fubfcription, for enlarging their ancient capital ftock, and for fitting out fhips to Tranquebar, Bengal, and China. Two years after, his Danifh majefty granted a new charter to his Eaft-India company, with vaft privileges; and for fome time its commerce was carried on with great vigour. I fhall juft mention, that the Danes likewife poffefs the iflands of St. Thomas and St. Croix, in the Weft-Indies; which are free ports, and celebrated for fmuggling; alfo the fort of Chriftianburg, on the coaft of Guinea; and carry on a confiderable commerce with the Mediterranean.

CURIOSITIES, NATURAL AND ARTIFICIAL. } Denmark Proper, affords fewer of thefe than the other parts of his Danifh majefty's dominions, if we except the contents of the Royal Mufeum at Copenhagen, which confifts of a numerous collection of both. Befides artificial fkeletons, ivory carvings, models, clock-work, and a beautiful cabinet of ivory and ebony, made by a Danifh artift who was blind, here are to be feen two famous antique drinking veffels; the one of gold, the other of filver, and both in the form of a hunting horn: that of gold feems to be of pagan manufacture; and from the raifed hieroglyphical figures on its outfide, it probably was made ufe of in religious ceremonies: it is about two feet nine inches long, weighs 102 ounces, contains two Englifh pints and a half; and was found in the diocefe of Ripen, in the year 1639. The other, of filver, weighs about four pounds, and is termed *Cornu Oldenburgicum*; which, they fay, was prefented to Otho I. duke of Oldenburg, by a Ghoft. Some, however, are of opinion, that this veffel was

made

made by order of Christiern I. king of Denmark, the first of the Oldenburg race, who reigned in 1448. I shall just mention in this place, that several vessels of different metals, and the same form, have been found in the north of England, and are probably of Danish original. This museum is likewise furnished with a prodigious number of astronomical, optical, and mathematical instruments; some Indian curiosities, and a set of medals antient and modern. Many curious astronomical instruments are likewise placed in the round tower at Copenhagen; which is so contrived, that a coach may drive to its top. The village of Anglen, lying between Flensburg and Sleswic, is also esteemed a curiosity, as giving its name to the Angles, or Anglo-Saxon inhabitants of Great-Britain, and the ancestors of the bulk of the modern English.

The greatest rarities in his Danish majesty's dominions are omitted, however, by geographers; I mean those antient inscriptions upon rocks, that are mentioned by antiquaries and historians; and are generally thought to be the old and original manner of writing, before the use of paper of any kind, and waxen tables, was known. These characters are Runic, and so imperfectly understood by the learned themselves, that their meaning is very uncertain; but they are imagined to be historical. Stephanus, in his notes upon Saxo Grammaticus, has exhibited specimens of several of those inscriptions.

CIVIL CONSTITUTION, GOVERNMENT AND LAWS. The civil constitution of Denmark, in its present despotic state, arises out of the ruins of the aristocratic powers which the nobility exercised over their inferiors with most intolerable tyranny. Formerly their kings were elective, and might be deposed by the convention of estates, which included the representatives of the peasants. The king's royalty gave him pre-eminence in the field and the courts of justice, but no revenues were attached to it; and unless he had a great estate of his own, he was obliged to live like a private nobleman. In process of time, however, the regal dignity became hereditary; or rather, the states tacitly acquiesced in that mode of government, to prevent the horrible ravages which they had experienced from civil wars and disputed successions. Their kings of the race of Oldenburg, the present royal family, though some of them were brave and spirited princes, did not chuse to abridge the nobility of their powers; and a series of unsuccessful wars rendered the nation in general so miserable, that the public had not money for paying off the army. The dispute came to a short question, which was, that the nobles should submit to taxes, from which they pleaded an exemption. The inferior people then, as usual,
threw

threw their eyes towards the king, for relief and protection from the oppressions of the intermediate order of nobility: in this they were encouraged by the clergy. In a meeting of the states, it was proposed that the nobles should bear their share in the common burden. Upon this, one Otta Craeg put the people in mind that the commons were no more than slaves to the lords.

This was the watch-word, which had been concerted between the leaders of the commons, the clergy, and even the court itself. Nanson, the speaker of the commons, catched hold of the term Slavery, the assembly broke up in a ferment; and the commons, with the clergy, withdrew to a house of their own, where they resolved to make the king a solemn tender of their liberties and services; and formally to establish in his family the hereditary succession to their crown. This resolution was executed the next day. The bishop of Copenhagen officiated as speaker for the clergy and commons. The king accepted of their tender, promising them relief and protection. The gates of Copenhagen were shut; and the nobility, finding the nerves of their power thus cut, submitted with the best grace they could, to confirm what had been done.

It is happy for the Danes, that ever since the year 1660, when this great revolution took place, few or no instances have happened, of abusing the despotic powers thus vested in the kings, which are at present perhaps more extensive than those of any crowned head in Europe. On the contrary, the administration of civil justice in Denmark is considered by many as a model for other nations; and some princes, his Prussian majesty particularly, have actually adopted great part of it. The code of the Danish laws, is a quarto volume, drawn up in the language of the country, in so plain and perspicuous a manner, and upon such simple principles of justice, that the most ignorant may learn it; and every man may plead his own cause: and no suit is to hang in suspence beyond one year and a month. But *the king hath privilege to explain, nay, to alter and change the same as he shall think good.* In Denmark there are two inferior courts, from which appeals lie to a High Right court in Copenhagen, where the king presides, assisted by his chief nobility. Judges are punished in cases of misbehaviour or corruption. Other tribunals are instituted for the affairs of the revenue, army, commerce, admiralty, and criminal matters. In short, it is allowed on all hands, that the civil policy of Denmark, and its executive powers, produce wonderful effects for the safety of the people as well as of the government.

DENMARK.

POLITICAL AND NATURAL INTERESTS OF DENMARK. } Since the acceſſion of his preſent majeſty, his court ſeems to have altered its maxims. His father, it is true, obſerved a moſt reſpectable neutrality during the late war; but never could get rid of French influence, notwithſtanding his connections with Great-Britain. The ſubſidies he received maintained his army; but his family-diſputes with Ruſſia, concerning Holſtein, and the aſcendency which the French had obtained over the Swedes, not to mention many other matters, did not ſuffer him to act that deciſive part in the affairs of Europe, to which he was invited by his ſituation; eſpecially about the time the treaty of Cloſter-ſeven was concluded. His preſent Daniſh majeſty's plan, ſeems to be that of forming his dominions into a ſtate of independency, by availing himſelf of their natural advantages. His friendſhip with Great-Britain, and the preſent divided deſpicable condition of the Swedes, together with the pacific diſpoſition of the princes of the empire, leave him at full leiſure to proſecute the great plans he has formed. The improvements his ſubjects have made ſince the reign of Frederic IV. who died in 1730, in manufactures and the mechanical arts, are aſtoniſhing; and the wiſe ſumptuary laws, eſpecially thoſe againſt imports of foreign manufactures, keep immenſe ſums in the kingdom.

With regard to the external intereſts of Denmark, they are certainly beſt ſecured by cultivating a friendſhip with the maritime powers. The preſent condition of her navy, renders her ſecure by ſea from Sweden and Ruſſia, whoſe marine, when united, falls ſhort of that of Denmark; for though the Ruſſians maintain a large number of ſhips, yet they are ſo poorly navigated, that Ruſſia cannot be conſidered as a maritime power. The exports of Denmark enables her to carry on a very profitable trade with France, Spain, and the Mediterranean; and ſhe is particularly courted by the Mahometan ſtates, on account of her ſhip-building ſtores. His preſent majeſty, like his father and grandfather, makes ſtrong efforts for drawing the trade of Hamburgh towards the favourite town of Altena; but hitherto with little apparent ſucceſs. This rivalſhip, however, never can embroil her with any European power, provided his Daniſh majeſty is ſo wiſe as to make no attempt upon the city of Hamburgh itſelf.

The preſent imperial family of Ruſſia has indeed many claims upon Denmark, on account of Holſtein; but as her poſſeſſions were guaranteed by his Britannic majeſty, there is but ſmall appearance of her being engaged in a war on that account. Were the Swedes to regain their military character, and to be commanded by so enterprising and despotic a prince as Charles XII. they probably would endeavour to repossess themselves, by arms, of the fine provinces torn from them by Denmark; but of this there is at present very small likelihood; and, whatever the arts of France may attempt, the Danes will always look with a jealous eye upon every measure taken for abolishing the present forms of the Swedish constitution. The greatest danger that can arise to Denmark from a foreign power is, when the Baltic sea (as has happened more than once) is so frozen over, as to bear not only men, but heavy artillery; in which case the Swedes have been known to march over great armies, and to threaten the conquest of the kingdom.

REVENUES.] His Danish majesty's revenues have three sources: the impositions he lays upon his own subjects; the duties paid by foreigners; and his own demesne lands, including confiscations. Wine, salt, tobacco, and provisions of all kinds, are moderately taxed. Marriages, paper, corporations, land, houses, and poll-money, raise a considerable sum. The expences of fortifications are borne by the people: and when the king's daughter is married, they pay about 100,000 rix-dollars towards her portion. The reader is to observe, that the internal taxes of Denmark are very uncertain, because they may be abated or raised at the king's will. Customs, and tolls upon exports and imports, are more certain. The tolls paid by strangers, arise chiefly from foreign ships that pass through the Sound into the Baltic, through the narrow strait between Schonen and the island of Zealand. These tolls are in proportion to the size of the ship and value of the cargo, exhibited in bills of lading. This tax, which forms a capital part of his Danish majesty's revenue, has more than once thrown the northern parts of Europe into a flame. It was often disputed by the English and Dutch; and the Swedes, who command the opposite side of the pass, for some time, refused to pay it; but in the treaty of 1720, between Sweden and Denmark, under the guarantee of his Britannic majesty, George I. the Swedes agreed to pay the same rates as are paid by the subjects of Great-Britain and the Netherlands. The toll is paid at Elsenore, a town seated on the Sound, at the entrance of the Baltic sea, and about 18 miles distant from Copenhagen. No estimate can be made of its produce, nor of the gross revenue of Denmark; though it is generally thought to amount at present to about 700,000 l. a year; a sum which, in that country, goes far, and maintains a splendid court, and powerful armaments both by sea and land.

ARMY AND NAVY.] The three last kings of Denmark, notwithstanding the degeneracy of their people in martial affairs,

fairs, were very respectable princes, by the number and discipline of their troops, which they have kept up with vast care. The present army of Denmark consists of 40,000 men, cavalry and infantry; most of whom are officered by foreigners. Though this army is burdensome to the nation, yet it costs little to the crown: great part of the infantry lie in Norway, where they live upon the boors at free quarter; and in Denmark, the peasantry are obliged to maintain the cavalry in victuals and lodging, and even to furnish them with money. His present majesty seems determined to re-establish the naval force of his kingdom, and to rank himself as a maritime power. It must be acknowledged that he has great invitation to such a conduct; his subjects in general are excellent seamen; Copenhagen has a noble capacious sea-port; and the present naval force of Denmark is said to consist of 30 ships of the line.

ORDERS OF KNIGHTHOOD IN DENMARK.] These are two; that of the Elephant, and that of Daneburg: the former was instituted by Christiern I. and is deemed the most honourable; its badge is an elephant surmounted with a castle, set in diamonds, and suspended to a sky-coloured watered ribbon; worn like the George in England: the number of its members, besides the sovereign, are thirty. The badges of the Daneburg order, which is said to be of the highest antiquity, consist of a white ribbon with red edges, worn over the left shoulder; from which depends a small cross of diamonds, and an embroidered star on the breast of the coat, surrounded with the motto, *Pietate & justitia*.

HISTORY.] We owe the chief history of Denmark, to a very extraordinary phænomenon; I mean, the revival of the purity of the Latin language in Scandinavia, in the person of Saxo Grammaticus, at a time (the 12th century) when it was lost over all other parts of the European continent. Saxo, like the other historians of his age, has adopted, and at the same time ennobled by his style, the most ridiculous absurdities of remote antiquity. We can, however, collect enough from him to conclude, that the antient Danes, like the Gauls, the Scots, the Irish, and other northern nations, had their bards; who recounted the military atchievements of their heroes; and that their first histories were written in verse. There can be no doubt that the Scandinavians (the inhabitants of Denmark, Norway, and Sweden) were Scythians by their original; but how far the tracts of land, called either Scythia * or Gaul, formerly reached, is uncertain.

Even

---

* By Scythia may be understood all those northern countries of Europe and Asia, now inhabited by the Danes, Norwegians, Swedes, Russians, and Tartars. See the Introduction.

DENMARK.

Even the name of the first Christian Danish king is uncertain; and those of the people whom they commanded were so blended together, that it is impossible for the reader to conceive a precise idea of the old Scandinavian history. This, undoubtedly, was owing to the remains of their Scythian customs, particularly that of removing from one country to another; and of several nations or septs joining together in expeditions by sea or land; and the adventurers being denominated after their chief leaders. Thus the terms Danes, Saxons, Jutes or Goths, Germans, and Normans, were promiscuously used long after the time of Charlemagne. Even the short revival of literature under that prince, throws very little light upon the Danish history. All we know is, that the inhabitants of Scandinavia, in their maritime expeditions, went generally under the name of Saxons with foreigners; that they were bold adventurers; that so far back as the year of Christ 500, they insulted all the sea coasts of Europe; that they settled in Ireland, where they built stone houses; and that they became masters of England, and some part of Scotland; both which kingdoms still retain proofs of their barbarity. When we read the history of Denmark and that of England, under the Danish princes who reigned over both countries, we meet with but a faint resemblance of events; but the Danes, as conquerors, always give themselves the superiority over the English.

Few very interesting events in Denmark preceded the year 1387, when Margaret mounted that throne; and partly by her address, and partly by hereditary right, she formed the union of Calmar; by which she was acknowledged sovereign of Sweden, Denmark, and Norway. She held her dignity with such firmness and courage, that she was justly stiled the Semiramis of the North. Her successors being destitute of her great qualifications, the union of Calmar fell to nothing; but Norway still continued annexed to Denmark. About the year 1448, the crown of Denmark fell to Christiern, count of Oldenburg, from whom the present royal family of Denmark is descended.

In 1513, Christiern II. king of Denmark, one of the most complete tyrants that modern times have produced, mounted the throne of Denmark; and having married the sister of the emperor Charles V. he gave a full loose to his innate cruelty. Being driven out of Sweden, for the bloody massacres he committed there, the Danes rebelled against him likewise; and he fled, with his wife and children, into the Netherlands. About the year 1536, the protestant religion was established in Denmark, by that wise and politic prince Christiern III.

Christiern IV. of Denmark, in 1629, was chosen for the head of the protestant league, formed against the house of Austria;

Auſtria ; but, though brave in his own perſon, he was in danger of loſing his dominions ; when he was ſucceeded in that command by Guſtavus Adolphus. The Dutch having obliged Chriſtiern, who died in 1648, to lower the duties of the Sound, his ſon, Frederic III. conſented to accept of an annuity of 150,000 florins for the whole. The Dutch, after this, perſuaded him to declare war againſt Charles Guſtavus, king of Sweden ; which had almoſt coſt him his crown in 1657. Charles ſtormed the fortreſs of Fredericſtadt ; and in the ſucceeding winter, he marched his army over the ice to the iſland of Funen, where he ſurpriſed the Daniſh troops, took Odenſee and Nyburg ; and marched over the Great Belt, to beſiege Copenhagen itſelf. Cromwell, the Engliſh uſurper, interpoſed ; and Frederic defended his capital with great magnanimity, till the peace of Roſchild ; by which Frederic ceded the provinces of Halland, Bleking, and Sconia, the iſland of Bornholm, and Bahus and Drontheim, in Norway, to the Swedes. Frederic ſought to elude thoſe ſevere terms ; but Charles took Cronenburg, and once more beſieged Copenhagen by ſea and land. The ſteady intrepid conduct of Frederic under theſe misfortunes, endeared him to his ſubjects ; and the citizens of Copenhagen made an admirable defence, till a Dutch fleet arrived in the Baltic, and beat the Swediſh fleet. The fortune of war was now entirely changed in favour of Frederic ; who ſhewed on every occaſion great abilities, both civil and military ; and having forced Charles to raiſe the ſiege of Copenhagen, might have carried the war into Sweden, had not the Engliſh fleet, under Montague, appeared in the Baltic. This enabled Charles to beſiege Copenhagen a third time ; but France and England offering their mediation, a peace was concluded in that capital ; by which the iſland of Bornholm returned to the Danes ; but the iſland of Rugen, Bleking, Halland, and Schonen, remained with the Swedes.

Though this peace did not reſtore to Denmark all ſhe had loſt, yet the magnanimous behaviour of Frederic, under the moſt imminent dangers, and his attention to the ſafety of his ſubjects, even preferably to his own, indeared him ſo much in their eyes, that they rendered him abſolute, in the manner and for the reaſons I have already mentioned. Frederic was ſucceeded, in 1670, by his ſon, Chriſtiern V. who obliged the duke of Holſtein Gottorp to renounce all the advantages he had gained by the treaty of Roſchild. He then recovered a number of places in Schonen ; but his army was defeated in the bloody battle of Lunden, by Charles XI. of Sweden. This defeat did not put an end to the war ; which Chriſtiern obſtinately continued, till he was defeated entirely at the battle of Landscroon: and he had almost exhausted his dominions in his military operations, till he was in a manner abandoned by all his allies, and forced to sign a treaty on the terms prescribed by France, in 1679. Christiern, however, did not desist from his military attempts; and at last he became the ally and subsidiary of Lewis XIV. who was then threatning Europe with chains. Christiern, after a vast variety of treating and fighting with the Holsteiners, Hamburghers, and other northern powers, died in 1699. He was succeeded by Frederic IV. who, like his predecessors, maintained his pretensions upon Holstein; and probably must have become master of that dutchy, had not the English and Dutch fleets raised the siege of Tonningen; while the young king of Sweden, Charles XII. who was no more than sixteen years of age, landed within eight miles of Copenhagen, to assist his brother-in-law, the duke of Holstein. Charles, probably, would have made himself master of Copenhagen, had not his Danish majesty agreed to the peace of Travendahl, which was entirely in the duke's favour. By another treaty concluded with the States General, Charles obliged himself to furnish a body of troops, who were to be paid by the confederates; and who afterwards did great service against the French.

Notwithstanding this peace, Frederic was perpetually engaged in wars with the Swedes; and while Charles was an exile at Bender, he made a descent upon the Swedish Pomerania; and another, in the year 1712, upon Bremen, and took the city of Stade. His troops, however, were totally defeated by the Swedes at Gadesbusch, who laid his favourite city of Altena in ashes. Frederic revenged himself, by seizing great part of the ducal Holstein, and forcing the Swedish general, count Steinbock, to surrender himself prisoner, with all his troops. In the year 1716, the successes of Frederic were so great, by taking Tonningen and Stralsund, by driving the Swedes out of Norway, and reducing Wismar, in Pomerania, that his allies began to suspect he was aiming at the sovereignty of all Scandinavia. Upon the return of Charles of Sweden from his exile, he renewed the war against Denmark, with a most embittered spirit; but on the death of that prince, who was killed at the siege of Fredericshal, Fredric durst not refuse the offer of his Britannic majesty's mediation between him and the crown of Sweden; in consequence of which, a peace was concluded at Stockholm, which left him in possession of the dutchy of Sleswic. Frederic died in the year 1730, after having, two years before, seen his capital reduced to ashes, by an accidental fire. His son and successor, Christiern Frederic, made no other use of his power, and the advantages

with

with which he mounted the throne, than to cultivate peace with all his neighbours, and to promote the happiness of his subjects; whom he eased of many oppressive taxes.

In 1734, after guarantying the Pragmatic Sanction, * Christiern sent 6000 men to the assistance of the emperor, during the dispute of the succession to the crown of Poland. Though he was pacific, yet he was jealous of his rights, especially over Hamburgh. He obliged the Hamburghers to call in the mediation of Prussia, to abolish their bank, to admit the coin of Denmark as current, and to pay him a million of silver marks. He had, two years after, viz. 1738, a dispute with his Britannic majesty, about the little lordship of Steinhorst, which had been mortgaged to the latter by a duke of Holstein Lawenburg, and which Christiern said belonged to him. Some blood was spilt during the contest; in which Christiern, it is thought, never was in earnest. It brought on, however, a treaty, in which he availed himself of his Britannic majesty's predilection for his German dominions; for he agreed to pay Christiern a subsidy of 70,000 l. sterling a year, on condition of keeping in readiness 7000 troops for the protection of Hanover: this was a gainful bargain for Denmark. And two years after, he seized some Dutch ships, for trading, without his leave, to Iceland; but the difference was made up by the mediation of Sweden. Christiern had so great a party in that kingdom, that it was generally thought he would revive the union of Calmar, by procuring his son to be declared successor to his then Swedish majesty. Some steps for that purpose were certainly taken: but whatever Christiern's views might have been, the design was frustrated by the jealousy of other powers, who could not bear the thoughts of seeing all Scandinavia subject to one family. Christiern died in 1746, with the character of being the father of his people.

His son and successor, Frederic V. had, in 1743, married the princess Louisa, daughter to his Britannic majesty. He improved upon his father's plan, for the happiness of his people; but took no concern, except that of a mediator, in the German war. For it was by his intervention, that the treaty of Closter-seven was concluded between his royal highness the late duke of Cumberland, and the French general Richlieu. Upon the death of his first queen, who was mother to his present Danish majesty, he married a daughter of the duke of Brunswic-Wolfenbuttel; and died in 1766. His son,

VOL. I.   H   Christiern

---

* An agreement by which the princes of Europe engaged to support the House of Austria in favour of the queen of Hungary, daughter of the emperor Charles VI. who had no male issue.

Chriſtiern VI. was born the 29th of January, 1749; and married his Britannic majeſty's youngeſt ſiſter, the princeſs Carolina-Matilda. I have already mentioned the many fair proſpects which this prince's reign has already opened for the good of his people; and can only add, from the ſpecimens he has given the public of his virtues, that he bids fair to be the greateſt king that ever filled the throne of Denmark.

His Danish Majesty's GERMAN DOMINIONS.

THOSE dominions are mentioned in a ſeparate article chiefly for the ſake of order, as the inhabitants differ little or nothing from other Germans; we ſhall therefore be more general in deſcribing them. The duchy of Sleſwic, which ſome ſay properly belongs to Denmark, is bounded by Jutland, the Baltic, the duchy of Holſtein, and the German ocean. It is well watered, and produces plenty of corn; but the capital city of Sleſwic, which ſtands upon a ſmall arm of the ſea, called the Sley, is much decayed both in trade and population. Gottorp ſtands likewiſe upon the Sley; and was once famous for the magnificent palace of its dukes, and for being the reſidence of the celebrated aſtronomer Tycho Brahe; ſome of his planetary machines and globes ſtill remaining in one of the ſummer-houſes of the palace.

Holſtein belongs partly to Denmark and partly to Ruſſia. The capital of the Daniſh Holſtein is Gluckſtadt, a well-built town and fortreſs, in a marſhy ſituation, on the right of the Elbe; in which is a Lutheran, a Calviniſt, a Romiſh church, and a Jews ſynagogue; and has ſome foreign commerce. Keyl is the capital of the Ducal Holſtein, and is well built, has a harbour, and neat public edifices.

The famous city of Hamburgh lies, in a geographical ſenſe, in Holſtein, but is now an imperial, free, and Hanſeatic city, lying on the verge of that part of Holſtein called Stormar: it has the ſovereignty of a ſmall diſtrict round it, of about ten miles circuit: it is one of the moſt flouriſhing commercial towns in Europe; and though the kings of Denmark ſtill lay claim to certain privileges within its walls, it may be conſidered as a well-regulated commonwealth. The number of its inhabitants are ſaid to amount to 180,000; and it is furniſhed with a vaſt variety of noble edifices, both public and private: it has two ſpacious harbours, formed by the river Elbe, which runs through the town, and 84 bridges are thrown over its canals. Hamburgh has the good fortune of having been peculiarly favoured in its commerce by Great-Britain, with whom
it

it still carries on a great trade. The Hamburghers maintain twelve companies of foot, and one troop of dragoons, besides an artillery company.

In Westphalia, the king of Denmark has the counties of Oldenburg and Delmenhorst; they lie near the south side of the Weser; their capitals, of the same name, are both regularly fortified: and Oldenburg gave a title to the first royal ancestor of his present Danish majesty.

LAPLAND.

THE northern situation of Lapland, and the division of its property, require, before I proceed farther, that I treat of it under a distinct head, and in the same method that I observe in other countries.

SITUATION, EXTENT, DIVISION AND NAME. } The whole country of Lapland extends, so far as it is known, from the North Cape in 71 30 N. lat. to the White-Sea, under the arctic circle. Part of Lapland belongs to the Danes, and is included in the government of Wardhuys; part to the Swedes, which is by far the most valuable; and some parts, in the east, to the Muscovites. It would be little better than wasting the reader's time, to pretend to point out the supposed dimensions of each. That belonging to the Swedes, may be seen in the table of dimensions given in the account of Sweden: but other accounts say, that it is about 100 German miles in length, and 90 in breadth; it comprehends all the country from the Baltic, to the mountains that separate Norway from Sweden. The Muscovite part lies towards the east, between the lake Enarak and the White-Sea. Those parts, notwithstanding the rudeness of the country, are divided into smaller districts; generally taking their names from rivers: but, unless in the Swedish part, which is subject to a prefect, the Laplanders can be said to be under no regular government. The Swedish Lapland therefore is the object considered by authors in describing this country. It has been generally thought, that the Laplanders are the descendants of Finlanders driven out of their own country, and that they take their name from *Lappes*, which signifies exiles. The reader, from what has been said in the Introduction, may easily conceive that in Lapland, for some months in the summer, the sun never sets; and during winter, it never rises: but the inhabitants are so well assisted by the twilight and the aurora borealis, that they never discontinue their work through darkness.

CLIMATE.] In winter, it is no unusual thing for their lips to be frozen to the cup in attempting to drink; and in some thermometers, spirits of wine are concreted into ice: the limbs of the inhabitants very often mortify with cold: drifts of snow threaten to bury the traveller, and cover the ground four or five feet deep. A thaw sometimes takes place, and then the frost that succeeds, presents the Laplander with a smooth level of ice, over which he travels in his sledge with inconceivable swiftness. The heats of summer are excessive for a short time; and the cataracts which dash from the mountains, often present to the eye the most picturesque appearances.

MOUNTAINS, RIVERS, LAKES, AND FORESTS.] The reader must form in his mind, a vast mass of mountains irregularly crowded together, to give him an idea of Lapland: they are, however, in some interstices, separated by rivers and lakes, which contain an incredible number of islands, some of which form delightful habitations; and are believed by the natives to be the terrestrial Paradise: even roses and flowers grow wild on their borders in the summer; but this is but a short gleam of temperature; for the climate in general is excessively severe. Dusky forests, and noisome, unhealthy morasses, cover great part of the flat country; so that nothing can be more uncomfortable than the state of the inhabitants.

METALS AND MINERALS.] Silver and gold mines, as well as those of copper and lead, have been discovered and worked in Lapland: beautiful chrystals are found here, as are some amethysts and topazes; also various sorts of mineral stones, surprizingly polished by the hand of nature; valuable pearls have been sometimes found in rivers, but never in the seas.

ANIMALS, QUADRUPEDS, BIRDS, FISHES, AND INSECTS.] We must refer to our accounts of Denmark and Norway for great part of this article, as its contents are in common with all the three countries. The zibelin, a creature resembling the marten, is a native of Lapland; and its skin, whether black or white, is so much esteemed, that it is frequently given as presents to royal and distinguished personages. The Lapland hares grow white in the winter; and the country produces a large black cat, which attends the natives in hunting. By far the most remarkable, however, of the Lapland animals, is the rein-deer; which nature seems to have provided to solace the Laplanders for the privation of the other comforts of life. This animal, the most useful perhaps of any in the creation, resembles the stag, only it somewhat droops the head, and the horns project forward. In summer, the rein-deer provide themselves with leaves and grass, and in the winter they live upon the moss already described:

scribed: they have a wonderful sagacity at finding it out, and when found, they scrape away the snow, that covers it, with their feet. The scantiness of their fare is inconceivable, as is the length of the journeys which they can perform without any other support. They fix the rein-deer to a kind of sledge, shaped like a small boat, in which the traveller, well secured from cold, is laced down, with the reins in one hand, and a kind of bludgeon in the other, to keep the carriage clear of ice and snow. The deer, whose harnessing is very simple, sets out, and continues the journey with prodigious speed; and is so safe and tractable, that the driver is at little or no trouble in directing him. At night they look out for their own provender; and their milk often helps to support their master. Their instinct in chusing their road and directing their course, can only be accounted for, by their being well acquainted with the country during the summer months, when they live in woods. Their flesh is a well-tasted food, whether fresh or dried: their skin forms excellent cloathing both for the bed and the body: their milk and cheese are nutritive and pleasant; and their intestines and tendons supply their masters with thread and cordage. When they run about wild in the fields, they may be shot at as other game. But it is said, that if one is killed in a flock, the survivors will gore and trample him to pieces; therefore single stragglers are generally pitched upon. Were I to recount every circumstance, related by the credulous, of this animal, the whole would appear fabulous. It is sufficient to observe further, that the number of tame rein-deers possessed by a Laplander, forms the chief part of his riches. With all their excellent qualities, however, the rein-deer have their inconveniences.

It is difficult in summer to keep them from straggling; they are sometimes buried in the snow; and they frequently grow restive, to the great danger of the driver and his carriage. His surprizing speed (for they are said to run at the rate of 200 miles a day) seems to be owing to his impatience to get rid of his incumbrance. None but a Laplander could bear the uneasy posture, when he is confined in one of those carriages or pulkhas; or believe that by whispering the rein-deer in the ear, they know the place of their destination. But after all those abatements, the natives would have difficulty to subsist without their rein-deer, which serves them for more purposes than I have room to mention.

PEOPLE, CUSTOMS, AND MANNERS.] The language of the Laplanders is barbarous, but it seems radically to have come from Finland. Learning has made no progress among them; and they practise such arts only as supply them with the means of living. Missionaries from the christianized parts of Scandinavia, introduced among them the Christian religion; but they cannot be said even yet to be Christians, though they have among them some religious seminaries, instituted by the king of Denmark. Upon the whole, the majority of the Laplanders practise as gross superstitions and idolatries, as are to be found among the most uninstructed pagans; and so absurd, that they scarcely deserve to be mentioned, were it not that the number and oddities of their superstitions, have induced the northern traders to believe that they are skilful in magic and divination. For this purpose their magicians, who are a peculiar set of men, make use of what they call a drum, made of the hollowed trunk of a fir, pine, or birch-tree, one end of which is covered with a skin; on this they draw, with a kind of red colour, the figures of their own gods, as well as of Jesus Christ, the apostles, the sun, moon, stars, birds, and rivers; on these they place one or two brass rings, which, when the drum is beaten with a little hammer, dance over the figures; and according to their progress, the sorcerer prognosticates. Those frantic operations are generally performed for gain; and the northern ship-masters are such dupes to the arts of the impostors, that they often buy from them a magic cord, which contains a number of knots, by opening of which, according to the magician's direction, they gain what wind they want. This is a very common traffic on the banks of the Red-Sea, and is managed with great address on the part of the sorcerer, who keeps up the price of his knotted talisman. The Laplanders still retain the worship of many of the Teutonic gods, but have among them great remains of the druidical institutions. They believe the transmigration of the soul; and have festivals set apart for the worship of certain genii, called Jeuhles, who they think inhabit the air, and have great power over human actions; but being without form or substance, they assign to them neither images nor statues.

Lapland is but poorly peopled, owing to the general barrenness of its soil. The whole number of its inhabitants may amount to about 60,000. Both men and women are in general shorter by the head than more southern Europeans. Maupertuis measured a woman, who was suckling her own child, whose height did not exceed four feet two inches and about a half; they make, however, a more human appearance than the men, who are ill-shaped and ugly, and their heads too large for their bodies.

When a Laplander intends to marry a female, he, or his friends, court her father with brandy; when, with some difficulty, he gains admittance to his fair one, he offers her a
beaver's

beaver's tongue, or some other eatable; which she rejects before company, but accepts of in private. Cohabitation often precedes marriage; but every admittance to the fair one is purchased from her father by the lover with a bottle of brandy, and this prolongs the courtship sometimes for three years. The priest of the parish at last celebrates the nuptials; but the bridegroom is obliged to serve his father-in-law for four years after. He then carries his wife and her fortune home.

COMMERCE.] Little can be said of the commerce of the Laplanders. Their exports consist of fish, rein-deer, furs, baskets, and toys; with some dried pikes, and cheeses made of rein-deer milk. They receive for these, rixdollars, woollen cloths, linen, copper, tin, flour, oil, hides, needles, knives, spirituous liquors, tobacco, and other necessaries. Their mines are generally worked by foreigners, and produce no inconsiderable profit. The Laplanders travel in a kind of caravan, with their families, to the Finland and Norway fairs. And the reader may make some estimate of the medium of commerce among them, when he is told, that fifty squirrel skins, or one fox-skin, and a pair of Lapland shoes, produce one rixdollar; but no computation can be made of the public revenue, the greatest part of which is allotted for the maintenance of the clergy. With regard to the security of their property, few disputes happen; and their judges have no military to enforce their decrees, the people having a remarkable aversion to war; and so far as we know, never employed in any army. The above is the latest and best account that has been received of this extraordinary people. As to the other particulars relating to them, they are in common with their neighbours the Danes, Norwegians, Swedes, and Russians.

SWEDEN.

EXTENT AND SITUATION.

Miles.
Length 800   between   { 56 and 69 north latitude.
Breadth 500   { 10 and 30 east longitude.

BOUNDARIES AND DIVISIONS.] THIS country is bounded by the Baltic Sea, the Sound, and the Categate, or Scaggerac, on the south; by the impassable mountains of Norway, on the west; by Danish or Norwegian Lapland, on the north; and by Muscovy on the east. It is divided into seven provinces: 1. Sweden Proper. 2. Gothland. 3. Livonia. 4. Ingria. (These two provinces belong now, however, to the Ruffians, having been conquered by Peter the Great, and ceded by pofterior treaties.) 5. Finland. 6. Swedifh Lapland: and 7. The Swedifh iflands. Great abatements muft be made for the lakes, and unimproved parts of Sweden; which are fo extenfive, that the habitable part is confined to narrow bounds. The following are the dimenfions given us of this kingdom.

Sweden.	Square miles. 76,835	Sum total. 228,715	Length.	Brdth.	Capital Cities.
Sweden Proper	47,900		342	194	STOCKHOLM N. L. 59 30. E. L. 19 15.
Gothland	25,975		253	160	Calmar
Schonen	2960	76,835	77	56	Lunden
Lapland, and W. Bothnia	76,000		420	340	Torne Uma
Finland, and E. Bothnia	73,000		395	225	Abo Cajenburg
Gothland I.	1000		80	23	Wifby
Oeland I.	560	150,560	55	10	Barkholm
Upper Saxony { Pomerania, P.	960		47	24	Stralfund
{ Rugen I.	360	1,320	24	21	Bergen

The face of Sweden is pretty fimilar to thofe of its neighbouring countries; only it has the advantage of navigable rivers.

CLIMATE AND SEASONS, SOIL AND PRODUCTIONS. } The fame may be faid with regard to this article. Summer burfts from winter; and vegetation is more fpeedy than in fouthern climates; for the fun is here fo hot, as fometimes to fet forefts on fire. Stoves and warm furs mitigate the cold of winter, which is fo intenfe, that the nofes and extremities of the inhabitants are fometimes mortified; and in fuch cafes, the beft remedy that has been found out, is rubbing the affected part with fnow. The Swedes, fince the days of Charles XII. have been at incredible pains to correct the native barrennefs of their country, by erecting colleges of agriculture, and in fome places with great fuccefs. The foil is much the fame with that of Denmark and fome parts of Norway, generally very bad, but in fome vallies furprizingly fertile. The Swedes, till of late years, had not induftry fufficient to remedy the one, nor improve the other. The peafants now follow the agriculture of France and England; and fome late accounts fay, that they rear almoft as much grain as maintains the natives. Gothland produces wheat, rye, barley, oats, peas and beans; and in cafe of deficiency, the people are fupplied from Livonia and

SWEDEN.

and the Baltic provinces. In summer, the fields are verdant, and covered with flowers, and produce strawberries, rasberries, currants, and other small fruits. The common people know, as yet, little of the cultivation of apricots, peaches, nectarines, pine-apples, and the like high-flavoured fruits; but melons are brought to great perfection in dry seasons.

MINERALS AND METALS.] Sweden produces chrystals, amethysts, topazes, porphyry, lapis-lazuli, agate, cornelian, marble, and other fossils. The chief wealth of Sweden, however, arises from her mines of silver, copper, lead, and iron. The last mentioned metal employs no fewer than 450 forges, hammering-mills, and smelting houses. A kind of a gold mine has likewise been discovered in Sweden, but so inconsiderable, that from the year 1741 to 1747, it produced only 2,398 gold ducats, each valued at 9s. 4d. sterling. The first gallery of one silver mine is 100 fathoms below the surface of the earth; the roof is supported by prodigious oaken beams; and from thence the miners descend about 40 fathoms to the lowest vein. This mine is said to produce 20,000 crowns a year. The product of the copper-mines is uncertain; but the whole is loaded with vast taxes and reductions to the government, which has no other resources for the exigencies of state. Those subterraneous mansions are astonishingly spacious, and at the same time commodious for their inhabitants, so that they seem to form a hidden world. The water-falls in Sweden afford excellent conveniency for turning mills for forges; and for some years, the exports of Sweden for iron, brought in 300,000l. sterling. Dr. Busching thinks that they constituted two-thirds of the national revenue. It must, however, be observed, that the extortions of the Swedish government, and the importation of American bar-iron into Europe, and some other causes, have greatly diminished this manufacture in Sweden; so that the Swedes very soon must apply themselves to other branches of trade and improvements, especially in agriculture.

ANTIQUITIES AND CURIOSITIES, NATURAL AND ARTIFICIAL.} A few leagues from Gottenburg, there is a hideous precipice, down which a dreadful cataract of water rushes with such impetuosity, from the height into so deep a bed of water, that large masts, and other bodies of timber, that are precipitated down it, disappear, some for half an hour, and others for an hour, before they are recovered: the bottom of this bed has never been found, though sounded by lines of several hundred fathoms. A remarkable slimy lake, which singes things put into it, has been found in the southern part of Gothland: and several parts of Sweden contain a stone,

which

which being of a yellow colour, intermixed with several streaks of white, as if composed of gold and silver, affords both sulphur, vitriol, allum, and minium. The Swedes pretend to have a manuscript copy of a translation of the Gospels into Gothic, done by a bishop 1300 years ago.

SEAS.] Their seas are the Baltic, and the gulphs of Bothnia and Finland, which are arms of the Baltic; and on the west of Sweden are the Categate sea, and the Sound, a strait about four miles over, which divides Sweden from Denmark.

These seas have no tides, and are frozen up usually four months in the year; nor are they so salt as the ocean, never mixing with it, because a current sets always out of the Baltic sea into the ocean.

ANIMALS, QUADRUPEDS, BIRDS, AND FISHES.] These differ little from those already described in Norway and Denmark, to which I must refer; only the Swedish horses are known to be more serviceable in war than the German. The Swedish hawks, when carried to France, have been known to revisit their native country; as appears from one that was killed in Finland, with an inscription on a small gold plate, signifying that he belonged to the French king. The fishes found in the rivers and lakes of Sweden, are the same with those in other northern countries, and taken in such quantities, that their pikes (particularly) are salted and pickled for exportation. The train-oil of the seals, taken in the gulph of Finland, is a considerable article of exportation.

INHABITANTS, MANNERS, AND CUSTOMS.] There is a great diversity of characters among the people of Sweden; and what is peculiarly remarkable among them, they have been known to have different characters in different ages. At present, their peasants seem to be a heavy plodding race of men, strong and hardy; but without any other ambition than that of subsisting themselves and their families as well as they can: the mercantile classes are much of the same cast; but great application and perseverance is discovered among them all. One could form no idea that the modern Swedes are the descendents of those, who, under Gustavus Adolphus and Charles XII. carried terror in their names through the most distant countries, and shook the foundations of the greatest empires. The intrigues of their senators dragged them to take part in the late war against Prussia; yet their behaviour was spiritless, and their courage contemptible. The principal nobility and gentry of Sweden are naturally brave, polite, and hospitable; they have high and warm notions of honour, and are jealous of their national interests. The dress, exercises, and

and diversions of the common people, are almost the same with those of Denmark: the better sort are infatuated with French modes and fashions. They are not fond of marrying their daughters when young, as they have little to spare in their own life-time. The women go to plough, thresh out the corn, row upon the water, serve the bricklayers, carry burthens, and do all the common drudgeries in husbandry.

RELIGION.] Christianity was introduced here in the 9th century. Their religion is Lutheran, which was propagated among them by Gustavus Vasa, about the year 1523. The Swedes are surprizingly uniform and unremitting in religious matters; and have such an aversion to popery, that castration is the fate of every Roman-catholic priest discovered in their country. The archbishop of Upsal has a revenue of about 400l. a year; and has under him 13 suffragans, besides superintendents, with moderate stipends. No clergyman has the least direction in the affairs of state; but their morals, and the sanctity of their lives, endear them so much to the people, that the government would repent making them its enemies. Their churches are neat, and often ornamented. A body of ecclesiastical laws and canons direct their religious œconomy. A conversion to popery, or a long continuance under excommunication, which cannot pass without the king's permission, is punished by imprisonment and exile.

LANGUAGE, LEARNING, AND LEARNED MEN.] The Swedish language is a dialect of the Teutonic, and resembles that of Denmark. The Swedish nobility and gentry are, in general, more conversant in polite literature than those of many other more flourishing states. They have of late exhibited some noble specimens of their munificence for the improvement of literature; witness their sending, at the expence of private persons, that excellent and candid natural philosopher Haselquist, into the eastern countries for discoveries, where he died. This noble spirit is eminently encouraged by the royal family; and her Swedish majesty purchased, at no inconsiderable expence for that country, all Haselquist's collection of curiosities. That able civilian, statesman, and historian, Puffendorff, was a native of Sweden; and so is the present Linnæus, who has carried natural philosophy, in some branches at least, to the highest pitch. The passion of the famous queen Christina for literature, is well known to the public; and she may be accounted a genius in many branches of knowledge. Even in the midst of the present distractions of Sweden, the fine arts, particularly drawing, sculpture, and architecture, are encouraged and protected. Agricultural learning, both in theory and practice, is now carried to a

great

great height in that kingdom; and the character given by some writers, that the Swedes are a dull heavy people, fitted only for bodily labour, is in a great measure owing to their having no opportunity of exerting their talents.

UNIVERSITIES.] These are the universities of Upsal, instituted near 400 years ago, and patronized by several successive monarchs, particularly by the great Gustavus Adolphus, and his daughter queen Christina. There is another at Abo, in Finland, but not so well endowed nor so flourishing: and there was a third at Lunden, in Schonen, which is now fallen into decay. Every diocese is provided with a free-school, in which boys are qualified for the university.

MANUFACTURES, TRADE, COMMERCE, AND CHIEF TOWNS.] The Swedish commonalty subsist by agriculture, mining, grazing, hunting, and fishing. Their materials for traffic, are the bulky and useful commodities of masts, beams, deal-boards, and other sorts of timber for shipping; tar, pitch, bark of trees, pot-ash, wooden utensils, hides, flax, hemp, peltry, furs, copper, lead, iron, cordage, and fish. Even the manufacturing of iron was introduced into Sweden so late as the 16th century; for till that time they sold their own crude ore to the Hanse towns, and bought it back again manufactured into utensils. About the middle of the 17th century, by the assistance of the Dutch and Flemings, they set up some manufactures of glass, starch, tin, woollen, silk, soap, leather-dressing, and saw-mills. Book-selling was at that time a trade unknown in Sweden. They have since had sugar-baking, tobacco-plantations, and manufactures of sail-cloth, cotton, fustian, and other stuffs; of linen, allum, brimstone, paper-mills, and gunpowder-mills; vast quantities of copper, brass, steel, and iron, are now wrought in Sweden. They have also founderies for cannon, forgeries for fire-arms and anchors, armories, wire and flatting-mills; mills also for fulling, and for boring, and stamping; and of late they have built many ships for sale.

Certain towns in Sweden, being 24 in number, are called Staple-towns, where the merchants are allowed to import and export commodities in their own ships. Those towns which have no foreign commerce, though lying near the sea, are called land-towns. A third kind are termed mine-towns, as belonging to mine districts. The Swedes, about the year 1752, had greatly encreased their exports, and diminished their imports, most part of which arrive, or are sent off in Swedish ships; the Swedes having now a kind of navigation-act, like that of the English. Those promising appearances were, however, blasted, by the madness and jealousies of the

Swedish

Swedish government; the form of which shall be hereafter described; and the people are now so opprest with taxes, that some important revolution is daily expected in that kingdom.

Stockholm is a staple-town, and the capital of the kingdom; it stands about 790 miles north-east from London, upon six contiguous islands, and built upon piles. The castle, though commodious, and covered with copper, has neither strength nor beauty; but accommodates the royal court, and the national courts and colleges. The number of housekeepers who pay taxes, are 60,000. The harbour is spacious and convenient, though difficult of access; and this city is furnished with all the exterior marks of magnificence, and erections for manufactures and commerce (particularly a national bank, the capital of which is 466,666l. 13s. 4d. sterling) that are common to other great European cities.

GOVERNMENT.] The government of Sweden, by which I mean its political constitutions, is of itself a study, occasioned by the checks which each order has upon another. The Swedes, like the Danes, were originally free; but after various revolutions, which will be hereafter mentioned, Charles XII. who was killed in 1718, became despotic. He was succeeded by his sister, Ulrica; who consented to the abolition of despotism, and restored the states to their former liberties; and they, in return, associated her husband, the landgrave of Hesse-Cassel, with her in the government. A new model of the constitution was then drawn up, by which the royal power was brought, perhaps, too low; for the king of Sweden can scarcely be called by that name, being limited in every exercise of government, and even in the education of his own children. The diet of the states appointed the great officers of the kingdom; and all employments of any value, ecclesiastical, civil, or military, are conferred by the king only with the approbation of the senate. The estates are formed of deputies from the four orders, nobility, clergy, burghers and peasants. The representatives of the nobility, which includes the gentry, amount to above 1000, those of the clergy to 200, the burghers to about 150, and the peasants to 250. Each order sits in its own house, and has its own speaker; and each chuses a secret committee for the dispatch of business. The states are to be convoked once in three years, in the month of January; and their collective body have greater powers than the parliament of Great-Britain; because, as it has been observed, the king's prerogative is far more bounded.

When the states are not sitting, the affairs of the public are managed by the king and the senate, which are no other than a committee of the states, but chosen in a particular manner; the nobility, or upper house, appoint 24 deputies, the clergy 12, and the burghers 12; these chuse three persons, who are to be presented to the king, that he may nominate one out of the three for each vacancy. The peasants have no vote in electing a senator. Almost all the executive power is lodged in the senate, which consists of 14 members, besides the chief governors of the provinces, the president of the chancery, and the grand marshal. Those senators, during the recess of the states, form the king's privy-council; but he has no more than a casting vote in their deliberations. Appeals lie to them from different courts of judicature; but each senator is accountable for his conduct to the states. Thus, upon the whole, the government of Sweden may be called republican, for the king's power is not so great as a stadtholder. The senate has even a power of imposing upon the king a sub-committee of their number, who is to attend upon his person, and to be a check upon all his proceedings, down to the very management of his family. It would be endless to recount the numerous subordinate courts, boards, commissions, and tribunals, which the jealousy of the Swedes have introduced into the administration of civil, military, commercial, and other departments; it is sufficient to say, that though nothing can be more plausible, yet nothing is less practicable than the whole plan of their distributive powers. Their officers and ministers, under the notion of making them checks upon one another, are multiplied to an inconvenient degree; many of their courts have little or nothing to do; and every operation of government is retarded or rendered ineffectual, by the tedious forms through which it must pass. This is seen in the present deplorable state of Sweden, where its whole system of government was lately in danger of annihilation; which must still be the consequence, if some material alterations are not introduced into it by the states; for the king and people equally complain of the senate.

POLITICAL INTERESTS OF SWEDEN. } The Swedes of late have been little better than pensioners to France. Through a strange medley of affairs, and views of interest, that crown has vast influence in all the deliberations of their senate; though it is evident, that the great scheme of the French is, to enlarge the royal powers so as that the king, who must depend upon them for support, may have it in his power to controul the resolutions of the senate. The imprudence of the majority of that body, by reducing the royal power into too narrow a compass, and, at the same time, oppressing the people, afford them a fair prospect of success. It
is,

is, however, to be hoped, that his Swedish majesty, the moment he is extricated from the present difficulties of his government, will apply himself to the true interests of his country, and be contented, under the guaranty of Great-Britain, to observe a strict neutrality with regard both to Denmark and Russia. The interest of Sweden even reaches as far as Turkey; for that empire found its account in balancing the power of Russia by that of Charles XII. At present, Sweden is crippled in every operation; and such are the public distractions, that her subjects are even disabled from availing themselves of the natural produce of their country in manufactures and exports.

REVENUE AND COIN.] The revenue of Sweden, since the unfortunate wars of Charles XII. has been greatly reduced. Her gold and silver specie, in the late reign, arose chiefly from the king's German dominions. Formerly, the crownlands, poll-money, tithes, mines, and other articles, are said to have produced a million sterling. The payments that are made in copper, which is here the chief medium of commerce, is extremely inconvenient; some of those pieces being as large as tiles; and a cart or wheelbarrow is often required to carry home a moderate sum. The Swedes, however, have gold ducats, and eight-mark pieces of silver, valued each at 5s. 2d. and the subsidies paid them by France helps to encrease their currency.

STRENGTH AND FORCES.] I have already hinted, that no country in the world has produced greater heroes, or braver troops, than the Swedes; and yet they cannot be said to maintain a standing army, as their forces consist of a regulated militia. The cavalry is cloathed, armed, and maintained, by a rate raised upon the nobility and gentry, according to their estates; and the infantry by the peasants. Each province is obliged to find its proportion of soldiers, according to the number of farms it contains; every farm of 60 or 70 l. per annum, is charged with a foot-soldier, furnishing him with diet, lodging, and ordinary cloaths, and about 20 s. a year in money; or else a little wooden house is built him by the farmer, who allows him hay and pasturage for a cow, and ploughs and sows land enough to supply him with bread. When embodied, they are subject to military law, but otherwise to the civil law of the country. It may therefore literally be said, that every Swedish soldier has a property in the country he defends. This national army is thought to amount to above 40,000 men; and Sweden formerly could have fitted out forty ships of the line.

ROYAL

ROYAL STILE.] The king's ſtile is, King of the Goths and Vandals, great prince of Finland, duke of Schonen, Pomeran, &c.

HISTORY OF SWEDEN.] The Goths, the ancient inhabitants of this country, joined by the Normans, Danes, Saxons, Vandals, &c. have had the reputation of ſubduing the Roman empire, and all the ſouthern nations of Europe. I ſhall not here follow the wild romances of Swediſh hiſtorians through the early ages. It is ſufficient to ſay, that Sweden has as good a claim to be an ancient monarchy, as any we know of. Nor ſhall I diſpute her being the paramount ſtate of Scandinavia (Sweden, Denmark, and Norway) and that ſhe borrowed her name from one of her princes. The introduction of Chriſtianity, however, by Anſgarius, biſhop of Bremen, in 829, ſeems to preſent the firſt certain period of the Swediſh hiſtory.

The hiſtory of Sweden, and indeed of all the northern nations, even during the firſt ages of Chriſtianity, is confuſed and unintereſting, and often doubtful; but ſufficiently replete with murders, maſſacres, and ravages. That of Sweden is void of conſiſtency, till about the middle of the fourteenth century, when it aſſumes an appearance more regular and conſiſtent; and affords wherewith to recompence the attention of thoſe who chooſe to make it an object of their ſtudies. At this time, however, the government of the Swedes was far from being clearly aſcertained, or uniformly adminiſtered. The crown was elective, though in this election the rights of blood were not altogether diſregarded. The great lords poſſeſſed the moſt conſiderable part of the wealth of the kingdom, which conſiſted chiefly in land; commerce being unknown or neglected, and even agriculture itſelf in a very rude and imperfect ſtate. The clergy, particularly thoſe of a dignified rank, from the great reſpect paid to their character, among the inhabitants of the north, had acquired an immenſe influence in all public affairs, and had obtained poſſeſſions of what lands had been left unoccupied by the nobility. Theſe two ranks of men, enjoying all the property of the ſtate, formed a council called the Senate, which was maſter of all public deliberations. This ſyſtem of government was extremely unfavourable to the national proſperity. The Swedes periſhed in the diſſentions between their prelates and lay-barons, or between thoſe and their ſovereign; they were drained of the little riches they poſſeſſed, to ſupport the indolent pomp of a few magnificent biſhops; and what was ſtill more fatal, the unlucky ſituation of their internal affairs, expoſed them to the inroads and oppreſſion of a foreign enemy. Theſe were the Danes, who, by

their

their neighbourhood and power, were always able to avail themselves of the diffentions in Sweden, and to subject under a foreign yoke, a country weakened and exhausted by its domestic broils. In this deplorable situation Sweden remained for more than two centuries; sometimes under their nominal subjection of its own princes, sometimes united to the kingdom of Denmark, and in either case equally oppressed and insulted.

Towards the year 1374, Margaret, daughter of Valdenar, king of Denmark, and widow of Huguin, king of Norway, reigned in both these kingdoms. That princess, to the ordinary ambition of her sex, added a penetration and enlargement of mind, which rendered her capable of conducting the greatest and most complicated designs. She has been called the Semiramis of the north, because, like Semiramis, she found means to reduce by arms or by intrigue, an immense extent of territory; and became queen of Denmark, Norway and Sweden. She projected the union of Calmar, so famous in the north, by which these kingdoms were for the future to remain under one sovereign, elected by each kingdom in its turn, and who should divide his residence between them all. Christiern II. the last king of Denmark, who, by virtue of this agreement, was also king of Sweden, had an ambition to become absolute. The barbarous policy, by which he attempted to effectuate this design no less barbarous, proved the destruction of himself, and afforded an opportunity for changing the face of affairs in Sweden. In order to establish his authority in that kingdom, he laid a plot for massacring the principal nobility. This horrid design was actually carried into execution, November 8, 1510. Of all those who could oppose the despotic purposes of Christiern, no one remained in Sweden, but Gustavus Vasa, a young prince, descended of the ancient kings of that country, and who had already signalized his arms against the king of Denmark. An immense price was laid on his head. The Danish soldiers were sent in pursuit of him; but by his dexterity and address, he eluded all their attempts, and escaped under the disguise of a peasant, to the mountains of Dalicarlia. This is not the place to relate his dangers and fatigues, how to prevent his discovery he wrought in the brass-mines, how he was betrayed by those in whom he reposed his confidence, and in fine, surmounting a thousand obstacles, engaged the savage but warlike inhabitants of Dalicarlia, to undertake his cause, to oppose, and to conquer his tyrannical oppressor. Sweden, by his means, again acquired independence. The antient nobility were mostly destroyed. Gustavus was at the head of a victorious army, who admired his valour, and were attached to his person. He was created, therefore,

therefore, first administrator, and afterwards king of Sweden, by the universal consent, and with the shouts of the whole nation. His circumstances were much more favourable than those of any former prince, who had possessed this dignity. The massacre of the nobles, had rid him of those proud and haughty enemies, who had so long been the bane of all regular government in Sweden. The clergy, indeed, were no less powerful and dangerous; but the opinions of Luther, which began at this time to prevail in the north, the force with which they were supported, and the credit which they had acquired among the Swedes, gave him an opportunity of changing the religious system of that country, and the exercise of the Roman catholic religion was prohibited, under the severest penalties, (which have never yet been relaxed) in the year 1544. Instead of a Gothic aristocracy, the most turbulent of all governments, and when empoisoned by religious tyranny, of all governments the most wretched, Sweden, in this manner, became a regular monarchy: the happy effects of this change were soon visible. Arts and manufactures were established and improved; navigation and commerce began to flourish; letters and civility were introduced; and a kingdom, known only by name to the rest of Europe, began to be known by its arms, and to have a certain weight in all public treaties or deliberations.

Gustavus, after a glorious reign, died in 1559; while his eldest son, Eric, was preparing to embark for England, to marry queen Elizabeth.

Under Eric, who succeded his father, Gustavus Vasa, the titles of count and baron were introduced into Sweden, and made hereditary. Eric's miserable and causeless jealousy of his brothers, forced them to take up arms; and the senate siding with them, he was deposed in 1566. His brother John succeeded him, and entered into a ruinous war with Russia. John attempted, by the advice of his queen, to re-establish the catholic religion in Sweden; but, though he made strong efforts for that purpose, and even reconciled himself to the pope, he was opposed by his brother Charles, and the scheme proved ineffectual. John's son, Sigismund, was, however, chosen king of Poland in 1587, upon which he endeavoured again to restore the Roman-catholic religion in his dominions, but he died in 1592.

Charles, brother to king John, was chosen administrator of Sweden; and being a strenuous protestant, his nephew, Sigismund, endeavoured to drive him from the administratorship, but without effect; till at last, he and his family were excluded from the succession to the crown, which was conferred upon Charles. The reign of Charles, through the
practices

practices of Sigifmund, who was himfelf a powerful prince, and at the head of a great party both in Sweden and Ruffia, was turbulent; which gave the Danes encouragement to invade Sweden. Their conduct was checked by the great Guftavus Adolphus, though then a minor, and heir apparent to Sweden. Upon the death of his father, which happened in 1611, he was declared of age by the ftates, though then only in his eighteenth year. Guftavus, foon after his acceffion, found himfelf, through the power and intrigues of the Poles, Ruffians, and Danes, engaged in a war with all his neighbours, under infinite difadvantages; all which he furmounted. He narrowly miffed being mafter of Ruffia; but the Ruffians were fo tenacious of their independency, that his fcheme was baffled. In 1617, he made a peace, under the mediation of James I. of England, by which he recovered Livonia, and four towns in the prefecture of Novogorod, with a fum of money befides.

The ideas of Guftavus began now to extend. He had feen a vaft deal of military fervice, and he was affifted by the counfels of La Gardie, one of the beft generals and wifeft ftatefmen of his age. His troops, by perpetual war, had become the beft difciplined and moft warlike in Europe; and he carried his ambition farther than hiftorians are willing to acknowledge. The princes of the houfe of Auftria were, it is certain, early jealous of his enterprizing fpirit, and fupported his antient implacable enemy Sigifmund, whom Guftavus defeated; and in 1627, he formed the fiege of Dantzic, in which he was unfuccefsful; but the attempt, which was defeated only by the fudden rife of the Viftula, added fo much to his military character, that the proteftant caufe placed him at the head of the confederacy for reducing the houfe of Auftria. His life, from that time, was a continued chain of the moft rapid and wonderful fucceffes: even the mention of each would exceed our bounds. It is fufficient to fay, that after taking Riga, and overrunning Livonia, he entered Poland, where he was victorious; and from thence, in 1630, he landed in Pomerania, drove the Germans out of Mecklenburgh, defeated the famous count Tilly, the Auftrian general, who was till then thought invincible; and over-ran Franconia. Upon the defeat and death of Tilly, Wallenftein, another Auftrian general, of equal reputation, was appointed to command againft Guftavus, who was killed upon the plain of Lutzen, after gaining a battle; which had he furvived, would probably have put a period to the Auftrian greatnefs.

SWEDEN.

The amazing abilities of Gustavus Adolphus, both in the cabinet and the field, never appeared so fully as after his death. He left behind him a set of generals, trained by himself, who maintained the glory of the Swedish army with most astonishing valour and success. The names of duke Bernard, Bannier, Torstenson, Wrangel, and others, and their prodigious actions in war, never can be forgotten in the annals of Europe. It is uncertain what course Gustavus would have pursued, had his life been prolonged, and his successes continued; but there is the strongest reasons to believe that he had in his eye somewhat more than the relief of the protestants, and the restoration of the Palatine family. His chancellor, Oxenstiern, was as consummate a politician as he was a warrior; and during the minority of his daughter Christina, he managed the affairs of Sweden with such success, that she in a manner dictated the peace of Westphalia, which threw the affairs of Europe into a new system.

Christina was but six years of age when her father was killed. She received a noble education; but her fine genius took an uncommon, and indeed romantic turn. She invited to her court Descartes, Salmasius, and other learned men; to whom she was not, however, extremely liberal. She expressed a value for Grotius; and she was an excellent judge of the polite arts: but illiberal, and indelicate in the choice of her private favourites. She at the same time discharged all the duties of her high station; and though her generals were basely betrayed by France, she continued to support the honour of her crown. Being resolved not to marry, she resigned her crown to her cousin, Charles Gustavus, son to the duke of Deux-Points, in 1654.

Charles had great success against the Poles: he drove their king, John Casimir, into Silesia; and received from them an oath of allegiance, which, with their usual inconstancy, they broke. His progress upon the ice against Denmark, has been already mentioned; and he died of a fever in 1660. His son and successor, Charles XI. was not five years of age at his father's death; and this rendered it necessary for his guardians to conclude a peace with their neighbours, by which the Swedes gave up the island of Bornholm, and Drontheim, in Norway. All differences were accommodated at the same time with Russia and Holland; and Sweden continued to make a very respectable figure in the affairs of Europe. When Charles came to be of age, he received a subsidy from the French king, Lewis XIV. but perceiving the liberties of Europe to be in danger from that monarch's ambition, he entered into the alliance with England and Holland against him. He afterwards joined with

France

France againſt the houſe of Auſtria; but being beaten in Germany at Felem-Bellin, a powerful confederacy was formed againſt him. The elector of Brandenburg made himſelf maſter of the Swediſh Pomerania; the biſhop of Munſter overran Bremen and Verden, and the Danes took Wiſmar, and ſeveral places in Schonen. They were afterwards beaten; and Charles, by the treaty of St. Germains, which followed that of Nimeguen, recovered all he had loſt, except ſome places in Germany. He then married Ulrica Leonora, the king of Denmark's ſiſter: but made a very bad uſe of the tranquillity he had regained; for he enſlaved and beggared his people, that he might render his power deſpotic, and his army formidable. The ſtates loſt all their power; and Sweden was reduced to the condition of Denmark. He ordered the brave Patkul, who was at the head of the Livonian deputies, to loſe his head and his right hand, for the boldneſs of his remonſtrance in favour of his countrymen, but he ſaved himſelf by flight; and Charles became ſo conſiderable a power, that the conferences for a general peace at Ryſwic were opened under his mediation.

Charles XI. died in 1697, and was ſucceeded by his minor ſon, the famous Charles XII. The hiſtory of no prince is better known than that of this hero. His father's will had fixed the age of his majority to eighteen, but it was ſet aſide for an earlier date by the management of count Piper; who became thereby his firſt miniſter. Soon after his acceſſion, the kings of Denmark and Poland, and the czar of Muſcovy, formed a powerful confederacy againſt him, encouraged by the mean opinion they had of his youth and abilities. He made head againſt them all; and beſieging Copenhagen, he dictated the peace of Travendahl to his Daniſh majeſty, by which the duke of Holſtein was re-eſtabliſhed in his dominions. The czar Peter was at this time ravaging Ingria, at the head of 80,000 men, and had beſieged Narva. The army of Charles did not exceed 20,000 men; but ſuch was his impatience, that he advanced at the head of 8000, entirely routed the main body of the Ruſſians, and raiſed the ſiege. Such were his ſucceſſes, and ſo numerous his priſoners, that the Ruſſians attributed his actions to necromancy. Charles from thence marched into Saxony, where his warlike atchievements equalled, if they did not excel, thoſe of Guſtavus Adolphus. He dethroned Auguſtus king of Poland: but he ſtained all his laurels, by putting the brave count Patkul to a death equally painful and ignominious. He raiſed Staniſlaus to the crown of Poland; and his name carried with it ſuch terror, that he was courted by all the powers of Europe; and among others,

by

by the duke of Marlborough, in the name of queen Anne, amidst the full career of her successes against France. His stubbornness and implacable disposition, however, was such, that he cannot be considered in a better light than that of an illustrious madman; for he lost, in the battle of Pultowa, which he fought in his march to dethrone the czar, more than all he had gained by his victories. His brave army was ruined, and he was forced to take refuge among the Turks at Bender. His actions there, in attempting to defend himself with 300 Swedes against 30,000 Turks, prove him to have been worse than frantic. The Turks found it, however, convenient for their affairs, to set him at liberty. But his misfortunes did not cure his military madness; and after his return to his dominions, he prosecuted his revenge against Denmark, till he was killed by a cannon-shot, at the siege of Fredericshal, in Norway, belonging to the Danes, in 1718, when he was no more than thirty-six years of age.

Charles XII. was succeeded, as I have already mentioned, by his sister, the princess Ulrica Eleonora, wife to the hereditary prince of Hesse. We have already seen in what manner the Swedes recovered their liberties; and given the substance of the capitulation signed by the queen and her husband, when they entered upon the exercise of government. Their first care was to make a peace with Great-Britain; which the late king intended to have invaded. The Swedes then, to prevent their farther losses by the progress of the Russian, the Danish, the Saxon, and other arms, made many great sacrifices to obtain peace from those powers. The French, however, about the year 1738, formed a dangerous party in the kingdom, under the name of the Hats; which not only broke the internal quiet of the kingdom, but led it into a ruinous war with Russia. Their Swedish majesties having no children, it was necessary to settle the succession; especially as the duke of Holstein was descended from the queen's eldest sister, and was, at the same time, the presumptive heir to the empire of Russia. Four competitors appeared; the duke of Holstein Gottorp; prince Frederic of Hesse-Cassel, nephew to the king; the prince of Denmark, and the duke of Deux-Points. The duke of Holstein would have carried the election, had he not embraced the Greek religion, that he might mount the throne of Russia. The czarina interposed, and offered to restore all the conquests she had made from Sweden, excepting a small district in Finland, if the Swedes would receive the duke of Holstein's uncle, the bishop of Lubec, as their hereditary prince, and successor to their crown. This was agreed to; and a peace was concluded at Abo, under the mediation of his

Britannic

Britannic majesty. This peace was so firmly adhered to by the czarina, that his Danish majesty thought proper to drop all the effects of his resentment, and the indignity done his son. The prince successor married the princess Ulrica, sister to the king of Prussia; and entered into the possession of his new dignity, which has proved to him a crown of thorns, in 1751. The reader, from what has been already premised, can be at no loss to know the sequel of the Swedish history to this present time.

GREAT RUSSIA, or MUSCOVY, in Europe.

Situation and Extent.

	Miles.		Degrees.
Length	1500	between	23 and 65 east long.
Breadth	1100		47 and 72 north lat.

DIVISIONS AND NAME. ACCORDING to the most authentic accounts of this mighty empire, it consists of fifteen (Mr. Voltaire says sixteen) provinces, or governments; besides part of Carelia, Esthonia, Ingria, and Livonia, which were conquered from Sweden.

The following are the dimensions of it, given us by Templeman.

	Russia.	Square miles.	Length	Brdth.	Chief cities.
Greek Church	Rus. or Mus.	784,650	1160	1050	Moscow,
	Belgorod,	72,900	475	285	Waronetz,
	Don Cossacks,	57,000	400	280	Panchina,
	Uk. Cossacks,	45,000	330	205	Kiow,
	Lapland,	72,000	405	270	Kola,
Conquered from Sweden since 1700.	Finland,	41,310	320	180	Petersburg,
	Livonia,	21,525	218	145	Riga,
	Ingria,	9,100	175	90	Nutteburg.
	Total—	1,103,485			

The reader, however, is to observe, that the knowledge the public has of this empire, is but lately acquired; and is still so doubtful, that it is very difficult to fix even the limits between the European and Asiatic Russia. As to the names of Russia and Muscovy, by which this empire is arbitrarily called, they probably are owing to the antient inhabitants, the Russi, or Borussi, and the river Mosca, upon which the antient capital Moscow was built; but of this we know nothing certain.

Climate, soil, productions, vegetables, mines, and minerals. In the southern parts of Russia, or Muscovy, the longest day does not exceed fifteen hours and a half; whereas in the most northern, the sun is seen in summer two months above the horizon. The reader from this will naturally conclude, that there is in Muscovy a vast diversity of soil as well as climate, and that the extremes of both are to be seen and felt in this vast empire. The quickness of vegetation here, is pretty much the same as has been described in Scandinavia. The snow is the natural manure of Russia, where grain grows in plenty, near Poland, and in the warmer provinces. The bulk of the people, however, are miserably fed; the soil produces a vast number of mushrooms for their subsistence; and in some places, besides oaks and firs, Russia yields rhubarb, flax, hemp, pasture for cattle, wax, honey, rice, and melons. The boors are particularly careful in the cultivation of honey, which yields them plenty of metheglin, their ordinary drink; they likewise extract a spirit from rye, which they prefer to brandy.

That a great part of Russia was populous in former days, is not to be disputed; though it is equally certain, that the inhabitants, till lately, were but little acquainted with agriculture; and supplied the place of bread, as the inhabitants of Scandinavia do now, with a kind of saw-dust and a preparation of fish-bones. Peter the Great, and his successors, down to the present empress, have been at incredible pains to introduce agriculture into their dominions; and though the soil is not every where proper for corn, yet its vast fertility in some provinces, bids fair to make grain as common in Russia as it is in the southern countries of Europe. The vast communications, by means of rivers, which the inland parts of that empire have with each other, serve to supply one province with those products of the earth in which another may be deficient. As to mines and minerals, they are as plentiful in Russia as in Scandinavia; and the people are daily improving in working them.

Mountains, rivers, forests, and face of the country. The Zimnopoias mountains, which lie in this empire, are thought to be the famous Montes Riphæi of the antients. The most considerable rivers are the Wolga, which, after traversing the greatest part of Muscovy, and winding a course of above 2000 English miles, discharges itself into the Caspian sea: it is not only reckoned the largest, but one of the most fertile rivers of Europe: it produces all kinds of fish; and fertilizes all the lands on each side with the richest trees, fruits, and vegetables. The Don, or Tanais, which divides
the

the most eastern part of Russia from Asia; and in its course towards the east, comes so near the Wolga, that the late czar had undertaken to have cut a communication between them by means of a canal: this grand project, however, was defeated by the irruptions of the Tartars. This river, exclusive of its turnings and windings, discharges itself into the Palus Mæotis, or sea of Asoph, about four hundred miles from its rise. The Boristhenes, or Dnieper, which is likewise one of the largest rivers in Europe, runs through Lithuania, the country of the Zaporog Cossacks, and that of the Nagaisch Tartars, which falls into the Euxine, or Black-sea, near Oczakow; it has thirteen cataracts within a small distance.

As to forests, they abound in this extensive country; and the northern and north-eastern provinces, are in a manner desart; nor can the few inhabitants they contain be called Christians rather than Pagans. Upon the whole, Muscovy is in general a flat level country.

ANIMALS, QUADRUPEDS, BIRDS, FISHES, AND INSECTS. } These do not differ greatly from those described in the Scandinavian provinces; to which we must refer the reader. The lynx, famous for its piercing eye, is a native of this empire; and makes prey of every creature it can master: they are said to be produced chiefly in the fir-tree forests. The hyænas, bears, wolves, foxes, and other creatures already described, afford their furs for cloathing the inhabitants; but the furs of the black foxes, and ermine, are more valuable in Russia than elsewhere. The dromedary and camel were formerly almost the only beasts of burden known in many parts of Russia. Czar Peter encouraged a breed of large horses for war and carriages; but those employed in the ordinary purposes of life are but small; as are their cows and sheep, which they salt for their winter provisions.

We know of few or no birds in Russia, that have not been already described. The same may be said of fishes; only the Russians are better provided than their neighbours are with sturgeon, cod, salmon, and belagas: the latter resemble a sturgeon, and is from twelve to fifteen feet in length; its flesh is white and delicious. Of the roe of the sturgeon and the belaga, the Russians make the famous caveär; so much esteemed for its richness and flavour, that it is often sent in presents to crowned heads.

POPULATION, MANNERS AND CUSTOMS. } Nothing can be more injudicious, or remote from truth, than the accounts we have from authors, of the population of this

this vast empire; the whole of which, they think, does not exceed, at most, seven millions. It is surprizing that such a mistake should have continued so long, when we consider the immense armies brought into the field by the sovereigns of Russia, and the bloody wars they maintained in Asia and Europe. Mr. Voltaire is, perhaps, the first author who has attempted to undeceive the public in this respect; and has done it upon very authentic grounds, by producing a list, taken in 1747, of all the males who paid the capitation, or poll-tax, and which amount to six million, six hundred and forty-six thousand, three hundred and ninety. In this number are included boys and old men; but girls and women are not reckoned, nor boys born between the making of one register of the lands and another. Now, if we only reckon triple the number of heads subject to be taxed, including women and girls, we shall find near twenty millions of souls. To this account may be added three hundred and fifty thousand soldiers, and two hundred thousand nobility and clergy; and foreigners of all kinds, who are likewise exempted from the poll-tax; as also (says Mr. Voltaire) the inhabitants of the conquered countries, namely, Livonia, Esthonia, Ingria, Carelia, and a part of Finland; the Ukraine, and the Don Cossacs, the Calmucs, and other Tartars; the Samojedes, the Laplanders, the Ostiacs, and all the idolatrous people of Siberia, a country of greater extent than China, are not included in this list. Upon the whole, this writer does not exaggerate, when he affirms, that the inhabitants of Russia do not amount to fewer than twenty-four millions.

As her imperial majesty of all the Russias possesses many of the countries from whence the prodigious swarms of barbarians who overthrew the Roman empire issued, there is the strongest reason to believe, that her dominions must have been better peopled formerly than they are at present; twenty-four millions being but a thin population for the immense tracts of country she possesses. As the like decrease of inhabitants is observable in many other parts of the globe, we are to look for the reason in natural causes, which we cannot discuss here. Perhaps the introduction of the small-pox and the venereal disease, may have assisted in the depopulation; and it is likely, that the prodigious quantity of strong and spirituous liquors, consumed by the inhabitants of the north, is unfriendly to generation.

The Russians, properly so called, are in general a personable people, hardy, vigorous, and patient of labour, especially in the field, to an incredible degree. Their complexions differ little from those of the English or Scots; but the women

men think that an addition of red heightens their beauty. Their eye-sight seems to be defective, occasioned, probably, by the snow, which for so long a time of the year is continually present to their eyes. Their officers and soldiers always possessed a large share of passive valour; but in the late war with the king of Prussia, they proved as active as any troops in Europe. They are implicitly submissive to discipline, let it be ever so severe; and on such occasions they appear to be void of the sensations to which other people are subject, especially in the meanness of their repasts, and hardness of their fare.

Before the days of Peter the Great, the Russians were barbarous, ignorant, mean, and much addicted to drunkenness; no fewer than 4000 brandy-shops have been reckoned in Moscow. Not only the common people, but many of the boyars, lived in a continued state of idleness and intoxication; and the most complete objects of misery and barbarity presented themselves upon the streets, while the court of Moscow was by far the most splendid of any upon the globe. The czar and the grandees dressed after the most superb Asiatic manner; and their magnificence exceeded every idea that can be conceived from modern examples. The earl of Carlisle, in the account of his embassy, says that he could see nothing but gold and precious stones in the robes of the czar and his courtiers. The manufactures, however, of those, and all other luxuries, were carried on by Italians, Germans, and other foreigners. Peter saw the bulk of his subjects, at his accession to the throne, little better than beasts of burden to support the pomp of the court. He forced his great men to lay aside their long robes, and dress in the European manner; and he even obliged the laity to cut off their beards. The other improvements, in learning and the arts, which he made, shall be mentioned elsewhere. The Russians, before his days, had not a ship upon their coasts. They had no conveniencies for travelling, no pavements in their streets, no places of public diversion; and they entertained a sovereign contempt for all improvements of the mind. At present, a French or English gentleman may make a shift to live as comfortably and sociably in Russia, as in any other part of Europe. Their stoves which they make use of, diffuse a more equal and genial warmth than our grates and chimnies. Their polite assemblies have, since the accession of the present emprefs, been put under proper regulations; and few of the antient usages remain, but such as are of public utility, and adapted to the nature of their country. It is, however, to be observed, that notwithstanding the severity of Peter, and the

prudence

prudence of succeeding governments, drunkenness still continues among all ranks; nor are even priests or ladies ashamed of it on holidays.

It is commonly thought that the Russian ladies are as submissive to their husbands in their families, as the latter are to their superiors in the field; and that they think themselves ill treated if they are not often reminded of their duty by the discipline of a whip, manufactured by themselves, which they present to their husbands on the day of their marriage. Their nuptial ceremonies are peculiar to themselves; and formerly consisted of some very whimsical rites, many of which are now disused. When the parents are agreed upon a match, though the parties perhaps have never seen each other, the bride is examined stark naked by a certain number of females, who are to correct, if possible, any defects they find in her person. On her wedding day she is crowned with a garland of wormwood; and after the priest has tied the nuptial knot, his clerk or sexton throws a handful of hops upon the head of the bride, wishing that she may prove as fruitful as that plant. She is then led home, with abundance of coarse, and indeed indecent ceremonies, which are now wearing off even by the lowest ranks; and the barbarous treatment of wives by their husbands, which extended even to scourging or broiling them to death, is either guarded against by the laws of the country, or by particular stipulations in the marriage contract.

FUNERALS.] The Russians entertain many fantastic notions with regard to the state of departed souls. After the dead body is drest, a priest is hired to pray for his soul, to purify it with incense, and to sprinkle it with holy water, while it remains above ground, which, among the better sort, it generally does for eight or ten days. When the body is carried to the grave, which is done with many gesticulations of sorrow, the priest produces a ticket, signed by the bishop and another clergyman, as the deceased's passport to heaven. When this is put into the coffin, the company returns to the deceased's house, where they drown their sorrow in intoxication; which lasts, among the better sort, with a few intervals, for forty days. During that time, a priest every day says prayers over the grave of the deceased; for though the Russians do not believe in purgatory, yet they imagine that their departed friend may be assisted by prayer, in his long journey, to the place of his destination after this life.

PUNISHMENTS.] The Russians are remarkable for the severity and variety of their punishments, which are both inflicted and endured with a wonderful insensibility. Peter the Great used to suspend the robbers upon the Wolga, and other parts

parts of his dominions, by iron hooks fixed to their ribs, on gibbets, where they writhed themselves to death, hundreds, nay, thousands at a time. The single and double knoute were lately inflicted upon ladies, as well as men of quality. Both of them are excruciating; but in the double knoute, the hands are bound behind the prisoner's back, and the cord being fixed to a pulley, lifts him from the ground, with the dislocation of both his shoulders; and then his back is in a manner scarified by the executioner, with a hard thong, cut from a wild ass's skin. This punishment has been so often fatal, that a surgeon generally attends the patient, to pronounce the moment that it should cease. The boring and cutting out the tongue, are likewise practised in Russia; and even the late empress Elizabeth, though she prohibited capital punishments, was forced to give way to the necessity of those tortures. From these particulars, many have concluded that the feelings of the Russians are different from those of mankind in general.

TRAVELLING.] Among the many conveniencies introduced of late into Russia, that of travelling is extremely remarkable, and the expence very trifling. Nothing strikes, either a reader or a stranger, more than the facility with which the Russians perform the longest and most uncomfortable journies. Like their Scandinavian neighbours, already described, they travel in sledges drawn by rein-deer, when the snow is frozen hard enough to bear them. In the internal parts of Russia, horses draw their sledges; and the sledge-way, towards February, becomes so well beaten, that they erect a kind of coach upon the sledges, in which they travel night and day; so that they often perform a journey of about 400 miles, such as that between Petersburg and Moscow, in three days and three nights. Her imperial majesty, in her journies, is drawn in a house which contains a bed, a table, chairs, and other conveniencies for four people, by 24 post-horses; and the house itself is fixed on a sledge.

COSSACS, AND OTHER NA-
TIONS SUBJECT TO RUSSIA. } As the present subjects of the Russian empire, in its most extensive sense, are the descendants of many different people, and inhabit prodigious tracts of country, so we find among them a vast variety of character and manners; and the great reformations introduced of late years, as well as the discoveries made, render former accounts to be but little depended upon. Many of the Tartars, who inhabit large portions of the Russian dominions, now live in fixed houses and villages, cultivate the land, and pay tribute like other subjects. Till lately, they were not admitted into the Russian armies; but they now make excellent soldiers. Other Russian Tartars retain their old wandering lives.

lives. Both sides of the Wolga are inhabited by the Zeremisses and Morduars; a peaceable industrious people. The Baskirs are likewise fixed inhabitants of the tract that reaches from Casan to the frontiers of Siberia; and have certain privileges, of which they are tenacious. The wandering Calmucs occupy the rest of this tract to Astracan and the frontiers of the Usbecs; and in consideration of certain presents they receive from her imperial majesty, they serve in her armies without pay, but are apt to plunder equally friends as foes.

As the Cossacs make now a figure in the military history of Europe, some account of them may not be unacceptable. They were originally Polish peasants, and served in the Ukrain as a militia against the Tartars. Being oppressed by their unfeeling lords, a part of them removed to the uncultivated banks of the Don, or Tanais, and there established a colony. They were soon after joined, in 1637, by two other detachments of their countrymen; and they reduced Asoph, which they were obliged to abandon to the Turks, after laying it in ashes. They next put themselves under the protection of the Russians, built Circasky, on an island in the Don; and their possessions, which consisted of thirty-nine towns on both sides that river, reached from Ribna to Asoph. They there lived in a fruitful country, which they took care to cultivate; and they were so wedded to their original customs, that they were little better than nominal subjects of the czars, till the time of Peter the Great. They professed the Greek religion; their inclinations were warlike, and occasionally served against the Tartars and Turks on the Palus Mæotis.

The internal government of the Cossacs approaches very near to the idea we form of that of the antient Germans, as described by Tacitus. The captains and officers of the nation chuse a chief, whom they call Hetman, and he resides at Circaska; but this choice is confirmed by the czar; and the hetman holds his authority during life. He acts as a superior over the other towns of the nation, each of which is formed into a separate commonwealth, governed by its own hetman, who is chosen annually. They serve in war, in consideration of their enjoying their laws and liberties. They indeed have several times rebelled, for which they suffered severely under Peter the Great. But the Russian yoke was so much easier than that of the Poles, that in 1654, the Cossacs of the Ukrain put themselves likewise under the protection of Russia. They complained, however, that their liberties had been invaded; and in the war between Charles XII. and Peter, their hetman, Mazeppa, joined the former; but he found himself unable to fulfil the magnificent promises he had made to Charles. He brought

brought over, however, some of the Zaparovian Cossacs, who are settled about the falls of the river Nieper, but most of them were cut in pieces.

The Russians were formerly noted for so strong an attachment to their native soil, that they seldom visited foreign parts. This, however, was only the consequence of their pride and ignorance; for Russian nobility, besides those who are in a public character, are now found at every court in Europe. Her imperial majesty even interests herself in the education of young men of quality, in the knowledge of the world, and foreign services, particularly that of the British fleet. No people have shewn a greater adventuring spirit than the Russians; witness the discovery of Kamtschatka, a country so little known, that it is doubtful to what quarter of the globe it pertains; but it certainly bids the fairest of any country in the world, to lie contiguous to America: and perhaps it may soon appear, that the Kamtschadales and the Americans are the same.

The best account we have of Kamtschatka is from Mr. Steller and Mr. Krasheninicoff, the latter of whom published their discoveries, under the sanction of the Petersburgh academy. The Kamtschadales, from being a people as wild as their country, are now in a fair way of becoming good Christians. They travel in small carriages drawn by dogs; and a complete Kamtschadalian equipage, dogs, harness and all, costs in that country 4 l. 10 s. or near twenty rubles. The Kamtschadales believed the immortality of the soul, before they were Christians. They are superstitious to extravagance; and extremely singular and capricious in the different enjoyments of life, particularly their convivial entertainments. They seem to be of Tartar original; and before they were humanized, their appearance and manners partook strongly of those of the Esquimaux in North America.

The Siberians are another nation of Russia, whose usages deserve to be mentioned; but we know less of them, than we do of the Kamtschadales. Many of them, as has been already hinted, are still gross pagans; and their manners were so barbarous, that Peter the Great thought he could not inflict a greater punishment upon his capital enemies the Swedes, than by banishing them to Siberia. The effect was, that the Swedish officers and soldiers introduced European usages and manufactures into the country, and thereby acquired a comfortable living. The Mahommetan Tartars form a considerable part of the natives: and according to the latest accounts, nature has been so kind to the country, that an exile to Siberia will hereafter be but a very slight punishment.

RELIGION.

RELIGION.] The established religion of Russia is that of the Greek church, the tenets of which are by far too numerous and complicated to be discussed here. It is sufficient to say, that they deny the pope's supremacy; and though they disclaim image-worship, they retain many idolatrous and superstitious customs. Their churches are full of pictures of saints whom they consider as mediators. They observe a number of fasts and lents, so that they live half the year very abstemiously; an institution which is extremely convenient for their soil and climate. They have many peculiar notions with regard to the sacraments and Trinity. They oblige their bishops, but not their priests, to celibacy. Peter the Great shewed his profound knowledge of government in nothing more, than the reformation of his church. He broke the dangerous powers of the patriarch, and the great clergy. He declared himself the head of the church; and preserved the subordinations of metropolitans, archbishops, and bishops. Their priests have no fixed income, but depend for subsistence upon the benevolence of their flocks and hearers. Peter, after establishing this great political reformation, left his clergy in full possession of all their idle ceremonies; nor did he cut off the beards of his clergy; that impolitic attempt was reserved for the late emperor, and greatly contributed to his fatal catastrophe. Before his days, an incredible number of both sexes were shut up in convents; nor has it been found prudent entirely to abolish those societies. The abuses of them, however, are in a great measure removed; for no male can become a monk till he is turned of thirty; and no female, or nun, till she is fifty; and even then not without the express permission of their superiors.

The conquered provinces, as I have already observed, retain the exercise of their own religion; but such is the extent of the Russian empire, that many of its subjects are Mahommetans, and more of them no better than pagans, in Siberia and the uncultivated countries. Many ill-judged attempts have been made to convert them by force, which have only tended to confirm them in their infidelity.

LANGUAGE.] The common language of Russia, is a mixture of the Polish and Sclavonian; their priests, however, and the most learned of their clergy, make use of what is called modern Greek; and they who know that language in its purity, are at no loss for understanding it in its corrupted state. The Russians have thirty-six letters, the forms of which have a strong resemblance to the old Greek alphabet.

LEARNING AND LEARNED MEN.] The Russians, hitherto, have made but an inconsiderable appearance in the republic of letters;

letters; but the great encouragement given by their sovereigns of late, in the institution of academies, and other literary boards, has produced sufficient proofs, that they are no way deficient as to intellectual abilities. The papers exhibited by them, at their academical meetings, have been favourably received all over Europe; especially those that relate to astronomy, the mathematics, and natural philosophy. The speeches pronounced by the bishop of Turer, the metropolitan of Novogorod, the vice-chancellor, and the marshal at the late opening of the commission for a new code of laws, are elegant and classical; and the progress which learning has made in that empire since the beginning of this century, is an evidence, that the Russians are as capable as any of their neighbours to shine in the arts and sciences.

UNIVERSITIES.] Three colleges were founded by Peter the Great at Moscow; one for classical learning and philosophy, the second for mathematics, and the third for navigation and astronomy. To these he added a dispensary, which is a magnificent building, and under the care of some able German chemists and apothecaries; who furnish medicines not only to the army, but all over the kingdom. And within these few years, Mr. de Shorealow, high chamberlain to the empress Elizabeth, daughter to Peter the Great, has founded an university in this city.

CITIES, TOWNS, PALACES, AND OTHER BUILDINGS.] Petersburgh naturally takes the lead in this division. It lies at the junction of the Neva with the lake Ladoga, already mentioned, in latitude 60; but the reader may have a better idea of its situation, by being informed that it stands on both sides the river Neva, between that lake and the bottom of the Finland gulph. In the year 1703, this city consisted of two small fishing huts, on a spot so waterish and swampy, that the ground was formed into nine islands; by which, according to Voltaire, its principal quarters are still divided. Without entering into too minute a description of this wonderful city, it is sufficient to say, that it extends about six miles every way; and contains every structure for magnificence, the improvement of the arts, revenue, navigation, war, commerce, and the like, that are to be found in the most celebrated cities in Europe. It may appear surprizing, that the latest authors who treat of that country, differ widely as to the population of Petersburgh. Voltaire tells us, that it is said to contain at present 400,000 souls. This seems to be an over-rate, even admitting the imperial troops, attendants, and officers of state to be included. Busching, whom I am rather inclined to follow, thinks that Petersburgh consists of about

8000 houses, and contains about 100,000 inhabitants: a number, however, that would seem to be disproportioned to that of the houses, did we not reflect on the great number of servants maintained by the Russian nobility and merchants. The new summer palace is reckoned one of the finest pieces of architecture in Europe. In the middle of the city (which has neither gates nor walls) is a strong, beautiful fort; and the admiralty and dock-yards are likewise well fortified.

As Petersburg is the emporium of Russia, the number of foreign ships trading to it in the summer time is surprising. In winter, 3000 one-horse sledges are employed for passengers in the streets. It contains twenty Russian, and four Lutheran churches, besides those of the Calvinists and Roman-Catholics; and is the seat of a university, and several academies. Petersburgh is the capital of the province of Ingria, one of Peter the Great's conquests from the Swedes.

The city of Moscow was formerly the glory of this great empire, and it still continues considerable enough to figure among the capitals of Europe. It stands, as has been already mentioned, on the river from whence it takes its name, in lat. 55 45, about 1414 miles north-east of London; and though its streets are not regular, it presents a very picturesque appearance, for it contains such a number of gardens, groves, lawns, and streams, that it seems rather to be a cultivated country than a city. The antient magnificence of this city would be incredible, were it not attested by the most unquestionable authors: but we are to make great allowances for the uncultivated state of the adjacent provinces, which might have made it appear with a greater lustre in a traveller's eyes. Neither Voltaire nor Busching gives us any satisfactory account of this capital; and little credit is to be given to the authors who divide it into regular quarters, and each quarter inhabited by a different order or profession. Busching speaks of it as the largest city in Europe; but that can be only meant as to the ground it stands on. It is generally agreed, that Moscow contains 1600 churches and convents, and forty-three places or squares. Busching makes the merchants exchange to contain about 6000 fine shops, which display a vast parade of commerce, especially to and from China. No city displays a greater contrast than Moscow, of magnificence and meanness in building. The houses of the inhabitants in general are miserable timber booths; but their palaces, churches, convents, and other public edifices, are spacious and lofty. The Krimlin, or grand imperial palace, is mentioned as one of the most superb structures in the world: it lies in the interior circle of the city, and contains the old imperial palace, pleasure-house, and stables, a victualling-house, the palace which formerly belonged to the patriarch, nine cathedrals, five convents, four parish churches, the arsenal, with the public colleges, and other offices. All the churches in the Krimlin have beautiful spires, most of them gilt, or covered with silver: the architecture is in the Gothic taste; but the insides of the churches are richly ornamented; and the pictures of the saints are decorated with gold, silver, and precious stones. Mention is made of the cathedral, which has no fewer than nine towers, covered with copper double gilt, and contains a silver branch with forty-eight lights, said to weigh 2800 pounds. A volume would scarcely suffice to recount the other particulars of this city's magnificence. Its sumptuous monuments of the great dukes and czars, the magazine, the patriarchal palace, the exchequer, and chancery, are noble structures. The public is no stranger to the barbarous anecdote, that the czar John Basilides ordered the architect of the church of Jerusalem to be deprived of his eyesight, that he might never contrive its equal. The story is improbable, and took its rise from the arbitrary disposition of that great prince. I shall have occasion hereafter to mention the great bell of Moscow; where the inhabitants are so distractedly fond of bells, that they are always tinkling in every quarter. The jewels and ornaments of an image of the virgin Mary, in the Krimlin church, and its other furniture, can be only equalled by what is seen at the famous Holy House of Loretto in Italy. Mr. Voltaire says, that Peter, who was attentive to every thing, did not neglect Moscow at the time he was building Petersburgh; for he caused it to be paved, adorned it with noble edifices, and enriched it with manufactures.

Nothing can be said with certainty as to the population of Moscow. When lord Carlisle was the English ambassador there, in the reign of Charles II. this city was 12 miles in compass, and the number of houses were computed at 40,000. Voltaire says, that Moscow was then twenty miles in circumference, and that its inhabitants amounted to 500,000; but it is almost impossible to make an estimate of its present population.

CURIOSITIES.] This article affords no great entertainment, as Russia has but lately been admitted into the rank of civilized nations. She can, however, produce many stupendous monuments of the public spirit of her sovereigns; particularly the canals made by Peter the Great, for the benefit of commerce. I have already hinted at the passion the Russians have for bell-ringing; and we are told, that the great bell of Moscow, the largest in the world, weighs 443,772 pounds weight; and was cast in the reign of the empress Anne; but the beam on which it hung being burnt, it fell, and a large piece is broke out of it; so that it lately lay in a manner useless. The building of Petersburgh, and raising it of a sudden from a few fishing-huts to be a populous and rich city, is perhaps a curiosity hardly to be paralleled since the erection of the Egyptian pyramids. The same may be said of the fortress of Kronstadt, in the neighbourhood of Petersburgh, which is almost impregnable. This fortress and city imployed, for some years, 300,000 men, in laying its foundations, and driving piles, night and day; a work which no monarch in Europe (Peter excepted) could have executed. The whole plan, with a very little assistance from some German engineers, was drawn by his own hand. Equally wonderful was the navy which he raised to his people, at the time when they could not be said to have possessed a ship in any part of the globe. What is more wonderful than all, he wrought in person in all those amazing works, with the same assiduity as if he had been a common labourer.

COMMERCE AND POLI-TICAL INTERESTS. } I have joined these two articles under one head, because such is the situation and strength of Russia, that she has nothing either to hope or to fear but from commerce. It is true, her territories are accessible on the side of Poland, and therefore it is her interest to preserve a strong party in that country; but even this policy has commerce chiefly for its object, because the greatest part of the Dissidents of Poland are the only traders in that great country; and three-fourths of them being of the Greek church, consider her imperial majesty as their patroness and protector.

In treating of the Russian commerce, former accounts are of little service at this time, because of its great improvements and variations. By the best and surest information, the annual exports of Russia at present amount to four millions of rubles; and her imports do not exceed three millions; so that the balance of trade is yearly 225000 l. sterling in her favour. This calculation, however, is subject to such uncertainties as time alone can remove, arising from Russia's commercial connections with Great-Britain, from whom, about fourteen years ago, she gained the greatest part of that balance. Great-Britain, however, has, within that time, given such encouragement to her American colonies, and to the Scotch and Irish linen manufacture, that her imports from Russia are greatly diminished. On the other hand, the vast advantages which by later treaties between England and Russia, her imperial majesty has been enabled to acquire upon the Caspian sea, and in the inland parts of Asia, will probably more than counterbalance all the diminution which the Russian exports to Great-Britain may have suffered.

Russia's productions and exports, in general, are many, and very valuable, viz. furs and peltry of various kinds, red leather, linen and thread, iron, copper, sail-cloth, hemp and flax, pitch and tar, wax, honey, tallow, ising-glass, linseed-oil, pot-ash, soap, feathers, train-oil, hogs bristles, musk, rhubarb, and other drugs; timber, and also raw-silk from China and Persia.

Her foreign commerce is much encreased since her conquests from Sweden, especially of Livonia and Ingria; and since the establishing of her new emporium of Petersburgh; whereby her naval intercourse with Europe is made much more short and easy.

Russia carries on a commerce over land, by caravans, to China, chiefly in furs: and they bring back from thence, tea, silks, cotton, gold, &c. To Bochara, near the river Oxus, in Tartary, Russia sends her own merchandize, in return for Indian silks, curled lamb-skins, and ready money; and also from the annual fair at Samarcand: she likewise trades to Persia, by Astracan, cross the Caspian sea, for raw and wrought silk.

Before the time of Peter the Great, Archangel, which lies upon the White-Sea, was the only port of naval communication which Russia had with the rest of Europe; but it was subject to a long and tempestuous voyage. This town is about three English miles in length, and one in breadth: built all of wood, excepting the exchange, which is of stone. Notwithstanding the decrease of the trade of Archangel, by building Petersburgh, it still exports a considerable quantity of merchandize.

The late and present empresses of Russia, were so sensible of the benefits arising to commerce through peace, that they seem to have postponed other valuable interests to that consideration; witness the sacrifices made by the empress Elizabeth, to preserve the tranquillity of the north, in settling the Swedish succession; and the moderation which her present majesty observed in her son's claims upon Denmark for the duchy of Holstein when her husband died. This difference, however, if not prudently prevented, may, some time or other, kindle a general flame in the north, if not all over Europe.

CONSTITUTION, LAWS, AND DISTINCTIONS OF RANK. } The constitution and laws of Russia, like those of other arbitrary governments, rest in the breast of the sovereign.

reign. The subjects, however, had some general rules to guide them, both in criminal and civil matters, which always took place, when no interposition of government happened to set them aside. The czar Alexis, who mounted the throne in 1645, drew up an imperfect code of laws; but he never could sufficiently enforce them, being perpetually engaged in war, either foreign or domestic; so that they became in a manner useless or unknown. Even Peter the Great never could bring his subjects into that state of civilization as to trust them with any law but his own will. In matters of importance, such as the trying and condemning his son to death, he generally appointed a commission, with some person of distinction at its head, for trying them; but this was only to save the appearance of despotism; for the commissioners always pronounced judgment according to what they knew to be his sentiments. The late empress, Elizabeth, made a law, but it only bound herself, that she would suffer no capital punishments to be inflicted in her reign. Were not the fact undoubted, posterity could not believe, that one of the most extensive governments in the world could subsist in peace and tranquillity within itself, under such an exception of justice. The truth is, the dreadful punishments incurred by delinquents, though not capital, were sufficient to deter them. Upon the whole, the virtues of the Russian sovereigns, since Peter's time, have supplied the deficiency of their laws.

The Russian monarchy is hereditary, but after a particular mode; for the senate and the great lords make themselves judges of the proximity of blood in their sovereigns; as may be seen in their history. The present empress was raised to the throne, by being wife to the emperor, and mother of his son; and she has sufficiently justified the partiality that has been shewed her, by the wisdom, patriotism, and vigour of her government; but in nothing so much as in her care to give her subjects a new code of laws. With this view, in 1768, she assembled deputies from all the districts and provinces of her dominions, so as to form, in effect, a Russian parliament. When they were met, they were presented with instructions, which contained her ideas of distributive justice; and which do the highest honour to her political and personal virtues. The code which has been drawn up, has not yet been made public, at least to the rest of Europe; but there can be no doubt that it is highly worthy of its imperial patroness.

The distinctions of rank, form a considerable part of the Russian constitution. The late empresses took the title of Autocratrix, which implies, that they owed their dignity to no earthly power. Their antient nobility were divided into knezes or knazeys, boyars, and vaivods. The knezes were sovereigns upon their own estates, till they were reduced by the czar; but they still retain the name. The boyars were nobility under the knezes; and the vaivods were governors of provinces. Those titles, however, so often revived the ideas of their antient power, that the present and late empresses have introduced among their subjects the titles of counts and princes, and the other distinctions of nobility that are common to the rest of Europe.

A senate, composed of the most respectable members of the empire, still subsists in Russia; but though the empress treats the institution with the highest regard and deference, and submits the greatest concerns of her empire to their deliberation, yet they are no better than her privy council; and they seldom or never give her any advice, but such as is conformable to her pleasure.

REVENUE AND EXPENCES.] Nothing certain can be said concerning the revenues of this mighty empire; but they are, undoubtedly, at present, far superior to what they were in former times, even under Peter the Great. The vast exertions for promoting industry, made by his successors, especially her present imperial majesty, must have greatly added to their income, which can scarcely be reckoned at less than four millions sterling annually. When the reader considers this sum relatively, that is, according to the high value of money in that empire, compared to its low value in Great-Britain, he will find it a very considerable revenue. That it is so, appears from the vast armies maintained and paid by the late and present empress, in Germany, Poland, and elsewhere, when no part of the money returned to Russia; nor do I find that they received any considerable subsidy from the houses of Bourbon and Austria, who, indeed, were in no condition to grant them any. Mr. Voltaire says, that in 1735, reckoning the tribute paid by the Tartars, with all taxes and duties in money, the sum total amounted to thirteen millions of rubles (each ruble amounting to about 4s. 6d. sterling.) This income was at that time sufficient to maintain 339,500, as well sea as land forces. The other expences, besides the payment of the army and navy of her present majesty, the number and discipline of which are at least equal to those of her greatest predecessors, is very considerable. Her court is elegant and magnificent; her guards and attendants splendid; and the encouragement she gives to learning, the improvement of the arts, and useful discoveries, costs her vast sums, exclusive of her ordinary expences of state.

Some of the Ruffian revenues arife from monopolies; which are often neceffary in the infancy of commerce. The moft hazardous enterprize undertaken by Peter the Great, was his imitating the conduct of Henry VIII. of England, in feizing the revenues of the church. He found, perhaps, that policy and neceffity required that the greateft part of them fhould be reftored, which was accordingly done; his great aim being to deprive the patriarch of his exceffive power. The clergy, however, are taxed in Ruffia: but the pecuniary revenues of the crown arife from taxes upon eftates, bagnios, bees, mills, fifheries, and other particulars.

The Ruffian armies are raifed at little or no expence *, and, while in their own country, fubfifted chiefly on provifions furnifhed them by the country people, according to their internal valuation.

HISTORY.] It is evident, both from ancient hiftory and modern difcoveries, that fome of the moft neglected parts of the Ruffian empire at prefent, were formerly rich and populous. The reader who throws his eyes on a general map of Europe and Afia, may fee the advantages of their fituation, and their communication by rivers with the Black Sea, and the richeft provinces in the Roman and Greek empires. In later times, the Afiatic part of Ruffia bordered with Samarcand, in Tartary, once the capital, under Jenghis khan and Tamerlane, of a far more rich and powerful empire, than any mentioned by hiftory; and nothing is more certain, than that the conqueft of Ruffia was among the laft attempts made by the former of thofe princes. We cannot, with the fmalleft degree of probability, carry our conjectures, with regard to the hiftory of Ruffia, higher than the introduction of Chriftianity, which happened about the tenth century; when a princefs of this country, called Olha, is faid to have been baptized at Conftantinople, and refufed the hand of the Greek emperor, John Zimifces, in marriage. This accounts for the Ruffians adopting the Greek religion, and part of their alphabet. Photius,

---

* On my return (fays a late traveller through Ruffia) from Tobolfky to St. Peterfburgh, going into a houfe where I was to lodge, I found a father chained to a poft in the middle of his family: by his cries, and the little regard his children paid to him, I imagined he was mad; but this was by no means the cafe. In Ruffia, people, who are fent to raife recruits, go through all the villages, and pitch upon the men proper for the fervice, as butchers, in all other parts, go into the folds to mark the fheep. This man's fon had been felected for the fervice, and made his efcape, without the father's knowledge; the father was made a prifoner in his own houfe; his children were his gaolers, and he was in daily expectation of receiving his fentence. I was fo much fhocked with this account, and with the fcene I beheld, that I was forced to feek another lodging immediately. Happy England!

the famous Greek patriarch, sent priests to baptize the Russians, who were for some time subject to the see of Constantinople; but the Greek patriarchs afterwards resigned all their authority over the Russian church; and its bishops erected themselves into patriarchs, who were in a manner independent of the civil power. It is certain, that till the year 1450, the princes of Russia were but very little considered, being chiefly subjected by the Tartars. It was about this time, that John, or Iwan Basilides, conquered the Tartars, and, among others, the duke of Great Novogorod; from whom he is said to have carried 300 cart loads of gold and silver.

His grandson, the famous John Basilowitz II. having cleared his country of the intruding Tartars, subdued the kingdoms of Casan and Astracan Tartary, in Asia, and annexed them to the Russian dominions. By his cruelty, however, he obliged the inhabitants of some of his finest provinces, particularly Livonia and Esthonia, to throw themselves under the protection of the Poles and Swedes. Before the time of this John II. the sovereign of Russia took the title of Welike Knez, i. e. great prince, great lord, or great chief; which the Christian nations afterwards rendered by that of great duke. The title of Tzar, or as we call it, czar, was added to that of the Russian sovereigns, but it seems to have been of Persian or Asiatic original; because, at first, it was applied only to Casan, Astracan, and the Asian Siberia. Upon the death of John Basilowitz, the Russian succession was filled up by a set of weak cruel princes, and their territories were torn in pieces by civil wars. In 1597, Boris Godonow, according to Voltaire, whose information I prefer, as it seems to be the most authentic, assassinated Demetri, or Demetrius, the lawful heir, and usurped the throne. A young monk took the name of Demetrius, pretending to be that prince, who had escaped from his murderers; and with the assistance of the Poles, and a considerable party (which every tyrant has against him) he drove out the usurper, and seized the crown himself. The imposture was discovered as soon as he came to the sovereignty, because the people were not pleased with him, and he was murdered. Three other false Demetrius's started up one after another.

These impostures prove the despicable state of ignorance in which the Russians were immerged. Their country became by turns a prey to the Poles and the Swedes; but was at length delivered by the good sense of the boyars, impelled by their despair, so late as the year 1613. The independency of Russia was then on the point of being extinguished. Udislaus, son

to Sigismund II. of Poland, had been declared czar; but the tyranny of the Poles was such, that it produced a general rebellion of the Russians, who drove the Poles out of Moscow, where they had for some time defended themselves with unexampled courage. Philaretes, archbishop of Rostow, whose wife was descended of the antient sovereigns of Russia, had been sent ambassador to Poland by Demetrius, one of the Russian tyrants; and there he was detained prisoner, under pretence, that his countrymen had rebelled against Uladislaus. The boyars met in a body; and such was their veneration for Philaretes and his wife, whom the tyrant had shut up in a nunnery, that they elected their son, Michael, a youth of 15 years of age, to be their sovereign. The father being exchanged for some Polish prisoners, returned to Russia; and being created patriarch by his son, he reigned in the young man's right with great prudence and success. He defeated the attempts of the Poles to replace Uladislaus upon the throne, and likewise the claims of a brother of Gustavus Adolphus, but submitted to young Michael without any terms. The claims of the Swedes and Poles upon Russia, occasioned a war between those two people, which gave Michael a kind of a breathing-time; and he made use of it for the benefit of his subjects. I find, that soon after the election of Michael, James I. of England sent, at his invitation, Sir John Meyrick, as his ambassador to Russia, upon some commercial affairs, and to reclaim a certain sum of money which James had advanced to Michael or his predecessors. The English court, however, was so ignorant of the affairs of that country, tho' a Russian company had been then established at London, that James was actually unacquainted with the czar's name and title, for he gave him no other denomination than that of Great duke and lord of Russia. Three years after, James and Michael became much better acquainted; and the latter concluded a commercial treaty with England, which shews him to have been not only well acquainted with the interests of his own subjects, but the laws and usages of nations. Before we take leave of Michael, who survived his father, I am to mention the modes of the czar's nuptials, which I could not introduce into the miscellaneous customs of their subjects, and which are as follow. His czarish majesty's intention to marry being known, the most celebrated beauties of his dominions were sent for to court, and there entertained. They were visited by the czar, and the most magnificent nuptial preparations were made, before the happy lady was declared, by sending her magnificent jewels, and a wedding robe. The rest of the candidates were then dismissed to their several homes, with
suitable

suitable presents. The name of the lady's father who pleased Michael, was Strefchnen; and he was ploughing his own farm, when it was announced to him, that he was father-in-law to the czar.

Alexis succeeded his father Michael, and was married in the same manner. He appears to have been a prince of great genius. He recovered Smolensko, Kiow, and the Ukraine; but was unfortunate in the wars with the Swedes. When the grand signior, Mahomet IV. haughtily demanded some possessions from him in the Ukraine, his answer was, "that he scorned to submit to a Mahometan dog, and that his scymitar was as good as the grand signior's sabre." He attempted to draw up a code of laws for the civil government of his subjects, which is said to be still in being. He cultivated a polite correspondence with the other powers of Europe; and even with the court of Rome, though he ordered his ambassadors not to kiss the pope's toe. He subdued a chief of the Don Cossacs, named Stenko Rasin, who endeavoured to make himself king of Astracan; and the rebel, with 12,000 of his adherents, were hanged on the high roads. He introduced linen and silk manufactures into his dominions: and instead of putting to death or enslaving his Lithuanian, Polish, and Tartar prisoners, he sent them to people the banks of the Wolga and the Kama. He died suddenly, at the age of 46, in the beginning of the year 1675, after shewing himself worthy of being father to Peter the Great.

Alexis left behind him three sons and a daughter, who was a woman of great intrigue and spirit. The names of the sons were Theodore, Iwan or John, and Peter, who was by a second marriage. Theodore mounted the throne, and shewed excellent dispositions for the improvement of his subjects; but his bodily infirmities prevented him from carrying them into execution. He died without any issue. His brother Iwan, being almost blind and dumb, and otherwise distempered, Theodore, before his death, named his younger brother, Peter, to the sovereignty; though then only 10 years of age. This destination was displeasing to the ambitious princess Sophia; and she found means to excite a horrible sedition among the Strelitzes, who then formed the standing army of Russia. Their excesses surpassed all description; but Sophia, by her management, replaced her brother Iwan in his birthright; and exercised the government herself, with the greatest severity and inhumanity; for all the Russian grandees who were related to Peter, or whom she supposed to favour him, were put to cruel deaths. The instances given by Voltaire, of her inhuman administration, are shocking to humanity. At length, in 1682, the

two

two princes, Iwan and Peter, were declared joint sovereigns, and their sister their associate and co-regent. Her administration was bloody and tumultuous; nor durst she venture to check the fury of the Strelitzes, and other insurgents. Finding this debility in her own person, she intended to have married prince Basil Galitzin, who is said to have been a man of sense and spirit, and some learning. Being placed at the head of the army by Sophia, he marched into Crim Tartary; but Peter was now about 17 years of age, and asserted his right to the throne. Sophia and Iwan were then at Moscow; and upon Peter's publishing aloud, that a conspiracy had been formed by his sister to murder him, he was joined by the Strelitzes, who defeated or destroyed Sophia's party, and forced herself to retire to a monastery. Galitzin's life was spared, but his great estate was confiscated; and the following curious sentence was pronounced as his punishment, "Thou art commanded by the most clement czar, to repair to Karga, a town under the pole, and there to continue the remainder of thy days. His majesty, out of his extreme goodness, allows thee three pence per day for thy subsistence." Upon the death of Iwan, which happened in 1696, Peter reigned alone.

It far exceeds the bounds prescribed to this work, to give even a summary detail of this great prince's actions. They may be collected from the histories of the northern nations, Poland, Germany, and other countries; some of which I have already exhibited, as I intend to do the rest. All therefore that is necessary in this place, is to give a general view of his power, and the vast reformation he introduced into his dominions.

Peter, towards the end of the last century, though he had been but very indifferently educated, through the jealousy of his sister, associated himself with Germans and Dutch; the former for the sake of their manufactures, which he early introduced into his dominions; and the latter, for their skill in navigation, which he practised himself. His inclinations for the arts were encouraged by his favourite Le Fort, a Piedmontese; and general Gordon, a Scotchman, disciplined the czar's own regiment, consisting of 5000 foreigners; while Le Fort raised a regiment of 12,000, among whom he introduced the French and German exercises of arms, with a view of employing them in curbing the insolences of the Strelitzes. Peter, after this, began his travels; leaving his military affairs in the hands of Gordon. He set out as an attendant upon his own ambassadors; and his adventures in Holland and England, and other courts, are too numerous, and too well known, to be inserted here. By working as a common ship-carpenter at Deptford

Deptford and Sardam, he completed himself in ship-building and navigation; and through the excellent discipline introduced among his troops by the foreigners, he not only over-awed or crushed all civil insurrections, but all his enemies on this side of Asia; and at last he even exterminated, all but two feeble regiments, the whole body of the Strelitzes. He rose gradually through every rank and service both by sea and land; and the many defeats which he received, especially by Charles XII. at Narva, seemed only to enlarge his ambition, and extend his ideas. The battles he lost rendered him a conqueror upon the whole, by adding experience to his courage: and the generous friendship he shewed to Augustus, king of Poland, both before and after he was dethroned by the king of Sweden, redounds greatly to his honour. He had no regard for rank, distinct from merit; and he at last married, by the name of Catharine, a young Lithuanian woman, who had been betrothed to a Swedish soldier; because, after long cohabitation, he found her possessed of a soul formed to execute his plans, and to assist his counsels. Catharine was so much a stranger to her own country, that her husband afterwards discovered her brother, who served as a common soldier in his armies. But military and naval triumphs, which succeeded one another after the battle of Pultowa with Charles XII. were not the chief glories of Peter's reign. He applied himself with equal assiduity, as I have already mentioned, to the cultivation of commerce, arts, and sciences: and, upon the whole, he made such acquisitions of dominion, even in Europe itself, that he may be said at the time of his death, which happened in 1725, to have been the most powerful prince of his age.

Peter the Great was unfortunate in his eldest son, who was called the czarewitz, and who marrying without his consent, entered, as his father alledged, into some dangerous practices against his person and government; for which he was tried and condemned to death. Under a sovereign so despotic as Peter was, we can say nothing as to the justice of the charge. It was, undoubtedly, his will, that the young prince should be found guilty; but he died, as is said, of a fever, before his sentence was put into execution, in 1722. Peter then ordered his wife Catharine to be crowned, with the same magnificent ceremonies as if she had been a Greek empress, and to be recognized as his successor; which she accordingly was, and mounted the Russian throne. She died, after a glorious reign, in 1727, and was succeeded by Peter II. a minor, son to the czarewitz. Many domestic revolutions happened in Russia during the short reign of this prince; but none was more remarkable than the disgrace and exile of prince Menzikoff,
the

the favourite general in the two late reigns, and efteemed the richeft fubject in Europe. Peter died of the fmall-pox in 1730.

Notwithftanding the defpotifm of Peter and his wife, the Ruffian fenate and nobility, upon the death of Peter II. ventured to fet afide the order of fucceffion which they had eftablifhed. The male iffue of Peter was now extinguifhed; and the duke of Holftein, fon to his eldeft daughter, was, by the deftination of the late emprefs, entitled to the crown: but the Ruffians, for political reafons, filled their throne with Anne, duchefs of Courland, fecond daughter to Iwan, Peter's eldeft brother; though her eldeft fifter, the duchefs of Mecklenburgh, was alive. Her reign was profperous and glorious; for though fhe accepted of the crown under limitations that were derogatory to her dignity, yet fhe broke them all, afferted the prerogative of her anceftors, and punifhed the afpiring Dolgoruki family, who had impofed upon her the limitations, that they themfelves might govern. She raifed her favourite, Biron, to the duchy of Courland; and was obliged to give way to many fevere executions on his account. Upon her death, in 1740, John, the fon of her niece, the princefs of Mecklenburgh, by Anthony Ulric, of Brunfwic Wolfenbuttel, was, by her will, entitled to the fucceffion: but being no more than two years old, Biron was appointed to be adminiftrator of the empire during his nonage. This deftination was difagreeable to the princefs of Mecklenburgh and her hufband, and unpopular among the Ruffians. Count Munich was employed by the princefs of Mecklenburgh to arreft Biron; who was tried, and condemned to die, but was fent in exile to Siberia.

The adminiftration of the princefs Anne of Mecklenburgh and her hufband, was, upon many accounts, but particularly that of their German connections, difagreeable, not only to the Ruffians, but to other powers of Europe; and notwithftanding a profperous war they carried on with the Swedes, the princefs Elizabeth, daughter, by Catharine, to Peter the Great, formed fuch a party, that in one night's time fhe was declared and proclaimed emprefs of the Ruffias; and the princefs of Mecklenburgh, her hufband, and fon, were made prifoners.

Elizabeth's reign may be faid to have been more glorious than that of any of her predeceffors, her father excepted. She abolifhed, as has been already hinted, capital punifhments; and introduced into all civil and military proceedings a moderation till her time unknown in Ruffia: but at the fame time fhe punifhed the counts Munich and Ofterman, who had the chief management of affairs during the late adminiftration, with exile. She made peace with Sweden; and fettled, as we have

have already seen, the succession to that crown, as well as to her own dominions, upon the most equitable foundation. Having gloriously finished a war, which had been stirred up against her, with Sweden, she replaced the natural order of succession in her own family, by declaring the duke of Holstein-Gottorp, who was descended from her elder sister, to be her heir. She gave him the title of grand duke of Russia; and soon after her accession to the throne, she called him to her court; where he renounced the succession to the crown of Sweden, which undoubtedly belonged to him, embraced the Greek religion, and married a princess of Anhalt-Zerbst, by whom he had a son, who is now heir to the Russian empire.

Few princes have had a more uninterrupted career of glory than Elizabeth. She was completely victorious over the Swedes. Her alliance was courted by Great-Britain, at the expence of a large subsidy; but many political, and some, as is said, private reasons, determined her to take part with the house of Austria against the king of Prussia in 1756. Her arms alone gave a turn to the success of the war, which was in disfavour of Prussia, notwithstanding that monarch's amazing abilities both in the field and cabinet. Her conquests were such, as portended the entire destruction of the Prussian power, which was saved only by her critical death, on January 5, 1762.

Elizabeth was succeeded by Peter III. grand prince of Russia, and duke of Holstein: a prince whose conduct has been variously represented. He mounted the throne possessed of an enthusiastic admiration of his Prussian majesty's virtues; to whom he gave peace, and whose principles and practices he seems to have adopted as the directories of his future reign. He might have surmounted the effects even of those peculiarities, unpopular as they then were in Russia; but it is said, that he aimed at reformations in his dominions, which even Peter the Great durst not attempt; and that he even ventured to cut off the beards of his clergy. His memory has been likewise accused of certain domestic infidelities, which were too provoking for a spirited princess to bear. Whatever there may be in those suggestions, it is certain that an universal conspiracy was formed against him, and that he scarcely knew an interval between the loss of his crown and his life, of which he was deprived while under an ignominious confinement. That his conduct with regard to Prussia, was not the sole cause of his deposition, seems pretty evident from the measures of his successor, who was his own wife, and now reigns by the title of Catharine III. That princess, with regard to Prussia, trod in her husband's steps, and now follows the plan he chalked out. The most remarkable domestic occurrence of

her

her reign hitherto, is the death of prince Iwan, son to the princess of Mecklenburgh, and, while he was in his cradle, emperor of Russia. That prince lost his life in an ill-concerted conspiracy, which had been formed by some private officers, to raise him to the throne.

As the internal tranquillity of Poland is a capital object with Russia, her present imperial majesty took a great concern in raising that king to the throne, and in securing the rights which the treaty of Oliva had given to the Greek and protestant subjects of the Polish republic. The umbrage which her armies gave to the Roman-catholic Poles, by their residence in Poland, produced first a civil war, and then confederacies against all that had been done during the late election; which rendered Poland a scene of blood and confusion. The Ottoman court, who had been long waiting for such an opportunity, availed itself of the occasion; they imprisoned, contrary to the law of nations, the Russian minister at Constantinople, declared war against Russia, and marched 500,000 troops to the confines of Poland and Russia.

Hostilities are now begun between these rival and mighty empires. The Russian arms have been victorious by sea and land, and the Turkish greatness has received a shock which seems to threaten an abridgment, if not the total dissolution of their power in Europe. In this quarrel the other nations of Europe have remained neutral. How far the rising greatness of the Russians may be consistent with the commercial interest of England, and the ballance of power established at the expence of so much blood and treasure, is a question which we shall leave to the speculation of politicians.

SCOTLAND, AND ITS ADJACENT ISLES.

ISLES OF SCOTLAND.

I Shall, according to the general plan I have laid down, treat of the islands belonging to Scotland, before I proceed to the description of that antient kingdom; and, to avoid prolixity, I shall comprehend under one head, those of Shetland, Orkney, and the Hebrides, or Western isles.

SITUATION AND EXTENT.] The islands of Shetland lie north-east of the Orcades, between 60 and 61 degrees of north latitude; and are part of the shire of Orkney.

The Orcades, or Orkney islands, lie north of Dungsby-head, between 59 and 60 degrees of north latitude; divided from the continent by Pentland Firth.

The

ISLES OF SCOTLAND.

The western isles are very numerous, and some of them large; situate between 55 and 59 degrees of north latitude.

CLIMATE.] There is very little difference in the climate of those islands, the air being keen, piercing, and salubrious; so that many of the natives live to a great age. In the Shetland and Orkney islands they see to read at midnight in June and July; and during four of the summer months, they have frequent communications, both for business and curiosity, with each other, and with the continent: the rest of the year, however, they are almost inaccessible, through fogs, darkness, and storms. It is a certain fact, that a Scotch fisherman was imprisoned in May, for publishing the account of the prince and princess of Orange being raised to the throne of England the preceding November; and, probably, would have been hanged, had not the news been confirmed by the arrival of a ship.

CHIEF ISLANDS AND TOWNS.] The largest of the Shetland islands, which are forty-six in number, (though many of them are uninhabited) is Mainland, which is 60 miles in length, and 20 in breadth. Its principal town is Larwick, which contains 300 families; the whole number of families in the island not exceeding 500. Skalloway is another town, where the remains of a castle are still to be seen, and is the seat of a presbytery. On this island the Dutch begin to fish for herrings at Midsummer, and their fishing season lasts six months.

The largest of the Orkney islands, which are about thirty in number, (though several of them are unpeopled) is called Pomona. Its length is twenty-four miles, and its breadth, in some places, nine. It contains nine parish churches, and four excellent harbours.

The isle of Mull, in the Hebrides, is twenty-four miles long, and, in some places, almost as broad. It contains two parishes, and a castle, called Duart, which is the chief place in the island. The other principal western islands are, Lewis, or Harries, (for they both form but one island) which belongs to the shire of Ross, and is 100 miles in length, and 13 or 14 in breadth. Sky, belonging to the shire of Inverness, is 40 miles long, and, in some places, 30 broad; fruitful, and well peopled. Bute, which is about 10 miles long, and 3 or 4 broad, is famous for containing the castle of Rothsay, which gave the title of duke to the eldest sons of the kings of Scotland; as it now does to the prince of Wales. Rothsay is likewise a royal burgh; and the islands of Bute and Arran, form the shire of Bute. The isles of Ila and Jura, are part of Argyleshire, but they have no towns worthy notice. North

Wift contains an excellent harbour, called Lochmaddy, famous for herring-fishing. I shall omit the mention of many other of the Hebrides islands, which are at present of small importance, either to the public or the proprietors; though, probably, they may, in future times, be of great consequence to both, by the very improveable fisheries upon their coasts. I cannot, however, avoid mentioning the famous isle of Iona, once the seat and sanctuary of western learning, and the burying-place of many kings of Scotland, Ireland, and Norway. It is still famous for its reliques of sanctimonious antiquity, as shall be hereafter mentioned. Some authors have been at great pains to describe the island of St. Kilda, or Hirt, for no other reason, that I can discover, but because it is the remotest of all the north-west islands, and very difficult of access; for it does not contain above thirty-five families, all of which are protestant, and know very little of the value of money.

INHABITANTS, CUSTOMS, POPULATION, LANGUAGE AND RELIGION. It is not to be imagined, that the inhabitants of the islands belonging to Scotland, can be so minutely described here, as they have been by some other authors; not so much on account of their importance, as their curiosity. Those of Shetland and Orkney were formerly subject to the crown of Denmark, who pledged them, and in the reign of James III. conveyed them in property to the crown of Scotland. The isles of Shetland and Orkney form a stewarty, or shire, which sends a member to parliament. At present, the people in general differ little from the Lowlanders of Scotland, only, perhaps, they are more honest and religious. Men of fortune there, have improved their estates wonderfully of late years; and have introduced into their families all the luxuries and elegancies that are to be found at the tables of their English and Scotch neighbours. They build their dwelling, and other houses, in the most fashionable taste; and are remarkable for the fineness of their linen. As to the common people, they live upon butter, cheese, fish, sea and land fowl (of which they have great plenty) particularly geese; and their chief drink is whey, which they have the art to ferment, so as to give it a vinous quality. In some of the northern islands, the Norwegian, which is called the Norse language, is still spoken. Their vast intercourse with the Dutch, during the fishing season, renders that language common in the Shetland and Orkney islands. The people there are as expert as the Norwegians, already described, in seizing the nests of sea-fowls, who build in the most frightful precipices and rocks. The people's temperance preserves them from many diseases known to luxury. They cure the scurvy and the jaundice, to which they are subject,

ject, with the powder of snail-shells and scurvy-grass, of which they have plenty. Their religion is protestant, according to the discipline of the church of Scotland; and their civil institutions are much the same with those of the country to which they belong.

Nothing certain can be mentioned as to the population of those three divisions of islands. We have the most undoubted evidences of history, that about 400 years ago, they were much more populous than they are now; for the Hebrides themselves were known often to send 10,000 fighting men into the field, without prejudice to their agriculture. At present, their numbers are said not to exceed 48,000. The people of the Hebrides are cloathed, and live like the Scotch Highlanders, who shall hereafter be described. They are similar in persons, constitutions, customs, and prejudices; but with this difference, that as the more polished manners of the Lowlanders are every day gaining ground in the Highlands, perhaps the descendents of the antient Caledonians, in a few years, will be discernible only in the Hebrides.

Those islands alone retain the antient usages of the Celts, as described by the oldest and best authors; but with a strong tincture of the feudal constitution. Their shanachies or story-tellers supply the place of the antient bards, so famous in history; and are the historians, or rather the genealogists, as well as poets, of the nation and family. The chief is likewise attended, when he appears abroad, with his musician, who is generally a bagpiper, and drest in the manner, but more sumptuously than the English minstrels of former times *. Notwithstanding the contempt into which that music is fallen, it is almost incredible with what care and attention it was cultivated among those islanders, so late as the beginning of the present century. They had regular colleges and professors, and the students took degrees according to their proficiency. Many of the Celtic rites, some of which were too barbarous to be retained, or even mentioned, are now abolished. The inhabitants, however, still preserve the most profound respect and affection for their several chieftains, notwithstanding all the pains that have been taken by the British legislature to break those connections, which experience has shewn to be so dangerous to government. The common people are but little better lodged than the Norwegians and Laplanders, already described; though they certainly fare better, for they have oatmeal, plenty of fish and fowl, cheese, butter-milk, and whey;

---

* See Percy's Reliques of antient English Poetry, in 3 vols.

whey; and, when they chufe it, plenty of mutton, beef, goat, kid, and venifon. They indulge themfelves, like their forefathers, in a romantic poetical turn, which is an enemy to induftry, and indeed to domeftic and perfonal cleanlinefs. The agility of both fexes in the exercifes of the field, and in dancing to their favourite mufic, is remarkable.

The reader would not pardon an author, who, in treating of this fubject, fhould omit that remarkable mantology, or gift of prophecy, which diftinguifhes the inhabitants of the Hebrides under the name of the fecond fight. It would be equally abfurd to attempt to difprove the reality of the inftances of this kind that have been brought by creditable authors, as to admit all that has been faid upon the fubject. The adepts of the fecond-fight pretend that they have certain revelations, or rather prefentations, either really or typically, which fwim before their eyes, of certain events that are to happen in the compafs of 24 or 48 hours. I do not, however, from the beft information, obferve that any two of thofe adepts agree as to the manner and forms of thofe revelations, or that they have any fixed method for interpreting their typical appearances. The truth feems to be, that thofe iflanders, by indulging themfelves in lazy habits, acquire vifionary ideas, and over-heat their imaginations, till they are prefented with thofe phantafms, which they miftake for fatidical manifeftations. They inftantly begin to prophecy; and it would be abfurd to fuppofe, that amidft many thoufands of predictions, fome did not happen to be fulfilled; and thefe being well attefted, gave a fanction to the whole.

Many learned men have been of opinion, that the Hebrides being the moft wefterly iflands where the Celts fettled, their language muft remain there in its greateft purity. This opinion, though very plaufible, has failed in experience. Many Celtic words, it is true, as well as cuftoms, are there found; but a vaft intercourfe which the Hebrides had with the Danes, the Norwegians, and other northern people, whofe language is mixed with the Sclavonian and Teutonic, which laft has no affinity with the Celtic, has rendered their language a compound; fo that it approaches in no degree to the purity of the Celtic, commonly called Erfe, which was fpoken by their neighbours in Lochaber and the oppofite coafts of Scotland, the undoubted defcendents of the Celts, among whom their language remains more unmixed.

The religion profeffed in the Hebrides, is chiefly prefbyterian, as eftablifhed in the church of Scotland; but popery and ignorance ftill prevail among fome of the iflanders, whilft fuperftitious perstitious practices and customs seem to be almost grafted in their nature.

Soil, mines and quarries.] Though it is not in the power of natural philosophy to account for the reason, yet it is certain that the soil both of the northern and western islands belonging to Scotland, has suffered an amazing alteration. It is evident to the eye-sight, that many of those islands have been the habitations of the Druids, whose temples are still visible in most of them; and those temples were surrounded by groves, though little or no timber now grows in the neighbourhood. The stumps of former trees, however, are discernible, as are many vestiges of grandeur, even since the admission of the Christian religion; which prove the decrease of the riches, power, and population, of the inhabitants. Experience daily shews, that if the soil of the northern and western islands till of late were barren, cold, and uncomfortable, it was owing to their want of culture; for such spots of them as are now cultivated, produce corn, vegetables, and gardenstuff, more than sufficient for the inhabitants; and even fruit-trees are now brought to maturity. Tin, lead, and silver mines; marl, slate, free-stone, and even quarries of marble, have been found upon those islands. They are not destitute of fine fresh water; and lakes, and rivulets that abound with excellent trout. At the same time it must be owned, that the present face of the soil is bare, and unornamented with trees, excepting a few that are reared in gardens.

Trade and manufactures.] These are all in their infancy in those islands. The reader can easily suppose, that their staple commodities consist of fish, especially herrings, which are the best in the world, and, when properly cured, are equal even to those of the Dutch. They carry on likewise a considerable trade in down and feathers; and their sheep affords them wool, which they manufacture into coarse cloths; and even the linen manufacture makes no small progress in those islands. They carry their black cattle alive to the adjacent parts of Scotland, where they are disposed of in sale or barter; as are large quantities of their mutton, which they salt in the hide. Upon the whole, application and industry, with some portion of public encouragement, are only wanting to render those islands at once ornamental and beneficial to their mother country, as well as to their inhabitants.

Beasts, birds, and fishes.] Little can be said on this head, that is peculiar to those islands. In the countries already described, mention has been made of most of the birds and fishes that have been discovered here; only it is thought that they contain a species of falcon or hawk, of a more noble and docile nature than any that are to be found elsewhere. The Shetland isles are famous for a small breed of horses, which are incredibly active, strong, and hardy, and frequently seen in the streets of London, yoked to the splendid carriages of the curious or wealthy. The coasts of those islands, till within these 20 years, seemed, however, to have been created not for the inhabitants, but for strangers. The latter furnish the former with wines, strong liquors, spice, and luxuries of all kinds, for their native commodities, at the gain of above 100 per cent. But it is to be hoped that this pernicious traffic now draws to an end. Three thousand busses have been known to be employed in one year by the Dutch in the herring fishery, besides those fitted out by the Hamburghers, Bremeners, and other northern ports.

RARITIES AND CURIOSITIES, ARTIFICIAL AND NATURAL. } Those islands exhibit many pregnant proofs, in their churches, the vestiges of old forts, and other buildings both sacred and civil, of what I have already observed, that they were formerly more populous than they are now. The use and construction of some of those works are not easily accounted for at present. In a gloomy valley belonging to Hoy, one of the western islands, is a kind of a hermitage, cut out of a stone called a dwarf-stone, 36 feet long, 18 broad, and nine thick; in which is a square hole, about two feet high, for an entrance, with a stone of the same size for a door. Within this entrance is the resemblance of a bed, with a pillow cut out of the stone, big enough for two men to lie on: at the other end is a couch, and in the middle a hearth, with a hole cut out above for a chimney. It would be endless to recount the various vestiges of the druidical temples remaining in those islands, some of which have required prodigious labour, and are stupendous erections, of the same nature as the famous Stonehenge near Salisbury, which I shall have occasion to describe: others seem to be memorials of particular persons, or actions, consisting of one large stone standing upright; some of them have been sculptured, and others have served as sepulchres, and are composed of stones cemented together. Barrows, as they are called in England, are frequent in those islands; and the monuments of Danish and Norwegian fortifications might employ an able antiquary to describe. The gigantic bones found in many burial places here, give room to believe, that the former inhabitants were of far larger size than the present. It is likewise probable, from some ancient remains, particularly catacombs, and nine silver fibulæ or clasps, found at Stennis, one of the Orkneys, that the Romans were well acquainted with those parts.

ISLES OF SCOTLAND.

The cathedral of Kirkwall, the capital of the Orkneys, is a fine Gothic building, dedicated to St. Magnus, but now converted into a parish church. Its roof is supported by 14 pillars on each side, and its steeple, in which is a good ring of bells, by four large pillars. The three gates of the church are chequered with red and white polished stones, embossed, and elegantly flowered.

The Hebrides are still more distinguished than the Orkney or Shetland isles for their remains of antiquity; and it would far exceed the bounds allotted to this head, were we even to mention every noted monument found upon them, dedicated to civil, religious, or warlike purposes. We cannot, however, avoid taking particular notice of the celebrated isle of Jona, called St. Columb-Kill. We shall not enter into the history or origin of the religious erections upon this island; it is sufficient to say, that it seems to have served as a sanctuary for St. Columba, and other holy men of learning, while Ireland, England, and Scotland, were desolated by barbarism. It appears that the northern pagans often landed here, and paid no regard to the sanctity of the place. The church of St. Mary, which is built in the form of a cathedral, is a beautiful fabric. It contains the bodies of some Scotch, Irish, and Norwegian kings, with some Gaelic inscriptions. The tomb of Columba, who lies buried here, is uninscribed. The steeple is large, the cupola 21 feet square, the doors and windows are curiously carved, and the altar is of the finest marble. Innumerable are the inscriptions of ancient customs and ceremonies that are discernible upon this island, and give countenance to the well-known observation, that when learning was extinct in the continent of Europe, it found a refuge in Scotland, or rather in those islands.

The islands belonging to Scotland, contain likewise some natural curiosities peculiar to themselves; the phaseoli, or Molucca beans, have been found in the Orkneys, driven, as is supposed, from the West-Indies, by the westerly winds, which often force ashore many curious shells and marine productions, highly esteemed by naturalists. In the parish of Harn, a large piece of stag's-horn was found very deep in the earth, by the inhabitants, who were digging for marl; and certain bituminous effluvia produce surprizing phenomena, which the natives believe to be supernatural.

LEARNING, LEARNED MEN, AND HISTORY. } See Scotland.

SCOTLAND.

EXTENT AND SITUATION.

	Miles.		Degrees.
Length	300	between	54 and 59 North latitude.
Breadth	150		1 and 6 Weſt longitude.

NAME.] THERE can be little doubt that the Scots were not the original inhabitants of this kingdom, which they invaded about the beginning of the fourth century, and having conquered the Picts, the territories of both were called Scotland; and that the word Scot, is no other than a corruption of Scuyth, or Scythian; being originally from that immenſe country, called Scythia by the ancients. It is termed, by the Italians, Scotia; by the Spaniards, Eſcotia; by the French, Eſcoſſe; by the Scots, Germans, and Engliſh, Scotland.

BOUNDARIES.] Scotland, which contains an area of 27,794 miles, is bounded on the ſouth by England; and on the north, eaſt, and weſt, by the Deucaledonian, German, and Iriſh ſeas, or more properly, the Atlantic Ocean.

DIVISIONS AND SUBDIVISIONS.] Scotland is divided into the counties ſouth of the Firth of Forth; the capital of which, and of all the kingdom, is Edinburgh; and thoſe to the north of the ſame river, where the chief town is Aberdeen. This was the antient national diviſion; but ſome modern writers, with leſs geographical accuracy, have divided it into Highlands and Lowlands, on account of the different habits, manners, and cuſtoms of the inhabitants of each.

Eighteen counties, or ſhires, are allotted to the ſouthern diviſion, and 15 to the northern; and thoſe counties are ſubdivided into ſherifdoms, ſtewarties, and bailiwicks, according to the antient tenures and privileges of the landholders.

Shires.	Counties and other ſubdiviſions.	Chief Towns.
1. Edinburgh	Mid-Lothian	Edinburgh, W. lon. 3. N. lat. 56. Muſſelburg, Leith, and Dalkeith.
2. Haddington	Eaſt-Lothian	Dunbar, Haddington, and North-Berwick.
3. Merſe, antiently Berwick *	The Merches, and Lauderdale	Duns, and Lauder.

* Berwick, on the north ſide of the Tweed, belonged formerly to Scotland, and gave name to a county in that kingdom; but it is now formed into a town and county of itſelf, in a political ſenſe diſtinct from England and Scotland, having its own privileges.

SCOTLAND. 169

Shires.	Counties and other subdivisions.	Chief Towns.
4. Roxborough	Tiviotdale, Lidsdale, Eskdale and Eusdale	Jedburgh, Kelso, and Melross.
5. Selkirk —	Ettrick Forest —	Selkirk.
6. Peebles —	Tweedale —	Peebles.
7. Lanerk —	Clydsdale —	Glasgow, W. lon. 4-5. N. lat. 55-52. Hamilton, Lanerk, & Rutherglen.
8. Dumfries —	Nithsdale, Annandale	Dumfries, Annand.
9. Wigtown	Galloway, West Part	Wigtown, Stanraer, & Whitehorn.
10. Kirkcudbright —	Galloway, East Part	Kirkudbright
11. Air —	Kyle, Carrick, and Cunningham —	Air, Kilmarnock, Irwin, Maybole, Stewarton, and Saltcots.
12. Dumbarton	Lenox — —	Dumbarton.
13. Bute and	Bute, Arran, and Cathness —	Rothsay.
14. Cathness		Wick, N. lat. 58-40. and Thurso.
15. Renfrew —	Renfrew ———	Renfrew, Paisley, Greenock, & Port-Glasgow.
16. Stirling.	Stirling ———	Stirling and Falkirk.
17. Linlithgow	West Lothian —	Linlithgow, Burroughstonness, and Queensferry.
18. Argyle —	Argyle, Cowal, Knapdale, Kintire, and Lorn, with Part of the Western Isles, particularly Isla, Jura, Mull, Wist, Terif, Col, and Lismore — —	Inverary, Dunstaffnag, Killonmer, and Campbletown.
19. Perth —	Perth, Athol, Gowry, Broadalbin, Monteith, Strathern, Glenshield, and Raynork — —	Perth, Scone, Dumblane, Blair, and Dunkeld.
20. Kincardin —	Merns — —	Bervie, Stonhive and Kinkardin.
21. Aberdeen —	Mar, Buchan, Garioch and Strathbogie —	Old Aberdeen, W. lon. 1-40. N. lat. 57-22. New Aberdeen, Fraserfburgh, Peterhead, Kintore, Inverurie, Strathbogie, and Old Meldrum.

SCOTLAND.

Shires.	Counties and other subdivisions.	Chief Towns.
22. Inverness	Aird, Strathglass, Sky, Harris, Badenoch, Lochaber, & Glenmorison	Inverness, Inverlochy, Fort Augustus, Boileau.
23. Nairne and 24. Cromartie	Western Part of Murray and Cromartie	Nairne, Cromartie.
25. Fife	Fife	St. Andrews, Couper, Falkland, Kirkaldy, Innerkythen, Ely, Burnt-Island, Dumfermlin, Dysart, Anstruther and Aberdour.
26. Forfar	Forfar, Angus	Montrose, Forfar, Dundee, Arbroth, and Brechin
27. Bamff	Bamff, Strathdovern, Boyne, Euzy, Balveny, Strathawin, and part of Bucan	Bamff and Cullen.
28. Sutherland	Strathnaver and Sutherland	Strathy and Dornoch.
29. Clacmanan & 30. Kinross	Fife Part	Culros, Clacmanan, Aloway and Kinross.
31. Ross	Easter and Wester Ross, Isle of Lewis, Lochbroom, Lochcarran, Ardmeanach, Redcastle, Ferrintosh, Strathpeffer, and Ferrindonald	Taine, Dingwall, Fortrose, Rosemarkie, and New Kelso.
32. Elgin	Murray & Strathspey	Elgin and Forres.
33. Orkney	Isles of Orkney and Shetland	Kirkwall, W. lon. 3. N. lat. 59-45. Skalloway, near the Meridian of London, N. lat. 61.

In all, thirty-three shires, which chuse thirty representatives to sit in the parliament of Great-Britain; Bute and Cathness chusing alternately, as do Nairne and Cromartie, and Clacmanan and Kinross.

The royal Boroughs which chuse representatives are,

Edinburgh — — — 1	Forfar, Perth, Dundee, Cowper, and St. Andrews } 1
Kirkwall, Wick, Dornoch, Dingwall, and Tayne } 1	Crail, Kilrenny, Anstruther East and West, and Pittenweem } 1
Fortrose, Inverness, Nairne, and Forres — — } 1	Dysert, Kirkaldy, Kinghorne, and Burnt Island } 1
Elgin, Cullen, Bamff, Inverury, and Kintore } 1	Innerkythen, Dumfermlin, Queensferry, Culross, and Sterling } 1
Aberdeen, Bervie, Montrose, Aberbrothe, and Brechin } 1	

Glasgow, Renfrew, Ruther-glen, and Dumbarton	1	Dumfries, Sanquehar, Annan, Lochmaban, and Kirkcudbright	1
Haddington, Dunbar, North-Berwick, Lawder, and Jedburgh	1	Wigtown, New Galloway, Stranrawer, and Whitehorn	1
Selkirk, Peebles, Linlithgow, and Lanerk	1	Air, Irwin, Rothfay, Campbeltown, and Inverary	1

CLIMATE, SOIL, AIR, AND WATER.] The climate all over Scotland is, from the variety of its hills, valleys, rivers, and lakes, for the most part, agreeable and healthy, exempted from the inconveniences that attend the northern countries already described, and even those of a more southerly situation. The air is, in general, moist and temperate; but in the neighbourhood of some high mountains, which are covered with eternal snow, it is keen and piercing for about nine months in the year. In the northern parts daylight, at Midsummer, lasts 18 hours and 5 minutes; and the day and night in winter, are in the same proportion. Late experience has proved, that industry, and skilful agriculture, can render the soil of Scotland, in sundry parts, as fruitful as that of England; though, perhaps, many of its vegetable and hortulane productions may not come so soon to maturity. The inequality of the soil of Scotland is surprizing; and cannot be accounted for by natural or apparent causes; some of the northern provinces being more fruitful and more early in their products than the southern: but those inequalities seem to be in common to all countries. The water of Scotland is pure, light, and easy to the stomach; and some mineral waters have been discovered.

MOUNTAINS.] The principal mountains in Scotland are the Grampian-hills, which run from east to west, from near Aberdeen to Cowal in Argyleshire, almost the whole breadth of the kingdom. Another chain of mountains, called the Pentland-Hills, runs through Lothian and join those of Tweedale. A third, called Lammer-Muir, rises near the eastern coast, and runs westward through the Merse. Besides those continued chains, among which we may reckon the Cheviot or Teviot-Hills, on the borders of England, Scotland contains many detached mountains, which, from their conical figure, sometimes go by the Celtic word Laws. Many of them are stupendously high, and of beautiful forms; but too numerous to be particularized here.

RIVERS, LAKES, AND FORESTS.] The largest river in Scotland is the Forth, which rises in Monteith near Callendar, and passing by Stirling, after describing a number of beautiful meanders, discharges itself near Edinburgh into that arm of the German sea to which it gives the name of Firth of Forth. Second to the Forth is the Tay, which issues out of Loch Tay, in Broadalbin, and, running south-east, passes the town of Perth, and falls into the sea at Dundee. The Spey, which is called the most rapid river in Scotland, issues from a lake of the same name in Badenoch, and, running from south-west to north-east, falls into the sea near Elgin; as do the rivers Dee and Don, which run from west to east, and disembogue themselves at Aberdeen. The Tweed rises on the borders of Lanerkshire, and, after many beautiful serpentine turnings, discharges itself into the sea at Berwick, where it serves as a boundary between Scotland and England, on the eastern side. The Clyde is a large river on the west of Scotland, has its rise in Annandale, runs north-west through the valley of that name, and, after passing by Lanerk, Hamilton, the city of Glasgow, Renfrew, Dumbarton, and Greenock, falls into the Firth of Clyde, opposite to the isle of Bute. Besides those capital rivers, Scotland contains many of an inferior sort, well provided with salmon, trout, and other fishes, which equally enrich and beautify the country. Several of those rivers go by the name of Esk, which is the old Celtic name for water. The greatest improvement for inland navigation that has been attempted in Great-Britain, is now (1771) carrying on at a very considerable expence, by a society of public-spirited gentlemen, for joining the rivers Forth and Clyde together; by which a communication will be opened between the east and west seas, to the immense advantage of the whole kingdom, as must be evident to every person who shall throw his eye upon the map of Scotland.

The lakes of Scotland (there called Lochs) are too many to be particularly described. Those called Loch Tay, Loch Lomond, Lochness, Loch Au, and one or two more, present us with such picturesque scenes as are not matched in Europe, if we except Ireland. Several of those lakes are beautifully fringed with woods, and contain plenty of fresh-water fish. The Scots sometimes give the name of a loch to an arm of the sea, for example, Loch Fyn, which is 60 miles long, and four broad, and is famous for its excellent herrings: the Loch of Spinie, near Elgin, is remarkable for its number of swans and cygnets, which often darken the air with their flights; owing, as some think, to the plant olorina, which grows in its waters, with a strait stalk and a cluster of seeds at the top. Near Lochness is a hill almost two miles perpendicular, on the top of which is a lake of cold fresh water, about 30 fathoms in length, too deep ever yet to be fathomed, and never freezes; whereas, but 17 miles from thence, the lake Lochanwyn, or Green Lake,

Lake, is covered with ice all the year round. The ancient province of Lochaber, receives that name from being the mouth of the lochs, by means of which the antient Caledonians, the genuine defcendents of the Celts, were probably enabled to preferve themfelves independent upon, and unmixed with, the Lowlanders. Befides thefe rivers and lochs, and others too numerous to mention, the coafts of Scotland are in many parts indented with large, bold, and navigable bays or arms of the fea; as the bay of Glenluce and Wigtoun Bay; fometimes they are called Firths, as the Solway Firth, which feparates Scotland from England on the weft; the Firth of Forth, Murray Firth, and thofe of Cromarty and Dornoch.

The face of Scotland, even where it is moft uninviting, prefents us with the moft uncontrovertible evidences of its having been formerly over-run with timber. The deepeft moffes, or moraffes, contain large logs of wood; and their waters being impregnated with turpentine have a preferving quality, as appears by the human bodies which have been difcovered in thofe moffes. The Sylva Caledonia, or Caledonian Foreft, the remains of which are now thought to be Etrick Wood, in the fouth of Scotland, famous in antiquity for its being the harbour of the Caledonian wild boars; but fuch an animal is not now to be feen in Scotland. Several woods, however, ftill remain in that country; and many attempts have been made for reducing them into charcoal, for the ufe of furnaces and founderies; but lying at a great diftance from water-carriage, though the work fucceeded perfectly in the execution, they were found impracticable to be continued. Fir-trees grow in great perfection almoft all over Scotland, and form beautiful plantations. The Scotch oak is excellent in the Highlands, where fome woods reach 20 or 30 miles in length, and four or five in breadth, but, through the inconveniency already mentioned, without being of much emolument to the proprietors.

METALS AND MINERALS.] Though Scotland does not at prefent boaft of its gold mines, yet, it is certain, that it contains fuch, or at leaft that Scotland afforded a confiderable quantity of that metal for its coinage. James V. and his father contracted with certain Germans for working the mines of Crawford-Moor; and it is an undoubted fact, that when James V. married the French king's daughter, a number of covered difhes, filled with coins of Scotch gold, were prefented to the guefts by way of deffert. The civil wars and troubles which followed, under his daughter and in the minority of his grandfon, drove thofe foreigners, the chief of whom was called Cornelius, from their works, which, fince that time, have never been recovered. Some fmall pieces of
gold

gold have been found in those parts washed down by the floods. It likewise appears by the public records, that those beautiful coins struck by James V. called bonnet-pieces, were fabricated of gold found in Scotland, as were other medals of the same metal.

Several landholders in Scotland derive a large profit from their lead mines, which are said to be very rich, and to produce large quantities of silver; but we know of no silver-mines that are worked at present. Some copper-mines have been found near Edinburgh; and many parts of Scotland, in the east, west, and northern counties, produce excellent coal of various kinds, large quantities of which are exported, to the vast emolument of the public. Lime-stone is here in great plenty, as is free-stone; so that the houses of the better sort are constructed of the most beautiful materials. The indolence of the inhabitants of many places in Scotland, where no coal is found, prevented them from supplying that defect by plantations of wood; and the peat-mosses being in many parts, of the north especially, almost exhausted, the inhabitants are put to great difficulties for fuel; however the taste for plantations, of all kinds, that now prevails, will soon remedy that inconveniency.

Lapis lazuli is said to be dug up in Lanerkshire; allum-mines have been found in Bamffshire; chrystal, variegated pebbles, and other transparent stones, which admit of the finest polish for seals, are found in many parts of Scotland; as are talc, flint, sea-shells, potters-clay, and fullers earth. The stones which the country people call elf-arrow-heads, and to which they assign a supernatural origin and use, were probably the flint-heads of arrows made use of by the Caledonians and ancient Scots. No country produces greater plenty of iron-ore, both in mines and stones, than Scotland; of which the proprietors now begin to taste the sweets, in their founderies and other metalline manufactures.

VEGETABLE AND ANIMAL PRODUCTIONS, BY SEA AND LAND. I have already observed that the soil of Scotland may be rendered in many parts as fruitful as that of England. Some large tracts of the low countries at present exceed in value English estates of the same extent, because they are far less exhausted, and worn out than those of the southern parts of the island; and agriculture is now perhaps as well understood, both in theory and practice, among many of the Scotch landlords and farmers, as it is in any part of Europe.

Such is the mutability of things, and the influence of commerce, that a very considerable part of the landed property has lately (perhaps happily for the public) fallen into new hands.
The

SCOTLAND. 175

The merchants of Glasgow, who are the life and soul of that part of the kingdom, while they are daily introducing new branches of commerce, are no less attentive to the progress of agriculture, by which they do their country in particular, and the whole island in general, the most essential service. The active genius of these people extends even to moors, rocks, and marshes, which being hitherto reckoned useless, were consequently neglected, but are now brought to produce certain species of grain or timber, for which the soil is best adapted.

But the fruits of skill and industry are chiefly perceiveable in the counties lying upon the river Forth, called the Lothians, where agriculture is thoroughly understood, and the farmers, who generally rent from 3 to 500 l. per ann. are well fed, well clothed, and comfortably lodged. The reverse, however, may be observed, of a very considerable part of Scotland, which still remains in a state of nature, and where the landlords, ignorant of their real interest, refuse to grant such leases as would encourage the tenant to improve his own farm. In such places, the husbandmen barely exist upon the gleanings of a scanty farm, seldom exceeding 20 or 30 l. per ann. the cattle are lean and small, the houses mean beyond expression, and the face of the country exhibits the most deplorable marks of poverty and oppression. Indeed, from a mistaken notion of the landed people in general, the greatest part of the kingdom lies naked and exposed, for want of such hedge-rows, and planting, as adorn the country of England. They consider hedges as useless and cumbersome, as occupying more room than what they call stone inclosures, which except in the Lothians already mentioned, are generally no other than low paultry walls, huddled up of loose stones, without lime or mortar, which yields a bleak and mean appearance.

The soil in general produces wheat, rye, barley, oats, hemp, flax, hay, and pasturage. In the southern counties the finest garden fruits, particularly apricots, nectarines, and peaches, fall little, if at all, short of those in England; and the same may be said of the common fruits. The uncultivated parts of the Highlands abound in various kinds of salubrious and pleasant-tasted berries; though it must be owned, that many extensive tracts are covered with a strong heath. The sea-coast produces the alga-marina, dulse, or dulish, a most wholesome nutritive weed, in great quantities, and other marine plants.

The fishes on the coast of Scotland are much the same with those of the islands and counties already described; but the Scots have improved in their fisheries as much as they have in their manufactures and agriculture, for societies have been

formed

formed, which have carried that branch of national wealth to a perfection that never was before known in that country; and bids fair to emulate, if not to excel, the Dutch themselves, in curing, as well as catching, their fish. In former times, the Scots seldom ventured to fish above a league's distance from the land, but they now ply in the deep waters as boldly and successfully as any of their neighbours. Their salmons, which they can send more early, when prepared, to the Levant and southern markets than the English or Irish can, are of great service to the nation, as the returns are generally made in specie, or beneficial commodities.

This country contains few or no kinds either of wild or domestic animals that are not common with their neighbours. The red-deer and the roe-buck are found in the Highlands, but their flesh is not comparable to English venison. Hares, and all other animals for game, are here plentiful; as are the grouse and heathcock, which is a most delicious bird, as likewise are the capperkaily, and the tarmacan, which is of the pheasant kind; but those birds are scarce even in the Highlands, and when discovered are very shy. The numbers of black cattle that cover the hills of Scotland towards the Highlands, and sheep that are fed upon the beautiful mountains of Tweedale, and other parts of the south, are almost incredible, and formerly brought large sums into the country; the black cattle especially, which, when fattened on the southern pastures, are reckoned superior to English beef. It is to be hoped, however, that this trade is now on its decline, by the vast increase of manufacturers, whose demands for butchers meat must lessen the exportation of cattle into England. Some are of opinion, that a sufficient stock, by proper methods, may be raised to supply both markets, to the great emolument of the nation.

Formerly the kings of Scotland were at infinite pains to mend the breed of the Scotch horses, by importing a larger and more generous kind from the continent; but the truth is, notwithstanding all the care that was taken, it was found that the climate and soil of Scotland were unfavourable to that noble animal, for they diminished both in size and spirit; so that about the time of the union, few horses, natives of Scotland, were of much value. Great efforts have been made of late to introduce the English and foreign breeds, and much pains have been taken for providing them with proper foods and management, but with what success time alone can discover.

POPULATION, INHABITANTS, MANNERS, AND CUSTOMS. } The population of Scotland is generally fixed at about a million and a half of souls. This calculation rests merely upon vague conjecture, as I know of no attempt that has

has been made to support even its probability. If we form an estimate upon any known principle, the inhabitants of Scotland are far more numerous. It is to be regretted that some public encouragement has not been given to bring this matter nearer to a certainty, which might be done by the returns of the clergy from their several parishes. The only records at present that can be appealed to, are those of the army; and, by the best information, they make the number of soldiers furnished by Scotland in the late war, which began in 1755, to amount to 80,000 men. We are, however, to observe, that above 60,000 of these were raised in the islands and Highlands, which form by far the least populous part of Scotland. It belongs, therefore, to political calculation to compute whether the population of Scotland does not exceed two millions and a half, as no country in the world, exclusive of the army, sends abroad more of its inhabitants. If we consult the most ancient and creditable histories, the population of Scotland, in the thirteenth century, must have been excessive, as it afforded so many thousands to fall by the swords of the English, without any sensible decrease (so far as I can find) of the inhabitants.

The people of Scotland are generally raw-boned; and a kind of a characteristical feature, that of high cheek bones, reigns in their faces; lean, but clean limbed, and can endure incredible fatigues. Their adventuring spirit was chiefly owing to their laws of succession, which invested the elder brother as head of the family with the inheritance, and left but a very scanty portion for the other sons. This obliged the latter to seek their fortunes abroad, though no people have more affection for their native soil than the Scots have in general. It is true, this disparity of fortune among the sons of one family prevails in England likewise; but the resources which younger brothers have in England are numerous, compared to those of a country so narrow, and so little improved, either by commerce or agriculture, as Scotland was formerly.

An intelligent reader may easily perceive, that the ridiculous family pride which is perhaps not yet entirely extinguished in Scotland, was owing to the feudal institutions which reigned there in all their horrors of blood and barbarity. Their family differences, especially the Highlanders, familiarized them to blood and slaughter; and the death of an enemy, however effected, was always a matter of triumph. These passions did not live in the breasts of the common people only, for they were authorised and cherished by their chieftains, many of whom were men who had seen the world, were conversant in the courts of Europe, masters of polite literature, and amiable in all the duties of civil and social life. Their kings, excepting some of them who were endued with extraordinary virtues, were considered in little other light than commanders of their army in time of war, for in time of peace their civil authority was so little felt, that every clan, or family, even in the most civilized parts of Scotland, looked upon its own chieftain as the sovereign. Those ideas were confirmed even by the laws, which gave those petty tyrants a power of life and death upon their own estates, and they generally executed in four and twenty hours after the party was apprehended. The pride which those chieftains had of out-vying each other, in the numbers of their followers, created perpetual animosities, which seldom or never ended without bloodshed; so that the common people, whose best qualification was a blind devotion to the will of their master, and the aggrandisement of his name, lived in a state of continual hostility.

The late Archibald, duke of Argyle, was the first chieftain we have heard of, who had the patriotism to attempt to reform his dependents, and to banish from them those barbarous ideas. His example has been followed by others; and there scarce can be a doubt, that a very few years will reconcile the Highlanders to all the milder habits of society.

Some Scotch gentlemen, who at this day pique themselves upon their family, or the antiquity of their descent, are the most dangerous as well as disagreeable animals upon earth; because, forgetting all the virtues of their ancestors, they imitate them only in their capricious vanity and revenge. Those who go abroad, and endeavour by industry to raise the lowness of their circumstances, excel in all the social, civil, commercial, and military duties. There is a kind of similarity in their personal characters, and by seeing one Scotchman who acquires a fortune abroad, you see the whole. They are hospitable, open, communicative, and charitable. They assimilate to the manners of the people with whom they live, with more ease and freedom than the natives of most other countries; and they have a surprizing facility in acquiring languages, particularly the French.

It remains perhaps a question, whether that lettered education, for which the Scots were noted by the neighbouring nations, was not of prejudice to their country, while it was of the utmost service to many of its natives. Their literature, however slight, rendered them acceptable and agreeable among foreigners; but at the same time, it drained their nation of that order of men, who are the best fitted for forming and executing the great plans of commerce and agriculture for the public emolument.

With regard to gentlemen who live at home, upon estates of 300 l. a year, and upwards, they differ little or nothing, in their manners, and stile of living, from their English neighbours of the like fortunes.

From what has been said, it appears that the antient modes of living among the Scotch nobility and gentry are as far from being applicable to the present time, as the forms of a Roman senate are to that of a conclave; and no nation, perhaps, ever underwent so quick and so sudden a transition of manners. The danger is, that it has been rather too rapid in a contrary extreme, before the resources of the luxuries and conveniencies of life have been fully established.

The peasantry have their peculiarities; their ideas are confined; but no people can conform their tempers better than they do to their stations. They are taught from their infancy to bridle their passions, to behave submissively to their superiors, and live within the bounds of the most rigid œconomy. Hence they save their money and their constitutions, and few instances of murder, perjury, robbery, and other atrocious vices occur at present in Scotland. They seldom enter singly upon any daring enterprize; but when they act in concert, the secrecy, sagacity and resolution, with which they carry on any desperate undertaking, is not to be paralleled; and their fidelity to one another, under the strongest temptations, arising from their poverty, is still more extraordinary. Their mobs are managed with all the caution of conspiracies, witness that which put Porteus to death, in 1735, in open defiance of law and government, and in the midst of 20,000 people; and, though the agents were well known, and some of them tried, with a reward of 500 l. annexed to their conviction, yet no evidence could be found sufficient to bring them to punishment. The fidelity of the Highlanders, of both sexes, under a still greater temptation, to the young Pretender, after his defeat at Culloden, could scarcely be believed were it not well attested.

They affect a fondness for the memory and language of their forefathers beyond, perhaps, any people in the world; but this attachment is seldom or never carried into any thing that is indecent or disgustful, though they retain it abroad as well as at home. They are fond of the antient Scotch dishes, such as the hoggice, the sheep's-head singed, the fish in sauce, the chicken broth, and minced collops. These dishes, in their original dressing, were savoury and nutritive for keen appetites; but the modern improvements that have been made in the Scotch cookery, have rendered them agreeable to the most delicate palates. The common use of oatmeal, undoubtedly, gave a hardness to the features of the vulgar of both sexes, besides some other disagreeable consequences it was attended with; but these unfavourable characteristics will wear out, by the introduction of wheaten bread, which now abounds in Scotland. The excessive use of oat-meal accounts for the common observation, that the faces of the lower women in Scotland are commonly very coarse; but it was owned at the same time, that among the higher rank of females, beauty was found in its utmost perfection. The reverse has been remarked of a neighbouring nation.

The inhabitants of those parts of Scotland, who live chiefly by pasture, have a natural vein for poetry; and the beautiful simplicity of the Scotch tunes is relished by all true judges of nature. Love is generally the subject, and many of the airs have been brought upon the English stage with variations, under new names, but with this disadvantage, that though rendered more conformable to the rules of music, they are mostly altered for the worse, being stripped of that original simplicity, which however irregular, is their most essential characteristic which is so agreeable to the ear, and has such powers over the human breast. Those of a more lively and merry strain have had better fortune, being introduced into the army in their native dress, by the fifes, an instrument for which they are remarkably well suited. It has been ridiculously supposed that Rizzio, the unhappy Italian secretary of Mary queen of Scots, reformed the Scotch music. This is a falshood invented by his countrymen in envy to the Scots. Their finest tunes existed long before Rizzio's arrival, in their church music; nor does it appear that Rizzio, who was entirely employed by his mistress in foreign dispatches, ever composed an air during the short time he lived in Scotland; but, were there no other evidences to confute this report, the original character of the music itself is sufficient.

The lower people in Scotland are not so much accustomed as the English are to clubs, dinners, and other convivial entertainments; but when they partake of them, for that very reason, they seem to enjoy them more completely. One institution there is, at once social and charitable, and that is, the contributions raised for celebrating the weddings of people of an inferior rank. Those festivities partake of the antient Saturnalia; but though the company consists promiscuously of the high and the low, the entertainment is as decent as it is jovial. Each guest pays according to his inclination or ability, but seldom under a shilling a head, for which they have a wedding dinner and dancing. When the parties happen to be servants in respectable families, the contributions are so liberal, that they often establish the young couple in the world.

The

The common people of Scotland retain the solemn decent manner of their anceſtors at burials. When a relation dies in a town, the pariſh beadle is ſent round with a paſſing bell; but he ſtops at certain places, and with a ſlow melancholy tone, announces the name of the party deceaſed, and the time of his interment, to which he invites all his fellow countrymen. At the hour appointed, if the deceaſed was beloved in the place, vaſt numbers attend. The proceſſion is ſometimes preceded by the magiſtrates and their officers, and the deceaſed is carried in his coffin, covered by a velvet pall, with chair poles, to the grave, where it is interred without any farther ceremony than the neareſt relation thanking the company for their attendance. The funerals of the nobility and gentry are performed in much the ſame manner as in England, but without the burial ſervice. The highland funerals were generally preceded by bagpipes, which played certain dirges, called coronachs, and were accompanied by the voices of the attendants of both ſexes.

Dancing is a favourite amuſement in this country, but little regard is paid to art or gracefulneſs; the whole conſiſts in agility, and in keeping time to their own tunes, which they do with great exactneſs. One of the peculiar diverſions practiſed by the gentlemen, is the Goff, which requires an equal degree of art and ſtrength: it is played by a bat and a ball; the latter is ſmaller and harder than a cricket ball; the bat is of a taper conſtruction, till it terminates in the part that ſtrikes the ball; which is loaded with lead, and faced with horn. The diverſion itſelf reſembles that of the Mall, which was common in England in the middle of the laſt century. An expert player will ſend the ball an amazing diſtance at one ſtroke; and each party follows his ball upon an open heath, and he who ſtrikes it in feweſt ſtrokes into a hole, wins the game. The diverſion of Curling is likewiſe, I believe, peculiar to the Scots. It is performed upon ice, with large flat ſtones, often from twenty to two hundred pounds weight each, which they hurl from a common ſtand, to a mark at a certain diſtance; and whoever is neareſt the mark is the victor. Theſe two may be called the ſtanding ſummer and winter diverſions of Scotland. The natives are expert at all the other diverſions common in England, the cricket excepted, of which they have no notion; the gentlemen look upon it as too athletic and mechanical.

LANGUAGE AND DRESS.] I place thoſe two articles under the ſame head, becauſe they had formerly an intimate relation to each other, both of them being evidently Celtic. The Highland plaid is compoſed of a woollen ſtuff, ſometimes very fine,

fine, called *tartan*. This stuff consists of various colours, forming stripes which cross each other at right angles; and the natives value themselves upon the judicious arrangement, or what they call sets, of those stripes and colours, which where skilfully managed, produce a wonderfully pleasing effect to the eye. Above the shirt, the Highlanders wear a waistcoat of the same composition with the plaid, which commonly consists of twelve yards in width, and which they throw over the shoulder into very near the form of a Roman toga, as represented in antient statues: sometimes it is fastened round the middle with a leather belt, so that part of the plaid hangs down before and behind like a petticoat, and supply the want of breeches. This they call being dressed in a phelig, but which the Lowlanders call a kilt, and I make no doubt is the same word with Celt. Sometimes they wear a kind of petticoat of the same variegated stuff, buckled round the waist, and this they term the philibeg, which seems to be of Milesian extraction. Their stockings were likewise of tartan, tied below the knee with tartan garters formed into tassels. The poorer people wear upon their feet, brogues made of untanned or undressed leather; for their heads a blue flat cap is used, called a bonnet, of a particular woollen manufacture. From the belt of the philibeg hung generally their knives, and a dagger, which they called a dirk, and an iron pistol, sometimes of fine workmanship, and curiously inlaid with silver. The introduction of the broad sword of Andrea Ferrara, a Spaniard (which was always part of the Highland dress) seems to be no earlier than the reign of James III. who invited that excellent workman to Scotland. A large leathern purse, richly adorned with silver, hanging before them, was always part of a Highland chieftain's dress.

The dress of the Highland women consisted of a petticoat and jerkin, with strait sleeves, trimmed or not trimmed, according to the quality of the wearer; over this they wore a plaid, which they either held close under their chins with the hand, or fastened with a buckle of a particular fashion. On the head they wore a kerchief of fine linen of different forms. The women's plaid has been but lately disused in Scotland by the ladies, who wore it in a graceful manner, the drapery falling towards the feet in large folds. A curious virtuoso may find a strong resemblance between the variegated and fimbriated draperies of the antients, and those of the Tuscans, (who were unquestionably of Celtic original) as they are to be seen in the monuments of antiquity.

The attachment of the Highlanders to this dress, rendered it a bond of union, which often proved dangerous to the government.

ment. Many efforts had been made by the legiflature, after the rebellion in 1715, to difarm them, and oblige them to conform to the Low-country dreffes. The difarming fcheme was the moft fuccefsful, for when the rebellion in 1745 broke out, the common people had fcarcely any other arms than thofe which they took from the king's troops. Their overthrow at Culloden, rendered it no difficult matter for the legiflature to force them into a total change of their drefs. Its conveniency, however, for the purpofes of the field, is fo great, that fome of the Highland regiments ftill retain it. Even the common people have of late refumed the ufe of it; and for its lightnefs and difcumbrance, many of the Highland gentlemen wear it in the fummer time.

The drefs of the higher and middling ranks in the Low-Country, differ little or nothing from the Englifh; but many of the peafantry ftill retain the bonnet, for the cheapnefs and lightnefs of the wear. The drefs of the women of all ranks are much the fame in both kingdoms.

I have already mentioned the language of the Highlanders, efpecially towards Lochaber and Badenoch, to be radically Celtic. The Englifh fpoken by the Scots, notwithftanding its provincial articulations, which are as frequent there as in the more fouthern counties, is written in the fame manner in both kingdoms. At prefent, the pronunciation of a Scotchman does not differ fo much from a Londoner, as that of a Londoner does from an inhabitant of Somerfetfhire, and fome parts of Worcefterfhire.

PUNISHMENTS.] Thefe are pretty much the fame in Scotland as in England, only that of beheading is performed by an inftrument called the Maiden: the model of which, it is well known, was brought from Hallifax in England to Scotland, by the regent earl of Morton, and it was hanfelled by his own execution.

RELIGION.] Antient Scottifh hiftorians, Bede, and other writers, generally agree that Chriftianity was firft taught in Scotland by fome of the difciples of St. John the apoftle, who fled to this northern corner to avoid the perfecution of Domitian, the Roman emperor; though it was not publicly profeffed till the beginning of the third century, when a prince, whom Scotch hiftorians call Donald the Firft, his queen, and feveral of his nobles, were folemnly baptized. It was further confirmed by emigrations from South Britain, during the perfecutions of Aurelius and Dioclefian, when it became the eftablifhed religion of Scotland, under the management of certain learned and pious men, named Culdees, who feem to have been the firft regular clergy in Scotland, and were governed by overseers or bishops chosen by themselves, from among their own body, but who had no pre-eminence or rank over the rest of their brethren.

Thus independant of the church of Rome, Christianity seems to have been taught, planted, and finally confirmed as a national church, where it flourished in its native simplicity, till the arrival of Palladius, a priest sent by the bishop of Rome in the fifth century, who found means to introduce the modes and ceremonies of the Romish church, which at last prevailed, and Scotland became involved in that darkness which for many ages overspread Europe; though their dependance upon the pope was very slender, when compared to the blind subjection of many other nations.

The Culdees, however, long retained their original manners, and remained a distinct order, notwithstanding the oppression of the Romish clergy, so late as the age of Robert Bruce, in the 14th century, when they disappeared. But it is worthy of observation, that the opposition to popery in this island, though it ceased in Scotland upon the extinction of the Culdees, was in the same age revived in England by John Wickliffe, a man of parts and learning, who was the forerunner, in the wo k of reformation, to John Huss, and Jerome of Prague, as the latter were to Martin Luther, and John Calvin. But though the doctrines of Wickliffe were nearly the same with those propagated by the Reformers in the 16th century, and the age seemed strongly disposed to receive them, affairs were not yet fully ripe for this great revolution; and the finishing blow to popery in England, was reserved to the age of Henry VIII.

Soon after that important event took place in England, when learning, arts and sciences began to revive in Europe, the absurdities of the church of Rome, as well as the profligate lives of her clergy, did not escape the notice of a free and enquiring people, and gave rise to the Reformation in Scotland; which began in the reign of James V. made great progress under that of his daughter Mary, and was at length compleated through the preaching of J hn Knox, who had adopted the doctrine of Calvin, and was become the apostle of Scotland. It was natural for his brethren to imagine, that, upon the abolition of the Roman Catholic religion, they were to succeed to the revenues of that clergy. The great nobility, who had parcelled out these possessions for themselves, did not at first discourage this notion; but no sooner had Knox succeeded in his designs, which, through the fury of the mob, destroyed some of the finest ecclesiastical buildings in the world, than the parliament, or rather the nobility, monopolized all the church livings,

livings, and moſt ſcandalouſly left the reformed clergy to live almoſt in a ſtate of beggary; nor could all their efforts produce any ſtruggle in their favour.

The nobility and great landholders, left the doctrine and diſcipline of the church to be modelled by the preachers, and they were confirmed by parliament. Succeeding times rendered the preſbyterian clergy of vaſt importance to the ſtate; and their revenues have been ſo much mended, that though no ſtipend there exceeds 150 l. a year, few fall ſhort of 60 l. and none of 50 l. If the preſent expenſive mode of living continues in Scotland, the eſtabliſhed clergy will have many unanſwerable reaſons to urge for the increaſe of their revenues.

The bounds of this work do not admit of entering at large upon the doctrinal and economical part of the church of Scotland. It is ſufficient to ſay, that its firſt principle is a parity of eccleſiaſtical authority among all its preſbyters; that it agrees in its cenſures with the reformed churches abroad in the chief heads of oppoſition to popery; but that it is modelled principally after the Calviniſtical plan eſtabliſhed at Geneva. This eſtabliſhment, at various periods, proved ſo tyrannical over the laity, by having the power of the greater and leſſer excommunication, which were attended by a forfeiture of eſtate, and ſometimes of life, that the kirk ſeſſions, and other bodies, have been abridged of all their dangerous powers over the laity, who are extremely jealous of their being revived. It is ſaid, that even that relic of popery, the obliging fornicators of both ſexes to ſit upon what they call a repenting-ſtool, in the church, and in full view of the congregation, begins to wear out; it having been found, that the Scotch women, on account of that penance, were the greateſt infanticides in the world. In ſhort, the power of the Scotch clergy is at preſent very moderate, or at leaſt very moderately exerciſed; nor are they accountable for the extravagancies of their predeceſſors. They have been, ever ſince the Revolution, firm adherents to civil liberty, and the houſe of Hanover; and acted with remarkable intrepidity during the rebellion in 1745. They dreſs without clerical robes; but ſome of them appear in the pulpit in gowns, after the Geneva form, and bands. They make no uſe of ſet forms in worſhip, but are not prohibited that of the Lord's Prayer. The rents of the biſhops, ſince the abolition of epiſcopacy, are paid to the king, who commonly appropriates them to pious purpoſes. A thouſand pounds a year is always ſent by his majeſty for the uſe of the proteſtant ſchools erected by act of parliament in North-Britain, and the Weſtern Iſles; and the Scotch clergy, of late, have planned out funds for the support of their widows and orphans. The number of parishes in Scotland are eight hundred and ninety, whereof thirty-one are collegiate churches, that is, where the cure is served by more than one minister.

The highest ecclesiastical authority in Scotland is the general assembly, which we may call the ecclesiastical parliament of Scotland. It consists of commissioners, some of which are laymen, under the title of ruling elders, from presbyteries, royal burghs, and universities. A presbytery, consisting of under twelve ministers, sends two ministers and one ruling elder: if it contains between twelve and eighteen ministers, it sends three, and one ruling elder: if it contains between eighteen and twenty-four ministers, it sends four ministers and two ruling elders: but if the presbytery has twenty-four ministers, it sends five ministers and two ruling elders. Every royal burgh sends one ruling elder, and Edinburgh two; whose election must be attested by the respective kirk-sessions of their own burghs. Every university sends one commissioner, usually a minister of their own body. The commissioners are chosen yearly, six weeks before the meeting of the assembly. The ruling elders are often of the first quality of the country.

The king presides by his commissioner (who is always a nobleman) in this assembly, which meets once a year: but he has no voice in their deliberations. The order of their proceedings is regular, though the number of members often create a confusion; which the moderator, who is chosen by them to be as it were speaker of the house, has not sufficient authority to prevent. Appeals are brought from all the other ecclesiastical courts in Scotland to the general assembly; and no appeal lies from its determinations in religious matters.

Provincial synods are next in authority to the general assembly. They are composed of a number of the adjacent presbyteries, over whom they have a power; and there are fifteen of them in Scotland; but their acts are reversible by the general assembly.

Subordinate to the synods, are presbyteries, sixty-nine of which are in Scotland, each consisting of a number of contiguous parishes. The ministers of these parishes, with one ruling elder, chosen half-yearly out of every kirk-session, compose a presbytery. These presbyteries meet in the head town of that division; but have no jurisdiction beyond their own bounds, though within these they have cognizance of all ecclesiastical causes and matters. A chief part of their business is the ordination of candidates for livings, in which they are regular and solemn. The patron of a living is bound to nominate

nate or prefent in fix months after a vacancy, otherwife the prefbytery fills the place *jure devoluto*; but that privilege does not hold in royal burghs.

A kirk-feffion is the loweft ecclefiaftical judicatory in Scotland, and its authority does not extend beyond its own parifh. The members confift of the minifter, elders, and deacons. The deacons are laymen, and act pretty much as church-wardens do in England, by having the fuperintendency of the poor, and taking care of other parochial affairs. The elder, or, as he is called, the ruling elder, is a place of great parochial truft, and he is generally a lay perfon of quality or intereft in the parifh. They are fuppofed to act in a kind of co-ordinancy with the minifter, and to be affifting to him in many of his clerical duties, particularly in catechifing, vifiting the fick, and at the communion-table.

The office of minifters, or preaching prefbyters, includes the offices of deacons and ruling-elders; they alone can preach, adminifter the facraments, catechife, pronounce church cenfures, ordain deacons and ruling elders, affift at the impofition of hands upon other minifters, and moderate or prefide in all ecclefiaftical judicatories.

It has already been obferved, that the eftablifhed religion in Scotland is prefbyterian: that it was formerly of a rigid nature, and partook of all the aufterities of Calvinifm, and intolerance of popery, by its perfecuting fpirit; but at prefent it is mild and gentle, and the moft rational Chriftian may accommodate himfelf to the doctrine and worfhip of the national church. It is to be wifhed, however, that this moderation was not too often interrupted by the fanaticifm not only of lay feceders, but of regular minifters. Thefe are induftrious to fix upon the abfurdities (and what church is without them) of former divines and vifionaries, and ecclefiaftical ordinances and difcipline, which were found to be incompatible with the nature of government. A vaft number of thefe feceding congregations are to be found in the Lowlands. They maintain their own preachers; though fcarcely any two congregations agree either in principle or practice with each other. We do not, however, find that they fly in the face of the civil power, or at leaft the inftances are rare and inconfiderable.

A different fet of diffenters in Scotland, confifts of the epifcopalians, a few quakers and papifts, and other fectaries, who are denominated from their preachers. Epifcopacy, from the time of the Reftoration in 1660, to that of the Revolution in 1688, was the eftablifhed church of Scotland; and would probably have continued fo, had not the bifhops, who were in
general

general very weak men, and creatures of the duke of York, afterwards James VII. and II. refused to recognize king William's title. The partizans of that unhappy prince retained the episcopal religion; and king William's government was so unpopular in Scotland, that in queen Anne's time, the episcopalians were more numerous in some parts than the presbyterians; and their meetings, which they held under the act of Toleration, as well attended. A Scotch episcopist thus becoming another name for a Jacobite, they received some checks after the rebellion in 1715; but they recovered themselves so well, that at the breaking out of the rebellion in 1745, they became again numerous; after which the government found means to invalidate the acts of their clerical order. Their meetings, however, still subsist, but thinly; and in a few years they will, probably, be reduced to nothing. In the mean while, the decline of the nonjurors is far from having suppressed episcopacy in Scotland: the English bishops supply them with clergy qualified according to law, whose chapels are chiefly filled by the English, and such Scotch hearers of that persuasion as have places under the government.

The defection of some great families from the cause of popery, and the extinction of others, have rendered its votaries very inconsiderable in Scotland. If any remain, they are confined to the northern parts, and the islands: but they appear to be as quiet and inoffensive as protestant subjects.

Scotland, during the time of episcopacy, contained two archbishoprics, St. Andrew's and Glasgow; and twelve bishoprics, which are, Edinburgh, Dunkeld, Aberdeen, Murray, Brichin, Dumblain, Ross, Caithness, Orkney, Galloway, Argyle, and the Isles.

LEARNING AND LEARNED MEN.] For this article we may refer to the literary history of Europe for these 1400 years past. The western parts and isles of Scotland produced St. Patric, the celebrated apostle of Ireland; and many others since, whose bare names would make a long article. The writings of Adamnanus, and other authors, who lived before, and at the time of the conquest of England, which are come to our hands, are specimens of their learning. Charles the Great, or Charlemagne, most unquestionably held a correspondence by letters with the kings of Scotland, with whom he formed a famous league; and employed Scotchmen in planning, settling, and ruling his favourite universities, and other seminaries of learning, in France, Italy, and Germany. It is an undoubted truth, though a seeming paradoxical fact, that Barbour, a Scotch poet, philosopher, and historian, though prior

in

in time to Chaucer, having flourished in the year 1368, wrote, according to the modern ideas, as pure English as that bard, and his versification is perhaps more harmonious. The destruction of the Scotch monuments of learning and antiquity, have rendered their early annals lame, and often fabulous; but the Latin stile of Buchanan's history is to this day the most classical of all modern productions. The letters of the Scotch kings to the neighbouring princes, are incomparably the finest compositions of the times in which they were written, and are free from the barbarisms of those sent them in answer. This is at least a manifest proof that classical learning was more cultivated at the court of Scotland, than at any other in Europe.

The discovery of the logarithms, a discovery, which in point both of ingenuity and utility, may vie with any that has been made in modern times, is the indisputable right of Napier of Merchiston. And since his time, the mathematical sciences have been cultivated in Scotland with amazing success. Keil, in his physico-mathematical works, to the clearness of his reasoning, has added the colours of a poet, which is the more remarkable, not only as the subject is little susceptible of ornament, but as he wrote in an ancient language. Of all writers on astronomy, Gregory is allowed to be one of the most perfect and elegant. Maclaurin, the companion and the friend of Sir Isaac Newton, was endowed with all that precision and force of mind, which rendered him peculiarly fitted for bringing down the ideas of that great man, to the level of ordinary apprehensions, and for diffusing that light thro' the world, which Newton had confined within the sphere of the learned. His Treatise on Fluxions is regarded by the best judges in Europe, as the clearest account of the most refined and subtile speculations on which the human mind ever exerted itself with success. While Maclaurin pursued this new career, a geometer no less famous, distinguished himself in the sure, but almost deserted tract of antiquity. This was the late Dr. Simpson, so well known over Europe, for his illustration of the ancient geometry. His Elements of Euclid, and above all, his Conic Sections, are sufficient of themselves to establish the literary reputation of his native country.

This, however, does not rest on the character of a few mathematicians and astronomers. The fine arts have been called sisters to denote their affinity. There is the same connection between the sciences, particularly those which depend on observation. Mathematicks, and physicks, properly so called, were in Scotland accompanied by the other branches of study to which they are allied. In medicine particularly, the names of Pitcairn, Arbuthnot, Monro, Smellie and White, hold a distinguished place.

Nor have the Scots been unsuccessful in cultivating the Belles Lettres. Foreigners, who inhabit warmer climates, and conceive the northern nations incapable of tenderness and feeling, are astonished at the poetic genius, and delicate sensibility of Thomson.

But of all literary pursuits, that of rendering mankind more virtuous and happy, which is the proper object of what is called morals, ought to be regarded with peculiar honour and respect. The philosophy of Dr. Hutcheson, not to mention other works more subtile and elegant, but less convincing and less instructive, deserves to be read by all who would know their duty, or who would wish to practise it. Next to the Essay on the Human Understanding, it is perhaps the best dissection of the human mind, that hath appeared in modern times; and it is likewise the most useful supplement to that essay.

It would be endless to mention all the individuals, who have distinguished themselves in the various branches of literature; particularly as those who are alive (some of them in high esteem for historical composition) dispute the merit with the dead, and cover their country with laurels, which neither envy can blast, nor time can destroy.

Universities.] The universities of Scotland are four, viz. Those of St. Andrews, Aberdeen, Edinburgh, and Glasgow.

Cities, towns, and other edifices public and private.] Edinburgh, the capital of Scotland, naturally takes the lead in this division, which the bounds of our work oblige us to contract. This castle, before the use of artillery, was deemed to be impregnable by force. It was probably built by the Saxon king Edwin, whose territories reached to the Firth of Forth, and who gave his name to Edinburgh, as it certainly did not fall into the hands of the Scots till the reign of Indulphus, who lived in the year 953. The town was built for the benefit of protection from the castle, and a more inconvenient situation for a capital can scarcely be conceived; the high-street, which is on the ridge of a hill, lying east and west; and the lanes running down its sides, north and south. In former times the town was surrounded by water, excepting towards the east; so that when the French landed in Scotland, during the regency of Mary of Guise, they gave it the name of Lislebourg. This situation suggested

the

the idea of building very lofty houses divided into stories, each of which contains a suite of rooms, generally large and commodious for the use of a family; so that the high street of Edinburgh, which is chiefly of hewn stone, broad and well paved, makes a most august appearance, especially as it rises a full mile in a direct line, and gradual ascent from the palace of Holyrood-house on the east, and is terminated on the west by the rude majesty of its castle, built upon a lofty rock, inaccessible on all sides, except where it joins to the city. The castle not only overlooks the city, its environs, gardens, the new town, and a fine rich neighbouring country, but commands a most extensive prospect of the river Forth, the shipping, the opposite coast of Fife, and even some hills, at the distance of 40 or 50 miles, which border upon the Highlands. This crouded population, however, was so shockingly inconvenient, that the English, who seldom went farther into the country, returned with the deepest impressions of Scotch nastiness, which became proverbial. The castle has some good apartments, a tolerable train of artillery, and has not only a large magazine of arms and ammunition, but contains the regalia, which were deposited here under the most solemn legal instruments of their never being removed from thence. All that is known at present of those regalia, is contained in the instrument which was taken at the time of their being deposited, where they are fully described.

Facing the castle, as I have already observed, at a mile's distance, stands the abbey, or rather palace, of Holyroodhouse. The inner quadrangular of this palace, was begun by James V. and finished by Charles I. is of magnificent modern architecture, built according to the plan, and under the direction of Sir William Bruce, a Scotch gentleman of family, and undoubtedly one of the greatest architects of that age. Round the quadrangle runs an arcade, adorned with pilasters; and the inside contains magnificent apartments for the duke of Hamilton, who is hereditary keeper of the palace, and other noblemen. Its long gallery contains figures, some of which are from portraits, but all of them painted by modern hands, of the kings of Scotland down to the time of the Revolution. James VII. when duke of York, intended to have made great improvements about this palace; for at present nothing can be more uncomfortable than its situation, at the bottom of bleak unimproved craggs and mountains, with scarce a single tree in its neighbourhood. The chapel belonging to the palace, as it stood when repaired and ornamented by that prince, is thought to have been a most elegant piece of Gothic architecture.

architecture. It had a very lofty roof, and two rooms of stone galleries supported by curious pillars. It was the conventual church of the old abbey. Its inside was demolished and rifled of all its rich ornaments, by the fury of the mob at the Revolution, which even broke into the repositories of the dead, and discovered a vault, till that time unknown, which contained the bodies of James V. his first queen, and Henry Darnley. The walls and roof of this antient chapel gave way and fell down on the 2d and 3d of December, 1768, occasioned by the enormous weight of a new stone roof, laid over it some years ago, which the walls were unable to support.

The hospital, founded by George Herriot, goldsmith to James VI. commonly called Herriot's work, stands to the south-west of the castle, in a noble situation. It is the finest and most regular specimen which Inigo Jones, whom James VI. of Scotland brought over from Denmark, has left us of his Gothic manner, and far exceeding any thing of that kind to be seen in England. One Balquhanan, a divine, whom Herriot left his executor, is said to have prevailed upon Jones to admit some barbarous devices into the building, particularly the windows, and to have insisted that the ornaments of each should be somewhat different from those of the others. It is, notwithstanding, upon the whole, a delightful fabric, and adorned with gardens, not inelegantly laid out. It was built for the maintenance and education of poor children belonging to the citizens and tradesmen of Edinburgh, and is under the direction of the city magistrates.

Among the other public edifices of Edinburgh before the Revolution, was the college, which claims the privileges of an university, founded by king James VI. and by him put under the direction of the magistrates; who have the power of chancellor and vice-chancellor. Little can be said of its buildings, which were calculated for the sober literary manners of those days; they are, however, improveable, and may be rendered elegant. What is of far more importance, it is supplied with excellent professors in the several branches of learning; and its schools for every part of the medical art are reckoned equal to any in Europe. This college is provided with a library, founded by one Clement Little, which is said to have been of late greatly augmented; and a museum belonging to it was given by Sir Andrew Balfour, a physician. It contains several natural, and some literary curiosities, which one would little expect to find at Edinburgh.

The Parliament-Square, or, as it is there called, Close, was formerly the most ornamental part of this city; it is formed
into

into a very noble quadrangle, part of which confists of lofty buildings; and in the middle is a very fine equeftrian ftatue of Charles II. The room built by Charles I. for the parliament-houfe, though not fo large, is better proportioned than Weft-minfter-hall; and its roof, though executed in the fame manner, is by many great judges held to be fuperior. It is now converted into a court of law, where a fingle judge, called the lord ordinary, prefides by rotation; in a room near it, fit the other judges; and adjoining are the public offices of the law, exchequer, chancery, fherivalty, and magiftracy of Edinburgh; and the lawyers valuable library. This equals any thing of the like kind to be found in England, or perhaps in any part of Europe, being at firft entirely founded and furnifhed by lawyers. The number of printed books it contains is amazing; and the collection has been made with exquifite tafte and judgment. It contains likewife the moft valuable manufcript remains of the Scotch hiftory, chartularies, and other papers of antiquity, with a feries of medals. Adjoining to the library, is the room where the public records are kept; but both it, and that which contains the library, though lofty in the roof, are miferably dark and difmal. It is faid that preparations are now carrying on, for lodging both the books and the papers in rooms far better fuited to their importance and value.

The High Church of Edinburgh, called that of St. Giles, is now divided into two or three churches, and a room where the general affembly fits. It is a large Gothic building, and its fteeple is furmounted by arches formed into an imperial crown, which has a good effect to the eye. The churches, and other edifices of the city, erected before the Union, contain little but what is common to fuch buildings; but the excellent pavement of the city, which was begun two centuries ago by one Merlin, a Frenchman, deferves particular attention.

The modern edifices in and near Edinburgh, fuch as the Exchange, its hofpitals, bridges, and the like, demonftrate the vaft improvement of the tafte of the Scots in their public works. On the north fide of the city, upon a rifing ground, the nobility, gentry, and principal citizens, have begun to build what is to be called the New Town, upon a plan which does honour to the prefent age. The ftreets and fquares are laid out with the utmoft regularity, and the houfes to be built of ftone, of an equal height, in the moft elegant tafte, with all the conveniences that render thofe of England fo delightful and commodious. The fronts of many already finifhed, are of afhler work, but fuch is the avarice of fome individuals, that here and there this beautiful place is already difgraced with
buildings,

buildings, raised up of rough unfinished stone, though the difference of expence in that country is very inconsiderable.

Edinburgh may be considered, notwithstanding its castle, and an open wall which encloses it on the south side, of a very modern fabric but in the Roman manner, as an open town; so that in fact, it would have been impracticable for its inhabitants to have defended it against the rebels, who took possession of it in 1745. A certain class of readers would perhaps think it unpardonable, should I omit mentioning that Edinburgh contains a playhouse, which has now the sanction of an act of parliament; and that concerts, assemblies, balls, music-meetings, and other polite amusements, are as frequent and brilliant here, as in any part of his majesty's dominions, London and Bath excepted.

Edinburgh is governed by a lord provost, four bailiffs, a dean of guild, and a treasurer, annually chosen from the common council. Every company, or incorporated trade, chooses its own deacon; and here are 14; namely, surgeons, goldsmiths, skinners, furriers, hammer-men, wrights or carpenters, masons, taylors, bakers, butchers, cordwainers, weavers, fullers, and bonnet-makers. The lord provost is colonel of the town-guard, a military institution to be found in no part of his majesty's dominions, but at Edinburgh: they serve for the city watch, and patrole the streets, are useful in suppressing small commotions, and attend the execution of sentences upon delinquents: they are divided into three companies, and wear an uniform; they are immediately commanded by three officers, under the name of captains. Besides this guard, Edinburgh raises 16 companies of trained bands, which serve as militia. The revenues of the city consist chiefly of that tax which is now common in most of the bodies corporate of Scotland, of two Scotch pennies, amounting in the whole to two thirds of a farthing, laid upon every Scotch pint of ale (containing two English quarts) consumed within the precincts of the city. This is a most judicious impost, as it renders the poorest people insensible of the burden. Its product, however, has been sufficient to defray the expence of supplying the city with excellent water, brought in leaden pipes at the distance of four miles; of erecting reservoirs, enlarging the harbour of Leith, and compleating other public works of great expence and utility.

Leith, though near two miles distant, may be properly called the harbour of Edinburgh, being under the same jurisdiction. It contains nothing remarkable, but the remains of two citadels (if they are not the same) fortified, and bravely defended by the French against the English, under Mary of Guise, and afterwards

afterwards repaired by Cromwell. The neighbourhood of Edinburgh is adorned with noble feats, which are daily encreafing; fome of them yield to few in England; but they are too numerous to be particularized here. I cannot however avoid mentioning the earl of Abercorn's, a fhort way from the city, the duke of Buccleugh's houfe at Dalkeith, that of the marquis of Lothian at Newbottle, and Hopton-houfe, fo called from the earl its owner. About four miles from Edinburgh is Roflin, noted for a ftately Gothic chapel, counted one of the moft curious pieces of workmanfhip in Europe; founded in the year 1440, by William St. Clair, prince of Orkney and duke of Oldenburgh.

Glafgow, in the fhire of Lanerk, fituated on a gentle declivity floping towards the river Clyde, 44 miles weft of Edinburgh, is for population, commerce, and riches, the fecond city of Scotland, and, confidering its fize, the firft in Great-Britain, and perhaps in Europe, as to elegance, regularity, and the beautiful materials of its buildings. The ftreets crofs each other at right angles, and are broad, ftrait, well paved, and confequently clean. Their houfes make a grand appearance, and are in general four or five ftories high, and many of them towards the center of the city are fupported by arcades, which form piazzas, and give the whole an air of magnificence. Some of the modern built churches are in the fineft ftile of architecture, and the cathedral is a ftupendous Gothic building, hardly to be parallelled in that kind of architecture. It contains three churches, one of which ftands above another, and is furnifhed with a very fine fpire fpringing from a tower; the whole being reckoned a mafterly and a matchlefs fabric. It was dedicated to St. Mungo or Kentigern, who was bifhop of Glafgow, in the 6th century. The cathedral is upwards of 600 years old, and was preferved from the fury of the Reformers by the refolution of the citizens. The town-houfe is a lofty building, and has very noble apartments for the magiftrates. The univerfity is efteemed the moft fpacious and beft built of any in Scotland, and is at prefent in a thriving ftate. In this city are feveral well endowed hofpitals; and it is particularly well fupplied with large and convenient inns, proper for the accommodation of the moft illuftrious ftranger. They are now building a handfome bridge acrofs the river Clyde, and a large piece of ground is purchafed near the crofs, where they intend to erect a magnificent Exchange; but our bounds do not allow us to particularize that, and the other public-fpirited undertakings of this city carrying on by the inhabitants, who do honour to the benefits arifing from their vaft commerce, both foreign and internal; which they carry on with amazing success. In Glasgow are seven churches, and eight or ten meeting-houses for sectaries of various denominations. The number of its inhabitants have been estimated at 50,000.

Aberdeen bids fair to be the third town in Scotland for improvement and population. It is the capital of a shire, to which it gives its name, and contains two towns, New and Old Aberdeen. The former is the shire town, and evidently built for the purpose of commerce. It is a large well built city, and has a good quay or tide-harbour: in it are three churches and several episcopal meeting-houses, a considerable degree of foreign commerce and much shipping, a well frequented university, and above 12,000 inhabitants. Old Aberdeen, near a mile distant, though almost joined to the new by means of a long village, has no dependance on the other; it is a moderately large market-town, but has no haven. In each of these two places there is a well endowed college, both together being termed the university of Aberdeen, although quite independent of each other. Perth, the capital town of Perthshire, lying on the river Tay, trades to Norway and the Baltic: it is finely situated, has an improving linen manufactory, and lies in the neighbourhood of one of the most fertile spots in Great-Britain, called the càrse of Gowry. Dundee, by the general computation, contains about 10,000 inhabitants: it lies near the mouth of the river Tay: it is a town of considerable trade, exporting much linen, grain, herrings and peltry, to sundry foreign parts: it has three churches. Montrose, Aberbrethick, and Brechin, lie in the same county of Angus: the first has a great and flourishing foreign trade, and the manufactures of the other two are upon the thriving hand.

It may be necessary again to put the reader in mind, that I write with great uncertainty with regard to Scotland, on account of its improving state. I have rather under than over-rated the number of inhabitants in the towns I have mentioned. Edinburgh certainly contains more than 60,000 souls, which is the common computation, to which I all along conform myself; but the influx of people, and the increase of matrimony in proportion to that of property, must create great alterations for the better, and few for the worse, because the inhabitants who are disposed to industry may always find employment. This uncertainty is the reason why I omit a particular description of Dumfries, Air, Greenock, Paisley, Sterling, and about 50 other burghs and towns of very considerable trade in Scotland.

The antient Scots valued themselves upon their trusting to their own valour, and not to fortifications, for the defence of their country: this was a maxim more heroical perhaps than prudent, as they have often experienced; and indeed to this day their forts would make but a sorry figure, if regularly attacked. The castles of Edinburgh, Sterling, and Dumbarton, formerly thought places of great strength, could not hold out 48 hours, if besieged by 6000 regular troops, with proper artillery. Fort William, which lies in the west Highlands, is sufficient to bridle the inhabitants of the neighbourhood, as are Fort George and Fort Augustus, in the north and northwest; but none of them can be considered as defences against a foreign enemy.

I shall not pretend to enter upon a description of the noble edifices that have, within the course of this and the last century, been erected by private persons in Scotland, because they are so numerous, that to particularize them exceeds the bounds of my plan. It is sufficient to say, that many of them are equal to the most superb buildings in England and foreign countries: and the reader's surprize at this will cease, when he is informed that the genius of no people in the world is more devoted to architecture than that of the nobility and gentry of Scotland; and that there is no country in Europe, on account of the cheapness of materials, where it can be gratified at so moderate an expence. This may likewise account for the stupendous Gothic cathedrals, and other religious edifices which antiently abounded in Scotland; but at the time of the Reformation were mostly demolished to the ground, by a furious and tumultuous mob, who, in these practices, received too much countenance from the reforming clergy.

ANTIQUITIES AND CURIOSITIES, NATURAL AND ARTIFICIAL. } The Roman, and other antiquities found in Scotland, have of themselves furnished matter for large volumes. The stations of the Roman legions, their castellas, their pretentures or walls, reaching across the island, have been traced with great precision by antiquaries and historians; so that, without some fresh discoveries, an account of them could afford no instruction to the learned, and but little amusement to the ignorant; because at present they can be discovered only by critical eyes. Some mention of the chief may, however, be proper. The course of the Roman wall, (or, as it is called by the country people, Graham's Dyke, from a tradition that a Scottish warrior of that name first broke over it) between the Clyde and Forth, which was first marked out by Agricola, and compleated by Antoninus Pius, is still discernible, as are several Roman camps in the neighbourhood. Agricola's camp, at the bottom of the Grampian hills, is a striking remain of Roman antiquity. It is situated at Ardoch, in Perthshire, and is generally thought to have been the camp occupied by Agricola before he fought the bloody battle, so well recorded by Tacitus, with the Caledonian king Galgacus, who was defeated. Some writers think, that this remain of antiquity at Ardoch was, on account of the numerous Roman coins and inscriptions found near it, a Roman castellum or fort. Be that as it will, it certainly is the most entire and best preserved of any Roman antiquity of that kind in Britain, having no less than five rows of ditches and six ramparts on the south side; and of the four gates which lead into the area, three of them are very distinct and plain, viz. the prætoria, decumana, and dextra: the prætorium is the place where the general's tent stood.

The Roman temple, or building in the form of the Pantheon at Rome, or the dome of St. Paul's at London, stood upon the banks of the river Carron, in Sterlingshire, but has been lately barbarously demolished, by a neighbouring Goth, for the purpose of mending a mill-pond. Its height was twenty-two feet, and its external circumference at the base was eighty-eight feet; so that upon the whole, it was one of the most compleat Roman antiquities in the world. It is thought to have been built by Agricola, or some of his successors, as a temple to the god Terminus, as it stood near the pretenture which bounded the Roman empire in Britain to the north. Near it are some artificial conical mounts of earth, which still retain the name of Duni-pace, or Duni-pacis; which serve to evidence, that there was a kind of solemn compromise between the Romans and Caledonians, that the former should not extend their empire farther to the northwards.

Innumerable are the coins, urns, utensils, inscriptions, and other remains of the Romans, that have been found in different parts of Scotland; some of them to the north of the wall, where, however, it does not appear that they made any establishment. By the inscriptions found near the wall, the names of the legions that built it, and how far they carried it on, may be learned. The remains of Roman highways are frequent in the southern parts.

Danish camps and fortifications are easily discernible in several northern counties, and are known by their square figures and difficult situations. Some houses of stupendous fabrics remain in Rofs-shire, but whether they are Danish, Pictish, or Scotish, does not appear. The elevations of two of them are to be seen in Gordon's Itinerarium Septentrionale. I am of opinion that they are Norwegian or Scandinavian structures, and built about the fifth century, to favour the descents of that people upon those coasts.

Two Pictish monuments, as they are thought to be, of a very extraordinary construction, were lately standing in Scotland, one of them at Abernethy in Perthshire, the other at Brechin in Angus: both of them are columns, hollow in the inside, and without a stair-case; that of Brechin is the most entire, being covered at the top with a spiral roof of stone, with three or four windows above the cornice: it consists of sixty regular courses of hewn free stone, laid circularly and regularly, and tapering towards the top. If those columns are really Pictish, that people must have had among them architects that far exceeded those of any coeval monuments to be found in Europe, as they have all the appearance of an order; and the building is neat, and in the Roman taste of architecture. It is, however, difficult to assign them to any but the Picts, as they stand in their dominions; and some sculptures upon that at Brechin, denote it to be of Christian original. It is not indeed impossible that those sculptures are of a later date. Besides those two pillars, many other Pictish buildings are found in Scotland, but not in the same taste.

The vestiges of erections by the antient Scots themselves, are not only curious but instructive, as they regard many important events of their history. That people had amongst them a rude notion of sculpture, in which they transmitted the actions of their kings and heroes. At a place called Aberlemno, near Brechin, four or five antient obelisks are still to be seen, called the Danish stones of Aberlemno. They were erected as commemorations of the Scotch victories over that people; and are adorned with bass-reliefs of men on horseback, and many emblematical figures and hieroglyphics, not intelligible at this day, but minutely described by Mr. Gordon. Many other historical monuments of the Scots may be discovered on the like occasions; but it must be acknowledged, that the obscurity of their sculptures have encouraged a field of boundless and frivolous conjectures, so that the interpretations of many of them are often fanciful. It would, however, be unpardonable if I should neglect to mention the stone near the town of Forres or Fortrose, in Murray, which far surpasses all the others in magnificence and grandeur, " and is (says Mr. Gordon) perhaps, one of the most stately monuments of that kind in Europe. It rises about 23 feet in height, above ground, and is, as I am credibly informed, no less than 12 or 15 feet below; so that the whole height is at least 35 feet, and its breadth near five. It is all one single and entire stone; great variety of figures in relievo are carved thereon, some of them still distinct and visible; but the injury of the weather has obscured those towards the upper part."

Though this monument has been generally looked upon as Danish, yet I have little doubt of its being Scotch, and that it was erected in commemoration of the final expulsion of the Danes out of Murray, where they held their last settlement in Scotland, after the defeat they received from Malcolm a few years before the conquest of England by the Normans.

Besides these remains of Roman, Pictish, Danish, and Scotch antiquities, many druidical monuments and temples are discernible in the northern parts of Scotland, as well as in the isles, where we may suppose that paganism took its last refuge. They are easily perceived by their circular forms; but though they are equally regular, yet none of them are so stupendous as the druidical erections in South-Britain. There is in Perthshire a barrow which seems to be a British erection, and the most beautiful of the kind perhaps in the world; it exactly resembles the figure of a ship with the keel uppermost. The common people call it Ternay, which some interpret to be *terræ navis*, the ship of earth. It seems to be of the most remote antiquity, and perhaps was erected to the memory of some British prince, who acted as auxiliary to the Romans; for it lies near Auchterarder, not many miles distant from the great scene of Agricola's operations.

Scotland affords few natural curiosities but those we have already mentioned in describing the lakes, rivers, and mountains. Mention is made of a heap of white stones, most of them clear like chrystal, together with great plenty of oyster and other sea-shells, that are found on the top of a mountain called Skorna Lappich, in Rossshire, twenty miles distant from the sea. Slains, in Aberdeenshire, is said to be remarkable for a petrifying cave, called the Dropping-cave, where water oozing through a spungy porous rock on the top, doth quickly consolidate after it drops to the bottom. Other natural curiosities belonging to Scotland have taken possession of its descriptions and histories, but they generally owe their extraordinary qualities to the credulity of the vulgar, and vanish when they are skilfully examined. Some caverns that are to be found in Fifeshire, and are probably natural, are of extraordinary dimensions, and have been the scenes of inhuman cruelties.

COMMERCE AND MANUFACTURES.] Scotland may hitherto be justly looked upon as a non-described country. All the writers, till within these few years, who have treated of that nation, represent it as being in the very same state as a century ago. In this they are not to blame, because the alteration which the people and country have undergone, has been inconceivably sudden. Without entering into the disputed point,
how

how far Scotland was benefited by its union with England, it is certain that the expedition of the Scots to take possession of Darien, and to carry on an East and West-India trade, was founded upon true principles of commerce, and (so far as it went) executed with a noble spirit of enterprize. The miscarriage of that scheme, after receiving the highest and most solemn sanctions, is a disgrace to the annals of that reign in which it happened; as the Scots had then a free, independent, and unconnected parliament. We are to account for the long languor of the Scottish commerce, and many other misfortunes which that country sustained, to the disgust the inhabitants conceived on that account, and some invasions of their rights, which they thought inconsistent with the articles of union. The intails and narrow settlements of family estates, and some remains of the feudal institutions, might contribute to the same cause.

Mr. Pelham, when at the head of the administration in England, after the extinction of the rebellion in 1745, was the first minister who discovered the true value of Scotland, which then became a more considerable object of governmental enquiry than ever. All the benefits received by that country, for the relief of the people from their feudal tyranny, were effected by that great man. The bounties and encouragements granted to the Scots, for the benefit of trade and manufactures, during his administration, made them sensible of their own importance; and had he been a Scotchman, must have ruined his ministry. Mr. Pitt, a succeeding minister, pursued Mr. Pelham's wise plan: and justly boasted in parliament, that he availed himself of the courage, good sense, and spirit of the Scots, in carrying on the most extensive war that Great Britain ever was engaged in. Let me add, to the honour of the British government, that whatever indecent and mean resentments have been expressed by the refuse of the English nation against the Scots, the latter have been suffered to avail themselves of all the benefits of commerce and manufactures they can claim, either in right of their former independency, the treaty of union, or posterior acts of parliament.

This is manifest in the extensive trade they carry on with the British settlements in America and the West-Indies, and with all the nations to which the English themselves trade; so that the increase of their shipping within these 25 years past, has been very considerable. The exports of those ships are composed chiefly of Scotch manufactures, fabricated from the produce of the soil, and the industry of its inhabitants. In exchange for those, they import tobacco, rice, cotton, sugar, and

and rum, from the British plantations; and from other countries. their products, to the immense saving of their nation.

The fisheries of Scotland are not confined to their own coasts, for they have a vast concern in the whale fishery carried on upon the coast of Spitsbergen; and their returns are valuable, as the government allows them a bounty of 40 s. for every ton of shipping employed in that article. The late improvement of their fisheries, which I have already mentioned, and which are daily encreasing, open inexhaustible funds of wealth; their cured fish being by foreigners, and the English planters in America, preferred to those of Newfoundland. The benefits of those fisheries are perhaps equalled by other manufactures carrying on at land, particularly that of iron at Carron, in Sterlingshire. Their linen manufactory, notwithstanding a strong rivalship from Ireland, supported underhand by some English, is in a flourishing state. The thread manufacture of Scotland is equal, if not superior, to any in the world; and the lace fabricated from it, has been deemed worthy of royal wear and approbation. It has been said some years ago, that the exports from Scotland to England, and the British plantations, in linen, cambrics, checks, Osnaburgs, inkle, and the like commodities, amounted annually to 400,000 l. exclusive of their home consumption; and there is reason to believe that the sum is considerably larger at present. The Scots are likewise making very promising efforts for establishing woollen manufactures; and their exports of caps, stockings, mittens, and other articles of their own wool, begin to be very considerable. The Scots, it is true, cannot pretend to rival the English in their finer cloths; but they make at present some broad cloth proper for the wear of people of fashion in an undress, and in quality and fineness equal to what is commonly called Yorkshire cloth. Among the other late improvements of the Scots, we are not to forget the vast progress they have made in working the mines, and smelting the ores of their country. Their coal trade to England is well known; and of late they have turned even their stones to account, by their contracts for paving the streets of London. If the great trade in cattle, which the Scots carried on of late with the English, is now diminished, it is owing to the best of national causes, that of an encrease of home consumption.

The trade carried on by the Scots with England, is chiefly from Leith, and the eastern ports of the nation; but Glasgow is the great emporium for the American commerce. I have already mentioned the great project now executing for joining the Forth to the Clyde, which will render the benefits of trade of mutual advantage to both parts of Scotland. In short,

short, the more that the seas, the situation, the soil, harbours, and rivers of this country are known, the better adapted it appears for all the purposes of commerce, both foreign and domestic.

With regard to other manufactures, not mentioned, some of them are yet in their infancy. The town of Paisley itself employs an incredible number of hands, in fabricating a particular kind of flowered and striped lawns, which are a reasonable and elegant wear. Sugar-houses, glass works of every kind, delf houses, and paper-mills are erected every where. The Scotch carpeting make neat and lasting furniture; and some essays have been lately made, with no inconsiderable degree of success, to carry that branch of manufacture to as great perfection as is found in any part of Europe. Even the fine arts begin to make some progress. An academy of painting, engraving, and statuary, is established at Glasgow, under the patronage of several noblemen, gentlemen, and principal merchants. After all that has been said, many years will be required before the trade and improvements of Scotland can be brought to maturity. In any event, they never can give umbrage to the English, as the interests of the two people are, or ought to be the same.

Having said thus much, I cannot avoid observing the prodigious disadvantages under which both the commercial and landed interest of Scotland lies, from her nobility and great landholders having too fond an attachment for England, and foreign countries, where they spend their ready money. This is one of the evils arising to Scotland from the union, which removed the seat of her legislature to London; but it is greatly augmented by the resort of volunteer absentees to that capital. While this partiality subsists, the Scots must always be distrest for a currency of specie. How far paper can supply that defect, depends upon an attention to the balance of trade; and the evil may, perhaps, be somewhat prevented, by money remitted from England for carrying on the vast manufactures and works now set on foot in Scotland. The gentlemen who reside in Scotland, have wisely abandoned French claret, (tho' too much of it is still made use of in the country) and brandy, for rum, and the liquors produced in the British plantations; and their own malt liquors are now come to as great perfection as those of England; and it has been said, that of late they export large quantities of their ale to London, Dublin, and the plantations.

REVENUES.] See England.

COINS.] In the reign of Edward II. of England, the value and denominations of coins were the same in Scotland

as

as in England. Towards the reign of James II. a Scotch shilling answered to about an English sixpence; and about the reign of queen Mary of Scotland, it was not more than an English groat. It continued diminishing in this manner till after the Union of the two crowns, under her son James VI. when the vast resort of the Scotch nobility and gentry to the English court, occasioned such a drain of specie from Scotland, that by degrees a Scotch shilling fell to the value of one twelfth of an English shilling, and their pennies in proportion. A Scotch penny is now very rarely to be found; and they were succeeded by bodles, which was double the value of a Scotch penny, and are still current, but are daily wearing out. A Scotch halfpenny was called a babie; some say, because it was first stamped with the head of James III. when he was a babe or baby; but perhaps it is only the corruption of two French words, *bas piece*, signifying a low piece of money. The same observation we have made of the Scotch shilling, holds of their pounds and marks; which are not coins, but denomination of sums. In all other respects, the currency of money in Scotland and England is the same; as very few people now reckon by the Scotch computation.

ORDER OF THE THISTLE.] This is a military order, instituted, as the Scotch writers assert, by their king Achaius, in the ninth century, upon his making an offensive and defensive league with Charlemagne, king of France. It has been frequently neglected and as often resumed. It consists of the sovereign, and 12 companions, who are called Knights of the Thistle, and have on their ensign this significant motto, *Nemo me impune lacessit*. None shall safely provoke me.

LAWS AND CONSTITUTION.] No government in Europe was better fitted for the enjoyment of liberty, than that of Scotland was by its original constitution; and if it was reprehensible in any respect, it was that it left more freedom to the subject than is consistent with civil subordination.

The ancient kings of Scotland, at their coronation, took the following oath, containing three promises, viz.

"In the name of Christ, I promise these three things to the Christian people my subjects: First, that I shall give order, and employ my force and assistance, that the church of God, and the Christian people, may enjoy true peace during our time, under our government. Secondly, I shall prohibit and hinder all persons, of whatever degree, from violence and injustice. Thirdly, in all judgments I shall follow the prescriptions of justice and mercy, to the end that our clement and merciful God, may shew mercy to me, and to you."

The parliament of Scotland antiently confisted of all who held any portion of land, however small, of the crown, by military service. This parliament appointed the times of its own meeting and adjournment, and committees to superintend the administration during the intervals of parliament; it had a commanding power in all matters of government; it appropriated the public money, ordered the keeping of it, and called for the accounts; it armed the people, and appointed commanders; it named and commissioned ambassadors, it granted and limited pardons; it appointed judges and courts of judicature; it named officers of state and privy-counsellors; it annexed and alienated the revenues of the crown, and restrained grants by the king. The king of Scotland had no negative voice in parliament; nor could he declare war, make peace, or conclude any other public business of importance, without the advice and approbation of parliament. The prerogative of the king was so bounded, that he was not even entrusted with the executive part of the government. And so late as the minority of James IV. who was cotemporary with and son-in-law to Henry VII. of England, the parliament pointed out to him his duty, as the first servant of his people; as appears by the acts still extant. In short, the constitution was rather aristocratical than monarchical. The abuse of these aristocratical powers, by the chieftains and great landholders, gave the king, however, a very considerable interest among the lower ranks; and a prince who had sense and address to retain the affections of his people, was generally able to humble the most overgrown of his subjects: when, on the other hand, a king of Scotland, like James III. shewed a disrespect to his parliament, the event was commonly fatal to the crown. The kings of Scotland, notwithstanding this paramount power in the parliament, found means to weaken and elude its force; and in this they were assisted by their clergy, whose revenues were immense, and who had very little dependence upon the pope, and were always jealous of the powerful nobility. This was done by establishing a select body of members, who were called *the lords of the articles*. These were chosen out of the clergy, nobility, knights, and burgesses. The bishops, for instance, chose eight peers, and the peers eight bishops; and those sixteen jointly chose eight barons; (or knights of the shire) and eight commissioners for burghs; and to all those were added eight great officers of state, the chancellor being president of the whole.

Their business was to prepare all questions and bills, and other matters brought into parliament; so that in fact, though the king could give no negative, yet being by his clergy, and the

the places he had to bestow, always sure of the lords of articles, nothing could come into parliament that could call for his negative. It must be acknowledged, that this institution seems to have prevailed by stealth; nor was it ever brought into any regular system: even its modes varied; and the greatest lawyers are ignorant when it took place. The Scots, however, never lost sight of their original principles: and tho' Charles I. wanted to form these lords of the articles into regular machines for his own despotic purposes, he found it impracticable; and the melancholy consequences are well known. At the Revolution, the Scots gave a fresh instance how much better they understood the principles of liberty than the English did, by omitting all pedantic debates about *abdication*, and the like terms, and voting king James at once to have forfeited his crown; which they gave to the prince and princess of Orange.

This spirit of resistance was the more remarkable, as the people had groaned under the most insupportable ministerial tyranny ever since the Restoration. It is asked, Why did they submit to that tyranny? The answer is, In order to preserve that independency upon England, which Cromwell and his parliament endeavoured to destroy, by uniting them with England: they therefore chose to submit to a temporal evil; but they took the first opportunity to get rid of their oppressors.

Scotland, when it was a separate kingdom, cannot be said to have had any peers, in the English sense of the word. The nobility, who were dukes, marquisses, earls, and lords, were by the king made hereditary barons of parliament; but they formed no distinct house, for they sat in the same room with the commons, who had the same deliberative and decisive vote with them in all public matters. A baron, though not a baron of parliament, might sit upon a lord's assize in matters of life and death; nor was it necessary for the assizers, or jury, to be unanimous in their verdict. The feudal customs, even at the time of the Restoration, were so prevalent, the rescue of a great criminal was commonly so much apprehended, that seldom above two days passed between the sentence and the execution.

Great uncertainty occurs in the Scotch history, by confounding parliaments with conventions; the difference was, that a parliament could enact laws as well as lay on taxes: a convention, or meeting of the states, only met for the purposes of taxation. Before the Union, the kings of Scotland had four great and four lesser officers of state; the great, were the lord high chancellor, high treasurer, privy-seal, and secretary:

tary: the four lesser were, the lords register, advocate, treasurer-depute, and justice-clerk. Since the Union none of these continue, excepting the lords privy-seal, register, advocate, and justice-clerk; a third secretary of state has occasionally been nominated by the king for Scottish affairs, but under the same denomination as the other two secretaries. The above officers of state sat in the Scotch parliament by virtue of their offices.

The officers of the crown were, the high-chamberlain, constable, admiral, and marshal. The officers of constable and marshal were hereditary. A nobleman has still a pension as admiral; and the office of marshal is exercised by a knight marshal.

The office of chancellor of Scotland differed little from the same in England. The same may be said of the lords treasurer, privy-seal, and secretary. The lord-register was head clerk to the parliament, convention, treasury, exchequer, and session, and keeper of all public records. Though his office was only during the king's pleasure, yet it was very lucrative, by disposing of his deputation, which lasted during life. He acted as teller to the parliament; and it was dangerous for any member to dispute his report of the numbers upon a division. The lord-advocate's office resembles that of the attorney-general in England, only his powers are far more extensive; because, by the Scotch laws, he is the prosecutor of all capital crimes before the justiciary, and likewise concurs in all pursuits before sovereign courts for breaches of the peace; and also in all matters civil, wherein the king, or his donator, has interest. Two sollicitors are named by his majesty, by way of assistants to the lord-advocate. The office of justice-clerk, entitles the possessor to preside in the criminal court of justice, while the justice-general, an office I shall describe hereafter, is absent.

The ancient constitution of Scotland admitted of many other offices both of the crown and state; but they are either now extinct or too inconsiderable to be described here. That of Lyon king at arms, or the rex fæcialium, or grand herald of Scotland, is still in being, and it was formerly an office of great splendour and importance, insomuch that the science of heraldry was preserved there in greater purity than in any other country in Europe. He was even crowned solemnly in parliament with a golden circle; and his authority, which is not the case in England, in all armorial affairs might be carried into execution by the civil law.

The privy-council of Scotland before the revolution, had, or assumed inquisitorial powers, even that of torture; but it is
now

now sunk in the parliament and privy-council of Great-Britain, and the civil and criminal causes there are chiefly cognizable by two courts of judicature.

The first is that of the college of justice, which was instituted by James V. after the model of the French parliament, to supply an ambulatory committee of parliament, who took to themselves the names of the lords of council and session, which the present members of the college of justice still retain. This court consists of a president and fourteen ordinary members, besides extraordinary ones named by the king, who may sit and vote, but have no salaries, and are not bound to attendance. This court may be called a standing jury in all matters of property that lie before them. Their forms of proceeding do not lie within my plan, neither does any enquiry how far such an institution, in so narrow a country as Scotland, is compatible with the security of private property. The civil law is their directory in all matters that come not within the municipal laws of the kingdom. It has been often matter of surprize, that the Scots were so tenacious of the forms of their courts and the essence of their laws, as to reserve them by the articles of the union. This, however, can be easily accounted for, because those laws and forms were essential to the possession of estates and lands, which in Scotland are often held by modes incompatible with the laws of England. I shall just add, that the lords of council and session act likewise as a court of equity; but their decrees are sometimes (fortunately perhaps for the subject) reversible by the British parliament, to which an appeal lies.

The justice court is the highest criminal tribunal in Scotland; but in its present form it was instituted so late as the year 1672, when a lord justice general, removeable at the king's pleasure, was appointed. This lucrative office still exists in the person of one of the chief nobility; but the ordinary members of the court, are the justice-clerk and five other judges, who are always nominated from the lords of session. In this court the verdict of a jury condemns or acquits, but, as I have already hinted, without any necessity of their being unanimous.

Besides those two great courts of law, the Scots, by the articles of the Union, have a court of exchequer. This court has the same power, authority, privilege, and jurisdiction, over the revenue of Scotland, as the court of exchequer in England has over the revenues there; and all matters and things competent to the court of exchequer of England relating thereto, are likewise competent to the exchequer of Scotland. The judges of the exchequer in Scotland exercise certain powers which

which formerly belonged to the treasury, and are still vested in that of England.

The court of admiralty in Scotland, was, in the reign of Charles II. by act of parliament, declared to be a supreme court, in all causes competent to its own jurisdiction; and the lord high admiral is declared to be the king's lieutenant and justice-general upon the seas, and in all ports, harbours, and creeks of the same; and upon fresh waters and navigable rivers, below the first bridge, or within flood-mark; so that nothing competent to his jurisdiction can be meddled with, in the first instance, but by the lord high admiral and the judges of his court. Sentences passed in all inferior courts of admiralty, may be brought again before his court; but no advocation lies from it to the lords of the session, or any other judicatory, unless in cases not maritime. Causes are tried in this court by the civil law, which, in such cases, is likewise the common law of Scotland, as well as by the laws of Oleron, Wisby, and the Hansetowns, and other maritime practices and decisions common upon the continent. The place of lord admiral of Scotland is little more than nominal, but the salary annexed to it is reckoned worth 1000 l. a year; and the judge of the admiralty is commonly a lawyer of distinction, with considerable perquisites pertaining to his office.

The college or faculty of advocates, which answers to the English inns of court, may be called the seminary of Scotch lawyers. They are within themselves an orderly court, and their forms require great precision and examination to qualify its candidates for admission. Subordinate to them is a body of inferior lawyers, or, as they may be called, attorneys, who call themselves writers to the signet, because they alone can subscribe the writs that pass the signet; they likewise have a bye government for their own regulation. Such are the different law-courts that are held in the capital of Scotland; we shall pass to those that are inferior.

The government of the counties in Scotland was formerly vested in sheriffs and stewards, courts of regality, baron courts, commissaries, justices of the peace, and coroners.

Formerly sheriffdoms were generally, though most absurdly, hereditable; but, by a late act of parliament, they are now all vested in the crown; it being there enacted, That all high-sheriffs, or stewards, shall, for the future, be nominated and appointed annually by his majesty, his heirs, and successors. In regard to the sheriff-deputes, and stewart-deputes, it is enacted, That there shall only be one in each county, or stewartry, who must be an advocate, of three years standing at least. For the space of seven years, these deputies are to be nominated by the king, with such continuance as his majesty shall think fit; after which they are to enjoy their offices *ad vitam aut culpam*, that is, for life, unless guilty of some offence. Some other regulations have been likewise introduced, highly for the credit of the sheriffs courts.

Stewartries were formerly part of the ancient royal domain; and the stewarts had much the same power in them, as the sheriff had in his county.

Courts of regality of old, were held by virtue of a royal jurisdiction vested in the lord, with particular immunities and privileges; but these were so dangerous, and so extravagant, that all the Scotch regalities are now dissolved by an act of parliament.

Baron courts belong to every person who holds a barony of the king. In civil matters, they extend to causes not exceeding forty shillings sterling; and in criminal cases, to petty actions of assault and battery; but the punishment is not to exceed twenty shillings sterling, or setting the delinquent in the stocks for three hours, in the day time. These courts, however petty, were, in former days, invested with the power of life and death, which they have now lost.

The courts of commissaries in Scotland, answer to those of the English diocesan chancellors, the highest of which is kept at Edinburgh; wherein, before four judges, actions are pleaded concerning matters relating to wills and testaments; the right of patronage to ecclesiastical benefices, tithes, divorces, and causes of that nature; but in almost all other parts of the kingdom, there sits but one judge on these causes.

According to the present institution, justices of the peace in Scotland exercise pretty much the same powers as those in England. In former times, their office, though of very old standing, was insignificant, being cramped by the powers of the great feudal tyrants, who obtained an act of parliament, that they were not to take cognizance of riots till fifteen days after the fact.

The institution of coroners is as old as the reign of Malcolm II. the great legislator of Scotland, who lived before the Norman conquest of England. They took cognizance of all breaches of the king's peace; and they were required to have clerks to register depositions and matters of fact, as well as verdicts of jurors: the office, however, is at present much disused in Scotland.

From the above short view of the Scotch laws and institutions, it is plain that they were radically the same with those of the English. The latter alledge indeed, that the Scots borrowed the contents of their *Regiam Majestatem*, their oldest law-book, from the work of Glanville, who was a judge under Henry II. of England. The Scots, on the other hand, with much better reason, and far greater appearance of truth, say, that Glanville's work was copied from their *Regiam Majestatem*, even with the peculiarities of the latter, which do not now, and never did, exist in the laws of England.

The royal burghs in Scotland form, as it were, a commercial parliament, which meets once a year at Edinburgh, consisting of a representative from each burgh, to consult upon the common good of the whole. Their powers are pretty extensive, and before the Union they made laws relating to shipping, to masters and owners of ships, to mariners and merchants, by whom they were freighted; to manufacturers, such as plaiding, linen, and yarn; to the curing and packing of fish, salmon, and herrings; to the importing and exporting several commodities: the trade between Scotland and the Netherlands is subject to their regulation: they fix the staple-port, which was formerly at Dort, and is now at Camphere. Their conservator is indeed nominated by the crown, but then their convention regulates his power, approves his deputies, and appoints his salary: so that, in truth, the whole staple trade is subjected to their management. Upon the whole, this is a very singular institution, and sufficiently proves the vast attention which the government of Scotland formerly paid to trade. It took its present form in the reign of James III. 1487, and had excellent consequences for the benefit of commerce.

Such are the laws and constitution of Scotland, as they exist at present, in their general view; but our bounds do not permit us to descend to farther particulars, which are various and complicated. The conformity between the practice of the civil law of Scotland, and that in England, is remarkable. The English law reports are of the same nature with the Scotch praticks; and their acts of federunt, answer to the English rules of court; the Scottish wadsets and reversions, to the English mortgages and defeazances: their ponding of woods, after letters of horning, is much the same as the English executions upon outlawries: and an appeal against the king's pardon, in cases of murder, by the next of kin to the deceased, is admitted in Scotland as well as in England. Many other usages are the same in both kingdoms. I cannot, however, dismiss this head without one observation, which proves the similarity between the English and Scotch constitutions, which I believe has been mentioned by no author. In old times, all the freeholders in Scotland met together in presence of the king, who was seated on the top of a hillock, which, in the old Scotch constitutions,

conſtitutions, is called the Moot, or Mute-hill; all national affairs were here tranſacted; judgements given, and differences ended. This Moot-hill I apprehend to be of the ſame nature as the Saxon Folc-mote, and to ſignify no more than the hill of meeting.

HISTORY.] Though the writers of ancient Scotch hiſtory are too fond of ſyſtem and fable, yet it is eaſy to collect, from the Roman authors, and other evidences, that Scotland was formerly inhabited by different people. The Caledonians were, probably, the firſt inhabitants; the Picts, undoubtedly, were the Britons, who were forced northwards by the Belgic Gauls, above fourſcore years before the deſcent of Julius Cæſar; and who, ſettling in Scotland, were joined by great numbers of their countrymen, who were driven northwards by the Romans. The Scots, moſt probably, were a nation of adventurers from the antient Scythia, who had ſerved in the armies on the continent, and, as has been already hinted, after conquering the other inhabitants, gave their own name to the country. The tract lying ſouthward of the Forth appears to have been inhabited by the Saxons, and by the Britons, who formed the kingdom of Alcuith, the capital of which was Dumbarton: but all theſe people, in proceſs of time, were ſubdued by the Scots.

Having premiſed thus much, it is unneceſſary for me to inveſtigate the conſtitution of Scotland from its fabulous, or even its early ages. It is ſufficient to add to what I have already ſaid upon that head, that they ſeem to have been as forward as any of their ſouthern neighbours in the arts of war and government.

It does not appear that the Caledonians, the antient Celtic inhabitants of Scotland, were attacked by any of the Roman generals before Agricola, anno 79. The name of the prince he fought with was Galdus, by Tacitus named Galgacus; and the hiſtory of that war is not only tranſmitted with great preciſion, but corroborated by the remains of the Roman encampments and forts, raiſed by Agricola in his march towards Dunkeld, the capital of the Caledonians. The brave ſtand made by Galdus againſt that great general, does honour to the valour of both people; and the ſentiments of the Caledonian, concerning the freedom and independency of his country, appear to have warmed the noble hiſtorian with the ſame generous paſſion. It is plain, however, that Tacitus thought it for the honour of Agricola to conceal ſome part of this war; for though he makes his countrymen victorious, yet they certainly returned ſouthward, to the province of the Horeſti,

which

which was the county of Fife, without improving their advantage.

Galdus, otherwise called Corbred, was, according to the Scotch historians, the twenty-first in a lineal descent from Fergus I. the founder of their monarchy; and though this genealogy has of late been disputed, yet nothing can be more certain, from the Roman histories, than that the Caledonians, or Scots, were governed by a succession of brave and wise princes, during the abode of the Romans in Britain. Their valiant resistance obliged Agricola himself, and after him the emperors Adrian and Severus, to build the two famous pretentures or walls, which will be described in our account of England, to defend the Romans from the Caledonians and Scots; and that the independence of the latter was never subdued.

Christianity was introduced into Scotland about the year 201 of the Christian æra, by Donald I. The Picts, who, as before mentioned, were the descendents of the antient Britons, who had been forced northwards by the Romans, had at this time gained a footing in Scotland; and being often defeated by the antient inhabitants, they joined with the Romans against the Scots and Caledonians, who were of the same original, and considered themselves as one people; so that the Scots monarchy suffered a short eclipse: but it broke out with more lustre than ever under Fergus II. who recovered his crown; and his successors gave many severe overthrows to the Romans and Britons.

When the Romans left Britain in 448, the Scots, as appears by Gildas, a British historian, were a powerful nation, and, in conjunction with the Picts, invaded the Britons; and having forced the Roman walls, drove them to the very sea; so that the Britons applied to the Romans for relief; and in the famous letter, which they called their groans, they tell them, that they had no choice left, but that of being swallowed up by the sea, or perishing by the swords of the barbarians; for so all nations were called who were not Roman or under the Roman protection.

Dongard was then king of Scotland; and it appears from the oldest histories, and those that are least favourable to monarchy, that the succession to the crown of Scotland still continued in the family of Fergus, but generally descended collaterally; till the inconveniencies of that mode of succession were so much felt, that by degrees it fell into disuse, and it was at last settled in the right line.

About the year 796, the Scots were governed by Achaius, a prince so much respected, that his friendship was courted by Charlemagne, and a league was concluded between them, which continued inviolate while the monarchy of Scotland had an existence. No fact of equal antiquity is better attested than this league, together with the great service performed by the learned men of Scotland, in civilizing the vast dominions of that great conqueror, as has been already observed under the article of learning. The Picts still remained in Scotland as a separate nation, and were powerful enough to make war upon the Scots; who, about the year 843, when Kenneth Mac Alpin was king of Scotland, finally subdued them, but not in the savage manner mentioned by some historians, by extermination. For he obliged them to incorporate themselves with their conquerors, by taking their name and adopting their laws. The successors of Kenneth Mac Alpin maintained almost perpetual wars with the Saxons on the southward, and the Danes and other barbarous nations towards the east; who being masters of the sea, harrassed the Scots by powerful invasions. The latter, however, were more fortunate than the English, for while the Danes were erecting a monarchy in England, they were every where overthrown in Scotland by bloody battles, and at last driven out of the kingdom. The Saxon and Danish monarchs, who then governed England, were not more successful against the Scots; who maintained their freedom and independency, not only against foreigners, but against their own kings, when they thought them endangered. The feudal law was introduced among them by Malcolm II.

Malcolm III. commonly called Malcolm Canmore, from two Gællic words which signify a large head, but most probably his great capacity, was the eighty-sixth king of Scotland, from Fergus I. the supposed founder of the monarchy; the forty-seventh from its restorer, Fergus II. and the twenty-second from Kenneth III. who conquered the kingdom of the Picts. Every reader who is acquainted with the tragedy of Macbeth, as written by the inimitable Shakespear, who keeps close to the facts delivered by historians, can be no stranger to the fate of Malcolm's father, and his own history previous to his mounting the throne in the year 1057. He was a wise and magnanimous prince, and in no respect inferior to his contemporary the Norman conqueror, with whom he was often at war. He married Margaret, daughter to Edward, sur-named the Outlaw, son to Edward Ironside, king of England. By the death of her brother, Edgar Etheling, the Saxon right to the crown of England devolved upon the posterity of that princess, who was one of the wisest and worthiest women of the age; and her daughter, Maud, was accordingly married to Henry I. of England. Malcolm, after a
glorious

glorious reign, was killed, with his son, treacherously, as it is said, at the siege of Alnwic, by the besieged.

Malcolm III. was succeeded by his brother, Donald VII. and he was dethroned by Duncan II. whose legitimacy was disputed. They were succeeded by Edgar, the son of Malcolm III. who was a wise and valiant prince; and upon his death, David I. mounted the throne.

Notwithstanding the endeavours of some historians to conceal what they cannot deny, I mean the glories of this reign, yet David was, perhaps, the greatest prince of his age, whether we regard him as a man, a warrior, or a legislator. The noble actions he performed in the service of his niece, the empress Maud, in her competition with king Stephen for the English crown, give us the highest idea of his virtues, as they could be the result only of duty and principle. To him Henry II. the mightiest prince of his age, owed his crown; and his possessions in England, joined to the kingdom of Scotland, placed David's power on an equality with that of England, when confined to this island. His actions and adventures, and the resources he always found in his own courage, prove him to have been a hero of the first rank. If he appeared to be too lavish to churchmen, and in his religious endowments, we are to consider, these were the only means by which he could then civilize his kingdom: and the code of laws I have already mentioned to have been drawn up by him, do his memory immortal honour. They are said to have been compiled under his inspection by learned men, whom he assembled from all parts of Europe in his magnificent abbey of Melross. He was succeeded by his grandson, Malcolm IV. and he, by William, sur-named, from his valour, the Lyon. William's son, Alexander II. was succeeded, in 1249, by Alexander III. who was a good king. He married, first, Margaret, daughter to Henry III. of England, by whom he had Alexander, the prince, who married the earl of Flanders's daughter; David and Margaret, who married Hangowan, or, as some call him, Eric, son to Magnus IV. king of Norway, who bare to him a daughter, named Margaret, commonly called the Maiden of Norway; in whom king William's whole posterity failed, and the crown of Scotland returned to the descendants of David, earl of Huntingdon, brother to king Malcolm IV. and king William.

I have been the more particular in this detail, because it was productive of great events. Upon the death of Alexander III. John Baliol, who was great-grandson to David earl of Huntingdon, by his elder daughter, Margaret, and Robert Bruce (grandfather to the great king Robert Bruce) grandson to the same earl of Huntingdon, by his younger daughter Isabel, became competitors for the crown of Scotland. The laws of succession, which were not then so well established in Europe as they are at present, rendered the case very difficult. Both parties were almost equally matched in interest; but after a confused interregnum of some years, the great nobility agreed in referring the decision to Edward I. of England, the most politic, ambitious prince of his age. He accepted the office of arbiter: but having long had an eye to the crown of Scotland, he revived some obsolete absurd claims of its dependency upon that of England; and finding that Baliol was disposed to hold it by that disgraceful tenure, Edward awarded it to him; but afterwards dethroned him, and treated him as a slave, without Baliol's resenting it.

After this, Edward used many bloody endeavours to annex their crown to his own; but tho' they were often defeated, the independent Scots never were conquered. They were indeed but few, compared to those in the interest of Edward and Baliol, which was the same; and for some time were obliged to temporize. Edward availed himself of their weakness and his own power. He accepted of a formal surrender of the crown from Baliol, to whom he allowed a pension, but detained him in England; and sent every nobleman in Scotland, whom he in the least suspected, to different prisons in or near London. He then forced the Scots to sign instruments of their subjection to him; and most barbarously carried off, or destroyed, all the monuments of their history, and the evidences of their independency; and particularly the famous fatidical stone, which is still to be seen in Westminster-Abbey.

Those severe proceedings, while they rendered the Scots sensible of their slavery, revived in them the ideas of their freedom; and Edward, finding their spirits were not to be subdued, endeavoured to caress them, and affected to treat them on the footing of an equality with his own subjects, by projecting an union, the chief articles of which have since taken place, between the two kingdoms. The Scotch patriots treated this project with disdain; and united under the brave William Wallace, the truest hero of his age, to expel the English. Wallace performed actions that entitle him to eternal renown, in executing this scheme. Being, however, no more than a private gentleman, and his popularity daily increasing, the Scotch nobility, among whom was Robert Bruce, the son of the first competitor, began to suspect that he had an eye upon the crown, especially after he had defeated the earl of Surry, Edward's viceroy of Scotland, in the battle of Stirling, and had reduced the garrisons of Berwick and Roxburgh, and was
declared

declared by the states of Scotland their protector. Their jealousy operated so far, that they formed violent cabals against the brave Wallace. Edward, upon this, once more invaded Scotland, at the head of the most numerous and best disciplined army England had ever seen, for it consisted of 80,000 foot, 3000 horsemen completely armed, and 4000 light armed; and was attended by a fleet to supply it with provisions. These, besides the troops who joined him in Scotland, formed an irresistible body; so that Edward was obliged to divide it, reserving the command of 40,000 of his best troops to himself. With these he attacked the Scotch army under Wallace at Falkirk, while their disputes ran so high, that the brave regent was deserted by Cumming, the most powerful nobleman in Scotland, and at the head of the best division of his countrymen. Wallace, whose troops did not exceed 30,000, being thus betrayed, was defeated with vast loss, but made an orderly retreat; during which he found means to have a conference with Bruce, and to convince him of his error in joining with Edward. Wallace still continued in arms, and performed many gallant actions against the English; but was betrayed into the hands of Edward, who most ungenerously put him to death at London as a traitor; but he died himself, as he was preparing to renew his invasion of Scotland with a still more desolating spirit of ambition, after having destroyed, according to the best historians, 100,000 of her inhabitants.

Bruce died soon after the battle of Falkirk; but not before he had inspired his son, who was a prisoner at large about the English court, with the glorious resolution of vindicating his own rights, and his country's independency. He escaped from London, and with his own hand killed Cumming, for his attachment to Edward; and after collecting a few patriots, among whom were his own four brothers, he assumed the crown; but was defeated by the English (who had a great army in Scotland) at the battle at Methven. After this defeat, he fled, with one or two friends, to the Western Isles, and parts of Scotland, where his fatigues and sufferings were as inexpressible, as the courage with which he and his few friends (the lord Douglas especially) bore them was incredible. Tho' his wife and daughter were sent prisoners to England, where the best of his friends, and two of his brothers, were put to death, yet, such was his persevering spirit, that he recovered all Scotland, excepting the castle of Sterling, and improved every advantage that was given him by the dissipated conduct of Edward II. who raised an army more numerous and better appointed still than that of his father, to make a total conquest of Scotland. It is said that it consisted of 300,000, but this

must

must be understood as including the foreigners attending the camp, which in those days were very numerous; but it is admitted on all hands, that it did not consist of so few as 100,000 fighting men, while that of Bruce did not exceed 30,000; but all of them heroes who had been bred up in a detestation of tyranny.

Edward, who was not deficient in point of courage, led this mighty host towards Sterling, then besieged by Bruce; who had chosen, with the greatest judgment, a camp near Bannock-burn. The chief officers under Edward were, the earls of Gloucester, Hereford, Pembroke, and Sir Giles Argenton. Those under Bruce were, his own brother Sir Edward, who, next to himself, was reckoned to be the best knight in Scotland; his nephew, Randolf, earl of Murray, and the young lord Walter, high-steward of Scotland. Edward's attack of the Scotch army was furious beyond dispute, and required all the courage and firmness of Bruce and his friends to resist it, which they did so effectually, that they gained one of the most complete victories that is recorded in history. The great loss of the English fell upon the bravest part of their troops, who were led on by Edward in person against Bruce himself. The Scotch writers make the loss of the English to amount to 50,000 men. Be that as it will, there certainly never was a more total defeat, though the conquerors lost 4000. The flower of the English nobility were either killed or taken prisoners. Their camp, which was immensely rich, and calculated for the purpose rather of a triumph than a campaign, fell into the hands of the Scots: and Edward himself, with a few followers, favoured by the goodness of their horses, were pursued by Douglas to the gates of Berwick, from whence he escaped in a fishing-boat. This great and decisive battle happened in the year 1314 *.

The remainder of Robert's reign was a series of the most glorious successes; and so well did his nobility understand the principles of civil liberty, and so unfettered they were by religious considerations, that in a letter they sent to the pope, they acknowledged that they had set aside Baliol, for debasing the crown by holding it of England; and that they would do the

---

* That the Scots of those days were better acquainted with Mars than the Muses, may be seen from a scoffing ballad, made on this memorable victory, which begins as follows.

Maydens of England sore may ye mourn,
For zour lemmons (laymens) zou have lost at Bannockburn.
         With heve a low!
What ho! ween'd the king of England,
So soon to have won all Scotland.
         With a rumby low!

the same by Robert if he should make the like attempt. Robert having thus delivered Scotland, sent his brother Edward to Ireland, at the head of an army, with which he conquered the greatest part of that kingdom, and was proclaimed its king; but by exposing himself too much, he was killed. Robert, before his death, which happened in 1328, made an advantageous peace with England; and when he died, he was acknowledged to be indisputably the greatest hero of his age.

The glory of the Scots may be said to have been in its zenith under Robert I. who was succeeded by his son, David II. He was a virtuous prince, but his abilities, both in war and peace, were eclipsed by his brother-in-law, and enemy, Edward III. of England, whose sister he married. Edward, who was as keen as any of his predecessors upon the conquest of Scotland, espoused the cause of Baliol, son to Baliol, the original competitor. His progress was at first amazingly rapid; and he and Edward defeated the royal party in many bloody battles; but Baliol was at last driven out of his usurped kingdom by the Scotch patriots. David had the misfortune to be taken prisoner by the English at the battle of Durham; and after continuing above eleven years in captivity, he paid 100,000 marks for his ransom; and died in peace, without issue, in the year 1371.

The crown of Scotland then devolved upon the family of Stuart, by its head having been married to the daughter of Robert I. The first king of that name was Robert II. a wise and brave prince. He was succeeded by his son, Robert III. whose age and infirmities disqualified him from reigning; so that he was forced to trust the government to his worthless relations. Robert, upon this, attempted to send his second son to France, but he was most ungenerously intercepted by Henry IV. of England; and after suffering a long captivity, he was obliged to pay an exorbitant ransom. During the imprisonment of James in England, the military glory of the Scots was carried to its greatest height in France, where they supported that tottering monarchy against England, and their generals obtained some of the first titles of the kingdom.

James, the first of that name, upon his return to Scotland, discovered great talents for government, enacted many wise laws, and was beloved by the people. He had received an excellent education in England during the reigns of Henry IV. and V. where he saw the feudal system refined from many of the imperfections which still adhered to it, in his own kingdom; he determined therefore to abridge the overgrown power of the nobles, and to recover such lands as had been unjustly wrested from the crown during his minority and the

pre-

preceding reigns; but the execution of these designs cost him his life, being murthered in his bed by some of the chief nobility, in 1437, and the 44th year of his age.

A long minority succeeded; but James II. would probably have equalled the greatest of his ancestors both in warlike and civil virtues, had he not been suddenly killed by the accidental bursting of a cannon, in the thirtieth year of his age, as he was besieging the castle of Roxburgh, which was defended by the English.

Suspicion, indolence, immoderate attachment to favourites, and many of the errors of a feeble mind, are visible in the conduct of James III. and his turbulent reign was closed by a rebellion of his subjects, being slain in battle in 1488, aged thirty-five.

His son, James IV. was the most accomplished prince of the age: he was naturally generous and brave; he loved magnificence, he delighted in war, and was eager to obtain fame. He encouraged and protected the commerce of his subjects, so that they rivalled the English in riches; and the court of James, at the time of his marriage with Henry VII's daughter, was splendid and respectable. Even this alliance could not cure him of his family distemper, a predilection for the French, in whose cause he rashly entered, and was killed, with the flower of his nobility, by the English, in the battle of Flodden, anno 1513, and the fortieth year of his age.

The minority of his son, James V. was long and turbulent: and when he grew up, he married two French ladies; the first being daughter to the king of France, and the latter of the house of Guise. He instituted the court of session, enacted many salutary laws, and greatly promoted the trade of Scotland, particularly the working of the mines. At this time the ballance of power was so equally poised between the contending princes of Europe, that James's friendship was courted by the pope, the emperor, the king of France, and his uncle Henry VIII. of England, from all whom he received magnificent presents. But James took no share in foreign affairs; he seemed rather to imitate his predecessors in their attempts to humble the nobility; and the doctrines of the reformation beginning to be propagated in Scotland, he gave way, at the instigation of the clergy, to a religious persecution, tho' it is generally believed that, had he lived, he would have seized all the church revenues in imitation of Henry; but he died in the thirty-first year of his age, anno 1542, of grief, for an affront which his arms had sustained in an ill-judged expedition against the English.

His daughter and successor, Mary, was but a few hours old at the time of her father's death. Her beauty, and her

her misfortunes, are alike famous in hiftory. It is fufficient here to fay, that during her minority, and while fhe was wife to Francis II. of France, the reformation advanced in Scotland: that being called to the throne of her anceftors while a widow, fhe married her own coufin-german, the lord Darnley, whofe untimely death has given rife to much controverfy, and the refult of which is highly in favour of her memory. The confequence of her hufband's death was a rebellion, by which fhe was driven into England, where fhe was bafely detained a prifoner for eighteen years, and afterwards beheaded by order of queen Elizabeth in 1586-7, and the forty-fixth year of her age.

Mary's fon, James VI. of Scotland, fucceeded in right of his blood from Henry VII. upon the death of queen Elizabeth, to the Englifh crown, after fhewing great abilities in the government of Scotland. This union of the two crowns, in fact, deftroyed the independency, as it impoverifhed the people of Scotland; for the feat of government being removed to England, their trade was checked, their agriculture neglected, and their gentry obliged to feek for bread in other countries. James, after a fplendid, but troublefome reign over his three kingdoms, left them, in 1625, to his fon, the unfortunate Charles I. It is well known, that the defpotic principles of that prince received the firft check from the Scots; and that, had it not been for them, he would eafily have fubdued his Englifh rebels, who implored the affiftance of the Scots; but afterwards, againft all the ties of honour and humanity, brought him to the block in 1648.

The Scots faw their error when it was too late; and made feveral bloody, but unfortunate attempts, to fave the father, and to reftore his fon, Charles II. That prince was finally defeated by Cromwell, at the battle of Worcefter; after which, to the time of his reftoration, the ufurper gave law to Scotland. I have, in another place, touched upon the moft material parts of Charles's reign, and that of his deluded brother, James VII. of Scotland, and II. of England, as well as of king William, who was fo far from being a friend to Scotland, that, relying on his royal word to her parliament, fhe was brought to the brink of ruin.

The ftate of parties in England, at the acceffion of queen Anne, was fuch, that the Whigs, once more, had recourfe to the Scots, and offered them their own terms, if they would agree to the incorporate Union as it now ftands. It was long before the majority of the Scotch parliament would liften to the propofal; but at laft, partly from conviction, and partly through the force of money diftributed among the needy nobility, it was agreed to; fince which event, the hiftory of Scotland becomes the fame with that of England.

ENGLAND.

EXTENT AND SITUATION.

Length 360 } between { 50 and 56 north latitude.
Breadth 300 }   { 2 east and 6-20 west longitude.
(Miles.)

CLIMATE AND BOUNDARIES. THE longest day in the northern parts, contains 17 hours 30 minutes; and the shortest, in the southern, near 8 hours. It is bounded on the north, by that part of the island called Scotland; on the east, by the German Ocean; on the west, by St. George's Channel; and on the south, by the English Channel, which parts it from France.

This situation, by the sea washing it on three sides, renders England liable to a great uncertainty of weather, so that the inhabitants on the sea coasts are often visited by agues and fevers. On the other hand, it prevents the extremes of heat and cold, to which other places, lying in the same degrees of latitude, are subject; and it is, on that account, friendly to the longevity of the inhabitants in general, especially those who live on a dry soil. To this situation likewise we are to ascribe that perpetual verdure for which England is admired and envied all over the world, occasioned by the refreshing showers and the warm vapours of the sea.

NAME AND DIVISIONS, ANCIENT AND MODERN. Antiquaries are divided with regard to the etymology of the word *England*; some derive it from a Celtic word, signifying a level country; but I prefer the common etymology, of its being derived, as I have already mentioned, from Anglen, a province now subject to his Danish majesty, which furnished a great part of the original Saxon adventurers into this island. In the time of the Romans, the whole island went by the name of *Britannia*. The word *Brit*, according to Mr. Camden, signified painted or stained; the antient inhabitants being famous for painting their bodies: other antiquaries, however, do not agree in this etymology. The western tract of England, which is almost separated from the rest by the rivers Severn and Dee, is called Wales, or the land of strangers, because inhabited by the Belgic Gauls, who were driven thither by the Romans, and were strangers to the old natives.

When the Romans provinciated England (for they never did Scotland) they divided it into,

1. Britannia Prima, which contained the southern parts of the kingdom.

2. Bri-

2. Britannia Secunda, containing the western parts, comprehending Wales; and,

3. Maxima Cæsariensis, which reached from the Trent as far northward as the wall of Severus, between Newcastle and Carlisle, and sometimes as far as that of Adrian in Scotland, between the Forth and Clyde.

To these divisions some add, the Flavia Cæsariensis, which they suppose to contain the midland counties.

When the Saxon invasion took place, about the year 450, and when they were established in the year 582, their chief leaders appropriated to themselves, after the manner of the other northern conquerors, the countries which each had been the most instrumental in conquering; and the whole formed a heptarchy, or political republic, consisting of seven kingdoms; but in time of war, a chief was chosen out of the seven kings; for which reason I call it a political republic, its constitution greatly resembling that of antient Greece.

Kingdoms erected by the Saxons, usually stiled the Saxon Heptarchy.

Kingdoms.	Counties.	Chief Towns.
1. Kent, founded by Hengist in 475, and ended in 823.	Kent	Canterbury
2. South Saxons, founded by Ella in 491, and ended in 600.	Sussex Surry	Chichester Southwark.
3. East-Angles, founded by Uffa in 575, and ended in 793.	Norfolk Suffolk Cambridge With the Isle of Ely	Norwich Bury St. Edmonds Cambridge Ely.
4. West-Saxons, founded by Cerdic in 512, and ended in 1060.	Cornwall Devon Dorset Somerset Wilts Hants Berks Lancaster	Launceston Exeter Dorchester Bath Salisbury Winchester Abingdon. Lancaster.
5. Northumberland, founded by Ida, in 574, and ended in 792.	York Durham Cumberland Westmoreland Northumberland, and Scotland to the Firth of Edinburgh	York Durham Carlisle Appleby Newcastle.

Kingdoms.	Counties.	Chief Towns.
6. Eaſt-Saxons, founded by Erchewin in 527, and ended in 746.	Eſſex — Middleſex, and part of Hertford	London
7. Mercia, founded by Cridda in 582, and ended in 874.	Glouceſter ——— Hereford ——— Worceſter ——— Warwick ——— Leiceſter ——— Rutland ——— Northampton ——— Lincoln ——— Huntingdon ——— Bedford ——— Buckingham ——— Oxford ——— Stafford ——— Derby ——— Salop ——— Nottingham ——— Cheſter ——— And the other part of Hertford ———	Glouceſter Hereford Worceſter Warwick Leiceſter Oakham Northampton Lincoln Huntingdon Bedford Ayleſbury Oxford Stafford Derby Shrewſbury Nottingham Cheſter Hertford.

I have been the more ſollicitous to preſerve thoſe diviſions, as they account for different local cuſtoms, and many very eſſential modes of inheritance, which, to this day, prevail in England, and which took their riſe from different inſtitutions under the Saxons. Since the Norman conqueſt, England has been divided into counties, a certain number of which, excepting Middleſex and Cheſhire, are comprehended in ſix circuits, or annual progreſſes of the judges for adminiſtering juſtice to the ſubjects who are at a diſtance from the capital. Theſe circuits are;

Circuits.	Counties.	Chief Towns.
1. Home Circuit.	Eſſex ———	Chelmsford, Colcheſter, Harwich, Malden, Saffron-Walden, Bocking, Braintree, and Stratford.
	Hertford	Hertford, St. Alban's, Royſton, Ware, Hitchin, Baldock, Biſhops-Stortford, Berkhamſted, Hemſted, and Barnet.
	Kent —	Maidſtone, Canterbury, Chatham, Rocheſter, Greenwich, Woolwich, Dover, Deal, Deptford, Feverſham, Dartford, Romney, Sandwich, Sheerneſs, Tunbridge, Margate, Graveſend, and Milton.

ENGLAND.

Circuits.	Counties.	Chief Towns.
1. Home Circuit continued.	Surry	Southwark, Kingston, Guildford, Croydon, Epsom, Richmond, Wansworth, Battersea, Putney, Farnham, Godalmin, Bagshot, Egham, and Darking.
	Sussex	Chichester, Lewes, Rye, East-Grinstead, Hastings, Horsham, Midhurst, Shoreham, Arundel, Winchelsea, Battel, Brighthelmstone, and Petworth.
2. Norfolk Circuit.	Bucks	Aylesbury, Buckingham, High-Wickham, Great-Marlow, Stony Stratford, and Newport-Pagnel.
	Bedford	Bedford, Ampthill, Wooburn, Dunstable, Luton, and Bigglefwade.
	Huntingdon	Huntingdon, St. Ives, Kimbolton, Godmanchester, St. Neot's, Ramsey, and Yaxley.
	Cambridge	Cambridge, Ely, Newmarket, Royston, and Wisbich.
	Suffolk	Bury, Ipswich, Sudbury, Leostoff, part of Newmarket, Aldborough, Bungay, Southwold, Brandon, Halesworth, Mildenhall, Beccles, Franglingham, Stow-market, Woodbridge, Lavenham, Hadley, Long-Melford, Stratford, and Easterbergholt.
	Norfolk	Norwich, Thetford, Lynn, and Yarmouth.
3. Oxford Circuit.	Oxon	Oxford, Banbury, Chippingnorton, Henley, Burford, Whitney, Dorchester, Woodstock, and Tame.
	Berks	Abingdon, Windsor, Reading, Wallingford, Newbury, Hungerford, Maidenhead, Farrington, Wantage, and Oakingham.
	Gloucester	Gloucester, Tewkibury, Cirencester, part of Bristol, Campden, Stow, Berkley, Durfley, Leechdale, Tetbury, Sudbury, Wotton, and Marshfield.
	Worcester	Worcester, Evesham, Droitwich, Bewdley, Stourbridge, Kidderminster, and Pershore.
	Monmouth	Monmouth, Chepstow, Abergavenny, Caerleon, and Newport.
	Hereford	Hereford, Lemster, Weobley, Ledbury, Kyneton, and Rofs.

Vol. I.   P

ENGLAND.

Circuits.	Counties.	Chief Towns.
3. Oxford Circuit continued.	Salop —	Shrewsbury, Ludlow, Bridgnorth, Wenlock, Bishop's-castle, Witchurch, Oswestry, Wem, and Newport.
	Stafford —	Stafford, Litchfield, Newcastle under Line, Woolverhampton, Rugeley, Burton, Utoxeter, and Stone.
4. Midland Circuit.	Warwick	Warwick, Coventry, Birmingham, Stratford upon Avon, Tamworth, Aulcester, Nuneaton, and Atherton.
	Leicester	Leicester, Melton-Mowbray, Ashby de la Zouch, Bosworth, and Harborough.
	Derby —	Derby, Chesterfield, Workſworth, Bakewel, and Balsover.
	Nottingham	Nottingham, Southwell, Newark, East and West Redford, Mansfield, Tuxford, Workſop, and Blithe.
	Lincoln	Lincoln, Stamford, Boston, Grantham, Croyland, Spalding, New Sleaford, Great Grimsby, Gainsborough, Louth, and Horncastle.
	Rutland —	Oakham and Uppingham.
	Northampt.	Northampton, Peterborough, Daventry, Higham-Ferrers, Brackley, Oundle, Wellingborough, Thorpſton, Towcester, Rockingham, Kettering, and Rothwell.
5. Western Circuit.	Hants —	Winchester, Southampton, Portsmouth, Andover, Basingstoke, Christchurch, Petersfield, Lymington, Ringwood, Rumsey, Arlesford; and Newport, Yarmouth, and Cowes, in the Isle of Wight.
	Wilts —	Salisbury, Devizes, Marlborough, Malmſbury, Wilton, Chippenham, Calne, Cricklade, Trowbridge, Bradford, and Warminster.
	Dorset —	Dorchester, Lyme, Sherborn, Shaftsbury, Pool, Blandford, Bridport, Weymouth, Melcombe, Wareham, and Winburn.
	Somerset —	Bath, Wells, Bristol in part, Taunton, Bridgwater, Ilchester, Minehead, Milbourn-Port, Glastenbury, Wellington, Dulverton, Dunſter, Watchet, Yeovil; Somerton, Axbridge, Chard, Bruton, Shepton-Mallet, Crofcomb, and Froome.

ENGLAND. 227

Circuits.	Counties.	Chief Towns.
5. Western Circuit continued.	Devon	Exeter, Plymouth, Barnstaple, Biddeford, Tiverton, Dartmouth, Tavistock, Topsham, Okehampton, Ashburton, Credeton, Moulton, Torrington, Totnes, Axminster, Plympton, Honiton, and Ilfracomb.
	Cornwall	Launceston, Falmouth, Truro, Saltash, Bodmyn, St. Ives, Padstow, Tregony, Fowey, Penryn, Kellington, Leskard, Lestwithiel, Helston, Penzance, and Redruth.
6. Northern Circuit.	York	York, Leeds, Wakefield, Halifax, Rippon, Pontefract, Hull, Richmond, Scarborough, Boroughbridge, Malton, Sheffield, Doncaster, Whitby, Beverly, Northallerton, Burlington, Knaresborough, Barnesley, Sherborn, Bradford, Tadcaster, Skipton, Wetherby, Ripley, Heydon, Howden, Thirske, Gisborough, Pickering, and Yarum.
	Durham	Durham, Stockton, Sunderland, Stanhope, Barnard-Castle, Darlington, Hartlepool, and Awkland.
	Northumb.	Newcastle, Tinmouth, North-Shields, Morpeth, Alnwick, and Hexham.
	Lancaster	Lancaster, Manchester, Preston, Liverpoole, Wiggan, Warrington, Rochdale, Bury, Ormskirk, Hawkshead, and Newton.
	Westmorel.	Appleby, Kendal, Lonsdale, Kirkby-Stephen, Orton, Ambleside, Burton, and Milthorpe.
	Cumberland	Carlisle, Penrith, Cockermouth, Whitehaven, Ravenglass, Egremont, Keswick, Workington, and Jerby.

Middlesex is not comprehended; and Cheshire is left out of these circuits, because, being a county palatine, it enjoys municipal laws and privileges. The same may be said of Wales, which is divided into four circuits.

Counties exclusive of the Circuits.	Middlesex	London, first meridian, N. Lat. 51-30. Westminster, Uxbridge, Brentford, Chelsea, Highgate, Hampstead, Kensington, Hackney, and Hampton-Court.
	Chester	Chester, Nantwich, Macclesfield, Malpas, Northwich, Middlewich, Sandbach, Congleton, Knotsford, Frodisham, and Haulton.

Circuits of WALES.

Circuit	Counties	Towns
North-East Circuit.	Flint —	Flint, St. Asaph, and Holywell.
	Denbigh —	Denbigh, Wrexham, and Ruthen.
	Montgomery	Montgomery, Llanvylin, and Welchpool.
North-West Circuit.	Anglesey	Beaumaris, Holyhead, and Newburgh.
	Caernarvon	Bangor, Conway, Caernarvon, and Pullilly.
	Merioneth	Delgelly, Bala, and Harlegh.
South-East Circuit.	Radnor —	Radnor, Prestean, and Knighton.
	Brecon —	Brecknock, Built, and Hay.
	Glamorgan	Llandaff, Cardiff, Cowbridge, Neath, and Swansey.
South-West Circuit.	Pembroke	St. David's, Haverfordwest, Pembroke, Tenby, Fiscard, and Milfordhaven.
	Cardigan	Cardigan, Aberistwith, and Llanbadarn-vawr.
	Caermarth.	Caermarthen, Kidwelly, Lanimdovery, Llandilovawr, Langharn, and Lanelthy.

In ENGLAND.

40 Counties, which send up to parliament — 80 knights.
25 Cities (Ely none, London four) — 50 citizens.
167 Boroughs, two each — 334 burgesses.
5 Boroughs, (Abingdon, Banbury, Bewdley, Highham-Ferrars, and Monmouth) one each — 5 burgesses.
2 Universities — 4 representatives.
8 Cinque ports, (Hastings, Dover, Sandwich, Romney, Hythe, and their three dependents, Rye, Winchelsea, and Seaford) two each — 16 barons.

WALES.

12 Counties — 12 knights.
12 Boroughs (Pembroke two, Merioneth none) one each — 12 burgesses.

SCOTLAND.

33 Shires — 30 knights.
67 Cities and Boroughs — 15 burgesses.

Total 558

SOIL, AIR, SEASONS, AND WATER. The soil of England and Wales differ in each county, not so much from the nature of the ground, though that must be admitted to occasion a very considerable alteration, as from the progress which the inhabitants of each county has made in the cultivation of land and garden, the draining of marshes, and many other local improvements, which are here carried to a much greater degree of perfection than they are perhaps in any other part of the world, if we except China. To enter upon particular specimens and proofs of these improvements, would require a large volume of itself. All that can be said therefore is in general, that if no unkindly seasons happen, England produces corn not only sufficient to maintain her own inhabitants, but to bring immense sums of ready money for her exports. The benefit, however, from those exports have sometimes tempted the inhabitants to carry out of the kingdom more grain than could be conveniently spared, and have laid the poor under distress; for which reason exportations have been sometimes checked by government. No nation in the world exceeds England in the productions of the garden, which have come to such perfection, that the rarest of foreign fruits have been cultivated there, and that with success. If any farther proof of this should be required, let it be remembered, that London, and its neighbourhood, though peopled by about 1,000,000 inhabitants, is plentifully supplied with all kinds of roots, fruits, and kitchen-stuff from grounds within 12 miles distance.

The soil of England seems to be particularly adapted for rearing timber, and the plantations of trees round the houses of noblemen and gentlemen, and even of peasants, are delightful and astonishing at the same time. Some have observed a decay of that oak timber which anciently formed the vast fleets that England put to sea; but as no public complaints of that kind have been heard, it may be supposed that great stores are still in reserve; unless it may be thought that our ship-yards are partly supplied from America or the Baltic.

As to air, I can add but little to what I have already said concerning the climate. In many places it is certainly loaded with vapours wafted from the Atlantic Ocean by westerly winds, but they are ventilated by winds and storms, so that in this respect England is to foreigners, and people of delicate constitutions, more disagreeable than unsalubrious. It cannot, however, be denied, that in England the weather is so excessively capricious, and unfavourable to certain constitutions, that many of the inhabitants are obliged to fly to foreign countries, for a renovation of their health. Many, especially foreigners,

foreigners, have attributed that remarkable self-dissatisfaction of the English, which too often proceeds to acts of suicide, to their air and climate; but however these may operate, the evil probably lies in the people's manner of living, which is more gross and luxurious, than that of any other nation.

After what we have observed in the English air, the reader may form some idea of its seasons, which are so uncertain, that they admit of no description. Spring, summer, autumn, and winter, succeed each other, but in what month their different appearances take place, is very undetermined. The spring begins sometimes in February, and sometimes in April. In May the face of the country is as often covered with hoary frost as with blossoms. The beginning of June is often as cold as the middle of December, yet sometimes the thermometer rises in that month as high as it does in Italy. Even August has its vicissitudes of heat and cold, and upon an average September, and next to it October, bid very fair to be the two most agreeable months in the year. The natives sometimes experience all the four seasons within the compass of one day, cold, temperate, hot, and mild weather. After saying thus much, it would be in vain to attempt any farther description of the English seasons. Their inconstancy, however, are not attended with the effects that may be naturally apprehended. A fortnight, very seldom three weeks, generally make up the difference with regard to the maturity of the fruits of the earth: and it is generally observed, that the inhabitants seldom suffer by a hot summer. Even the greatest irregularity, and the most unfavourable appearances of the seasons, is not, as in other countries, attended with famine, and very seldom with scarcity. Perhaps this, in a great measure, may be owing to the vast improvements of agriculture, for when scarcity itself has been complained of, it generally, if not always, proceeded from the excessive exportations of grain, on account of the drawback, and the profit of the returns.

In speaking of water, I do not intend to include rivers, brooks, or lakes; I mean waters for the common conveniencies of life, and those that have mineral qualities. The champain parts of England are generally supplied with excellent springs and fountains, though a discerning palate may perceive, that they commonly contain some mineral impregnation. In many high lying parts of the country, the inhabitants are greatly distrest for water, and supply themselves by trenches, or digging deep wells. The constitutions of the English, and the various diseases to which they are liable, have rendered them extremely inquisitive after salubrious waters, for the recovery and preservation

preservation of their health, so that England contains as many mineral wells, of known efficacy, as perhaps any country in the world. The most celebrated are the hot baths of Bath and Bristol, in Somersetshire, and of Buxton, in Derbyshire; the mineral waters of Tunbridge, Epsom, Dulwich, Acton, Harrowgate, and Scarborough. Sea water is used as commonly as any other for medicinal purposes, and so delicate are the tones of the English fibres, that the patients can perceive both in drinking and bathing, a difference between the sea-water of one coast, and that of another.

FACE OF THE COUNTRY AND MOUNTAINS.] The industry of the English is, and has been such as to supply the absence of those favours which nature has so lavishly bestowed upon some foreign climates, and in many respects even to exceed them. No nation in the world can equal the cultivated parts of England in beautiful scenes. The variety of high-lands and low-lands, the former gently swelling, and both of them forming prospects equal to the most luxuriant imagination, the corn and meadow ground, the intermixtures of enclosures and plantations, the noble seats, comfortable houses, chearful villages, and well-stocked farms, often rising in the neighbourhood of populous towns and cities, decorated with the most vivid colours of nature, are inexpressible. The most barren spots are not without their verdure, but nothing can give us a higher idea of the English industry, than by observing that some of the most beautiful counties in the kingdom, are naturally the most barren, but rendered fruitful by labour. Upon the whole, it may be safely affirmed, that no country in Europe equals England in the beauty of its prospects, or the opulence of its inhabitants.

Though England is full of delightful rising grounds, and the most enchanting slopes, yet it contains few mountains. The most noted are the Peak in Derbyshire, the Endle in Lancashire, the Wolds in Yorkshire, the Cheviot-hills on the borders of Scotland, the Chiltern in Bucks, Malvern in Worcestershire, Cotswold in Gloucestershire, the Wrekin in Shropshire; with those of Plinlimmon and Snowden in Wales. In general, however, Wales, and the northern parts, may be termed mountainous.

RIVERS AND LAKES.] The rivers in England add greatly to its beauty, as well as its opulence; the Thames, the noblest perhaps in the world, rises on the confluence of Gloucestershire, and after receiving the many tributary streams of other rivers, it passes to Oxford, then by Wallingford, Reading, Marlow, and Windsor. From thence to Kingston, where formerly it met the tide, which, since the building of Westminster bridge, is said to flow no higher than Richmond; from whence it flows to London, and after dividing the counties of Kent and Essex, it widens in its progress, till it falls into the sea at the Nore, from whence it is navigable for large ships to London bridge; but for a more particular description the reader must consult the map. It was formerly a matter of reproach to England, among foreigners, that so capital a river should have so few bridges; those of London and Kingston (which is of wood) being the only two it had from the Nore, to the last mentioned place, for many ages. This inconveniency was in some measure owing to the dearness of materials for building stone bridges; but perhaps more to the fondness which the English, in former days, had for water carriage, and the encouragement of navigation. The vast increase of riches, commerce, and inland trade, are now multiplying bridges, and some think the world cannot parallel for commodiousness, architecture, and workmanship, those lately erected at Westminster, and Black Friars. Putney, Kew, and Hampton-court, have now bridges likewise over the Thames, and others are projecting by public spirited proprietors of the grounds on both sides.

The river Medway, which rises near Tunbridge, falls into the mouth of the Thames at Sheerness, and is navigable for the largest ships as far as Chatham, where the men of war are laid up. The Severn, reckoned the second river for importance in England, and the first for rapidity, rises at Plinlimmon-hill in north Wales; becomes navigable at Welch-Pool; runs east to Shrewsbury; then turning south, visits Bridgenorth, Worcester, and Tewkesbury, where it receives the Upper Avon; after having passed Gloucester, it takes a south-west direction; is near its mouth increased by the Wye and Ustre, and discharges itself into the Bristol-channel, near King-road; and there the great ships, which cannot get up to Bristol, lie. The Trent rises in the Moorlands of Staffordshire, and running south-east by Newcastle-under-line, divides that county into two parts; then turning north-east on the confines of Derbyshire, visits Nottingham, running the whole length of that county to Lincolnshire, and being joined by the Ouse, and several other rivers towards the mouth, obtains the name of the Humber, falling into the sea south-east of Hull.

The other principal rivers in England, are the Ouse (which is a Gaelic word signifying water in general) which falls into the Humber, after receiving the water of many other rivers. Another Ouse rises in Bucks, and falls into the sea near Lynn in Norfolk. The Tine runs from west to east through Northumberland, and falls into the German sea at Tinmouth below

low Newcaſtle. The Tees runs from weſt to eaſt, dividing Durham from Yorkſhire, and falls into the German ſea below Stockton. The Tweed runs from weſt to eaſt on the borders of Scotland, and falls into the German ſea at Berwick. The Eden runs from ſouth to north through Weſtmoreland and Cumberland, and paſſing by Carliſle, falls into Solway Frith below that city. The Lower Avon runs weſt through Wiltſhire to Bath, and then dividing Somerſetſhire from Gloucesterſhire, runs to Briſtol, falling into the mouth of the Severn below that city. The Derwent, which runs from eaſt to weſt through Cumberland, and paſſing by Cockermouth, falls into the Iriſh ſea a little below. The Ribble, which runs from eaſt to weſt through Lancaſhire, and paſſing by Preſton, diſcharges itſelf into the Iriſh ſea. The Merſey, which runs from the ſouth-eaſt to the north-weſt through Cheſhire, and then dividing Cheſhire from Lancaſhire, paſſes by Liverpool, and falls into the Iriſh ſea a little below that town; and the Dee riſes in Wales, and divides Flintſhire from Cheſhire, falling into the Iriſh channel below Cheſter.

The lakes of England are but few, though it is plain from hiſtory and antiquity, and indeed, in ſome places from the face of the country, that meres and fens have been very frequent in England, till drained and converted into arable land by induſtry. The chief lakes now remaining, are Soham mere, Wittleſea mere, and Ramſay mere, in the iſle of Ely, in Cambridgeſhire. All theſe meres in a rainy ſeaſon are overflowed, and form a lake of 40 or 50 miles in circumference. Winander mere lies in Weſtmoreland, and ſome ſmall lakes in Lancaſhire, go by the name of Derwent waters.

FORESTS.] The firſt Norman kings of England, partly for political purpoſes, that they might the more effectually enſlave their new ſubjects, and partly from the wantonneſs of power, converted immenſe tracts of ground into foreſts, for the benefit of hunting, and theſe were governed by laws peculiar to themſelves, ſo that it was neceſſary about the time of paſſing the Magna Charta, to form them into a ſort of a code, called the foreſt-laws; and juſtices in Eyre, ſo called from their ſitting in the open air, were appointed to ſee them obſerved. By degrees thoſe vaſt tracts were disforeſted, and the chief foreſts, properly ſo called, remaining out of no fewer than 69, are thoſe of Windſor, New Foreſt, the Foreſt of Dean, and Sherwood Foreſt. Thoſe foreſts produced formerly great quantities of excellent oak, elm, aſh, and beech, beſides walnut-trees, poplar, maple, and other kinds of wood. In ancient times England contained large woods, if not foreſts, of cheſnut-trees, which exceeded all other kinds of timber,

for

for the purposes of building, as appears from many great houses still standing, in which the chesnut beams and roofs remain still fresh, and undecayed, though some of them above 600 years old.

METALS AND MINERALS.] Among the minerals, the tin mines of Cornwall deservedly take the lead. They were known to the Greeks and Phenicians, the latter especially, some ages before that of the Christian Æra; and since the English have found the method of manufacturing their tin into plates, and white iron, they are of immense benefit to the nation. An ore called Mundic is found in the beds of tin, which was very little regarded, till about 60 years ago, Sir Gilbert Clark discovered the art of manufacturing it, and it is said now to bring in 150,000l. a year, and to equal in goodness the best Spanish copper, yielding a proportionable quantity of lapis caliminaris for making brass. Those tin-works are under peculiar regulations, by what are called the stannary laws, and the miners have parliaments and privileges of their own, which are in force at this time. The number of Cornish miners alone are said to amount to 100,000. Some gold has likewise been discovered in Cornwall, and the English lead is impregnated with silver. The English coined silver is particularly known by roses, and that of Wales by that prince's cap of feathers. Devonshire, and other counties of England, produces marble, but the best kind, which resembles Egyptian granite, is excessively hard to work. Quarries of freestone are found in many places. Northumberland and Cheshire yields allum and salt pits. The English fullers earth is of such infinite consequence to the cloathing trade, that its exportation is prohibited under the severest penalties. Pit and sea coal is found in many counties of England, but the city of London, to encourage the nursery of seamen, is chiefly supplied from the pits of Northumberland, and the bishopric of Durham. The cargoes are shipped at Newcastle and Sunderland, and the exportation of coals to other countries, is a valuable article.

VEGETABLE AND ANIMAL PRODUCTIONS BY SEA AND LAND.] This is so copious an article, and such improvements have been made in gardening and agriculture, ever since the best printed accounts we have had of both, that much must be left to the reader's own observation and experience. I have already touched, in treating on the soil, upon the corn trade of England, but nothing can be said with any certainty concerning the quantities of wheat, barley, rye, peas, beans, vetches, oats, and other horse grain growing in the kingdom. Excellent institutions for the improvement of agriculture, are now common in England, and their members are so public spirited

ENGLAND.

spirited as to print periodical accounts of their discoveries and experiments, which serve to shew that both agriculture and gardening can admit to be carried to a much higher state of perfection, than they are in at present. Honey and saffron are natives of England. It is almost needless to mention to the most uninformed reader, in what plenty the most excellent fruits, apples, pears, plums, cherries, peaches, apricots, nectarines, currants, gooseberries, rasberries, and other hortulane productions, grow here, and what vast quantities of cyder, perry, metheglin, and the like liquors, are made in some counties. The cyder, when kept, and made of proper apples, and in a particular manner, is often preferred, by judicious palates, to French white wine. It is not enough to mention those improvements, did we not observe that the natives of England have made the different fruits of all the world their own, sometimes by simple culture, but often by hot beds, and other means of forcing nature. The English pine-apples are delicious, and now plentiful. The same may be said of other natives of the East and West Indies, Persia and Turkey. The English grapes are pleasing to the taste, but their flavour is not exalted enough for making of wine, and indeed wet weather injures the flavour of all the other fine fruits raised here. Our kitchen gardens abound with all sorts of greens, roots, and sallads, in perfection, such as artichokes, asparagus, cauliflowers, cabbage, coleworts, brocoli, peas, beans, kidney beans, spinage, beets, lettuce, cellary, endive, turnips, carrots, potatoes, mushrooms, leeks, onions and shallots.

Woad for dying is cultivated in Bucks and Bedfordshire, as hemp and flax is in other counties. In nothing, however, have the English been more successful, than in the cultivation of clover, cinquefoil, trefoil, saintfoin, lucern, and other meliorating grasses for the soil. It belongs to a botanist to recount the various kinds of useful and salutary herbs, shrubs and roots, that grow in different parts of England. The soil of Kent, Essex, Surry, and Hampshire, is most favourable to the difficult and tender culture of hops, which is now become a very considerable article of trade.

With regard to animal productions, I shall begin with the quadrupeds. The English oxen are large and fat, but some prefer for the table the smaller breed of the Scotch, and the Welch cattle, after grazing in English pastures. The English horses, upon the whole, are the best of any in the world, whether we regard their spirit, strength, swiftness, or docility. Incredible have been the pains taken by all ranks, from the monarch down to the peasant, for improving the breed of this

favourite

favourite and noble animal, and the fuccefs has been anfwerable, for they now unite all the qualities and beauties of Indian, Perfian, Arabian, Spanifh, and other foreign horfes. It is no uncommon thing for an Englifh horfe, mare, or gelding, though not of the race kind, to run above 20 miles within the hour, and they have been known to do it in a carriage. The irrefiftible fpirit and weight of the Englifh cavalry, renders them the beft in the world in war: and an Englifh hunter will perform incredible things in a fox or ftag-chace. Thofe which draw equipages on the ftreets of London, are particularly beautiful, and a fet often cofts 1000l. a ftronger and a heavier breed is employed for other draughts. I muft not omit that the exportation of horfes to France, and other countries, where they fell for large prices, has of late become a confiderable article of commerce. It is hard to fay how far this traffic with our natural enemies is allowable, but there is certainly lefs danger attending it, as the animals are commonly gelded. The breed of affes and mules begin likewife to be improved and encouraged in England.

The Englifh fheep are of two kinds, thofe that are valuable for their fleece, and thofe that are proper for the table. The former are very large, and their fleeces conftitute the original ftaple commodity of England. I have been credibly informed, that in fome counties the inhabitants are as curious in their breed of rams, as in thofe of their horfes and dogs, and that in Lincolnfhire, particularly, it is no uncommon thing for one of thofe animals to fell for 30l. It muft, however, be owned, that thofe large fat fheep are very rank eating. It is thought that in England twelve millions of fleeces are fhorn annually, which, at a medium of 2s. a fleece, makes 1,200,000l. It is fuppofed, however, that by the fall of the value of the fleeces, a fourth part of this fum ought to be deducted at prefent. The other kind of fheep, which are fed upon the downs, fuch as thofe of Banftead, Bagfhot-heath, and Devonfhire, where they have, what the farmers call, a fhort bite, is little, if at all, inferior in flavour and fweetnefs, to venifon.

The Englifh maftiffs and bulldogs, are the ftrongeft and fierceft of the canine fpecies in the world, but either from the change of foil, or feeding, they degenerate in foreign climates. James I. of England, by way of experiment, turned out two Englifh bulldogs, upon one of his moft terrible lions in the Tower, and they laid him on his back. The maftiff, however, is the preferable creature, having all the courage of the bulldog, without its ferocity, and he is particularly diftinguifhed for his fidelity and docility. All the different fpecies of dogs, which abound in other countries (and are needless to be enumerated here) for the field, as well as domestic uses, are to be found in England.

What I have observed of the degeneracy of the English dogs in foreign countries, is applicable to the English game cocks, which afford much barbarous diversion to our sportsmen. The courage and ferocity of those birds is astonishing, and one of the true breed never leaves the pit alive without victory. The proprietors and feeders of this generous animal, are likewise extremely curious as to his blood and pedigree.

Tame fowls are pretty much the same in England, as in other countries; turkies, peacocks, common poultry, such as cocks, pullets, and capons, geese, swans, ducks, and tame pigeons. The wild sort are bustards, wild geese, wild ducks, teal, wigeon, plover, pheasants, partridges, woodcocks, in the season, growse, quail, landrail, snipe, wood-pigeons, hawks of different kinds, kites, owls, herons, crows, rooks, ravens, magpies, jackdaws and jays, blackbirds, thrushes, nightingales, gold-finches, linnets, larks, and a great variety of small birds, particularly canary birds, which breed in England. The wheat-ear is by many preferred to the ortolan, for the delicacy of its flesh and flavour, and is peculiar to England.

Few countries are better supplied than England with river and sea-fish. Her rivers and ponds contain plenty of salmon, trout, eels, pike, perch, smelts, carp, tench, barble, gudgeons, roach, dace, mullet, bream, plaice, flounders, and craw-fish, besides a delicate lake fish, called char, which is found in some fresh water lakes of Wales and Cumberland, and as some say no where else. The sea-fish are cod, mackarel, haddock, whiting, herrings, pilchards, skaite, soles. The John Dory, found towards the western coast, is reckoned a great delicacy, as is the red mullet. Several other fish are found on the same coasts. As to shell-fish, they are chiefly oysters, the propagation of which, upon their proper banks, requires a peculiar culture. Lobsters, crabs, and shrimps, and escallops, one of the most delicious of shell-fishes, cockles, wilks, or periwinkles, and muscles, with many other small shell-fish, abound in the English seas. The whales chiefly visit the northern coast, but great numbers of porpusses and seals appear in the channel. After all, the English have been, perhaps, with great justice, accused of not paying proper attention to their fisheries, which are confined to a few inconsiderable towns in the west of England. The best fish that comes to the tables of the great in London, are sold by the Dutch to English boats, and that industrious people even take them upon the English coast. Great attention, it is true, has been

paid

paid within these 30 years past, by the English, to this important concern. Many public spirited noblemen, and gentlemen, formed themselves into a company for carrying on a British fishery. Large sums were subscribed, and paid with unbounded generosity. Busses and other vessels were built, and the most pleasing prospects of success presented themselves to the public. They were, however, unaccountably disappointed, though it is hard to say from what cause, unless it was, that the price of English labour was too dear for bringing the commodity to the market, upon the same terms as the Dutch, whose herrings were actually surpassed in the curing by the British.

With regard to reptiles, such as adders, vipers, snakes, and worms, and insects, such as ants, gnats, wasps, and flies, England is pretty much upon a par with the rest of Europe, and the difference, if any, becomes more proper for natural history, than geography.

POPULATION, INHABITANTS, MANNERS, CUSTOMS, AND DIVERSIONS. } The exemption of the English constitution, from the despotic powers exercised in foreign nations, not excepting republics, is one great reason why it is very difficult to ascertain the number of inhabitants in England, and yet it is certain that this might occasionally be done, by parliament, without any violation of public liberty. With regard to political calculations, they must be very fallible, when applied to England. The prodigious influx of foreigners, who settle in the nation, the evacuations of inhabitants to America, their return from thence, the vast numbers of hands employed in shipping, and the late demand of men for the East Indies, and for settling our new conquests, are all of them matters that render any calculation extremely precarious. Upon the whole, I am apt to think that England is more populous, than the estimators of her inhabitants are willing to allow. The late war, which broke out with France and Spain, annually employed above 200,000 Englishmen, exclusive of Scotch and Irish, by sea and land, and in its progress carried off, by various means, very near that number. The decay of population was indeed sensibly felt, but not in comparison to what it was during the wars in queen Anne's reign, though not half of the numbers were then employed in the sea and land service. Great-Britain indeed was obliged to furnish large contingents of men to the confederate army, yet not above half of them were her own subjects. I mention those conjectures, partly on the strength of the public accounts, and partly from undisputed facts, which some now alive may remember, as the nobility, and even ministers of state, often had their servants pressed from behind

behind their coaches, to supply the sea and land-service, an expedient to which we were not reduced in the late war.

At the same time I am not of opinion, that England is at present naturally more populous, than it was in the reign of Charles I. though she is accidentally so. The English, of former ages, were strangers to the excessive use of spirituous liquors, and other modes of living, that are destructive of propagation. On the other hand, the vast quantities of cultivated lands in England, since those times, undoubtedly must have been favourable to mankind, though upon an average, perhaps, a married couple has not such a numerous progeny now, as formerly. I will take the liberty to make another observation, which falls within the cognizance of almost every man, and that is the incredible encrease of foreign names upon our parish books, and public lists, compared to what they were even in the reign of George I.

After what has been premised, it would be presumptuous to pretend to ascertain the number of inhabitants in England and Wales, but in my own private opinion, there cannot be fewer than seven millions, and that they are daily encreasing. The fallibility of political calculations, appears in a very striking light in those of the population of London, because it is impossible to fix it upon any of the known rules or proportions of births and burials. Calculators have been not only mistaken in applying those rules to London, and, as they are called, the bills of mortality, but even in topical matters, because about 100,000 inhabitants, at the very gates of London, do not lie within the bills of mortality.

Englishmen, in their persons, are generally well-sized, regularly featured, commonly fair, rather than otherwise, and florid in their complexions. It is, however, to be presumed, that the vast numbers of foreigners that are intermingled and intermarried with the natives, have given a cast to their persons and complexions, different from those of their ancestors, 150 years ago. The women, in their shapes, features, and complexion, appear so graceful and lovely, that England may be termed the native country of female beauty; and it has been also observed, that the women of Lancashire and some other counties, display a manifest superiority in these respects. But besides the external graces so peculiar to the women in England, they are still more to be valued for their prudent behaviour, thorough cleanliness, and a tender affection for their husbands and children. Of all people in the world the English keep themselves the most cleanly. Their nerves are so delicate, that people of both sexes are sometimes forcibly, nay mortally affected by imagination, insomuch, that before the practice of inoculation for the small-pox took place, it was thought improper to mention that loathsome disease, by its true name, in any polite company.

This over sensibility is one of the sources of those oddities, which so strongly characterize the English nation. An apprehension of dying a beggar, often kills them in the midst of plenty and prosperity. They magnify the slightest appearances into realities, and bring the most distant dangers immediately home to themselves; and yet when real danger approaches, no people face it with greater resolution, or constancy of mind. A groundless paragraph, in a news-paper, has been known to affect the stocks, and consequently public credit, to a considerable degree, and their credulity goes so far, that England may be termed the paradise of quacks and empirics, in all arts and professions. In short, the English feel, as if it really existed, every evil in mind, body, and estate, which they form in their imagination. At particular intervals, they are sensible of this absurdity, and run into a contrary extremity, striving to banish it by dissipation, riot, intemperance, and diversions. They are fond, for the same reason, of clubs, and convivial associations, and when these are kept within the bounds of temperance and moderation, they prove the best cures for those mental evils, which are so peculiar to the English, that foreigners have pronounced them to be national.

The same observations hold with regard to the higher orders of life, which must be acknowledged to have undergone a remarkable change since the accession of the House of Hanover, especially of late years. The English nobility and gentry, of great fortunes, now assimilate their manners to those of foreigners, with whom they cultivate a more frequent intercourse than their forefathers did. They do not now travel only as pupils, to bring home the vices of the countries they visit, under the tuition, perhaps, of a despicable pedant, or family dependant. They travel for the purposes of society, and at the more advanced ages of life, while their judgments are mature, and their passions regulated. This has enlarged society in England, which foreigners now visit as commonly as Englishmen visited them, and the effects of the intercourse become daily more visible, especially as it is not now, as formerly, confined to one sex.

Such of the English noblemen and gentlemen, as do not strike into those high walks of life, affect rather what we call a snug, than a splendid way of living. They study and understand better than any people in the world, conveniency in their houses, gardens, equipages, and estates, and they spare no cost to purchase it. It has, however, been observed, that

this

this turn renders them less communicative than they ought to be, but, on the other hand, the few connections they form, are sincere, chearful, and indissoluble. The like habits descend pretty far into the lower ranks, and are often discernible among tradesmen. This love of snugness and conveniency, may be called the ruling passion of the English people, and is the ultimate end of all their application, labours and fatigues, which are incredible. A good œconomist, with a brisk run of trade, is generally, when turned of 50, in a condition to retire from business, that is, either to purchase an estate, or to settle his money in the funds. He then commonly resides in a comfortable house in the country, often his native county, buys a good gelding, wears a laced hat, and expects to be treated on the footing of a gentleman; his stile of living, however, being always judiciously suited to his circumstances.

Few people in the world know better than tradesmen, and men of business, in England, how to pay their court to their customers, and employers, nay even by bribes, and sometimes becoming tributary to their servants. Those arts they consider only as the means of acquiring that independence, the pride of which too commonly leads them into a contrary extreme, even that of thinking themselves under no obligation from the rules of decency, duty and subordination. This carries them to that petulance, which is so offensive to strangers, and though encouraged through the want of education, has its root in the noblest of principles, badly understood, I mean that right which the laws of England give to every man over his own property. The same laws, at the same time, take no cognizance of the abuse of liberty, if not carried into an actual breach of the peace, so that every Englishman has a copious range for unpunished ill-manners, and unprovoked insolence. This licentiousness, or abuse of freedom, is carried in England to an astonishing height, and seems to be epidemical. It is the only public evil, that instead of losing, gathers strength, and what is to be lamented, its violence is always in proportion to the mildness of the government, and its cautious execution of the laws, so that it may be properly considered as a mode of that riotous dissipation I have already mentioned.

The over sensibility of the English, is discovered in nothing more than in the vast subscriptions for public charities, raised by all degrees of both sexes. An Englishman feels all the pains which a fellow creature suffers, and poor and miserable objects are relieved in England with a liberality that sometime or other may prove injurious to industry, because it takes from the lower ranks the usual motives of labour, that they may save somewhat for themselves and families, against the days of pain or sickness. The very people who contribute to those collections, are assessed in proportion to their property for their parochial poor, who have a legal demand for a maintenance, insomuch that there can be no beggar in England but through choice or indolence; and upwards of three millions sterling is said to be collected yearly in this country for charitable purposes. The institutions however of extra-parochial infirmaries, hospitals, and the like, are in some cases reprehensible. The vast sums bestowed in building them, the contracts made by their governors, and even the election of physicians, who thereby acquire credit, which is the same as profit, very often begets heats and cabals, which are very different from the purposes of disinterested charity, owing to the violent attachments and prepossessions of friends, and too often even to party considerations.

Notwithstanding those noble provisions which would banish poverty from any other country, the streets of London, and the highways of England, abound with objects of distress, who beg in defiance of the laws which render the practice severely punishable. This is owing to the manner in which the common people live, who consider the food to be uneatable which in other countries would be thought luxurious.

The English, though irascible, are the most placable people in the world, and will often sacrifice part of their interest rather than proceed to extremity. They are easily prevailed upon to forgive by submission, and they carry this lenity too far, by accepting of professions of sorrow published in advertisements by those who offend them, and who seldom are sincere; nay, often laugh at the easiness of their prosecutors, for dismissing them so gently. The unsuspecting nature of the English, and their honest open manners, especially of those in the mercantile way, render them dupes in several respects. They attend to projectors, and no scheme is so ridiculous that will not find abettors in England. They listen to the voice of misfortunes in trade, whether real or pretended, deserved or accidental, and generously contribute to the relief of the parties even by replacing them, often in a more creditable condition than ever. The lowest bred of the English, are capable of those and the like generous actions, but they often make an ostentatious display of their own merits, which diminishes their value. There is among the English of all ranks, a most unpardonable preference given to wealth, over all other considerations. Riches, both in public and private, compensate for the absence of every good quality. This offensive failing arises partly from the democratical part of their constitution, which makes the possession of property a qualification for the legiflature, and almoft every other species of magiftracy, government, honours, and diftinctions.

The fame attention to property operates in many other shapes among the lower claffes, who think it gives them a right to be rude and difregardful of all about them, nor are the higher orders exempt from the fame failing. The fame principle often influences their exterior appearances. Noblemen of the firft rank have been often feen laying bets with butchers and coblers at horfe-races and boxing-matches. Gentlemen and merchants of vaft property are not to be diftinguifhed either by their drefs or converfation from the meaneft of their fervants, and a wager offered to be ftaked in ready money againft a pennylefs antagonift, is generally a decifive argument in public company.

An Englifhman of thorough education and reading, is the moft accomplifhed gentleman in the world, and underftands arts and fciences the beft. He is however fhy and retentive in his communications even to difguft, and a man may be in company with him for months without difcovering that he knows any thing beyond the verge of a farm yard, or above the capacity of a horfe jockey. This unamiable coldnefs is fo far from being affected, that it is a part of their natural conftitution. Living learning and genius meets with very little regard, even from the firft rate of Englifhmen: and it is not unufual for them to throw afide the beft productions of literature, if they are not acquainted with the author. While the ftate diftinction of Whig and Tory fubfifted, the heads of each party affected to patronize men of literary abilities, but the pecuniary encouragements given them were but very moderate, and the very few who met with preferment in the ftate, might have earned them by a competent knowledge of bufinefs, and that pliability which the dependents in office generally poffefs. We fcarce have an inftance even in the munificent reign of queen Anne, or of her predeceffors, who owed fo much to the prefs, of a man of genius being, as fuch, made eafy in his circumftances. Mr. Addifon had about 300 l. a year of the public money to affift him in his travels, and Mr. Pope though a Roman catholic was offered, but did not accept of, the like penfion from Mr. Craggs, the whig fecretary of ftate, when it was remarked that his tory friend and companion the earl of Oxford, when fole minifter, did nothing for him, but bewail his misfortune in being a papift. This reproach upon governmental munificence is now wearing off under the patronage of his majefty and his minifters.

The unevenneſs of the Engliſh in their converſation is very remarkable: ſometimes it is delicate, ſprightly, and replete with true wit; ſometimes it is ſolid, ingenious and argumentative; ſometimes it is cold and phlegmatic, and borders upon diſguſt, and all in the ſame perſon. In their convivial meetings they are generally noiſy, and their wit is often offenſive, while the loudeſt are the moſt applauded. Courage is a quality that ſeems to be congenial to the Engliſh nation. Boys, before they can ſpeak, diſcover that they know the proper guards in boxing with their fiſts; a quality that perhaps is peculiar to the Engliſh, and is ſeconded by a ſtrength of arm that few other people can exert. This gives the Engliſh ſoldiers an infinite ſuperiority in all battles that are to be decided by the bayonet ſcrewed upon the muſquet. The Engliſh courage has likewiſe the property, under able commanders, of being equally paſſive as active. Their ſoldiers will keep up their fire in the mouth of danger, but when they deliver it, it has a moſt dreadful effect upon their enemies; and in naval engagements they are unequalled. The Engliſh are not remarkable for invention, though they are for their improvements upon the inventions of others, and in the mechanical arts, they excell all nations in the world. The intenſe application which an Engliſhman gives to a favourite ſtudy is incredible, and, as it were, abſorbs all his other ideas. This creates the numerous inſtances of mental abſences that are to be found in the nation.

All I have ſaid concerning the Engliſh, is to be underſtood of them in general as they are at preſent, for it is not to be diſſembled that every day produces ſtrong indications of great alterations in their manners. The vaſt fortunes made during the late and the preceding wars, the immenſe acquiſitions of territory by peace, and above all the amazing encreaſe of territorial as well as commercial property in the Eaſt Indies, have introduced a ſpecies of people among the Engliſh, who have become rich without induſtry, and by diminiſhing the value of gold and ſilver have created a new ſyſtem of finances in the nation. Time alone can ſhew the event: Hitherto the conſequences ſeem to have been unfavourable, as it has introduced among the commercial ranks a ſpirit of luxury and gaming that is attended with the moſt fatal effects, and an emulation among merchants and traders of all kinds, to equal, or ſurpaſs the nobility and the courtiers. The plain frugal manners of men of buſineſs which prevailed ſo lately as the acceſſion of the preſent family to the crown, are now diſregarded for taſteleſs extravagance in dreſs and equipage, and the moſt expenſive amuſements and diverſions, not only in the capital but all over the trading towns of the kingdom.

Even

ENGLAND.

Even the customs of the English have, since the beginning of this century, undergone an almost total alteration. Their antient hospitality subsists but in few places in the country, or is revived only upon electioneering occasions. Many of their favourite diversions are now disused. Those remaining are operas, dramatic exhibitions, ridottos, and sometimes masquerades in or near London; but concerts of music, and card and dancing assemblies are common all over the kingdom. I have already mentioned stag and fox hunting and horse-races, of which the English of all denominations are fond, even to infatuation. Somewhat however may be offered by way of apology for those diversions: The intense application which the English give to business, their sedentary lives, and luxurious diet require exercise, and some think that their excellent breed of horses is encreased and improved by those amusements. The English are remarkably cool, both in losing and winning at play, but the former is often attended with acts of suicide. An Englishman will rather murder himself than bring a sharper, who he knows has fleeced him, to condign punishment, even though warranted by law. Next to horse-racing, and hunting, cock-fighting, to the reproach of the nation, is a favourite diversion, among the great, as well as the vulgar. Multitudes of both assemble round the pit, at one of those matches, and enjoy the pangs and death of the generous animal, every spectator being concerned in a bet, sometimes of high sums. The athletic diversion of cricket is still kept up in the southern and western parts of England, and is sometimes practised by people of the highest rank. It is performed by a person who with a clumsy wooden bat, defends a wicket raised of two slender sticks, with one across, which is attacked by another person, who endeavours to beat it down, with a hard leather ball, from a certain stand. The farther the distance is to which the ball is driven, the oftener the defender is able to run between the wicket and the stand. This is called gaining so many notches, and he who gets the most is the victor. Many other pastimes are common in England, some of them of a very robust nature, such as cudgelling, wrestling, bowls, skittles, quoits, and prison-base; not to mention duck-hunting, foot, and ass-races, dancing, puppet-shews, May garlands, and above all, ringing of bells, a species of music, which the English boast they have brought into an art. The barbarous diversions of boxing and prize-fighting, which were as frequent in England, and equally inhuman, as the shews of gladiators in Rome, are now prohibited, and all places of public diversions, excepting the royal theatres, are under regulations by act of parliament. Other diversions, which are common to other countries, such as tennis, fives, billiards, cards, swimming, angling, fowling, coursing, and the like, are familiar to the English. Two kinds, and those highly laudable, are perhaps peculiar to them, and these are rowing and sailing. The latter, if not introduced, was patronized and encouraged, by his present majesty's father, the late prince of Wales, and may be considered as a national improvement. The English are excessively fond of skaiting, in which, however, they are not very expert, but they are adventurous in it often to the danger and loss of their lives. The game acts have taken from the common people a great fund of diversion, though without answering the purposes of the rich, for the farmers, and the country people destroy the game in their nets, which they dare not kill with the gun. This monopoly of game, among so free a people as the English, has been considered in various lights.

DRESS.] In the dress of both sexes, before the present reign of George III. they followed the French; but that of the military officers partook of the German, in compliment to his late majesty. The English, at present, bid fair to be the dictators of dress to the French themselves, at least with regard to elegance, neatness, and richness of attire. People of quality and fortune, of both sexes, appear on high occasions, in cloth of gold and silver, the richest brocades, sattins, silks, and velvets, both flowered and plain, and it is to the honour of the court, that the foreign manufactures of all those are discouraged. Some of those rich stuffs are said to be brought to as great perfection in England, as they are in France, or any other nation. The quantities of jewels that appear on public occasions are incredible, especially since the vast acquisitions of the English in the East-Indies. The same nobility, and persons of distinction, on ordinary occasions, dress like creditable citizens, that is, neat, clean, and plain, in the finest cloth, and the best of linen. The full dress of a clergyman consists of his gown, cassock, scarf, beaver-hat and rose, all of black; his undress is a dark grey frock, and plain linen. The physicians, the formality of whose dress, in large tie perukes, and swords, was formerly remarkable, if not ridiculous, begin now to dress like other gentlemen, and men of business, that is, to wear a plain suit of superfine cloth, excellent linen and wigs, that suit their complections, and the form of their faces. Few Englishmen, tradesmen, merchants and lawyers, as well as men of landed property, are without some passion for the sports of the field, on which occasions they dress with remarkable propriety, in a light frock, narrow brimmed hat, a short bob wig, jockey boots, and buckskin, or shag breeches. The people of England love rather to be neat than fine in

their

their apparel; but since the accession of his present majesty, the dresses at court, on solemn occasions, are superb beyond description. Few even of the lowest tradesmen, on Sundays, carry about them less than 10 l. in cloathing, comprehending hat, wig, stockings, shoes and linen, and even many beggars in the street appear decent in their dress. In short, none but the most abandoned of both sexes are otherwise; and the appearance of a man in holiday times, is commonly an indication of his industry and morals.

RELIGION.] Eusebius and other antient writers, positively assert, that Christianity was first preached in South Britain by the apostles and their disciples. It is unnecessary to repeat what has been said in the Introduction respecting the rise and fall of the church of Rome in Europe. I shall only observe in this place, that John Wickliffe, an Englishman, educated at Oxford in the reign of Edward III. has the honour of being the first person in Europe who publicly called in question, and boldly refuted those doctrines which had passed for certain during so many ages; and that the established religion in England, which had its rise under Henry VIII. is reformed from the errors of popery, and approaches nearer to the primitive christianity, being equally removed from superstition and indelicacy in its worship, and as void of bigotry, as of licentiousness, in its practice. The constitution of the church is episcopal, and is governed by bishops, whose benefices were converted, by the Norman conqueror, into temporal baronies, in right of which, every bishop has a seat and vote in the house of peers. The benefices of the inferior clergy, are now freehold, but in many places their tithes are impropriated in favour of the laity. The œconomy of the church of England, has been accused for the inequality of its livings; some of them, especially in Wales, being too small to maintain a clergyman, especially if he has a family, with any tolerable decency; but this, perhaps, is unavoidable, and very probably never can be entirely remedied, though the crown, as well as private persons, has done great things towards the augmentation of poor livings.

The dignitaries of the church of England, such as deans, prebends, and the like, have generally large incomes; some of them exceeding in value those of bishoprics, for which reason the revenues of a rich deanery, or other living, is often annexed to a poor bishopric. At present, the clergy of the church of England, as to temporal matters, are in a most flourishing situation, because the value of their tithes encreases with the improvements of lands, which of late has been amazing in England. The sovereigns of England, ever since the reign of

Henry VIII. have been called in public writs, the supreme heads of the church; but this title conveys no spiritual meaning, as it only denotes the regal power, to prevent any ecclesiastical differences, or in other words, to substitute the king in place of the pope, before the reformation, with regard to temporalities, and the internal œconomy of the church. The kings of England never intermeddle in ecclesiastical disputes, and are contented to give a sanction to the legal rights of the clergy.

The church of England, under this description, of the monarchical power over it, is governed by two archbishops, and twenty-four bishops, besides the bishop of Sodor and Man, who not being possessed of an English barony, does not sit in the house of peers*. The two archbishops, are those of Canterbury and York, who are both dignified with the address of ' your grace.' The former is the first peer of the realm, as well as metropolitan of the English church. He takes precedence next to the royal family, of all dukes and officers of state. He is enabled to hold ecclesiastical courts upon all affairs that were formerly cognizable in the court of Rome, when not repugnant to the law of God, or the king's prerogative. He has the privilege consequently of granting, in certain cases, licenses and dispensations, together with the probate of wills, when the party dying is worth upwards of five pounds. Besides his own diocese, he has under him the bishops of London, Winchester, Ely, Lincoln, Rochester, Litchfield and Coventry, Hereford, Worcester, Bath and Wells, Salisbury, Exeter,

---

* To the following list, I have subjoined the sum each see is charged in the king's books; for though that sum is far from being the real annual value of the see, yet it assists in forming a comparative estimate between the revenues of each see with those of another.

ARCHBISHOPRICS,

Canterbury, — £2682 : 12 : 2 | York, — — £1610 : 0 : 0

BISHOPRICS,

London, — —	1000 : 0 : 0	Chichester, — —	677 : 1 : 3
Durham, —	1821 : 1 : 3	St. Asaph, —	187 : 11 : 8
Winchester —	2873 : 18 : 1	Salisbury, — —	1385 : 5 : 9
These three bishoprics take precedency of all others in England, and the others according to the seniority of their consecrations.		Bangor, — —	131 : 16 : 3
		Norwich, — —	834 : 11 : 7
		Gloucester, — —	315 : 7 : 3
		Landaff, — —	154 : 14 : 2
Ely, — —	2134 : 18 : 6	Lincoln, — —	894 : 18 : 1
Bath and Wells,	533 : 1 : 3	Bristol, — —	294 : 11 : 0
Hereford, —	768 : 11 : 0	Carlisle, — —	531 : 4 : 9
Rochester, —	358 : 4 : 0	Exeter, — —	500 : 0 : 0
Litchfield & Coventry	559 : 17 : 3	Peterborough, —	414 : 17 : 8
Chester, — —	420 : 1 : 8	Oxford, — —	381 : 11 : 0
Worcester, — —	929 : 13 : 3	St. David's, — —	426 : 2 : 1

Exeter, Chichester, Norwich, Gloucester, Oxford, Peterborough, Bristol; and, in Wales, St. David's, Landaff, St. Asaph and Bangor.

The archbishop of Canterbury has, by the constitution and laws of England, such extensive powers, that ever since the death of archbishop Laud (whose character will be hereafter given) the government of England has thought proper to raise to that dignity, none but men of very moderate principles, and of very inoffensive abilities. This practice has been attended with excellent effects, with regard to the public tranquillity of the church, and consequently of the state.

The archbishop of York takes place of all dukes, not of the blood royal, and of all officers of state, the lord chancellor excepted. He has in his province, besides his own diocese, the bishoprics of Durham, Carlisle, Chester, and Sodor and Man. In Northumberland, he has the power of a palatine, and jurisdiction in all criminal proceedings.

The bishops are addressed Your lordships, stiled Right reverend fathers in God, and precede as barons on all public occasions. They have all the privileges of peers, and the bishoprics of London, Winchester, Durham, Salisbury, Ely and Lincoln, require no additional revenues to support their prelates in the rank of noblemen. English bishops are to examine and ordain priests and deacons, to consecrate churches and burying-places, and to administer the rite of confirmation. Their jurisdiction relates to the probation of wills; to grant administration of goods of such as die intestate; to take care of perishable goods when no one will administer; to collate to benefices; to grant institutions to livings; to defend the liberties of the church; and to visit their own dioceses once in three years.

Deans and prebends of cathedrals, have been already mentioned, but it would perhaps be difficult to assign their utility in the church, farther than to add to the pomp of worship, and to make provision for clergymen of eminence and merit. England contains about sixty archdeacons, whose office is to visit the chuches twice or thrice every year, but their offices are less lucrative than they are honourable. Subordinate to them are the rural deans, formerly stiled arch presbyters, who signify the bishop's pleasure to his clergy, the lower clafs of which consists of priests and deacons.

The ecclesiastical government of England is, properly speaking, lodged in the convocation, which is a national representative or synod, and answers pretty near to the ideas we have of a parliament. They are convoked at the same time with every parliament, and their business is to consider of the state of the church, and to call those to an account who have advanced new opinions, inconsistent with the doctrines of the church of England. Some high flying clergymen, during the reign of queen Ann, and in the beginning of that of George I. raised the powers of the convocation to a height that was inconsistent with the principles of religious tolerancy, and indeed of civil liberty; so that the crown was obliged to exert its prerogative of calling the members together, and of dissolving them, and ever since they have not been permitted to sit for any time, in which they could do business.

The court of arches is the most ancient consistory of the province of Canterbury, and all appeals in church matters, from the judgment of the inferior courts, are directed to this. The processes run in the name of the judge, who is called dean of the arches; and the advocates, who plead in this court, must be doctors of the civil law. The court of audience has the same authority with this, to which the archbishop's chancery was formerly joined. The prerogative court is that wherein wills are proved, and administrations taken out. The court of peculiars, relating to certain parishes, have a jurisdiction among themselves, for the probate of wills, and are therefore exempt from the bishop's courts. The see of Canterbury has no less than fifteen of these peculiars. The court of delegates receives its name from its consisting of commissioners delegated or appointed by the royal commission; but it is no standing court. Every bishop has also a court of his own, called the consistory court. Every archdeacon has likewise his court, as well as the dean and chapter of every cathedral.

The church of England is, beyond any other church, tolerant in its principles. Moderation is its governing character, and it excludes no sect of Christians from the exercise of their respective religious worship. Without entering upon the motives of its reformation under Henry VIII. it is certain, that episcopal government, excepting under the time of usurpation, has ever since prevailed in England. The wisdom of acknowledging the king the head of the church, is conspicuous in discouraging all religious persecution and intolerancy, and if religious sectaries have multiplied in England, it is from the same principle that civil lincentiousness has prevailed; I mean a tenderness in matters that can affect either conscience or liberty. The bias which the clergy had towards popery, in the reign of Henry VIII. and his son, and even so late as that of Elizabeth, occasioned an interposition of the civil power, for a farther reformation. Thence arose the puritans, so called from their affecting a singular purity of life and manners. Many of them were worthy pious men, and some of them good patriots.

patriots. Their descendants are the modern presbyterians, who retain the same character, and have true principles of civil and religious liberty, only with some differences as to church discipline, and the modes of worship. Their doctrine, like the church of Scotland, was originally derived from the Geneva plan, instituted by Calvin, and tended to an abolition of episcopacy, and to vesting the government of the church in a parity of presbyters. The presbyterians, however, are now considered as being dissenters. The baptists form another sect of dissenters. These do not believe that infants are proper objects of baptism, and in the baptism of adults, they practise immersion into water. Blended with these are the independents, but it is hard to say what are the particular tenets of those sects, so much have they deviated from their original principles, and so greatly do their professors differ from each other. The moderate clergy of the church of England, treat the presbyterians with affection and friendship; and though the hierarchy of their church, and the character of bishops, are capital points in their religion, they consider their differences with the presbyterians, and even with the baptists, as not being very material to salvation, nor indeed do many of the established church think that they are strictly and conscientiously bound to believe the doctrinal parts of the thirty-nine articles, which they are obliged to subscribe before they can enter into holy orders. Some of them have of late contended in writings, that all subscriptions to religious systems are repugnant to the spirit of Christianity, and to reformation.

The methodists are a sect of a late institution, and their founder is generally looked upon to be Mr. George Whitefield, a divine of the church of England, but it is difficult to describe the tenets of this numerous sect. All we know is, that they pretend to great fervour and devotion, that their founder, who died lately, thought that the form of ecclesiastical worship, and prayers, whether taken from a common prayer book, or poured forth extempore, was a matter of indifference, and he accordingly made use of both forms. His followers are rigid observers of the thirty-nine articles, and many of them profess themselves to be calvinists. But even this sect is split among themselves, some of them acknowledging Mr. Whitefield, and others Mr. Wesley, for their leader; not to mention a variety of subordinate sects (some of whom are from Scotland) who have their separate followers, both at London, and in the country of England. I am to observe, that there seems at present to be among those sectaries, and dissenters, a vast relaxation of ecclesiastical discipline, which is chiefly owing to disunion among themselves, and in some measure to the principle

of

of free-thinking, the professors of which are presbyterians or independents, and consider all systems of religious government, and tests of faith, as so many fetters upon reason and conscience.

The quakers form a numerous sect of dissenters in England, and perhaps if their profest principles were to undergo a very strict examination, they would appear to be founded in free-thinking, though they pretend to be guided by internal revelation, dictated by the spirit of God. That revelation, and that spirit, however, are just what they please to make them, and if they mean any thing, it is an abstraction from all sensual ideas, in treating of the Christian religion, and its mysteries, for they attempt to allegorize all the facts in the gospel. They disclaim all religious creeds made use of by other Christians, and all the modes of worship practised in other churches. They disregard the authority of the clergy, and refuse to pay tithes unless they are compelled by law. They neither use baptism, nor partake of the Lord's Supper. They affect a peculiar plainness of dress, both as to the form and the colours of their cloaths, and they publickly declaim against resistance, and the legality of going to war on any account. With regard to the resurrection of the body, and the doctrines of rewards and punishments hereafter, and many other capital points of Christianity, they have not yet explained themselves authentically.

Were all the other peculiarities of this sect to be described, a reader, not acquainted with it, would be apt to think it impossible, that it should associate with other Christians. Nothing however is more certain, than that the quakers are most excellent members of the community. The strictness of their morality makes amends for the oddities of their principles, and the simplicity of their living, for the wildness of their opinions. Their œconomy is admirable, for though none of them pretend to any coercive power, yet their censures are submitted to as implicitly, as if they were Romish bigots under an inquisition. The highest punishment is a kind of excommunication, which I shall not pretend to describe, but which is taken off upon repentance and amendment, and the party is readmitted into all the privileges of their body. Their government is truly republican, and admirably well adapted to their principles. They have an annual meeting, which is generally held at London, in the month of May, and this is resorted to by deputies from all parts of Great-Britain, Ireland, Holland, Germany, and the British plantations. In this meeting is examined the proceedings of their other meetings, which are monthly and quarterly. Indecencies of every kind are censured,

sured, contributions are received, accounts are examined, and discourses, exhortations, and sermons are delivered suitable to the exigency of the times, and their prevailing vices and immoralities. The good sense for which this sect is remarkable, renders their leaders more respectable, than those which royalty or power appoint over other communities. This, with the mildness of their behaviour, sobriety, and great industry, have raised them high in the esteem of the legislature, which has even indulged them by admitting of their affirmation, instead of an oath in the courts of justice.

I shall not here enter into their political history, or in what manner one of their number, William Penn, formed that admirable establishment of their order, which still subsists in Pensylvania. It is sufficient to observe, that it was found by experience, during the two last wars with France, that their principles were incompatible, with either civil or military government; and consequently, that, unless their enemies had been quakers likewise, they must have been masters of their country. This created great trouble with the mother country, and it unfortunately happened, that the quakers were as tenacious of their property, as of their principles. Necessity and danger, however, at last compelled them to contribute for their own defence, by their purses, though we do not find that they did it in their persons; from all which it appears that it would be impracticable to form quakers into a civil government of any kind.

The ignorance of Fox, and the first leaders of this sect, led the quakers into a thousand extravagancies, by agitations and convulsions of the body, which they termed the workings of the spirit. Barclay, Keith, and some other metaphysical heads, defended the doctrine, though they dropt the singularities of the profession. This softened the ridicule of the public, and Barclay's successors have omitted in their behaviour and appearance many of those unmeaning singularities. The quakers, it is true, in general, still retain the appellation of Friend, instead of Sir, and make use of Thou and Thee in discourse; neither are they very ready to pull off their hats, by way of civility or respect. They know, however, how to accommodate themselves to the common usages of life, upon particular emergencies, and the singularities of a quaker of address are now but just discernible, and can give no offence to politeness, unless they are affected.

It is impossible to say any thing with certainty concerning the number of quakers in England. In the beginning of the late reign they were estimated at 50,000; and I am apt to believe,

lieve, they are encreafed, though that encreafe is not perceptible, by their laying afide moſt of their fingularities. The regularity of their meetings is furprizing, and the admonitions which they give to their brethren, by circular letters, from their yearly meetings, are worthy imitation by the moſt civilized government. The payment of tithes is a kind of a ſtanding grievance, becauſe it is renewed every year. They are however ſteady in their oppoſition to it. They who pay them voluntarily, are always cenfured. The books relating to their religion, which they print, muſt be licenfed by a committee before they are difperfed.

Many families in England ſtill profefs the Roman catholic religion, and its exercife is under very mild and gentle reſtrictions. Though the penal laws againſt papiſts in England appear at firſt to be fevere, yet they are executed with fo much lenity, that a Roman catholic feels himſelf under few hardſhips. Legal evaſions are found out for their double taxes, upon their landed property, and, as they are fubject to none of the expences and troubles (unlefs voluntary) attending public offices, parliamentary elections, and the like burdens, the Engliſh Roman catholics are in general in good circumſtances, as to their private fortunes. The truth is, they know that a change of government, inſtead of bettering, would hurt their fituation, becauſe it would encreafe the jealoufy of the legiſlature, which would undoubtedly expofe them daily to greater burdens, and heavier penalties. This fenfible confideration has of late rendered the Roman catholics as dutiful and zealous fubjects as any his majeſty has, and their intereſt in election of members of parliament, which is confiderable, has for thefe 30 years paſt, commonly gone for the court. Scarcely any Engliſh Roman catholic, excepting thofe who were bred, or had ferved abroad, were engaged in the rebellion of the year 1745, and though thofe at home were moſt carefully obferved, few or none of them were found guilty of difloyal practices.

I fhould here take my leave of the ſtate of religion in England, were it not neceſſary to mention thofe who profefs no religion at all, and yet have a vaſt influence upon the circumſtances and ſtate of the eſtabliſhed church. Thefe go under the name of Free-thinkers, and they are divided into as many fects as Chriſtianity itſelf. Arians and Socinians, words well known to imply a difbelief of the doctrines of the church of England, with regard to the Trinity, ſhelter themfelves under the name of Free-thinkers. The Deiſt ſhakes himfelf loofe of all religious inſtitutions, by pleading Free-thinking. The Fatalift, who is a branch of deifm, and in fact fignifies the fame as a deist, does the like, and what is still worse, free-living is often the consequence of free-thinking, as is seen in the unbounded dissipation, debauchery and impiety of its professors. What the effects of this irreligion may prove, is hard to say, but it seems not to be so general at present as in any one reign since the revolution. This is in a great measure owing to the discouragement it meets with from the royal example, which has brought an attendance upon religious ordinances into credit, at the court and capital. Another circumstance, in favour of religion, is the noble provision, which the enjoyment of a bishopric, or a dignified station in the church makes, for the younger sons of noble families. The bench of bishops has, at no time since the reformation, been possessed by so many men of birth and quality; nor has it ever been known that so many young persons of rank and family, have been educated to the church, as at present.

LANGUAGE.] The English language is known to be a compound of almost every other language in Europe, particularly the Saxon, the French, and the Celtic. The Saxon, however, predominates, and the words that are borrowed from the French, being radically Latin, are common to other nations, particularly the Spaniards and the Italians. To describe it abstractedly, would be superfluous to an English reader, but relatively it enjoys all the properties, without many of the defects of other European languages. It is more energic, manly, and expressive, than either the French, or the Italian; more copious than the Spanish, and more eloquent than the German, or the other northern tongues. It is subject, however, to great provincialities in its accent, for the people of one county can scarcely understand those of another; but this happens in other countries. People of fortune and education in England, of both sexes, commonly either speak, or understand the French, and many of them, the Italian and Spanish; but it has been observed, that foreign nations have great difficulty in understanding the few English who talk Latin, which is perhaps the reason why that language is disused in England, even by the learned professions.

LEARNING AND LEARNED MEN.] England may be looked upon as another word for the seat of learning and the Muses. Her great Alfred cultivated both in the time of the Saxons, when barbarism and ignorance overspread the rest of Europe, nor has there since his time been wanting a continual succession of learned men, who have distinguished themselves by their writings or studies. These are so numerous, that a bare catalogue of their names, down to this day, would form a moderate volume.

The English institutions, for the benefit of study, partake of the character of their learning. They are solid and substantial, and provide for the ease, the disencumbrance, the peace, the plenty, and the conveniency of its professors; witness the two universities of Oxford and Cambridge, institutions that are not to be matched in the world, and which were respected even amidst the barbarous rage of civil war. The industrious Leland, who was himself a moving library, was the first who made a short collection of the lives and characters of those learned persons, who preceded the reign of his master Henry VIII. among whom he has inserted several of the blood royal of both sexes, particularly a son and daughter of the great Alfred, Editha, the queen of Edward the Confessor, and other Saxon princes, some of whom were equally devoted to Mars as the Muses.

In speaking of the dark ages, it would be unpardonable, if I should omit the mention of that prodigy of learning, and natural philosophy, Roger Bacon, who was the forerunner in science to the great Bacon, lord Verulam, as the latter was to Sir Isaac Newton. Among the other curious works ascribed to him by Leland, we find treatises upon the flux and reflux of the British sea, upon metallurgy, upon astronomy, cosmography, and upon the impediments of knowledge. He lived under Henry III. and died at Oxford in 1248. The honourable Mr. Walpole has preserved the memory of some noble and royal English authors, who have done honour to learning and the Muses, and to his work I must refer. Since the Reformation, England resembles a galaxy of literature *, and it is but doing justice to the memory of cardinal Wolsey, though otherwise a dangerous and profligate minister, to acknowledge that both his example and encouragement, laid the foundation of the polite arts, and the revival of classical learning in England. As many of the English clergy had different sentiments in religious matters, at the time of the reformation, encouragement was given to learned foreigners, to settle in England. Edward VI. during his short life, did a great deal for the encouragement of these foreigners, and shewed dispositions for cultivating the most useful parts of learning, had he lived. Learning, as well as liberty, suffered an almost total eclipse in England, during the bloody bigotted reign of queen Mary. Elizabeth, her sister, was herself a learned princess. She advanced many persons of consummate abilities, to high ranks, both in church and state, but she seems to have considered their literary accomplishments to have been only secondary to their civil.

---

* See the Biographia Britannica.

In this she shewed herself a great politician, but she would have been a more amiable queen, had she raised genius from obscurity; for though she was no stranger to Spencer's Muse, she suffered herself to be so much imposed upon, by an unfeeling minister, that the poet languished to death in obscurity. Though she tasted the beauties of the divine Shakespear, yet we know not that they were distinguished by any particular acts of her munificence, but her parsimony was nobly supplied by her favourite the earl of Essex, the politest scholar of his age, and his friend the earl of Southampton, who were patrons of genius.

The encouragement of learned foreigners in England, continued to the reign of James I. who was very munificent to Casaubon, and other foreign authors of distinction, even of different principles. He was himself no great author, but his example had a wonderful effect upon his subjects, for in his reign were formed those great masters of polemic divinity, whose works are almost inexhaustible mines of knowledge. Nor must it be forgot, that the second Bacon, whom I have already mentioned, was by him created viscount Verulam, and lord high chancellor of England. He was likewise the patron of Camden, and other historians, as well as antiquaries, whose works are to this day standards in those studies. Upon the whole, therefore, it cannot be denied, that English learning is under great obligations to James I.

His son Charles I. had a taste for the polite arts, especially sculpture, painting, and architecture. He was the patron of Rubens, Vandyke, Inigo Jones, and other eminent artists, so that had it not been for the civil wars, he would probably have converted his court and capital, into a second Athens, and the collections he made for that purpose, considering his pecuniary difficulties, were stupendous. His favourite, the duke of Buckingham, imitated him in that respect, and laid out the amazing sum of 400,000l. sterling, upon his cabinet of paintings and curiosities. The earl of Arundel was, however, the great Mæcenas of that age, and by the immense acquisitions he made of antiquities, especially his famous marble inscriptions, may stand upon a footing, as to the encouragement and utility of literature, with the greatest of the Medicean princes. Charles, and his court, had little or no relish for poetry. But such was his generosity in encouraging genius and merit of every kind, that he increased the salary of his poet laureat, the famous Ben Johnson, from 100 marks to 100l. per annum, and a tierce of Spanish wine; which salary is continued to this day.

The public encouragement of learning, and the arts, suffered indeed an eclipse, during the time of the civil wars, and the succeeding usurpation. Many very learned men, however, found their situations under Cromwell, though he was no stranger to their political sentiments, so easy, that they followed their studies, to the vast benefit of every branch of learning, and many works of vast literary merit, appeared even in those times of distraction. Usher, Willis, Harrington, Wilkins, and a prodigious number of other great names, were unmolested by that usurper, and he would even have filled the universities with literary merit, could he have done it with any degree of safety to his government.

The reign of Charles II. was chiefly distinguished by the great proficiency to which it carried natural knowledge, especially by the institution of the royal society. The king himself was an excellent judge of those studies, and though irreligious himself, England never abounded more with learned and able divines, than in his reign. He loved painting and poetry, but was far more munificent to the former than the latter. The incomparable Paradise Lost by Milton, was published in his reign, but so little read, that the impression did not pay the expence of 15 l. given by the bookseller for the copy. The reign of Charles II. notwithstanding the bad taste of his court in several of the polite arts, by some is reckoned the Augustan age in England, and is dignified with the names of Boyle, Halley, Hook, Sydenham, Harvey, Temple, Tillotson, Butler, Cowley, Waller, Dryden, Wycherley, and Otway. The pulpit assumed more majesty, a better stile, and truer energy, than it ever had known before. Classic literature recovered many of its native graces, and though England could not under him boast of a Jones, and a Vandyke, yet Sir Christopher Wren introdued a more general regularity, than ever had been known before in architecture, and many excellent English painters (for Lely and Kneller were foreigners) flourished in this reign.

That of James II. though he likewise had a taste for the fine arts, is chiefly distinguished in the province of literature, by those compositions that were published by the English divines against popery, and which, for strength of reasoning, and depth of erudition, never were equalled in any age or country.

The names of Newton and Locke adorned the reign of William III. a prince, who neither understood, nor loved learning, or genius in any shape. It flourished, however, in his reign, merely by the excellency of the soil, in which it had

had been planted. It has been obferved, that metaphyfical reafoning, and a fqueamifh fcepticifm in religious matters, prevailed too much, and this has been generally attributed to his indifference as to facred fubjects. Argumentation, however, thereby acquired, and has ftill preferved a far more rational tone in every province of literature, than it had before, efpecially in religion and philofophy.

The moft uninformed readers are not unacquainted with the improvements which learning, and all the polite arts, received under the aufpices of queen Anne, and which put her court at leaft on a footing with that of Lewis XIV. in its moft fplendid days. Many of the great men, who had figured in the reigns of the Stuarts and William, were ftill alive, and in the full exercife of their faculties, when a new race fprung up, in the republic of learning and the arts. Addifon, Prior, Pope, Swift, lord Bolingbroke, lord Shaftefbury, Arbuthnot, Congreve, Steele, Rowe, and many other excellent writers, both in verfe and profe, need but be mentioned to be admired, and the Englifh were as triumphant in literature as in war. Natural and moral philofophy kept pace with the polite arts, and even religious and political difputes contributed to the advancement of learning, by the unbounded liberty which the laws of England allow in fpeculative matters.

The minifters of George I. were the patrons of erudition, and fome of them were no mean proficients themfelves. I have already obferved, that in this reign a poet held the pen of firft fecretary of ftate, though Mr. Addifon's talents were very inadequate to the poft, and his temper ftill more.

Though George II. was himfelf no Mecænas, yet his reign yielded to none of the preceding, in the numbers of learned and ingenious men it produced. The bench of bifhops was never known to be fo well provided with able prelates, as it was in the early years of his reign, a full proof that his nobility and minifters were judges of literary qualifications. In other departments of erudition, the favour of the public generally fupplied the coldnefs of the court. After the rebellion in the year 1745, when Mr. Pelham was confidered as being firft minifter, this fcreen between government and literature, was in a great meafure removed, and men of genius began then to tafte the royal bounty.

The reign of his grandfon promifes to renew a golden age to learning and all the arts. The noble inftitution of a royal academy, and his majefty's generous munificence to men of merit, in every ftudy, have already thrown an illuftrious refulgence

fulgence round his court, which must endear his memory to future generations.

Besides learning, and the fine arts in general, the English excel, in what we call, the learned professions. Their courts of justice are adorned with greater abilities and virtues, perhaps, than those which any other country can boast of. A remarkable instance of which, occurs in the appointments for the last 200 years of their lord chancellors, who hold the highest and the most uncontroulable judicial seat in the kingdom, and yet it is acknowledged by all parties, that during that time, their bench has remained unpolluted by corruption, or partial affections. The few instances that may be alledged to the contrary, fix no imputation of wilful guilt upon the parties. The great lord chancellor Bacon was censured indeed for corrupt practices, but malevolence itself does not say that he was guilty any farther than in too much indulgence to his servants. The case of one of his successors is still more favourable to his memory, as his censure reflects disgrace only upon his enemies, and his lordship was, in the eyes of every man of candour and conscience, acquitted, not only of actual but intentional guilt. Even Jefferies, infernal as he was in his politics, never was accused of partiality in the causes that came before him as chancellor.

It must be acknowledged, that neither pulpit, nor bar-eloquence, has been much studied in England; but this is owing to the genius of the people, and their laws. The sermons of their divines are often learned, and always found as to the practical and doctrinal part, but the many religious sects in England, require to be opposed rather by reasoning than eloquence. An unaccountable notion has however prevailed even among the clergy themselves, that the latter is incompatible with the former, as if the arguments of Cicero and Demosthenes were weakened by those powers of language, with which they are adorned. A short time, perhaps, may remove this prepossession, and convince the clergy, as well as laity, that true eloquence is the first and fairest hand-maid of argumentation. The reader, however, is not to imagine that I am insinuating, that the preachers of the English church are destitute of the graces of elocution, so far from that, no clergy in the world can equal them, in the purity and perspicuity of language, though I think that if they consulted more than they do the powers of elocution, they would preach with more effect. If the semblance of those powers, coming from the mouths of ignorant enthusiasts, are attended with the amazing effects we daily see, what must not be the consequence, if
they

they were exerted in reality, and supported with spirit and learning.

The laws of England are of so peculiar a cast, that the several pleadings at the bar, do not admit, or but very sparingly, of the flowers of speech, and I am apt to think that a pleading in the Ciceronian manner, would make a ridiculous appearance in Westminster-hall. The English lawyers, however, though they deal little in eloquence, are well versed in rhetoric and reasoning.

Parliamentary speaking not being bound down to that precedent which is required in the courts of law, no nation in the world can produce so many examples of true eloquence, as the English senate in its two houses, witness the fine speeches made by both parties, in parliament, in the reign of Charles I. and those that have been printed since the accession of the present family.

Medicine and surgery, botany, anatomy, and all the arts or studies for preserving life, have been carried into great perfection by the English, and every member of the medical profession, is sure of an impartial hearing at the bar of the public. The same may be said of music, and theatrical exhibitions. Even agriculture and mechanism, are now reduced in England to sciences, and that too without any public encouragement, but that given by private noblemen and gentlemen, who associate themselves for that purpose. In ship-building, clock work, and the various branches of cutlery, they stand unrivalled.

UNIVERSITIES.] I have already mentioned the two universities of Cambridge and Oxford, which have been the seminaries of more learned men than any in Europe, and some have ventured to say, than all other literary institutions. It is certain that their magnificent buildings, which of late years, in splendour and architecture, rival the most superb royal edifices, the rich endowments, the liberal ease and tranquillity enjoyed by those who inhabit them, surpass all the ideas which foreigners, who visit them, conceive of literary societies. So respectable are they in their foundations, that each university sends two members to the British parliament, and their chancellors and officers have ever a civil jurisdiction over their students, the better to secure their independency. Their colleges, in their revenues and buildings, exceed those of many other universities. In Oxford there are 20, besides five halls, that are not endowed, and where the students maintain themselves. The colleges of Oxford are University, founded as some say by Alfred the Great. Baliol, founded by John Baliol, king of Scots, in 1262. Merton, founded by Walter of

Merton, bishop of Rochester, and high chancellor of England, in 1267. Exeter, founded in 1316, by Walter Stapleton, bishop of Exeter, and lord treasurer of England. Oriel, founded by Edward II. in the year 1324. Queen's, founded by Robert Eglesfield, chaplain to queen Philippa, consort to Edward III. in her honour. New college, founded in 1386, by William of Wickham, bishop of Winchester, but finished by Thomas de Rotheram, archbishop of York, and lord high chancellor, in the year 1475. All Souls, founded by Henry Chicheley, archbishop of Canterbury, in 1437. Magdalen, was founded by William Patten, alias Wainfleet, bishop of Winchester, and lord chancellor, in the year 1458. Brazen Nose, founded in 1509, by William Smith, bishop of Lincoln. Corpus Christi, founded in 1516, by Richard Fox, bishop of Winchester. Christ Church, founded by cardinal Wolsey, in 1515, but compleated by others, and is now the cathedral of the diocese. Trinity, founded by Sir Thomas Pope, soon after the reformation. St. John Baptist was founded in 1555, by Sir Thomas White, lord mayor of London. Jesus, was begun by Hugh Price, prebendary of Rochester, and appropriated to the Welch. Wadham, so called from its founder Nicholas Wadham, of Somersetshire, Esq. It was begun by him in the year 1609, but finished after his death, by his lady, in 1613. Pembroke, so called in honour of the earl of Pembroke, then lord high chancellor, was founded by Thomas Tesdale, Esq; Richard Wrightwick, B. D. in 1624. Worcester, was erected into a college, by Sir Thomas Cooke of Astley, in Worcestershire.

To these 19 may be added Hertford college, formerly Hart-Hall; but a patent having passed the great seal in the year 1740, for erecting it into a college, that design is now carrying into execution.

The five halls are these following: Alban hall, Edmund hall, St. Mary's hall, New-inn hall, and St. Mary Magdalen hall.

The colleges of Cambridge are Peter-house, founded by Hugh Balsham, prior of Ely, in 1257, who was afterwards bishop of that see. Clare hall, founded in 1340, by a benefaction of lady Elizabeth Clare, countess of Alstor. Pembroke hall, founded seven years after, by a countess of Pembroke. St. Bennet's, or Corpus Christi, founded about the same time, by the united guilds, or fraternities of Corpus Christi, and the Blessed Virgin. Trinity hall, founded by Bateman, bishop of Norwich, about the year 1548. Gonvil and Caius, founded by Edmund de Gonvil in 1348, completed by bishop Bateman, and additionally endowed 200 years after,

by

by John Caius, a physician. King's college, founded by Henry VI. and completed by his successors. Queen's college, was founded by the same king's consort, but finished by Elizabeth, wife to Edward IV. Catharine hall, founded by Richard Woodlark in 1475. Jesus college, founded by John Alcock, bishop of Ely, in the reign of Henry VII. Christ college was founded about the same time, by that king's mother, Margaret, countess of Richmond. St. John's college was founded by the same lady. Magdalen college was founded by Thomas Audley, baron of Walden, in the reign of Henry VIII. Trinity college was founded by Henry VIII. Emanuel college, by Sir Walter Mildmay, in 1584. Sidney college was founded by Thomas Ratcliff, earl of Sussex, in 1588, and had its name from his wife Frances Sidney.

CITIES, TOWNS, FORTS, AND OTHER EDIFICES, PUBLIC AND PRIVATE. } This head is so very extensive, that I can only touch upon objects that can assist in giving the reader some idea of its importance, grandeur, or utility.

* London, the metropolis of the British empire, naturally takes the lead in this division'; it appears to have been founded between the reigns of Julius Cæsar and Nero, but by whom is uncertain; for we are told by Tacitus, that it was a place of great trade in Nero's time, and soon after became the capital of the island. It was first walled about with hewn stones, and British bricks, by Constantine the Great, and the walls formed an oblong square, in compass about three miles, with seven principal gates. The same emperor made it a bishop's see; for it appears that the bishop of London was at the council of Arles, in the year 314: he also settled a mint in it, as is plain from some of his coins.

London, in its large sense, including Westminster, Southwark, and part of Middlesex, is a city of a very surprizing extent, of prodigious wealth, and of the most extensive trade. This city, when considered with all its advantages, is now what ancient Rome once was; the seat of liberty, the encourager of arts, and the admiration of the whole world. London is the centre of trade; it has an intimate connection with all the countries in the kingdom; it is the grand mart of the nation, to which every part send their commodities, from whence they

---

* London is situated in 51° 31' north latitude, 400 miles south of Edinburgh, and 270 south-east of Dublin; 180 miles west of Amsterdam, 210 north-west of Paris, 500 south-west of Copenhagen, 600 north-west of Vienna, 790 south-west of Stockholm, 800 north-east of Madrid, 820 north-west of Rome, 850 north-east of Lisbon, 1360 north-west of Constantinople, and 1414 south-west of Moscow.

they again are sent back into every town in the nation, and to every part of the world. From hence innumerable carriages, by land and water, are constantly employed; and from hence arises that circulation in the national body, which renders every part healthful, vigorous, and in a prosperous condition; a circulation that is equally beneficial to the head, and the most distant members. Merchants are here as rich as noblemen; witness their incredible loans to government; and there is no place in the world where the shops of tradesmen make such a noble and elegant appearance, or are better stocked.

It is situated on the banks of the Thames, a river, which, though not the largest, is the richest and most commodious for commerce of any in the world. It being continually filled with fleets, sailing to or from the most distant climates; and its banks being from London-bridge to Blackwall, almost one continued great magazine of naval stores, containing three large wet docks, 32 dry docks, and 33 yards for the building of ships, for the use of the merchants, beside the places allotted for the building of boats and lighters; and the king's yards lower down the river for the building men of war. As this city is about 60 miles distant from the sea, it enjoys, by means of this beautiful river, all the benefits of navigation, without the danger of being surprized by foreign fleets, or of being annoyed by the moist vapours of the sea. It rises regularly from the water-side, and extending itself on both sides along its banks, reaches a prodigious length from east to west in a kind of amphitheatre towards the north, and is continued for near 20 miles on all sides, in a succession of magnificent villas, and populous villages, the country seats of gentlemen and tradesmen; whither the latter retire for the benefit of the fresh air, and to relax their minds from the hurry of business. The regard paid by the legislature to the property of the subject, has hitherto prevented any bounds being fixed for its extension.

The irregular form of this city makes it difficult to ascertain its extent. However, its length from east to west, is generally allowed to be above seven miles from Hyde-park corner to Poplar, and its breadth, in some places, three, in other two; and in other again not much above half a mile. Hence the circumference of the whole is almost 18 miles. But it is much easier to form an idea of the large extent of a city so irregularly built, by the number of the people, who are computed to be near a million; and from the number of edifices devoted to the service of religion.

beside St. Paul's cathedral, and the collegiate minster, there are 102 parish churches, and
69 cha-

69 chapels of the eftablifhed religion; 21 French proteftant chapels; 11 chapels belonging to the Germans, Dutch, Danes, &c. 33 baptift meetings; 26 independent meetings; 28 prefbyterian meetings; 19 popifh chapels, and meeting-houfes for the ufe of foreign ambaffadors, and people of various fects; and 3 Jews fynagogues. So that there are 326 places devoted to religious worfhip, in the compafs of this vaft pile of buildings, without reckoning the 21 out-parifhes, ufually included within the bills of mortality.

There are alfo in and near this city 100 alms-houfes, about 20 hofpitals and infirmaries, 3 colleges, 10 public prifons, 15 flefh-markets; 1 market for live cattle, 2 other markets more particularly for herbs; and 23 other markets for corn, coals, hay, &c. 15 inns of court, 27 public fquares, befide thofe within any fingle buildings, as the Temple, &c. 3 bridges, 49 halls for companies, 8 public fchools, called free-fchools; and 131 charity-fchools, which provide education for 5034 poor children; 207 inns, 447 taverns, 551 coffee-houfes, 5975 alehoufes; 800 hackney coaches; 400 ditto chairs; 7000 ftreets, lanes, courts, and alleys, and 130,000 dwelling-houfes, containing, as has been already obferved, about 1,000,000 inhabitants, who, according to a late eftimate, confume annually the following articles of provifions.

Black cattle	98,244
Sheep and lambs	711,123
Calves	194,760
Swine	186,932
Pigs	52,000
Poultry, and wild fowl innumerable	
Mackarel fold at Billingfgate	14,740,000
Oyfters, bufhels	115,536
Small boats with cod, haddock, whiting, &c. over and above thofe brought by land-carriage, and great quantities of river and falt-fifh	1,398
Butter, pounds weight, about	16,000,000
Cheefe, ditto, about	20,000,000
Gallons of milk	7,000,000
Barrels of ftrong beer	1,172,494
Barrels of fmall beer	798,495
Tons of foreign wines	30,044
Gallons of rum, brandy, and other diftilled waters, above	11,000,000
Pounds weight of candles, above	11,000,000

London bridge was first built of stone in the reign of Henry II. about the year 1163, by a tax laid upon wool, which in course of time gave rise to the notion that it was built upon wool-packs; from that time it has undergone many alterations and improvements, particularly since the year 1756, when the houses were taken down, and the whole rendered more convenient and beautiful. The passage for carriages is 31 feet broad, and 7 feet on each side for foot passengers. It crosses the Thames, where it is 915 feet broad, and has at present 19 arches of about 20 feet wide each, but the centre one is considerably larger.

Westminster-bridge is reckoned one of the most compleat and elegant structures of the kind in the known world. It is built entirely of stone, and extended over the river at a place where it is 1,223 feet broad; which is above 300 feet broader than at London-bridge. On each side is a fine balustrade of stone, with places of shelter from the rain. The width of the bridge is 44 feet, having on each side a fine foot way for passengers. It consists of 14 piers, and 13 large, and two small arches, all semi-circular, that in the center being 76 feet wide, and the rest decreasing four feet each from the other; so that the two least arches of the 13 great ones, are each 52 feet. It is computed that the value of 40,000 l. in stone, and other materials is always under water. This magnificent structure was begun in 1738, and finished in 1750, at the expence of 389,000 l. defrayed by the parliament.

Black-friars-bridge falls nothing short of that of Westminster, either in magnificence or workmanship; but the situation of the ground on the two shores, obliged the architect to employ elliptical arches; which, however, have a very fine effect; and many unquestionable judges, prefer it to Westminster-bridge. This bridge was begun in 1760, and finished in 1770, at the expence of 120,000 l. to be discharged by a toll upon the passengers. It is situated almost at an equal distance between those of Westminster and London, commands a view of the Thames from the latter to Whitehall, and discovers the majesty of St. Paul's in a very striking manner.

The cathedral of St. Paul's is the most capacious, magnificent, and regular Protestant church in the world. The length within is 500 feet; and its height, from the marble pavement to the cross, on the top of the cupola, is 340. It is built of Portland stone, according to the Greek and Roman orders, in the form of a cross, after the model of St. Peter's at Rome, to which in some respects it is superior. St. Paul's church is the principal work of Sir Christopher Wren, and undoubtedly the only work of the same magnitude, that ever was compleated by one man. He lived to a great age, and finished the building 37 years

years after he himself laid the first stone. It takes up six acres of ground, though the whole length of this church measures no more than the width of St. Peter's. The expence of rebuilding it after the fire of London, was defrayed by a duty on coals, and is computed at a million sterling.

Westminster-abbey, or the collegiate church of Westminster, is a venerable pile of building, in the Gothic taste. It was first built by Edward the Confessor; king Henry III. rebuilt it from the ground, and Henry VII. added a fine chapel to the east end of it; this is the repository of the deceased British kings and nobility; and here are also monuments erected to the memory of many great and illustrious personages, commanders by sea and land, philosophers, poets, &c. In the reign of queen Anne, 4000l. a year, out of the coal duty, was granted by parliament for keeping it in repair.

The inside of the church of St. Stephen's Walbrook, is admired for its lightness and elegance, and does honour to the memory of Sir Christopher Wren. The same may be said of the steeples of St. Mary-le-Bow, and St. Bride's, which are supposed to be the most complete in their kind of any in Europe, though architecture has laid down no rules for such erections. Few churches in or about London are without some beauty. The simplicity of the portico in Covent-Garden is worthy the purest ages of antient architecture. That of St. Martin's in the Fields would be noble and striking, could it be seen from a proper point of view. Several of the new churches are built in an elegant taste, and even some of the chapels have gracefulness and proportion to recommend them. The Banqueting-house at Whitehall, is but a very small part of a noble palace, designed by Inigo Jones, for the royal residence, and as it now stands, under all its disadvantages, its symmetry, and ornaments, are in the highest stile and execution of architecture.

Westminster-hall, though on the outside it makes a mean, and no very advantageous appearance, is a noble Gothic building, and is said to be the largest room in the world, it being 220 feet long, and 70 broad. Its roof is the finest of its kind that can be seen. Here are held the coronation feasts of our kings and queens; also the courts of chancery, king's-bench, and common-pleas, and above stairs, that of the exchequer.

That beautiful column, called the Monument, erected at the charge of the city, to perpetuate the memory of its being destroyed by fire, is justly worthy of notice. This column, which is of the Doric order, exceeds all the obelisks and pillars of the antients, it being 202 feet high, with a stair-case in the middle to ascend to the balcony, which is about 30 feet short of the top, from whence there are other steps, made for

persons

persons to look out at the top of all, which is fashioned like an urn, with a flame issuing from it. On the base of the Monument, next the street, the destruction of the city, and the relief given to the sufferers by Charles II. and his brother, is emblematically represented in bas relief. The north and south sides of the base have each a Latin inscription, the one describing its dreadful desolation *, and the other its splendid resurrection; and on the east side is an inscription, shewing when the pillar was begun and finished. The charge of erecting this monument, which was begun by Sir Christopher Wren in 1671, and finished by him in 1677, amounted to upward of 13,000l.

The Royal Exchange is a large noble building, and is said to have cost above 80,000 l.

We might here give a description of the Tower †, Bank of England, the New-treasury, the Admiralty-office, and the Horse-guards

---

* Which may be thus rendered : " In the year of Christ, 1666, Sept. 2, eastward from hence, at the distance of 202 feet (the height of this column) a terrible fire broke out about midnight; which driven on by a high wind, not only wasted the adjacent parts, but also very remote places, with incredible crackling and fury. It consumed 89 churches, the city-gates, Guildhall, many public structures, hospitals, schools, libraries, a vast number of stately edifices, 13,000 dwelling-houses, and 400 streets. Of the 26 wards it utterly destroyed 15, and left eight others shattered and half burnt. The ruins of the city were 436 acres, from the Tower by the Thames side to the Temple church; and from the north-east along the wall to Holborn-bridge. To the estates and fortunes of the city it was merciless, but to their lives very favourable, that it might in all things resemble the last conflagration of the world. The destruction was sudden; for in a small space of time the city was seen most flourishing, and reduced to nothing. Three days after, when this fatal fire had baffled all human counsels and endeavours; in the opinion of all, it stopped, as it were by a command from heaven, and was on every side extinguished."

† In examining the curiosities of the Tower of London, it will be proper to begin with those on the outside the principal gate; the first thing a stranger usually goes to visit is the wild beasts; which, from their situation, first present themselves: for having entered the outer gate, and passed what is called the spur-guard, the keeper's house presents itself before you, which is known by a painted lion on the wall, and another over the door which leads to their dens. By ringing a bell, and paying sixpence each person, you may easily gain admittance.

The next place worthy of observation is the Mint, which comprehends near one-third of the Tower, and contains houses for all the officers belonging to the coinage. On passing the principal gate you see the White Tower, built by William the Conqueror. This is a large, square, irregular stone building, situated almost in the center, no one side answering to another, nor any of its watch towers, of which there are four at the top, built alike. One of these towers is now converted into an observatory. In the first story are two noble rooms, one of which is a small armoury for the sea-service, it having various sorts of arms, very curiously laid up, for above 10,000 seamen. In the other room are many closets and presses, all filled with warlike engines and instruments of death. Over this are two other floors, one principally filled with arms; the other with arms and other warlike instruments, as spades, shovels, pick-axes, and cheveaux de frize. In the upper story, are kept match, sheep-skins, tanned hides, &c. and in a little-room, called Julius Cæsar's chapel, are deposited some records, containing perhaps the antient usages and customs of the place. In this building are also preserved the models of the new-invented engines of destruction, that have from time to time been presented to the government. Near the southwest angle of the White-Tower, is the Spanish armoury,

m

guards at White-hall, the Mews, where the king's horses are kept; the Mansion-house of the lord-mayor, the Custom-house,

in which are deposited the spoils of what was vainly called the Invincible Armada; in order to perpetuate to latest posterity, the memory of that signal victory, obtained by the English over the whole naval power of Spain, in the reign of Philip II.

You now come to the grand store-house, a noble building, to the northward of the White Tower, that extends 245 feet in length, and 60 in breadth. It was begun by king James II. who built it to the first floor; but it was finished by king William III. who erected that magnificent room called the New, or Small Armoury, in which that prince, with queen Mary, his consort, dined in great form, having all the warrant workmen and labourers to attend them, dressed in white gloves and aprons, the usual badges of the order of masonry. To this noble room you are led by a folding door, adjoining to the east end of the Tower chapel, which leads to a grand staircase of 50 easy steps. On the left side of the uppermost landing-place is the work-shop, in which are constantly employed about 14 furbishers, in cleaning, repairing, and new-placing the arms. On entering the armoury, you see what they call a wilderness of arms, so artfully disposed, that at one view you behold arms for near 80,000 men, all bright, and fit for service: a sight which it is impossible to behold without astonishment; and beside those exposed to view, there were, before the late war, 16 chests shut up, each chest holding about 1,200 muskets. The arms were originally disposed by Mr. Harris, who contrived to place them in this beautiful order, both here and in the guard chamber of Hampton-court. He was a common gun-smith; but after he had performed this work, which is the admiration of people of all nations, he was allowed a pension from the crown for his ingenuity.

Upon the ground floor under the small armoury, is a large room of equal dimensions with that, supported by 20 pillars, all hung round with implements of war. This room, which is 14 feet high, has a passage in the middle 16 feet wide. At the sight of such a variety of the most dreadful engines of destruction, before whose thunder the most superb edifices, the noblest works of art, and number of the human species, fall together in one common and undistinguished ruin; one cannot help wishing that those horrible inventions had still lain, like a false conception, in the womb of nature, never to have been ripened into birth.

The horse armoury is a plain brick building, a little to the eastward of the White Tower; and is an edifice rather convenient than elegant, where the spectator is entertained with a representation of those kings and heroes of our own nation, with whose gallant actions it is to be supposed he is well acquainted; some of them equipped and sitting on horseback, in the same bright and shining armour they were used to wear when they performed those glorious actions that give them a distinguished place in the British annals.

You now come to the line of kings, which your conductor begins by reversing the order of chronology; so that in following them we must place the last first.

In a dark, strong, stone room, about 20 yards to the eastward of the grand store-house, or new armoury, the crown jewels are deposited. 1. The imperial crown, with which it is pretended that all the kings of England have been crowned since Edward the Confessor, in 1042. It is of gold, enriched with diamonds, rubies, emeralds, saphires and pearls: the cap within is of purple velvet, lined with white taffety, turned up with three rows of ermine. They are however mistaken in shewing this as the ancient imperial diadem of St. Edward; for that, with the other most ancient regalia of this kingdom, was kept in the arched room in the cloisters in Westminster Abbey, till the grand rebellion; when in 1642, Harry Martin, by order of the parliament, broke open the iron chest in which it was secured, took it thence, and sold it, together with the robes, sword, and scepter, of St. Edward. However, after the restoration, king Charles II. had one made in imitation of it, which is that now shewn. II. The golden orb or globe, put into the king's right hand before he is crowned; and borne in his left hand with the sceptre in his right, upon his return into Westminster-Hall after he is crowned. It is about six inches in diameter, edged with pearl, and enriched with precious stones. On the top is an amethyst, of a violet colour, near an inch and an half in height, set with a rich cross of gold, adorned with diamonds, pearls, and precious stones.

The

house, India-house, and a vast number of other public buildings; beside the magnificent edifices raised by our nobility; as Charlton-

---

The whole height of the ball and cup is 11 inches. III. The golden scepter, with its cross set upon a large amethyst of great value, garnished round with table diamonds. The handle of the scepter is plain; but the pummel is set round with rubies, emeralds and small diamonds. The top rises into a *fleur de lis* of six leaves, all enriched with precious stones, from whence issues a mound or ball, made of the amethyst already mentioned. The cross is quite covered with precious stones. IV. The scepter with the dove, the emblem of peace, perched on the top of a small Jerusalem cross, finely ornamented with table diamonds and jewels of great value. This emblem was first used by Edward the Confessor, as appears by his seal; but the ancient scepter and dove was sold with the rest of the regalia, and this now in the Tower was made after the restoration. V. St. Edward's staff, four feet seven inches and a half in length, and three inches three quarters in circumference, all of beaten gold, which is carried before the king at his coronation. VI. The rich crown of state, worn by his majesty in parliament; in which is a large emerald seven inches round; a pearl esteemed the finest in the world, and a ruby of inestimable value. VII. The crown belonging to his royal highness the prince of Wales. The king wears his crown on his head while he sits upon the throne; but that of the prince of Wales is placed before him, to shew that he is not yet come to it. VIII. The late queen Mary's crown, globe, and scepter, with the diadem she wore at her coronation with her consort king William III. IX. An ivory scepter, with a dove on the top, made for king James II.'s queen, whose garniture is gold, and the dove on the top gold, enamelled with white. X. The *curtana*, or sword of mercy, which has a blade thirty-two inches long, and near two broad, is without a point, and is borne naked before the king at his coronation, between the two swords of justice, spiritual and temporal. XI. The golden spurs, and the armillas, which are bracelets for the wrists. These, though very antique, are worn at the coronation. XII. The *ampulla*, or eagle of gold, finely engraved, which holds the holy oil the kings and queens of England are anointed with; and the golden spoon that the bishop pours the oil into. These are two pieces of great antiquity. The golden eagle, including the pedestal, is about nine inches high, and the wings expand about seven inches. The whole weighs about ten ounces. The head of the eagle screws off about the middle of the neck, which is made hollow, for holding the holy oil; and when the king is anointed by the bishop, the oil is poured into the spoon out of the bird's bill. XIII. A rich salt-seller of state, in form like the square White Tower, and so exquisitely wrought, that the workmanship of modern times is in no degree equal to it. It is of gold, and used only on the king's table at the coronation. XIV. A noble silver font, double gilt, and elegantly wrought, in which the royal family are christened. XV. A large silver fountain, presented to king Charles II. by the town of Plymouth, very curiously wrought; but much inferior in beauty to the above. Besides these, which are commonly shewn, there are in the jewel office, all the crown jewels worn by the prince and princesses at coronations, and a great variety of curious old plate.

The Record Office consists of three rooms, one above another, and a large round room, where the rolls are kept. These are all handsomely wainscoted, the wainscot being framed into presses round each room, within which are shelves, and repositories for the records; and for the easier finding of them, the year of each reign is inscribed on the inside of these presses, and the records placed accordingly. Within these presses, which amount to 56 in number, are deposited all the rolls, from the first year of the reign of king John, to the beginning of the reign of Richard III. but those after this last period are kept in the rolls chapel. The records in the Tower, among other things, contain, the foundation of abbies, and other religious houses; the ancient tenures of all the lands in England, with a survey of the manors; the original of laws and statutes; proceedings of the courts of common law and equity; the rights of England to the dominion of the British seas; leagues and treaties with foreign princes; the atchievements of England in foreign wars; the settlement of Ireland, as to law and dominion; the

forms

ENGLAND. 271

Charlton-houſe, Marlborough-houſe, and Buckingham-houſe, in St. James's park; the duke of Montague's, and the duke of Richmond's, in the Privy-garden ; the earl of Cheſterfield's houſe, near Hyde-park; the duke of Devonſhire's, and the late earl of Bath's, in Piccadilly ; lord Shelburne's, in Berkeley-Square; Northumberland-houſe, in the Strand; the houſes of the dukes of Newcaſtle and Queenſberry ; of lord Bateman; of general Wade in Saville-row ; the earl of Granville's, Mr. Pelham's, the duke of Bedford's, and Montague houſe*, in Bloomſbury; with a great number of others of the nobility and gentry; but theſe would be ſufficient to fill a large volume.

This great city is happily ſupplied with abundance of freſh water from the Thames and the New River ; which is not only of inconceivable ſervice to every family, but by means of fire-plugs every where diſperſed, the keys of which are depoſited with the pariſh officers, the city is, in a great meaſure, ſecured from

---

forms of ſubmiſſion of ſome Scottiſh kings, for territories held in England; ancient grants of our kings to their ſubjects; privileges and immunities granted to cities and corporations during the period above-mentioned; enrollments of charters and deeds made before the conqueſt; the bounds of all the foreſts in England, with the ſeveral reſpective rights of the inhabitants to common paſture, and many other important records, all regularly diſpoſed, and referred to in near a thouſand folio indexes. This office is kept open, and attendance conſtantly given, from ſeven o'clock till one, except in the months of December, January and February, when it is open only from eight to one, Sundays and holidays excepted. A ſearch here is half a guinea, for which you may peruſe any one ſubject a year.

* The Britiſh Muſeum is depoſited in Montague houſe. Sir Hans Sloane, bart. (who died in 1753) may not improperly be called the founder of the Britiſh Muſeum; for its being eſtabliſhed by parliament, was only in conſequence of his leaving by will his noble collection of natural hiſtory, his large library, and his numerous curioſities, which coſt him 50,000 l. to the uſe of the public on condition that the parliament would pay 20,000 l. to his executors. To this collection were added the Cottonian library, the Harleian manuſcripts, collected by the Oxford family, and purchaſed likewiſe by the parliament, and a collection of books given by the late major Edwards. His late majeſty, in conſideration of its great uſefulneſs, was graciouſly pleaſed to add thereto, the royal libraries of books and manuſcripts collected by the ſeveral kings of England.

The Sloanian collection conſiſts of an amazing number of curioſities; among which are, the library, including books of drawings, manuſcripts, and prints, amounting to about 50,000 volumes. Medals, and coins, ancient and modern, 23,000. Cameos and intaglios, about 700. Seals 268. Veſſels, &c. of agate, jaſper, &c. 542. Antiquities, 1,125. Precious ſtones, agates, jaſper, &c. 2,256. Metals, minerals, ores, &c. 2,725. Cryſtals, ſpars, &c. 1,864. Foſſils, flints, ſtones, 1,275. Earths, ſands, ſalts, 1,035. Bitumens, ſulphurs, ambers, &c. 399. Talcs, micæ, &c. 388. Corals, ſpunges, &c. 1,421. Teſtacea, or ſhells, &c. 5,843. Echini, echinitæ, &c. 659. Aſteriai trochi, entrochi, &c. 241. Cruſtaceæ, crabs, lobſters, &c. 363. Stellæ, marinæ, ſtar-fiſhes, &c. 173. Fiſh, and their parts, &c. 1,555. Birds, and their parts, eggs, and neſts, of different ſpecies, 1,172. Quadrupeds, &c. 1,886. Vipers, ſerpents, &c. 521. Inſects, &c. 5,439. Vegetables, 12,506. Hortus, ſiccus, or volumes of dried plants, 334. Humani, as calculi, anatomical preparations, 756. Miſcellaneous things, natural, 2,098. Mathematical inſtruments, 55. A catalogue of all the above is written in a number of large volumes.

from the spreading of fire; for these plugs are no sooner opened than there is vast quantities of water to supply the engines.

This plenty of water has been attended with another advantage, it has given rise to several companies, who insure houses and goods, from fire; an advantage that is not to be met with in any other nation on earth: the premium is small *, and the recovery, in case of loss, is easy and certain. Every one of these offices, keep a set of men in pay, who are ready at all hours to give their assistance in case of fire; and who are on all occasions extremely bold, dexterous, and diligent; but though all their labours should prove unsuccessful, the person who suffers by this devouring element, has the comfort that must arise from a certainty of being paid the value (upon oath) of what he has insured.

If the use and advantage of public magnificence is considered as a national concern, it will be found to be of the utmost consequence, in promoting the welfare of mankind, as that attention to it, which encouragement will produce, must necessarily stimulate the powers of invention and ingenuity, and of course create employment for great numbers of artists, who, exclusive of the reward of their abilities, cannot fail of striking out many things which will do honour to themselves, and to their country. This consideration alone, is without doubt highly worthy of a commercial people; it is this which gives the preference to one country, in comparison with another, and it is this which distinguishes the genius of a people, in the most striking manner.

London, before the conflagration in 1666, when that great city (which like most others had arisen from small beginnings) was totally inelegant, inconvenient, and unhealthy, of which latter misfortune, many melancholy proofs are authenticated

in

---

* The terms of insurance are as follows, viz. every person insuring, shall

	s.	d.
pay for every 100 l. insured on goods, inclosed in brick or stone	2	0
If half hazardous, as to situation, or kind of goods	3	0
If hazardous	4	0
If hazardous, and half hazardous	5	0
If hazardous, and hazardous	6	0
For every 100 l. insured on goods, inclosed in part brick, and part timber	2	6
If half hazardous, as to situation, or kind of goods	3	9
If hazardous	5	0
If hazardous, and half hazardous	6	3
If hazardous and hazardous	7	6
For every 100 l. insured on goods, inclosed in timber	3	0
If half hazardous, as to situation, or kind of goods	4	6
If hazardous	6	0
If hazardous, and half hazardous	7	6
If hazardous, and hazardous	9	0

The premium is double upon any sum between one and two thousand, and treble between two and three thousand pounds.

in history, and which, without doubt, proceeded from the narrowness of the streets, and the unaccountable projections of the buildings, that confined the putrid air, and joined with other circumstances, such as the want of water, rendered the city scarce ever free from pestilential devastation. The fire which consumed the greatest part of the city, dreadful as it was to the inhabitants at that time, was productive of consequences, which made ample amends for the losses sustained by individuals; a new city arose on the ruins of the old, but, tho' more regular, open, convenient, and healthful than the former, yet by no means answered to the characters of magnificence or elegance, in some particulars, as shall be hereafter mentioned, and it is ever to be lamented (such was the infatuation of those times) that the magnificent, elegant and useful plan of the great Sir Christopher Wren, was totally disregarded and sacrificed to the mean and selfish views of private property; views which did irreparable injury to the citizens themselves, and to the nation in general; for had that great architect's plan been followed, what has often been asserted, must have been the result, the metropolis of this kingdom would incontestably have been the most magnificent and elegant city in the universe, and of consequence must from the prodigious resort of foreigners of distinction, and taste, who would have visited it, have become an inexhaustible fund of riches to this nation. But as the deplorable blindness of that age, has deprived us of so valuable an acquisition, it is become absolutely necessary, that some efforts should be made to render the present plan in a greater degree answerable to the character of the richest and most powerful people in the world.

The plan of London in its present state, will in many instances appear, to very moderate judges, to be as injudicious a disposition, as can possibly be conceived for a city of trade and commerce, on the borders of so noble a river as the Thames. The wharfs and quays on its banks are despicable and inconvenient beyond conception. Let any one who has a tolerable taste, and some idea of public magnificence, give himself the trouble of considering the state of the buildings, quays, and wharfs, on both sides the river Thames, from Chelsea to Blackwall, on the one hand, and from Battersea to Greenwich on the other; and he will be immediately convinced that there is not one convenient, well-regulated spot (as the buildings thereon are at present disposed) either for business or elegance, in that whole extent. After he has considered the state of the banks of the river, he may continue his observation upon the interior parts of the town, and naturally turn his eyes upon those useful places to the trading part of the world,

Wapping,

Wapping, Rotherhithe, and Southwark, all contiguous to the Thames, and all entirely destitute of that useful regularity, convenience, and utility, so very desirable in commercial cities. The observer may from hence direct his view to Tower-hill, the Custom-house, Thames-street, Watling-street, and the passages to London-bridge; thence to the miserably contrived avenues into Spitalfields, Whitechapel, and Moorfields. He may consider the situation of St. Paul's, and other churches, that of the Monument, the Companies halls, and other public buildings, that are thrust up in corners, and placed in such a manner as must tempt every foreigner to believe that they were designed to be concealed. The observer may next take in all those wretched parts which he will find on both sides the Fleet-market; necessity will oblige him to proceed into Smithfield, for the sake of breathing a fresher air; and when he has considered a spot, capable of the greatest advantages, but destitute of any, he may plunge into the deplorable avenues and horrid passages in that neighbourhood. He may thence proceed to Baldwin's Gardens, through the ruins of which if he escapes without hurt, he may reach Gray's-Inn lane; which, though one of the principal avenues to this metropolis, is despicable beyond conception. From thence he may travel into Holborn, where the first object that presents itself to view, is Middle-row, a nuisance universally detested, but suffered to remain a public disgrace to the finest street in London. He may hobble on with some satisfaction, until he arrives at Broad St. Giles's, where, if he can bear to see a fine situation covered with ruinous buildings, and inhabited by the most deplorable objects that human nature can furnish, he may visit the environs. From hence he may proceed along Oxford-road, and striking into the town on which hand he pleases, he will observe the finest situation covered with a profusion of deformity, that has been obtruded on the public, for want of a general, well regulated, limited plan, which should have been enforced by commissioners appointed by authority, men of sound judgment, taste, and activity; had that happily been the case, all the glaring absurdities, which are perpetually staring in the faces, and insulting the understandings of persons of science and taste, would never have had existence. But private property, and pitiful, mean understandings, suited to the capacities of the projectors, have taken place of that regularity and elegance, which a general plan would have produced; and nothing seems to have been considered for 20 years past, but the interest of a few tasteless builders, who have entered into a combination, with no other view than fleecing the public, and of extending and distorting the town, till they have rendered

rendered it completely ridiculous. From hence the obferver, in his road to the city of Weftminfter, may have a peep at St. James's, the refidence of the moft powerful and refpectable monarch in the univerfe: a prince, who is himfelf a lover of the arts, and under whofe happy aufpices artifts of real merit and ingenuity can never doubt of obtaining patronage and encouragement. The obferver will not be better fatisfied when he has reached Weftminfter, when he confiders what might have been done, and how little has been done, when fo fine an opportunity prefented itfelf. From Weftminfter-bridge he may conduct himfelf into St. George's Fields; one of the few fpots about London which has not yet fallen a facrifice to the depraved tafte of modern builders; here he may indulge himfelf with the contemplation of what advantageous things may yet be done for this hitherto neglected metropolis.

From what has been faid of the cities of London and Weftminfter, there cannot remain the leaft doubt but that their ftate, with regard to magnificence, elegance, or conveniency, is in fuch places very defpicable; but we have the pleafure to find, that the neceffity of rendering them otherwife is now become a matter of ferious concern to perfons in power; and that fome general plan is likely to be formed and obferved for their improvement. In the cities of Paris, Edinburgh, Rotterdam, and other places, the government takes cognizance of all public buildings, both ufeful and ornamental.

We might in this place take notice of the very elegant, ufeful, and neceffary improvement, by the prefent method of paving and enlightning the ftreets, upon the plan of the High-ftreet of Edinburgh; an improvement which is felt in the moft fenfible manner by all ranks and degrees of people. The roads are continued for feveral miles round upon the fame plan; and, exclufive of lamps regularly placed on each fide, at fhort diftances, are rendered more fafe by watchmen placed within a call of each other, who are protected from the weather by proper boxes. Nothing can appear more brilliant than thofe lights when viewed at a diftance, efpecially where the roads run acrofs; and even the principal ftreets, fuch as Pall-Mall, New Bond-ftreet, &c. convey an idea of elegance and magnificence; upon the whole, there never was, in any age or country, a public fcheme adopted which reflects more glory upon government, or does greater honour to the perfon who originally propofed and fupported it.

The embanking the river, and many other improvements now in agitation, as well as the tafte and public fpirit of fome ruling men, give reafon to hope, that this hitherto neglected metropolis will become, in point of beauty, conveniency, and elegance,

elegance, what it is in wealth and commerce, the glory of the island, the admiration of every stranger, and the first city on earth.

Windsor castle is the only fabric that deserves the name of a royal palace in England; and that chiefly through its beautiful and commanding situation; which, with the form of its construction, rendered it, before the introduction of artillery, impregnable. Hampton Court was the favourite residence of king William. It is built in the Dutch taste, and has some good apartments, and like Windsor lies near the Thames. Both these places have some good pictures; but nothing equal to the magnificent collection made by Charles I. and dissipated in the time of the civil wars. The cartoons of Raphael, which, for design and expression, are reckoned the master-pieces of painting, have by his present majesty been removed from the gallery built for them at Hampton-Court, to the queen's palace, formerly Buckingham-house, in St. James's Park. The palace of St. James's is commodious, but has the air of a convent; and that of Kensington, which was purchased from the Finch family by king William, is remarkable only for its gardens, which are laid out in a grand taste. Other houses, though belonging to the king, are far from deserving the name of royal.

Foreigners have been puzzled to account how it happens that the monarchs of the richest nation in Europe should be so indifferently lodged, especially as Charles I. whose finances were but low, compared to some of his successors, had he lived undisturbed, would more than probably have completed the august plan which Inigo Jones drew for a royal palace, and which would have been every way suitable to an English monarch's dignity. The truth is, his son Charles II. though he had a fine taste for architecture, dissipated his revenues upon his pleasures. The reign of his brother was too short for such an undertaking. Perpetual wars during the reigns of king William and queen Ann, left the parliament no money to spare for a palace. The two succeeding monarchs were indifferent as to such a piece of grandeur in England; and though several schemes were drawn up for that purpose, yet they came to nothing, especially as three millions of money were necessary for carrying it into execution. We have, however, every thing to expect during the present reign, when architecture and magnificence shine out in their full lustre.

It would be needless, and, indeed, endless, to attempt even a catalogue of the houses of the nobility and gentry in the neighbourhood of London, and all over the kingdom. They are by far more superb and elegant than the subjects of any other

other nation can difplay; witnefs thofe of the duke of Devonfhire, the countefs of Leicefter, lord Scarfale, the earl Temple, and earl Pembroke, where more remains of antiquity are to be found than are in the poffeffion of any fubject in the world; Sir Gregory Page, the earl of Tilney, and hundreds of others equally grand and fumptuous. But thofe capital houfes of the Englifh nobility and gentry have an excellency diftinct from what is to be met with in any other part of the globe, which is, that all of them are complete without and within, all the apartments and members being fuitable to each other, both in conftruction and furniture, and all kept in the higheft prefervation. It often happens, that the houfe, however elegant and coftly, is not the principal object of the feat, which confifts in its hortulane and rural decorations. Viftas, opening landfcapes, temples, all of them the refult of that enchanting art of imitating nature, and uniting beauty with magnificence.

It cannot be expected that I fhould here enter into a detail of the chief towns of England; which, to fay the truth, have little befides their commerce, and the conveniency of their fituation, to recommend them, though fome of them have noble public buildings and bridges. Briftol is thought to be the largeft city in the Britifh dominions, after London and Dublin, and to contain about 100,000 inhabitants. No nation in the world can fhew fuch dock-yards, and all conveniencies for the conftruction and repairs of the royal navy, as Portfmouth (the moft regular fortification in England) Plymouth, Chatham, Woolwich, and Deptford. The royal hofpital at Greenwich for fuperannuated feamen, is fcarcely exceeded by any royal palace for its magnificence and expence. In fhort, every town in England is noted for fome particular production or manufacture, to which its building and appearance are generally fitted; and though England contains many excellent and commodious fea-ports, yet all of them have an immediate connection with London, which is the common centre of national commerce.

ANTIQUITIES AND CURIOSITIES } The antiquities of
NATURAL AND ARTIFICIAL. } England are either Britifh, Roman, Saxon, or Danifh, and Anglo-Normannic; but thefe, excepting the Roman, throw no great light upon antient hiftory. The chief Britifh antiquities, are thofe circles of ftones, particularly that called Stonehenge, in Wiltfhire, which probably were places of facred worfhip in the times of the Druids. Stonehenge is, by Inigo Jones, Dr. Stukeley, and others, defcribed as a regular circular ftructure. The body of the work confifts of two circles, and two ovals,

which are thus composed. The upright stones are placed at three feet and a half distance from each other, and joined at top by over-thwart stones, with tennons fitted to the mortises in the uprights, for keeping them in their due position. Some of these stones are vastly large, measuring two yards in breadth, one in thickness, and above seven in height; others are less in proportion. The uprights are wrought a little with a chissel, and something tapered; but the transomes, or over-thwart stones, are quite plain. The outside circle is near one hundred and eighty feet in diameter; between which, and the next circle, there is a walk of three hundred feet in circumference, which has a surprizing and awful effect on the beholders. After all the descriptions of, and dissertations upon, this celebrated antiquity, by ingenious writers, it is not to be denied, that it has given rise to many extravagant ridiculous conjectures, from the time of Leland, who has been very particular on the subject, down to Stukeley, who, on a favourite point of antiquity, sometimes formed the most enthusiastic conjectures. The barrows that are near this monument, were certainly graves of persons of both sexes, eminent in peace or war; some of them having been opened, and bones, arms, and antient trinkets, found within them.

Monuments of the same kind as that of Stonehenge, are to be met with in Cumberland, Oxfordshire, Cornwall, Devonshire, and many other parts of England, as well as in Scotland, and the isles, which have been already mentioned.

The Roman antiquities in England, consist chiefly of altars, and monumental inscriptions, which instruct us as to the legionary stations of the Romans in Britain, and the names of some of their commanders. The Roman military ways give us the highest idea of the civil as well as military policy of those conquerors. Their vestiges are numerous; one is mentioned by Leland, as beginning at Dover, and passing through Kent to London, from thence to St. Alban's, Dunstable, Stratford, Towcester, Littleburn, St. Gilbert's hill near Shrewsbury, then by Stratton, and so through the middle of Wales to Cardigan. The great Via Militaris called Hermen-street, passed from London through Lincoln, where a branch of it, from Pomfret to Doncaster, strikes out to the westward, passing through Tadcaster to York, and from thence to Aldby, where it again joined Hermen-street. There would, however, be no end of describing the vestiges of the Roman roads in England, many of which serve as foundations to our present highways. The great earl of Arundel, the celebrated English antiquary, had formed a noble plan for describing those which pass through Sussex and Surry towards London;

but

but the civil war breaking out, put an end to the undertaking. The remains of many Roman camps are difcernible all over England. Their fituations are generally fo well chofen, and their fortifications appear to have been fo complete, that there is fome reafon to believe, that they were the conftant habitations of the Roman foldiers in England, though it is certain from the baths and tefferated pavements, that have been found in different parts, that their chief officers and magiftrates, lived in towns or villas. Roman walls have likewife been found in England; and, perhaps, upon the borders of Wales, many remains of their fortifications and caftles, are blended with thofe of a later date; and it is difficult for the moft expert architect to pronounce that fome halls and courts are not entirely Roman. The private cabinets of noblemen and gentlemen, as well as the public repofitaries, contain a vaft number of Roman arms, coins, fibulæ, trinkets, and the like, that have been found in England; but the moft amazing monument of the Roman power in England, is the prætenture, or wall of Severus, commonly called the Picts wall, running through Northumberland and Cumberland, beginning at Tinmouth, and ending at Solway Firth, being about eighty miles in length. The wall at firft confifted only of ftakes and turf, with a ditch, but Severus built it with ftone forts, and turrets, at proper diftances, fo that each might have a fpeedy communication with the other, and it was attended all along by a deep ditch, or vallum, to the north, and a military high way to the fouth. This prodigious work, however, was better calculated to ftrike the Scots and Picts with terror, than to give any real fecurity to the Roman poffeffions. In fome places, the wall, the vallum, and the road, are plainly difcernible, and the latter ferves as a foundation for a modern work of the fame kind, carried on at the public expence. A critical account of the Roman antiquities in England, is among the defiderata of hiftory, but perhaps it is too great a defign for any one man to execute, as it cannot be done without vifiting every place, and every object in perfon.

The Saxon antiquities in England confift chiefly in ecclefiaftical edifices, and places of ftrength. At Winchefter is fhewn the round table of king Arthur, with the names of his knights. The antiquity of this table has been difputed by Cambden, and later writers, perhaps with reafon; but if it is not Britifh, it certainly is Saxon. The cathedral of Winchefter, ferved as the burying place of feveral Saxon kings, whofe bones were collected together by bifhop Fox, in fix large wooden chefts. Many monuments of Saxon antiquity, prefent themfelves all over the kingdom, though they are often not to be difcerned from the Normannic; and the Britifh Mufeum contains feveral ftriking original fpecimens of their learning. Many Saxon charters figned by the king, and his nobles, with a plain crofs inftead of their names, are ftill to be met with. The writing is neat and legible, and was always performed by a clergyman, who affixed the name and quality of every donor, or witnefs, to his refpective crofs. The Danifh erections in England, are hardly difcernible from the Saxon. The form of their camps are round, and generally built upon eminences, but their forts are fquare.

All England is full of Anglo Normannic monuments, which I chufe to call fo, becaufe, though the princes, under whom they were raifed, were of Norman original, yet the expence was defrayed by Englifhmen, with Englifh money. York-minfter, and Weftminfter-hall, and abbey, are perhaps the fineft fpecimens to be found in Europe, of that Gothic manner, which prevailed in building, before the recovery of the Greek and Roman architecture. All the cathedrals, and old churches in the kingdom, are more or lefs in the fame tafte, if we except St. Paul's. In fhort, thofe erections are fo common, that they fcarcely deferve the name of curiofities. It is uncertain, whether the artificial excavations, found in fome parts of England, are Britifh, Saxon, or Norman. That under the old caftle of Ryegate in Surry, is very remarkable, and feems to have been defigned for fecreting the cattle and effects of the natives, in times of war and invafion. It contains an oblong fquare hall, round which runs a bench, cut out of the fame rock, for fitting upon; and tradition fays, that it was the room in which the barons of England met, during their wars with king John. The rock itfelf is foft, and very practicable; but it is hard to fay, where the excavation, which is continued in a fquare paffage, about fix feet high, and four wide, terminates, becaufe the work is fallen in in fome places.

The natural curiofities of England are fo various, that I can touch upon them only in general; as there is no end of defcribing the feveral medicinal waters and fprings, which are to be found in every part of the country. They have been analyfed with great accuracy and care, by feveral learned naturalifts, who, as their interefts, or inclinations led them, have not been fparing in recommending their falubrious qualities. England, however, is not fingular in its medicinal waters, though in fome countries the difcovering and examining them is fcarce worth while. In England, a much frequented well or fpring, is a certain eftate to its proprietor. The moft remarkable of thefe wells have been divided into thofe for

bathing,

bathing, and thofe for purging. The chief of the former lie in Somerfetſhire; and the Bath waters are famous through all the world, both for drinking and bathing. Spaws of the fame kind are found at Scarborough, and other parts of Yorkſhire; at Tunbridge in Kent; Epfom and Dulwich in Surry; Acton and Iflington in Middlefex. Here alfo are many remarkable fprings; whereof fome are impregnated either with falt, as that at Droitwich in Worcefter; or fulphur, as the famous well of Wigan in Lancaſhire; or bituminous matter, as that at Pitchford in Shropſhire. Others have a petrifying quality, as that near Lutterworth in Leicefterfhire; and a dropping well in the weft riding of Yorkſhire. And finally, fome ebb and flow, as thofe of the Peak in Derbyſhire, and Laywell near Torbay, whofe waters rife and fall feveral times in an hour. To thefe we may add that remarkable fountain near Richard's caftle in Herefordſhire, commonly called Bonewell, which is generally full of fmall bones, like thofe of frogs or fiſh, though often cleared out. At Ancliff, near Wigan in Lancaſhire, is the famous burning well; the water is cold, neither has it any fmell; yet there is fo ftrong a vapour of fulphur iffuing out with the ftream, that upon applying a light to it, the top of the water is covered with a flame, like that of burning fpirits, which lafts feveral hours, and emits fo fierce a heat that meat may be boiled over it. The fluid itfelf will not burn when taken out of the well.

Derbyſhire is celebrated for many natural curiofities. The Mam Tor, or Mother Tower, is faid to be continually mouldering away, but never diminifhes. The Elden Hole, about four miles from the fame place: this is a chafm in the fide of a mountain, near feven yards wide, and fourteen long, diminiſhing in extent within the rock, but of what depth is not known. A plummet once drew 884 yards of line after it, whereof the laft 80 were wet, without finding a bottom. The entrance of Poole's hole near Buxton, for feveral paces, is very low, but foon opens into a very lofty vault, like the infide of a Gothic cathedral. The height is certainly very great, yet much fhort of what fome have afferted, who reckon it a quarter of a mile perpendicular, though in length it exceeds that dimenfion: a current of water, which runs along the middle, adds, by its founding ftream, re-ecchoed on all fides, very much to the aftoniſhment of all who vifit this vaft concave. The drops of water which hang from the roof, and on the fides, have an amufing effect; for they not only reflect numberlefs rays from the candles carried by the guides, but as they are of a petrifying quality, they harden in feveral places into various forms, which, with the help of a ftrong
imagination,

imagination, may pass for lions, fonts, organs, and the like. The entrance into that natural wonder, which is from its hideousness, named the Devil's Arse, is wide at first, and upwards of thirty feet perpendicular. Several cottagers dwell under it, who seem in a great measure to subsist by guiding strangers into the cavern, which is crossed by four streams of water, and then is thought impassable. The vault, in several places, makes a noble appearance, which is particularly beautiful, by being chequered by various coloured stones. These are the most celebrated natural excavations in England, where they are beheld with great wonder, but are nothing comparable to those that exist in Germany, and other parts, both of Europe and Asia.

Some spots of England are said to have a petrifying quality. We are told, that near Whitby in Yorkshire, are found certain stones, resembling the folds and wreaths of a serpent; also other stones of several sizes, and so exactly round, as if artificially made for cannon balls, which being broke, do commonly contain the form and likeness of serpents, wreathed in circles, but generally without heads. In some parts of Gloucestershire, stones are found, resembling cockles, oisters, and other testaceous marine animals. Those curiosities, however, in other countries, would, as such, make but a poor appearance, and even in England they are often magnified by ignorance and credulity.

COMMERCE AND MANUFACTURES.] This article is so copious, and has been so well discussed in former publications, many of which are master-pieces in their kind, that the reader, I hope, will not expect that I enter into minutiæ. It is well known that commerce and manufactures have raised the English to be at this day the first and most powerful people in the world. Historical reviews, on this head, would be tedious. It is sufficient then to say, that it was not till the reign of Elizabeth, that England began to feel her true weight in the scale of commerce. She planned some settlements in America, Virginia particularly, but left the expence attending them to be defrayed by her subjects; and indeed she was too parsimonious to carry her own notions of trade into execution. James I. entered upon great and beneficial schemes for the English trade. The East-India company owes to him their success and existence, and the British America saw her most flourishing colonies rise under him and his family. The spirit of commerce went hand in hand with that of liberty, and their gradations have terminated in the present glorious state of the nation. It is not within my design to follow commerce through all her fluctuations and states. This would

would be an idle attempt, and it has already taken up large volumes. The nature of a geographical work, requires only a reprefentation of the prefent ftate of commerce in every country; and in this light I flatter myfelf that I fhall be able to treat of it with more precifion, than former writers upon the fame fubject.

The prefent fyftem of Englifh politics may properly be faid to have taken rife in the reign of queen Elizabeth. At this time the Proteftant religion was eftablifhed, which naturally allied us to the reformed ftates, and made all the Popifh powers our enemies.

We began in the fame reign to extend our trade, by which it became neceffary for us alfo to watch the commercial progrefs of our neighbours; and, if not to incommode and obftruct their traffic, to hinder them from impairing ours.

We then likewife fettled colonies in America, which was become the great fcene of European ambition; for, feeing with what treafures the Spaniards were annually enriched from Mexico and Peru, every nation imagined, that an American conqueft or plantation would certainly fill the mother country with gold and filver.

The difcoveries of new regions, which were then every day made, the profit of remote traffic, and the neceffity of long voyages, produced, in a few years, a great multiplication of fhipping. The fea was confidered as the wealthy element; and, by degrees, a new kind of fovereignty arofe, called naval dominion.

As the chief trade of Europe, fo the chief maritime power was at firft in the hands of the Portuguefe and Spaniards, who, by a compact, to which the confent of other princes was not afked, had divided the newly difcovered countries between them; but the crown of Portugal having fallen to the king of Spain, or being feized by him, he was mafter of the fhips of the two nations, with which he kept all the coafts of Europe in alarm, till the Armada, he had raifed at a vaft expence for the conqueft of England, was deftroyed; which put a ftop, and almoft an end, to the naval power of the Spaniards.

At this time the Dutch, who were oppreffed by the Spaniards, and feared yet greater evils than they felt, refolved no longer to endure the infolence of their mafters; they therefore revolted; and after a ftruggle, in which they were affifted by the money and forces of Elizabeth, erected an independant and powerful common-wealth.

When the inhabitants of the Low Countries had formed their fyftem of government, and fome remiffion of the war gave them leifure to form fchemes of future profperity; they

eafily

easily perceived that, as their territories were narrow, and their numbers small, they could preserve themselves only by that power, which is the consequence of wealth; and that by a people whose country produced only the necessaries of life, wealth was not to be acquired, but from foreign dominions, and by the transportation of the products of one country into another.

From this necessity, thus justly estimated, arose a plan of commerce, which was for many years prosecuted with an industry and success, perhaps never seen in the world before; and by which the poor tenants of mud-walled villages and impassible bogs, erected themselves into high and mighty states, who set the greatest monarchs at defiance, whose alliance was courted by the proudest, and whose power was dreaded by the fiercest nations. By the establishment of this state, there arose to England a new ally, and a new rival.

At this time, which seems to be the period destined for the change of the face of Europe, France began first to rise into power, and from defending her own provinces with difficulty and fluctuating success, to threaten her neighbours with incroachments and devastations. Henry IV. having, after a long struggle, obtained the crown, found it easy to govern nobles, exhausted and wearied by a long civil war; and having composed the disputes between the Protestants and Papists, so as to obtain, at least, a truce for both parties, was at leisure to accumulate treasure, and raise forces which he proposed to have employed in a design of settling for ever the balance of Europe. Of this great scheme he lived not to see the vanity, or feel the disappointment; for he was murdered in the midst of his mighty preparations.

The French, however, were in this reign taught to know their own power; and the great designs of a king, whose wisdom they had so long experienced, even though they were not brought to actual experiment, disposed them to consider themselves as masters of the destiny of their neighbours; and from that time he that shall nicely examine their schemes and conduct, will find that they began to take an air of superiority, to which they had never pretended before; and that they have been always employed more or less openly, upon schemes of dominion, though with frequent interruptions from domestic troubles.

When queen Elizabeth entered upon the government, the customs produced only 36,000 l. a year; at the restoration, they were let to farm for 400,000 l. and produced considerably above double that sum before the revolution. The people of London, before we had any plantations, and but very little trade,

trade, were computed at about 100,000; at the death of queen Elizabeth, they were increafed to 150,000, and are now above fix times that number. In thofe days, we had not only our naval ftores, but our fhips from our neighbours. Germany furnifhed us with all things made of metal, even to nails; wine, paper, linen, and a thoufand other things came from France. Portugal furnifhed us with fugars; all the produce of America was poured upon us from Spain; and the Venetians and Genoefe retailed to us the commodities of the Eaft-Indies at their own price. In fhort, the legal intereft of money was 12 per cent. and the common price of our land 10 or 12 years purchafe. We may add, that our manufactures were few, and thofe but indifferent; the number of Englifh merchants very fmall, and our fhipping much inferior to what now belong to our American colonies.

Such was the ftate of our trade when this great princefs came to the throne; but, as we have already obferved, the limits of our undertaking do not permit us to give a detail of the gradual progrefs of commerce fince that reign, we flatter ourfelves that the Britifh reader will not be difpleafed with the following view of our extenfive trade, at prefent carried on through the various nations of the globe.

Great-Britain is, of all other countries, the moft proper for trade; as well from its fituation, as an ifland, as from the freedom and excellency of its conftitution, and from its natural products, and confiderable manufactures. For exportation: our country produces many of the moft fubftantial and neceffary commodities, as butter, cheefe, corn, cattle, wool, iron, lead, tin, copper, leather, copperas, pitcoal, alum, faffron, &c. Our corn fometimes preferves other countries from ftarving. Our horfes are the moft ferviceable in the world, and highly valued by all nations, for their hardinefs, beauty, and ftrength. With beef, mutton, pork, poultry, bifcuit, we victual not only our own fleets, but many foreigners that come and go. Our iron we export manufactured in great guns, carcafes, bombs, &c. Prodigious, and almoft incredible, is the value likewife of other goods from hence exported; viz. hops, flax, hemp, hats, fhoes, houfhold-ftuff, ale, beer, red-herrings, pilchards, falmon, oyfters, faffron, liquorice, watches, ribbands, toys, &c.

There is fcarce a manufacture in Europe, but what is brought to great perfection in England; and therefore it is perfectly unneceffary to enumerate them all. The woollen manufacture is the moft confiderable, and exceeds in goodnefs and quantity that of any other nation. Hard-ware is another capital article; locks, edge-tools, guns, swords, and other arms, exceed any thing of the kind; houshold utensils of brass, iron, and pewter, also are very great articles; our clocks and watches are in very great esteem. There are but few manufactures we are defective in. In those of lace and paper we do not seem to excel; but we import much more than we should, if the duty on British paper were taken off. As to foreign traffic, the woollen manufacture is still the great foundation and support of it.

Our American colonies are the objects that naturally first present themselves for our discussion, and they may be divided into two classes, our possessions on the continent, and those in the islands, which go under the name of the West-Indies.

I shall rank the English possessions in North-America, under the heads of the following colonies, viz. Hudson's Bay, Labrador, Newfoundland, Canada, Nova-Scotia, New-England, Rhode-Island, Connecticut, and New-Hampshire, (the three last forming one colony) New York, Pensylvania, and Maryland, (originally but one colony) North-Carolina, South-Carolina, Georgia, East and West Florida. The chief commodities exported from Great-Britain to those colonies, are wrought iron, steel, copper, pewter, lead, and brass, cordage, hemp, sail-cloth, ship-chandlery, painter's colours, millinery, hosiery, haberdashery, gloves, hats, broad cloths, stuffs, flannels, Colchester bays, long ell silks, gold and silver lace, Manchester goods, British, foreign, and Irish linens, earthen wares, grind-stones, Birmingham and Sheffield wares, toys, sadlery, cabinet wares, seeds, cheese, strong beer, smoaking pipes, snuffs, wines, spirits, and drugs, East-India goods, books, paper, leather, besides many other articles, according to the different wants and exigencies of the different colonies, impossible to be enumerated here.

The commodities exported from America to Great Britain, and other markets, are tobacco, rice, flour, biscuit, wheat, beans, peas, oats, Indian corn, and other grain; honey, apples, cyder, and onions; salt-beef, pork, hams, bacon, venison, tongues, butter and cheese, prodigious quantities of cod, mackarel, and other fish, and fish oil; furs and skins of wild beasts, such as bear, beaver, otter, fox, deer, and racoon; horses, and live stock; timber planks, masts, boards, staves, shingles, pitch, tar, and turpentine; ships built for sale; flax, flax-seed, and cotton; indigo, pot-ash, bees-wax, tallow, copper ore, and iron in bars and in pigs; besides many other commodities peculiar to the climes and soil of different provinces. As to those, which have been acquired by the last general peace, they are certainly very improveable, nor can we form any judgment of them,

them, in their present infantine unsettled state. It does not enter within my design, nor indeed does it fall within my subject, to recapitulate the differences that unhappily subsist at present between those colonies, and their mother country. It is sufficient if I exhibit a state of the trade between them, as it existed when those differences took place, marking at the same time the commercial strength and shipping of the colonies.

Colonies.	Ships.	Seamen.	Exports from Great Britain.	Exports from the Colonies.
Hudson's Bay	4	130	L. 16,000	L. 29,340
Labrador, American vessels 120				49,050
Newfoundland (3000 boats)	380	20,560	273,400	345,000
Canada	34	408	105,000	105,500
Nova Scotia	6	72	26,500	38,000
New England	46	552	395,000	370,500
Rhode Island, Connecticut, and New Hampshire	3	36	12,000	114,500
New York	30	330	531,000	526,000
Pensylvania	35	390	611,000	705,500
Virginia and Maryland	330	3,960	865,000	1,040,000
North Carolina	34	408	18,000	68,350
South Carolina	140	1,680	365,000	395,666
Georgia	24	240	49,000	74,200
East Florida	2	24	7,000	
West ditto	10	120	97,000	63,000
	1,078	28,910	3,370,900	3,924,606

The principal islands belonging to the English, in the West Indies, are the Bermudas, or Summer islands; the Bahama, or Lucayan islands; Jamaica, Anguilla, Berbuda, St. Christopher's, Nevis, Antigua, Montserrat, Dominica, St. Vincent, Barbados, Tobago, and Granada, and the Grenadines, or Grenadillos. Of these, Dominica, St. Vincent, Tobago, and Granada, were ceded by France to Great-Britain, by the definitive treaty of 1763.

The English trade with their West India islands, consists chiefly in sugars, rum, cotton, logwood, cocoa, coffee, pimento, ginger, indigo, materials for dyers, mahogany, and manchineel planks, drugs and preserves; for these the exports from England are osnaburgs, a coarse kind of linen, with which the West-Indians now clothe their slaves; linen of all sorts, with broadcloth, and kersies, for the planters, their overseers and families; silks and stuffs for their ladies and houshold servants; red caps for their slaves of both sexes; stockings and shoes of all sorts; gloves and hats; millinery ware, and perukes; laces for linen, woollen, and silks; strong beer, pale beer, pickles, candles, butter, and cheese; iron ware, as saws, files, axes, hatchets, chissels, adzes, hoes, mattocks, gouges, planes,

planes, augres, nails; lead, powder, and shot; brass and copper wares; toys, coals, and pantiles; cabinet wares, snuffs, and in general whatever is raised or manufactured in Great Britain; also negroes from Africa, and all sorts of India goods. Formerly the English West India islands, sent home large quantities of money in specie, which they got upon the balance of trade with the French, Spaniards, and Portuguese. We cannot, however, speak with any precision, as to the particulars of the trade between the English West Indies, and the mother country, though undoubtedly it is highly for the benefit of the latter, because of the cessions made of new islands there by the late peace, which, when fully peopled, must have a very sensible influence upon the former system of commerce in those parts, as I shall have occasion to observe in its proper place.

The trade of England to the East Indies constitutes one of the most stupendous, political, as well as commercial machines, that is to be met with in history. The trade itself is exclusive, and lodged in a company, which has a temporary monopoly of it, in consideration of money advanced to the government. Without entering into the history of the East India trade, within these twenty years past, and the company's concerns in that country, it is sufficient to say, that besides their settlements on the coast of India, which they enjoy under proper restrictions, by act of parliament, they have, through the various internal revolutions which have happened at Indostan, acquired such territorial possessions, as renders them the most formidable commercial republic (for so it may be called in its present situation) that has been known in the world since the demolition of Carthage. Their revenues are only known, and that but imperfectly, to the directors of the company, who are chosen annually by the proprietors of the stock; but it has been publicly affirmed, that it amounts annually to above three millions and a half sterling. The expences of the company in forts, fleets, and armies, for maintaining those acquisitions, are certainly very great; but after these are defrayed, the company not only clears a vast sum, but is able to pay to the government four hundred thousand pounds yearly, for a certain time, partly by way of indemnification, for the expences of the public in protecting the company, and partly as a tacit tribute for those possessions that are territorial and not commercial. This republic therefore cannot be said to be independent, and it is hard to say what form it may take when the term of the bargain with the government is expired.

This company exports to the East Indies all kinds of woollen manufacture, all sorts of hard-ware, lead, bullion, and

and quickfilver. Their imports confift of gold, diamonds, raw-filk, drugs, tea, pepper, arrack, porcelain, or China ware, faltpetre for home confumption; and of wrought filks, muflins, callicoes, cottons, and all the woven manufactures of India, for exportation to foreign countries. I fhall now proceed to a concife view of the Englifh trade to other countries, according to the lateft, and moft authentic accounts.

To Turkey England fends, in her own bottoms, woollen cloths, tin, lead, and iron, hard-ware, iron utenfils, clocks, watches, verdegris, fpices, cochineel, and logwood. She imports from thence raw-filks, carpets, fkins, dying drugs, cotton, fruits, medicinal drugs, coffee, and fome other articles. Formerly the balance of this trade was about 500,000 l. annually, in favour of England. The Englifh trade was afterwards diminifhed through the practices of the French: but the Turkey trade at prefent is at a very low ebb with the French as well as the Englifh. It is to be prefumed, if the Ruffians are fuffered to drive the Turks out of Europe, that Great-Britain will fecure to herfelf a port in one of the numerous fine iflands of the Levant.

England exports to Italy, woollen goods of various kinds, peltry, leather, lead, tin, fifh, and Eaft India goods; and brings back raw and thrown filk, wines, oil, foap, olives, oranges, lemons, pomegranates, dried fruits, colours, anchovies, and other articles of luxury: the balance of this trade in favour of England, is annually about 200,000 l.

To Spain, England fends all kinds of woollen goods, leather, tin, lead, fifh, corn, iron and brafs manufactures; haberdafhery wares, affortments of linen from Germany, and elfewhere, for her American colonies: and receives in return, wines, oils, dried fruits, oranges, lemons, olives, wools, indico, cochineal, and other dying drugs, colours, gold and filver coin.

Portugal, till of late, was, upon commercial accounts, the favourite ally of England, whofe fleets and armies have more than once faved her from deftruction. Of late her miniftry have changed their fyftem, and have fallen in with the views of the houfe of Bourbon. They have eftablifhed courts, which are inconfiftent with the treaties between Portugal and England, and defraud the Englifh merchants of great parts of their capitals, which they find it impoffible to recover. They have likewife erected two Brazil companies; the one for Maranham, and Gran Para, the other for Perambuco, greatly to the detriment of the Englifh rights. The court of London is, at this time, by its minifters, making the ftrongeft efforts for redrefs, and it is to be hoped they will be attended with success, as Portugal itself cannot exist even as a kingdom, but by the protection of the English. Before these misunderstandings happened, the English trade to Portugal was highly beneficial for both nations. England sent to that country almost the same kind of merchandizes as to Spain, and they received in return vast quantities of wines, with oils, salt, dried and moist fruits, dying drugs, and gold coins.

To France, England sends much tobacco, lead, tin, flannels, horns, and sometimes corn; and always much money at the long run; and brings home, in a smuggling way, a much greater value in wines, brandies, linen, cambrics, lace, velvets, and many other prohibited fopperies, and brocades; always very considerably to England's disadvantage. But as there is no commercial treaty subsisting between England and France, not even in time of peace, England's just loss cannot be ascertained.

England sends to Flanders, serges, flannels, tin, lead, sugars, and tobacco; and receives in return, laces, linen, cambrics, and other articles of luxury, by which England loses upon the balance 250,000 l. sterling yearly. To Germany, England sends cloths and stuffs, tin, pewter, sugars, tobacco, and East India merchandize; and brings thence vast quantities of linen, thread, goat-skins, tinned plates, timbers for all uses, wines, and many other articles. Before the late war, the balance of this trade was thought to be 500,000 l. annually, to the prejudice of England, but that sum is now greatly reduced, as most of the German princes now find it their interest to clothe their armies in English manufactures. I have already mentioned the trade with Denmark, Norway, Sweden, and Russia, which formerly was against England, but the balance is now vastly diminished by the great improvements of her American colonies, in raising hemp, flax, making pot-ashes, iron-works, and tallow, all which used to be furnished to her by the northern powers.

To Holland, England sends an immense quantity of many sorts of merchandize; such as all kinds of woollen goods, hides, corn, coals, East India and Turkey merchandize, tobacco, tar, sugar, rice, ginger, and other American productions; and makes returns in fine linen, lace, cambrics, thread, tapes, incle, madder, boards, drugs, whalebone, train-oil, toys, and many other things; and the balance is usually supposed to be much in favour of England. I shall forbear to mention the trade between England and Ireland, till I come to treat of the latter kingdom.

The acquisitions which the English have made upon the coast of Guinea, particularly their settlement at Senegal, have
opened

opened new sources of commerce with Africa. The French, when in possession of Senegal, traded there for gold, slaves, hides, ostrich feathers, bees-wax, millet, ambergris, and, above all, for that useful commodity, gum Senegal, which was monopolized by them and the Dutch. At present England sends to the coast of Guinea, sundry sorts of coarse woollen and linen, iron, pewter, brass and hardware manufactures, lead-shot, swords, knives, fire-arms, gunpowder, and glass manufactures. And, besides its drawing no money out of the kingdom, it supplies her American colonies with negro slaves, amounting in number to above 100,000 annually. The other returns are in gold dust, gum, dying and other drugs, red wood, Guinea grains, and ivory.

To Arabia, Persia, China, and other parts of Asia, England sends much foreign silver coin and bullion, and sundry English manufactures of woollen goods, and of lead, iron, and brass; and brings home from those remote regions, muslins and cottons of many various kinds, callicoes, raw and wrought silk, chints; teas, porcelain, gold dust, coffee, salt-petre, and many other drugs. And so great a quantity of those various merchandize are re-exported to foreign European nations, as more than abundantly compensates for all the silver bullion which England carries out.

During the infancy of commerce with foreign parts, it was judged expedient to grant exclusive charters to particular bodies or corporations of men; hence the East-India, South-Sea, Hudson's-Bay, Turkey, Russia, and Royal African companies; but the trade to Turkey, Russia, and Africa, is now laid open, though the merchant who proposes to trade thither, must become a member of the company, be subject to their laws and regulations, and advance a small sum at admission, for the purposes of supporting consuls, forts, &c.

With regard to the general account of England's foreign balance, the exports have been computed at seven millions sterling, and its imports at five, of which above one million is re-exported; so that if this calculation is true, England gains, annually, three millions sterling in trade; but this is a point upon which the most experienced merchants, and ablest calculators, differ. After all that has been said, it must be acknowledged, that many exceptions lie to particular estimates. The vast improvements at home, in iron, silk, linen, and other manufactures, and the growing imports from America, must greatly diminish the English imports from abroad. On the other hand, some of the other European nations are making vigorous efforts for rivalling the English manufactures. With what success they may be attended, time alone can determine;

determine; but hitherto, the appearances on their side are not very promising.

Yet our foreign trade does not amount to one sixth part of the inland; the annual produce of the natural products and manufactures of England amounting to above forty-two millions. The gold and silver of England is received from Portugal, Spain, Jamaica, the American colonies, and Africa; but great part of this gold and silver we again export to Holland, and the East Indies; and it is supposed that two-thirds of all the foreign traffic of England is carried on in the port of London.

We shall conclude this account of our trade, with the following comparative view of shipping, which, till a better table can be formed, may have its uses.

If the shipping of Europe be divided into twenty parts, then,

Great Britain, &c. is computed to have	6
The United Provinces	6
Denmark, Sweden, and Russia	2
The trading cities of Germany, and the Austrian Netherlands	1
France	2
Spain and Portugal	2
Italy, and the rest of Europe	1

My bounds will not afford room to enter into a particular detail of the places where those English manufactures, which are mentioned in the above account, are fabricated; a few general strictures, however, may be proper.

Cornwall and Devonshire supply tin and lead, and woollen manufactures are common to almost all the western counties. Dorsetshire manufactures cordage for the navy, feeds an incredible number of sheep, and has large lace manufactures. Somersetshire, besides furnishing lead, copper, and lapis calaminaris, has large manufactures of bone lace, stockings and caps. Bristol, which is both a city and county, is said by some to employ 2000 maritime vessels of all sizes, coasters as well as ships employed in foreign voyages: it has many very important manufactures; its glass-bottle and drinking-glass one alone occupying fifteen large houses: its brass-wire manufactures are also very considerable. Vast manufactures of all kinds, glass in particular, are carried on in London and its neighbourhood; the gold and silver manufactures of London and Spitalfields, through the encouragement given them by the court and the nobility, already equal, if they do not exceed, those of any country in Europe. Colchester is famous for its manufactures of bays and serges; and Norwich for its excellent

excellent stuffs, camblets, druggets, and stockings. Birmingham, though no corporation, is one of the largest and most populous towns in England, and carries on an amazing trade, in excellent and ingenious hard-ware manufactures, particularly snuff and tobacco-boxes, buttons, shoe-buckles, etwees, and many other sorts of steel and brass wares: it is here, and in Sheffield, which is famous for cutlery, that the true genius of English art and industry is to be seen; for such are their excellent inventions for fabricating hard wares, that they can afford them for the fourth part of the price at which other nations can furnish the same or an inferior kind: the cheapness of coals, and all necessaries, and the conveniency of situation, no doubt, contribute greatly to this.

The northern counties of England carry on a prodigious trade in the coarser and slighter woollen manufactures; witness those of Hallifax, Leeds, Wakefield and Richmond, and, above all, Manchester; which, by its variety of beautiful cottons, dimities, tickens, checks, and the like stuffs, is become a large and populous place, though it is only a village, and its highest magistrate a constable. I might mention Coventry, Nottingham, Leicester, Derby, Kendal, and many other manufacturing towns and places of England, each of which is noted for some particular commodity, but the detail would become too bulky. I must not, however, dismiss this head, without observing the beautiful porcelane and earthen ware that has of late years been manufactured in different places of England, particularly in Worcestershire and Staffordshire. The English carpets, particularly those of Wilton and Kidderminster, though but a late manufacture, greatly exceed in beauty any imported from Turkey, and are extremely durable; and consequently, is a vast saving to the nation. Paper, which till very lately, was imported in vast quantities from France and Holland, is now made in every corner of the kingdom, and is a most necessary as well as beneficial manufacture. The parliament, of late, has given encouragement for reviving the manufacture of salt-petre, which was first attempted in England by Sir Walter Raleigh, but was dropt afterwards in favour of the East-India company: the success of such an undertaking would be of immense benefit, as well as security to the nation.

After all that has been said on this head, the seats of manufactures, and consequently of trade, in England, are fluctuating; they will always follow those places where living is cheap, and taxes are easy: for this reason, they have been observed of late to move towards the northern counties, where provisions are in plenty, and the land-tax very low; add to this, that probably, in a few years, the inland navigations which are opening

opening in many parts of England, will make vast alterations as to its internal state.

Many sensible but speculative Englishmen, daily express their apprehensions, lest the weight of taxes and dearness of living in England, should enable other nations to ruin the English trade at foreign markets, by underworking them. This objection is of a long standing, and would have great weight, did not experience prove that it is not founded in fact. An English workman, it is true, lives much better than a foreigner, but then he will do double, if not triple the work, in the same time; and other nations are taxed deeply as well as England.

A short view of the STOCKS, *or public Funds in England, with an historical account of the East-India, the Bank, and South-Sea Companies.*

As there are few subjects of conversation more general than the value of stocks, and hardly any thing so little understood, nothing can be more useful than a short account of them, which we shall here give in as clear and concise a manner as possible; presenting our readers with the rationale of the stocks, and a short history of the several companies, describing the nature of their separate funds, the uses to which they are applied, and the various purposes they answer, both with respect to the government, the companies themselves, and the community in general.

In order to give a clear idea of the money transactions of the several companies, it is proper we should say something of money in general, and particularly of paper money, and the difference between that and the current specie. Money is the standard of the value of all the necessaries and accommodations of life, and paper-money is the representative of that standard to such a degree, as to supply its place, and to answer all the purposes of gold and silver coin. Nothing is necessary to make this representative of money supply the place of specie, but the credit of that office or company, who delivers it; which credit consists in its always being ready to turn it into specie whenever required. This is exactly the case of the Bank of England; the notes of this company are of the same value as the current coin, as they may be turned into it whenever the possessor pleases. From hence, as notes are a kind of money, the counterfeiting them is punished with death, as well as coining.

The method of depositing money in the Bank, and exchanging it for notes (though they bear no interest) is attended with many conveniencies; as they are not only safer than money

money in the hands of the owner himfelf; but as the notes are more portable, and capable of a much more eafy conveyance: fince a bank note for a very large fum, may be fent by the poft, and to prevent the defigns of robbers, may, without damage, be cut in two, and fent at two feveral times. Or bills, called Bank poft-bills, may be had by application at the Bank, which are particularly calculated to prevent loffes by robberies, they being made payable to the order of the perfon who takes them out, at a certain number of days after fight; which gives an opportunity to ftop bills at the Bank, if they fhould be loft, and prevents their being fo eafily negociated by ftrangers as common Bank notes are : and whoever confiders the hazard, the expence and trouble, there would be in fending large fums of gold and filver to and from diftant places, muft alfo confider this as a very fingular advantage. Befides which, another benefit attends them ; for if they are deftroyed by time, or other accident, the Bank will, on oath being made of fuch accident, and fecurity being given, pay the money to the perfon who was in poffeffion of them.

Bank notes differ from all kinds of ftock in thefe three particulars ; 1. They are always of the fame value. 2. They are paid off without being transferred ; and, 3. They bear no intereft; while ftocks are a fhare in a company's funds, bought without any condition of having the principal returned. India bonds indeed (by fome perfons, though erroneoufly, denominated ftock) are to be excepted, they being made payable at fix months notice, either on the fide of the company or of the poffeffor.

By the word STOCK was originally meant, a particular fum of money contributed to the eftablifhing a fund to enable a company to carry on a certain trade, by means of which the perfon became a partner in that trade, and received a fhare in the profit made thereby, in proportion to the money employed. But this term has been extended farther, though improperly, to fignify any fum of money which has been lent to the government, on condition of receiving a certain intereft till the money is repaid, and which makes a part of the national debt. As the fecurity both of the government and of the public companies is efteemed preferable to that of any private perfon, as the ftocks are negotiable and may be fold at any time, and as the intereft is always punctually paid when due, fo they are thereby enabled to borrow money on a lower intereft than what might be obtained from lending it to private perfons, where there is often fome danger of lofing both principal and intereft.

But as every capital stock or fund of a company is raised for a particular purpose, and limited by parliament to a certain sum, it necessarily follows, that when that fund is compleated, no stock can be bought of the company; though shares already purchased, may be transferred from one person to another. This being the case, there is frequently a great disproportion between the original value of the shares, and what is given for them when transferred; for if there are more buyers than sellers, a person who is indifferent about selling, will not part with his share without a considerable profit to himself; and on the contrary, if many are disposed to sell, and few inclined to buy, the value of such shares will naturally fall, in proportion to the impatience of those who want to turn their stock into specie.

These observations may serve to give our readers some idea of the nature of that unjustifiable and dishonest practice called Stock-jobbing, the mystery of which consists in nothing more than this: the persons concerned in that practice, who are denominated Stock-jobbers, make contracts to buy or sell, at a certain distant time, a certain quantity of some particular stock, against which time they endeavour, according as their contract is, either to raise or lower such stock, by raising rumours and spreading fictitious stories, in order to induce people either to sell out in a hurry, and consequently cheap, if they are to deliver stock; or to become unwilling to sell, and consequently to make it dearer, if they are to receive stock.

The persons who make these contracts are not in general possessed of any real stock, and when the time comes that they are to receive or deliver the quantity they have contracted for, they only pay such a sum of money as makes the difference between the price the stock was at when they made the contract, and the price it happens to be at when the contract is fulfilled; and it is no uncommon thing for persons not worth 100 l. to make contracts for the buying or selling 100,000 l. stock. In the language of Exchange-Alley, the buyer in this case is called the Bull, and the seller the Bear.

Besides these, there are another set of men, who though of a higher rank, may properly enough come under the same denomination. These are the great monied men, who are dealers in stock, and contractors with the government whenever any new money is to be borrowed. These indeed are not fictitious, but real buyers and sellers of stock; but by raising false hopes, or creating groundless fears, by pretending to buy or sell large quantities of stock on a sudden, by using the forementioned set of men as their instruments, and other like practices,

tices, are enabled to raife or fall the ftocks one or two per cent. at pleafure.

However, the real value of one ftock above another, on account of its being more profitable to the proprietors, or any thing that will really, or only in imagination, affect the credit of a company, or endanger the government, by which that credit is fecured, muft naturally have a confiderable effect on the ftocks. Thus, with refpect to the intereft of the proprietors, a fhare in the ftock of a trading company which produces 5 l. or 6 l. per cent. per ann. muft be more valuable than an annuity with government fecurity, that produes no more than 3 l. or 4 l. per cent. per annum; and confequently fuch ftock muft fell at a higher price than fuch an annuity. Though it muft be obferved, that a fhare in the ftock of a trading company producing 5 l. or 6 l. per cent. per annum, will not fetch fo much money at market as a government annuity producing the fame fum, becaufe the fecurity of the company is not reckoned equal to that of the government, and the continuance of their paying fo much per annum, is more precarious, as their dividend is, or ought to be, always in proportion to the profits of their trade.

As the ftocks of the Eaft-India, the Bank, and South-Sea companies, are diftinguifhed by different denominations, and are of a very different nature, we fhall give a fhort hiftory of each of them, together with an account of the different ftocks each is poffeffed of, beginning with the Eaft-India company, as the firft eftablifhed.

PUBLIC TRADING COMPANIES.] Of thefe the Eaft-India company takes the lead; and I have already given fome account of it, as being the capital commercial object in England. The firft idea of it was formed in queen Elizabeth's time, but it has fince admitted of vaft alterations. Its fhares, or fupfcriptions, were originally only 50 l. fterling; and its capital only 369,891 l. 5 s. but the directors having a confiderable dividend to make in 1676, it was agreed to join the profits to the capital, by which the fhares were doubled, and, confequently, each became of 100 l. value, and the capital 739,782 l. 10 s. to which capital, if 963,639 l. the profits of the company to the year 1685, be added, the whole ftock will be found to be 1,703,402 l. Though the eftablifhment of this company was vindicated in the cleareft manner by Sir Jofiah Child, and other able advocates, yet the partiality which the duke of York, afterwards James II. had for his favourite African trade, the loffes it fuftained in wars with the Dutch, and the revolutions which had happened in the affairs of Indoftan, damped the ardour of the public to fupport it; fo that

at

at the time of the Revolution, when the war broke out with France, it was in a very indifferent situation. This was in a great measure owing to its having no parliamentary sanction, whereby its stock often sold for one half less than it was really worth; and it was resolved that a new company should be erected, under the authority of parliament.

The opposition given to all the public spirited measures of king William by faction, rendered this proposal a matter of vast difficulty; but at last, after many parliamentary enquiries, the new subscription prevailed; and the subscribers, upon advancing two millions to the public at 8 per cent. obtained an act of parliament in their favour. The old company, however, retained a vast interest both in the parliament and nation; and the act being found in some respects defective, so violent a struggle between the two companies arose, that in the year 1702, they were united by an indenture tripartite. In the year 1708, the yearly fund of 8 per cent. for two millions, was reduced to 5 per cent. by a loan of 1,200,000 l, to the public, without any additional interest; for which consideration the company obtained a prolongation of its exclusive privileges; and a new charter was granted to them, under the title of The United Company of Merchants trading to the East Indies. Its exclusive right of trade was prolonged from time to time; and a farther sum was lent by the company in 1730, by which, though the company's privileges were extended for thirty-three years, yet the interest of their capital, which then amounted to 3,200,000 l. was reduced to three per cent. and called the India 3 per cent. annuities.

Those annuities are different from the trading stock of the company, the proprietors of which, instead of receiving a regular annuity, have, according to their different shares, a dividend of the profits arising from the company's trade; and that dividend rises or falls according to the circumstances of the company, either real, or, as is too often the case, pretended. A proprietor of stock to the amount of 500 l. whether man or woman, native or foreigner, has a right to be a manager, and to give a vote in the general council. Two thousand pounds is the qualification for a director: the directors are twenty-four in number, including the chairman and deputy-chairman, who may be re-elected for four years successively. The chairman has a salary of 200 l. a year, and each of the directors 150 l. The meetings, or court of directors, are to be held at least once a week; but are commonly oftener, being summoned as occasion requires. Out of the body of directors are chosen several committees, who have the peculiar inspection of certain branches of the company's business;

bufinefs; as the committee of correfpondence, a committee of buying, a committee of treafury, a houfe committee, a committee of warehoufes, a committee of fhipping, a committee of accounts, a committee of law-fuits, and a committee to prevent the growth of private trade; who have under them a fecretary, cafhier, clerks, and warehoufe-keepers.

The amazing territorial acquifitions of this company, which are attended with a proportionable encreafe of trade, joined to the diffentions among its managers both at home and abroad, have of late engaged the attention of the legiflature fo much, that a reftriction has been laid for their dividends for a certain time, not to exceed 12 and a half per cent. As to the vaft fortunes acquired by their governors and officers abroad, the ftate in which they live, and their other economical regulations, they are foreign to this head.

Other officers of the company are governors and factors abroad, fome of whom have guards of foldiers, and live in all the ftate of fovereign princes.

BANK OF ENGLAND.] The company of the Bank was incorporated by parliament, in the 5th and 6th years of king William and queen Mary, by the name of the Governors and Company of the Bank of England; in confideration of the loan of 1,200,000 l. granted to the government; for which the fubfcribers received almoft 8 per cent. By this charter, the company are not to borrow under their common feal, unlefs by act of parliament; they are not to trade, or fuffer any perfon in truft for them, to trade in any goods, or merchandize; but they may deal in bills of exchange, in buying or felling bullion, and foreign gold and filver coin, &c.

By an act of parliament paffed in the 8th and 9th year of Will. III. they were impowered to enlarge their capital ftock to 2,201,171 l. 10s. It was then alfo enacted, that bank ftock fhould be a perfonal, and not a real eftate; that no contract either in word or writing, for buying or felling Bank ftock, fhould be good in law, unlefs regiftered in the books of the Bank within feven days; and the ftock transferred in fourteen days, and that it fhould be felony, without benefit of clergy, to counterfeit the common feal of the Bank, or any fealed Bank bill, or any Bank note, or to alter or erafe fuch bills or notes.

By another act paffed in the 7th of queen Anne, the company were impowered to augment their capital to 4,402,343 l. and they then advanced 400,000 l. more to the government; and in 1714, they advanced another loan of 1,500,000 l.

In the third year of the reign of king George I. the intereft of their capital ftock was reduced to 5 per cent. when the

Bank

Bank agreed to deliver up as many Exchequer bills as amounted to 2,000,000 l. and to accept an annuity of 100,000 l. and it was declared lawful for the Bank to call from their members, in proportion to their interests in the capital stock, such sums of money as in a general court should be found necessary. If any member should neglect to pay his share of the monies so called for, at the time appointed by notice in the London Gazette, and fixed upon the Royal Exchange, it should be lawful for the Bank, not only to stop the dividend of such member, and to apply it toward payment of the money in question; but also to stop the transfers of the share of such defaulter, and to charge him with an interest of 5 per cent. per annum, for the money so omitted to be paid: and if the principal and interest should be three months unpaid, the Bank should then have power to sell so much of the stock belonging to the defaulter as would satisfy the same.

After this, the Bank reduced the interest of the 2,000,000 l. lent to the government, from 5 to 4 per cent. and purchased several other annuities, which were afterwards redeemed by the government, and the national debt due to the Bank, reduced to 1,600,000 l. But in 1742, the company engaged to supply the government with 1,600,000 l. at 3 per cent. which is now called the 3 per cent. annuities; so that the government was now indebted to the company 3,200,000 l. the one half carrying 4, and the other 3 per cent.

In the year 1746, the company agreed that the sum of 986,800 l. due to them in the Exchequer bills unsatisfied, on the duties for licences to sell spirituous liquors by retail, should be cancelled, and in lieu thereof to accept of an annuity of 39,442 l. the interest of that sum at 4 per cent. The company also agreed to advance the further sum of 1,000,000 l. into the Exchequer, upon the credit of the duties arising by the malt and land-tax, at 4 per cent. for Exchequer bills to be issued for that purpose; in consideration of which, the company were enabled to augment their capital with 986,800 l. the interest of which, as well as that of the other annuities, was reduced to 3 and a half per cent. till the 25th of December 1757, and from that time to carry only 3 per cent.

And in order to enable them to circulate the said Exchequer bills, they established what is now called Bank circulation. The nature of which not being well understood, we shall take the liberty to be a little more particular in its explanation than we have been with regard to the other stocks.

The company of the Bank are obliged to keep cash sufficient to answer not only the common, but also any extraordinary demand

demand that may be made upon them; and whatever money they have by them, over and above the sum supposed necessary for these purposes, they employ in what may be called the trade of the company; that is to say, in discounting bills of exchange, in buying of gold and silver, and in government securities, &c. But when the Bank entered into the above-mentioned contract, as they did not keep unemployed a larger sum of money than what they deemed necessary to answer their ordinary and extraordinary demands, they could not conveniently take out of their current cash so large a sum as a million, with which they were obliged to furnish the government, without either lessening that sum they employed in discounting, buying gold and silver, &c. (which would have been very disadvantageous to them) or inventing some method that should answer all the purposes of keeping the million in cash. The method which they chose, and which fully answers their end, was as follows.

They opened a subscription, which they renew annually, for a million of money; wherein the subscribers advance 10 per cent. and enter into a contract to pay the remainder, or any part thereof, whenever the Bank shall call upon them, under the penalty of forfeiting the 10 per cent. so advanced; in consideration of which, the Bank pays the subscribers 4 per cent. interest for the money paid in, and one fourth per cent. for the whole sum they agree to furnish; and in case a call should be made upon them for the whole, or any part thereof, the Bank farther agrees to pay them at the rate of 5 per cent. per annum for such sum till they repay it, which they are under an obligation to do at the end of the year. By this means the Bank obtains all the purposes of keeping a million of money by them; and though the subscribers, if no call is made upon them (which is in general the case) receive 6 and a half per cent. for the money they advance, yet the company gains the sum of 23,500 l. per annum by the contract; as will appear by the following account.

The Bank receives from the government for the advance of a million — — — £. 30,000

The Bank pays to the subscribers who advance 100,000 l. and engage to pay (when called for) 900,000 l. more — — 6,500

The clear gain to the Bank therefore is — — 23,500

This is the state of the case, provided the company should make no call on the subscribers, which they will be very unwilling

willing to do, becaufe it would not only leffen their profit, but affect the public credit in general.

Bank ftock may not improperly be called a trading ftock, fince with this they deal very largely in foreign gold and filver, in difcounting bills of exchange, &c. Befides which, they are allowed by the government very confiderable fums annually for the management of the annuities paid at their office. All which advantages, render a fhare in their ftock very valuable; though it is not equal in value to the Eaft-India ftock. The company make dividends of the profits half yearly, of which notice is publicly given; when thofe who have occafion for their money, may readily receive it: but private perfons, if they judge convenient, are permitted to continue their funds, and to have their intereft added to the principal.

This company is under the direction of a governor, deputy-governor, and twenty-four directors, who are annually elected by the general court, in the fame manner as in the Eaft-India company. Thirteen, or more, compofe a court of directors for managing the affairs of the company.

The officers of this company are very numerous.

SOUTH-SEA COMPANY.] During the long war with France, in the reign of queen Anne, the payment of the failors of the royal navy being neglected, and they receiving tickets inftead of money, were frequently obliged, by their neceffities, to fell thefe tickets to avaritious men at a difcount of 40 l. and fometimes 50 l. per cent. By this, and other means, the debts of the nation unprovided for by parliament, and which amounted to 9,471,321 l. fell into the hands of thefe ufurers. On which Mr. Harley, at that time chancellor of the Exchequer, and afterwards earl of Oxford, propofed a fcheme to allow the proprietors of thefe debts and deficiencies 6 l. per cent. per annum, and to incorporate them, in order to their carrying on a trade to the South-fea; and they were accordingly incorporated under the title of the Governor and Company of Merchants of Great-Britain, trading to the South-Seas, and other parts of America, and for encouraging the Fifhery, &c.

Though this company feem formed for the fake of commerce, it is certain the miniftry never thought ferioufly, during the courfe of the war, about making any fettlements on the coaft of South America, which was what flattered the expectations of the people; nor was it indeed ever carried into execution, or any trade ever undertaken by this company, except the Affiento, in purfuance of the treaty of Utrecht, for furnifhing the Spaniards with negroes; of which this company was deprived upon receiving 100,000 l. in lieu of all claims upon Spain,

Spain, by a convention between the courts of Great-Britain and Spain, soon after the treaty of Aix la Chapelle, in 1748.

Some other sums were lent to the government in the reign of queen Anne, at 6 per cent. In the third of George I. the interest of the whole was reduced to 5 per cent. and they advanced two millions more to the government at the same interest. By the statue of the 6th of George I. it was declared, that this company might redeem all or any of the redeemable national debts; in consideration of which, the company were empowered to augment their capital according to the sums they should discharge: and for enabling the company to raise such sums for purchasing annuities, exchanging for ready money new Exchequer bills, carrying on their trade, &c. the company might, by such means as they should think proper, raise such sums of money as in a general court of the company should be judged necessary. The company were also empowered to raise money on the contracts, bonds, or obligations under their common seal, on the credit of their capital stock. But if the sub-governor, deputy-governor, or other members of the company, should purchase lands or revenues of the crown, upon account of the corporation, or lend money by loan or anticipation, on any branch of the revenue, other than such part only on which a credit of loan was granted by parliament, such sub-governor, or other member of the company, should forfeit treble the value of the money so lent.

The fatal South-Sea scheme, transacted in the year 1720, was executed upon the last mentioned statute. The company had at first set out with good success, and the value of their stock, for the first five years, had risen faster than that of any other company, and his majesty, after purchasing 10,000 l. stock, had condescended to be their governor. Things were in this situation, when taking advantage of the above statute, the South-Sea bubble was projected. The pretended design of which was to raise a fund for carrying on a trade to the South-Sea, and purchasing annuities, &c. paid to the other companies: and proposals were printed and distributed, shewing the advantages of the design, and inviting persons into it. The sum necessary for carrying it on, together with the profits that were to arise from it, were divided into a certain number of shares, or subscriptions, to be purchased by persons disposed to adventure therein. And the better to carry on the deception, the directors engaged to make very large dividends; and actually declared that every 100 l. original stock would yield 50 l. per annum: which occasioned so great a rise of their stock, that a share of 100 l. was sold for upwards of 800 l. This was in the month of July; but before the end of of September, it fell to 150 l. by which multitudes were ruined, and such a scene of distress occasioned, as is scarcely to be conceived. But the consequences of this infamous scheme are too well known. We shall pass over all the other transactions of this company in the reign of king George I. as not material to our present purpose.

By a statute of the 6th of George II. it was enacted, that from and after the 24th of June, 1733, the capital stock of this company, which amounted to 14,651,103 l. 8 s. 1 d. and the shares of the respective proprietors, should be divided into four equal parts, three-fourths of which should be converted into a joint stock, attended with annuities, after the rate of 4 per cent. until redemption by parliament, and should be called, the new South-Sea annuities; and the other fourth part should remain in the company as a trading capital stock, attended with the residue of the annuities or funds payable at the Exchequer to the company for their whole capital, till redemption; and attended with the same sums allowed for the charge of management, and with all effects, profits of trade, debts, privileges, and advantages, belonging to the South-Sea company. That the accomptant of the company should, twice every year, at Christmas and Midsummer, or within one month after, state an account of the company's affairs, which should be laid before the next general court, in order to their declaring a dividend: and all dividends should be made out of the clear profits, and should not exceed what the company might reasonably divide, without incurring any farther debt; provided that the company should not at any time divide more than 4 per cent. per annum, until their debts were discharged; and that the South-Sea company, and their trading stock, should, exclusively from the new joint stock of annuities, be liable to all the debts and incumbrances of the company; and that the company should cause to be kept, within the city of London, an office and books, in which all transfers of the new annuities should be entered, and signed by the party making such transfer, or his attorney; and the person to whom such transfer should be made, or his attorney, should underwrite his acceptance; and no other method of transferring the annuities should be good in law.

The annuities of this company, as well as the other, are now reduced to 3 l. per cent.

This company is under the direction of a governor, sub-governor, deputy-governor, and twenty-one directors; but no person is qualified to be governor, his majesty excepted, unless such governor has in his own name and right, 5000 l. in the trading stock; the sub-governor is to have 4000 l. the deputy 3000 l. and a director 2000 l. in the same stock. In every general court, every member, having in his own name and right, 500 l. in trading stock, has one vote; if 2000 l. two votes; if 3000 l. three votes, and if 5000 l. four votes.

The East-India company, the Bank of England, and the South-Sea company, are the only incorporated bodies to which the government is indebted, except the Million-Bank, whose capital is only one million, constituted to purchase the reversion of the long Exchequer orders.

The interest of all the debts owing by the government, is now reduced to 3 per cent. excepting only the annuities for the years 1756, and 1758, the life annuities, and the Exchequer orders: but the South-Sea company still continues to divide 4 per cent. on their present capital stock; which they are enabled to do from the profits they make on the sums allowed to them for management of the annuities paid at their office, and from the interest of annuities which are not claimed by the proprietors.

As the prices of the different stocks are continually fluctuating above and below *par*, so when a person who is not acquainted with transactions of that nature, reads in the papers the prices of stocks, where Bank stock is marked perhaps 127, India ditto 134 a 134¼, South-Sea ditto 97½, &c. he is to understand, that 100 l. of those respective stocks sell at such a time for those several sums.

In comparing the prices of the different stocks one with another, it must be remembered, that the interest due on them from the time of the last payment, is taken into the current price, and the seller never receives any separate consideration for it, except in the case of India bonds, where the interest due is calculated to the day of the sale, and paid by the purchaser, over and above the premium agreed for. But as the interest on the different stocks is paid at different times, this, if not rightly understood, would lead a person, not well acquainted with them, into considerable mistakes in his computation of their value; some always having a quarter's interest due on them more than others, which makes an appearance of a considerable difference in the price, when, in reality, there is none at all. Thus, for instance, old South-Sea annuities sell at present for £. 85 ½, or £. 85 10 s. while new South-Sea annuities fetch only £. 84 ¼, or £ 84 15 s. though each of them produce the same annual sum of 3 per cent. but the old annuities have a quarter's interest more due on them than the new annuities, which amount to 15 s. the exact difference. There is, however, one or two causes that will always make one species of annuities sell somewhat lower than another, though of the same real value ; one of which is, the annuities making but a small capital, and there not being, for that reason, so many people at all times ready to buy into it, as into others, where the quantity is larger; because it is apprehended that whenever the government pays off the national debt, they will begin with that particular species of annuity, the capital of which is the smallest.

A stock may likewise be affected by the court of Chancery ; for if that court should order the money which is under their direction, to be laid out in any particular stock, that stock, by having more purchasers, will be raised to a higher price than any other of the like value.

By what has been said, the reader will perceive how much the credit and the interest of the nation depends on the support of the public funds.—While the annuities, and interest for money advanced, is there regularly paid, and the principal insured by both prince and people, (a security not to be had in other nations) foreigners will lend us their property, and all Europe be interested in our welfare; the paper of the companies will be converted into money and merchandize, and Great-Britain can never want cash to carry her schemes into execution.

In other nations, credit is founded on the word of the prince, if a monarchy ; or that of the people, if a republic ; but here it is established on the interests of both prince and people, which is the strongest security : for however lovely and engaging honesty may be in other respects, interest in money-matters will always obtain confidence ; because many people pay great regard to their interest, who have but little veneration for virtue.

ENGLAND.

The Amount of the Capitals at the Bank, Threadneedle-street, South-Sea, ditto; and India-House, Leadenhall-street.	Interest per annum.	When due.	When transferred.	Holidays.
BANK STOCK.	£10,780,000			Jan. 1, 6, 18, 25, 30
—4 per cent. con. an.	20,240,000	5 April & 10 Oct.	Tues. Thurs. & Frid.	Feb. 2, 24.
*4 per cent. 1763	3,500,000	Ditto	Mon. Tu. Th. & Fr.	March 25.
4 per cent. navy	140,000	Ditto	Wedn. & Satur.	April 23, 25.
3½ per cent. 1756	1,741,527 3 9	25 March & 29 Sept.	Ditto	May 1, 29.
*3½ per cent. 1758	1,500,000	5 Jan. & 5 July	Tues. & Thurs.	June 4, 11, 24, 29.
—3 per cent. conf.	4,500,000	Ditto	Mon. Wed. & Frid.	July 25.
—3 per cent. red.	35,127,821 5 1	Ditto	M.Tu.We.Th.&Fr.	August 12, 24.
—3 per cent. 1726	19,201,323 16 4	5 April & 10 Oct.	Tu. Wed. Th. & Fr.	Sept. 2, 21, 22, 29.
Long ann. for 99 years com. 5 Jan. 1761	1,000,000	5 Jan. & 5 July	Wed. & Satur.	Oct. 18, 25, 28.
				Nov. 1, 4, 5, 9, 30.
	248,150	Ditto	Ditto	Dec. 21, 25, 26, 27, 28
SOUTH-SEA STOCK.	3,652,784 8 6	Ditto	Mon. Wed. & Frid.	MOVEABLE.
—3 per cent. old an.	12,404,270 2 7	5 April & 10 Oct.	Ditto	Shrove Tu. Ash. Wed
—3 per cent. new	8,958,255 2 10	5 Jan. & 5 July	Tues. Thurs. & Sat.	Good Friday.
—3 per cent. 1751	2,100,000	Ditto	Tues. & Thurs.	East. Mo. Tu. & Wed.
IND. STOCK, 12 perC.	3,200,000	Ditto	Do. & Sat. till 12 o'cl.	Holy Thursday.
—3 per cent. ann.	3,000,000	5 April & 10 Oct.	Mon. Wed. & Fri.	Whit. M. T. & Wed.
N. B. Interest on India bonds due 31ft March and 30th of September.	£130,915,931 19 1	£4,982,458 13	N. B. Dividends paid at the Bank from 9 to 11, and 1 to 3 ⎫ Saturday Transfers from 11 to 1 ⎬ after 1 Div. at the So. Sea & Ind. H. from 9 to 12 ⎭ excepted. Transfers from 12 to 1	

☞ These marked with a * were paid off between the years 1765 and 1771.

ENGLAND.

CONSTITUTION AND LAWS.] Tacitus, in describing such a constitution as that of England, seems to think, that however beautiful it may be in theory, it will be found impracticable in the execution. Experience has proved his mistake, for by certain checks, that operate mutually, and which did not fall within his ideas, the English constitution has continued in its full vigour for above 500 years. It must, at the same time, be admitted, that it has received, during that time, many amendments, and some interruptions, but its principles are the same, with those described by the above-mentioned historian, as belonging to the Germans, and the other northern ancestors of the English nation, and which are very improperly blended under the name of Gothic. On the first invasion of England by the Saxons, who came from Germany, and the neighbouring countries, their laws and manners were pretty much the same, as those mentioned by Tacitus. The people had a leader in time of war. The conquered lands, in proportion to the merits of his followers, and their abilities to serve him, were distributed among them, and the whole was considered as the common property which they were to unite in defending against all invaders. Fresh adventurers coming over, under separate leaders, the old inhabitants were driven into Wales, and those leaders, at last, assumed the title of kings over the several districts they had conquered. This change of appellation made them more respectable among the Britons, and their neighbours the Scots and Picts, but did not encrease their power, the operations of which continued to be confined to military affairs.

All civil matters were proposed in a general assembly of the chief officers, and the people, till, by degrees, sheriffs, and other civil officers, were appointed. The country was divided into wapentakes, and hundreds, names that still subsist in England, and overseers were chosen to direct them for the good of the whole. The sheriff was the judge of all civil and criminal matters, within the county, and to him, after the introduction of Christianity, was added the bishop. In process of time, as business multiplied, itinerant, and other judges, were appointed; but by the earliest records, it appears, that all civil matters were decided by 12 or 16 men, living in the neighbourhood of the place where the dispute lay, and here we have the original of English juries.

Before the introduction of Christianity, we know not whether the Saxons admitted of juries in criminal matters, but we are certain that there was no action so criminal, as not to be compensated for by money*. A mulct was imposed

in

---

* Called by the Saxons GUELT, and thence the word *guilty* in criminal trials.

in proportion to the guilt, even if it was the murder of the king, upon the malefactor, and by paying it, he purchased his pardon. Those barbarous usages seem to have ceased soon after the Saxons were converted to Christianity, and cases of murder and felony were then tried, even in the king's court, by a jury.

Royalty, among the Saxons, was not, strictly speaking, hereditary, though in fact it came to be rendered so through the affection which the people bore for the blood of their kings, and for preserving the regularity of government. Even estates and honours were not strictly hereditary, till they were made so by William the Conqueror.

That prince new modelled the English constitution. He divided the conquered lands among his followers, as had been agreed before the time of the invasion, in perpetual property. He partitioned out the lands into knight's fees, an indetermined number of which formed a barony, and those baronies were given to the great noblemen, who composed what is called the King's Court, or Court of Peers, from every baron being a peer, or equal to another. In this court all civil as well as military matters, and the proportions of knights and men, which each baron was to raise for the king's service, were settled. Even bishoprics were converted into lay baronies, and were obliged, as others, to furnish their quotas. In other respects, the Conqueror, and the first princes of the Norman line, did all they could to efface from the minds of the people, the remembrance of the Saxon constitution, but the attempt was to no purpose. The nobility, as well as the people, had their complaints against the crown, and after much war and blood-shed, the famous charter of English liberties, so well known by the name of Magna Charta, was forcibly, in a manner, obtained from king John, and confirmed by his son Henry III. who succeeded to the crown in 1216. It does not appear, that till this reign, and after a great deal of blood had been spilt, the commons of England were represented in parliament, or the great council of the nation; so entirely had the barons engrossed to themselves the disposal of property.

The precise year, when the house of commons was formed, is not known, but we are certain, that it began in the reign of Henry III. though we shall not enter into any disputes about their specific powers. We shall therefore proceed to describe the constitution, as it stands at present.

In all states there is an absolute supreme power, to which the right of legislation belongs; and which, by the singular constitution of these kingdoms, is here vested in the king, lords, and commons.

OF THE KING.] The supreme executive power of Great Britain and Ireland, is vested by our constitution in a single person, king, or queen; for it is indifferent to which sex the crown descends: the person entitled to it, whether male or female, is immediately intrusted with all the ensigns, rights, and prerogatives of sovereign power.

The grand fundamental maxim upon which the right of succession to the throne of these kingdoms depends, is: "that the crown, by common law and constitutional custom, is hereditary; and this in a manner peculiar to itself: but that the right of inheritance may from time to time be changed or limited by act of parliament: under which limitations the crown still continues hereditary."

That the reader may enter more clearly into the deduction of the following royal succession, by its being transferred from the house of Tudor, to that of Stuart, it may be proper to inform him that on the death of queen Elizabeth, without issue, it became necessary to recur to the other issue of her grandfather Henry VII. by Elizabeth of York his queen: whose eldest daughter Margaret, having married James IV. king of Scotland, king James the Sixth of Scotland, and of England the First, was the lineal descendant from that alliance. So that in his person, as clearly as in Henry VIII. centered all the claims of the different competitors, from the Norman conquest downward; he being indisputably the lineal heir of the conqueror. And, what is still more remarkable, in his person also centered the right of the Saxon monarchs, which had been suspended from the conquest till his accession. For Margaret, the sister of Edgar Atheling, the daughter of Edward the Outlaw, and granddaughter of king Edmund Ironside, was the person in whom the hereditary right of the Saxon kings, supposing it not abolished by the conquest, resided. She married Malcolm III. king of Scotland; and Henry II. by a descent from Matilda their daughter, is generally called the restorer of the Saxon line. But it must be remembered, that Malcolm, by his Saxon queen, had sons as well as daughters; and that the royal family of Scotland, from that time downward, were the offspring of Malcolm and Margaret. Of this royal family king James I. was the direct lineal descendant; and therefore united in his person every possible claim, by hereditary right, to the English as well as Scottish throne, being the heir both of Egbert, and William the Conqueror.

At the revolution in 1688, the convention of estates, or representative body of the nation, declared, that the misconduct of
king

king James II. amounted to an abdication of the government, and that the throne was thereby vacant.

In consequence of this vacancy, and from a regard to the ancient line, the convention appointed the next Protestant heirs of the blood royal of king Charles I. to fill the vacant throne, in the old order of succession; with a temporary exception, or preference, to the person of king William III.

On the impending failure of the Protestant line of king Charles I. (whereby the throne might again have become vacant) the king and parliament extended the settlement of the crown to the Protestant line of king James I. viz. to the princess Sophia of Hanover, and the heirs of her body, being protestants: and she is now the common stock, from whom the heirs of the crown must descend *.

The

---

* A Chronology of English KINGS, from the time that this country became united under one monarch, in the person of Egbert, who subdued the other princes of the Saxon heptarchy, and gave the name of Angle-land to this part of the island, the Saxons and Angles having, about four centuries before, invaded and subdued the ancient Britons, whom they drove into Wales and Cornwall.

Began to reign.

800 Egbert
838 Ethelwulf
857 Ethelbald
860 Ethelbert
866 Ethelred
871 Alfred the Great
901 Edward the Elder
925 Athelstan } Saxon Princes.
941 Edmund
946 Edred
955 Edwy
959 Edgar
975 Edward the Martyr
978 Ethelred II.
1016 Edmund II.

1017 Canute, king of Denmark
1035 Harold } Danish.
1039 Hardicanute

1041 Edward the Confessor } Saxon.
1065 Harold, Usurper

1066 William I. { (Commonly called the Conqueror, from his conquering England) duke of Normandy, a province facing the south of England, now annexed to the French monarchy.

1087 William II. } Sons of the Conqueror.
1100 Henry I.

1135 Stephen, grandson to the Conqueror, by his fourth daughter Adela.

1154 Henry II. { (Plantagenet) grandson of Henry I. by his daughter the empress Maud, and her second husband Geoffroy Plantagenet.

1189 Richard I. } Sons of Henry II.
1199 John

1216 Henry III. son of John.
1272 Edward I. son of Henry III.

1307 Ed-

The true ground and principle, upon which the revolution proceeded, was an entirely new case in politics, which had never before happened in our history; the abdication of the reigning monarch, and the vacancy of the throne thereupon. It was not a defeazance of the right of succession, and a new limitation of the crown, by the king and both houses of parliament: it was the act of the nation alone, upon a conviction that there was no king in being. For in a full assembly of the lords and commons, met in convention upon the supposition of this vacancy, both houses came to this resolution; "that king James II. having endeavoured to subvert the constitution of the kingdom, by breaking the original contract between king and people; and by the advice of jesuits, and other wicked persons, having violated the fundamental laws; and having

Began to reign.

1307 Edward II. son of Edward I.
1327 Edward III. son of Edward II.
1377 Richard II. grandson of Edward III. by his eldest son, the black prince.
1399 Henry IV. { Son to John of Gaunt, duke of Lancaster, 4th son to Edward III. }
1413 Henry V. son of Henry IV. } House of Lancaster.
1422 Henry VI. son of Henry V.
1461 Edward IV. descended from Edw. III. by Lionel his 3d son
1483 Edward V. son of Edward IV. } House of York.
1483 Richard III. brother of Edward IV.
1485 Henry VII. { ('Tudor) son of the countess of Richmond, of the House of Lancaster. } House of Tudor, in whom were united the houses of Lancaster and York, by Henry VII's marriage with Elizabeth, daughter of Edward IV.
1509 Henry VIII. son of Henry VII.
1547 Edward VI. son of Henry VIII.
1553 Mary } Daughters of Henry VIII.
1558 Elizabeth
1603 James I. { Great grandson of James IV. king of Scotland, by Margaret, daughter of Henry VII. and first of the Stuart family in England.
1625 Charles I. son of James I.
Usurpation by commonwealth and Cromwell.
1649 Charles II. } Sons of Charles I.
1685 James II.
1688 { William III. nephew and son-in-law of James II.
and Mary } Daughters of James II. in whom ended the Protestant line of
1702 Anne } Charles I. for James II. upon his abdicating the throne, carried with him his infant son (the late pretender) who was excluded by act of parliament, which settled the succession in the next Protestant heirs of James I. The surviving issue of James, at the time of his death, were a son and a daughter, viz. Charles, who succeeded him, and the princess Elizabeth, who married the elector palatine, who took the title of king of Bohemia, and left a daughter, the princess Sophia, who married the duke of Brunswick Lunenburg, by whom she had George, elector of Hanover, who ascended the throne, by act of parliament, expressly made in favour of his mother.

1714 George I.
1727 George II. son of George I. } House of Hanover.
1760 George III. grandson of George II.

having withdrawn himself out of this kingdom, has abdicated the government, and that the throne is thereby vacant." Thus ended at once, by this sudden and unexpected vacancy of the throne, the old line of succession: which from the conquest had lasted above 600 years, and from the union of the Saxon heptarchy in king Egbert, almost 900.

Though in some points (owing to the peculiar circumstances of things and persons) the revolution was not altogether so perfect as might have been wished; yet from thence a new æra commenced, in which the bounds of prerogative and liberty have been better defined, the principles of government more thoroughly examined and understood, and the rights of the subject more explicitly guarded by legal provisions, than in any other period of the English history. In particular, it is worthy observation, that the convention, in this their judgment, avoided with great wisdom the wild extreams into which the visionary theories of some zealous republicans would have led them. They held that this misconduct of king James amounted to an endeavour to subvert the constitution, and not to an actual subversion, or total dissolution of the government. They therefore very prudently voted it to amount to no more than an abdication of the government, and a consequent vacancy of the throne; whereby the government was allowed to subsist, though the executive magistrate was gone: and the kingly office to remain, though king James was no longer king. And thus the constitution was kept intire; which, upon every sound principle of government, must otherwise have fallen to pieces, had so principal and constituent a part as the royal authority been abolished, or even suspended.

Hence it is easy to collect, that the title to the crown is at present hereditary, tho' not quite so absolutely hereditary as formerly; and the common stock or ancestor, from whom the descent must be derived, is also different. Formerly the common stock was king Egbert; then William the Conqueror; afterward, in James I.'s time, the two common stocks united, and so continued till the vacancy of the throne in 1688: now it is the princess Sophia, in whom the inheritance was vested by the new king and parliament. Formerly the descent was absolute, and the crown went to the next heir without any restriction; but now, upon the new settlement, the inheritance is conditional; being limited to such heirs only, of the body of the princess Sophia, as are Protestant members of the church of England, and are married to none but Protestants.

And in this due medium consists the true constitutional notion of the right of succession to the imperial crown of these kingdoms.

kingdoms. The extremes, between which it steers, are each of them equally destructive of those ends for which societies were formed, and are kept on foot. Where the magistrate, upon every succession, is elected by the people, and may by the express provision of the laws be deposed (if not punished) by his subjects, this may sound like the perfection of liberty, and look well enough when delineated on paper; but in practice will be ever productive of tumult, contention, and anarchy. And, on the other hand, divine indefeasible hereditary right, when coupled with the doctrine of unlimited passive obedience, is surely of all constitutions the most thoroughly slavish and dreadful. But when such an hereditary right, as our laws have created and vested in the royal stock, is closely interwoven with those liberties, which are equally the inheritance of the subject; this union will form a constitution, in theory the most beautiful of any, in practice the most approved, and, in all probability, will prove in duration the most permanent. This constitution, it is the duty of every Briton to understand, to revere, and to defend.

The principal duties of the king are expressed in his oath at the coronation, which is administered by one of the archbishops, or bishops of the realm, in the presence of all the people; who, on their parts, do reciprocally take the oath of allegiance to the crown. This coronation oath is conceived in the following terms:

" *The archbishop, or bishop, shall say,* Will you solemnly promise and swear, to govern the people of this kingdom of England, and the dominions thereunto belonging, according to the statutes in parliament agreed on, and the laws and customs of the same?—*The king or queen shall say,* I solemnly promise so to do.

Archbishop or bishop. Will you to your power cause law and justice, in mercy, to be executed in all your judgments? —*King or queen.* I will.

Archbishop or bishop. Will you to the utmost of your power maintain the laws of God, the true profession of the gospel, and the Protestant reformed religion established by the law? And will you preserve unto the bishops and clergy of this realm, and to the churches committed to their charge, all such rights and privileges as by the law do or shall appertain unto them, or any of them?—*King or queen.* All this I promise to do.

After this the king or queen, laying his or her hand upon the holy gospels, shall say, The things which I have here before promised, I will perform and keep: so help me God. *And then shall kiss the book."*

This is the form of the coronation oath, as it is now prescribed by our laws: and we may observe, that in the king's part in this original contract, are expressed all the duties that a monarch can owe to his people; viz. to govern according to law: to execute judgment in mercy: and to maintain the established religion. With respect to the latter of these three branches, we may farther remark, that by the act of union, 5 Ann. c. 8. two preceding statutes are recited and confirmed; the one of the parliament of Scotland, the other of the parliament of England: which enact; the former, that every king at his succession shall take and subscribe an oath, to preserve the Protestant religion, and Presbyterian church government in Scotland: the latter, that at his coronation, he shall take and subscribe a similar oath, to preserve the settlement of the church of England within England, Ireland, Wales, and Berwick, and the territories thereunto belonging.

The king of Great Britain, notwithstanding the limitations of the power of the crown, already mentioned, is one of the greatest monarchs reigning over a free people. His person is sacred in the eye of the law, which makes it high treason so much as to imagine or intend his death; neither can he, in himself, be deemed guilty of any crime, the law taking no cognizance of his actions, but only in the persons of his ministers, if they infringe the laws of the land. As to his power, it has no bounds (except where it breaks in upon the liberty and property of his subjects, as in making new laws, or raising new taxes) for he can make war or peace; send and receive ambassadors; make treaties of league and commerce; levy armies, fit out fleets, employ them as he thinks proper; grant commissions to his officers both by sea and land, or revoke them at pleasure; dispose of all magazines, castles, &c. summon the parliament to meet, and, when met, adjourn, prorogue, or dissolve it at pleasure; refuse his assent to any bill, tho' it hath passed both houses; which, consequently, by such a refusal, has no more force than if it had never been moved. He possesseth the right of chusing his own council; of nominating all the great officers of state, of the household, and the church; and, in fine, is the fountain of honour, from whom all degrees of nobility and knighthood are derived. Such is the dignity and power of a king of Great Britain.

OF THE PARLIAMENT.] Parliaments, in some shape, are, as has been observed, of as high antiquity as the Saxon government in this island; and have subsisted, in their present form, at least 500 years.

The parliament is assembled by the king's writs, and its sitting must not be intermitted above three years. Its constituent parts are, the king sitting there in his royal political capacity,

pacity, and the three estates of the realm; the lords spiritual, the lords temporal, (who sit together with the king, in one house) and the commons, who sit by themselves in another. The king and these three estates, together, form the great corporation or body politic of the kingdom, of which the king is said to be *caput, principium, et finis*. For upon their coming together the king meets them, either in person, or by representation; without which there can be no beginning of a parliament; and he also has alone the power of dissolving them.

It is highly necessary for preserving the balance of the constitution, that the executive power should be a branch, tho' not the whole, of the legislature. The crown cannot begin of itself any alterations in the present established law; but it may approve or disapprove of the alterations suggested and consented to by the two houses. The legislative therefore cannot abridge the executive power of any rights which it now has by law, without its own consent: since the law must perpetually stand as it now does, unless all the powers will agree to alter it. And herein indeed consists the true excellence of the English government, that all the parts of it form a mutual check upon each other. In the legislature, the people are a check upon the nobility, and the nobility a check upon the people; by the mutual privilege of rejecting what the other has resolved: while the king is a check upon both, which preserves the executive power from encroachments.

The lords spiritual consist of two archbishops and 24 bishops. The lords temporal consist of all the peers of the realm, the bishops not being in strictness held to be such, but merely lords of parliament. Some of the peers sit by descent, as do all antient peers; some by creation, as do all the new-made ones: others, since the union with Scotland, by election, which is the case of the 16 peers, who represent the body of the Scots nobility. The number of peers is indefinite, and may be increased at will by the power of the crown.

A body of nobility is more peculiarly necessary in our mixed and compounded constitution, in order to support the rights of both the crown and the people; by forming a barrier to withstand the encroachments of both. It creates and preserves that gradual scale of dignity, which proceeds from the peasant to the prince; rising like a pyramid from a broad foundation, and diminishing to a point as it rises. The nobility therefore are the pillars, which are reared from among the people, more immediately to support the throne: and if that falls, they must also be buried under its ruins. Accordingly, when in the last century the commons had determined to extirpate monarchy, they also voted the house of lords to be useless and dangerous.

The commons confist of all such men of any property in the kingdom, as have not seats in the house of lords; every one of which has a voice in parliament, either personally, or by his representatives. In a free state, every man, who is supposed a free agent, ought to be, in some measure, his own governor; and therefore a branch at least of the legislative power should reside in the whole body of the people. In so large a state as ours, it is very wisely contrived, that the people should do that by their representatives, which it is impracticable to perform in person: representatives, chosen by a number of minute and separate districts, wherein all the voters are, or easily may be, distinguished. The counties are therefore represented by knights, elected by the proprietors of lands: the cities and boroughs are represented by citizens and burgesses, chosen by the mercantile part, or supposed trading interest of the nation. The number of English representatives is 513, and of Scots 45; in all 558. And every member, though chosen by one particular district, when elected and returned, serves for the whole realm. For the end of his coming thither is not particular, but general; not barely to advantage his constituents, but the common wealth, and to advise his majesty, as appears from the writ of summons.

These are the constituent parts of a parliament, the king, the lords spiritual and temporal, and the commons. Parts, of which each is so necessary, that the consent of all three is required to make any new law that should bind the subject. Whatever is enacted for law by one, or by two only, of the three, is no statute; and to it no regard is due, unless in matters relating to their own privileges.

The power and jurisdiction of parliament, says Sir Edward Coke, is so transcendent and absolute, that it cannot be confined, either for causes or persons, within any bounds. It hath sovereign and uncontrolable authority in making, confirming, enlarging, restraining, abrogating, repealing, reviving, and expounding of laws, concerning matters of all possible denominations, ecclesiastical, or temporal, civil, military, maritime, or criminal: this being the place where that absolute despotic power, which must in all governments reside somewhere, is entrusted by the constitution of these kingdoms. All mischiefs and grievances, operations and remedies, that transcend the ordinary course of the laws, are within the reach of this extraordinary tribunal. It can regulate or new model the succession to the crown; as was done in the reign of Henry VIII. and William III. It can alter the established religion of the land; as was done in a variety of instances, in the reigns of king Henry VIII. and his three children. It can change

change and create afresh even the constitution of the kingdom, and of parliaments themselves; as was done by the act of union, and the several statutes for triennial and septennial elections. It can, in short, do every thing that is not naturally impossible; and therefore some have not scrupled to call its power, by a figure rather too bold, the omnipotence of parliament. True it is, that what the parliament doth, no authority upon earth can undo. So that it is a matter most essential to the liberties of this kingdom, that such members be delegated to this important trust, as are most eminent for their probity, their fortitude, and their knowledge; for it was a known apothegm of the great lord treasurer Burleigh, "that England could never be ruined but by a parliament:" and, as Sir Matthew Hale observes, this being the highest and greatest court, over which none other can have jurisdiction in the kingdom, if by any means a misgovernment should any way fall upon it, the subjects of this kingdom are left without all manner of remedy.

In order to prevent the mischiefs that might arise, by placing this extensive authority in hands that are either incapable, or else improper, to manage it, it is provided that no one shall sit or vote in either house of parliament, unless he be twenty-one years of age. To prevent innovations in religion and government, it is enacted, that no member shall vote or sit in either house, till he hath, in the presence of the house, taken the oaths of allegiance, supremacy, and abjuration; and subscribed and repeated the declaration against transubstantiation, the invocation of saints, and the sacrifice of the mass. To prevent dangers that may arise to the kingdom from foreign attachments, connexions, or dependencies, it is enacted, that no alien, born out of the dominions of the crown of Great-Britain, even though he be naturalized, shall be capable of being a member of either house of parliament.

Some of the more notorious privileges of the members of either house are, privilege of speech, of person, of their domestics, and of their lands and goods. As to the first, privilege of speech, it is declared by the statute of 1 W & M. st. 2. c. 2. as one of the liberties of the people, "that the freedom of speech, and debates, and proceedings in parliament, ought not to be impeached or questioned in any court or place out of parliament." And this freedom of speech is particularly demanded of the king in person, by the speaker of the house of commons, at the opening of every new parliament. So likewise are the other privileges, of person, servants, lands and goods. This includes not only privilege from illegal violence, but also from legal arrests, and seisures by process from the courts of law. To assault by violence a member of either house, or his menial servants, is a high contempt of parliament, and there punished with the utmost severity. Neither can any member of either house be arrested and taken into custody, nor served with any process of the courts of law; nor can his menial servants be arrested; nor can any entry be made on his lands; nor can his goods be distrained or seized, without a breach of the privilege of parliament *.

The house of lords have a right to be attended, and consequently are, by the judges of the court of king's bench and common-pleas, and such of the barons of the exchequer, as are of the degree of the coif, or have been made serjeants at law; as likewise by the masters of the court of chancery; for their advice in point of law, and for the greater dignity of their proceedings.

The speaker of the house of lords is generally the lord chancellor, or lord-keeper of the great seal, which dignities are commonly vested in the same person.

Each peer has a right, by leave of the house, as being his own representative, when a vote passes contrary to his sentiments, to enter his dissent on the journals of the house, with the reasons for such dissent; which is usually stiled his protest. Upon particular occasions, however, these protests have been so bold as to give offence to the majority of the house, and have therefore been expunged from the journals.

The house of commons may be properly stiled the grand inquest of Great Britain, impowered to enquire into all national grievances, in order to see them redressed.

The peculiar laws and customs of the house of commons relate principally to the raising of taxes, and the elections of members to serve in parliament.

With regard to taxes: it is the antient indisputable privilege and right of the house of commons, that all grants of subsidies, or parliamentary aids, do begin in their house, and are first bestowed by them; although their grants are not effectual to all intents and purposes, until they have the assent of the other two branches of the legislature. The general reason given for this exclusive privilege of the house of commons, is, that the supplies are raised upon the body of the people, and therefore it is proper that they alone should have the right of taxing themselves. And so reasonably jealous are the commons

---

* This exemption from arrests for lawful debts, was always considered by the public as a grievance. The lords and commons therefore generously relinquished their privilege by act of parliament 1770; and members of both houses may now be sued like other debtors.

mons of this privilege, that herein they will not suffer the other house to exert any power but that of rejecting; they will not permit the least alteration or amendment to be made by the lords to the mode of taxing the people by a money bill. Under this appellation are included all bills, by which money is directed to be raised upon the subject, for any purpose, or in any shape whatsoever; either for the exigencies of government, and collected from the kingdom in general, as the land tax; or for private benefit, and collected in any particular district, as by turnpikes, parish rates, and the like.

The method of making laws is much the same in both houses. In each house the act of the majority binds the whole: and this majority is declared by votes openly and publicly given: not as at Venice, and many other senatorial assemblies, privately, or by ballot. This latter method may be serviceable, to prevent intrigues and unconstitutional combinations, but is impossible to be practised with us, at least in the house of commons, where every member's conduct is subject to the future censure of his constituents, and therefore should be openly submitted to their inspection.

To bring a bill into the house of commons, if the relief sought by it is of a private nature, it is first necessary to prefer a petition; which must be presented by a member, and usually sets forth the grievance desired to be remedied. This petition (when founded on facts that may be in their nature disputed) is referred to a committee of members, who examine the matter alleged, and accordingly report it to the house; and then (or, otherwise, upon the meer petition) leave is given to bring in the bill. In public matters, the bill is brought in upon motion made to the house, without any petition. (In the house of lords, if the bill begins there, it is, when of a private nature, referred to two of the judges, to examine and report the state of the facts alledged, to see that all necessary parties consent, and to settle all points of technical propriety.) This is read a first time, and, at a convenient distance, a second time; and after each reading, the speaker opens to the house the substance of the bill, and puts the question, whether it shall proceed any farther. The introduction of the bill may be originally opposed, as the bill itself may at either of the readings; and, if the opposition succeeds, the bill must be dropt for that session; as it must also, if opposed with success in any of the subsequent stages.

After the second reading, it is committed, that is, referred to a committee; which is either selected by the house in matters of small importance, or else, if the bill is a matter of great, or national consequence, the house resolves itself into a
committee

committee of the whole houſe. A committee of the whole houſe is compoſed of every member; and, to form it, the ſpeaker quits the chair, (another member being appointed chairman) and may ſit and debate as a private member. In theſe committees, the bill is debated clauſe by clauſe, amendments made, the blanks filled up, and ſometimes the bill entirely new modelled. After it has gone through the committee, the chairman reports it to the houſe, with ſuch amendments as the committee have made; and then the houſe reconſider the whole bill again, and the queſtion is repeatedly put upon every clauſe and amendment. When the houſe have agreed or diſagreed to the amendments of the committee, and ſometimes added new amendments of their own, the bill is then ordered to be engroſſed, or written in a ſtrong groſs hand, on one or more long rolls of parchments ſewed together. When this is finiſhed, it is read a third time, and amendments are ſometimes then made to it; and, if a new clauſe be added, it is done by tacking a ſeparate piece of parchment on the bill, which is called a rider. The ſpeaker then again opens the contents; and, holding it up in his hands, puts the queſtion, whether the bill ſhall paſs. If this is agreed to, the title to it is then ſettled. After this, one of the members is directed to carry it to the lords, and deſire their concurrence; who, attended by ſeveral more, carries it to the bar of the houſe of peers, and there delivers it to their ſpeaker, who comes down from his woolſack to receive it. It there paſſes through the forms, as in the other houſe, (except engroſſing, which is already done) and, if rejected, no more notice is taken, but it paſſes *ſub ſilentio*, to prevent unbecoming altercations. But if it is agreed to, the lords ſend a meſſage by two maſters in chancery (or, ſometimes in matters of high importance, by two of the judges) that they have agreed to the ſame: and the bill remains with the lords, if they have made no amendment to it. But if any amendments are made, ſuch amendments are ſent down with the bill to receive the concurrence of the commons. If the commons diſagree to the amendments, a conference uſually follows between members deputed from each houſe; who, for the moſt part, ſettle and adjuſt the difference: but, if both houſes remain inflexible, the bill is dropped. If the commons agree to the amendments, the bill is ſent back to the lords by one of the members, with a meſſage to acquaint them therewith. The ſame forms are obſerved, *mutatis mutandis*, when the bill begins in the houſe of lords. But, when an act of grace or pardon is paſſed, it is firſt ſigned by his majeſty, and then read once only in each of the houſes, without any new engroſſing or amendment. And when both houses have done with any bill, it always is deposited in the house of peers, to wait the royal assent; except in the case of a money-bill, which, after receiving the concurrence of the lords, is sent back to the house of commons. It may be necessary here to acquaint the reader, that both in the houses, and in their committees, the slightest expression, or most minute alteration, does not pass, till the speaker, or the chairman, puts the question; which, in the house of commons, is answered by *aye* or *no*; and, in the house of peers, by *content* or *not content*.

The giving the royal assent to bills, is a matter of great form. When the king is to pass bills in person, he appears on his throne in the house of peers, in his royal robes, with the crown on his head, and attended by his great officers of state and heralds. A seat on the right hand of the throne, where the princes of Scotland, when peers of England, formerly sate, is reserved for the prince of Wales. The other princes of the blood sit on the left hand of the king; and the chancellor on a close bench removed a little backwards. The viscounts and temporal barons, or lords, face the throne, on benches, or wool-packs, covered with red cloth or baize. The bench of bishops runs along the house to the bar on the right hand of the throne; as the dukes and earls do on the left. The chancellor and judges, on ordinary days, sit upon wool-packs between the barons and the throne. The common opinion is, that the house sitting on wool is symbolical of wool being formerly the staple commodity of the kingdom. Many of the peers, on solemn occasions, appear in their parliamentary robes. None of the commons have any robes, excepting the speaker, who wears a long black silk gown; and when he appears before the king, it is trimmed with gold.

The royal assent may be given two ways: 1. In person. When the king sends for the house of commons to the house of peers, the speaker carries up the money-bill or bills in his hand; and, in delivering them, he addresses his majesty in a solemn speech, in which he seldom fails to extol the generosity and loyalty of the commons, and to tell his majesty how necessary it is to be frugal of the public money. It is upon this occasion, that the commons of Great-Britain appear in their highest lustre. The titles of all bills that have passed both houses are read; and the king's answer is declared by the clerk of the parliament in Norman-French: a badge, it must be owned, (now the only one remaining) of conquest; and which one could wish to see fall into total oblivion; unless it be reserved as a solemn *momento* to remind us that our liberties

ties are mortal, having once been deſtroyed by a foreign force. If the king conſents to a public bill, the clerk uſually declares, *le roy le veut*, "the king wills it ſo to be;" if to a private bill, *ſoit fait come il eſt deſire*, "be it as it is deſired." If the king refuſes his aſſent, it is in the gentle language of *le roy s' aviſera*, "the king will adviſe upon it." When a money-bill is paſſed, it is carried up and preſented to the king by the ſpeaker of the houſe of commons, and the royal aſſent is thus expreſſed, *le roy remercie ſes loyal ſubjects, accepte lour benevolence, et auſſi le veut*, "the king thanks his loyal ſubjects, accepts their benevolence, and wills it ſo to be." In caſe of an act of grace, which originally proceeds from the crown, and has the royal aſſent in the firſt ſtage of it, the clerk of the parliament thus pronounces the gratitude of the ſubject; *les prelats, ſeigneurs, et commons, en ce preſent parliament aſſemblies, au nom de touts vous autres ſubjects, remercient tres humblement votre majeſte, et prient a Dieu vous donner en ſante bone vie et longue*; "the prelates, lords and commons, in this preſent parliament aſſembled, in the name of all your other ſubjects, moſt humbly thank your majeſty, and pray to God to grant you in health and wealth long to live." 2. By the ſtatute 33 Hen. VIII. c. 21. the king may give his aſſent by letters patent under his great ſeal, ſigned with his hand, and notified, in his abſence, to both houſes aſſembled together in the high houſe, by commiſſioners conſiſting of certain peers, named in the letters. And, when the bill has received the royal aſſent in either of theſe ways, it is then, and not before, a ſtatute or act of parliament.

This ſtatute or act is placed among the records of the kingdom; there needing no formal promulgation to give it the force of a law, as was neceſſary by the civil law with regard to the emperor's edicts; becauſe every man in England is, in judgment of law, party to the making of an act of parliament, being preſent thereat by his repreſentatives. However, copies thereof are uſually printed at the king's preſs, for the information of the whole land.

An act of parliament, thus made, is the exerciſe of the higheſt authority that this kingdom acknowledges upon earth. It hath power to bind every ſubject in the land, and the dominions thereunto belonging; nay, even the king himſelf, if particularly named therein. And it cannot be altered, amended, diſpenſed with, ſuſpended, or repealed, but in the ſame forms, and by the ſame authority of parliament: for it is a maxim in law, that it requires the ſame ſtrength to diſſolve, as to create an obligation.

Such is the parliament of Great-Britain; the source and guardian of our liberties and properties, the strong cement which binds the foundation and superstructure of our government, and the wisely concerted balance maintaining an equal poise, that no one part of the three estates overpower or distress either of the other.

From the above general view of the English constitution, it appears that no security for its permanency, which the wit of man can devise, is wanting. If it should be objected, that parliaments may become so corrupted, as to give up or betray the liberties of the people, the answer is, that parliaments, as every other body politic, are supposed to watch over their political existence, as a private person does his natural life. If a parliament was to act in that manner, it must become *felo de se*, an evil that no human provisions can guard against. But there are still such resources of liberty in England, that no such fatal effect is now to be apprehended; and though the constitution has been even overturned, and sometimes dangerously wounded, yet, its own innate powers have recovered and still preserve it. Monf. Mezeray, the famous historian, said to a countryman of ours, in the close of the last century, " We had once in France the same happiness and the same privileges which you have; *our laws were then made by representatives of* OUR OWN *chusing, therefore our money was not taken from us; but granted by us.* Our kings were then subject to the rules of law and reason—now, alas! we are miserable, and all is lost. Think nothing, Sir, too dear to maintain these precious advantages; if ever there should be occasion, venture your life and estate rather then basely and foolishly submit to that abject condition to which you see us reduced."—

The king of England, besides his high court of parliament, has subordinate officers and ministers to assist him, and who are responsible for their advice and conduct. They are made by the king's nomination, without either patent or grant; and on taking the necessary oaths, they become immediately privy-counsellors, during the life of the king that chooses them; but subject to removal at his direction.

The duty of a privy-counsellor appears from the oath of office, which consists of seven articles: 1. To advise the king according to the best of his cunning and discretion. 2. To advise for the king's honour and good of the public, without partiality through affection, love, meed, doubt or dread. 3. To keep the king's counsel secret. 4. To avoid corruption. 5. To help and strengthen the execution of what shall be there resolved. 6. To withstand all persons who would attempt the contrary. And, lastly, in general, 7. To observe, keep, and do all that a good and true counsellor ought to do to his sovereign lord.

As no government can be so complete as to be provided with laws that may answer every unforeseen emergency, the privy-council, in such cases, can supply the deficiency. It has even been known, that upon great and urgent occasions, such as that of a famine, they can supersede the operation of the law, if the parliament is not sitting; but this is considered as illegal, and an act of parliament must pass for the pardon and indemnification of those concerned.

Among the privy-counsellors, the two secretaries of state are more officially so than the others, as they are entrusted with the king's signet, and are supposed to advise him in acts of government that may not be proper to be communicated even to a privy-counsellor; such as giving orders for secret expeditions, correspondence with spies or other agents, securing traitors, and the like. The secretaryship of state is now held by two noblemen or gentlemen; formerly the king nominated three, but the office was not then of that consequence which it is now. Since the accession of the family of Hanover, we have likewise known three principal secretaries of state; but one of them was supposed to transact the affairs of Scotland, which are now committed to other ministers. Upon the vast increase of the British colonies, a new board of trade was erected, and the first commissioner acts as secretary for the American affairs, but without that title. Till this erection took place, all American dispatches came first to the hands of a principal secretary of state, who corresponded with the American governors, and sent them directions in his majesty's name. The office itself is at present divided into a southern and a northern department. The southern contains France, Spain, Portugal, Italy, the Swiss Cantons, Constantinople, and, in short, all the states in the southern parts. The northern comprehends the different states of Germany, Prussia, Poland, Russia, Sweden, Denmark, Holland, Flanders, and the Hanseatic towns.

With regard to the capital acts of government, which were formerly entrusted with the secretaries of state, a committee of the privy-council, commonly called a cabinet-council, are chiefly entrusted. This cabinet generally consists of a select number of ministers and noblemen, according to the king's opinion of their integrity and abilities; but though its operations are powerful and extensive, a cabinet-council is not essential to the constitution of England.

This observation naturally leads me to mention the person who is so well known by the name of the first minister; a term unknown to the English constitution, though the office, in effect, is perhaps necessary. The constitution points out the lord high chancellor as minister, but the affairs of his own courts give him sufficient employment. When the office of first lord of the treasury is united with that of chancellor of the exchequer (offices which I am to explain hereafter) in the same person, he is considered as first minister. The truth is, his majesty may make any of his servants his first minister. But though it is no office, yet there is a responsibility annexed to the name and common repute, that renders it a post of difficulty and danger. I shall now take a short review of the nine great officers of the crown, who by their posts take place next to the princes of the royal family and the two primates.

The first is the lord high steward of England. This is an office so great, that it is now exercised only occasionally, that is, at a coronation, or to sit judge on a peer or peeress, when tried for a capital crime. In coronations, it is held, for that day only, by some high nobleman. In cases of trials, it is exercised generally by the lord chancellor, or lord keeper; whose commission, as high steward, ends with the trial, by breaking his white rod, the badge of his office.

The lord high chancellor presides in the court of chancery, to moderate the severities of the law, in all cases where the property of the subject is concerned; and he proceeds according to the dictates of equity and reason.

The post of lord high treasurer has of late been vested in a commission, consisting of five persons, who are called lords of the treasury; but the first commissioner is supposed to possess the power of lord high treasurer. He has the management and charge of all the revenues of the crown kept in the Exchequer; as also the letting of the leases of all crown lands, and the gift of all places belonging to the customs in the several ports of the kingdom. From this short view of his office, its importance may be easily understood; as he has, in fact, the public finances in his hands, besides the disposal of so great a number of lucrative places, both in England and America, that the bare catalogue of them would exceed the bounds we allot to a long article.

The lord president of the council, was an officer formerly of great power: his duty is to propose all the business transacted at the council-board, and to report to the king, when his majesty is not present, all its debates and proceedings. It is a place of great dignity as well as difficulty, on account of the

vast

vast number of American and West-Indian causes, captures, and the like affairs, that come before the board; all which may be abridged to the vast conveniency of the subject by an able president.

The office of lord privy seal, consists in his putting the king's seal to all charters, grants, and the like, which are signed by the king, in order to their passing the great seal. The lord privy seal has likewise under his cognizance several other affairs, which do not require the great seal. He is to take care that the crown is not imposed upon in any transaction passing through his hands; and he is responsible if he should apply the privy seal to any thing against the law of the land.

The office of lord great chamberlain of England is hereditary in the duke of Ancaster's family. He attends the king's person, on his coronation, to dress him: he has likewise charge of the house of lords during the sitting of parliament; of fitting up Westminster-hall for coronations, or trials of peers.

The office of lord high constable has been disused since the year 1521, but is occasionally revived for a coronation. It was formerly a place of the highest trust, as it commanded all the king's forts and garrisons, and took place of all officers in the field.

The duke of Norfolk is hereditary earl marshal of England. Before England became so commercial a country, as it has been for a hundred years past, this office required great abilities, learning, and knowledge of the English history for its discharge. In war time, he was judge of army causes, and decided according to the principles of the civil law. If the cause did not admit of such decision, it was left to a personal combat, which was attended with a vast variety of ceremonies, the arrangement of which, even to the smallest trifle, fell within the marshal's province. To this day, he, or his deputy, regulates all points of precedency according to the archives kept in the herald's office, which is entirely within his jurisdiction. He directs all solemn processions, coronations, proclamations, funerals, general-mournings, and the like. He is supposed to be judge of the Marshalsea-court; and in those reigns where proclamations had the force of law, he had a censorial power in all cases of usurping false names, designations, armorial bearings, and the like; but this power is now disputed, and reduced to a conformity with the common law. As his grace is disqualified by his religion from the exercise of many parts of his office, some nobleman, generally one of his own friends or family, is deputed to act for him; and he wears, as his badge, a gold baton tipped with ebony.

The office of lord high admiral of England is * now, likewise held by commission, and is equal in its importance to any of the preceding, especially since the growth of the British naval power. The English admiralty is a board of direction as well as execution, and is in its proceedings independent of the crown itself. All trials upon life and death, in maritime affairs, are appointed and held under a commission immediately issuing from that board; and the members must sign even the death warrants for execution: but it may be easily conceived, that as they are removeable at pleasure, they do nothing that can clash with the prerogative of the crown, and conform themselves to the directions they receive from his majesty. The board of admiralty regulates the whole naval force of the realm, and names all its officers, or confirms them when named; so that its jurisdiction is very extensive. They appoint vice-admirals under them; but an appeal from them lies to the high court of admiralty, which is of a civil nature: London is the place where it is held; and all its processes and proceedings run in the lord high admiral's name, or those of the commissioners, and not in that of the king. The judge of this court is commonly a doctor of the civil law; but all criminal matters, relating to piracies, and other capital offences committed at sea, are tried and determined according to the laws of England, by witnesses and a jury, ever since the reign of Henry VIII. It now remains to treat of the courts of law in England.

COURTS OF LAW.] The court of Chancery, which is a court of equity, is next in dignity to the high court of parliament, and is designed to relieve the subject against frauds, breaches of trust, and other oppressions; and to mitigate the rigour of the law. The lord high chancellor sits as sole judge, and in his absence the master of the Rolls. The form of proceeding is by bills, answers, and decrees, the witnesses being examined in private: however, the decrees of this court are only binding to the persons of those concerned in them, for they do not affect their lands and goods; and consequently, if a man refuses to comply with the terms, they can do nothing more than send him to the prison of the Fleet. This court is always open; and if a man be sent to prison, the lord chancellor, in any vacation, can, if he sees reason for it, grant a *habeas corpus*.

The clerk of the crown likewise belongs to this court, he, or by his deputy, being obliged always to attend on the lord chancellor

---

* The last Lord High Admiral was George, prince of Denmark, and husband of queen Anne.

chancellor as often as he sits for the dispatch of business; through his hands pass all writs for summoning the parliament or chusing of members; commissions of the peace, pardons, &c.

The King's Bench, so called either from the kings of England sometimes sitting there in person, or because all matters determinable by common law between the king and his subjects, are here tried; except such affairs as properly belong to the court of Exchequer. This court is, likewise, a kind of cheque upon all the inferior courts, their judges, and justices of the peace. Here preside four judges, the first of whom is stiled lord chief justice of the King's bench, or, by way of eminence, lord chief justice of England, to express the great extent of his jurisdiction over the kingdom: for this court can grant prohibitions in any cause depending either in spiritual or temporal courts; and the house of peers does often direct the lord chief justice to issue out his warrant for apprehending persons under suspicion of high crimes. The other three judges are called justices, or judges, of the king's bench.

The court of Common Pleas takes cognizance of all pleas debateable between subject and subject; and in it, beside all real actions, fines and recoveries are transacted, and prohibitions are likewise issued out of it, as well as from the King's Bench. The first judge of this court is stiled lord chief justice of the common pleas, or common bench; beside whom there are likewise three other judges, or justices, of this court. None but serjeants at law are allowed to plead here.

The court of Exchequer was instituted for managing the revenues of the crown, and has a power of judging both according to law and according to equity. In the proceedings according to law, the lord chief baron of the Exchequer, and three other barons, preside as judges. They are stiled barons, because formerly none but barons of the realm were allowed to be judges in this court. Beside these, there is a fifth, called cursitor baron, who has not a judicial capacity, but is only employed in administring the oath to sheriffs and their officers, and also to several of the officers of the custom-house.—But when this court proceeds according to equity, then the lord treasurer and the chancellor of the Exchequer preside, assisted by the other barons. All matters touching the king's treasury, revenue, customs, and fines, are here tried and determined.— Beside the officers already mentioned, there belong to the Exchequer, the king's remembrancer, who takes and states all accounts of the revenue, customs, excise, parliamentary aids and subsidies, &c. except the accounts of the sheriffs and their officers.

officers. The lord treasurer's remembrancer, whose business it is to make out processes against sheriffs, receivers of the revenue, and other officers.

For putting the laws effectually in execution, an high-sheriff is annually appointed for every county (except Westmoreland and Middlesex) by the king; whose office is both ministerial and judicial. He is to execute the king's mandates, and all writs directed to him out of the king's courts of justice; to impannel juries, to bring causes and malefactors to trial, to see the sentences, both in civil and criminal affairs, executed. And at the assize to attend the judges, and guard them all the time they are in his county. It is also part of his office to collect all public fines, distresses, and amerciaments, into the Exchequer, or where the king shall appoint, and to make such payments out of them as his majesty shall think proper.

As his office is judicial, he keeps a court, called the county court, which is held by the sheriff, or his under-sheriffs, to hear and determine all civil causes in the county under forty shillings; this, however, is no court of record; but the court, formerly called the sheriff's turn, was one; and the king's leet, through all the county: for in this court, enquiry was made into all criminal offences against the common law, where by the statute law there was no restraint. This court, however, has been long since abolished.

Under the sheriff are various officers, as the under-sheriff, clerks, stewarts of courts, bailiffs, (in London called serjeants) constables, gaolers, beadles, &c.

The next officer to the sheriff, is the justice of peace, several of whom are commissioned for each county: and to them is entrusted the power of putting great part of the statute law in execution, in relation to the highways, the poor, vagrants, treasons, felonies, riots, the preservation of the game, &c. &c. and they examine and commit to prison all who break or disturb the peace, and disquiet the king's subjects. In order to punish the offenders, they meet every quarter at the county-town, when a jury of twelve men, called the grand inquest of the county, is summoned to appear. This jury, upon oath, is to inquire into the cases of all delinquents, and to present them by bill guilty of the indictment, or not guilty: the justices commit the former to gaol for their trial at the next assizes, and the latter are acquitted. This is called the quarter-sessions for the county. The justice of peace ought to be a person of great good sense, sagacity, and integrity, and to be not without some knowledge of the law; for as much power is lodged in his hands, and as nothing is so intoxicating,

toxicating, without thefe qualifications he will be apt to make miftakes, and to ftep beyond his authority, for which he is liable to be called to an account at the court of king's bench.

Each county contains two coroners, who are to enquire, by a jury of neighbours, how and by whom any perfon came by a violent death, and to enter it on record as a plea of the crown.

The civil government of cities is a kind of fmall independent policy of itfelf; for every city hath, by charter from the king, a jurifdiction within itfelf, to judge in all matters civil and criminal; with this reftraint only, that all civil caufes may be removed from their courts to the higher courts at Weftminfter; and all offences that are capital, are committed to the judge of the affize. The government of cities differs according to their different charters, immunities, and conftitutions. They are conftituted with a mayor, aldermen, and burgeffes, who together make the corporation of the city, and hold a court of judicature, where the mayor prefides as judge. Some cities are counties, and chufe their own fheriffs, and all of them have a power of making bye-laws, for their own government. Some have thought the government of cities, by mayor, aldermen, and common-council, is an epitome of the Englifh government, by king, lords, and commons.

The government of incorporated boroughs is much after the fame manner: in fome there is a mayor, and in others two bailiffs. All which, during their mayoralty, or magiftracy, are juftices of the peace within their liberties, and confequently efquires.

The Cinque-ports are five havens, that lie on the eaft part of England towards France, and were endowed with particular privileges by our antient kings, upon condition that they fhould provide a certain number of fhips at their own charge, to ferve in the wars for forty days, as often as they were wanted. See the table of divifions and counties.

For the better government of villages, the lords of the foil, or manor (who were formerly called barons) have generally a power to hold courts, called courts-leet, and courts-baron, where their tenants are obliged to attend and receive juftice. The bufinefs of courts-leet is chiefly to prefent and punifh nuifances; and at courts-baron, the conveyances and alienations of the copyhold tenants are enrolled, and they are admitted to their eftates on a defcent or purchafe.

A conftable is a very antient and refpectable office of the peace, under the Englifh conftitution. Every hundred has a high conftable, and every parifh in that hundred a conftable, and they are to attend the high conftable upon occafions.

They

They are affisted by another antient officer, called the tything-man, who formerly superintended the tenth part of a hundred, or ten free burgs, as they were called in the time of the Saxons, and each free burg consisting of ten families. The business of a constable is to keep the peace in all cases of quarrels and riots. He can imprison offenders till they are brought before a justice of peace; and it is his duty to execute, within his district, every warrant that is directed to him from that magistrate, or a bench of justices. The neglect of the old Saxon courts, both for the preservation of the peace, and the more easy recovery of small debts, has been regretted by many eminent lawyers, and it has of late been found necessary to revive some of them, and to appoint others of a similar nature.

Besides these, there are courts of conscience settled in many parts of England for the relief of the poor, in the recovery or payment of small debts, not exceeding forty shillings.

There neither is, nor ever was, any constitution provided with so many fences, as that of England is, for the security of personal liberty. Every man imprisoned has a right to bring a writ before a judge in Westminster-hall, called his Habeas Corpus.

If that judge, after considering the cause of commitment, shall find that the offence is bailable, the party is immediately admitted to bail, till he is condemned, or acquitted, in a proper court of justice.

The rights of individuals are so attentively considered, that the subject may, without the least danger, sue his sovereign, or those who act in his name, and under his authority; he may do this in open court, where the king may be cast, and be obliged to pay damages to his subject. He cannot take away the liberty of the least individual, unless he has, by some illegal act, accused or suspected upon oath, to have forfeited his right to liberty, or except when the state is in danger, and the representatives of the people think the public safety makes it necessary that he should have the power of confining persons, on a suspicion of guilt: such as that of an act of rebellion within the kingdom, the legislature has thought proper to pass a temporary suspension of the Habeas Corpus Act; but this never has been done but with great difficulty and caution, and when the national safety absolutely required it. The king has a right to pardon, but neither he nor the judges, to whom he delegates his authority, can condemn a man as a criminal, except he be first found guilty, by twelve men, who must be his peers or his equals. That the judges may not be influenced by the king, or his ministers, to misrepresent the case to the jury, they have their salaries for life, and not during the pleasure of their sovereign. Neither can the king take away, nor endanger the life of any subject, without trial, and the persons being first chargeable with a capital crime, as treasons, murder, felony, or some other act injurious to society: nor can any subject be deprived of his liberty, for the highest crime, till some proof of his guilt be given upon oath before a magistrate; and he has then a right to insist upon his being brought, the first opportunity, to a fair trial, or to be restored to liberty on giving bail for his appearance. If a man is charged with a capital offence, he must not undergo the ignominy of being tried for his life, till the evidences of his guilt are laid before the grand jury of the town or county in which the fact is alledged to be committed, and not without twelve of them agreeing to a bill of indictment against him. If they do this, he is to stand a second trial before twelve other men, whose opinion is definitive. In some cases, the man (who is always supposed innocent till there is sufficient proof of his guilt) is allowed a copy of his indictment, in order to help him to make his defence. He is also furnished with the pannel, or list of the jury, who are his true and proper judges, that he may learn their characters, and discover whether they want abilities, or whether they are prejudiced against him. He may in open court peremptorily object to twenty of the number *, and to as many more as he can give reason for their not being admitted as his judges; till at last twelve unexceptionable men, the neighbours of the party accused, or living near the place where the supposed fact was committed, are approved of, who take the following oath that they *shall well and truly try, and true deliverance make, between the king and the prisoners whom they shall have in charge, according to the evidence.* By challenging the jury, the prisoner prevents all possibility of bribery, or the influence of any superior power: by their living near the place where the fact was committed, they are supposed to be men who knew the prisoner's course of life, and the credit of the evidence. These only are the judges, from whose sentence the prisoner is to expect life or death, and upon their integrity and understanding, the lives of all that are brought in danger ultimately depend; and from their judgment there lies no appeal: they are therefore to be all of one mind, and after they have fully heard the evidence, are to be confined without meat, drink, or candle, till they are unanimous in acquitting, or condemning the prisoner. Every juryman is therefore invested with a solemn and awful trust: if he without evidence

submits

---

* The party may challenge thirty-five in case of treason.

submits his opinion to that of any of the other jury, or yields in complaisance to the opinion of the judge; if he neglects to examine with the utmost care; if he questions the veracity of the witnesses, who may be of an infamous character; or after the most impartial hearing has the least doubt upon his mind, and yet joins in condemning the person accused; he will wound his own conscience, and bring upon himself the complicated guilt of perjury and murder. The freedom of Englishmen consists in its being out of the power of the judge on the bench to injure them, for declaring a man innocent, whom he wishes to be brought in guilty. Were not this the case, juries would be useless; so far from being judges themselves, they would only be the tools of another, whose province it is not to guide, but to give a sanction to their determination. Tyranny might triumph over the lives and liberties of the subject, and the judge on the bench be the minister of the prince's vengeance.

These are the glorious privileges which we enjoy above any other nation upon earth. Juries have always been considered as giving the most effectual check to tyranny; for in a nation like this, where a king can do nothing against law, they are a security that he shall never make the laws, by a bad administration, the instruments of cruelty and oppression. Were it not for juries, the advice given by father Paul, in his maxims of the republic of Venice, might take effect in its fullest latitude. "When the offence is committed by a nobleman against a subject, says he, let all ways be tried to justify him; and if that is not possible to be done, let him be chastised with greater noise than damage. If it be a subject that has affronted a nobleman, let him be punished with the utmost severity, that the subject may not get too great a custom of laying their hands on the patrician order." In short, was it not for juries, a corrupt nobleman might, whenever he pleased, act the tyrant, while the judge would have that power which is now denied to our kings. But by our happy constitution, which breathes nothing but liberty and equity, all imaginary indulgence is allowed to the meanest, as well as the greatest. When a prisoner is brought to take his trial, he is freed from all bonds; and though the judges are supposed to be counsel for the prisoner, yet, as he may be incapable of vindicating his own cause, other counsel are allowed him; he may try the validity and legality of the indictment, and may set it aside, if it be contrary to law. Nothing is wanting to clear up the cause of innocence, and to prevent the sufferer from sinking under the power of corrupt judges, and the oppression of the great. The racks and tortures that are cruelly made use of in other parts of Europe, to make a man accuse himself, are here unknown, and none punished without conviction, but he who refuses to plead in his own defence.

As the trial of malefactors in England is very different from that of other nations, the following account thereof may be useful to foreigners and others, who have not seen those proceedings.

The court being met, and the prisoner called to the bar, the clerk commands him to hold up his hand, then charges him with the crime of which he is accused, and asks him whether he is *guilty* or *not guilty*. If the prisoner answers *guilty*, his trial is at an end; but if he answers *not guilty*, the court proceeds on the trial, even though he may before have confessed the fact: for the law of England takes no notice of such confession; and unless the witnesses, who are upon oath, prove him guilty of the crime, the jury must acquit him, for they are directed to bring in their verdict according to the evidence given in court. If the prisoner refuses to plead, that is, if he will not say in court, whether he is *guilty* or *not guilty*, he is by the law of England to be pressed to death.

When the witnesses have given in their evidence, and the prisoner has, by himself or his counsel, cross examined them, the judge recites to the jury the substance of the evidence given against the prisoner, and bids them discharge their conscience; when, if the matter be very clear, they commonly give their verdict without going out of court; and the foreman, for himself and the rest, declares the prisoner *guilty*, or *not guilty*, as it may happen to be. But if any doubt arises among the jury, and the matter requires debate, they all withdraw into a room with a copy of the indictment, where they are locked up, till they are unanimously agreed on the verdict; and if any one of the jury should die during this their confinement, the prisoner will be acquitted.

When the jury have agreed on the verdict, they inform the court thereof by an officer who waits without, and the prisoner is again set to the bar, to hear his verdict. This is unalterable, except in some doubtful cases, when the verdict is brought in special, and is therefore to be determined by the twelve judges of England.

If the prisoner is found guilty, he is then asked what reason he can give why sentence of death should not be passed upon him? There is now no benefit of clergy—it is changed to transportation, or burning in the hand. Upon a capital conviction the sentence of death, after a summary account of the trial, is pronounced on the prisoner, in these words: *The law is, That thou shalt return to the place from whence thou camest, and from thence be carried to the place of execution, where thou shalt hang by the neck, till thy body be dead, and the Lord have mercy on thy soul:* whereupon the sheriff is charged with the execution.

All the prisoners found *not guilty* by the jury, are immediately acquitted and discharged, and in some cases obtain a copy of their indictment from the court to proceed at law against their prosecutors.

OF PUNISHMENTS.] Though the laws of England are esteemed more merciful, with respect to offenders, than those which at present subsist in any other part of the known world; yet the punishment of such who at their trial refuse to plead guilty or not guilty, is here very cruel. In this case the prisoner is laid upon his back, and his arms and legs being stretched out with cords, and a considerable weight laid upon his breast, he is allowed only three morsels of barley bread, which is given him the next day without drink, after which he is allowed nothing but foul water till he expires. This, however, is a punishment which is scarcely inflicted once in an age; but some offenders have chose it to preserve their estates for their children. Those guilty of this crime are not now suffered to undergo such a length of torture, but have so great a weight placed upon them, that they soon expire. In case of high treason, though the criminal stands mute, judgment is given against him, as if he had been convicted, and his estate is confiscated.

The law of England includes all capital crimes under high treason, petty treason, and felony. The first consists in plotting, conspiring, or rising up in arms against the sovereign, or in counterfeiting the coin. The traitor is punished by being drawn on a sledge to the place of execution, when, after being hanged upon a gallows for some minutes, the body is cut down alive, the heart taken out and exposed to public view, and the entrails burnt: the head is then cut off, and the body quartered, after which the head is usually fixed on some conspicuous place. All the criminal's lands and goods are forfeited, his wife loses her dowry, and his children both their estates and nobility.

But though coining of money is adjudged high treason, the criminal is only drawn upon a sledge to the place of execution, and there hanged.

Though the sentence passed upon all traitors is the same, yet with respect to persons of quality, the punishment is generally altered to beheading: a scaffold is erected for that purpose, on which the criminal placing his head upon a block, it is struck off with an axe †.

The punishment for misprision of high treason, that is, for neglecting or concealing it, is imprisonment for life, the forfeiture of all the offender's goods, and the profits arising from his lands.

Petty treason is when a child kills his father, a wife her husband, a clergyman his bishop, or a servant his master or mistress. This crime is punished by being drawn in a sledge to the place of execution, and there hanged upon a gallows till the criminal is dead. Women guilty both of this crime, and of high treason, are sentenced to be burnt alive, but instead of suffering the full rigour of the law, they are strangled at the stake before the fire takes hold of them.

Felony includes murders, robberies, forging notes, bonds, deeds, &c. These are all punished by hanging, only * murderers are to be executed soon after sentence is passed; and then delivered to the surgeons in order to be publicly dissected. Persons guilty of robbery, when there are some alleviating circumstances, are sometimes transported for a term of years to his majesty's plantations. And in all such felonies where the benefit of the clergy is allowed, as it is in many, the criminal is burnt in the hand with a hot iron.

Other crimes punished by the laws are,

Manslaughter, which is the unlawful killing of a person without premeditated malice, but with a present intent to kill; as when two who formerly meant no harm to each other, quarrel, and the one kills the other; in this case, the criminal is allowed the benefit of his clergy for the first time, and only burnt in the hand.

Chance-medley, is the accidental killing of a man without an evil intent, for which the offender is also to be burnt in the hand; unless the offender was doing an unlawful act, which last circumstance makes the punishment death.

Shop-lifting, and receiving goods knowing them to be stolen, are punished with transportation to his majesty's colonies, or burning in the hand.

Perjury, or keeping disorderly houses, are punished with the pillory and imprisonment.

---

† This is not to be considered as a different punishment; but as a remission of all the parts of the sentence mentioned before, excepting the article of beheading.

* By a late act, murderers are to be executed within twenty-four hours after sentence is pronounced; but as Sunday is not reckoned a day, they are generally tried on a Saturday, so that they obtain a respite till Monday.

Petty-larceny, or small theft, under the value of twelve-pence, is punished by whipping.

Libelling, using false weights and measures, and forestalling the market, are commonly punished with standing on the pillory, or whipping.

For striking, so as to draw blood, in the king's court, the criminal is punished with losing his right hand.

For striking in Westminster-hall, while the courts of justice are sitting, is imprisonment for life, and forfeiture of all the offender's estate.

Drunkards, vagabonds, and loose, idle, disorderly persons, are punished by being set in the stocks, or by paying a fine.

OF HUSBAND AND WIFE.] The first private relation of persons is that of marriage, which includes the reciprocal rights and duties of husband and wife; or, as most of our elder law books call them, *baron* and *feme*. The holiness of the matrimonial state is left entirely to the ecclesiastical law; the punishment therefore, or annulling, of incestuous, or other unscriptural marriages, is the province of spiritual courts.

The first legal disability is a prior marriage, or having another husband or wife living; in which case, besides the penalties consequent upon it as a felony, the second marriage is to all intents and purposes void: polygamy being condemned both by the law of the New Testament, and the policy of all prudent states, especially in these northern climates. The second legal disability is want of age. This is sufficient to avoid all other contracts, on account of the imbecillity of judgment in the parties contracting. Therefore if a boy under fourteen, or a girl under twelve years of age, marries, this marriage is imperfect; and, when either of them comes to the age of consent aforesaid, they may disagree, and declare the marriage void, without any divorce or sentence in the spiritual court. This is founded on the civil law. But the canon law pays a greater regard to the constitution, than the age of the parties: for if they are *habiles ad matrimonium*, it is a good marriage, whatever their age may be. And in our law it is so far a marriage, that if at the age of consent they agree to continue together, they need not be married again. If the husband be of years of discretion, and the wife under twelve, when she comes to years of discretion, he may disagree as well as she may; for in contract, the obligation must be mutual; both must be bound, or neither; and so it is, *vice versa*, when the wife is of years of discretion, and the husband under.

Another incapacity arises from want of consent of guardians. By the common law, if the parties themselves were of age of consent, there wanted no other concurrence to make the marriage valid: and this was agreeable to the canon law. But by several statutes, penalties of 100l. are laid on every clergyman, who marries a couple either without publication of banns (which may give notice to parents or guardians) or without a licence, to obtain which the consent of parents or guardians must be sworn to. And it has been lately thought proper to enact, that all marriages celebrated by licence (for banns suppose notice) where either of the parties is under twenty-one (not being a widow, or widower, who are supposed free) without the consent of the father, or, if he be not living, of the mother or guardians, shall be absolutely void. A provision is made, as in the civil law, when the mother or guardian is *non compos*, beyond the sea, or unreasonably froward, to dispense with such consent at the discretion of the lord chancellor; but no provision is made, in case the father should labour under any mental, or other incapacity. Much may be, and much has been said, both for and against this innovation upon our ancient laws and constitution. On the one hand, it prevents the clandestine marriage of minors, which are often a terrible inconvenience to those private families wherein they happen. On the other hand, restraints upon marriages, especially among the lower class, are evidently detrimental to the public, by hindering the increase of people; and to religion and morality, by encouraging licentiousness and debauchery, among the single of both sexes; and thereby destroying one end of society and government.

A fourth incapacity is want of reason; without a competent share of which, as no other, so neither can the matrimonial contract, be valid.

Lastly, the parties must not only be willing, and able to contract, but actually must contract themselves in due form of law, to make it a good civil marriage. Verbal contracts are now of no force, to compel a future marriage. Neither is any marriage at present valid, that is not celebrated in some parish church, or public chapel, unless by dispensation from the archbishop of Canterbury. It must also be proceded by publication of banns, or by licence from the spiritual judge. It is held to be also essential to marriage, that it be performed by a person in orders: though in the times of the grand rebellion, all marriages were performed by the justices of the peace; and these marriages were declared valid in the succeeding reign. But, as the law now stands, we may upon the whole collect, that no marriage by the temporal law is void, that is celebrated by a person in orders,—in a parish church, or public chapel (or elsewhere, by dispensation)—in pursuance of banns or a licence,—between single persons,—consenting,—of sound mind,—and of the age of twenty-one years; —or of the age of fourteen in male, and twelve in female, with consent of parents or guardians, or without it, in case of widowhood.

There are two kinds of divorce, the one total, the other partial. The total divorce must be for some of the canonical causes of impediment, and those existing before the marriage; as consanguinity, affinity, or corporal imbecility. The issue of such marriage, as is thus entirely dissolved, are bastards.

The other kind of divorce is when the marriage is just and lawful, and therefore the law is tender of dissolving it; but, for some supervenient cause, it becomes improper, or impossible, for the parties to live together: as in the case of intolerable ill temper, or adultery, in either of the parties. In this case the law allows alimony to the wife (except when for adultery, the parliament grants a total divorce, as has happened frequently of late years) which is that allowance, which is made to a woman, for her support, out of the husband's estate; being settled at the discretion of the ecclesiastical judge, on consideration of all the circumstances of the case, and the rank and quality of the parties.

Having thus shewn how marriages may be made, or dissolved, I come now, lastly, to speak of the legal consequences of such making, or dissolution.

By marriage, the husband and wife are one person in law; that is, the very being, or legal existence of the woman, is suspended during the marriage, or at least is incorporated and consolidated into that of the husband: under whose wing, protection, and *cover*, she performs every thing, and is therefore called in our law French, a *feme-covert*, under the protection and influence of her husband, her *baron*, or lord; and her condition, during her marriage, is called her *coverture*. Upon this principle, of an union of person in husband and wife, depend almost all the legal rights, duties, and disabilities, that either of them acquire by the marriage. I speak not at present of the rights of property, but of such as are merely *personal*. For this reason a man cannot grant any thing to his wife, or enter into covenant with her; for the grant would be to suppose her separate existence; and the covenant with her would be only to covenant with himself; and therefore it is generally true, that all compacts made between husband and wife, when single, are voided by the intermarriage. A woman indeed may be attorney for her husband; for that implies no separation from, but is rather a representation

tion of her lord. And a husband may also bequeath any thing to his wife by will; for that cannot take effect till the coverture is determined by his death. The husband is bound to provide his wife with necessaries by law, as much as himself; and if she contracts debts for them, he is obliged to pay them; but, for any thing, besides necessaries, he is not chargeable. Also if a wife elopes, and lives with another man, the husband is not chargeable even for necessaries: at least, if the person who furnishes them, is sufficiently apprized of her elopement. If the wife be indebted before marriage, the husband is bound afterwards to pay the debt; for he has adopted her and her circumstances together. If the wife be injured in her person or property, she can bring no action for redress without her husband's concurrence, and in his name as well as her own; neither can she be sued, without making the husband a defendant; except when the husband has abjured the realm, or is banished; for then he is dead in law. In criminal prosecutions, it is true, the wife may be indicted, and punished separately; for the union is only a civil union. But, in trials of any sort, they are not allowed to be evidences for, or against, each other; partly because it is impossible their testimony should be indifferent; but principally because of the union of person. But where the offence is directly against the person of the wife, this rule has been usually dispensed with; and, therefore, in case a woman be forcibly taken away, and married, she may be a witness against such her husband, in order to convict him of felony.

In the civil law, the husband and the wife are considered as two distinct persons; and may have separate estates, contracts, debts, and injuries; and, therefore, in our ecclesiastical courts, a woman may sue, and be sued, without her husband.

But, though our law in general considers man and wife as one person, yet there are some instances in which she is separately considered, as inferior to him, and acting by his compulsion. And therefore all deeds executed, and acts done, by her, during her coverture, are void; except it be a fine, or the like matter of record, in which case she must be solely and secretly examined, to learn if her act be voluntary. She cannot by will devise land to her husband, unless under special circumstances; for at the time of making it, she is supposed to be under his coercion. And in some felonies, and other inferior crimes, committed by her, through constraint of her husband, the law excuses her: but this extends not to treason or murder.

The husband also (by the old, and likewise by the civil law) might give his wife moderate correction. For, as he is to answer for her misbehaviour, the law thought it reasonable to entruſt him, with this power of reſtraining her, by domeſtic chaſtiſement, in the ſame moderation that a man is allowed to correct his ſervants or children; for whom the maſter or parent is alſo liable in ſome caſes to anſwer. But in the politer reign of Charles II. this power of correction began to be doubted; and a wife may now have ſecurity of the peace againſt her huſband; or, in return, a huſband againſt his wife: yet the lower rank of people, who were always fond of the old common law, ſtill claim and exert their antient privilege; and the courts of law will ſtill permit a huſband to reſtrain a wife of her liberty, in caſe of any groſs miſbehaviour.

These are the chief legal effects of marriage during the coverture; upon which we may obſerve, that even the diſabilities, which the wife lies under, are for the moſt part intended for her protection and benefit. So great a favourite is the female ſex with the laws of England.

REVENUES OF THE BRITISH GOVERNMENT. } The king's eccleſiaſtical revenue conſiſts in, 1. The cuſtody of the temporalities of vacant biſhoprics; from which he receives little or no advantage. 2. Corodies and penſions, formerly ariſing from allowances of meat, drink, and cloathing, due to the king from an abbey or monaſtery, and which he generally beſtowed upon favourite ſervants; but now, I believe, diſuſed. 3. Extra-parochial tithes. 4. The firſt fruits and tenths of benefices. At preſent, ſuch has been the bounty of the crown to the church, that thoſe four branches afford little or no revenue.

The king's ordinary temporal revenue conſiſts in, 1. The demeſne lands of the crown. 2. The hereditary exciſe; being part of the conſideration for the purchaſe of his feodal profits, and the prerogatives of purveyance and pre-emption. 3. An annual ſum iſſuing from the duty on wine licences; being the reſidue of the ſame conſideration. 4. His foreſts. 5. His courts of juſtice, &c.

The extraordinary grants are uſually called by the ſynonimous names of aids, ſubſidies, and ſupplies; and are granted, as has been before hinted, by the commons of Great-Britain, in parliament aſſembled: who, when they have voted a ſupply to his majeſty, and ſettled the *quantum* of that ſupply, uſually reſolve themſelves into what is called a committee of ways and means, to conſider of the ways and means of raiſing the ſupply ſo voted. And in this committee every member (though it is looked upon as the peculiar province of the chancellor of the exchequer) may propoſe ſuch ſcheme of taxation as he thinks will be leaſt detrimental to the public. The reſolutions of this committee (when approved by a vote of the houſe) are in general eſteemed to be (as it were) final and conclusive. For, though the supply cannot be actually raised upon the subject till directed by an act of the whole parliament, yet no monied man will scruple to advance to the government any quantity of ready cash, on the credit of a bare vote of the house of commons, tho' no law be yet passed to establish it.

The annual taxes are, 1. The land tax, or the ancient subsidy raised upon a new assessment. 2. The malt tax, being an annual excise on malt, mum, cyder, and perry.

The perpetual taxes are, 1. The customs, or tonnage and poundage of all merchandize exported or imported. 2. The excise duty, or inland imposition, on a great variety of commodities. 3. The salt duty. 4. The * post office, or duty for the carriage of letters. 5. The stamp duty on paper, parchment, &c. 6. The duty on houses and windows. 7. The duty on licences for hackney coaches and chairs. 8. The duty on offices and pensions.

The clear neat produce of these several branches of the revenue, after all charges of collecting and management paid, amounts annually to about seven millions and three quarters sterling; besides two millions and a quarter raised annually, at an average, by the land and malt tax. How these immense sums are appropriated, is next to be considered. And this is, first and principally, to the payment of the interest of the national debt.

In order to take a clear and comprehensive view of the nature of this national debt, it must be first premised, that after the revolution, when our new connections with Europe introduced a new system of foreign politics; the expences of the nation, not only in settling the new establishment, but in maintaining long wars, as principals, on the continent, for the security of the Dutch barrier, reducing the French monarchy, settling the Spanish succession, supporting the house of Austria, maintaining the liberties of the Germannic body, and other purposes, increased to an unusual degree: insomuch that it was not thought adviseable to raise all the expences of any one year by taxes to be levied within that year, left the unaccustomed weight of them should create murmurs among the people. It was therefore the policy of the times, to anticipate the revenues of their posterity, by borrowing immense sums for the current service of the state, and to lay no more taxes upon the subject than would suffice to pay the annual interest of the sums so borrowed: by this means converting the principal debt into a new species of property, transferable from

---

* From the year 1715 to 1763, the annual amount of franked letters gradually increased from 23,000 l. to 170,700 l.

from one man to another, at any time and in any quantity. A system which seems to have had its original in the state of Florence, A. D. 1344: which government then owed about 60,000 l. sterling: and, being unable to pay it, formed the principal into an aggregate sum, called metaphorically a mount or bank: the shares whereof were transferable like our stocks. This laid the foundation of what is called the national debt: for a few long annuities created in the reign of Charles II. will hardly deserve that name. And the example then set has been so closely followed, during the long wars in the reign of queen Anne, and since; that the capital of the national debt (funded and unfunded) amounted, in January 1765, to upward of 145,000,000 l. to pay the interest of which, and the charges for management, amounting annually to about four millions and three quarters, the extraordinary revenues just now enumerated (excepting only the land-tax and annual malt-tax) are in the first place mortgaged, and made perpetual by parliament; but still redeemable by the same authority that imposed them: which, if it at any time can pay off the capital, will abolish those taxes which are raised to discharge the interest.

It is indisputably certain, that the present magnitude of our national incumbrances very far exceeds all calculations of commercial benefit, and is productive of the greatest inconveniencies. For, first, the enormous taxes that are raised upon the necessaries of life, for the payment of the interest of this debt, are a hurt both to trade and manufactures; by raising the price, as well of the artificer's subsistence, as of the raw material; and of course, in a much greater proportion, the price of the commodity itself. Secondly, if part of this debt be owing to foreigners, either they draw out of the kingdom annually a considerable quantity of specie for the interest; or else it is made an argument to grant them unreasonable privileges, in order to induce them to reside here. Thirdly, if the whole be owing to subjects only, it is then charging the active and industrious subject, who pays his share of the taxes, to maintain the indolent and idle creditor who receives them. Lastly, and principally, it weakens the internal strength of a state, by anticipating those resources which should be reserved to defend it in case of necessity. The interest we now pay for our debts would be nearly sufficient to maintain any war, that any national motives could acquire. And if our ancestors in king William's time had annually paid, so long as their exigencies lasted, even a less sum than we now annually raise upon their accounts, they would, in time of war, have borne no greater burdens than they have bequeathed to, and settled upon, their posterity in time of peace; and might have been eased the instant the exigence was over.

The produce of the several taxes before-mentioned were originally separate and distinct funds; being securities for the sums advanced on each several tax, and for them only. But at last it became necessary, in order to avoid confusion, as they multiplied yearly, to reduce the number of these separate funds, by uniting and blending them together; superadding the faith of parliament for the general security of the whole. So that there are now only three capital funds of any account: the aggregate fund, and the general fund, so called from such union and addition; and the South Sea fund, being the produce of the taxes appropriated to pay the interest of such part of the national debt as was advanced by that company and its annuitants. Whereby the separate funds, which were thus united, are become mutual securities for each other; and the whole produce of them, thus aggregated, liable to pay such interest or annuities as were formerly charged upon each distinct fund; the faith of the legislature being moreover engaged to supply any casual deficiencies.

The customs, excises, and other taxes, which are to support these funds, depending on contingencies, upon exports, imports, and consumptions, must necessarily be of a very uncertain amount: but they have always been considerably more than sufficient to answer the charge upon them. The surplusses therefore of the three great national funds, the aggregate, general, and South-Sea funds, over and above the interest and annuities charged upon them, are directed by statute 3 Geo. 1. c. 7. to be carried together, and to attend the disposition of parliament; and are usually denominated the sinking fund, because originally destined to sink and lower the national debt. To this have been since added many other intire duties, granted in subsequent years; and the annual interest of the sums borrowed on their respective credits, is charged on, and payable out of the produce of the sinking fund. However the neat surplusses and savings, after all deductions paid, amount annually to a very considerable sum; particularly in the year ending at Christmas 1764, to about two millions and a quarter. For, as the interest on the national debt has been at several times reduced, (by the consent of the proprietors, who had their option either to lower their interest, or be paid their principal) the savings from the appropriated revenues must needs be extremely large. This sinking fund is the last resort of the nation; its only domestic resource, on which must chiefly depend all the hopes we can entertain of ever discharging or moderating our incumbrances. And therefore the prudent application of the large sums, now arising from this fund, is a point of the utmost importance, and well worthy the serious attention of parliament; which was thereby enabled, in the year 1765, to reduce above two millions sterling of the public debt.

But, before any part of the aggregate fund (the surplusses whereof are one of the chief ingredients that form the sinking fund) can be applied to diminish the principal of the public debt, it stands mortgaged by parliament to raise an annual sum for the maintenance of the king's houshold and the civil list. For this purpose, in the late reigns, the produce of certain branches of the excise and customs, the post-office, the duty on wine-licences, the revenues of the remaining crown lands, the profits arising from courts of justice, (which articles include all the hereditary revenues of the crown) and also a clear annuity of 120,000l. in money, were settled on the king for life, for the support of his majesty's houshold, and the honour and dignity of the crown. And, as the amount of these several branches was uncertain, (though in the last reign they were computed to have sometimes raised almost a million) if they did not arise annually to 800,000l. the parliament engaged to make up the deficiency. But his present majesty having, soon after his accession, spontaneously signified his consent, that his own hereditary revenues might be so disposed of, as might best conduce to the utility and satisfaction of the public; and having graciously accepted the limited sum of 800,000 l. *per annum*, for the support of his civil list, (and that also charged with three life annuities, to the princess of Wales, the duke of Cumberland, and princess Amelia, to the amount of 77,000 l.) the said hereditary, and other revenues, are now carried into, and made a part of, the aggregate fund; and the aggregate fund is charged with the payment of the whole annuity to the crown of 800,000 l. *per annum*. Hereby the revenues themselves, being put under the same care and management as the other branches of the public patrimony, will produce more, and be better collected than heretofore; and the public is a gainer of upward of 100,000l. *per annum*, by this disinterested bounty of his majesty. The civil list, thus liquidated, together with the four millions and three quarters, interest of the national debt, and the two millions and a quarter produced from the sinking fund, make up the seven millions and three quarters *per annum*, neat money, which was before stated to be the annual produce of our perpetual taxes: beside the immense, though uncertain sums, arising from the annual taxes on land and malt, but which, at an average, may be calculated at more than two millions and a quarter; and which, added to the preceding sum, make the clear produce of the taxes, exclusive of the charge of collecting, which are raised yearly on the people of this country,

amount

amount to upward of ten million sterling; to which may be further added, the sum of 400,000 l. which the East India company have agreed to pay to the public for a certain time.

The expences defrayed by the civil list, are those that in any shape relate to civil government; as the expences of the houshold, all salaries to officers of state, to the judges, and every one of the king's servants; the appointments to foreign ambassadors, the maintenance of the queen and royal family, the king's private expences, or privy purse, and other very numerous outgoings; as secret service-money, pensions, and other bounties. These sometimes have so far exceeded the revenues appointed for that purpose, that application has been made to parliament, to discharge the debts contracted on the civil list; as particularly in 1724, when one million was granted for that purpose by the statute 11 Geo. I. c. 17.

The civil list is indeed properly the whole of the king's revenue in his own distinct capacity; the rest being rather the revenue of the public, or its creditors, though collected, and distributed again, in the name, and by the officers of the crown; it now standing in the same place, as the hereditary income did formerly; and, as that has gradually diminished, the parliamentary appointments have encreased.

MILITARY AND MARINE STRENGTH OF GREAT BRITAIN. } The military state includes the whole of the soldiery; or, such persons as are peculiarly appointed among the rest of the people, for the safe-guard and defence of the realm.

In a land of liberty it is extremely dangerous to make a distinct order of the profession of arms. In such, no man should take up arms, but with a view to defend his country and its laws: he puts not off the citizen when he enters the camp; but it is because he is a citizen and would wish to continue so, that he makes himself for a while a soldier. The laws, therefore, and constitution of these kingdoms know no such state, as that of a perpetual standing soldier, bred up to no other profession than that of war: and it was not till the reign of Henry VII. that the kings of England had so much as a guard about their persons.

It seems universally agreed by all historians, that king Alfred first settled a national militia in this kingdom, and by his prudent discipline made all the subjects of his dominions soldiers.

In the mean time we are not to imagine that the kingdom was left wholly without defence, in case of domestic insurrections, or the prospect of foreign invasions. Besides those, who by their military tenures were bound to perform 40 days service in the field, the statute of Winchester obliged every man, according to his estate and degree, to provide a determinate quantity of

such

such arms as were then in use, in order to keep the peace: and constables were appointed in all hundreds, to see that such arms were provided. These weapons were changed by the statute 4 and 5 Ph. and M. c. 2. into others of more modern service; but both this and the former provision were repealed in the reign of James I. While these continued in force, it was usual from time to time, for our princes to issue commissions of array, and send into every county officers in whom they could confide, to muster and array (or set in military order) the inhabitants of every district; and the form of the commission of array was set in parliament in the 5 Henry IV. But at the same time it was provided, that no man should be compelled to go out of the kingdom at any rate; nor out of his shire, but in cases of urgent necessity; nor should provide soldiers unless by consent of parliament. About the reign of king Henry VIII. and his children, lord lieutenants began to be introduced, as standing representatives of the crown, to keep the counties in military order; for we find them mentioned as known officers in the statute 4 and 5 Ph. and M. c. 3. tho' they had not been then long in use; for Camden speaks of them in the time of queen Elizabeth, as extraordinary magistrates, constituted only in times of difficulty and danger.

Soon after the restoration of king Charles II. when the military tenures were abolished, it was thought proper to ascertain the power of the militia, to recognize the sole right of the crown to govern and command them, and to put the whole into a more regular method of military subordination: and the order in which the militia now stands by law, is principally built upon the statutes which were then enacted. It is true, the two last of them are apparently repealed; but many of their provisions are re-enacted, with the addition of some new regulations, by the present militia-laws; the general scheme of which is to discipline a certain number of the inhabitants of every county, chosen by lot for three years, and officered by the lord lieutenant, the deputy lieutenants, and other principal landholders, under a commission from the crown. They are not compellable to march out of their counties, unless in case of invasion, or actual rebellion, nor in any case compellable to march out of the kingdom. They are to be exercised at stated times; and their discipline in general is liberal and easy; but, when drawn out into actual service, they are subject to the rigours of martial law, as necessary to keep them in order. This is the constitutional security which our laws have provided for the public peace, and for protecting the realm against foreign or domestic violence; and which the statutes declare, is essentially necessary to the safety and prosperity of the kingdom.

But,

ENGLAND. 349

But, as the fashion of keeping standing armies has universally prevailed over all Europe of late years (though some of its potentates, being unable themselves to maintain them, are obliged to have resource to richer powers, and receive subsidiary pensions for that purpose) it has also for many years past been annually judged necessary by our legislature, for the safety of the kingdom, the defence of the possessions of the crown of Great-Britain, and the preservation of the balance of power in Europe, to maintain, even in time of peace, a standing body of troops, under the command of the crown; who are, however, *ipso facto*, disbanded at the expiration of every year, unless continued by parliament. The land forces * of these king-

* The land forces consist of 2 Troops of horse-guards raised in 1660.—2 Troops of horse-grenadier-guards raised in 1693 and 1702.—1 Royal regiment of horse-guards, ditto 1661.—4 Regiments of horse-guards, ditto 1685 and 1688.—3 Regiments of dragoon-guards, ditto 1685.—14 Regiments of dragoons, including light-horse, raised between 1683 and 1759.—3 Regiments of foot-guards, raised in 1660.—76 Regiments of foot; the first or royal Scots, raised in 1663, the others between 1661 and 1762.—8 Independent companies of invalids.

Daily Pay of each Rank in his Majesty's Land Forces on the *British* Establishment.

	Royal Reg. of Horse-guards		Dragoons		Foot Guards		Foot	
	F. Pay	Subsist.	F. Pay	Subsist.	F. Pay	Subsist.	F. Pay	Subsist.

kingdoms, in time of peace, amount to about 40,000 men, including troops and garrisons in Ireland, Gibraltar, Minorca, and America; but in time of war, there have been in British pay, natives and foreigners, above 150,000. The regiftered militia in England confifts of near 200,000. To keep this body of troops in order, an annual act of parliament paffes, " to punifh mutiny and defertion, and for the better payment of the army and their quarters." This regulates the manner in which they are to be difperfed among the feveral innkeepers and victuallers throughout the kingdom; and eftablifhes a law martial for their government. By this, among other things, it is enacted, that if any officer and foldier fhall excite, or join any mutiny, or, knowing of it, fhall not give notice to the commanding officer; or fhall defert, or lift in any other regiment, or fleep upon his poft, or leave it before he is relieved, or hold correfpondence with a rebel or enemy; or ftrike or ufe violence to his fuperior officer, or fhall difobey his lawful command; fuch offender fhall fuffer fuch punifhment as a court martial fhall inflict, though it extend to death itfelf.

Officers and foldiers that have been in the king's fervice, are by feveral ftatutes, enacted, at the clofe of feveral wars, at liberty to ufe any trade or occupation they are fit for, in any town of the kingdom (except the two univerfities) notwithftanding any ftatute, cuftom, or charter to the contrary. And foldiers in actual military fervice, may make verbal wills, and difpofe of their goods, wages, and other perfonal chattels, without thofe forms, folemnities, and expences, which the law requires in other cafes.

The maritime ftate is nearly related to the former; though much more agreeable to the principles of our free conftitution. The royal navy of England hath ever been its greateft defence and ornament; it is its ancient and natural ftrength; the floating bulwark of the ifland; an army, from which, however ftrong and powerful, no danger can ever be apprehended to liberty: and accordingly it has been affiduoufly cultivated, even from the earlieft ages. To fo much perfection was our naval reputation arrived in the twelfth century, that the code of maritime laws, which are called the laws of Oleron, and are received by all nations in Europe, as the ground and fubftruction of all the marine conftitutions, was confeffedly compiled by our king Richard I. at the ifle of Oleron, on the coaft of France, then part of the poffeffions of the crown of England. And yet, fo vaftly inferior were our anceftors in this point, to the prefent age, that even in the maritime reign of queen Elizabeth, Sir Edward Coke thinks it matter of boaft, that the royal navy of England then confifted of 33 fhips. The prefent condition of our marine is in great meafure owing to the falutary provifions of the ftatutes, called the navigation acts; whereby the conftant increafe of Englifh fhipping and feamen, was not only encouraged, but rendered unavoidably neceffary. The moft beneficial ftatute for the trade and commerce of thefe kingdoms, is that navigation-act, the rudiments of which were firft framed in 1650, with a narrow partial view: being intended to mortify the fugar iflands, which were difaffected to the parliament, and ftill held out for Charles II. by ftopping the gainful trade which they then carried on with the Dutch; and at the fame time to clip the wings of thofe our opulent and afpiring neighbours. This prohibited all fhips of foreign nations from trading with any Englifh plantations without licence from the council of ftate. In 1651, the prohibition was extended alfo to the mother country; and no goods were fuffered to be imported into England, or any of its dependencies, in any other than Englifh bottoms; or in the fhips of that European nation, of which the merchandize imported was the genuine growth or manufacture. At the reftoration, the former provifions were continued, by ftatute 12 Car. II. c. 18. with this very material improvement, that the mafter, and three fourths of the mariners fhall alfo be Englifh fubjects.

The complement of feamen, in time of peace, ufually amounts to 12 or 15,000. In time of war, they have amounted to no lefs than 80,000 men.

This navy is commonly divided into three fquadrons, namely, the red, white, and blue, which are fo termed from the differences of their colours. Each fquadron has its admiral; but the admiral of the red fquadron has the principal command of the whole, and is ftiled vice-admiral of Great Britain. Subject to each admiral is alfo a vice and a rear-admiral. But the fupreme command of our naval force is, next to the king, in the lords commiffioners of the admiralty. Notwithftanding our favourable fituation for a maritime power, it was not until the vaft armament fent to fubdue this nation by Spain, in 1588, that the nation, by a vigorous effort, became fully fenfible of its true intereft and natural ftrength, which it has fince fo happily cultivated.

We may venture to affirm that the Britifh navy, during the late war, was able to cope with all the other fleets in Europe. In the courfe of a few years it entirely vanquifhed the whole naval power of France, difabled Spain, and kept the Dutch and other powers in awe.

For the protection of the British empire, and the annoyance of our enemies, it was then divided into several powerful squadrons, so judiciously stationed, as at once to appear in every quarter of the globe, and while some fleets were humbling the pride of Spain in Asia and America, others were employed in frustrating the designs of France, and escorting home the riches of the eastern and western worlds.

Many laws have been made for the supply of the royal navy with seamen; for their regulation when on board; and to confer privileges and rewards on them, during, and after their service.

1. For their supply. The power of impressing men, for the sea-service, by the king's commission, has been a matter of some dispute, and submitted to with great reluctance; tho' it hath very clearly and learnedly been shewn by Sir Michael Foster, that the practice of impressing, and granting powers to the admiralty for that purpose, is of very antient date, and hath been uniformly continued by a regular series of precedents to the present time; whence he concludes it to be a part of the common law. The difficulty arises from hence, that no statute, or act of parliament, has expressly declared this power to be in the crown, though many of them very strongly imply it.

Besides this method of impressing (which is only defensible from public necessity, such as an actual rebellion or invasion of the kingdom, to which all private considerations must give way) the principal trading cities, and sometimes the government, offer bounty money to seamen who enter voluntarily into his majesty's service; and every foreign seaman, who, during a war, shall serve two years in any man of war, merchantman, or privateer, is naturalized *ipso facto*.

But as impressing is generally considered as a gross violation of the natural rights of mankind, so has the bounty money, which seldom exceeds 40s. proved ineffectual. The wages of seamen on board of merchantmen, in time of war, is usually 50s. or upwards, per month; on board of the royal navy, they only receive 22 s. They are flattered indeed with the hopes of prize money, which, if divided in a more equal and equitable manner, would produce the happiest effects to this nation. There would then be less occasion for bounty money or pressing; our fleets would be speedily manned, and regularly supplied with experienced and able seamen. Since under Providence, not only the very existence of this nation, its commerce and foreign settlements; but the liberties of Europe, and security of the Protestant religion, solely depend on the strength and success of the British navy, which is the only

mode

mode of war we ought ever to engage in; it has been matter of surprize to every thinking, disinterested subject of these kingdoms, that neither the above-mentioned regulation, nor any other satisfactory scheme has yet taken place. That to enrich a few superior officers, we should deprive those very men of their rights and liberty, to whose valour and intrepidity alone, in the day of public danger, we look for preservation.

2. The method of ordering seamen in the royal fleet, and keeping up a regular discipline there, is directed by certain express rules, articles, and orders, first enacted by the authority of parliament, soon after the restoration; but since new modelled and altered, after the peace of Aix-la-Chapelle, to remedy some defects which were of fatal consequence in conducting the preceding war. In these articles of the navy, almost every possible offence is set down, and the punishment thereof annexed, in which respect the seamen have much the advantage over their brethren in the land service; whose articles of war are not enacted by parliament, but framed from time to time at the pleasure of the crown.

3. With regard to the privileges conferred on sailors, they are pretty much the same with those conferred on soldiers; with regard to relief, when maimed or wounded, or superannuated, either by county rates, or the royal hospital at Greenwich; with regard also to the exercise of trades, and the power of making testaments; and, farther, no seaman aboard his majesty's ships can be arrested for any debt, unless the same be sworn to amount to at least 20 pounds; though by the annual mutiny act, a soldier may be arrested for a debt which extends to half that value, but not to less amount.

I shall close this account of the military and maritime strength of England, or rather of Great Britain, by observing, that though sea officers and sailors, are subject to a perpetual act of parliament, which answers the annual military act, which is passed for the government of the army, yet neither of those bodies are exempted from legal jurisdiction in civil or criminal cases, but in a few instances of no great moment. The soldiers, particularly, may be called upon by a civil magistrate, to enable him to preserve the peace, against all attempts to break it. The military officer, who commands the soldiers on those occasions, is to take his directions from the magistrate, and both he and they, if their proceedings are regular, are indemnified against all consequences, be they ever so fatal. The civil magistrate, giftrate, however, is extremely cautious in calling for the military on these occasions, upon any commotion, whatever *.

COINS.]

* The Royal Navy of GREAT BRITAIN, as it stood at the close of the Year 1762.

N. B. Those in *Italics* were taken from the French or Spaniards.

FIRST RATES.

Guns.
- 100 Britannia
- 100 Royal George
- 100 R. Sovereign

SECOND RATES.

- 90 Blenheim
- 90 Duke
- 90 St. George
- 90 Namur
- 90 *Neptune*
- 90 Ocean
- 90 Prince
- 90 Princess Royal
- 84 Royal William
- 90 Sandwich
- 90 Union

THIRD RATES.

- 64 Africa
- 64 *Alcide*
- 74 Arrogant
- 64 Bedford
- 64 *Belliqueux*
- 74 Bellona
- 64 Belleisle
- 64 *Bienfaisant*
- 70 Buckingham
- 70 Burford
- 80 Cambridge
- 64 Captain
- 74 Centaur
- 70 Chichester
- 74 Cornwall
- 74 Culloden
- 64 Defiance
- 66 Devonshire
- 70 Dorsetshire
- 74 Dragon
- 74 Dublin
- 64 Elizabeth
- 64 Essex
- 74 Fame
- 80 *Foudroyant*
- 70 Grafton
- 64 Hampton-Court
- 74 Hercules
- 74 Hero

Guns.
- 74 Kent
- 74 Lenox
- 74 *Magnanime*
- 68 Marlborough
- 74 Mars
- 64 *Modeste*
- 64 Monmouth
- 64 Nassau
- 80 Newark
- 74 Norfolk
- 70 Northumberland
- 70 Orford
- 64 Pr. Frederick
- 80 Princess Amelia
- 60 Princess Mary
- 64 Revenge
- 74 Shrewsbury
- 70 Somerset
- 74 Sterling-Castle
- 74 *Superb*
- 70 Swiftsure
- 74 *Temeraire*
- 70 Temple
- 74 Terrible
- 74 Thunderer
- 74 Torbay
- 64 *Trident*
- 74 Valiant
- 70 Vanguard
- 74 Warspight

FOURTH RATES.

- 60 Achilles
- 60 America
- 60 Anson
- 50 Antelope
- 50 Assistance
- 50 Centurion
- 50 Chatham
- 50 Chester
- Dreadnought
- 50 Deptford
- 60 Dunkirk
- 60 Edgar
- 50 Falkland
- 50 Falmouth
- 60 *Firme*
- 60 *Florentine*
- 50 Guernsey
- 50 Hampshire
- 60 Jersey

Guns.
- 60 *Intrepide*
- 50 *Isis*
- 60 Lion
- 60 Medway
- 60 Montague
- 50 Norwich
- 50 *Oriflame*
- 60 Panther
- 60 Pembroke
- 50 Portland
- 50 Preston
- 60 Prince of Orange
- 60 Rippon
- 50 Romney
- 50 Rochester
- 50 Salisbury
- 50 Sutherland
- 60 Weymouth
- 50 Winchester
- 60 Windsor
- 60 York

FIFTH RATES.

- 32 Adventurer
- 32 Alarm
- 32 *Arethusa*
- 32 Æolus
- 32 *Bologne*
- 32 Boston
- 32 *Blonde*
- 36 Brilliant
- 32 *Crescent*
- 38 *Danae*
- 32 Diana
- 44 Dover
- 32 Emerald
- 44 Enterprize
- 32 *Flora*
- 44 Gosport
- 32 Juno
- 32 Lark
- 44 Launceston
- 30 Looe
- 44 Lynn
- 36 *Melampe*
- 32 Minerva
- 32 Montreal
- 32 *Niger*
- 36 Pallas
- 44 Penzance

Guns.
- 44 Phœnix
- 44 Prince Edw.
- 32 Quebec
- 44 *Rainbow*
- 36 *Renown*
- 32 Repulse
- 32 Richmond
- 32 Saphire
- 32 Southampton
- 32 Stagg
- 32 Thames
- 32 *Thetis*
- 30 Torrington
- 32 Tweed
- 36 Venus
- 32 *Vestal*
- 44 Woolwich

SIXTH RATES.

- 28 Actæon
- 28 Active
- 20 Aldborough
- 24 *Amazon*
- 28 *Aquilon*
- 28 Argo
- 24 Arundel
- 28 Boreas
- 28 Cerberus
- 24 Coventry
- 20 Deal-Castle
- 24 Dolphin
- 24 Echo
- 20 Flamborough
- 24 Fowey
- 24 Garland
- 20 Gibraltar
- 20 Glasgow
- 20 Greyhound
- 24 Hind
- 24 Kennington
- 28 Levant
- 24 Lively
- 28 Liverpool
- 28 Lizard
- 24 Ludlow-Castle
- 28 Maidstone
- 24 Mercury
- 28 Milford
- 24 Nightingale
- 24 Portmahon
- 20 Rose
- 24 Rye

ENGLAND. 355

COINS.] In Great Britain money is computed by pounds, shillings, and pence, twelve pence making a shilling, and twenty shillings one pound, which is only an imaginary coin.

The

Guns.	Guns.	Guns.	Furnace
24 Rye	14 Dispatch	18 Postillion	Infernal
20 Scarborough	10 Druid	8 Ranger	
20 Seaford	14 Escorte	Racehorse	Fire-St. no Guns,
20 Seahorse	16 Favourite	14 Saltash	
28 Shannon	18 Ferret	8 Savage	Ætna
24 Sheerness	8 Flambro's Prize	14 Senegal	Cormorant
24 Solebay	8 Fly	14 Sardome	Grampus
20 Syren	14 Fortune	8 Speedwell	Lightning
24 Surprize	14 Grampus	10 Spy	Pluto
28 Tartar	10 Granado	14 Swallow	Raven
24 Terpsichore	8 Gorce	14 Swift	Roman Emperor
28 Trent	8 Happy	14 Swan	Proserpine
28 Valeur	8 Hazard	16 Tamer	Salamander
28 Unicorn	14 Hornet	Terror	Strombolo
24 Wager	14 Hound	10 Thunder	Vesuvius
	10 Hunter	14 Trial	
SLOOPS.	14 Jamaica	14 Vulture	YACHTS.
	10 King's Fisher	8 Wasp	
14 Albany	8 Laurel	16 Weazle	Guns.
10 Alderney	6 Lurcher	8 Wolf	10 Dorset
10 Antigua	18 Merlin	10 Zephir	8 Fubbs
12 Badger	16 Mortar		8 Katharine
16 Baltimore	18 Nautilus	BOMB Vessels.	Augusta
10 Barbadoes	8 Peggy		
10 Bonetta	10 Pomona	Basilisk	STORESHIPS.
8 Cruzier	10 Otter	Blast	
18 Cygnet	14 Pelican	Carcass	20 Crown
10 Diligence	14 Porcupine	Firedrake	24 South Sea Castle.

Ships out of Commission and Building.

Rates.	Guns.	Names.	Rates.	Guns.	Names.	Rates.	Guns.	Names.
3	74	Albion	5	44	Eltham	3	84	Ramillies
3	64	Asia	5	44	Expedition	3	64	Royal Oak
4	60	Augusta	3	80	Formidable	4	60	Rupert
5	44	Anglesea	4	50	Gloucester	4	50	Ruby
5	32	Aurora	5	44	Glory			R. Charlotte Yacht
2	90	Barfleur	6	28	Guadalupe			
		Ditto, a new ship	5	44	Hastings	3	64	Suffolk
3	80	Boyne	5	44	Hector	4	60	St. Alban's
4	50	Bristol	5	30	Jason	6	24	Sphinx
6	24	Blandford	2	90	London	3	74	Triumph
	90	Blenheim	5	44	Mary Galley		28	Vengeance
		Hospital-ship			Martin Sloop		10	Viper
3	74	Canada			Mary Yacht	1	100	Victory
4	60	Canterbury	3	74	Monarch			Vulture Sloop
3	74	Courageux	4	40	Nonsuch	4		Warwick
4	50	Colchester	3	80	Pr. Carolina	5		Winchelsea
3	74	Defiance	4	60	Pr. Louisa	4	60	Worcester
	24	Experiment	4	60	Plymouth			William and Mary Yacht
	60	Eagle	5	44	Poole			
	64	Edinburgh	1	90	Queen	3	64	Yarmouth
6	60	Exeter	1	100	Royal Anne			

Com.

The gold pieces confist only of guineas, halves, and quarters: the filver, of crowns, half-crowns, fhillings, fixpences, groats, and even down to a filver penny; and the copper money, only of half-pence, and farthings. In a country like England, where the intrinfic value of the filver is very near equal, and in fome coins, crown pieces particularly, fuperior to the nominal, the coinage of filver money is a matter of great confequence; and yet the prefent ftate of the national currency, feems to demand a new coinage of fhillings and fixpences, the intrinfic value of the latter being many of them worn down to half their nominal value. This can only be done by an act of parliament, and by the public lofing the difference between the bullion of the new and the old money. Befides the coins already mentioned, five and two guinea pieces are coined at the Tower of London, but they are not generally current, nor is any filver coin that is lower than fixpence. The coins of the famous Simon, in the time of Cromwell, and in the beginning of Charles II.'s reign, are remarkable for their beauty.

ROYAL TITLES, ARMS, AND ORDERS.} The title of the king of England, is, By the Grace of God, of Great-Britain, France, and Ireland, King, Defender of the Faith. The defignation of the kings of England was formerly, his or her Grace, or Highnefs, till Henry VIII. to put

Complement of Men, and Weight of Metal, in the Royal Navy.

Ships of three Decks.					Guns.	Men.	Metal.		
Guns.	Men.	Metal.			60	420	24	12	6
100	850	42	24	12 6	60	400	24	9	6
90	750	32	18	12 6	50	350	24	12	6
80	600	32	13	9 6	50	300	18	9	6
Ships of two Decks.					44 40	250	18	9	6
80 74	650	32	18	9	Frigates of one Deck.				
70	520	32	18	9	36	240	12	6	
68	Ditto				32	220	12	6	
66	Ditto				28	200	9	4	
64	480	24	12	6	20	160	9	4	

When a fhip of war becomes old or unfit for fervice, the fame name is transferred to another, which is built, as it is called, upon her bottom. While a fingle beam of the old fhip remains, the name cannot be changed unlefs by act of parliament.

The Pay of the Officers of the Royal Navy in each Rate. FLAG OFFICERS, and the CAPTAINS to Flags. per day.

						£	s	d
Admirals and Commanders in Chief of the Fleet					—	5	0	0
An Admiral	—	—	—	—	—	3	10	0
Vice Admiral	—	—	—	—		2	10	0
Rear Admiral	—	—	—			1	15	0
Firft Captain to the Commander in Chief				—	—	1	15	0
Second ditto, and Captain to other Admirals					—	1	0	0
—to V. Admirals ⎫ if firft or fecond Rates, to ⎧					—	0	16	0
—to R. Admirals ⎭ have the pay of fuch Rates ⎩					—	0	13	6

ENGLAND. 357

put himself on a footing with the emperor Charles V. assumed that of Majesty, but the old designation was not abolished, till towards the end of queen Elizabeth's reign.

Since the accession of the present royal family of Great-Britain, anno 1714, the royal atchievement is marshalled as follows: quarterly, in the first grand quarter, *Mars, three lions passant guardant, in pale, Sol,* the imperial ensigns of England, impaled, with the royal arms of Scotland, which are, *Sol, a lion rampant within a double tressure flowered and counterflowered, with fleurs-de-lis, Mars.* The second quarter is the royal arms of France, viz. *Jupiter, three fleurs-de-lis, Sol.* The third, the ensigns of Ireland; which is, *Jupiter,*

Z 3 *an*

OFFICERS.	First.			Second.			Third.			Fourth.			Fifth.			Sixth.		
	l.	*s.*	*d.*	*l.*	*s.*	*d.*	*l.*	*s.*	*d.*	*l.*	*s.*	*d.*	*l.*	*s.*	*d.*	*l.*	*s.*	*d.*
Captain *per day*	1	0	0	0	16	0	0	13	6	0	10	0	0	8	0	0	8	0
Lieutenant *per day*	0	5	0	0	5	0	0	4	0	0	4	0	0	4	0	0	4	0
Master *per month*	9	2	0	8	8	0	7	6	0	6	12	0	6	2	8	5	0	0
2d master & pilots of yachts each 3*l* 10*s*																		
Master's mate	3	6	0	3	0	0	2	16	2	2	7	10	2	2	0	2	2	0
Midshipman	2	5	0	2	0	0	1	17	6	1	13	9	1	10	0	1	10	0
Schoolmaster	0	0	0	0	0	0	1	17	6	1	13	9	1	10	0			
Captain's clerk	2	5	0	2	0	0	1	17	6	1	13	9						
Quarter-master	1	15	0	1	15	0	1	12	0	1	10	0	1	8	0	1	6	0
Quar. master's mate	1	10	0	1	10	0	1	8	0	1	8	0	1	6	0	1	5	0
Boatswain	4	0	0	3	10	0	3	0	0	2	10	0	2	5	0	2	0	0
Boatswain's mate	1	15	0	1	15	0	1	12	0	1	10	0	1	8	0	1	6	0
Yeoman of the sheets	1	12	0	1	10	0	1	8	0	1	8	0	1	6	0	1	6	0
Coxswain	1	12	0	1	10	0	1	8	0	1	8	0	1	6	0	1	6	0
Master sail maker	1	15	0	1	15	0	1	15	0	1	14	0	1	12	0	1	10	0
Sail maker's mate	1	8	0	1	8	0	1	8	0	1	8	0	1	8	0	1	8	0
Sail maker's crew	1	5	0	1	5	0	1	5	0	1	5	0	1	5	0	1	5	0
* Gunner	4	0	0	3	10	0	3	0	0	2	10	0	2	5	0	2	0	0
Gunner's mate	1	15	0	1	15	0	1	12	0	1	10	0	1	8	0	1	6	0
Yeo. of powder room	1	15	0	1	15	0	1	12	0	1	10	0	1	8	0	1	6	0
Quarter gunner *	1	6	0	1	6	0	1	5	0	1	5	0	1	5	0	1	5	0
Armourer	2	5	0	2	0	0	1	17	6	1	13	9	1	10	0	1	10	0
Armourer's mate	1	10	0	1	10	0	1	8	0	1	8	0	1	6	0	1	5	0
Gunsmith	1	5	0	1	5	0												
Carpenter	4	0	0	3	10	0	3	0	0	2	10	0	2	5	0	2	0	0
Carpenter's mate	2	0	0	2	0	0	1	16	0	1	14	0	1	12	0	1	10	0
Carpenter's crew	1	6	0	1	6	0	1	5	0	1	5	0	1	5	0	1	5	0
Purser	4	0	0	3	10	0	3	0	0	2	10	0	2	5	0	2	0	0
Steward	1	5	0	1	5	0	1	5	0	1	3	4	1	0	8	1	0	0
Steward's mate	1	0	8	1	0	8	1	0	8	1	0	8						
Cook	1	5	0	1	5	0	1	5	0	1	5	0	1	5	0	1	4	0
Surgeon †	5	0	0	5	0	0	5	0	0	5	0	0	5	0	0	5	0	0
Surgeon's first mate	3	0	0	3	0	0	3	0	0	3	0	0	3	0	0	3	0	0
—— second mate	2	10	0	2	10	0	2	10	0	2	10	0	2	10	0			
—— third mate	2	0	0	2	0	0	2	0	0									
—— fourth and fifth	1	10	0	1	10	0	1	10	0									
Chaplain ‡	0	19	0	0	19	0	0	19	0	0	19	0						

* *One to every four guns.* † *Besides 2d. a month from each man.*
‡ *Besides 4d. a month from each man.*

an harp, Sol, ſtringed Luna. And the fourth grand quarter is his preſent majeſty's own coat, viz. *Mars, two lions paſſant guardant, Sol,* for Brunſwick, impaled with Lunenburg, which is, *Sol, ſenée of hearts, proper, a lion rampant, Jupiter,* having antient Saxony, viz. *Mars, an horſe currant Luna ente* (or grafted) *in baſe;* and, *in a ſhield ſurtout, Mars, the diadem, or crown of Charlemagne;* the whole, within a garter, as ſovereign of that moſt noble order of knighthood.

The motto of *Dieu et mon Droit,* that is, *God and my Right,* is as old as the reign of Richard I. who aſſumed it to ſhew his independency upon all earthly powers. It was afterwards revived by Edward III. when he laid claim to the crown of France. Almoſt every king of England had a particular badge or cognizance: ſometimes a white hart, ſometimes a fetlock with a falcon, by which it is ſaid Edward IV. alluded to the infidelity of one of his miſtreſſes, and ſometimes a portcullis, which was that of the houſe of Lancaſter; many of the princes of which were born in the caſtle of Beaufort. The white roſe was the bearing of the houſe of York; and that of Lancaſter, by way of contra-diſtinction, adopted the red. The thiſtle, which is now part of the royal armorial bearings, belonged to Scotland, and was very ſignificant when joined to its motto, *Nemo me impune laceſſit.* None ſhall ſafely provoke me.

The titles of the king's eldeſt ſon, are, Prince of Wales, duke of Cornwall and Rothſay, earl of Cheſter, electoral prince of Brunſwick and Lunenburg, earl of Carrick, baron of Renfrew, lord of the iſles, great ſteward of Scotland, and captain general of the artillery company.

The order of the garter, the moſt honourable of any in the world, was inſtituted by Edward III. It conſiſts of the ſovereign, who is always the king or queen of England, of 25 companions, called Knights of the Garter, who wear a medal of St. George killing the dragon, ſuppoſed to be the tutelar ſaint of England, commonly enamelled on gold, ſuſpended from a blue ribband, which was formerly worn about their necks, but now croſſes their bodies from the ſhoulder. The garter, however, which is buckled under the left knee, gives the name to the order, and on it was embroidered the words, *Honi ſoit qui mal y penſe.* Evil to him who evil thinks. Authors are divided as to the original of that motto, but it certainly alluded to the bad faith of the French king John, Edward's contemporary. This order is ſo reſpectable, that it has a prelate, who is the biſhop of Wincheſter, and a chancellor, who is the biſhop of Saliſbury, for the time being. It has likewiſe a regiſter, who is dean of Windſor, and a principal king at arms, called garter, whoſe office is to marſhal and

and manage the solemnities at the installation, and feasts of the knights. The place of installation is Edward III.'s chapel, at Windsor, on which occasion the knights appear in magnificent robes, appropriated to their order, and in their collars of SS.

Knights of the Bath, so called from their bathing at the time of their creation, are supposed to be instituted by Henry IV. about the year 1399, but the order seems to be more ancient. For many reigns they were created at the coronation of a king or queen, or other solemn occasions, and they wear a scarlet ribband hanging from the left shoulder, with an enamelled medal of three crowns, and the motto, *Tria juncta in unum*. Three joined in one. This order being discontinued, was revived by king George I. on the 17th of June, 1725, when 18 noblemen, and as many commoners of the first rank, were installed knights of the order, with great ceremony, at Westminster, where the place of installment is Henry VII.'s chapel. Their robes are splendid and shewy, and the number of the knights is undetermined. The bishop of Rochester is perpetual dean of the order, which has likewise a register and other officers.

The order of the Thistle, as belonging to Scotland, is mentioned in the account of that kingdom.

The origin of the English peerage, or nobility, has been already mentioned. Their titles, and order of dignity, are dukes, marquises, earls, viscounts, and lords or barons.

Baronets can scarce be said to belong to an order, having no other badge than a bloody hand in a field, argent, in their arms. They are the only hereditary honour under the peerage, and would take place even of the knights of the garter, were it not that the latter are always privy counsellors, there being no intermediate honour between them and the parliamentary barons of England. They were instituted by James I. about the year 1615. Their number was then two hundred, and each paid about 1000l. on pretence of reducing and planting the province of Ulster in Ireland: but, at present, the number of these knights amount to 700.

A knight is a term used almost in every nation in Europe, and in general signifies a soldier serving on horseback, a rank of no mean estimation in antient armies, and entitling the party himself to the appellation of Sir. In the common laws they are called milites or soldiers, and they are made by the king laying a sword upon their shoulders, and desiring them to rise by the title of Sir. It is a mark of personal regard from the crown, and therefore the title does not descend to posterity. Other knighthoods formerly took place in England, such as those of bannerets, batchelors, knights of the carpet, and the like, but they are now disused.

It is somewhat difficult to account for the original of the word esquire, which formerly signified a person bearing the arms of a nobleman or knight, and they were therefore called armigeri. This title denoted any person, who, by his birth or property, was entitled to bear arms; but it is at present applied promiscuously to any man, who can afford to live in the character of a gentleman without trade, and even a tradesman, if he is a justice of peace, demands the appellation. This degree, so late as in the reign of Henry IV. was an order, and conferred by the king, by putting about the party's neck, a collar of SS. and giving him a pair of silver spurs. Gower, the poet, appears from his effigies on his tomb in Southwark, to have been an esquire by creation. Serjeants-at-law, and other serjeants belonging to the king's houshold, justices of the peace, doctors in divinity, law and physic, take place of other esquires, and it is remarkable, that all the sons of dukes, marquises, earls, viscounts, and barons, are in the eye of the law no more than esquires, though commonly designed by noble titles. The appellation of gentleman, tho' now confounded with the mean ranks of people, is the root of all English honour, for every nobleman is presumed to be a gentleman, though every gentleman is not a nobleman.

History.] It is generally agreed, that the first inhabitants of Britain were a tribe of the Gauls, or Celtæ, that settled on the opposite shore: a supposition founded upon the evident conformity in their language, manners, government, religion, and complexion.

In the account I have given of the laws and constitution, may be found great part of the history of England, which I shall not here repeat, but confine myself to the different gradations of events, in a chronological order, connected with the improvement of arts, sciences, commerce, and manufactures, at their proper periods, and that in a manner suitable to the proposed brevity of this work.

When Julius Cæsar, about fifty-two years before the birth of Christ, meditated a conquest of Britain, the natives, undoubtedly, had great connections with the Gauls, and other people of the continent, in government, religion, and commerce, rude as the latter was. Cæsar wrote the history of his two expeditions, which he pretended were accompanied with vast difficulties, and attended by such advantages over the islanders, that they agreed to pay tribute. It plainly appears, however, from contemporary, and other authors, as well as Cæsar's own narrative, that his victories were incomplete and indecisive;

decisive; nor did the Romans receive the least advantage from his expedition, but a better knowledge of the island than they had before. The Britons, at the time of Cæsar's descent, were governed, in time of war, by a political confederacy, of which Cassibelan, whose territories lay in Hertfordshire, and some of the adjacent counties, was the head; and this form of government continued among them for some time.

In their manner of life, as described by Cæsar, and the best authors, they differed little from the rude inhabitants of the northern climates that have been already mentioned; but they certainly sowed corn, though, perhaps, they chiefly subsisted upon animal food and milk. Their cloathing was skins, and their fortifications beams of wood. They were dexterous in the management of their chariots beyond credibility, and they fought with lances, darts, and swords. Women sometimes led their armies to the field, and were recognized as sovereigns of their particular districts. They favoured a primogeniture, or seniority, in their succession to royalty, but set it aside on the smallest inconveniency attending it. They painted their bodies with woad, which gave them a bluish or greenish cast; and they are said to have had figures of animals, and heavenly bodies on their skins. In their marriages they were not very delicate, for they formed themselves into what we may call matrimonial clubs. Twelve or fourteen men married as many wives, and each wife was in common to them all, but her children belonged to the original husband.

The Britons lived, during the long reign of Augustus Cæsar, rather as the allies than the tributaries of the Romans; but the communications between Rome and Great-Britain being then extended, the emperor Claudius Cæsar, about forty-two years after the birth of Christ, undertook an expedition in person, in which he seems to have been succesful against Britain. His conquests, however, were imperfect; Caractacus, and Boadicia, though a woman, made noble stands against the Romans. The former was taken prisoner, after a desperate battle, and carried to Rome, where his undaunted behaviour before Claudius gained him the admiration of the victors, and is celebrated in the histories of the times. Boadicia being oppressed in a manner that disgraces the Roman name, and defeated, disdained to survive the liberties of her country; and Agricola, general to Domitian, after subduing South-Britain, carried his arms, as has been already seen in the history of Scotland, northwards, into Caledonia, where his successors had no reason to boast of their progress, every inch of ground being bravely defended. During the time

time the Romans remained in this island, they erected those walls I have so often mentioned, to protect the Britons from the invasions of the Caledonians, Scots, and Picts; and we are told, that the Roman language, learning, and customs, became familiar in Britain. There seems, however, to be no great foundation for this assertion; and it is more probable, that the Romans considered Britain chiefly as a nursery for their armies abroad, on account of the superior strength of body and courage of the inhabitants, when disciplined. That this was the case, appears plainly enough from the defenceless state of the Britons, when the government of Rome recalled her forces from that island. I have already taken notice, that during the abode of the Romans in Britain, they introduced into it all the luxuries of Italy; but it is certain, that under them the South Britons became the most abject slaves, and that the genius of liberty retreated northwards, where the natives had made a brave resistance against the tyrants of the world. For though the Britons were unquestionably very brave, when incorporated with the Roman legions abroad, yet we know of no struggle they made, in later times, for their independency at home, notwithstanding the many favourable opportunities that presented themselves. The Roman emperors and generals, while in this island, assisted by the Britons, were entirely employed in repelling the attacks of the Caledonians and Picts (the latter are thought to have been the southern Britons retired northwards) and they appeared to have been in no pain about the southern provinces.

Upon the mighty inundations of those barbarous nations, which, under the names of Goths and Vandals, invaded the Roman empire, with infinite numbers, fury, and danger to Rome itself *, the Roman legions were withdrawn out of Britain, with the flower of the British youth, for the defence of the capital and center of the empire. As the Roman forces decreased in Britain, the Scots and Picts, who had always opposed the progress of the Romans in this island, advanced the more boldly into the southern parts, carrying terror and desolation over the whole country. The effeminated Britons were so habituated to slavery, and accustomed to have recourse to the Romans for defence, that they again and again implored the return of the Romans, who as often drove back the invaders to their mountains and antient limits beyond the walls. But these enterprises served only to protract the miseries of the Britons; and the Romans, now reduced to extremities

* See the Introduction.

mities at home, and fatigued with these distant expeditions, acquainted the Britons, that they must no longer look to them for protection, exhorted them to arm in their own defence; and, that they might leave the island with a good grace, they assisted the Britons in rebuilding with stone the wall of Severus, between Newcastle and Carlisle, which they lined with forts and watch towers; and having done this good office, took their last farewell of Britain, about the year 448, after having been masters of the most fertile parts of it, if we reckon from the invasion of Julius Cæsar, 500 years.

The Scots and Picts, finding the whole island finally deserted by the Roman legions, now regarded the whole as their prize, attacked Severus's wall with redoubled forces, ravaged all before them with a rage and fury peculiar to northern nations in those ages, and which a remembrance of former injuries could not fail to inspire. The poor Britons, like a helpless family, deprived of their parent and protector, already subdued by their own fears, had again recourse to Rome, and sent over their miserable epistle for relief (still upon record) which was addressed in these words: *To Aetius, thrice consul: The groans of the Britons*; and told them, after other lamentable complaints, *That the barbarians drove them to the sea, and the sea back to the barbarians; and they had only the hard choice left of perishing by the sword or by the waves.* But having no hopes given them by the Roman general, of any succours from that side, they began to consider what other nation they might call over to their relief: and we have from Gildas, who was himself a Briton (and describes the degeneracy of his countrymen in lamentable strains) but very dark confused hints of their officers, and the names of some of their kings, particularly one Vortigern, who struck a bargain with two Saxon chiefs, Hengist and Horsa, to protect them from the Scots and Picts. The Saxons were in those days masters of what is now called the English channel, and their native countries, comprehending Scandinavia, and the northern parts of Germany, being overstocked with inhabitants, they readily accepted the invitation of the Britons; whom they relieved by checking the progress of the Scots and Picts; and had the island of Thanet allowed them for their residence. But their own country was so populous and barren, and the fertile lands of Britain so agreeable and alluring, that in a very little time, Hengist and Horsa began to meditate a settlement for themselves; and fresh supplies of their countrymen arriving daily, the Saxons soon became formidable to the Britons, whom, after a violent struggle of near 150 years, they subdued, or drove into Wales, where their language and descendants still remain.

Literature at this time in England was so rude, that we know but little of its history. The Saxons were ignorant of letters, and public transactions among the Britons were recorded only by their bards and poets, a species of men whom they held in great veneration. Nennius, who seems to have been contemporary with Gildas, mentions, indeed, a few facts, but nothing that can be relied on, or that can form a connected history. We can, therefore, only mention the names of Merlin, a reputed prince and prophet; Pendragon, the celebrated Arthur, and Thaliessin, whose works are said to be extant, with others of less note. All we know upon the whole is, that after repeated bloody wars, in which the Britons were sometimes the enemies, and sometimes the allies of the Scots and Picts, the Saxons became masters of all England, to the south of Adrian's, or rather, Severus's wall; but the Scots and Picts seem to have been masters of all the territory to the north of that, though they suffered the Britons, who had been driven northwards, to be governed by their own tributary kings; an intermixture that has created great doubts and confusions in history, which I shall not here pretend to unravel.

I have already given a sketch of the constitution and government which the Saxons imported into England, and which form by far the most valuable part of their antient history.

We have no account of their conversion to Christianity but from Popish writers, who generally endeavour to magnify the merits of their superiors. According to them, Ethelbert, king of Kent, who claimed pre-eminence in the heptarchy, as being descended from Hengist, married the king of France's daughter, and she being a Christian, Pope Gregory the Great seized that opportunity to enforce the conversion of her husband to Christianity, or rather to Popery. For that purpose, about the year 596, he sent over to England the famous Austin, the monk, who probably found no great difficulty in converting the king and his people; and also Sebert, king of the East Saxons, who was baptized, and founded the cathedral of St. Paul in London. The monk then, by his master's order, attempted to bring the churches of the Britons in Wales to a conformity with that of Rome, particularly as to the celebration of Easter; but finding a stout resistance on the part of the bishops and clergy, he persuaded his Christian converts to massacre them, which they did to the number of 1200 priests and monks, and reduced the Britons, who were found in the heptarchy, to a state of slavery, which some think gave rise to the antient villenage in England. Austin is accounted the first archbishop archbifhop of Canterbury, and died in 605, as his convert Ethelbert did foon after.

It does not fall within my defign to relate the feparate hiftory of every particular nation that formed the heptarchy. It is fufficient to fay, that the pope, in Auftin's time, fupplied England with about 400 monks, and that the popifh clergy took care to keep their kings and laity under the moft deplorable ignorance, but always magnifying the power and fanctity of his holinefs. Hence it was, that the Anglo-Saxons, during their heptarchy, were governed by priefts and monks; and as they faw convenient, perfuaded their kings either to fhut themfelves up in cloifters, or to undertake pilgrimages to Rome, where they finifhed their days; no lefs than thirty Anglo-Saxon kings, during the heptarchy, refigned their crowns in that manner, and among them was Ina, king of the Weft Saxons, though in other refpects he was a wife and brave prince. The bounty of thofe Anglo-Saxon kings to the fee of Rome, was therefore unlimited; and Ethelwald, king of Mercia, whom I have already mentioned, impofed an annual tax of a penny upon every houfe, which was afterwards known by the name of Peter's pence.

The Anglo-Saxon kings, during the heptarchy, commonly chofe one who was to be the head of their political confederacy, for regulating their concerns, but without any jurifdiction in the dominions of others. The clergy, we may eafily fuppofe, had great influence on thofe occafions; and the hiftory of the Saxon heptarchy is little more than that of crimes, treafons, and murders, committed by the inftigations of priefts and monks. Even their criminal law, as I have already inferred, admitted of a pecuniary compenfation for murder, and regicide itfelf.

Under all thofe difadvantages of bigotry and barbarity, the Anglo-Saxons were happy in comparifon of the nations on the continent; becaufe they were free from the Saracens, or fucceffors of Mahomet, who had erected an empire in the Eaft, upon the ruins of the Roman, and began to extend their ravages over Spain and Italy. London was then a place of very confiderable trade; and, if we are to believe the Saxon chronicles, quoted by Tyrrel, Withred, king of Kent, paid at one time to Ina, king of Weffex, a fum in filver equal to 90,000 l. fterling, in the year 694. England, therefore, we may fuppofe to have been about this time a refuge for the people of the continent. The venerable Bede then compofed his church hiftory of Britain. The Saxon Chronicle is one of the oldeft and moft authentic monuments of hiftory that any nation can produce. An architecture, fuch as it was, with stone and glass working, was introduced into England; and we read, in 709, of a Northumbrian prelate who was served in silver plate. It must, however, be owned, that the Saxon coins, which are generally of copper, are many of them illegible, and all of them mean. Ale and alehouses are mentioned in the laws of Ina, about the year 728; and in this state was the Saxon heptarchy in England, when, about the year 800, the Anglo-Saxons, tired out with the tyranny of their petty kings, united in calling to the government of the heptarchy, Egbert, who was the eldest remaining branch of the race of Cerdic, one of the Saxon chiefs who first arrived in Britain.

Charles the Great, otherwise Charlemaigne, was then king of France, and emperor of Germany; and I have, in a former part of this work, mentioned the commercial treaty between him and Offa, king of Mercia, to whom he sent in a present, a Hungarian sword, a belt, and two silken vests. Egbert had been obliged, by state jealousies, to fly to the court of Charles for protection from the persecutions of Eadburga, daughter of Offa, wife to Brithric, king of the West Saxons. Egbert acquired at the court of Charles, the arts both of war and government, and soon united the Saxon heptarchy in his own person, but without subduing Wales. He changed the name of his kingdom into that of Engle-lond, or England; but there is reason to believe that some part of England continued still to be governed by independent princes of the blood of Cerdic, though they paid, perhaps, a small tribute to Egbert. His prosperity excited the envy of the northern nations, who, under the name of Danes, then infested the seas, and were no strangers to the coasts of England; for about the year 832 they made descents upon Kent and Dorsetshire, where they defeated Egbert in person, and carried off abundance of booty to their ships. About two years after they landed in Cornwall, and, though they were joined by the Cornish Britons, they were driven out of England by Egbert, who died in the year 838, at Winchester, his chief residence.

Egbert was succeeded by his son Ethelwolf, who divided his power with his eldest son Athelstan. By this time England had become a scene of blood and ravages, through the renewal of the Danish invasions; and Ethelwolf, after some time bravely opposing them, retired in a fit of devotion to Rome, to which he carried with him his youngest son, afterwards the famous Alfred, the father of the English constitution. The gifts which Ethelwolf made to the clergy on this occasion (copies of which are still remaining) are so prodigious, that they shew his brain to have been touched by his devotion.

Upon

Upon his death, after his return from Rome, he divided his dominions between two of his sons (Athelstan being then dead) Ethelbald and Ethelbert, but we know of no patrimony that was left to young Alfred. Ethelbert, who was the surviving son, left his kingdom, in 866, to his brother Ethelred; in whose time, notwithstanding the courage and conduct of Alfred, the Danes became masters of the sea-coasts, and the finest counties in England. Ethelred being killed, his brother Alfred mounted the throne in 871. He was one of the greatest princes, both in peace and war, mentioned in history. He fought seven battles with the Danes, with various success, and when defeated, he found resources that rendered him as terrible as before. He was, however, at one time, reduced to an uncommon state of misery, being forced to live in the disguise of a cowherd. He still, however, kept up a secret correspondence with his brave friends, whom he collected together, and by their assistance he gave the Danes many signal overthrows, till at last he recovered the kingdom of England, and obliged the Danes, who had been settled in it, to swear obedience to his government: even part of Wales courted his protection; so that he is thought to have been the most powerful monarch that before his time ever reigned in England.

Among the other glories of Alfred's reign, was that of raising a maritime power in England, by which he secured her coasts from future invasions. He rebuilt the city of London, which had been burnt down by the Danes, and founded the university of Oxford about the year 895: He divided England into counties, hundreds and tythings; or rather he revived those divisions, and the use of juries, which had fallen into desuetude by the ravages of the Danes. Having been educated at Rome, he was himself not only a scholar, but an author, and he tells us himself, that upon his accession to the throne he had scarcely a lay subject who could read English, or an ecclesiastic who understood Latin. He introduced stone and brick buildings to general use in palaces as well as churches, though it is certain that his subjects for many years after his death were fond of timber buildings. His encouragement of commerce and navigation may seem incredible to modern times, but he had merchants who traded in East-India jewels; and William of Malmsbury says, that some of their gems were reposited in the church of Sherborne in his time. He received from one Octher, about the year 890, a full discovery of the coasts of Norway and Lapland, as far as Russia; and he tells the king, in his memorial printed by Hakluyt, " that he sailed " along the Norway coast, so far north as commonly the
" whale

"whale hunters use to travel." He invited numbers of learned men into his dominions, and found faithful and useful allies in the two Scotch kings his contemporaries, Gregory and Donald, against the Danes. He is said to have fought no less than fifty-six pitched battles with those barbarians. He was inexorable against his corrupt judges, whom he used to hang up on public highways, as a terror to evil doers. He died in the year 901, and his character is so completely amiable and heroic, that he is justly dignified with the epithet of the Great. I have been the more diffuse on the history of Alfred's reign, as it is the most glorious of any in the English annals, though it did not extend to foreign conquests.

Alfred was succeeded by his son Edward the Elder, under whom, though a brave prince, the Danes renewed their barbarities and invasions. He died in the year 925, and was succeeded by his eldest son Athelstan. This prince was such an encourager of commerce as to make a law, that every merchant who made three voyages, on his own account, to the Mediterranean, should be put upon a footing with a thane, or nobleman of the first rank. He encouraged coinage, and we find by his laws that archbishops, bishops, and even abbots, had then the privilege of minting money. His dominions appear, however, to have been confined towards the north by the Danes, although his vassals still kept a footing in those counties. He was engaged in perpetual wars with his neighbours, the Scots in particular, and died in 941. The reigns of his successors, Edmund, Edred, and Edwy, were weak and inglorious, being either engaged in wars with the Danes, or disgraced by the influence of priests. Edgar, who mounted the throne about the year 959, revived the naval glory of England, but, like his predecessors, he was the slave of priests, particularly St. Dunstan. His reign, however, was pacific and glorious, though he was obliged to cede to the Scots all the territory to the north of the Tine. He was succeeded, in 975, by his eldest son Edward, who was barbarously murdered by his step-mother, whose son Ethelred mounted the throne in 978. The English nation, at that time, by the help of priests, was over-run with barbarians, and the Danes by degrees became possessed of the finest part of the country, while their countrymen made sometimes dreadful descents in the western parts. In the year 1002 they had made such settlements in England, that Ethelred was obliged to give way to a general massacre of them by the English, but it is improbable that it was ever put into execution. Some attempts of that kind, however, were undoubtedly made in particular counties, but they served only to enrage the Danish king,

Swein,

Swein, who, in 1013, drove Ethelred, his queen, and two sons, out of England into Normandy, a province of France, facing the south-east coast of England, at that time governed by its own princes, stiled the dukes of Normandy. Swein being killed, was succeeded by his son Canute the Great, whom I have already mentioned, but Ethelred returning to England, forced Canute to retire to Denmark, from whence he invaded England with a vast army, and obliged Edmund Ironside, Ethelred's son, to divide with him the kingdom. Upon Edmund's being assassinated, Canute succeeded to the undivided kingdom; and dying in 1035, his son, Harold Harefoot, did nothing memorable, and his successor, Hardicanute, was so degenerate a prince that the Danish royalty ended with him in England.

The family of Ethelred was now called to the throne; and Edward, who is commonly called the Confessor, mounted it, though Edgar Etheling, by being descended from an elder branch, had the lineal right, and was alive. Edward the Confessor was a soft, good-natured prince, a great benefactor to the church, and excessively fond of the Normans, with whom he had resided. He was governed by his minister, earl Godwin, and his sons, the eldest of whom was Harold. He durst not resent, though he felt, their ignominious treatment; and perceiving his kinsman Edgar Etheling to be of a soft disposition, neither he nor the English paid much regard to Etheling's hereditary right; so that the Confessor, as is said, devised the succession of his crown upon his death to William duke of Normandy. Be that as it will, it is certain, that upon the death of the Confessor, in the year 1066, Harold, son to Godwin earl of Kent, mounted the throne of England.

William duke of Normandy, though a bastard, was then in the unrivalled possession of that great dutchy, and resolved to assert his right to the crown of England. For that purpose he invited the neighbouring princes, as well as his own vassals, to join him, and by way of anticipation, he parcelled out the territory of England to each in proportion to the number of men he brought into the field, making it thereby their interest to assist him effectually. By these means he collected 40,000 of the bravest and most regular troops in Europe, and while Harold was embarrassed with fresh invasions from the Danes, William landed in England without opposition. Harold, returning from the north, encountered William at Hastings in Sussex, with a superior army, but Harold being killed, the crown of England devolved upon William, in the year 1066.

I cannot find any great improvements, either in arts or arms, which the Saxons had made in England since the first invasion of the Danes. Those barbarians seem to have carried off with them almost all the bullion and ready money of the Anglo-Saxons, for I perceive that Alfred the Great left no more to his two daughters for their portions than 100 l. each. The return of the Danes to England, and the victories which had been gained over them, had undoubtedly brought back great part of the money and bullion they had carried off; for we are told that Harold, in his last victory over the Danes, regained as much treasure as twelve lusty men could carry off. We have, indeed, very particular accounts of the value of provisions and manufactures in those days; a palfrey cost 10 s. an acre of land (according to bishop Fleetwood in his Chronicon Pretiosum) 1 s. and a hide of land, containing 120 acres, 100 s. but there is great difficulty in forming the proportion of value which those shillings bore to the present standard of money, though many ingenious treatises have been written on that head. A sheep was estimated at 1 s. an ox was computed at 6 s. a cow at 4 s. a man at 3 l. The board wages of a child, the first year, was 8 s. The tenants of Shireburne were obliged at their choice to pay either 6 d. or four hens. Silk and cotton were quite unknown. Linen was not much used. In the Saxon times, land was divided among all the male children of the deceased. Entails were sometimes practised in those times.

With regard to the manners of the Anglo-Saxons, we can say little, but that they were in general a rude, uncultivated people, ignorant of letters, unskilful in the mechanical arts, untamed to submission under law and government, addicted to imtemperance, riot, and disorder. Even so low as the reign of Canute, they sold their children and kindred into foreign parts. Their best quality was their military courage, which yet was not supported by discipline or conduct. Even the Norman historians, notwithstanding the low state of the arts in their own country, speak of them as barbarians, when they mention the invasion made upon them by the duke of Normandy. Conquest put the people in a situation of receiving slowly from abroad the rudiments of science and cultivation, and of correcting their rough and licentious manners. Their uncultivated state might be owing to the clergy, who always discouraged manufactures.

We are, however, to distinguish between the secular clergy, and the regulars or monks. Many of the former, among the Anglo-Saxons, were men of exemplary lives, and excellent magistrates. The latter depended upon the see of
Rome,

Rome, and directed the consciences of the king and the great men, and were generally ignorant, and often a bloody set. A great deal of the Saxon barbarism was likewise owing to their continual intercourse with the continent: and the Danish invasions, which left little room for civil or literary improvements. Amidst all those defects, public and personal liberty were well understood and guarded by the Saxon institutions; and we owe to them, at this day, the most valuable privileges of English subjects.

The loss which both sides suffered at the battle of Hastings is uncertain. Anglo-Saxon authors say, that Harold was so impatient to fight, that he attacked William with half of his army, so that the advantage of numbers was on the side of the Norman; and, indeed, the death of Harold seems to have decided the day; and William, with very little further difficulty, took possession of the throne, and partly new modelled the whole constitution of England in the manner I have already described, by converting all the lands into knights fees [*], which are said to have amounted to 62,000, which were held of the Norman and other great persons who had assisted him in his conquest, and who were bound to attend him with their knights and their followers in his wars. He gave, for instance, to one of his barons, the whole county of Chester, which he erected into a palatinate, and rendered by his grant almost independant of the crown: and here, according to some historians, we have the rise of the feudal law in England. William found it no easy matter to keep possession of his crown. Edgar Etheling, and his sister, the next Anglo-Saxon heirs, were affectionately received in Scotland, and many of the Saxon lords took arms and formed conspiracies in England. William got the better of all difficulties, especially after he had made a peace with Malcolm, king of Scotland, who married Etheling's sister; but not without exercising horrible cruelties upon the Anglo-Saxons, whom he obliged to put out their candles and fires every evening at eight o'clock, upon the ringing of a bell, called the *courfeu*. He introduced Norman laws and language. He built the stone square tower at London, commonly called the White Tower; and bridled the country with forts, and disarmed the old inhabitants; in short, he attempted every thing possible to obliterate every trace of the Anglo-Saxon constitution.

He caused a general survey of all the lands of England to be made, or rather to be compleated, (for it was begun in Edward

---

[*] Four hides of land made one knight's-fee; a barony was twelve times greater than that of a knight's-fee: and when Doomsday-book was framed, the number of great barons amounted to 700.

the Confessor's time) and an account to be taken of the villains, slaves, and live stock upon each estate; all which were recorded in a book called Doomsday-book, which is now kept in the Exchequer. But the repose of this fortunate and victorious king was disturbed in his old age, by the rebellion of his eldest son Robert, who had been appointed governor of Normandy, but now assumed the government as sovereign of that province, in which he was favoured by the king of France. And here we have the rise of the wars between England and France; which have continued longer, drawn more noble blood, and been attended with more memorable atchievements, than any other national quarrel we read of in antient or modern history. William seeing a war inevitable, entered upon it with his usual vigour, and, with incredible celerity, transporting a brave English army, invaded France, where he was every where victorious, but died before he had finished the war, in the year 1087, the sixty-first of his age, and twenty-first of his reign in England, and was buried in his own abbey at Caen in Normandy.

The above are the most material transactions of William's reign; and it may be further observed, that by the Norman conquest, England not only lost the true line of her antient Saxon kings, but also her principal nobility, who either fell in battle in defence of their country and liberties, or fled to foreign countries, particularly Scotland, where being kindly received by king Malcolm, they established themselves; and what is very remarkable, introduced the Saxon or English, which has been the prevailing language in the Lowlands of Scotland to this day.

On the other hand, England, by virtue of the conquest, became much greater, both in dominion and power, by the accession of so much territory upon the continent. For though the Normans, by the conquest of England, gained much of the English lands and riches, yet England gained the large and fertile dukedom of Normandy, which became a province to this crown. England likewise gained much by the great increase of naval power, and multitude of ships, wherein Normandy then abounded. This, with the perpetual intercourse between England and the continent, gave us an increase of trade and commerce, and of treasure to the crown and kingdom, as appeared soon afterwards. England, by the conquest, gained likewise a natural right to the dominion of the Channel, which had been before acquired only by the great naval power of Edgar, and other Saxon kings. But the dominion of the narrow seas seems naturally to belong, like that of rivers, to those who possess the banks or coasts on both sides;

and so to have strengthened the former title, by so long a coast as that of Normandy on one side, and of England on the other side of the Channel. This dominion of the Channel, though we have long ago lost all our possessions in France, we continue to defend and maintain by the bravery of our seamen, and the superior strength of our navy to any other power.

The succession to the crown of England was disputed between the Conqueror's sons Robert and William, (commonly called Rufus) and was carried in favour of the latter. He was a brave and intrepid prince, but no friend to the clergy, who have, therefore, been unfavourable to his memory. He was likewise hated by the Normans, who loved his elder brother, and consequently was engaged in perpetual wars with his brothers, and rebellious people. About this time the crusades to the Holy Land began, and Robert, who was among the first to engage, accommodated matters with William for a sum of money, which he levied from the clergy. William behaved with great generosity towards Edgar Etheling and the court of Scotland, notwithstanding all the provocations he had received from that quarter, but was accidentally killed as he was hunting in New Forest, in the year 1100, and the forty-fourth year of his age. He is chiefly accused of rapaciousness and oppression; but the circumstances of his reign had great demands for money, which he had no other means of raising but from a luxurious, over-grown clergy, who had engrossed all the riches of the kingdom.

This prince built Westminster-hall as it now stands, and added several works to the Tower, which he surrounded with a wall and ditch. In the year 1100 happened that inundation of the sea, which overflowed great part of earl Godwin's estate in Kent, and formed those shallows in the Downs, now called the Goodwin Sands.

He was succeeded by his brother Henry I. surnamed Beauclerc, on account of his learning, though his brother Robert was returning from the Holy Land. Henry may be said to have purchased the throne, first by his brother's treasures, which he seized at Winchester; and, secondly, by a charter, in which he restored his subjects to the rights and privileges they had enjoyed under the Anglo-Saxon kings: thirdly, by his marriage with Matilda, daughter of Malcolm III. king of Scotland, and niece to Edgar Atheling, of the antient Saxon line. His reign in a great measure restored the clergy to their influence in the state, and they formed as it were a separate body dependent upon the pope, which afterwards created great convulsions in England. Henry, partly by force,

force, and partly by ſtratagem, made himſelf maſter of his brother Robert's perſon, and dutchy of Normandy; and, with a moſt ungenerous meanneſs, detained him a priſoner for twenty-eight years, till the time of his death; and in the mean while Henry quieted his conſcience by founding an abbey. He was afterwards engaged in a bloody but ſucceſsful war with France; and before his death he ſettled the ſucceſſion upon his daughter the empreſs Matilda, widow to Henry IV. emperor of Germany, and her ſon Henry, by her ſecond huſband Geoffrey Plantagenet, earl of Anjou. Henry died of a ſurfeit, in the ſeventy-eighth year of his age, in 1135.

Notwithſtanding the late ſettlement of ſucceſſion, the crown of England was claimed, and ſeized by Stephen, earl of Blois, the ſon of Adela, fourth daughter to William the Conqueror. Matilda and her ſon were then abroad; and Stephen was aſſiſted in his uſurpation by his brother the biſhop of Wincheſter, and the other great prelates, that he might hold his crown dependent as it were upon them. Matilda, however, found a generous protector in her uncle, David, king of Scotland, and a worthy ſubject in her natural brother Robert, earl of Glouceſter, who headed her party before her ſon grew up. A long and bloody war enſued, the clergy having abſolved Stephen and all his friends from their guilt of breaking the act of ſucceſſion; but at length the barons, who dreaded the power of the clergy, inclined towards Matilda; and Stephen, who depended chiefly on foreign mercenaries, having been abandoned by the clergy, was defeated and taken priſoner in 1141; and being carried before Matilda, ſhe impotently upbraided him, and ordered him to be put in chains.

Matilda was proud and weak; the clergy were bold and ambitious; and when joined with the nobility, who were factious and turbulent, they were an overmatch for the crown. Being now maſters of the ſoil of England, they forgot the principles of their Normannic conſtitution, becauſe it rendered them dependent upon the crown. They demanded to be governed by the Saxon laws, according to the charter that had been granted by Henry I. upon his acceſſion; and finding Matilda refractory, they drove her out of England in 1142. Stephen having been exchanged for the earl of Glouceſter, who had been taken priſoner likewiſe, upon his obtaining his liberty, found that his clergy and nobility had, in fact, excluded him from the government, by building 1100 caſtles (though they owed all their rights to the king) where each owner lived as an independent prince. We do not, however, find that this alleviated the feudal ſubjection of the inferior ranks. Stephen was ill enough adviſed to attempt to force them into a compliance with his will, by declaring his ſon Euſtace heir apparent to the kingdom; and

exaſperated

exafperated the clergy fo much, that they invited over young Henry of Anjou, who had been acknowledged duke of Normandy, and was fon to the emprefs; and he accordingly landed in England with an army of foreigners.

This meafure divided the clergy from the barons, who were apprehenfive of a fecond conqueft; and the earl of Arundel, with the heads of the lay ariftocracy, propofed an accommodation, to which both parties agreed. Stephen, who about that time loft his fon Euftace, was to retain the name and office of king; but Henry, who was in fact invefted with the chief executive power, was acknowledged his fucceffor. Tho' this accommodation was only precarious and imperfect, yet it was received by the Englifh, who had bled at every pore during the late civil wars, with raptures of joy; and Stephen dying very opportunely, Henry mounted the throne without a rival in 1154.

Henry II. furnamed Plantagenet, was by far the greateft prince of his time. It is true, he owed his crown to the arms and valour of his grand uncle, David king of Scotland, and the virtues and wifdom of the earl of Gloucefter; but Henry, as he grew up, difcovered amazing abilities for government, having performed, in the fixteenth year of his age, actions that would have dignified the moft experienced warriors. At his acceffion to the throne, he found the condition of the Englifh boroughs greatly bettered by the privileges granted them in the ftruggles between their late kings and the nobility. Henry perceived the good policy of this, and brought the boroughs to fuch a height, that if a bondman or fervant remained in a borough a year and a day, he was by fuch refidence made free. He erected Wallingford, Winchefter, and Oxford, into free boroughs, for the fervices the inhabitants had done to his mother and himfelf; by difcharging them from every burden, excepting the fixed fee-farm rent of fuch town; and this throughout all England, excepting London. This gave a vaft acceffion of power to the crown, becaufe the crown alone could fupport the boroughs againft their feudal tyrants, and enabled Henry to reduce his overgrown nobility.

Without being very fcrupulous in adhering to his former engagements, he refumed the exceffive grants of crown lands by Stephen, on pretence of his being an ufurper. He demolifhed the rebellious caftles that had been built; but when he came to touch the clergy, he found their ufurpations not to be fhaken. He perceived that the root of all their enormous diforders lay in Rome, where the popes had exempted churchmen, not only from lay courts, but civil taxes. The bloody cruelties and diforders, occafioned by thofe exemptions, all over the kingdom, would be incredible, were they not attested by the most unexceptionable evidences. Unfortunately for Henry, the head of the English church, and chancellor of the kingdom, was the celebrated Thomas Becket. This man, powerful from his offices, and still more so by his popularity, arising from a pretended sanctity, was violent, intrepid, and a determined enemy to temporal power of every kind, but withal, cool and politic. The king assembled his nobility at Clarendon, the name of which place is still famous for the constitutions there enacted; which, in fact, abolished the authority of the Romish see over the English clergy. Becket finding it in vain to resist the stream, signed those constitutions, till they could be ratified by the pope; who, as he foresaw, rejected them. Henry, though a prince of the most determined spirit of any of his time, was then embroiled with all his neighbours; and the see of Rome was at the same time in its meridian grandeur. Becket having been arraigned and convicted of robbing the public, while he was chancellor, fled to France, where the pope and the French king espoused his quarrel. The effect was, that all the English clergy who were on the king's side were excommunicated, and the subjects absolved from their allegiance. This disconcerted Henry so much, that he submitted to treat, and even to be insulted by his rebel prelate, who returned triumphantly through the streets of London in 1170. His return swelled his pride, and encreased his insolence, till both became insupportable to Henry, who was then in Normandy. Finding that he was in fact only the first subject of his own dominions, he was heard to say, in the anguish of his heart, " Is there none who will revenge his monarch's cause upon this audacious priest?" These words reached the ears of four knights, Hugh Norvil, William Tracy, Hugh Brito, and Richard Fitzwise; and, without acquainting Henry of their intentions, they went over to England, where they beat out Becket's brains before the altar of his own church at Canterbury. Henry was in no condition to second the blind obedience of his knights; and the public resentment rose so high, on the supposition that he was privy to the murder, that he submitted to be scourged by monks at the tomb of the pretended martyr.

Henry, in consequence of his well known maxim, endeavoured to cancel all the grants which had been made by Stephen to the royal family of Scotland, and actually resumed their most valuable possessions in the north of England. This occasioned a war between the two kingdoms, in which William king of Scotland was taken prisoner, and forced to pay for his ransom 100,000 l, As the money and coins of Scotland

land were at that time of the same intrinsic value with those of England, and as one half of the ransom was paid in ready money, and the other at a time appointed, it has been observed by bishop Nicholson, and other very accurate authors, that, considering the vast difficulties which England, in the next reign, had to pay the ransom of king Richard, Scotland must have then possessed more ready money than England, a fact, which tho' undoubted, is not easily accounted for upon any historical system hitherto formed.

Henry likewise distinguished his reign by the conquest of Ireland, which I shall have occasion to mention when I treat of that island; and by marrying Eleanor, the divorced queen of France, but the heiress of Guienne and Poictou, he became almost as powerful as the French king himself in his own dominions, and the greatest prince in Christendom. Henry, however, in his old age was far from being fortunate. He had a turn for pleasure, and embarrassed himself in intrigues with women, particularly the fair Rosamond, which were resented by his queen Eleanor, by her seducing her sons, Henry, (whom his father had unadvisedly caused to be crowned in his own life-time) Richard and John, into repeated rebellions, which at last broke the old man's spirit, and he died obscurely at Chinou, in France, in the year 1189, and 58th of his age. The sum he left in ready money, at his death, has, perhaps, been exaggerated, but the most moderate accounts make it amount to 200,000 l. of our money.

During the reign of Henry, corporation charters were established all over England, by which, as I have already hinted, the power of the barons was greatly reduced. Those corporations encouraged trade; but manufactures, especially those of silk, seem still to have been confined to Spain and Italy; for the silk coronation robes, made use of by young Henry and his queen, cost 87 l. 10 s. 4 d. in the sheriff of London's account, printed by Mr. Madox; a vast sum in those days. Henry introduced the use of glass in windows into England, and stone arches in building. Malmsbury, and other historians who lived under him, are remarkable for their Latin stile, which in some places is both pure and elegant.

In this reign, and in those barbarous ages, it was a custom in London for great numbers, to the amount of a hundred or more, of the sons and relations of eminent citizens, to form themselves into a licentious confederacy, to break into rich houses, and plunder them, to rob and murder passengers, and to commit with impunity all sorts of disorders.

Henry so far abolished the barbarous and absurd practice of forfeiting ships, which had been wrecked on the coast, that if one man or animal were alive in the ship, the vessel and goods

goods were restored to the owners. This prince was also the first who levied a tax on the moveable or personal estates of his subjects, nobles as well as people. Their zeal for the holy wars made them submit to this innovation; and a precedent being once obtained, this taxation became, in following reigns, the usual method of supplying the necessities of the crown. It was a usual practice of the kings of England to repeat the ceremony of their coronation thrice a year, on assembling the states at the three great festivals. Henry, after the first years of his reign, never renewed this ceremony, which was found to be very expensive and very useless. None of his successors ever revived it. Since we are here collecting some detached instances, which show the genius of these ages, it may not be improper to mention the quarrel between Roger, archbishop of York, and Richard, archbishop of Canterbury. We may judge of the violence of military men and laymen, when ecclesiastics could proceed to such extremities. The pope's legate having summoned an assembly of the clergy at London; and as both the archbishops pretended to sit on his right hand, this question of precedency begot a controversy between them. The monks and retainers of archbishop Richard fell upon Roger in the presence of the cardinal and of the synod, threw him on the ground, trampled him under foot, and so bruised him with blows, that he was taken up half dead, and his life was with difficulty saved from their violence.

Richard I. surnamed Cœur de Lion, was the third, but eldest surviving son of Henry II. The clergy had found means to gain him over, and for their own ends they persuaded him to make a most magnificent ruinous crusade to the Holy Land, where he took Ascalon, and performed actions of valour that give countenance even to the fables of antiquity. After several glorious, but fruitless campaigns, he made a truce of three years with Saladin, emperor of the Saracens; and in his return to England he was treacherously surprized by the duke of Austria; who, in 1193, sent him prisoner to the emperor Henry VI. His ransom was fixed by the sordid emperor at 150,000 marks, about 300,000 l. of our present money. According to contemporary authors, the raising of this ransom proved to be a matter of so much difficulty, that all the church plate was melted down, and a tax was laid on all persons, both ecclesiastical and secular, of one fourth part of their income, for one year; and twenty shillings on every knight's-fee; also one year's wool borrowed of the Cistercians, besides money raised upon the clergy of the king's French dominions; and 2000 marks, which were furnished by William king of Scotland, in gratitude for Richard's generous behaviour to
him

him before his departure. Though all those sums are well authenticated, yet it is not easy to reconcile them with certain other money transactions of this reign, but by supposing that Richard carried off with him, and expended abroad, all the visible specie in the kingdom; and that the people had reserved vast hoards, which they afterwards produced, when commerce took a brisker turn.

Upon Richard's return from his captivity, he held a parliament at Nottingham; whither William king of Scotland came, and demanded the counties of Northumberland, Cumberland, Westmoreland, and Lancaster, as his predecessors had enjoyed the same. Richard put him off for the present with fair words, yet by advice of his council he granted William, by charter, the following honours and benefits for him and his successors, viz. " That whenever a king of Scotland was to be summoned to the court of England, to do homage for the lands he held in England, he should be, at the river Tweed, received by the bishop of Durham, and the sheriff of Northumberland, and they should conduct him to the river Tees, where the archbishop and sheriff of York should receive him; and so in like sort the bishop, and sheriffs of the other shires, till he arrived at court. On his journey he had 100 shillings (15 l. of our money) per day, allowed him for charges. At court thirty shillings per day; twelve wastels, and twelve simnels of the king's, (two sorts of fine bread in use then) four quarts of the king's best wine; six quarts of ordinary wine; two pound weight of pepper; and four pound weight of cinnamon: four wax lights: forty great long perches of the king's best candles; and twenty-four of the ordinary ones. And on his return he was to be conducted as before, with the same allowances."

Whilst the Scottish kings enjoyed their lands in England, they found it their interest, once generally in every king's reign, to perform the said homage; but when they were deprived of their said lands, they paid no more homage.

Woollen broad-cloths were made in England at this time. An ox sold for three shillings, which answers to nine shillings of our money, and a sheep at four pence, or one shilling. Richard, upon his return, found his dominions in great disorder, through the practices of his brother John, whom he however pardoned; and by the invasions of the French, whom he repelled, but was slain in besieging the castle of Chalons, in the year 1199, the 42d of his age and 10th of his reign.

The reign of his brother John, who succeeded him, is infamous in the English history. He is said to have put to death Arthur, the eldest son of his brother Geoffrey, who had the hereditary right to the crown. The young prince's mother,

ther, Constance, complained to Philip, the king of France, who, upon John's non-appearance at his court, as a vassal, deprived him of Normandy. John notwithstanding in his wars with the French, Scotch, and Irish, gave many proofs of personal valour, but became at last so apprehensive of a French invasion, that he rendered himself a tributary to the pope, and laid his crown and regalia at the foot of the legate Pandulph, who kept them for five days. The great barons resented his meanness by taking arms, but he repeated his shameful submissions to the pope, and after experiencing various fortunes of war, John was at last brought so low, that the barons obliged him, in 1216, to sign the great deed, so well known by the name of Magna Charta. Though this charter is deemed the foundation of English liberty, yet it is in fact no other than a renewal of those immunities which the barons and their followers had possessed under the Saxon princes, and which they claimed by the charter of Henry I. As the principles of liberty, however, came to be more enlarged, and property to be better secured; this charter, by various subsequent acts and explanations, came to be applicable to every English subject, as well as to the barons, knights, and burgesses. John had scarce signed it, when he retracted, and called upon the pope for protection, when the barons withdrew their allegiance from John, and transferred it to Lewis, the eldest son of Philip Augustus, king of France. This gave umbrage to the pope, and the barons being apprehensive of their country becoming a province to France, they returned to John's allegiance, but he was unable to protect them, till the pope refused to confirm the title of Lewis. John died in 1216, and the 49th year of his reign, just as he had a glimpse of resuming his authority. Without disputing what historians have said of his arbitrary, inconstant, and cruel disposition, it is evident, from the same relations, that he had great provocations from the clergy and the barons, who in their turns attempted to annihilate the regal prerogative. It is undeniable, at the same time, that under John the commons of England laid the foundation of all the wealth and privileges they now enjoy; and the commerce of England received a most surprizing encrease. He may be called the father of the privileges of free boroughs, which he established, and endowed all over his kingdom; and it was under him that the stone bridge, as it stood some years ago, was erected cross the Thames at London. The city of London owes her privileges to him. The office of mayor, before his reign, was for life; but he gave them a charter to chuse a mayor out of their own body, annually, and to elect their sheriffs and common-council annually, as at present.

England

England was in a deplorable situation when her crown devolved upon Henry III. the late king's son, who was but nine years of age. The earl of Pembroke was chosen his guardian; and the pope taking part with the young prince, the French were defeated, and driven out of the kingdom, and their king obliged to renounce all claims upon the crown of England. The regent earl of Pembroke, who had thus retrieved the independency of his country, died in 1219, and the regency devolved upon the bishop of Winchester. The French king all this time kept possession of Normandy; but at home the pope was now become king of England, and sent no fewer than 300 of his rapacious clergy at one time to take possession of its best benefices, and to load the people with taxes. This evil was encreased, by Henry marrying the daughter of the king of Provence, a needy prince, whose poor relations engrossed the best estates and places in the kingdom. The king was of a soft, pliable disposition, and had been persuaded to violate the Great Charter. An association of the barons was formed against him and his government, and a civil war breaking out, Henry seemed to be abandoned by all but his Gascons, and foreign mercenaries. His profusion brought him into inexpressible difficulties, and the famous Stephen Montfort being chosen general of the association, the king and his two sons were defeated, and taken prisoners, at the battle of Lewes. A difference happening between Montfort, and the earl of Gloucester, a nobleman of great authority, prince Edward, Henry's eldest son, obtained his liberty, and assembling as many as he could of his father's subjects, who were jealous of Montfort, and weary of the tyranny of the barons, he gave battle to the rebels, whom he defeated at Evesham, and killed Montfort. The representatives of the commons of England, both knights and burgesses, formed now part of the English legislature, in a separate house, and this gave the first blow to feudal tenures in England, but historians are not agreed in what manner the commons, before this time, formed any part of the English parliaments, or great councils. Prince Edward being afterwards engaged in a crusade, Henry, during his absence, died in 1272, the 64th year of his age and 56th of his reign, which was uncomfortable and inglorious. During his reign, the principal customs arose from the importation of French and Rhenish wines, the English being as yet strangers to those of Spain, Portugal and Italy. Interest had in that age mounted to an enormous height, as might be expected from the barbarism of the times, and mens ignorance of commerce, which was still very low, though it seems rather to have encreased since the conquest. There are instances of 50 l.

per cent. paid for money, which tempted the Jews to remain in England, notwithstanding the grievous oppressions they laboured under, from the bigotry of the age, and Henry's extortions. In 1255 Henry made a fresh demand of 8000 marks from the Jews, and threatened to hang them, if they refused compliance. They now lost all patience, and desired leave to retire with their effects out of the kingdom. But the king replied, " How can I remedy the oppression you complain of? I am myself a beggar; I am despoiled; I am stripped of all my revenues; I owe above 200,000 marks; and if I had said 300,000, I should not exceed the truth; I am obliged to pay my son, prince Edward, 15,000 marks a year; I have not a farthing; and I must have money from any hand, from any quarter, or by any means." King John, his father, once demanded 10,000 marks from a Jew of Bristol: and on his refusal, ordered one of his teeth to be drawn every day till he should consent. The Jew lost seven teeth, and then paid the sum required of him.

Edward returning to England, on the news of his father's death, invited all who held of his crown *in capite*, to his coronation dinner, which consisted (that the reader may have some idea of the luxury of the times) of 278 bacon hogs, 450 hogs, 440 oxen, 430 sheep, 22,600 hens and capons, and 13 fat goats; (see Rymer's Fœdera).

Edward was a brave and a politic prince, and being perfectly well acquainted with the laws, interests, and constitution of his kingdom, his regulations and reformations of his laws, have justly given him the title of the English Justinian. He passed the famous mortmain act, whereby all persons were restrained from giving, by will or *otherwise*, their estates to those *so called*, religious purposes, and the societies that never die, without a licence from the crown." He granted certain privileges to the cinque-ports, which, though now very inconsiderable, were then obliged to attend the king when he went beyond sea, with fifty-seven ships, each having twenty armed soldiers on board, and to maintain them at their own costs for the space of fifteen days. He reduced the Welch to pay him tribute, and annexed its principality to his crown, and was the first who gave the title of prince of Wales to his eldest son. Though he encouraged foreigners to trade with England, yet the aggregate body of every particular nation residing here, became answerable for the misdmeanors of every individual person of their number. He regulated the forms of parliment, and their manner of giving aids towards the nation's defence, as they now stand, with very little variation. Perceiving that the indolence of his subjects rendered them a prey to the Jews, who were the great ufurers and money dealers of the times, he expelled them out of England, and feized all their immoveable eftates. I have in the article of Scotland mentioned the unjuftifiable manner in which he abolifhed the independency of that kingdom; but, on the other hand, it muft be acknowledged that he held the balance of power in Europe, and employed the vaft fums he raifed from his fubjects, for the aggrandizement of his crown and people. He had frequent wars abroad, efpecially with France, in which he was not very fuccefsful, and would willingly have abridged the power of the barons, and great nobility, had they not been fo ftrong.

His vaft connections with the continent were productive of many benefits to his fubjects, particularly by the introduction of reading glaffes and fpectacles, though they are faid to have been invented in the late reign, by the famous friar Bacon, whom I have already mentioned. Windmills were erected in England, about the fame time, and the regulation of gold and filver workmanfhip was afcertained by an affay, and mark of the goldfmiths company. After all, Edward's continental wars were unfortunate both to himfelf and the Englifh, by draining them of their wealth, and it is thought that he too much neglected the woollen manufactures of his kingdom. He was often embroiled with the pope, efpecially upon the affairs of Scotland, and he died in 1307, the 69th year of his age and 35th of his reign, while he was upon a frefh expedition to exterminate that people.

His fon and fucceffor Edward II. fhewed early difpofitions for encouraging favourites, but Gavefton, his chief minion, being banifhed by his father Edward, he mounted the throne, with vaft advantages, both political and perfonal, all which he foon forfeited by his own imprudence. He recalled Gavefton, and loaded him with honours, and married Ifabella, daughter to the French king, who reftored to him part of the territories, which Edward I. had loft in France. The knights templars were fuppreffed in his reign, and the barons obliged him once more to banifh his favourite, and to confirm the great charter, while king Robert Bruce recovered all Scotland, excepting the caftle of Stirling, near to which, Bannockburn, Edward in perfon received the greateft defeat that England ever fuffered, in 1314. Gavefton being beheaded by the barons, Edward fixed upon young Hugh Spencer for his favourite, but he was banifhed, together with his father, an aged nobleman of great honour and courage. His queen, a furious ambitious woman, perfuaded her hufband to recall the Spencers, while the common people, from their hatred to the barons, joined the king's ftandard, and after defeating them, reftored him to the exercife of all his prerogatives. A cruel use was made of those successes, and many noble patriots, with their estates, fell victims to the queen's revenge, but at last she became enamoured with Roger Mortimer, who was her prisoner, and had been one of the most active of the antiroyalist lords. A breach between her and the Spencers soon followed, and going over to France with her lover, she found means to form such a party in England, that returning with some French troops, she put the eldest Spencer to an ignominious death, made her husband prisoner, and forced him to abdicate his crown, in favour of his son Edward III. then fifteen years of age. Nothing now but the death of Edward II. was wanting to complete her guilt, and he was most barbarously murdered in Berkeley-castle, by ruffians, supposed to be employed by her and her paramour Mortimer, in the year 1327.

The fate of Edward II. was in some measure as unjust as it was cruel. His chief misfortune lay in not being a match for Robert Bruce, king of Scotland, the greatest military and political genius of his age, by which the English lost that kingdom. It cannot, at the same time, be denied, that he was too much engrossed by favourites, who led him into sanguinary measures. In other respects he was a far better friend than his father had been to public liberty. He even voluntarily limited his own prerogative, in a parliament held at London in 1324, and he secured the tenants of great barons, from being oppressed by their lords. None of his predecessors equalled him in his encouragement of commerce, and he protected his trading subjects with great spirit against the Hanseatic league, and the neighbouring powers. Upon an average, the difference of living then and now seems to be nearly as 5 or 6 is to 1, always remembering that their money contained thrice as much silver as our money or coin of the same denomination does. Thus, for example, if a goose then cost 2 d. ½, that is 7 d. ½ of our money, or according to the proportion of 6 to 1, it would now cost 3 s. 9 d.

Edward III. mounted the throne in 1327. He was then under the tuition of his mother, who cohabited with Mortimer, and they endeavoured to keep possession of their power, by executing many popular measures, and putting an end to all national differences with Scotland. Edward, young as he was, was soon sensible of their designs. He surprized them in person at the head of a few chosen friends in the castle of Nottingham. Mortimer was ignominiously put to a public death, and the queen herself was shut up in confinement. It was not long before Edward found means to quarrel with David, king of Scotland, who had married his sister, and who was driven to France by Edward Baliol, who acted as Edward's tributary king of Scotland, and general. Soon after, upon the death of Charles the Fair, king of France (without issue) who had succeeded by virtue of the Salic law, which the French pretended cut off all female succession to that crown, Philip of Valois claimed it, as being the next heir male by succession, but he was opposed by Edward, as being the son of Isabella, who was sister to the three last mentioned kings of France, and first in the female succession. The former was preferred, but the case being doubtful, Edward pursued his claim, and invaded France with a powerful army.

On this occasion, the vast difference between the feudal constitutions of France, which were then in full force, and the government of England, more favourable to public liberty, appeared. The French officers knew no subordination. They and their men were equally undisciplined, and disobedient, though far more numerous than their enemies in the field. The English freemen, on the other hand, having now vast property to fight for, which they could call their own, independent of a feudal law, knew its value, and had learned to defend it by providing themselves with proper armour, and submitting to military exercises, and proper subordination in the field. The war, on the part of Edward, was therefore a continued scene of success and victory. At Cressy, in 1346, above 100,000 French were defeated, chiefly by the valour of the prince of Wales, who was but sixteen years of age (his father being no more than thirty-four) though the English did not exceed 30,000. The loss of the French far exceeded the number of the English army, whose loss consisted of no more than three knights, and one esquire, and about fifty private men. The battle of Poictiers was fought in 1356, between the prince of Wales, and the French king John, but with superior advantages of numbers on the part of the French, who were totally defeated, and their king and his favourite son Philip taken prisoners. It is thought that the number of French killed in this battle, was double that of all the English army, but the modesty and politeness with which the prince treated his royal prisoners, formed the brightest wreath in his garland.

Edward's glories were not confined to France. Having left his queen Philippa daughter to the earl of Hainault, regent of England, she had the good fortune to take prisoner David, king of Scotland, who had ventured to invade England, about six weeks after the battle of Cressy was fought. Thus Edward, on his return, had the glory to see two crowned heads his captives at London. Both kings were afterwards ransomed,

ransomed, but John returned to England, and died at the palace of the Savoy. After the treaty of Bretigni, into which Edward III. is said to have been frightened by a dreadful storm, his fortunes declined. He had resigned his French dominions entirely to the prince of Wales, and he sunk in the esteem of his subjects at home, on account of his attachment to his mistress, one Alice Piers. The prince of Wales, commonly called the Black Prince, while he was making a glorious campaign in Spain, where he reinstated Peter the Cruel on that throne, was seized with a consumptive disorder, which carried him off in the year 1372. His father did not long survive him, for he died dispirited, and obscure, at Shene, in Surry, in the year 1377, the 65th of his age and 51st of his reign.

No prince ever understood the balance and interests of Europe better than Edward did. Having set his heart on the conquest of France, he gratified the more readily his people in their demands for protection, and security to their liberties and properties, but he thereby exhausted his regal dominions; neither was his successor, when he mounted the throne, so powerful a prince as he was, in the beginning of his reign. He has the glory of establishing the woollen manufacture among the English, who, till his time, generally exported the unwrought commodity. The rate of living in his reign, seems to have been much the same as in the late reign, and few of the English ships, even of war, exceeded forty or fifty tons. But notwithstanding the vast encrease of property in England, villainage still continued in the royal, episcopal, and baronial manors. Historians are not agreed, whether Edward made use of artillery, in his first invasion of France, but it certainly was well known before his death. The magnificent castle of Windsor, was built by Edward III. and his method of conducting that work may serve as a specimen of the condition of the people in that age. Instead of alluring workmen by contracts and wages, he assessed every county in England to send him so many masons, tilers, and carpenters, as if he had been levying an army. Soldiers were enlisted only for a short time; they lived idle all the rest of the year, and commonly all the rest of their lives; one successful campaign, by pay and plunder, and the ransom of prisoners, was supposed to be a small fortune to a man: which was a great allurement to enter into the service. The wages of a master carpenter was limited through the whole year to three-pence a day, a common carpenter to two-pence, money of that age. John Wickliffe, a secular priest, educated at Oxford, began, in the latter end of this reign, to spread the doctrines of reformation by his discourses, sermons, and writings; and he made many disciples of all ranks and stations. He seems to have been a man of parts and learning; and has the honour of being the first person in Europe, who publickly called in question those doctrines, which had universally passed for certain and undisputed, during so many ages.

The doctrines of Wickliffe, being derived from his search into the scriptures, and into ecclesiastical antiquity, were nearly the same with those propagated by the reformers in the sixteenth century. But though the age seemed strongly disposed to receive them, affairs were not yet fully ripe for this great revolution, which was reserved for a more free and enquiring period, that gave the finishing blow to Romish superstition in this and many other kingdoms of Europe. His disciples were distinguished by the name of Wickliffites or Lollards.

Richard II. was no more than eleven years of age, when he mounted the throne. The English arms were then unsuccessful, both in France and Scotland. The doctrines of Wickliffe had taken root under John of Gaunt, duke of Lancaster, the king's uncle, and one of his guardians, and gave enlarged notions of liberty to the villains, and lower ranks of people. The truth is, agriculture was then in so flourishing a state, that corn, and other victuals, were suffered to be transported, and the English had fallen upon a way of manufacturing for exportation, likewise their leather, horns, and other native commodities, and with regard to the woollen manufactures, they seem from records to have been exceeded by none in Europe. John of Gaunt's foreign connections with the crowns of Portugal and Spain, were of prejudice to England, and so many men were employed in unsuccessful wars, that the commons of England, like powder receiving a spark of fire, all at once flamed out into rebellion, under the conduct of Ball, a priest, Wat Tyler, and others, the scum of the people. Their profest principles were those of levelling, but it soon appeared, that their real intention was to have murdered the king, and seized upon the government.

Richard was not then above sixteen, but he acted with great spirit and wisdom. He faced the storm of the insurgents, at the head of the Londoners, while Walworth the mayor, and Philpot an alderman, had the courage to put Tyler, the arch traitor, to death, in the midst of his rabble. This, with the seasonable behaviour of Richard, quelled the insurrection for that time, but it broke out with the most bloody effects in other parts of England, and though it was suppressed by making many examples of severity and justice among the insurgents, yet the common people never after that lost sight of their own importance, till by degrees they obtained those privileges which they now enjoy. Had Richard been a prince of real abilities, he might, after the suppression of those insurgents, have established the tranquillity of his dominions on a sure foundation, but he delivered himself up to worthless favourites, particularly Sir Michael de la Pole, whom he created lord chancellor, judge Tresilian, and above all, Robert de Vere, earl of Oxford, whom he created duke of Ireland. They were obnoxious both to the parliament and people, and Richard stooped to the most ignoble measures to save them; but he found that it was not in his power. They were attainted and condemned to suffer as traitors; but Pole, and the duke of Ireland escaped abroad, where they died in obscurity. Richard associated to himself a new set of favourites. His people, and great lords, again took arms, and being headed by the duke of Gloucester, the king's uncle, they forced Richard once more into their terms; but being insincere in all his compliances, he was upon the point of becoming more despotic than any king of England ever had been, when he lost his crown and life by a sudden catastrophe.

A quarrel happened between the duke of Hereford, son to the duke of Lancaster, and the duke of Norfolk, and Richard banished them both, with particular marks of injustice to the former, who now became duke of Lancaster by his father's death. Richard carrying over a great army to quell a rebellion in Ireland, a strong party was formed in England, who offered the duke of Lancaster the crown. He landed at Ravenspur in Yorkshire, and was soon at the head of 60,000 men, all of them English. Richard hurried back to England, where his troops refusing to fight, he was made prisoner, with no more than twenty attendants, and being carried to London, he was deposed in full parliament, upon a formal charge of misconduct, and soon after he was starved to death in prison, in the year 1399, the 34th of his age, and the 23d of his reign.

Though the nobility of England were possessed of great power at the time of this revolution, yet we do not find that it abated the influence of the commons. They had the courage to remonstrate boldly in parliament against the usury, which was but too much practised in England, and other abuses of both clergy and laity, and the destruction of the feudal powers soon followed.

Henry the fourth, * son of John of Gaunt, duke of Lancaster, fourth son of Edward III. being settled in the throne of

---

* The throne being now vacant, the duke of Lancaster stepped forth, and having crossed himself on his forehead, and on his breast, and called upon the name of Christ,

ENGLAND.

of England, in prejudice to the elder branches of Edward III's family, the great nobility were in hopes that this glaring defect of his title would render him dependent upon them. At first some conspiracies were formed against him among his great men, but he crushed them by his activity and steadiness, and laid a plan for reducing their overgrown powers. This was understood by the Piercy family, the greatest in the north of England, who complained of Henry having deprived them of some Scotch prisoners, whom they had taken in battle, and a dangerous rebellion broke out under the old earl of Northumberland, and his son, the famous Henry Piercy, surnamed the Hotspur, but it ended in the defeat of the rebels, chiefly by the valour of the prince of Wales. With equal good fortune Henry suppressed the insurrections of the Welch, under Owen Glendower; and by his prudent concessions to his parliament, to the commons particularly, he at last conquered all opposition, while, to salve the defect of his title, the parliament entailed the crown upon him, and the heirs male of his body, lawfully begotten, thereby shutting out all female succession. The young duke of Rothsay, heir to the crown of Scotland, (afterwards James I. of that kingdom) falling a prisoner into Henry's hands about this time, was of infinite service to his government; and before his death, which happened in 1413, in the 46th year of his age, and 13th of his reign, he had the satisfaction to see his son, and successor, the prince of Wales, disengage himself from many youthful follies, which had till then disgraced his conduct.

The English marine was now so greatly encreased, that we find an English vessel of 200 tons in the Baltic, and many other ships of equal burden, carrying on an immense trade all over Europe, but with the Hanse towns in particular. With regard to public liberty, Henry IV. as I have already hinted, was the first prince who gave the different orders in parliament, especially that of the commons, their due weight. It is however a little surprizing, that learning was at this time at a much lower pass in England, and all over Europe, than it had been 200 years before. Bishops, when testifying synodal acts, were often forced to do it by proxy in the following terms,

---

Christ, he pronounced these words, which I shall give in the original language, because of their singularity.

In the name of Fadher, Son, and Holy Ghost, I Henry of Lancaster, challenge this rewme of Ynglande, and the croun, with all the membres, and the appurtenances; als I that am descendit by right line of the blode (meaning a claim in right of his mother) *coming fro the gude king Henry therde, and throge that right that God of his grace hath sent me, with helpe of kyn, and of my friendes, to recover it; the which rewme was in poynt to be ondone by defaut of governance, and undoying of the gude lawes.*

terms, viz. " As I cannot read myself, N. N. hath subscribed for me; or, As my lord bishop cannot write himself, at his request I have subscribed."

The balance of trade with foreign parts was against England, at the accession of Henry V. in 1413, so greatly had luxury encreased. The Lollards, or the followers of Wickliff, were excessively numerous, and had chosen Sir John Oldcastle for their head, but Henry dispersed them, and executed their leader. Henry next turned his eyes towards France, which he had many incitements for invading. He demanded a restitution of Normandy, and other provinces that had been ravished from England in the preceding reigns; also the payment of certain arrears due for king John's ransom since the reign of Edward III. and availing himself of the distracted state of that kingdom, he invaded it, where he first took Harfleur, and then defeated the French in the battle of Agincourt, which equalled those of Cressy and Poictiers in glory to the English, but exceeded them in its consequences, on account of the vast number of French princes of the blood, and other great noblemen, who were there killed. Henry, who was as great a politician as a warrior, made such alliances, and divided the French among themselves so effectually, that he forced the queen of France, whose husband Charles VI. was a lunatic, to agree to his marrying her daughter, the princess Catharine, to disinherit the dauphin, and to declare Henry regent of France during her husband's life, and him and his issue successors to the French monarchy, which must at this time have been exterminated, had not the Scots (tho' their king still continued Henry's captive) furnished the dauphin with vast supplies, and preserved the French crown for his head. Henry, however, made a triumphal entry into Paris, where the dauphin was proscribed; and after receiving the fealty of the French nobility, he returned to England to levy a force that might crush the dauphin and his Scotch auxiliaries. He probably would have been successful, had he not died of a pleuritic disorder, in 1422, the 34th year of his age, and the 10th of his reign.

Henry V's vast successes in France revived the trade of England, and at the same time encreased and established the privileges and liberties of the English commonalty. As he died when he was only thirty-four years of age, it is hard to say, if he had lived, whether he might not have given the law to all the continent of Europe, which was then greatly distracted by the divisions among its princes: but whether this would have been of service or prejudice to the growing liberties of his English subjects we cannot determine,

By

By an authentic and exact account of the ordinary revenues of t e crown during this reign, it appears that they amounted only to 55,714 l. a year, which is nearly the same with the revenues in Henry III's time, and the kings of England had neither become much richer nor poorer in the courſe of 200 years. The ordinary expences of the government amounted to 52,507 l. ſo that the king had of ſurplus only 3,207 l. for the ſupport of his houſhold, for his wardrobe, for the expence of embaſſies, and other articles. This ſum was nowiſe ſufficient even in time of peace; and to carry on his wars, this great conqueror was reduced to many miſerable ſhifts: he borrowed from all quarters; he pawned his jewels, and ſometimes the crown itſelf; he ran in arrears to his army; and he was often obliged to ſtop in the midſt of his career of victory, and to grant truce to the enemy. I mention theſe particulars, that the reader may judge of the ſimplicity and temperance of our predeceſſors three centuries ago, when the expences of the greateſt king in Europe were not ſo high as the penſion of a ſuperannuated courtier of the preſent age.

It required a prince equally able as Henry IV. and V. to confirm the title of the Lancaſter houſe to the throne of England. Henry VI. ſurnamed of Windſor, was no more than nine months old, when in conſequence of the treaty of Troyes, concluded by his father with the French court, he was proclaimed king of France, as well as of England. He was under the tuition of his two uncles, the dukes of Bedford and Glouceſter, both of them princes of great accompliſhments, virtues, and courage, but unable to preſerve their brother's conqueſts. Upon the death of Charles VI. the affections of the French for his family revived in the perſon of his ſon and ſucceſſor, Charles VII. The duke of Bedford, who was regent of France, performed many glorious actions, and at laſt laid ſiege to Orleans, which, if taken, would have completed the conqueſt of France. The ſiege was raiſed by the valour and good conduct of the Maid of Orleans, a phenomenon hardly to be paralleled in hiſtory, being born of the loweſt extraction, and bred a cow-keeper, and ſometimes a helper in ſtables at public inns. She muſt, notwithſtanding, have poſſeſſed an amazing fund of ſagacity as well as valour. After an unparalleled train of glorious actions, and placing the crown upon her ſovereign's head, ſhe was accidentally taken priſoner by the Engliſh, who burnt her alive for being a witch and a heretic.

The death of the duke of Bedford, and the agreement of the duke of Burgundy, the great ally of the Engliſh, with Charles VII. contributed to the entire ruin of the Engliſh intereſt in

France, and the loss of all their fine provinces in that kingdom, notwithstanding the amazing courage of Talbot, the first earl of Shrewsbury, and their other officers. The capital misfortune of England, at this time, was its disunion at home. The duke of Gloucester lost his authority in the government, and the king married Margaret, daughter to the needy king of Sicily; a woman of a high spirit, but an implacable disposition; while the cardinal of Winchester, who was the richest subject in England, if not in Europe, presided at the head of the treasury, and by his avarice ruined the interest of England, both at home and abroad. Next to the cardinal, the duke of York, who was lord lieutenant of Ireland, was the most powerful subject in England. He was descended by the mother's side from Lionel, an elder son of Edward III. and prior in claim to the reigning king, who was descended from John of Gaunt, Edward's youngest son, and he affected to keep up the distinction of a white rose, that of the house of Lancaster being red. It is certain, he paid no regard to the parliamentary entail of the crown upon the reigning family, and he lost no opportunity of forming a party to assert his right, but acted at first with a most profound dissimulation. The duke of Suffolk was a favourite of the queen, who was a profest enemy to the duke of York, but being impeached in parliament, he was banished for five years, and had his head struck off on board a ship by a common sailor. This was followed by an insurrection of 20,000 Kentishmen, headed by one Jack Cade, a man of low condition, who sent to the court a list of grievances, but was suppressed by the valour of the citizens of London, and the queen seemed to be perfectly secure against the duke of York. The inglorious management of the English affairs in France befriended him, and upon his arrival in England from Ireland, he found a strong party of the nobility his friends, but being considered as the fomenter of Cade's rebellion, he profest the most profound reverence to Henry.

The persons in high power and reputation in England, next to the duke of York, were the earl of Salisbury, and his son the earl of Warwick. The latter had the greatest land estate of any subject in England, and his vast abilities, joined to some virtues, rendered him equally popular. Both father and son were secretly on the side of York; and during a fit of illness of the king, that duke was made protector of the realm. Both sides now prepared for arms, and the king recovering, the queen, with wonderful activity, assembling an army, the royalists were defeated in the first battle of St. Alban's, and the king himself was taken prisoner. The duke of York was once

once more declared protector of the kingdom, but it was not long before the queen resumed all her influence in the government, and the king, though his weakness became every day more and more visible, recovered all his authority.

The duke of York upon this threw off the mask, and in 1459, he openly claimed the crown, and the queen was again defeated by the earl of Warwick, who was now called the King-maker. A parliament upon this being assembled, it was enacted, that Henry should possess the throne for life, but that the duke of York should succeed him, to the exclusion of all Henry's issue. All, excepting the magnanimous queen, agreed to this compromise. She retreated northwards, and the king being still a prisoner, she pleaded his cause so well, that assembling a fresh army, she fought the battle of Wakefield, where the duke of York was defeated and slain in 1460.

It is pretty extraordinary, that though the duke of York, and his party, openly asserted his claim to the crown, they still professed allegiance to Henry; but the duke of York's son, afterwards Edward IV. prepared to revenge his father's death, and obtained several victories over the royalists. The queen, however, advanced towards London, and defeating the earl of Warwick, in the second battle of St. Alban's, she delivered her husband; but the disorders committed by her northern troops disgusted the Londoners so much, that she durst not enter London, where the duke of York was received on the 28th of February, 1461, while the queen and her husband were obliged to retreat northwards. She soon raised another army, and fought the battle of Towton, the most bloody perhaps that ever happened in any civil war. After prodigies of valour had been performed on both sides, the victory remained with young king Edward, and near 40,000 men lay dead on the field of battle. Margaret and her husband were once more obliged to fly to Scotland, where they met with a generous protection.

It may be proper to observe, that this civil war was carried on with greater animosity, than any perhaps ever known. Margaret was as blood thirsty as her opponents, and when prisoners of either side were made, their deaths, especially if they were of any rank, were deferred only for a few hours.

Margaret, by the concessions she made to the Scots, soon raised a fresh army there, and in the north of England, but met with defeat upon defeat, till at last her husband, the unfortunate Henry, was carried prisoner to London.

The duke of York, now Edward IV. being crowned on the 29th of June, fell in love with, and privately married Elizabeth, the widow of Sir John Gray, though he had some

time

time before sent the earl of Warwick to demand the king of France's sister in marriage, in which embassy he was successful, and nothing remained but the bringing over the princess into England. When the secret of Edward's marriage broke out, the haughty earl, deeming himself affronted, returned to England, inflamed with rage and indignation; and from being Edward's best friend became his most formidable enemy, and gaining over the duke of Clarence, Edward was made prisoner, but escaping from his confinement, the earl of Warwick, and the French king Lewis XI. declared for the restoration of Henry, who was replaced on the throne, and Edward narrowly escaped to Holland. Returning from thence, he advanced to London, under pretence of claiming his dukedom of York, but being received into the capital, he resumed the exercise of royal authority, made king Henry once more his prisoner, and defeated and killed Warwick, in the battle of Barnet. A few days after he defeated a fresh army of Lancastrians, and made queen Margaret prisoner, together with her son, prince Edward, whom Edward's brother, the duke of Gloucester, murdered in cold blood, as he is said (but with no great shew of probability) to have done his father Henry VI. then a prisoner in the Tower of London, a few days after, in the year 1471. Edward being now settled on the throne, was guilty of the utmost cruelty to all the Lancastrian party, whom he put to death, whenever he could find them, so that they were threatened with utter extermination.

The great object of his vengeance was Henry, earl of Richmond. He was descended from John Beaufort, the eldest son of the earl of Somerset, who was the eldest son of John of Gaunt, by his last wife Catharine Swineford, but born in adultery, during her husband's life-time. This disability, however, was afterwards removed, both by the pope and by the parliament, and the descendants of John of Gaunt, by that lady, as far as could be done, were declared legitimate. The last lord, John, duke of Somerset, left a daughter, Margaret, who was married to Edmund Tudor, earl of Richmond, and their son was Henry, earl of Richmond (afterwards Henry VII.) who, at the time I treat of, lived in France, to secure himself from the cruelty of Edward. The reader may see, from the detail of this important genealogy, that the young earl of Richmond had not the smallest claim in blood (even supposing the illegitimacy of his ancestors had been removed) to the crown of England.

The kingdom of England was, in 1474, in a deplorable situation. The king was immersed in expensive and criminal luxuries,

luxuries, in which he was imitated by his great men, who, to support their extravagancies, became pensioners to the French king. The parliament seemed to act only as the executioners of Edward's bloody mandates. The best blood in England was shed on scaffolds, and even the duke of Clarence fell a victim to his brother's jealousy. Edward, partly to amuse the public, and partly to supply the vast expence of his court, pretended sometimes to quarrel, and sometimes to treat, with France, but his irregularities brought him to his death (1483) in the twenty-third year of his reign, and forty-second of his age.

Notwithstanding the turbulence of the times, the trade and manufactures of England encreased during the reigns of Henry VI. and Edward IV. So early as 1440, a navigation act was thought of, by the English, as the only means to preserve to themselves the benefit of being the sole carriers of their own merchandize, but foreign influence prevented Henry's passing the bill for that purpose. The invention of printing, which was imported into England by William Caxton, and received some countenance from Edward, is the chief glory of his reign, but learning in general was then in a poor state in England. The lord Tiptoft was its great patron, and seems to have been the first English nobleman, who cultivated what are now called the belles lettres. The books printed by Caxton, are mostly re-translations or compilations from the French, or Monkish Latin; but it must be acknowledged, at the same time, that literature, after this period, made a more rapid and general progress among the English, than it did in any other European nation.

Edward IV. left two sons by his queen, who had exercised her power with no great prudence, by having nobilitated many of her obscure relations. Her eldest son, Edward V. was about thirteen, and his uncle, the duke of Gloucester, taking advantage of the queen's unpopularity among the great men, found means to bastardize her issue, by act of parliament, under the scandalous pretext of a pre-contract between their father and another lady. The duke, at the same time, was declared guardian of the kingdom, and, at last, accepted of the crown, which was offered him by the Londoners, having first put to death all the nobility and great men, whom he thought to be well affected to the late king's family. Whether the king, and his brother, were murdered in the Tower, by his direction, is doubtful. The most probable opinion is, that they were clandestinely sent abroad by his orders, and that the elder died, but that the younger survived, and was the same who was afterwards well known by the name of Perkin Warbeck.

Warbeck. Be this as it will, the English were prepossessed so strongly against Richard, as being the murderer of his nephews, that the earl of Richmond, who still remained in France, carried on a secret correspondence with the remains of Edward IV's friends, and by offering to marry his eldest daughter, he was encouraged to invade England, at the head of about 2000 foreign troops, but they were soon joined by 7000 English and Welch. A battle between him and Richard, who was at the head of 15,000 men, ensued at Bosworth-field, in which Richard, after displaying most astonishing acts of personal valour, was killed, having been first abandoned by a main division of his army, under lord Stanley, and his brother in the year 1485.

There can scarcely be a doubt, that the crimes of Richard have been exaggerated by historians. He was exemplary in his distributive justice. He kept a watchful eye over the great barons, whose oppressions he abolished, and was a father to the common people. He founded the society of heralds, an institution, which, in his time, was found necessary to prevent disputes among great families. During his reign, short as it was, we have repeated instances of his relieving cities and corporations that had gone into decay. He was remarkable for the encouragement of the hardware manufactures of all kinds, and for preventing their being imported into England, no fewer than seventy-two different kinds being prohibited importation by one act. He was the first English king who appointed a consul for the superintendency of English commerce abroad, one Strozzi being nominated for Pisa, with an income of the fourth part of one per cent. on all goods of Englishmen imported to or exported from thence. I shall not enter into the subject of the concern he had in the supposed murder of his two nephews, but only observe, that the temporizing parliament, by bastardizing them, cut them off from the succession to the crown.

Though the same act of bastardy affected the daughters, as well as the sons of the late king, yet no disputes were raised upon the legitimacy of the princess Elizabeth, eldest daughter to Edward IV. and who, as had been before concerted, married Henry of Lancaster, earl of Richmond, thereby uniting both houses, which happily put an end to the long and bloody wars between the contending houses of York and Lancaster. Henry, however, rested his right upon conquest, and seemed to pay no regard to the advantages of his marriage. He was the most sagacious monarch that ever had reigned in England; but, at the same time, the most jealous of his power, for he shut up the earl of Warwick, son to the

duke

duke of Clarence, brother to Edward IV. a close prisoner in the Tower, though he was but a boy, and though nothing was alledged against him but his propinquity to the house of York. He was the first who instituted that guard called Yeomen, which still subsists, and in imitation of his predecessor, he gave an irrecoverable blow to the dangerous privileges assumed by the barons, in abolishing liveries, and retainers, by which every malefactor could shelter himself from the law, by assuming a nobleman's livery, and attending his person. Some rebellions happened in the beginning of his reign, but they were easily suppressed, as was the imposture of Lambert Simnel, who pretended to be the imprisoned earl of Warwick. The despotic court of star chamber, owed its original to Henry, but, at the same time, it must be acknowledged, that he passed many acts, especially for trade and navigation, that were highly for the benefit of his subjects. They expressed their gratitude, by the great supplies and benevolences they afforded him, and as a finishing stroke to the feudal tenures, an act passed by which the barons and gentlemen of landed interest were at liberty to sell and mortgage their lands, without fines or licences for the alienation.

This, if we regard its consequences, is perhaps the most important act that ever passed in an English parliament, tho' its tendency seems only to have been known to the politic king. Luxury, by the increase of trade, and the discovery of America, had broken with irresistible force into England, and monied property being chiefly in the hands of the commons, the estates of the barons became theirs, but without any of their dangerous privileges, and thus the baronial powers were soon extinguished in England.

Henry, after encountering and surmounting many difficulties both in France and Ireland, was attacked in the possession of his throne, by a young man, one Perkin Warbeck, who pretended to be the duke of York, second son to Edward IV. and was acknowledged as such by the duchess of Burgundy, Edward's sister. We shall not follow the adventures of this young man, which were various and uncommon, but it is certain that many of the English, with the courts of France and Scotland, believed him to be what he pretended. Henry endeavoured to prove the death of Edward V. and his brother, but never did it to the public satisfaction; and though James IV. of Scotland dismissed Perkin out of his dominions, being engaged in a treaty of marriage with Henry's eldest daughter, yet by the kind manner in which he entertained and dismissed him, it is plain that he believed him to be the real duke of York, especially as he refused to deliver up his person, which

he

he might have done with honour, had he thought him an impostor. Perkin, after various unfortunate adventures, fell into Henry's hands, and was shut up in the Tower of London, from whence he endeavoured to escape along with the innocent earl of Warwick, for which Perkin was hanged, and the earl beheaded. It is said, that Perkin made a confession of his impostors before his death, but if he did, it might have been extorted from him, either upon the hope of pardon, or the fear of torture. In 1499, Henry's eldest son, Arthur, prince of Wales, was married to the princess Catharine, of Arragon, daughter to the king and queen of Spain, and he dying soon after, such was Henry's reluctance to refund her great dowry, that he consented to her being married again to his second son, then prince of Wales, on pretence that the first match had not been consummated. Soon after, Henry's eldest daughter, the princess Margaret, was sent with a most magnificent train to Scotland, where she was married to James IV. Henry, at the time of his death, which happened in 1509, the 52d year of his age, and 24th of his reign, was possessed of 1,800,000l. sterling, which is equivalent to five millions at present, so that he may be supposed to have been master of more ready money than all the kings in Europe besides possessed, the mines of Peru and Mexico being then only beginning to be worked.

I have already mentioned the vast alteration which happened in the constitution of England, during Henry VII's reign. His excessive love of money was the probable reason why he did not become master of the West-Indies, he having the first offer of the discovery from Columbus, whose proposals being rejected by Henry, that great man applied to the court of Spain, and he set out upon the discovery of a new world, in the year 1492, which he effected after a passage of 33 days, and took possession of the country in the name of the king and queen of Spain. Henry however made amends by encouraging Cabot, who discovered the main land of North America, in 1498, and we may observe, to the praise of this king, that sometimes, in order to promote commerce, he lent to merchants sums of money, without interest, when he knew, that their stock was not sufficient for those enterprizes, which they had in view. From the proportional prices of living produced by Madox, Fleetwood, and other writers, agriculture and breeding of cattle must have been prodigiously advanced, before Henry's death; an instance of this is given in the case of lady Anne, sister to Henry's queen, who had an allowance of 20s. per week, for her exhibition, sustentation, and convenient diet of meat and drink; also, for two gentlewomen,

women, one woman child, one gentleman, one yeoman, and three grooms (in all eight perſons) 51 l. 11 s. 8 d. per annum, for their wages, diet, and cloathing; and for the maintenance of ſeven horſes yearly, 16 l. 9 s. 4 d. *i. e.* for each horſe 2 l. 7 s. 0 d. ¼ yearly, money being ſtill 1 ½ times as weighty as our modern ſilver coin. Wheat was that year no more than 3 s. 4 d. a quarter, which anſwers to 5 s. of our money, conſequently it was about ſeven times as cheap as at preſent; ſo that had all other neceſſaries been equally cheap, ſhe could have lived as well as on 1260 l. 10 s. 6 d. of our modern money, or ten times as cheap as at preſent.

The fine arts were as far advanced in England at the acceſſion of Henry VIII. 1509, as in any European country, if we except Italy, and perhaps no prince ever entered with greater advantages than he did on the exerciſe of royalty. Young, vigorous, and rich, without any rival, he held the balance of power in Europe, but it is certain, that he neglected theſe advantages in commerce, with which his father became too lately acquainted. Imagining he could not ſtand in need of a ſupply, he did not improve Cabot's diſcoveries, and he ſuffered the Eaſt and Weſt Indies to be engroſſed by Portugal and Spain. His vanity engaged him too much in the affairs of the continent, and his flatterers encouraged him to make preparations for the conqueſt of all France. Theſe projects, and his eſtabliſhing what is properly called a navy royal, for the permanent defence of the nation (a moſt excellent meaſure) led him into incredible expences. He was on all occaſions the dupe of the emperor Maximilian, the pooreſt prince in Europe, and early in his reign he gave himſelf almoſt entirely up to the guidance of the celebrated cardinal Wolſey. While involved in a war with France, his lieutenant, the earl of Surry, conquered and killed James IV. of Scotland, who had invaded England, and he became a candidate for the German empire, during its vacancy, but ſoon reſigned his pretenſions to Francis I. of France, and Charles of Auſtria, king of Spain, who was elected in 1519. Henry's conduct, in the long and bloody wars between thoſe princes, was directed by Wolſey's views upon the popedom, which he hoped to gain by the intereſt of Charles, but finding himſelf twice deceived, he perſuaded his maſter to declare himſelf for Francis, who had been taken priſoner at the battle of Pavia. Henry, however, continued to be the dupe of all parties, and to pay great part of their expences, till at laſt he was forced to lay vaſt burdens upon his ſubjects.

Henry continued all this time the great enemy of the reformation, and the champion of the popes, and the Romiſh church.

church. He wrote a book against Luther, about the year 1521, for which the pope gave him the title of *Defender of the Faith*, which his successors retain to this day; but about the year 1527, he began to have some scruples with regard to the validity of his marriage with his brother's widow. I shall not say, how far on this occasion he might be influenced by the charms of the famous Anne Bullen, maid of honour to the queen, whom he married, before he had obtained from Rome the proper bulls of divorce from the pope. The difficulties he met with in this process, ruined Wolsey, who died of heart-break, after being stript of his immense power and possessions; and had introduced into the king's favour Cranmer, who was afterwards archbishop of Canterbury.

A perplexing, though nice conjuncture of affairs, it is well known, induced Henry at last to throw off all relation to or dependence upon the church of Rome, and to bring about a reformation, in which, however, many of the Romish errors and superstitions were retained. Henry never could have effected this mighty measure, had it not been for his despotic disposition, which broke out on every occasion. Upon a slight suspicion of his queen's inconstancy, and after a sham trial, he cut off her head, and put to death some of her nearest relations, and he was declared arbitrary by repeated acts of parliament, which assembled only as a board to execute his pleasures. The dissolution of the religious houses, and the immense wealth that came to Henry, by seizing all the ecclesiastical property in his kingdom, enabled him to give full scope to his sanguinary disposition, so that the best and most innocent blood of England was daily shed on scaffolds, and few days passed that were not marked with some illustrious victim of his tyranny. Among others was the aged countess of Salisbury, descended immediately from Edward IV. and mother to the cardinal Pole, the marquis of Exeter, the lord Montague, and others of the blood royal, for holding a correspondence with that cardinal.

His third wife was Jane Seymour, daughter to a gentleman of fortune and family; but she died in bringing Edward VI. into the world. His fourth wife was Anne, sister to the duke of Cleves. He disliked her so much, that he scarce bedded with her, and obtaining a divorce, he suffered her to reside in England, on a pension of 3000 l. a year. His fifth wife was Catharine Howard, niece to the duke of Norfolk, whose head he cut off for ante-nuptial incontinency. His last wife was queen Catherine Par, in whose possession he died, after narrowly escaping being brought to the stake for her religious opinions, which favoured the reformation. Henry's cruelty
encreased

encreased with his years, and was now exercised promiscuously on Protestants and Catholics. He put the brave earl of Surry to death without a crime being proved against him; and his father, the duke of Norfolk, must have suffered next day, had he not been saved by Henry's own death, in the year 1547, in the 56th year of his age, and the 38th of his reign.

The state of England, during the reign of Henry VIII. is, by the help of printing, too well known to be enlarged upon here. His attention to the naval security of England is highly commendable; and it is certain that he employed the despotic power he was possessed of, in many respects for the glory and interest of his subjects. Without enquiring into his religious motives, it must be candidly confessed, that had the reformation gone through all the forms prescribed by the laws, and the courts of justice, it probably never could have taken place, or at least not for many years; and whatever Henry's personal crimes or failings might have been, the partition he made of the church's property among his courtiers and favourites, and thereby rescuing it from dead hands, undoubtedly promoted the present greatness of England. With regard to learning and the arts, Henry was a generous encourager of both. He gave a pension to Erasmus, which is another name for learning itself. He brought to England, encouraged, and protected Hans Holbein, that excellent painter and architect; and in his reign noblemen's houses began to have the air of Italian magnificence and regularity. He was a constant and generous friend to Cranmer: and though he was, upon the whole, rather whimsical than settled in his own principles of religion, he advanced and encouraged many who became afterwards the instruments of a more pure reformation.

In this reign the Bible was ordered to be printed in English. Wales was united and incorporated with England. Ireland was created into a kingdom, and Henry took the title of king of Ireland.

Edward VI. was but nine years of age at the time of his father's death; and after some disputes were over, the regency was settled in the person of his uncle the earl of Hertford, afterwards the protector and duke of Somerset, a declared friend and patron of the reformation, and a bitter enemy to the see of Rome. Much of the popish leaven, however, still remained in the council, which was embroiled at once with France and Scotland. The protector marched with an army into Scotland, to force that people to give their young queen Mary, only child of James V. in marriage to Edward, with a view to unite the two kingdoms, a measure which the late king had recommended with his dying breath to his executors. The protector defeated the Scots at Pinkey, but the match never took place; and the factions now forming against the protector, obliged him to return with his army to England. His own brother, who had married the queen dowager, was at the head of his enemies, and she dying, he made his addresses to the princess Elizabeth, afterwards queen. This gave a handle to the protector to bring his brother, who was lord admiral, to the block, where he lost his head.

The reader is to observe in general, that the reformation was not effected without many public disturbances. The common people, during the reign of Henry and Edward, being deprived of the vast relief they had from abbeys and religious houses, and being ejected from their small corn-growing farms, had often taken arms, but had been as often suppressed by the government; and several of these insurrections were crushed in this reign. A war, which was not very happily managed, broke out with Scotland; and the protector, who was, upon the whole, a weak, but conscientious man, was so intent upon religion, that he was first driven from the helm of state, and then lost his head upon a scaffold, by a faction formed equally of papists and pretended protestants. Dudley, who was created duke of Northumberland, then took the lead in the government, and drove Edward, who, though young, meant extremely well, and was a sincere protestant, into many impolitic acts, so that upon the whole England never made a poorer figure than it did in this reign.

The reformation, however, went on rapidly, through the zeal of Cranmer, and other, some of them foreign, divines. In some cases, particularly with regard to the princess Mary, they lost sight of that moderation, which the reformers had before so strongly recommended; and some cruel sanguinary executions, on account of religion, took place. Edward's youth excuses him from blame, and his charitable endowments, which still exist and flourish, shew the goodness of his heart. He died of a deep consumption in 1553, in the 16th year of his age, and the 7th of his reign.

Edward, on his death bed, from his zeal for religion, had made a very unconstitutional will, for he set aside his sister Mary from the succession, which was claimed by lady Jane Grey, daughter to the duchess of Suffolk, younger sister to Henry VIII. This lady, though she had scarcely reached her 17th year, was a prodigy of learning and virtue; but the bulk of the English nation recognized the claim of the princess Mary, who cut off lady Jane's head, and that of her husband lord Guilford Dudley, son to the duke of Northumberland, who suffered in the same manner.

Mary

Mary being thus settled on the throne, suppressed an insurrection under Wyat, and proceeded like a female fury to re-establish popery, which she did all over England. She recalled cardinal Pole from banishment, made him the principal instrument of her cruelties, and lighted up the flames of persecution, in which archbishop Cranmer, the bishops Ridley, Hooper, and Latimer, and many other illustrious confessors of the English reformed church, were consumed; not to mention a vast number of other sacrifices of both sexes, and all ranks, that suffered through every quarter of the kingdom. Bonner, bishop of London, and Gardiner bishop of Winchester, were, under Pole, the chief executioners of her bloody mandates; and had she lived, she would have endeavoured to exterminate all her protestant subjects.

Mary was married to Philip II. king of Spain, who, like herself, was an unfeeling bigot to popery; and the chief praise of her reign is, that by the marriage articles provision was made for the independency of the English crown. By the assistance of troops, which she furnished to her husband, he gained the important battle of St. Quintin; but that victory was so ill improved, that the French, under the duke of Guise, soon after took Calais, the only place then remaining to the English in France. This loss, which was chiefly owing to cardinal Pole's secret connections with the French court, is said to have broken Mary's heart, who died in 1558, in the 42d year of her life, and 6th of her reign. " In the heat of her persecuting flames, (says a contemporary writer of credit) were burnt to ashes, 5 bishops, 21 divines, 8 gentlemen, 84 artificers, and 100 husbandmen, servants, and labourers, 26 wives, 20 widows, 9 virgins, 2 boys, and 2 infants; one of them whipped to death by Bonner, and the other, springing out of the mother's womb from the stake as she burned, thrown again into the fire."

Elizabeth, daughter to Henry VIII. by Anne Bullen, mounted the throne under the most discouraging circumstances, both at home and abroad. Popery was the established religion of England; her title to the crown, on account of the circumstances attending her mother's marriage and death, was disputed by Mary queen of Scots, grand-child to Henry VII's eldest daughter, and wife to the dauphin of France; and the only ally she had on the continent was Philip king of Spain, who was the life and soul of the popish cause, both abroad and in England. Elizabeth was no more than 25 years of age, at the time of her inauguration, but her sufferings under her bigotted sister, joined to the superiority of her genius, had taught her caution and policy, and she soon conquered all difficulties. Even to mention every glorious action of her reign, would far exceed my bounds, I shall therefore here only touch on the great lines of her government.

In matters of religion she succeeded with surprizing facility, for in her first parliament, in 1559, the laws establishing popery were repealed, her supremacy was restored, and an act of uniformity passed soon after. With regard to her title, she took advantage of the divided state of Scotland, and formed a party there, by which Mary, now become the widow of Francis II. of France, was obliged to renounce, or rather to suspend her claim. Elizabeth, not contented with this, sent troops and money, which supported the Scotch malecontents, till Mary's unhappy marriage, and her other misfortunes drove her to take refuge in Elizabeth's dominions, where she had been often promised a safe and an honourable asylum. It is well known how unfaithful Elizabeth was to this profession of friendship, and that she detained the unhappy prisoner 18 years in England, then brought her to a sham trial, pretending that Mary aimed at the crown, and, without the least proof of guilt, cut off her head, an action which must have tarnished all the glories of her reign had it been a thousand times more splendid than it was.

As to Elizabeth's affairs with Spain, which formed, in fact, the main business of her government, they exhibit different scenes of wonderful events, partly arising from her own masterly conduct, partly from the sagacity of her statesmen, and partly from the intrepid of her forces by sea and land.

The same Philip, who had been the husband of her late sister, upon Elizabeth's accession to the throne, offered to marry her, but she dextrously avoided his addresses; and by a train of skilful negociations between that court and that of France, she kept the balance of Europe undetermined, that she had leisure to unite her people at home, and to establish an excellent internal policy in her dominions. She sometimes supported the protestants of France; and she sometimes gave the dukes of Anjou and Alenzon the strongest assurances that one or other of them should be her husband; by which she kept that court, who dreaded Spain, at the same time in so good humour with her government, that it shewed no resentment when she cut off queen Mary's head.

When Philip was no longer to be imposed upon by Elizabeth's arts, which had amused and baffled him in every quarter; it is well known that he made use of the immense sums which he drew from Peru and Mexico, in equipping the most formidable armament that perhaps ever had been put to sea, and a numerous army of veterans, under the prince of Parma, the
best

best captain of that age; and that he procured a papal bull for absolving Elizabeth's subjects from their allegiance. No reader can be so uninformed as to be ignorant of the consequences, that the largeness of the Spanish ships proved disadvantageous to them on the seas where they engaged; that the lord admiral Howard, and the brave sea-officers under him, engaged, beat, and chased the Spanish fleet for several days, and that the seas and tempests finished the destruction which the English arms had begun, and that few of the Spanish ships recovered their ports. Next to the admiral lord Howard of Effingham, Sir Francis Drake, captain Hawkins, and captain Forbisher, distinguished themselves against this formidable invasion, in which the Spaniards are said to have lost 81 ships of war, large and small, and 13,500 men.

Elizabeth had for some time supported the revolt of the Hollanders from Philip, and had sent them her favourite, the earl of Leicester, who acted as her viceroy and general in the Low Countries. Though Leicester behaved ill, yet her measures were so wise, that the Dutch established their independency upon Spain, and then she sent forth her fleets under Drake, Raleigh, the earl of Cumberland, and other gallant naval officers, into the East and West Indies, from whence they brought prodigious treasures taken from the Spaniards into England.

After the death of the earl of Leicester, the young earl of Essex became Elizabeth's chief favourite, and commanded the land forces in a joint expedition with the lord admiral Howard, in which they took and plundered the city of Cadiz in Spain, destroyed the ships in the harbour, and did other damage to the Spaniards, to the amount of twenty millions of ducats.

Elizabeth in her old age grew distrustful, peevish, and jealous. Though she undoubtedly loved the earl of Essex, she teized him by her capriciousness into the madness of taking arms, and then cut off his head. She complained that she had been betrayed into this sanguinary measure, and this occasioned a sinking of her spirits, which brought her to her grave in 1603, the 70th year of her age, and 45th of her reign, having previously named her kinsman James VI. king of Scotland, and son to Mary, for her successor.

The above, as I have already hinted, form the great lines of Elizabeth's reign, and from them may be traced, either immediately or remotely, every act of her government. She supported the protestants in Germany against the house of Austria, of which Philip, king of Spain, was the head. She crushed the papists in her own dominions for the same reason, and made a further reformation in the church of England, in which state it has remained ever since. In 1600 the English East-India company received its first formation, that trade being then in the hands of the Portuguese (in consequence of their having first discovered the passage to India by the cape of Good Hope) who at that time were subjects to Spain; and factories were established in China, Japan, India, Amboyna, Java, and Sumatra.

Before queen Elizabeth's reign, the kings of England had usually recourse to the city of Antwerp for voluntary loans; and their credit was so low, that, besides the exorbitant interest of 10 or 12 per cent. they were obliged to make the city of London join in the security. The trade to Turkey was begun about 1583; and that commerce was immediately confined to a company by queen Elizabeth. Before that time, the Grand Signior had always conceived England to be a dependant province of France. About 1590 there were in London four persons only rated in the subsidy book so high as 400 l. In 1567 there were found on enquiry to be 4851 strangers of all nations in London, of whom 3838 were Flemings, and only 58 Scots.

As to Elizabeth's internal government, the successes of her reign have disguised it, for she was far from being a friend to personal liberty, and she was guilty of many stretches of power against the most sacred rights of Englishmen. Before I close this short account of her reign, I am to observe, that through the practices of the Spaniards with the Irish Roman catholics, she found great difficulty to keep that island in subjection, and at the time of her death her government there had gone into great disorder.

We can scarce require a stronger proof that the English began to be tired of Elizabeth, than the joy testified by all ranks at the accession of her successor, notwithstanding the long inveterate animosities between the two kingdoms. James was far from being destitute of natural abilities for government, but he had received wrong impressions of the regal office, and too high an opinion of his own dignity, learning, and political talents. It was his misfortune that he mounted the English throne under a full conviction that he was entitled to all the unconstitutional powers that had been exercised by Elizabeth, and the house of Tudor; and while he was boasting of an almost unlimited prerogative, there was not so much as a single regiment in England to maintain his extensive claims; a sufficient proof that he sincerely believed his pretensions to be well grounded. He made no allowance for the glories of Elizabeth; which, as I have observed, disguised her most arbitrary acts; and none for the free, liberal

sentiments

sentiments which the improvement of knowledge and learning had diffused through England. It is needless, perhaps, to point out the vast encrease of property through trade and navigation, which enabled the English at the same time to defend their liberties. James's first attempt of great consequence was to effect an union between England and Scotland; but though he failed in this through the aversion of the English to that measure, he shewed no violent resentment at the disappointment. It was an advantage to him at the beginning of his reign that the courts of Rome and Spain were thought to be his enemies; and this opinion was increased by the discovery and defeat of the gun-powder treason *.

I have taken notice, in several preceding parts of this work, of the vast obligations which commerce and colonization owed to this prince; and, in fact, he laid the foundations of all the advantages which the English have reaped from either. That his pedantry was ridiculous cannot be denied; and it is certain that he had no just ideas of the English constitution and liberties. This led him into many absurd disputes with his parliament, and has thrown a most disagreeable shade upon his memory. Without enquiring from what motive his love of peace proceeded, I may venture to affirm that it was productive of many blessings to England; and though his perpetual negociations have given rise to much satire against his person and government, yet they were less expensive and destructive

---

* This was a scheme of the Roman catholics to cut off at one blow the king, lords, and commons, at the meeting of parliament, when it was also expected that the queen, and prince of Wales, would be present. The manner of enlisting any new conspirator was by oath, and administring the sacrament; and this dreadful secret, after being religiously kept near 18 months, was happily discovered in the following manner: about ten days before the long wished for meeting of parliament, a Roman catholic peer received a letter, which had been delivered to his servant by an unknown hand, earnestly advising him to shift off his attendance on parliament at that time, but which contained no kind of explanation. The nobleman, though he considered the letter as a foolish attempt to frighten and ridicule him, thought proper to lay it before the king, who studying the contents with more attention, began to suspect some dangerous contrivance by gun-powder; and it was judged advisable to inspect all the vaults below the houses of parliament, but the search was purposely delayed till the night immediately preceding the meeting, when a justice of peace was sent with proper attendants, and before the door of the vault under the upper house, finding one Fawkes, who had just finished all his preparations, he immediately seized him, and at the same time discovered in the vault 36 barrels of powder, which had been carefully concealed under faggots and piles of wood. The match, with every thing proper for setting fire to the train, were found in Fawkes's pocket, whose countenance bespoke his savage disposition, and who, after regretting that he had lost the opportunity of destroying so many heretics, made a full discovery; and the conspirators, who never exceeded 80 in number, being seized by the country people, confessed their guilt, and were executed in different parts of London. Notwithstanding this horrid crime, the bigotted catholics were so devoted to Garnet, a jesuit, one of the conspirators, that they fancied miracles to be wrought by his blood, and in Spain he was considered as a martyr.

structive to his people than any wars he could have entered into. He restored to the Dutch their cautionary towns, upon discharging part of the mortgage that was upon them; but he procured from Spain at the same time an acknowledgment of their independency.

James gave his daughter the princess Elizabeth in marriage to the elector palatine, the most powerful protestant prince in Germany, and he soon after assumed the crown of Bohemia. The memory of James has been much abused for his tame behaviour after that prince had lost his kingdom and electorate by the imperial arms; but it is to be observed that he always opposed his son-in-law's assuming the crown of Bohemia; that had he kindled a war to reinstate him in that and his electorate, he probably would have stood single in the same, excepting the feeble and uncertain assistance he might have received from the elector's dependents and friends in Germany. Nothing, however, is more certain than that James furnished the elector with large sums of money to retrieve them, and that he actually raised a regiment of 2200 men, under Sir Horace Vere, who carried them over to Germany, where the Germans, under the marquis of Anspach, refused to second them against Spinola the Spanish general, and that the elector hurt his own cause by not giving the brave count Mansfield the command of his troops instead of Anspach.

James has been greatly and justly blamed for his partiality to favourites. His first was Robert Car, a private Scotch gentleman, who was raised to be first minister and earl of Somerset. He married the countess of Essex, who had obtained a divorce from her husband, and was with her found guilty of poisoning Sir Thomas Overbury in the Tower; but James, contrary as is said to a solemn oath he made, pardoned them both. His next favourite was George Villiers, a private English gentleman, who, upon Somerset's disgrace, was admitted to an unusual share of favour and familiarity with his sovereign. James had at that time formed a system of policy for attaching himself intimately to the court of Spain, that it might assist him in recovering the palatinate; and to this system he had sacrificed the brave Sir Walter Raleigh, on a charge of having committed hostilities against the Spanish settlements in the West-Indies. James having lost his eldest son Henry, prince of Wales, who had an invincible antipathy to a popish match, threw his eyes upon the infanta of Spain, as a proper wife for his son Charles, who had succeeded to that principality. Buckingham, who was equally a favourite with the son as with the father, fell in with the prince's romantic humour, and against the king's will they travelled in disguise to Spain,
where

where a moſt ſolemn farce of courtſhip was played, but the prince returned without his bride, and, had it not been for the royal partiality in his favour, the earl of Briſtol, who was then ambaſſador in Spain, would probably have brought Buckingham to the block.

James was all this while perpetually jarring with his parliament, whom he could not perſuade to furniſh money equal to his demands; and at laſt he agreed to his ſon's marrying the princeſs Henrietta Maria, ſiſter to Lewis XIII. and daughter to Henry the Great of France. James died before the completion of this match, and it is thought that had he lived, he would have diſcarded Buckingham. His death happened in 1625, in the 59th year of his age, after a reign over England of 22 years. As to the progreſs of the arts and learning under his reign, it has been already deſcribed. James encouraged and employed that excellent painter Sir Peter Paul Rubens, as well as Inigo Jones, who reſtored the pure taſte of architecture in England. His was the golden reign for theological learning; and under him poetical genius, though not much encouraged at court, arrived at its vertical point.

Charles I. was unfortunate in his marriage with the princeſs Henrietta Maria. He ſeems to have been but a cold lover, and he quarrelled with and ſent back her favourite attendants a few days after her arrival in England. On the other hand ſhe had a high ſpirit, diſdained and diſliked every thing that was incompatible in government with her Italian and arbitrary education, and was a diſagreeable wife, notwithſtanding her huſband's ſubmiſſion and tenderneſs. The ſpirit of the people had forced the late king into a breach with Spain, and Charles early gave ſuch indications of his partiality for Buckingham, and his own deſpotic temper, that the parliament was remiſs in furniſhing him with money for carrying on the war. In a ſhort time Buckingham perſuaded Charles to take the part of the French Hugonots, in their quarrel with that crown. They were ſo ill ſupported, though Charles was ſincere in ſerving them, that Rochelle was reduced to extremity, by which the proteſtant intereſt received an irrecoverable blow in France. The blame of all the public miſcarriages and diſgraces was thrown by, the almoſt, unanimous voice both of the parliament and people upon the favourite; but he ſheltered himſelf from their vengeance under the royal protection till he was murdered by one Felton, a ſubaltern officer, as he was ready to embark for the relief of Rochelle, which ſoon after ſurrendered to cardinal Richlieu.

The death of the duke of Buckingham, which happened in 1628, did not deter Charles from his arbitrary proceedings, which the English patriots in that enlightened age considered as so many acts of tyranny. He, without authority of parliament, laid arbitrary impositions upon trade, which were refused to be paid by many of the merchants and members of the house of commons. Some of them were imprisoned, and the judges were checked for admitting them to bail. The house of commons resented those proceedings by drawing up a protest, and denying admittance to the gentleman-usher of the black rod, who came to adjourn them, till it was finished. This served only to widen the breach, and the king dissolved the parliament, after which he exhibited informations against nine of the most eminent members, among whom was the great Mr. Selden. They objected to the jurisdiction of the court, but their plea was over-ruled, and they were sent to prison during the king's pleasure.

Every thing now operated towards the destruction of Charles. The commons had voted him no money even for the maintenance of his houshold, and presuming on what had been practised in reigns when the principles of liberty were imperfectly, or not at all understood, he levied money upon monopolies of salt, soap, and such necessaries, and other obsolete claims, particularly for knighthood. His government becoming every day more and more unpopular, Burton, a divine, Prynne, a lawyer, and Bostwick, a physician, all of them men of mean parts, but desperately resolute and fiery, founded the trumpet of sedition, and their punishments were so severe that they encreased the unpopularity of the government. Unfortunately for Charles, he put his conscience into the hands of Laud, archbishop of Canterbury, who was as great a bigot as himself, both in church and state. Laud advised him to persecute the puritans, and to introduce the religion of the church of England into Scotland. The Scots upon this formed secret connections with the discontented English, and invaded England, where Charles was so ill-served by his officers and his army, that he was forced to agree to an inglorious peace with the Scots; but neither party being sincere in observing the terms, and Charles discovering that some of their great men had offered to throw themselves under the protection of the French king, he raised a fresh army by virtue of his prerogative. All his preparations, however, were baffled by the Scots, who made themselves masters of Newcastle and Durham, and being now openly befriended by the house of commons, they obliged the king to comply with their demands.

Charles did this with so bad a grace, though he took a journey to Scotland for that purpose, that it did him no service; on the contrary it encouraged the commons to rise in
their

their demands. He had made Wentworth earl of Strafford, a man of great abilities, prefident of the council of the north, and lord lieutenant of Ireland; and he was generally believed to be the firſt miniſter of ſtate. Strafford had been at the head of the oppoſition, and by changing his party he became ſo much the object of public deteſtation, that they forced Charles in an illegal and imperious manner to conſent to the cutting off his head; and Laud loſt his ſoon after in like manner.

Charles, upon various occaſions, faw the neceſſity of moderation, and ſought to recover the affections of his people, firſt by paſſing the Petition of Right, and afterwards agreeing to other popular demands made by the commons. Theſe compliances did him no ſervice. A rebellion broke out in Ireland, where the proteſtants were maſſacred by the papiſts, and great pains were taken to perſuade the public that Charles ſecretly favoured them out of hatred to his Engliſh ſubjects. The biſhops were expelled the houſe of peers, and the leaders of the Engliſh houſe of commons ſtill kept up a correſpondence with the diſcontented Scots. Charles was ill enough adviſed to go in perſon to the houſe of commons, and demanded that lord Kimbolton, Mr. Pym, Mr. Hampden, Mr. Hollis, Sir Arthur Haſelrig, and Mr. Stroud, ſhould be apprehended, but they previouſly had made their eſcape. This act of Charles was reſented as high treaſon againſt his people, and the commons rejected all the offers of ſatisfaction he could make them. The city of London took the alarm, and the accuſed members into its protection. The train-bands were raiſed, and the mobs were ſo unruly, that Charles removed from Whitehall to Hampton-court, and from thence into Yorkſhire, where he raiſed an army to face that which the parliament, or rather the houſe of commons, had raiſed in and about London.

That the nation in general did not think their liberties in danger, or that the king was a tyrant, appears from the alacrity and numbers with which he was ſerved, and which was compoſed of three-fourths of the landed property of England. The parliament, however, took upon themſelves the executive power, and were favoured by many of the trading towns and corporations, but its great reſource lay in London. The king's general was the earl of Lindſey, a brave, but not an enterprizing commander, but he had great dependence on his nephews the princes Rupert and Maurice, ſons to the elector palatine, by his ſiſter the princeſs Elizabeth. In the beginning of the war the ſenſe of honour which prevailed among the king's officers was too ſtrong for the principles on which the parliament forces fought, but a ſpirit of enthuſiaſm catching the latter, it became too powerful for honour. The earl of

Essex was made general under the parliament, and the first battle was fought at Edge-hill in Warwickshire, in October 1642; but both parties claimed the victory, though the advantage lay with Charles, for the parliament was so much distressed, that they invited the Scots to come to their assistance, and they accordingly invaded England anew, with about 20,000 horse and foot. Charles attempted to remove the parliament to Oxford, where many members of both houses met; but his enemies continued still sitting at Westminster, where they prosecuted their animosities against the royalists with great fury. The independent party, which had scarcely before been thought of, began now to unmask themselves and to figure at Westminster. They equally hated the presbyterians, who till then had conducted the rebellion, as they did the royalists, and such was their management, under the direction of the famous Oliver Cromwell, that a plan was formed, for dismissing the earls of Essex, and Manchester, and the heads of the presbyterians, from the parliament's service, and for introducing Fairfax, who was an excellent officer, but more manageable, though a presbyterian, and some independent officers. In the mean while, the war went on with unremitting fury on both sides. Two battles were fought at Newbury, in which the advantage inclined to the king. He had likewise many other successes, and having defeated Sir William Waller, he pursued the earl of Essex, who remained still in command, into Cornwall, from whence he was obliged to escape by sea, but his infantry surrendered themselves prisoners to the royalists, though his cavalry delivered themselves by their valour.

The first fatal blow the king's army received, was at Marston-moor, where, through the imprudence of prince Rupert, the earl of Manchester defeated the royal army, of which 4000 were killed, and 1500 taken prisoners. This victory was owing chiefly to the courage and conduct of Cromwell, and tho' it might have been retrieved by the successes of Charles in the west, yet his whole conduct was a string of mistakes, till at last, his affairs became irretrievable. It is true, many treaties of peace, particularly one at Uxbridge, were set on foot during the war, and the heads of the presbyterian party would have agreed to terms, that would have bounded the king's prerogative. They were outwitted, betrayed, and overruled, by the independents, who were assisted by the stiffness, and unamiable behaviour of Charles himself. In short, the independents at last succeeded, in persuading the members at Westminster, that Charles was not to be trusted, whatever his concessions might be. From that moment the affairs of the royalists rushed into ruin. Sir Thomas Fairfax, whose father, lord Fairfax,

Fairfax, remained in the north, was at the head of the army, which was now new modelled, so that Charles by piecemeal lost all his towns and forts, and was defeated by Fairfax and Cromwell, at the decisive battle of Naseby, owing partly as usual to the misconduct of prince Rupert. This battle was followed by fresh misfortunes to Charles, who retired to Oxford, the only place where he thought he could be safe.

The Scots were then besieging Newark, and no good understanding subsisted between them and the English parliamentarians, but the best and most loyal friends Charles had, thought it prudent to make their peace. In this melancholy situation of his affairs, he escaped in disguise from Oxford to the Scotch army before Newark, upon a promise of protection. The Scots, however, were so intimidated, by the resolutions of the parliament at Westminster, that they put the person of Charles into the hands of the parliament's commissioners, not suspecting the fatal consequences.

The presbyterians now saw, more than ever, the necessity of making peace with the king, but they were no longer masters, being forced to receive laws from the army, and the independents. The latter now avowed their intentions. They first by force took Charles out of the hands of the commissioners in June 1647, and then dreading that a treaty might still take place with the king, they imprisoned 41 of the presbyterian members, voted the house of peers to be useless, and that of the commons was reduced to 150 independents, and most of them officers of the army. In the mean while Charles, who unhappily promised himself relief from those dissentions, was carried from prison to prison, and sometimes cajoled by the independents, with hopes of deliverance, but always narrowly watched. Several treaties were set on foot, but all miscarried, and he had been imprudent enough, after his effecting an escape, to put himself into colonel Hammond's hands, the parliament's governor of the isle of Wight. A fresh negociation was begun and almost finished, when the independents, dreading the general disposition of the people for peace, once more seized upon the king's person, brought him a prisoner to London, carried him before a mock court of justice, of their own erecting, and after a sham trial, his head was cut off, before his own palace at Whitehall, on the 30th of January, 1648-9, being the 49th year of his age, and the 24th of his reign.

Charles is allowed to have had many virtues, and there is reason to believe, that affliction had taught him so much wisdom and moderation, that had he been restored to his throne, he would have become a most excellent prince. This undoubtedly was the sense of his people, at the time of his murder,

murder, as it was univerſally deteſted by all but the parricides, who brought him to the block, and were heated by enthuſiaſm. Many, in the courſe of the rebellion, who had been his great opponents in parliament, became ſincere converts to his cauſe, in which they loſt their lives and fortunes, and never did any prince die more generally lamented, than he did, by his people. We cannot reflect upon the great loſs of lives, to the amount at leaſt of 100,000 fighting men, during the ſix years of the civil war, without being inclined to think that England was more populous then, than it is now. Though the hiſtory of that period has been minutely related, by writers of all parties, who had the very beſt opportunities to know the true ſtate of the nation, yet we do not find that the loſs of men had any influence upon agriculture or commerce, or the exerciſe of the common arts of life, and proviſions rather ſunk than roſe in their value. The ſurviving children of Charles, were Charles and James, who were ſucceſſively kings of England, Henry, duke of Glouceſter, who died ſoon after his brother's reſtoration; the princeſs Mary, married to the prince of Orange, and mother to William, prince of Orange, who was afterwards king of England, and the princeſs Henrietta Maria, who was married to the duke of Orleans, and whoſe daughter was married to Victor Amadeus, duke of Savoy, and king of Sardinia.

They who brought Charles to the block, were men of different perſuaſions and principles, but many of them poſſeſſed moſt amazing abilities for government. They omitted no meaſure that could give a perpetual excluſion to kingly power in England, and it cannot be denied, that after they erected themſelves into a commonwealth, they did prodigious things, for retrieving the glory of England by ſea. They were joined by many of the preſbyterians, and both factions hated Cromwell and Ireton, though they were forced to employ them in the reduction of Ireland, and afterwards againſt the Scots, who had received Charles II. as their king. By cutting down the timber upon the royal domains, they produced, as it were by magic, all at once, a fleet ſuperior to any that had ever been ſeen in Europe. Their general, Cromwell, invaded Scotland, and though he was there reduced to great difficulties, he totally defeated the Scots, at the battles of Dunbar and Worceſter. The ſame commonwealth paſſed an act of navigation, and declaring war againſt the Dutch, who were thought till then invincible at ſea, they effectually humbled thoſe republicans in repeated engagements.

By this time Cromwell, who hated the republic, had the addreſs to get himſelf declared commander in chief of the

English army. Admiral Blake, and the other English admirals, carried the terror of the English name by sea, to all quarters of the globe; and Cromwell having now but little employment, began to be afraid that his services would be forgotten, for which reason he went without any ceremony, with a file of musqueteers, dissolved the parliament, and opprobriously drove all the members out of their house. He next annihilated the council of state, with whom the executive power was lodged, and transferred the administration of government to about 140 persons, whom he summoned to Whitehall, on the 4th of July, 1653.

The war with Holland, in which the English were again victorious, still continued. Seven bloody engagements by sea, were fought in little more than the compass of one year, and in the last, which was decisive in favour of England, the Dutch lost their brave admiral Van Tromp. Cromwell all this while wanted to be declared king, but he perceived that he must encounter unsurmountable difficulties from Fleetwood, and his other friends, if he should persist in his resolution. He was however declared lord protector of the common wealth of England, a title, under which he exercised all the power that had been formerly annexed to the regal dignity. He next proceeded to new model the government, and various were the schemes that were proposed, established, and proved abortive. Those schemes, however, were temporary, and suited to each juncture, nor have we any high idea of Cromwell's political capacity, but in his management of the army, by which he did every thing. He was openly or secretly thwarted by people of property all over England, and however dazzled historians have been with his amazing fortune and power, it appears, from the best evidences, that during the continuance of his protectorate, he was perpetually distrest for money, to keep the wheels of his government going.

His wants at last led him into the fatal error of taking part with France against Spain, in hopes that the rich Spanish prizes would supply him with ready money. He lent the French court 6000 men, and Dunkirk being taken by their assistance from the Spaniards, he took possession of it. Finding that his usurpation gave as much discontent to his own party, as terror to the royalists, he had thoughts of renewing the model of the constitution, and actually erected a house of lords out of his own creatures. No king ever acted either in England, or Scotland, more despotically than he did, yet no tyrant ever had fewer real friends, and even those few threatened to oppose him, if he should take upon him the title of king. Historians, in drawing a character of Cromwell, have

been

been imposed upon by his amazing success, and dazzled by the lustre of his fortune; but when we consult Thurloe's, and other state papers, the imposition in a great measure vanishes. After a most uncomfortable usurpation of four years, eight months, and thirteen days, he died surrounded by enthusiasts, on the 3d of September, 1658, in the 60th year of his age.

It is not to be denied that England acquired much more respect from foreign powers, between the death of Charles I. and that of Cromwell, than she had been treated with since the death of Elizabeth. This was owing to the great men who formed the republic, which Cromwell abolished, and who as it were instantaneously called forth the naval strength of the kingdom. Neither they nor Cromwell had formed any fixed plan of legislation, and his safety was owing to the different sentiments of government, that prevailed among the heads of the republic. In the year 1656, the charge of the public amounted to one million, three hundred thousand pounds, of which a million went to the support of the navy and army, and the remainder to that of the civil government. In the same year, Cromwell abolished all tenures *in capite*, by knight's service, and soccage in chief, and likewise the courts of wards and liveries. Several other grievances that had been complained of, during the late reigns, were likewise removed. Next year the total charge, or public expence of England, amounted to two millions, three hundred twenty six thousand, nine hundred and eighty-nine pounds. The collections by assessments, excise, and customs, paid into the Exchequer, amounted to two millions, three hundred and sixty-two thousand pounds, four shillings.

Upon the whole it appears, that England, from the year 1648, to the year 1658, was improved equally in riches as in power. The legal interest of money was reduced from 8 to 6 per cent. a sure symptom of encreasing commerce. The navigation act, that palladium of the English trade, was planned and established, though afterwards confirmed under Charles II. Monopolies of all kinds were abolished, and liberty of conscience to all sects was granted to the vast advantage of population and manufactures, which had suffered greatly by Laud's intolerant schemes having driven numbers of handicrafts to America, and foreign countries. To the above national meliorations, we may add the modesty and frugality, introduced among the common people, and the citizens in particular, by which they were enabled to increase their capitals. It appears however that Cromwell, had he lived, and been firmly settled in the government, would have broken thro' the sober maxims of the republicans; for, some time before his death, he affected great magnificence in his person, court, and attendants. We know of no art, or science, that was patronized by the usurper, and yet he had the good fortune to meet in the person of Cooper, an excellent miniature painter, and his coins done by Simons, exceed in beauty and workmanship any of that age. He is likewise said to have paid some regard to men of learning, and particularly to those entrusted with the care of youth at the universities.

The fate of Richard Cromwell, who succeeded his father Oliver, as protector, sufficiently proves the little forecast, which the latter had in matters of government, and his being almost totally unbefriended. Richard was placed in his dignity by those who wanted to make him the tool of their own government, and he was soon after driven without the last struggle of opposition into contempt and obscurity. It is in vain for historians of any party to ascribe the restoration of Charles II. (who with his mother and brothers, during the usurpation, had lived abroad on a very precarious subsistence) to the merits of any particular persons. It was effected by the general concurrence of the people, who found by experience, that neither peace nor protection were to be obtained, but by restoring the ancient constitution of monarchy. General Monk, a man of military abilities, but of no principles, excepting such as served his ambition or interest, had the sagacity to observe this, and after temporizing in various shapes, being at the head of the army, he made the principal figure in restoring Charles II. For this he was created duke of Albemarle, confirmed in the command of the army, and loaded with honours and riches.

Charles II. being restored in 1660, in the first year of his reign, seemed to be under no influence, but that of his people's happiness. Upon his confirming the abolition of all the feudal tenures, he received from the parliament a gift of the excise for life, and in this act, coffee and tea are first mentioned. By his long residence, and that of his friends abroad, he imported into England, the culture of many elegant vegetables, such as that of asparagus, artichokes, cauliflowers, and several kinds of beans, peas, and sallads. Under him, Jamaica, which had been conquered, but neglected, by the English, during the late usurpation, was improved, and made a sugar colony. The Royal Society was instituted, and many popular acts respecting trade and colonization were passed. In short, Charles knew, and cultivated the true interests of his kingdom, till he was warped by pleasure, and sunk in indolence, failings that had the same consequences as despotism itself. He took a paternal concern in the sufferings of his citizens, when London was burnt down in 1666, and its being rebuilt with greater luſtre and conveniences, is a proof of the encreaſe of her trade; but there was no bound of Charles's love of pleaſure, which led him into the moſt extravagant expences. He has been ſeverely, but perhaps unjuſtly cenſured, for ſelling Dunkirk to the French king, to ſupply his neceſſities, after he had ſquandered the immenſe ſums granted him by parliament. The price was about 250,000 l. ſterling. In this he is more defenſible, than he was with his ſecret connections with France. Theſe are ſuppoſed to have brought on a war with the Dutch, but their behaviour and ingratitude to England, merited the ſevereſt chaſtiſement.

The firſt ſymptoms of his degeneracy as a king, appeared in his giving way to the popular clamour againſt the lord Clarendon, one of the wiſeſt and moſt diſintereſted ſtateſmen, that ever England could boaſt of, and ſacrificing him to the ſycophants of his pleaſurable hours. The firſt Dutch war, which began in 1665, was carried on, with great reſolution and ſpirit, under the duke of York, but through Charles's miſapplication of the public money, which had been granted for the war, the Dutch, while a treaty of peace was depending at Breda, found means to inſult the royal navy of England, by ſailing up the Medway, as far as Chatham, and deſtroyed ſeveral capital ſhips of war. Soon after this a peace was concluded at Breda, between Great Britain, and the States general, for the preſervation of the Spaniſh Netherlands, and Sweden having acceded to the treaty, it was called the triple alliance.

If we look into the hiſtory of thoſe times, we ſhall find that the humbling the power of France, was the ruling paſſion of almoſt all the reſt of Europe; but at the ſame time every ſtate at enmity with her, had particular views of its own, which defeated every plan of confederacy againſt the French power. The ſituation of Charles, in this reſpect, was delicate. The inſults and rivalſhip of the Dutch, were intolerable to the trading part of his people, but his parliament thought that all conſiderations ought to give way to the humiliation of the French king. Charles found ſuch oppoſition from his parliament, and ſuch difficulties in raiſing money, that he was perſuaded by his French miſtreſs, the ducheſs of Portſmouth, to throw himſelf into the arms of the French king, who promiſed to ſupply him with money, ſufficient to enable him to rule without a parliament. This has always been a capital charge againſt Charles II. and it had, I am apt to think, too great a weight with his parliament, whoſe conduct, in ſome particulars, is not to be vindicated.

In

ENGLAND.

In 1671, Charles was so ill advised, as to seize upon the money of the bankers, which had been lent him at 8 l. per cent. and to shut up the Exchequer. This was an indefensible step, and Charles pretended to justify it by the necessity of his affairs, being then on the eve of a fresh war with Holland. This was declared in 1672, and had almost proved fatal to that republic. In this war the English fleet, and army, acted in conjunction with those of France. The duke of York commanded the English fleet, and displayed great gallantry in that station. The duke of Monmouth, the eldest and favourite natural son of Charles, commanded 6000 English forces, who joined the French in the Low Countries, and all Holland must have fallen into the hands of the French, had it not been for the vanity of their monarch, Lewis XIV. who was in a hurry to enjoy his triumph in his capital, and some very unforeseen circumstances.

All confidence was now lost between Charles and his parliament, notwithstanding the glory which the English fleet obtained by sea against the Dutch. The popular clamour at last obliged Charles to give peace to that republic, in consideration of 200,000 l. which was paid him; but in some things Charles acted very despotically. He complained of the freedom taken with his prerogative in coffee-houses, and ordered them to be shut up, but in a few days after to be opened. His parliament addressed him, but in vain, to make war with France, in the year 1677, for he was entirely devoted to that crown, and regularly received its money as a pensioner. It is not however to be denied, that the trade of England was now incredibly encreased, and Charles entered into many vigorous measures for its protection and support.

This gave him no merit in the eyes of his parliament, which grew every day more and more furious, and untractable, against the French and the Papists; at the head of whom was the king's eldest brother, and presumptive heir of the crown, the duke of York. Charles, notwithstanding the opposition he met with in parliament, knew that he had the affections of his people, but was too indolent to take advantage of that circumstance. He dreaded the prospect of a civil war, and offered any concessions to avoid it. The conduct of his parliament on this occasion is indefensible. Many of the members were bent upon such a revolution as afterwards took place, and were secretly determined, that the duke of York never should reign. In 1678, the famous Titus Oates, and some other miscreants, forged a plot, charging the papists with a design to murder the king, and to introduce popery by means of Jesuits in England, and from St. Omer's. Though nothing could be more ridiculous, and more self-contradictory, than the whole of this forgery, yet it was supported by even a frantic zeal, on the part of the parliament. The aged and innocent lord Stafford, Coleman, secretary to the duke of York, with many Jesuits, and other papists, were publickly executed on perjured evidences. The queen herself escaped with difficulty: the duke of York was obliged to retire into foreign parts, and Charles, though convinced that the whole was an infamous imposture, yielded to the torrent. At last it spent its force. The earl of Shaftesbury, who was at the head of the opposition, pushed on the total exclusion of the duke of York from the throne. He was seconded by the ill advised duke of Monmouth, and the bill, after passing the commons, miscarried in the house of peers. All England was again in a flame, but the king, by a well-timed adjournment of the parliament to Oxford, recovered the affections of his people, to an almost incredible degree.

The duke of York, and his party, made a scandalous use of their victory. They trumped up on their side a plot of the protestants for killing or seizing the king, and altering the government. This plot was as false as that which had been forged against the papists. The excellent lord Russel, who had been remarkable in his opposition to the popish succession, Algernon Sidney, and several distinguished protestants, were tried, condemned, and suffered death, and the king set his foot upon the neck of opposition. Even the city of London was intimidated into the measures of the court, as were almost all the corporations in the kingdom. The duke of Monmouth, and the earl of Shaftesbury, were obliged to fly, and the duke of York returned in triumph to Whitehall. It was thought, however, that Charles intended to have recalled the duke of Monmouth, and to have executed some measures for the future quiet of his reign, when he died in February, 1684-5, in the 55th year of his age, and 25th of his reign. He had married Catharine, infanta of Portugal, by whom he received a large fortune in ready money, besides the town and fortress of Tangier in Africa, but he left behind him no lawful issue. The descendents of his natural sons and daughters, are now among the most distinguished of the British nobility.

In recounting the principal events of this reign, I have been sufficiently explicit as to the principles, both of the king and the opposition to his government. The heads of the latter were presbyterians, and had been greatly instrumental in the civil war against the late king, and the usurpations that followed. They had been raised and preferred by Charles, in hopes of their being useful in bringing their party into his measures, and he would probably have succeeded, had not the remains of
the

the old royalists, and the dissipated part of the court, fallen in with the king's foible for pleasure. The presbyterians, however, availed themselves of their credit, in the early part of his reign, when the fervour of loyalty was abated, to bring into parliament such a number of their friends, as rendered the reign of Charles very uneasy, and it was owing, perhaps, to them, that civil liberty, and protestantism, now exist in the English government. On the other hand, they seem to have carried their jealousy of a popish successor too far, and the people, without doors, certainly thought that the parliament ought to have been satisfied with the legal restraints and disabilities, which Charles offered to impose upon his successor. This gave such a turn to the affections of the people, as left Charles, and his brother, at the time of his death, masters of the laws and liberties of England.

The reign of Charles has been celebrated for wit and galantry, but both were coarse and indelicate. The court was the nursery of vice, and the stages exhibited scenes of impurity. Some readers, however, were found, who could admire Milton, as well as Dryden, and never perhaps were the pulpits of England so well supplied with preachers, as in this reign. Our language was harmonized, refined, and rendered natural, witness the stile of their sermons; and the days of Charles may be called the Augustan age of mathematics, and natural philosophy. Charles loved, patronized and understood the arts, more than he encouraged, or rewarded them, especially those of English growth, but this neglect proceeded not from narrow-mindedness but indolence, and want of reflection. If the memory of Charles II. has been traduced for being the first English prince, who formed a body of standing forces, as guards to his person, it ought to be remembered, at the same time, that he carried the art of ship-building to the highest perfection; and that the royal navy of England, at this day, owes its finest improvements to his, and his brother's complete knowledge of naval affairs and architecture.

All the opposition which, during the late reign, had shaken the throne, seems to have vanished, at the accession of James II. The popular affection towards him was encreased by the early declaration he made in favour of the church of England, which, during the late reign, had formally pronounced all resistance to the reigning king to be unlawful. This doctrine proved fatal to James, and almost ruined protestantism. The army and people supported him, in crushing an ill-formed and indeed wicked rebellion of the duke of Monmouth, who pretended to be the lawful son of Charles II. and, as such, had assumed the title of king. That duke's head being cut off

James desperately resolved to try how far the practice of the church of England would agree with her doctrine of non-resistance. The experiment failed him. He made the most provoking steps to render popery the established religion of his dominions. He pretended to a power of dispensing with the known laws; he instituted an illegal ecclesiastical court, he openly received and admitted into his privy-council, the pope's emissaries, and gave them more respect than was due to the ministers of a sovereign prince. The encroachments he made upon both the civil and religious liberties of his people, are almost beyond description, and were disapproved of by the pope himself, and all sober Roman catholics. His sending to prison, and prosecuting for a libel, seven bishops, for presenting a petition against reading his declaration, and their acquittal upon a legal trial, alarmed his best protestant friends.

In this extremity, many great men in England and Scotland, though they wished well to James, applied for relief to William, prince of Orange, in Holland, a prince of great abilities, and the inveterate enemy of Lewis XIV. who then threatened Europe with chains. The prince of Orange was the nephew and son-in-law of James, having married the princess Mary, that king's eldest daughter, and he embarked with a fleet of 500 sail for England, on pretence of restoring church and state to their due rights. Upon his arrival in England, he was joined not only by the Whigs, but many whom James had considered as his best friends; and even his daughter the princess Anne, and her husband, George, prince of Denmark, left him and joined the prince of Orange, who soon discovered that he expected the crown. James might still have reigned, but he was surrounded with French emissaries, and ignorant Jesuits, who wished him not to reign rather than not restore popery. They secretly persuaded him to send his queen and son, then but six months old, to France, and to follow them in person, which he did; and thus in 1688, ended his reign in England, which event in English history is termed *the revolution*.

This short reign affords little matter for the national progress in its true interests. James is allowed, on all hands, to have understood them, and that had it not been for his bigotry, he would have been a most excellent king of England. The writings of the English divines against popery, in this reign, are esteemed to be the most masterly pieces of controversy that ever were published on that subject.

Had it not been for the baleful influence of the Jesuits over James, the prince of Orange might have found his views upon the crown frustrated. The conduct of James gave him advantages,

vantages, he could not have hoped for. Few were in the prince's fecret, and when a convention of the ftates was called, it was plain, that had not James abdicated his throne, it would not have been filled by the prince and princefs of Orange. Even that was not done without long debates. It is well known that king William's chief object, was to humble the power of France, and his reign was fpent in an almoft uninterrupted courfe of hoftilities with that power, which were fupported by England, at an expence fhe had never known before. The nation had grown cautious, through the experience of the two laft reigns, and he gave his confent to the *bill of rights*, which contained all the people could claim, for the prefervation of their liberties. The two laft kings had made a very bad ufe of the whole national revenue, which was put into their hands, and which was found to be fufficient to raife and maintain a ftanding army. The revenue was therefore divided, part was allotted for the current national fervice of the year, and was to be accounted for to parliament, and part, which is ftill called the civil lift money, was given to the king, for the fupport of his houfe and dignity.

It was the juft fenfe the people had of their civil and religious rights alone, that could provoke the people of England to agree to the late revolution, for they never in other refpects had been at fo high a pitch of wealth and profperity, as in the year 1688. The tonage of their merchant fhips, as appears from Dr. Davenant, was, that year, near double to what it had been in 1666; and the tonage of the royal navy, which in 1660, was only 62,594 tons, was in 1688 encreafed to 101,032 tons. The encreafe of the cuftoms, and the annual rental of England, was in the fame proportion. It was therefore no wonder, if a ftrong party, both in the parliament and nation, was formed againft the government, which was hourly encreafed by the king's predilection for the Dutch. The war with France, which, on the king's part, was far from being fuccefsful, required an enormous expence, and the Irifh continued in general, faithful to king James. Many Englifh, who wifhed well to the Stuart family, dreaded their being reftored by conqueft, and the parliament enabled the king to reduce Ireland, and to gain the battle of the Boyn againft James, who there loft all the military honour he had acquired before. The marine of France, however, proved fuperior to that of England, in the beginning of the war; but in the year 1692, that of France received an irrecoverable blow in the defeat at La Hogue, which the French feel to this day.

Invafions were threatened, and confpiracies difcovered every day againft the government, and the fupply of the continental war forced the parliament to open new resources for money. A land-tax was imposed, and every subject's lands were taxed, according to their valuations given in by the several counties. Those who were the most loyal, were the heaviest taxed, and this preposterous burthen still continues; but the greatest and boldest operation in finances, that ever took place, was established in this reign, which was carrying on the war by borrowing money upon parliamentary securities, which form what are now called the public funds. The chief projector of this scheme, is said to have been Charles Montague, afterwards lord Halifax. His chief argument for such a project was, that it would oblige the moneyed part of the nation to befriend the revolution interest, because after lending their money, they could have no hopes of being repaid, but by supporting that interest, and that the weight of taxes would oblige the commercial people to be more industrious. How well those views have been answered, is needless to observe, as I have already mentioned the present state of public credit.

William, notwithstanding the vast service he had done to the nation, and the public benefits which took place under his auspices, particularly in the establishment of the bank of England, and the recoining the silver money, met with so many mortifications from his parliament, that he actually resolved upon an abdication, and had drawn up a speech for that purpose, which he was prevailed upon to suppress. He long bore the affronts he met with in hopes of being supported in his war with France, but at last, in 1697, he was forced to conclude the peace of Ryswick with the French king, who acknowledged his title to the crown of England. By this time William had lost his queen, but the government was continued in his person. After peace was restored, the commons obliged him to disband his army, all but an inconsiderable number, and to dismiss his favourite Dutch guards. Towards the end of his reign his fears of seeing the whole Spanish monarchy in possession of France at the death of the catholic king Charles II. which was every day expected, led him into a very impolitic measure, which was the Partition treaty with France, by which that monarchy was to be divided between the houses of Bourbon and Austria. This treaty was highly resented by the parliament, and some of his ministry were impeached for advising it. It is thought that William saw his error when it was too late. His ministers were acquitted from their impeachment, and the death of king James discovered the insincerity of the French court, which immediately proclaimed his son king of Great Britain.

This

This perfidy rendered William again popular in England. The two houses passed the bill of abjuration, and an address for a war with France. The last and most glorious act] of William's reign was his passing the bill for settling the succession to the crown in the house of Hanover, on the twelfth of June, 1701. His death was hastened by a fall he had from his horse, soon after he had renewed the grand alliance against France, on the eighth of March, 1702, the 52d year of his age, and the 14th of his reign in England. This prince was not made by nature for popularity. His manners were cold and forbidding. His notions of national government inclined towards despotism; and it was observed, that though he owed his royalty to the whigs, yet he favoured the tories, as often as he could do it with safety. The rescue and preservation of religion and public liberty were the chief glories of William's reign, for England under him suffered severely both by sea and land, and the public debt, at the time of his death, amounted to the then unheard of sum of 14,000,000. I have nothing to add after this, as to the general state of England in the beginning of the 18th century.

Anne, princess of Denmark, being the next protestant heir to her father James II. succeeded king William in the throne. As she had been ill treated by the late king, it was thought she would have deviated from his measures, but the behaviour of the French in acknowledging the title of her brother, who has since been well known by the name of the pretender, left her no choice, and she resolved to fulfil all William's engagements with his allies, and to employ the earl of Marlborough, who had been imprisoned in the late reign on a suspicion of Jacobitism, and whose wife was her favourite, as her general. She could not have made a better choice of a general and a statesman, for that earl excelled in both. No sooner was he placed at the head of the English army abroad, than his genius and activity gave a new turn to the war, and he became as much the favourite of the Dutch as his wife was of the queen.

Charles II. of Spain, in consequence of the intrigues of France, and at the same time resenting the Partition treaty, in which his consent had not been asked, left his whole dominions by will to Philip, duke of Anjou, grandson of Lewis XIV. and Philip was immediately proclaimed king of Spain, which laid the foundation of the family alliance, that still subsists, between France and that nation. Philip's succession was however disputed by the second son of the emperor of Germany, who took upon himself the title of Charles III. and his cause was favoured by the empire, England, Holland,

land, and other powers who joined in a confederacy against the house of Bourbon, now become more dangerous than ever by the acquisition of the whole Spanish dominions.

The capital measure of continuing the war against France being fixed, the queen found no great difficulty in forming her ministry, who were for the most part tories, and the earl of Godolphin, who (though afterwards a leading whig) was thought all his life to have a predilection for the late king James and his queen, was placed at the head of the treasury. His son had married the earl of Marlborough's eldest daughter, and the earl could trust no other with that important department.

I shall hereafter have occasion to mention the glorious victories obtained by the earl, who was soon made duke of Marlborough. Those of Blenheim and Ramilies gave the first effectual checks to the French power. By that of Blenheim, the empire of Germany was saved from immediate destruction. Though prince Eugene was that day joined in command with the duke, yet the glory of the day was confessedly owing to the latter. The French general Tallard was taken prisoner, and sent to England; and 20,000 French and Bavarians were killed, wounded, or drowned in the Danube, besides about 13,000 who were taken, and a proportionable number of cannon, artillery, and trophies of war. About the same time, the English admiral, Sir George Rook, reduced Gibraltar, which still remains in our possession. The battle of Ramilies was fought and gained under the duke of Marlborough alone. The loss of the enemy there has been variously reported; it is generally supposed to have been 8000 killed or wounded, and 6000 taken prisoners; but the consequences shewed its importance.

After the battle of Ramilies, the states of Flanders assembled at Ghent, and recognized Charles for their sovereign, while the confederates took possession of Louvain, Brussels, Mechlin, Ghent, Oudenarde, Bruges, and Antwerp; and several other considerable places in Flanders and Brabant, and acknowledged the title of king Charles. The next great battle gained over the French was at Oudenarde, where they lost 3000 on the field, and about 7000 were taken prisoners; and the year after, September 11, 1709, the allies forced the French lines at Malplaquet, near Mons, with the loss of about 20,000 men. Thus far I have recounted the flattering successes of the English, but they were attended with many potions of bitter alloy.

The queen had sent a very fine army to assist Charles III. in Spain, under the command of lord Galway; but in 1707, after

after he had been joined by the Portuguese, the English were defeated in the plains of Almanza, chiefly through the cowardice of their allies. Though some advantages were obtained at sea, yet that war in general was carried on to the detriment if not to the disgrace of England. Prince George of Denmark, husband to the queen, was then lord high admiral, but he had trusted the affairs of that board to underlings, who were either corrupted or ignorant, and complaints coming from every quarter, with regard to that department, the house of commons were put in very bad humour, nor did things seem to be much better managed after the prince's death. The immense sums raised for the current service of the year being severely felt, and but indifferently accounted for, it appeared that England had borne the chief burden of the war; that neither the Austrians, Germans, nor Dutch, had furnished their stipulated quotas, and that they trusted to the English parliament for making them good. A noble design, which had been planned at the court, and was to have been executed by the assistance of the fleet of England, for taking Toulon, at a vast expence, miscarried through the selfishness of the court of Vienna, whose chief object of attention was their own war in Naples. At the same time England felt severely the scarcity of hands in carrying on her trade and manufactures, and the French king, the haughty Lewis XIV. now professed his readiness to agree to almost any terms the English should prescribe.

These and many other internal disputes about the prerogative, the succession, religion, and other public matters, had created great ferments in the nation and parliament. The queen stuck close to the duke of Marlborough and his friends, who finding that the tories inclined to treat with France, put themselves at the head of the whigs, who were for continuing the war, from which the duke and his dependents received immense emoluments. The failures of the Germans and Dutch could not however be longer dissembled, and the personal interest of the duchess of Marlborough with the queen began to be shaken by her own insolence.

The whigs at last were forced to give way to a treaty, and the conferences were held at Gertruydenburg. They were managed on the part of England by the duke of Marlborough and the lord Townshend, and by the marquis de Torcy for the French. It soon appeared that the English plenipotentiaries were not in earnest, and that the Dutch were entirely guided by the duke of Marlborough. The French king was gradually brought to comply with all the demands of the allies, excepting that of employing his own troops against the duke of

Anjou,

Anjou, in Spain, where the fortune of war continued still doubtful. All his offers were rejected by the duke and his associate, and the war was continued.

The unreasonable haughtiness of the English plenipotentiaries at Gertruydenburg saved France, and affairs from that day took a turn in their favour. Means were found to convince the queen, who was not destitute of sense, and faithfully attached to the church of England, that the war in the end, if continued, must prove ruinous to her and her people, and that the whigs were no friends to the national religion. The general cry of the people was that the church was in danger, which, though groundless, had great effects. One Sacheverel, an ignorant, worthless preacher, had espoused this clamour in one of his sermons, with the ridiculous, impracticable doctrines of passive obedience and non-resistance. It was, as it were, agreed by both parties to try their strength in this man's case. He was impeached by the commons, and found guilty by the lords, who ventured to pass upon him only a very small censure. After this trial the queen's affections were entirely alienated from the duchess of Marlborough, and the whig administration. Her friends lost their places, which were supplied by tories, and even the command of the army was taken from the duke of Marlborough, and given to the duke of Ormond, who produced orders for a cessation of arms; but they were disregarded by the queen's allies in the British pay.

Conferences were opened for a peace at Utrecht, to which the queen and the French king sent plenipotentiaries, and the allies being defeated at Denain, they grew sensible that they were no match for the French, now that they were abandoned by the English. In short, the terms were agreed upon between France and England. The reader needs not be informed of the particular cessions made by the French, especially that of Dunkirk; but after all, the peace would have been indefensible had it not been for the death of the emperor Joseph, by which his brother Charles III. for whom the war was chiefly undertaken, became emperor of Germany, as well as king of Spain, and the bad faith of the English allies, in not fulfilling their engagements, and throwing upon the British parliament almost the whole weight of the war, not to mention the exhausted state of the kingdom. Mr. Harley, who was created earl of Oxford, and lord high treasurer of England, was then considered as the queen's first minister, but the negociations for the peace went through the hands of Mr. Harley and lord Bolingbroke, one of the principal secretaries of state. The ministry endeavoured to stifle the complaints of the whigs,
and

and the remonstrances of prince Eugene, who arrived in England on the part of the allies, by falling upon the contractors, foragers, and other agents of the fleet and army, whom they accused of corrupt practices.

The queen was at this time in a critical situation. The whigs, without attempting to answer the arguments of the tories for peace, condemned it as shameful. The majority of the house of lords was of that party, but that of the house of commons were tories. The queen was afraid that the peers would reject the peace, and by an unprecedented exercise of her prerogative she created twelve peers at one time, which secured the approbation of the parliament for the peace. Such was the state of affairs at this critical period; and I am apt to think from their complexion that the queen had by some secret influence, which never has yet been discovered, and was even concealed from her ministers, inclined to call her brother to the succession. The rest of the queen's life was rendered uneasy by the jarring of parties. The whigs demanded a writ for the electoral prince of Hanover, as duke of Cambridge, to come to England, and she was obliged to dismiss her lord treasurer, when she fell into a lethargic disorder, which carried her off the first of August 1714, in the fiftieth year of her age, and the thirteenth of her reign*. I have nothing to add to what I have already said of her character, but that though she was a favourite with neither party in her parliament till towards the end of her reign, when the tories affected to idolize her, yet her people dignified her with the name of the Good queen Anne. Notwithstanding all I have said of the exhausted state of England before the peace of Utrecht was concluded, yet the public credit was little or nothing affected by her death, though the national debt then amounted to about fifty millions, so firm was the dependence of the people upon the security of parliament.

Anne had no strength of mind, by herself, to carry any important resolve into execution; and she left public measures in so indecisive a state, that upon her death the succession took place in terms of the act of settlement, and George I. elector of Hanover, was proclaimed king of Great Britain, his mother, who would have been next in succession, having died but a few days before. He came over to England with strong prepossessions against the tory ministry, most of whom he displaced; but this did not make any great alteration to his prejudice in England; while the Scots were driven into rebellion in 1715, which was happily suppressed the beginning of the next year

---

* And with her ended the House of Stewart, which from the accession of James I. anno 1603, had swayed the sceptre of England 111 years, and that of Scotland 343 years, from the accession of Robert II. anno 1371.

year. Some deluded noblemen and gentlemen in the north of England joined a party of the Scotch rebels, but they were surrounded at Preston, where they delivered up their arms, and their leaders were sent prisoners to London, where some of them suffered. The tories and Jacobites, however, raised mobs and commotions at London, Oxford, and other parts of England, but they were soon suppressed by making their ringleaders examples of justice. Lord Oxford was imprisoned for three years, but the capital prosecution of him by the whigs for the hand he had in the peace of Utrecht, was secretly disapproved of by the king, and dropped.

After all, the nation was in such a disposition that the ministry durst not venture to call a new parliament, and the members of that which was sitting voted a continuance of their duration from three to seven years, which is thought to have been the greatest stretch of parliamentary power ever known. Several other extraordinary measures took place about the same time. Mr. Shippen, an excellent speaker, and member of parliament, was sent to the Tower for saying that the king's speech was calculated for the meridian of Hanover rather than of London; and one Matthews, a young journeyman printer, was hanged for composing a silly pamphlet, that in later times would not have been thought worthy of animadversion. The truth is, the whig ministry were excessively jealous of every thing that seemed to affect their master's title, and George I. though a sagacious, moderate prince, undoubtedly rendered England too subservient to his continental connections, which were various and complicated. He quarrelled with the czar of Muscovy about their German concerns, and had not Charles XII. king of Sweden been killed so critically as he was, Great Britain probably would have been invaded by those northern conquerors, great preparations being made for that purpose.

In 1718 he quarrelled with Spain on account of the quadruple alliance, that had been formed by Great Britain, France, Germany, and the states general; and his admiral, Sir George Byng, by his orders, destroyed the Spanish fleet near Syracuse. A trifling war with Spain then commenced, but it was soon ended by the Spaniards delivering up Sardinia and Sicily, the former to the duke of Savoy and the latter to the emperor.

A national punishment different from plague, pestilence, and famine, overtook England in the year 1720, by the sudden rise of the South-Sea Stock, one of the trading companies. This company was but of late erection, and was owing to a scheme of carrying on an exclusive trade, and making a settlement in the South-Seas, which had been formed in 1711. In 1720 the company obtained an act to encrease their capital stock

stock by redeeming the public debts; and was then invested with the assiento of negroes, which had been stipulated between Great Britain and Spain. In short, it became so favourite a company, that by the twentieth of June this year, their stock rose to 890 per cent. and afterwards to 1000; but before the end of September it fell to 150, by which thousands were involved in ruin. Though this might be owing to the inconsiderate avarice of the subscribers, yet the public imagined that the ministry had contributed to the calamity; and some of the directors insinuated as if the ministers and their friends had been the chief gainers. The latter, however, had the address to escape without censure, but the parliament passed a bill which confiscated the estates of the directors, with an allowance for their maintenance; a poor reparation for the public injuries.

The Jacobites thought to avail themselves of the national discontent of the South-Sea scheme, and England's connections with the continent, which every day encreased. One Layer, a lawyer, was tried and executed for high-treason. Several persons of great quality and distinction were apprehended on suspicion, but the storm fell chiefly on Francis Atterbury, lord bishop of Rochester, who was deprived of his see and seat in parliament, and banished for life. This must have been at best an idle plot, and the reality of it has never been discovered, so that the justice of the bishop's censure has been questioned. After the ferment of this plot had subsided, the ministry, who were all in the interest of Hanover, ventured upon several bold measures, in some of which the national interest if not honour was evidently sacrificed to that electorate. The crown of Great Britain was engaged in every continental dispute, however remote it was from her interest; and a difference still subsisting between the courts of Madrid and Vienna, it was agreed that it should be determined by a congress to be held at Cambray, under the auspices of France. This congress proved abortive, and England was involved in fresh difficulties on account of Hanover. So fluctuating was the state of Europe at this time, that in September 1725, a fresh treaty was concluded at Hanover between the kings of Great Britain, France, and Prussia, to counterbalance an alliance that had been formed between the courts of Vienna and Madrid. A squadron was sent to the Baltic, another to the Mediterranean; and a third, under admiral Hosier, to the West Indies to watch the Spanish plate fleets. This last was a fatal as well as an inglorious expedition. The admiral and most of his men perished by epidemical diseases, and the hulks of his ships rotted so as to render them unfit for service. The management

management of the Spaniards was little better. They lost near 10,000 men in the siege of Gibraltar, which they were obliged to raise. The king, in his speech to the parliament, publicly accused the emperor of a design to place the pretender upon the throne of Great Britain, but this was strenuously denied by baron Palmer, the imperial resident at London, who was therefore ordered to leave the kingdom.

A quarrel with the imperor was the most dangerous to Hanover of any that could happen; but though an opposition in the house of commons was formed by Sir William Wyndham and Mr. Pulteney, the parliament continued to be more and more lavish in granting money, and raising enormous subsidies for the protection of Hanover, to the kings of Denmark and Sweden, and the landgrave of Hesse Cassel. Such was the state of affairs in Europe, when George I. suddenly died on the eleventh of June 1727, at Osnaburgh, in the sixty-eighth year of his age, and the thirteenth of his reign. This period is too late to offer any thing new by way of observation on national improvements. The reign of George I. is remarkable for the incredible number of bubbles and cheating projects, to which it gave rise, and for the great alteration of the system of Europe, by the concern which the English took in the affairs of the continent. The institution of the sinking fund for diminishing the national debt, is likewise owing to this period. The value of the northern parts of the kingdom began now to be better understood than formerly, and the state of manufactures began to shift. This was chiefly owing to the unequal distribution of the land tax, which rendered it difficult for the poor to subsist in certain counties, which had been forward in giving in the true value of their estates when that tax took place.

Sir Robert Walpole was considered as first minister of England when George I. died, and some differences having happened between him and the prince of Wales, it was generally thought upon the accession of the latter to the crown that Sir Robert would be displaced. That might have been the case could another person have been found equally capable, as he was, to manage the house of commons, and to gratify that predilection for Hanover which George II. inherited from his father. No minister ever understood better the temper of the people of England, and none perhaps ever tried it more. He filled all places of power, trust, and profit, and almost the house of commons itself, with his own creatures; but peace was his darling object, because he thought that war must be fatal to his power. The times are too recent for me to enter upon particulars. It is sufficient to say, that during his long administration

administration he never lost a question that he was in earnest to carry. The excise scheme was the first measure that gave a shock to his power, and even that he could have carried, had he not been afraid of the spirit of the people without doors, which might have either produced an insurrection, or endangered his interest in the next general election. Having compromised all differences with Spain, he filled all the courts of Europe with embassies and negociations, and the new parliament gratified him with the means of performing his engagements. He continued and enlarged the subsidies paid to the German princes for the security of Hanover, and had even the address to obtain from time to time votes of credit for fulfilling his intermediate engagements, and in the mean while, to amuse the public, he suffered enquiries into the state of the jails, and other matters that did not affect his own power, to proceed.

His pacific system brought him, however, into inconveniencies both at home and abroad. He encouraged the Spaniards to continue their depredations upon the British shipping in the American seas, and the French to treat the English court with insolence and neglect. At home, many of the great peers thought themselves slighted, and they interested themselves more than ever they had done in elections. This, together with the disgust of the people at the proposed excise scheme, about the year 1736 and 1737, encreased the minority in the house of commons to 130, some of whom were as able men and as good speakers as ever had sat in a parliament, and taking advantage of the encreasing complaints against the Spaniards, they gave the minister great uneasiness. Having thus shewn Walpole's administration in the unfavourable, it is but just we turn to the most advantageous light it will admit of.

He filled the courts of justice with able and upright judges, nor was he ever known to attempt any perversion of the known laws of the kingdom. He was so far from checking the freedom of debate, that he bore with equanimity the most scurrilous abuse that was thrown out to his face. He gave way to one or two prosecutions for libels, in complaisance to his friends, who thought themselves affected by them, and it cannot be denied that the press of England never was more open or free than during his administration. If he managed the majority of parliament by corruption, which is the main charge against him, it is not to be denied that his enemies were often influenced by no very laudable motives, and that the attempt they made, without specifying any charge, to remove him from his majesty's councils and presence for ever, was illegal and unjust. As to his pacific system, it certainly more than repaid to the nation all that was required to support it, by the encreafe of her trade and the improvement of her manufactures.

With regard to the king's own perfonal concern in public matters, Walpole was rather his minifter than his favourite, and his majefty often hinted to him, as Walpole himfelf has been heard to acknowledge, that he was refponfible for all the meafures of government. The debates concerning the Spanifh depredations in the Weft Indies, and the proofs that were brought to fupport the complaints of the merchants, made at laft an impreffion even upon many of Walpole's friends. The heads of the oppofition in both houfes of parliament accufed the minifter of having by the treaty of Seville, and other negotiations, introduced a branch of the houfe of Bourbon into Italy, and depreffed the houfe of Auftria, the antient and natural ally of England. They expofed, with invincible force of eloquence and reafoning, the injuftice and difgrace as well as lofs arifing from the Spanifh depredations, and the neceffity of repelling force by force. Sir Robert adhered to his pacific fyftem, and concluded a fhameful and indefenfible compromife, under the title of a convention, with the court of Spain, which produced a war with that nation.

Queen Caroline, confort to George II. had been always a firm friend to the minifter, but fhe died when a variance fubfifted between the king and his fon the prince of Wales. The latter complained, that through Walpole's influence he was deprived not only of the power but the provifion to which his birth entitled him, and he put himfelf at the head of the oppofition with fo much firmnefs, that it was generally forefeen that Walpole's power was drawing to a crifis. Admiral Vernon, who hated the minifter, was fent with a fquadron of fix fhips to the Weft Indies, where he took and demolifhed Porto Bello; but being a hot, impracticable man, he mifcarried in his other attempts, efpecially that upon Carthagena, in which many thoufands of Britifh lives were wantonly thrown away. The oppofition exulted in Vernon's fuccefs, and imputed his mifcarriages to the minifter's ftarving the war, by with-holding the means for carrying it on. The general election approaching, fo prevalent was the intereft of the prince of Wales in England, and that of the duke of Argyle in Scotland, that a majority was returned to parliament who were no friends to the minifter, and after a few trying divifions he retired from the houfe, refigned his employments, and fome days after was created earl of Orford.

George II. bore the lofs of his minifter with the greateft equanimity, and even conferred titles of honour and pofts of diftinction upon the heads of the oppofition. By this time,

the

the death of the emperor Charles VI. the danger of the pragmatic fanction (which meant the fucceffion of his daughter to the Auftrian dominions) through the ambition of France, who had filled all Germany with her armies, and many other concurrent caufes, induced George to take the leading part in a continental war. He was encouraged to this by lord Carteret, afterwards earl of Granville, an able, but a headftrong minifter, whom George had made his fecretary of ftate, and, indeed, by the voice of the nation in general. George accordingly put himfelf at the head of his army, fought and gained the battle of Dettingen, and his not fuffering his general, the earl of Stair, to improve the blow, was thought to proceed from tendernefs for his electoral dominions. This partiality created a univerfal flame in England, and the clamour raifed againft his lordfhip's meafures was encreafed by the duke of Newcaftle and his brother, lord chancellor Hardwicke, the lord Harrington, and other minifters, who refigned, or offered to refign their places if lord Carteret fhould retain his influence in the cabinet. His majefty was obliged to give way to what he thought was the voice of his people, and he indulged them with accepting the fervices of fome gentlemen who never had been confidered as zealous friends to the houfe of Hanover. After various removals, Mr. Pelham was placed at the head of the treafury, and appointed chancellor of the exchequer, and confequently was confidered as firft minifter, or rather the power of the premierfhip was divided between him and his brother the duke of Newcaftle.

Great Britain was then engaged in a very expenfive war both againft the French and Spaniards, and her enemies fought to avail themfelves of the general difcontent that had prevailed in England on account of Hanover, and which, even in parliamentary debates, exceeded the bounds of duty. This naturally fuggefted to them the idea of applying to the pretender, who refided at Rome, and he agreed that his fon Charles, who was a fprightly young man, fhould repair to France, from whence he fet fail, and narrowly efcaped with a few followers in a frigate to the weftern coafts of Scotland, between the iflands of Mull and Skey, where he difcovered himfelf, affembled his followers, and publifhed a manifefto exciting the nation to a rebellion. It is neceffary, before we relate the unaccountable fuccefs of this enterprize, to make a fhort retrofpect to foreign parts.

The war of 1741 proved unfortunate in the Weft Indies, through the fatal divifions between admiral Vernon and general Wentworth, who commanded the land troops, and it was thought that above 20,000 Britifh foldiers and feamen perifhed in the impracticable attempt of Carthagena, and the inclemency of the air and climate during other idle expeditions. The year 1742 had been spent in negociations with the courts of Petersburgh and Berlin, which, though expensive, proved of little or no service to Great Britain, so that the victory of Dettingen left the French troops in much the same situation as before. A difference between the admirals Matthews and Lestock had suffered the Spanish and French fleets to escape out of Toulon with but little loss; and soon after the French, who had before acted only as allies to the Spaniards, declared war against Great Britain, who, in her turn, declared war against the French. The Dutch, the natural allies of England, during this war carried on a most lucrative trade, nor could they be brought to act against the French, till the people entered into associations and insurrections against the government. Their marine was in a miserable condition, and when they at last sent a body of troops to join the British and Austrian armies, which, indeed, had been wretchedly commanded for one or two campaigns, they did it with so bad a grace, that it was plain they did not intend to act in earnest. When the duke of Cumberland took upon himself the command of the army, the French, to the great reproach of the allies, were almost masters of the barrier in the Netherlands, and were besieging Tournay. The duke attempted to raise the siege, but by the coldness of the Austrians, the cowardice of the Dutch, whose government all along held a secret correspondence with France, and misconduct somewhere else, he lost the battle of Fontenoy, and 7000 of his best men, though it is generally allowed that his dispositions were excellent, and both he and his troops behaved with unexampled intrepidity. To counterbalance such a train of misfortunes, admiral Anson returned this year to England, with an immense treasure, which he had taken from the Spaniards, in his voyage round the world; and the English commodore Warren, with colonel Pepperel, took from the French the important town and fortress of Louisbourg in the island of Cape Breton.

Such was the state of affairs abroad in August 1745, when the pretender's eldest son, at the head of some Highland followers, surprized and disarmed a party of the king's troops in the western Highlands, and advanced with great rapidity to Perth. I shall only add to what I have already said of the progress and suppression of this rebellion, that it spread too great an alarm through England. The government never so thoroughly experienced, as it did at that time, the benefit of the public debt for the support of the revolution. The French and

and the Jacobite party (for such there was at that time in England) had laid a deep scheme for distressing the Bank; but common danger abolished all distinctions, and united them in the defence of one interest, which was private property. The merchants undertook, in their address to the king, to support it, by receiving bank-notes in payment. This seasonable measure saved public credit; but the defeat of the rebels by the duke of Cumberland at Culloden, and the executions that followed, did not restore tranquillity to Europe. Though the prince of Orange, son-in-law to his majesty George II. was, by the credit of his majesty and the spirit of the people of the United Provinces, raised to be their stadtholder, the Dutch never could be brought to act heartily in the war. The allies were defeated at Val, near Maestricht, and the duke of Cumberland was in danger of being made prisoner. Bergen-op-zoom was taken in a manner that has never yet been accounted for. The allies suffered other disgraces on the continent; and it now became the general opinion in England, that peace was necessary to save the duke and his army from total destruction. By this time, however, the French marine and commerce were in danger of being annihilated by the English at sea, under the commands of the admirals Anson, Warren, Hawke, and other gallant officers; but the English arms were not so successful as could have been wished under rear admiral Boscawen in the East-Indies. In this state of affairs, the successes of the French and English during the war, may be said to have been balanced, and both ministries turned their thoughts to peace. The question is not yet decided which party had the greatest reason to desire it, the French and Spaniards for the immense losses they had sustained by sea, or the allies for the disgraces they had suffered by land.

Whatever may be in this, preliminaries for peace were signed in April 1748, and a definitive treaty was concluded at Aix-la-Chapelle, in October, the basis of which was the restitution on both sides of all places taken during the war. The number of prizes taken by the English in this war, from its commencement to the signing the preliminaries of peace, was 3434; namely, 1249 from the Spaniards, and 2185 from the French; and that they lost during the war, 3238; 1360 being taken by the Spaniards, and 1878 by the French. Several of the ships taken from the Spaniards were immensely rich; so that the balance upon the whole amounted to almost two millions, in favour of the English. Such is the gross calculation on both sides, but the consequences plainly proved that the losses of the French and Spaniards must have been much greater.

greater. The vast fortunes made by private persons in England all of a sudden, sufficiently shewed that immense sums had not been brought to the public account; but the greatest proof was, that next year the interest of the national debt was reduced from four to three and a half per cent. for seven years, after which the whole was to stand reduced to three per cent.

This was the boldest stroke of financing that ever was attempted perhaps in any country, consistently with public faith; for the creditors of the government, after a small ineffectual opposition, continued their money in the funds, and a few who sold out even made interest to have it replaced on the same security, or were paid off their principal sums out of the sinking fund. This was an æra of improvements; Mr. Pelham's candour and rectitude of administration leaving him few or no enemies in parliament, and he omitted no opportunity of carrying into execution every scheme for the improvement of commerce, manufactures, and the fisheries; the benefits of which were felt during the succeeding war, and are to this day. Every intelligent person, however, considered the peace of Aix-la-Chapelle as no better than an armed cessation of hostilities. The French employed themselves in recruiting and repairing their marine, and had laid a deep scheme for possessing themselves of the British back settlements in America, and for cutting off all communication between the English and the native Indians, in which case our colonies must have been reduced to a narrow slip on the coasts, without the means of getting any subsistence but from the mother country. Fortunately for Great-Britain, they disclosed their intention by entering upon hostilities before they had power to support them.

In the mean while, a new treaty of commerce was signed at Madrid, between Great-Britain and Spain, by which, in consideration of 100,000 l. the South-Sea company gave up all their future claims to the assiento contract, by virtue of which, that company had supplied the Spanish West-Indies with negroes. In March, 1750, died, universally lamented, his royal highness Frederic prince of Wales. In May 1751, an act passed for regulating the commencement of the year, by which the old stile was abolished, and the new stile established, to the vast conveniency of the subject. This was done by sinking eleven days in September 1752, and thereafter beginning the year on the first of January. In 1753 the famous act passed for preventing clandestine marriages; but whether it is for the benefit of the subject is a point that is still very questionable. The public of England about this time

time sustained an immense loss by the death of Mr. Pelham, who was indisputably the honestest, wisest, the most popular, and therefore the most successful minister England had ever seen.

The barefaced encroachments of the French, who had built forts on our back settlements in America, and the dispositions they made for sending over vast bodies of veteran troops to support those encroachments, produced a wonderful spirit in England, especially after admiral Boscawen was ordered with eleven ships of the line, besides a frigate and two regiments, to sail to the banks of Newfoundland, where he came up with and took two French men of war, the rest of their fleet escaping up the river St. Lawrence, by the straits of Belleisle. No sooner was it known that hostilities were begun, than the public of England poured their money into the government's loan, and orders were issued for making general reprisals in Europe as well as in America; and that all the French ships, whether outward or homeward bound, should be stopped and brought into British ports. These orders were so effectual, that before the end of the year 1755, above 300 of the richest French merchant ships, and above 8000 of their best sailors were brought into British ports. This well-timed measure had such an effect, that the French had neither hands to navigate their merchant-men, nor to man their ships of war, for about two years after near 30,000 French seamen were found to be prisoners in England.

In July 1755, general Braddock, who had been injudiciously sent from England to attack the French and reduce the forts on the Ohio, was defeated and killed, by falling into an ambuscade of the French and Indians near Fort du Quesne; but major general Johnson defeated a body of French near Crown Point, of whom he killed about 1000.

The English at this time could not be said to have any first minister; some great men agreed in nothing but in opposing the measures of the cabinet, which had been undertaken without their consent. The English navy in 1755 consisted of one ship of 110 guns, five of 100 guns each, thirteen of 90, eight of 80, five of 74, twenty-nine of 70, four of 66, one of 64, thirty-three of 60, three of 54, twenty-eight of 50, four of 44, thirty-five of 40, and forty-two of 20; four sloops of war of 18 guns each, two of 16, eleven of 14, thirteen of 12, and one of 10; besides a great number of bomb-ketches, fireships, and tenders; a force sufficient to oppose the united maritime strength of all the powers of Europe. Whilst that of the French, even at the end of this year, and including the ships then upon the stocks, amounted to no more than six ships

ships of 80 guns, twenty-one of 74, one of 72, four of 70, thirty-one of 64, two of 60, six of 50, and thirty-two frigates.

In proportion as the spirits of the public were elevated by those invincible armaments, they were sunk with an account that the French had landed 11,000 men in Minorca, to attack fort St. Philip there, that admiral Byng, who had been sent out with a squadron at least equal to that of the French, had been baffled if not defeated by their admiral Galissoniere, and that at last Minorca was surrendered by general Blakeney. The English were far more alarmed than they ought to have been at those events. The loss of Minorca was more shameful than detrimental to the kingdom, but the public outcry was such, that the king gave up Byng to public justice, and he was shot to death at Portsmouth for cowardice.

It was about this time that Mr. Pitt was placed, as secretary of state, at the head of the administration. He had been long known to be a bold speaker, and he soon proved himself to be as spirited a minister. The miscarriages in the Mediterranean had no consequence but the loss of fort St. Philip, which was more than repaired by the vast success of the English privateers, both in Europe and America. The successes of the English in the East-Indies, under colonel Clive, are almost incredible. He defeated Suraja Dowla, nabob of Bengal, Bahar, and Orixa, and placed Jaffier Ally Cawn in the antient seat of the nabobs of those provinces. Suraja Dowla, who was in the French interest, was a few days after his being defeated taken by the new nabob Jaffier Ally Cawn's son, and put to death. This event laid the foundation of the present amazing extent of riches and territory, which the English now possess in the East Indies.

Mr. Pitt introduced into the cabinet a new system of operations against France, than which nothing could be better calculated to restore the spirits of his countrymen, and to alarm their enemies. Far from dreading an invasion, he planned an expedition for carrying the arms of England into France itself, and the descent was to be made at Rochefort, under general Sir John Mordaunt, who was to command the land troops. Nothing could be more promising than the dispositions for this expedition. It failed on the 8th of September 1757, and admiral Hawke brought both the sea and land forces back on the 6th of October to St. Helen's, without the general making an attempt to land on the coast of France. He was tried and acquitted without the public murmuring, so great an opinion had the people of the minister, who, to do him justice,

did

did not suffer a man or a ship belonging to the English army or navy to lie idle.

The French having attacked the electorate of Hanover with a most powerful army, merely because his Britannic majesty refused to wink at their encroachments in America, the English parliament, in gratitude, voted large supplies of men and money in defence of the electoral dominions. The duke of Cumberland had been sent thither to command an army of observation, but he had been so powerfully pressed by a superior army, that he found himself obliged to lay down his arms, and the French, under the duke of Richelieu, took possession of that electorate, and its capital. At this time, a scarcity next to a famine raged in England; and the Hessian troops, who, with the Hanoverians, had been sent to defend the kingdom from an invasion intended by the French, remained still in England. So many difficulties concurring, in 1758 a treaty of mutual defence was agreed to between his majesty and the king of Prussia; in consequence of which, the parliament voted 670,000 l. to his Prussian majesty; and also voted large sums, amounting in the whole to near two millions a year, for the payment of 50,000 of the troops of Hanover, Hesse-Cassel, Saxe-Gotha, Wolfenbuttel, and Buckeburg. This treaty, which proved afterwards so burdensome to England, was intended to unite the protestant interest in Germany.

George II. with the consent of his Prussian majesty, pretending that the French had violated the convention concluded between them and the duke of Cumberland at Closterseven, ordered his Hanoverian subjects to resume their arms under prince Ferdinand of Brunswick, a Prussian general, who instantly drove them out of Hanover; and the duke of Marlborough, after the English had repeatedly insulted the French coasts, by destroying their stores and shipping at St. Maloes and Cherbourg, marched into Germany, and joined prince Ferdinand with 12,000 British troops, which were afterwards encreased to 25,000. A sharp war ensued. The English every where performed wonders, and according to the accounts published in the London Gazette, they were every where victorious, but nothing decisive followed, and the enemy opened every campaign with advantage. Even the battle of Minden, the most glorious, perhaps, in the English annals, in which about 7000 English defeated 80,000 of the French regular troops in fair battle, contributed nothing to the conclusion of the war, or towards weakening the French in Germany,

The

ENGLAND.

The English bore the expence of the war with chearfulness, and applauded Mr. Pitt's administration, because their glorious successes in every other part of the globe demonstrated that he was in earnest. Admiral Boscawen and general Amherst, in August 1758, reduced and demolished Louisbourg, in North America, which had been restored to the French by the treaty of Aix-la-Chapelle, and was become the scourge of the British trade, and took five or six French ships of the line; Frontenac and Fort du Quesne, in the same quarter, fell also into the hands of the English: acquisitions that far overbalanced a check which the English received at Ticonderago, and the loss of about 300 of the English guards, as they were returning under general Bligh from the coast of France.

The English affairs in the East Indies this year proved equally fortunate, and the lords of the admiralty received letters from thence, with an account that admiral Pocock engaged the French fleet near Fort St. David's on the 29th of March, in which engagement a French man of war, called the Bien Aime, of 74 guns, was so much damaged that they run her on shore. The French had 600 men killed and wounded on this occasion, and the English only 29 killed, and 89 wounded. That on the third of August following, he engaged the French fleet a second time, near Pondicherry; when, after a brisk firing of ten minutes, the French bore away with all the sail they could make, and got safe into the road of Pondicherry. The loss of the French in this engagement was 540 killed and wounded; and that of the English only 147 killed and wounded. And that on the 14th of December following, general Lally, commander of the French army in those parts, marched to besiege Madrass, which was defended by the English colonels Laurence and Draper; and after a brisk cannonade, which lasted till the 16th of February following, the English having received a reinforcement of 600 men, general Lally thought proper to raise the siege and retire with precipitation, leaving behind him forty pieces of cannon.

The year 1759 was introduced by the taking of the island of Goree, on the coast of Africa, by commodore Keppel. Three capital expeditions had been planned for this year in America, and all of them proved successful. One of them was against the French islands in the West Indies, where Guadaloupe was reduced. The second expedition was against Quebec, the capital of the French Canada. The command was given, by the minister's advice, to general Wolfe, a young officer of a truly military genius. Wolfe was opposed with far superior forces by Moncalm, the best and most successful cefsful general the French had. Though the situation of the country which Wolfe was to attack, and the works the French threw up to prevent a defcent of the Englifh, were deemed impregnable, yet Moncalm never relaxed in his vigilance. Wolfe's courage and perfeverance, however, furmounting incredible difficulties, he gained the heights of Abraham, near Quebec, where he fought and defeated the French army, but was himfelf killed; and general Monckton, who was next in command, being wounded, the completion of the French defeat, and the glory of reducing Quebec, was referved for brigadier general (now lord vifcount) Townfhend.

General Amherft, who was the firft Englifh general on command in America, conducted the third expedition. His orders were to reduce all Canada, and to join the army under general Wolfe on the banks of the river St. Laurence. It is to the honour of the minifter that Mr. Amherft in this expedition was fo well provided with every thing that could make it fuccefsful, that there fcarcely appeared any chance for its mifcarriage, and thus the French empire in North America became fubject to Great Britain.

The affairs of the French being now defperate, and their credit ruined, they refolved upon an attempt to retrieve all by an invafion of Great Britain: but, on the 18th of Auguft, 1759, admiral Bofcawen attacked the Toulon fquadron, commanded by M. de la Clue, near the ftraits of Gibraltar, took Le Centaure of 74, Le Temeraire of 74, and Le Modefte of 74 guns; and burnt L'Ocean of 80, and Le Redoubtable of 74 guns. The reft of the fleet, confifting of feven fhips of the line, and three frigates, made their efcape in the night. And on November 20, Sir Edward Hawke defeated the Breft fleet, commanded by admiral Conflans, off the ifland of Dumet, in the bay of Bifcay. The Formidable, a French man of war of 80 guns, was taken; the Thefée of 74, and the Superbe of 70 guns, were funk; and the Soleil Royal of 80, and the Heros of 74, were burnt. Seven or eight French men of war of the line got up the river Villaine, by throwing their guns overboard; and the reft of the fleet, confifting of five fhips of the line, and three frigates, efcaped in the night. The Englifh loft on this occafion, the Effex of 64, and the Refolution of 74 guns. After this engagement, the French gave over all thoughts of their intended invafion of Great-Britain.

In February 1760, Captain Thurot, a French marine adventurer, who had with three floops of war alarmed the coafts of Scotland, and actually made a defcent at Carrickfergus in Ireland, was, on his return from thence, met, defeated, and killed by captain Elliot, who was the commodore of three
fhips

ships, inferior in force to the Frenchman's squadron. Every day's gazette added to the accounts of the successes of the English, and the utter ruin of the French finances, which that government did not blush publicly to avow. In short, Great-Britain now reigned as sole mistress of the main, and had succeeded in every measure that had been projected for her own safety and advantage.

The war in Germany, however, continued still as undecisive as it was expensive, and many in England began to consider it now as foreign to the internal interests of Great-Britain. The French again and again shewed dispositions for treating, and the charges of the war, which began now to amount to little less than eighteen millions sterling yearly, inclined the British ministry to listen to their proposals. A negotiation was accordingly entered upon, which proved abortive, as did many other projects for accommodation, but on the 25th of October 1760, George II. died suddenly, full of years and glory, in the 77th of his age and 33d of his reign, and was succeeded by his grandson, now George III. eldest son to the late prince of Wales.

The memory of George II. is reprehensible on no head but his predilection for his electoral dominions. He never could separate an idea that there was any difference between them and his regal dominions, and he was sometimes ill enough advised to declare so much in his speeches to parliament. We are, however, to remember, that his people gratified him in this partiality, and that he never acted by power or prerogative. He was just rather than generous, and in matters of œconomy, either in his state or his houshold, he was willing to connive at abuses, if they had the sanction of law and custom. By this means those mismanagements about his court were multiplied to an enormous degree, and even under-clerks in offices amassed fortunes ten times greater than their legal salaries or perquisites could raise. He was not very accessible to conversation, and therefore it was no wonder that having left Germany after he had attained to man's estate, he still retained foreign notions both of men and things. In government he had no favourite, for he parted with Sir Robert Walpole's administration with great indifference, and shewed very little concern at the subsequent revolutions among his servants. This quality may be deemed a virtue, as it contributed greatly to the internal quiet of his reign, and prevented the people from loading the king with the faults of his ministers. In his personal disposition he was passionate, but placable, fearless of danger, fond of military parade, and enjoyed the memory of the campaigns in which he served when young.

young. His affections, either public or private, were never known to interfere with the ordinary course of justice; and though his reign was distracted by party, the courts of justice were never better filled than under him: this was a point in which all factions were agreed.

The brighter the national glory was at the time of George II's death, the more arduous was the province of his successor, George III. Born and bred in England, he had no prepossessions but for his native country, and an excellent education gave him true notions of its interests, therefore he was not to be imposed upon by flattering appearances. He knew that neither the finances, nor the population of England could furnish men and money for supplying the necessities of the war, successful as it was, and yet he was obliged to continue it, so as to bring it to a happy period. He chose for his first minister the earl of Bute, whom he had known ever since he began to know himself, and among the first acts of his reign was to convince the public that the death of his predecessor should not relax the operations of the war. Accordingly, in 1761, the island of Belleisle, on the coast of France, surrendered to his majesty's ships and forces under commodore Keppel and general Hodgson; as did the important fortress of Pondicherry in the East Indies to colonel Coote and admiral Stevens. The operations against the French West Indies still continued under general Monckton, lord Rollo, and Sir James Dowglass; and in 1762, the island of Martinico, hitherto deemed impregnable, with the islands of Grenada, Grenadillas, St. Vincent, and others of less note, were subdued by the British arms, with inconceivable rapidity.

By this time the famous family compact among all the branches of the Bourbon family had been concluded, and it was found necessary to declare war against Spain, who having been hitherto no principals in the quarrel, had scandalously abused their neutrality in favour of the French. A respectable armament was fitted out under admiral Pocock, having the earl of Albemarle on board to command the land forces, and the vitals of the Spanish monarchy were struck at, by the reduction of the Havannah, the strongest and most important fort which his catholic majesty held in the West Indies. The capture of the Hermione, a large Spanish register ship, bound from Lima to Cadiz, the cargo of which was valued at a million sterling, preceded the birth of the prince of Wales, and the treasure passed in triumph through Westminster to the Bank, the very hour he was born. The loss of the Havannah, with the ships and treasures there taken from the Spaniards,

niards, was succeeded by the reduction of Manilla in the East Indies, by general Draper and admiral Cornish, with the capture of the Trinidad, reckoned worth three millions of dollars. To counteract those dreadful blows given to the family compact, the French and Spaniards opened their last resource, which was to quarrel with and invade Portugal, which had been always under the peculiar protection of the British arms. Whether this quarrel was real or pretended is not for me to decide. It certainly embarrassed his Britannic majesty, who was obliged to send thither armaments both by sea and land.

The negotiations for peace were now resumed, and the necessity of concluding one was acknowledged by all his majesty's ministers and privy counsellors excepting two. Many difficulties were surmounted, but the romantic and useless war in Germany was continued between the French and English with greater fury than ever. The enemy, however, at last granted such terms as the British ministry thought admissible and adequate to the occasion. A cessation of arms took place in Germany, and in all other quarters, and on the 10th of February 1763, the definitive treaty of peace between his Britannic majesty, the king of France, and the king of Spain, was concluded at Paris, and acceded to by the king of Portugal; March 10, the ratifications were exchanged at Paris. The 22d, the peace was solemnly proclaimed at the usual places in Westminster and London; and the treaty having on the 18th been laid before the parliament, it met with the approbation of a majority of both houses.

By this treaty, the extensive province of Canada, with the islands of Newfoundland, Cape Breton, and St. John, were confirmed to Great Britain; also the two Floridas, containing the whole of the continent of North America, on this side the Mississippi, except the town of New Orleans, with a small district round it, was surrendered to us by France and Spain, in consideration of our restoring to Spain the island of Cuba; and to France the islands of Martinico, Guadaloupe, Mariegalante, and Desirade; and in consideration of our granting the French the two small islands of St. Pierre and Miquelon, on the coast of Newfoundland, and quitting our pretensions to the neutral island of St. Lucia, they yielded to us the islands of Grenada and the Grenadilles, and quitted their pretensions to the neutral islands of St. Vincent, Dominica, and Tobago. In Africa we retained the settlement of Senegal, by which we engross the whole gum trade of that country; but we returned Goree, a small island of little value. The article that relates to the East Indies, was dictated by the directors of the English company,

company, which restores to the French all the places they had at the beginning of the war, on condition that they shall maintain neither forts nor forces in the province of Bengal. And the city of Manilla was restored to the Spaniards; but they granted to us the liberty of cutting logwood in the Bay of Honduras in America. In Europe, likewise, the French restored to us the island of Minorca, and we restored to them the island of Belleisle. In Germany, after six years spent in marches and counter-marches, numerous skirmishes and bloody battles, Great Britain acquired much military fame, but, at the expence of 30 millions sterling! As to the objects of that war, it was agreed that a mutual restitution and oblivion should take place, and each party sit down at the end of the war in the same situation in which they began it. And peace was restored between Portugal and Spain, both sides to be upon the same footing as before the war.

Thus ended a war (such were the effects of unanimity at home) the most brilliant in the British annals. No national prejudices, nor party disputes then existed. The same truly British spirit by which the minister was animated, fired the breast of the soldier and seaman. The nation had then arrived at a pitch of wealth unknown to former ages, and the monied man, pleased with the aspect of the times, confiding in the abilities of the minister, and courage of the people, chearfully opened his purse. The incredible sums of 18, 19, and 22 millions, raised by a few citizens of London, upon a short notice, for the service of the years 1759, 1760, and 1761, was no less astonishing to Europe, than the success which attended the British fleets and armies in every quarter of the globe.

GENEALOGICAL LIST OF THE ROYAL FAMILY OF GREAT BRITAIN.

George William Frederic III. born June 4, 1738; proclaimed king of Great Britain, France and Ireland, and elector of Hanover, October 26, 1760; and married, September 8, 1761, to the princess Sophia Charlotte, of Mecklenburgh Strelitz, born May 16, 1744, crowned September 22, 1761, and now have issue;

1. George Augustus Frederick, prince of Wales, born August 12, 1762.
2. Prince Frederick, born August 16, 1763, elected bishop of Osnaburg February 27, 1764.
3. Prince William Henry, born August 21, 1765.
4. Princess Charlotte, born September 29, 1766.
5. Prince Edward, born November 2, 1767.
6. Princess Augusta Sophia, born November 8, 1768.
7. Princess Elizabeth, born May 22, 1770.

Augusta, daughter to Frederic II. duke of Saxe Gotha, now princess dowager of Wales, was born November 30, 1719.

Her issue by the late prince of Wales:

1. Her royal highness Augusta, born August 11, 1737, married to the hereditary prince of Brunswick Lunenburgh, January 16, 1764.
2. His present majesty.
3. Prince

WALES.

THOUGH this principality is politically included in England, yet as it has distinctions in language, and manners, I have, in conformity with the common custom, assigned it a separate article.

NAME AND LANGUAGE.] The Welch are descendants, according to the best antiquaries, of the Belgic Gauls, who made a settlement in England about fourscore years before the first descent of Julius Cæsar, and thereby obtained the name of Galles or Walles (the G and W being promiscuously used by the antient Britons) that is, Strangers. Their language has a strong affinity with the Celtic or Phœnician, and is highly commended for its pathetic and descriptive powers by those who understand it.

SITUATION, BOUNDARIES, AND EXTENT.] Wales was formerly of greater extent than it is at present, being bounded only by the Severn and the Dee; but after the Saxons had made themselves masters of all the plain country, the Welsh or antient Britons were shut up within more narrow bounds, and obliged gradually to retreat westward. It does not, however, appear that the Saxons ever made any farther conquests in their country, than Monmouthshire and Herefordshire, which are now reckoned part of England. This country is divided into four circuits. See ENGLAND.

CLIMATE, SOIL, AND WATER.] The seasons are pretty much the same as in Scotland and the northern parts of England, and the air is sharp but wholesome. The soil of Wales, especially towards the north, is mountainous, but contains rich vallies, which produce crops of wheat, rye, and other corn. Wales contains many quarries of free-stone and slate, several mines of lead, and abundance of coal-pits. This country is well supplied with wholesome springs, and its chief rivers are the Clywd, the Wheeler, the Dee, the Severn, the Elwy, and the Alen, which furnish Flintshire with great quantities of fish. Holywell contains an excellent mineral water

---

3. Prince William Henry, duke of Gloucester, born November 25, 1743.
4. Prince Henry Frederic, duke of Cumberland, born November 7, 1745.
5. Princess Caroline Matilda, born July 22, 1751; married at St. James's Oct. 1, 1766, by proxy, to Christian VII. king of Denmark.

His late majesty's issue by queen Caroline, now living:
1. Princess Amelia Sophia, born June 10, 1711.
2. Princess Mary, born March 5, 1723-4, married to the prince of Hesse Cassel, July 19, 1740.

water, the virtues of which are attributed by the common people to the female martyr St. Winifred.

MOUNTAINS.] It would be endless to particularize the mountains of this country. Snowdon, in Carnarvonshire, and Plinlimmon, which lies partly in Montgomery, and partly in Cardiganshire, are the most famous; and it was probably by their mountainous situation that the natives made so noble and long a struggle against the Roman, Anglo-Saxon, and Norman powers.

VEGETABLE AND ANIMAL PRODUCTIONS BY SEA AND LAND.} In these particulars Wales differs little from England. Their horses are smaller, but can endure vast fatigue, and their black cattle are small likewise, but excellent beef, and their cows are remarkable for yielding large quantities of milk. Great numbers of goats feed on the mountains. As for the other productions of Wales, see England and Scotland. Some very promising mines of silver, copper, lead, and iron, have been discovered in Wales. The Welch silver may be known by its being stamped with the ostrich feathers, the badge of the prince of Wales.

POPULATION, INHABITANTS, MANNERS, AND CUSTOMS.} The inhabitants of Wales are supposed to amount to about 300,000, and though not in general wealthy, they are provided with all the necessaries, and many of the comforts of life. The land-tax of Wales brought in some years ago about forty-three thousand seven hundred and fifty-two pounds a year. The Welch are, if possible, more jealous of their liberties than the English, and far more irascible, but their anger soon abates, and they are remarkable for fidelity and attachment, especially to their own countrymen. They are very fond of carrying back their pedigrees to the most remote antiquity, but we have no criterion for the authenticity of their manuscripts, some of which they pretend to be coeval with the incarnation. It is however certain, that great part of their antient history, especially the ecclesiastical, is more antient, and better attested than that of the Anglo-Saxons. Wales was formerly famous for its bards and poets, particularly Thaliessin, who lived about the year 450, and whose works were certainly extant at the time of the reformation, and clearly evinces that Geoffrey of Monmouth was not the inventor of the history which makes the present Welch the descendants of the antient Trojans. This poetical genius seems to have influenced the antient Welch with an enthusiasm for independency, for which reason Edward I. is said to have made a general massacre of the bards, an inhumanity which was characteristical of that ambitious prince. The Welch may be called an unmixed people, as may be proved by keeping up their antient hospitality, and a strict adherence to their antient customs and manners. This appears even among gentlemen of fortune, who in other countries commonly follow the stream of fashion. We are not, however, to imagine that many of the nobility and gentry of Wales do not comply with the modes and manner of living in England and France. All the better sort of the Welch speak the English language, though numbers of them understand the Welch.

Religion.] I have already mentioned the massacre of the Welch clergy by Augustine, the popish apostle of England, because they would not conform to the Romish ritual. Wales, after that, fell under the dominion of petty princes, who were often weak and credulous. The Romish clergy insinuated themselves into their favour, by their pretended power of absolving them from crimes, and the Welch, when their antient clergy were extinct, conformed themselves to the religion of Rome. The Welch clergy, in general, are but poorly provided for, and in many of the country congregations they preach both in Welch and English. Their poverty was formerly a vast discouragement to religion and learning, but the measures taken by the society for propagating christian knowledge has effectually removed the reproach of ignorance from the poorer sort of the Welch. In the year 1749 a hundred and forty-two schoolmasters were employed in removing from place to place for the instruction of the inhabitants, and their scholars amounted to 72,264. No people have distinguished themselves more, perhaps, than the Welch have done by acts of national munificence. They print at a vast expence bibles, common-prayers, and other religious books, and distribute them gratis to the poorer sort. Few of their towns are unprovided with a free-school.

The established religion in Wales is that of the church of England, but their common people in many places are so tenacious of their antient customs, that they retain several of the Romish superstitions, and some antient families among them, are still Roman catholics. It is likewise said, that Wales abounds with Romish priests in disguise.

For bishoprics (See England.) We are however to observe, that in former times Wales contained more bishoprics than it does now, and about the time of the conquest of England, the religious foundations there, far exceeded the wealth of all the other parts of the principality.

Learning and learned men.] Wales was the seat of learning when England knew not the use of letters. It suffered, as I have already hinted, an eclipse, by their repeated
massacres

massacres of the clergy and bards. Wickliffism took shelter in Wales, when it was persecuted in England. The Welch and Scotch dispute about the nativity of certain learned men, particularly four of the name of Gildas. Giraldus Cambrensis, whose history was publ.shed by Camden, is thought to have been a Welchman, and Leland mentions several learned men of the same country, who flourished before the reformation. The discovery of the famous king Arthur's, and his wife's burying place, was owing to some lines of Thaliessin, which were repeated before Henry II. of England, by a Welch bard. Since the reformation, Wales has produced several excellent antiquaries and divines. Among the latter was Hugh Broughton and Hugh Holland, who was a Roman catholic, and is mentioned by Fuller in his Worthies. Among the former were several gentlemen of the name of Llhuyd, particularly the author of that invaluable work the Archæologia. Rowland, the learned author of the Mona Antiqua, was likewise a Welchman, as was that great statesman and prelate, the lord keeper Williams, archbishop of York, in the time of king Charles I. After all, I must be of opinion, that the great merit of the Welch learning, in former times, lay in the knowledge of the antiquity, language, and history of their own country. Wales, notwithstanding all that Dr. Hickes, and other antiquaries, have said to the contrary, furnished the Anglo-Saxons with an alphabet. This is clearly demonstrated by Mr. Llhuyd, in his Welch preface to his Archæologia, and is confirmed by various monumental inscriptions of undoubted authority (See Rowland's Mona Antiqua.) I must not however omit, the excellent history of Henry VIII. written by lord Herbert of Cherbury.

With regard to modern Welchmen of learning, they are so numerous, that it would be unjust to particularise any. It is sufficient to say that their clergy are now excellent scholars, and the Welch make as good a figure in literature as any of their neighbours. The Welch Pater-noster is as follows.

Ein Tad, yr hwn wyt yn y nefoedd, sancteiddier dy enw ; deued dy deyrnas ; bydded dy ewyllys ar y ddaear, megis y mae yn y nefoedd : dyro i ni heddyw ein bara beunyddiol ; a maddeu i ni ein dyledion, fel y maddeuwn ni i'n dyledwyr ; ac nac arwain ni i brofedigaeth, eithr gwared ni rhag drwg : canys eiddot ti yw'r deyrnas, a'r gallu, a'r gogoniant, yn oes oesoedd. Amen.

CITIES, TOWNS, FORTS, AND OTHER EDIFICES, PUBLIC AND PRIVATE. } Wales contains no cities or towns that are remarkable, either for populousness or magnificence. Beaumaris is the chief town of Anglesey, and has a harbour for ships. Brecknock trades in cloathing.

cloathing. Cardigan is a large populous town, and lies in the neighbourhood of lead and silver mines. Caermarthen has a large bridge, and is governed by a mayor, two sheriffs and aldermen, who wear scarlet gowns, and other ensigns of state. Pembroke is well inhabited by gentlemen and tradesmen, and part of the county is so fertile, and pleasant, that it is called Little England. As to the other towns of Wales, I shall not mention them. I am however to observe, that Wales, in ancient times, was a far more populous and wealthy country, than it is at present; and though it contains no regular fortifications, yet many of its old castles are so strongly built, and so well situated, that they might be turned into strong forts, by a little expence; witness the vigorous defence which many of them made in the civil wars, between Charles I. and his parliament.

ANTIQUITIES AND CURIOSITIES, NATURAL AND ARTIFICIAL. } Wales abounds in remains of antiquity. Several of its castles are stupendously large; and in some the remains of Roman architecture are plainly discernible. The architecture of others are doubtful, and some appear to be partly British, and partly Roman. In Brecknockshire are some rude sculptures, upon a stone six feet high, called the Maiden-Stone; but the remains of the druidical institutions, and places of worship, are chiefly discernible in the isle of Anglesey, the ancient Mona, mentioned by Tacitus, who describes it as being the chief seminary of the druidical rites and religion. To give a description of the Roman altars, antiquities and utensils, which have been discovered in Wales, would be endless; but future antiquaries may make great discoveries from them. Among the other artificial curiosities, is king Offa's dyke, which is said to have been a boundary between the Saxons, and the Welch or Britons. Cherphilly-castle in Glamorganshire, is said to have been the largest in Great-Britain, excepting Windsor, and the remains of it shew it to have been a most beautiful fabric. One half of a round tower has fallen quite down, but the other over-hangs its basis more than nine feet, and is as great a curiosity as the leaning tower of Pisa in Italy.

Some curious coins of Welch princes are said to be found in the cabinets of the curious, but I do not find that they have been very serviceable in ascertaining the ancient history of the country.

The chief natural curiosities are as follow. At a small village, called Newton in Glamorganshire, is a remarkable spring nigh the sea, which ebbs and flows contrary to the sea. In Merionethshire is Kader Idris, a mountain remarkable for
its

its height, which affords variety of Alpine plants. In Carnarvonshire is the high mountain of Penmanmooer, across the edge of which the public road lies, and occasions no small terror to many travellers; from one hand the impending rock seems ready every minute to crush them to pieces, and the great precipice below, which hangs over the sea, is so hideous, and, till very lately when a wall was raised on the side of the road, full of danger, that one false step was of dismal consequence. Snowdon hill is by triangular measurement 1240 yards perpendicular height.

COMMERCE AND MANUFACTURES.] The Welch are on a footing as to their commerce and manufactures, with many of the western and northern counties of England. Their trade is mostly inland, or with England, into which they import numbers of black cattle. Milfordhaven, which is reckoned the finest in Europe, lies in Pembrokeshire, but the Welch have hitherto reaped no great benefit from it, though of late considerable sums have been granted by parliament for its fortifications. It lies under two capital disadvantages. The first is, that by making it the rendezvous of all the English marine, a bold attempt of an enemy might totally destroy the shipping, however strongly they may be defended by walls and forts. The same objection however lies to every harbour that contains ships of war and merchantmen. The second, and perhaps the chief disadvantage it lies under, is the strong opposition to rendering it the capital harbour of the kingdom, that it must meet with in parliament, from the numerous Cornish and West-country members, the benefit of whose estates must be greatly lessened by the disuse of Plymouth and Portsmouth, and other harbours. The town of Pembroke employs near 200 merchant ships, and its inhabitants carry on an extensive trade. In Brecknockshire are several woollen manufactures, and Wales in general carries on a great coal trade with England and even Ireland.

CONSTITUTION AND GOVERNMENT.] Wales was united, and incorporated with England, in the 27th of Henry VIII. when, by act of parliament, the government of it was modelled according to the English form; all laws, customs, and tenures, contrary to those of England, being abrogated, and the inhabitants admitted to a participation of all the English liberties and privileges, particularly that of sending members to parliament, viz. a knight for every shire, and a burgess for every shire-town, except Merioneth. By the 34th and 35th of the same reign, there were ordained four several circuits, for the administration of justice in the said shires, each of which was to include three shires; so that the chief justice of Chester has

has under his jurisdiction the three several shires of Flint, Denbigh and Montgomery. The shires of Caernarvon, Merioneth, and Anglesey, are under the justices of North Wales. Those of Caermarthen, Pembrokeshire and Cardigan, have also their justices, as have likewise those of Radnor, Brecknock and Glamorgan. By the eighteenth of queen Elizabeth, one other justice-assistant was ordained to the former justices; so that now every one of the said four circuits has two justices, viz. one chief justice, and a second justice-assistant.

REVENUES.] As to the revenues, I have already mentioned the land-tax, and the crown has a certain, though small property, in the product of the silver and lead-mines; but it is said that the revenue accruing to the prince of Wales for his principality, does not exceed 7 or 8000 l. a year.

ARMS.] The arms of the prince of Wales differ from those of England, only by the addition of a label of three points. His cap, or badge of ostrich feathers, was occasioned by a trophy of that kind, which Edward the Black Prince took from the king of Bohemia, when he was killed at the battle of Poictiers, and the motto is *Ich dien*, I serve. St. David, commonly called St. Taffy, is the tutelar saint of the Welch, and his badge is a leek, which is wore on his day, the 1st of March, and for which various reasons have been assigned.

HISTORY.] The ancient history of Wales is uncertain, on account of the number of petty princes who governed it. That they were sovereign and independent, appears from the English history. It was formerly inhabited by three different tribes of the Britons, the Silures, the Dimetæ, and the Ordovices. These people cut out so much work for the Romans, that they do not appear ever to have been entirely subdued, though part of their country, as appears from the ruins of castles, was bridled by garrisons. Though the Saxons, as I have already observed, conquered the counties of Monmouth and Hereford, yet they never penetrated farther, and the Welch remained an independent people, governed by their own princes, and their own laws. About the year 870, Roderic, king of Wales, divided his dominions among his three sons; and the names of these divisions were, Deemetia, or South Wales; Povesia, or Powis-Land; and Venedotia, or North Wales. This division gave a mortal blow to the independency of Wales. About the year 1112, Henry I. of England planted a colony of Flemings on the frontiers of Wales, to serve as a barrier to England, none of the Welch princes being powerful enough to oppose them. They made, however, many vigorous brave attempts against the Norman kings of England, to maintain their liberties, and even the

English

English historians admit the injustice of their claims. In 1237, the crown of England was first supplied with a handle for the future conquest of Wales; their old and infirm prince Llewellin, in order to be safe from the persecutions of his undutiful son Griffyn, having put himself under subjection and homage to king Henry III.

But no capitulation could satisfy the ambition of Edward I. who resolved to annex Wales to the crown of England; and Llewellin, prince of Wales, disdaining the subjection to which old Llewellin had submitted, Edward raised an irresistible army at a prodigious expence, with which he penetrated as far as Flint, and taking possession of the isle of Anglesey, he drove the Welch to the mountains of Snowdon, and obliged them to submit to pay a tribute. The Welch however made several efforts under young Llewellin, but at last, in 1285, he was killed in battle. He was succeeded by his brother David, the last independent prince of Wales, who, falling into Edward's hands through treachery, was by him most barbarously and unjustly hanged, and Edward, from that time, pretended that Wales was annexed to his crown of England. It was about this time, probably, that Edward perpetrated the inhuman massacre of the Welch bards. Perceiving that his cruelty was not sufficient to complete his conquest, he sent his queen to be delivered in Carnarvon castle, that the Welch, having a prince born among themselves, might the more readily recognize his authority. This prince was the unhappy Edward II. and from him the title of prince of Wales has always descended to the eldest sons of the English kings. The history of Wales and England becomes now the same. It is proper, however, to observe, that the kings of England have always found it their interest to soothe the Welch, with particular marks of their regard. Their eldest sons not only held the titular dignity, but actually kept a court at Ludlow, and a regular council with a president was named by the crown, for the administration of all the affairs of the principality. This was thought so necessary a piece of policy, that when Henry VIII. had no son, his daughter Mary was created princess of Wales.

IRELAND.

SITUATION, BOUNDARIES, AND EXTENT.

THE island of Ireland is situated on the west side of England, between 6 and 10 degrees west longitude, and between 51 and 55 degrees 20 minutes north latitude, or between the middle parallel of the eighth clime, where the longest day is 16¼ hours, and the 24th parallel, or the end of the tenth clime, where the longest day is 17½ hours.

The extent, or superficial content of this kingdom is, from the nearest computation and survey, found to be in length 285 miles from Fairhead north, to Missenhead south; and from the east part of Down, to the west part of Mayo, its greatest breadth, 160 miles, and to contain 11,067,712 Irish plantation acres, which makes 17,927,864 acres of English statute measure, and is held to bear proportion to England and Wales as 18 to 30. Mr. Templeman, who makes the length 275, and the breadth 159 miles, gives it an area of 27,457 square miles. From the east part of Wexford to St. David's in Wales, it is reckoned 45 miles, but the passage between Donaghadee and Portpatrick in Scotland is little more than twenty miles.

NAME AND DIVISIONS, ANCIENT AND MODERN. } More conjectures as to the Latin (Hibernia) Irish (Erin) as well as the English name of this island, have been formed than the subject deserves. It probably takes it rise from a Phœnician or Gallic term, signifying the farthest habitation westward.

It is pretty extraordinary, that even modern authors are not agreed as to the divisions of Ireland; some dividing it into five circuits, and some into four provinces, those of Leinster, Ulster, Connaught, and Munster. I shall follow the last division, as being the most common, and likewise the most antient.

	Counties.	Chief Towns.
Leinster, 12 counties.	Dublin	Dublin
	Louth	Drogheda
	Wicklow	Wicklow
	Wexford	Wexford
	Longford	Longford
	East Meath	Trim
	West Meath	Mullinger
	King's County	Phillipstown
	Queen's County	Maryborough
	Kilkenny	Kilkenny
	Kildare	Kildare
	Carlow	Carlow

IRELAND. 457

	Counties.	Chief Towns.
Ulster, 9 Counties.	Down	Down
	Armagh	Charlemont
	Monaghan	Monaghan
	Cavan	Cavan
	Antrim	Carrickfergus
	Londonderry	Derry
	Tyrone	Omagh
	Fermanagh	Enniskillen
	Donegall	Donegall
Connaught, 6 Count.	Leitrim	Leitrim
	Roscommon	Roscommon
	Mayo	Ballinrobe
	Sligo	Sligo
	Galway	Galway
	Clare	Ennis
Munster, 5 Counties.	Cork	Cork
	Kerry	Tralee
	Limerick	Limerick
	Tipperary	Clonmel
	Waterford	Waterford

CLIMATE, SEASONS, AND SOIL. } The climate of Ireland differs little from that of England, with which it would almost perfectly agree, were the soil equally improved. Uncultivated swamps, bogs, and forests, and uninhabited banks of rivers, naturally produce fogs and an unwholsome thickness of air, as is the case with some parts of England itself; but upon the whole the air of the cultivated part of Ireland is as mild and salubrious, and as friendly to human nature as that of England; some have thought that it is even more so.

The soil of Ireland in general is fruitful, perhaps beyond that of England itself, when properly cultivated. Pasturage, tillage, and meadow ground abound in this kingdom; but till of late tillage was too much discountenanced, though the ground is excellent for the culture of all grains; and in some of the northern parts of the kingdom abundance of hemp and flax are raised, a cultivation of infinite advantage to the linen manufacture. Ireland rears vast numbers of black cattle and sheep. The Irish wool is excellent, but many have thought that the prohibition of exporting it to any other nation but England, is of detriment to both kingdoms, because it encourages the inhabitants to smuggle it into France. The prodigious, and, indeed, incredible supplies of salt provisions (fish excepted)

excepted) shipped at Cork, and carried to all parts of the world, are proofs scarcely to be exhibited in any other country, of the natural fertility of the Irish soil. As to the seasons of Ireland, they differ little from those of Great Britain, in the same latitude. I must not here forget that Ireland is remarkable for breeding and nourishing no venomous creatures.

RIVERS, BAYS, HARBOURS, AND LAKES.} Nor has nature been less favourable to Ireland in the numerous rivers, enchanting lakes, spacious bays, commodious havens, harbours and creeks, which enrich and beautify this country. The Shannon issues from Lough Allen, in the county of Leitrim, serves as a boundary between Connaught and the three other provinces, and after a course of 150 miles, forming in its progress many beautiful lakes, it falls into the Atlantic ocean, between Kerry-point and Loophead, where it is nine miles broad. The navigation of this river is interrupted by a ridge of rocks spreading quite across it, south of Killaloe, but this might be remedied by a short canal, at the expence of 10, or 12,000 l. and communications might also be made with other rivers, to the great benefit of the nation. The Ban falls into the ocean near Colerain, the Boyne falls into St. George's channel at Drogheda, as does the Liffey at the bay of Dublin, and is only remarkable for watering that capital, where it forms a spacious harbour. The Barrow, the Noer, and the Suir, water the south part of the kingdom, and after uniting their streams below Ross, they fall into the channel at Waterford haven.

But the bays, havens, harbours, and creeks, which every where indent the coast, form the chief glory of Ireland, and render that country, beyond any other in Europe, the best fitted for foreign commerce. The most considerable are those of Carrickfergus, Strangford, Dundrum, Carlingford, Dundalk, Dublin, Waterford, Dungarvan, Cork, Kinsale, Baltimore, Glandore, Dunmanus, Bantry, Kilmare, Dingle, Shannon-mouth, Galway, Sligoe, Donegall, Killebegs, Lough-Swilly, and Lough-Foyle.

Ireland contains a vast number of lakes, or, as they were formerly called, loughs, particularly in the provinces of Ulster and Connaught. Many of them produce large quantities of fine fish; and the great lake Neagh, between the counties of Antrim, Down and Armagh, is remarkable for its petrifying quality. Though those loughs in the main have but few properties that are not in common with the like bodies of water in other countries, yet they have given rise to many traditionary accounts among the natives, which disfigure and disgrace

disgrace their true history, and even modern geographers have been more copious on that head than either truth or the subject can admit of. The Irish are so fond of loughs, that, like the Scots, they often give that term to inlets of the sea.

INLAND NAVIGATION.] The inland navigation of Ireland is very improveable, as appears from the canals that have lately been cut through different parts of the kingdom, one in particular (See the Map) reaching an extent of 60 miles, between the Shannon and the Liffey at Dublin, which opens a communication from the Channel to the Atlantic ocean. In surveying the grounds for this canal, however, it was found necessary to carry it through a bog 24 miles over, which, from the spungy nature of that soil, became a work of incredible labour and expence, in strengthening the sides, and other works, to prevent falling in.

MOUNTAINS.] The Irish language has been more happy in distinguishing the size of mountains than perhaps any other. A knock signifies a low hill, unconnected with any other eminence; a slieve marks a craggy high mountain, gradually ascending and continued in several ridges; a beinn or bin signifies a pinnacle or mountain of the first magnitude, ending in a sharp or abrupt precipice. The two last are often seen and compounded together in one and the same range. Ireland, however, when compared with some other countries, is far from being mountainous. The mountains of Mourne and Ifeah, in the county of Down, are reckoned among some of the highest in the kingdom, of which Slieu-Denard has been calculated at a perpendicular heighth of 1056 yards. Many other mountains are found in Ireland, but they contain little or nothing particular, if we except the fabulous histories that are annexed to some of them. Some of these mountains contain in their bowels beds of mines, minerals, coals, quarries of stone, slate and marble, with veins of iron, lead, and copper.

FORESTS.] The chief forests in Ireland lie in Leinster, the King's and Queen's counties, and those of Wexford and Carlow. In Ulster there are great forests, and in the county of Donegall and in the north part of Tyrone; also in the county of Fermanagh, along Loughlin Earne, and in the north part of the county of Down, wherein is some good timber, and the oak is esteemed as good as any of the English growth, and as fit for ship-building.

METALS AND MINERALS.] The mines of Ireland are late discoveries. Several contain silver and lead, and it is said that 30 pounds of their lead ore produce a pound of silver; but the richest silver mine is at Wicklow. A copper and lead mine

have

have been discovered at Tipperary, as likewise iron ore, and excellent free-stone for building. Some of the Irish marble quarries contain a kind of porphyry, being red striped with white. Quarries of fine slate are found in most counties. The coals that are dug at Kilkenny emit very little smoke, and it contains a christalline stream which has no sediment. Those peculiarities, with the serenity of the air in that place, have given rise to the well known proverb, That Kilkenny contains fire without smoke, water without mud, and air without fog.

VEGETABLE AND ANIMAL PRODUC-TIONS, BY SEA AND LAND. } There is little that falls under this head that is peculiar to Ireland, her productions being much the same as in England and Scotland. Ireland affords excellent turf and moss, which are of vast service for firing, where wood and coals are scarce. A few wolves were formerly found in Ireland, but they are now almost exterminated by their wolf dogs, which are much larger than mastiffs, shaped like greyhounds, yet as gentle and governable as spaniels. What I have already observed about the Irish exportation of salt provisions, sufficiently evinces the prodigious numbers of hogs, sheep, as well as black cattle, bred in that kingdom. Rabbits are said to be more plentiful there than in England. The fish that are caught upon the coasts of Ireland are likewise in greater plenty than on those of England, and some of them larger and more excellent in their kind.

POPULATION, INHABITANTS, MAN-NERS, CUSTOMS, AND DIVERSIONS. } Ireland is said to contain two millions and a half of inhabitants; but I suspect that the calculation is over-charged by near half a million. As it is of great consequence to ascertain as near as possible the numbers of inhabitants of Ireland of both religions, we shall give them according to the best accounts, as they stood in the four provinces in 1733.

	Protestant families.		Popish families.
In Ulster	—	62,620	— — 38,459
Leinster	—	25,238	— — 92,424
Munster	—	13,337	— — 106,407
Connaught	—	4,299	— — 44,133
	Total	105,494	Total 281,423

Which, at five to each family in the country, and ten for Dublin, and seven for Cork city, makes in all 2,015,229 souls. I am apt to think, when we consider the waste of war by sea and

and land, and the vast emigrations of the Irish to Britain, the British colonies, and other nations; that the above calculation may nearly serve for the present times, though the balance of number is certainly greatly risen on the side of protestantism; and in some late debates in the Irish parliament it has been asserted that the number of inhabitants of Ireland amount to three millions.

The old Irish, or, as they are termed by the protestants, the *mere Irish*, are generally represented as an ignorant, uncivilized, and blundering sort of people. Impatient of abuse, and injury, they are implacable and violent in all their affections, but quick of apprehension, courteous to strangers, and patient of hardships. Though in these respects there is, perhaps, little difference between them and the more uninformed part of their neighbours, yet their barbarisms are more easy to be accounted for from accidental than natural causes. By far the greatest number of them are papists, and it is the interest of their priests, who govern them with an absolute sway, to keep them in the most profound ignorance. They also lie under many legal disabilities, which in their own country discourages the exertion both of their mental and bodily faculties; but when employed in the service of foreign princes, they are distinguished for intrepidity, courage, and fidelity. Many of their surnames have an *O*, or *Mac*, placed before them, which signify grandson and son: formerly the *O* was used by their chiefs only, or such as piqued themselves upon the antiquity of their families. Their music is the bagpipe, but their tunes are generally of a melancholy strain; though some of the latest airs are lively, and when sung by an Irishman, extremely diverting. The old Irish is generally spoken in the interior parts of the kingdom, where some of the old uncouth customs still prevail, particularly their funeral howlings; but this custom may be traced in many countries of the continent. Their custom of placing a dead corpse before their doors, laid out upon tables, having a plate upon the body to excite the charity of passengers, is practised even in the skirts of Dublin, which one could wish to see abolished. And their convivial meetings on Sunday afternoon, dancing to the bagpipe, but more often quarrelling among themselves, is offensive to every stranger. But, as we have already observed, these customs are chiefly confined to the more unpolished provinces of the kingdom, particularly Connaught; the common people there having the least sense of law and government of any in Ireland, except their tyrannical landlords or leaseholders, who squeeze the poor without mercy. The common Irish, in their manner of living, seem to resemble the antient Britons, as described by Roman authors, or the present Indian inhabitants of America. Mean huts or cabbins built of clay and straw, partitioned in the middle by a wall of the same materials, serve the double purposes of accommodating the family, who live and sleep promiscuously, having their fires of turf in the middle of the floor, with an opening through the roof for a chimney; the other being occupied by a cow, or such pieces of furniture as are not in immediate use.

Their wealth consists of a cow, sometimes a horse, some poultry, and a spot for potatoes. Coarse bread, potatoes, eggs, milk, and sometimes fish, constitute their food. For however plentifully the fields may be stocked with cattle, these poor natives seldom taste butcher's meat of any kind. Their children, plump, robust, and hearty, scarcely know the use of cloaths, and are not ashamed to gaze upon strangers, or make their appearance upon the roads in that primitive manner.

In this idle and deplorable state, many thousands are in a manner lost to the community and to themselves, who, if they had an equal chance with their neighbours of being instructed in the real principles of Christianity, inured and incouraged to industry and labour, and obedience to their sovereign, would add considerable strength to government. The Spaniards and French, particularly the latter, have not failed to avail themselves of the uncomfortable situation of the Irish at home, by alluring them to enter their service, and in this they have hitherto been assisted by priests and jesuits, whose interest it is to infuse into the minds of their credulous disciples an aversion to the British government; but we have now the pleasing prospect of a happy reformation among these people, from the numerous English protestant working schools, lately established over the kingdom, which institution will undoubtedly strike deeper at the root of popery than all the endeavours of the British monarchs to reduce them.

The descendants of the English and Scots, since the conquest of Ireland by Henry II. though not the most numerous, form the wealthiest part of the nation. Of these are most of the nobility, gentry, and principal traders, who inhabit the eastern and northern coasts, where most of the trade of Ireland is carried on, especially Belfast, Londonderry, and other parts of the province of Ulster, which, though the poorest soil, is, next to Dublin, and its neighbourhood, by far the best cultivated and most flourishing part of the kingdom. Here a colony of Scots, in the reign of James I. and other presbyterians, who fled from persecution in that country in succeeding reigns, planted themselves, and established that

great

great staple of Irish wealth the linen manufactory, which they have since carried on and brought to the utmost perfection. From this short review it appears that the present inhabitants are composed of three distinct classes of people; the old Irish, poor, ignorant, and depressed, who inhabit, or rather exist upon the interior and western parts; the descendants of the English, who inhabit Dublin, Waterford, and Cork, and who gave a new appearance to the whole coast facing England, by the introduction of arts, commerce, science, and more liberal and cultivated ideas of the true God and primitive Christianity. Thirdly, as I have already observed, emigrants from Scotland in the northern provinces, who like the others are so zealously attached to their own religion and manner of living, that it will require some ages before the inhabitants of Ireland are so thoroughly consolidated and blended as to become one people. The gentry and better sort of the Irish nation in general differ little in language, dress, manners and customs, from those of the same rank in Great Britain, whom they imitate. Their hospitality is well known, but in this they are sometimes suspected of more ostentation than real friendship.

RELIGION.] The established religion and ecclesiastical discipline of Ireland is the same with that of England. I have already observed, that among the bulk of the people, in the most uncultivated parts, popery, and that too of the most absurd, illiberal kind, is prevalent. The Irish papists still retain their nominal bishops and dignitaries, who subsist on the voluntary contributions of their votaries. But even the blind submission of the latter to their clergy, does not prevent protestantism from making a very rapid progress there in towns and communities. How far it may be the interest of England that some kind of balance between the two religions should be kept up, I shall not here enquire.

Ireland contains at least as many sectaries as England, particularly presbyterians, anabaptists, quakers, and methodists, who are all of them connived at and tolerated. Great efforts have been made ever since the days of James I. in erecting free-schools for civilizing and converting the Irish papists to protestantism. The institution of the incorporated society for promoting English protestant working-schools, though of no older date than 1717, has been amazingly successful, as have many institutions of the same kind, in introducing industry and knowledge among the Irish; and no country in the world can shew greater public spirited efforts than have been made by the government of Ireland, since that time, for these purposes.

ARCH-

464 IRELAND.

ARCHBISHOPRICS AND BISHOPRICS.] The archbishoprics are four, Armagh, Cashel, Dublin, and Tuam.

The bishops are eighteen, viz. Clogher, Clonfert, Cloyne, Cork, Derry, Down, Drumore, Elphin, Kildare, Killaloe, Leighlin, Limeric, Meath, Ossory, Raphoe, and Waterford.

LANGUAGE.] The language of the Irish is fundamentally the same with the British and Welch, and a dialect of the Celtic, which is made use of by the Scotch Highlanders, opposite the Irish coasts. It is, however, in a great measure defaced by provincial alterations, but not so altered as to render the Irish, Welch, and Highlanders, unintelligible to each other. The usage of the Irish language occasions among the common people, who speak both that and the English, a disagreeable tone in speaking, which diffuses itself among the vulgar in general, and even among the better sort who do not understand Irish. It is probable, however, that a few ages hence the latter will be accounted among the dead languages.

LEARNING AND LEARNED MEN.] If we are to believe the fabulous accounts of Ireland, learning flourished there while she was dormant in all the other parts of the globe. The truth is, that the Irish writers, in several branches of learning, arts, and sciences, are equal to those of their neighbours. Archbishop Usher does honour to literature itself. Dean Swift, who was a native of Ireland, has perhaps never been equalled in the walks of wit, humour, and satire. The sprightliness of Farquhar's wit is well known to all lovers of the drama : and to particularize other Irish writers of learning and genius, many of whom are living at this day, would far exceed my bounds.

UNIVERSITIES.] Ireland contains but one university (if a college can be called such) which is that of Dublin, founded by queen Elizabeth, under the title of the College of the holy and undivided Trinity, near Dublin, with a power of conferring degrees of batchelors, masters, and doctors, in all the arts and faculties. At present it consists of a provost, seven senior, thirteen junior fellows, and seventy scholars of the house, who have maintenance upon the foundation. The visitors are the chancellor or vice chancellor, and the archbishop of Dublin.

ANTIQUITIES AND CURIOSITIES, } I have already mentioned the wolf-dogs
    NATURAL AND ARTIFICIAL.

in Ireland, and her exemption from all venomous animals. The Irish gos-hawks and gerfalcons are celebrated for their shape and beauty. The moose-deer is thought to have been formerly a native of this island, their horns being sometimes dug up of so great a size, that one pair has been found near

eleven

eleven feet from the tip of the right horn to the tip of the left; but the greatest natural curiosity in Ireland is the Giant's Causeway in the county of Antrim, about eight miles from Colerain, which is thus described by Dr. Pococke, late bishop of Ossory, a celebrated traveller and antiquary. He says, "that he measured the most westerly point at high water, to the distance of 360 feet from the cliff; but was told, that at low water it extended 60 feet further upon a descent, till it was lost in the sea. Upon measuring the eastern point, he found it 540 feet from the cliff; and saw as much more of it as of the other, where it winds to the east, and is like that lost in the water.

"The causeway is composed of pillars all of angular shapes, from three sides to eight. The eastern point, where it joins the rock, terminates in a perpendicular cliff, formed by the upright sides of the pillars, some of which are thirty-three feet four inches high. Each pillar consists of several joints or stones, lying one upon another, from six inches to about a foot in thickness; and what is very surprizing, some of these joints are so convex, that their prominences are nearly quarters of spheres, round each of which is a ledge, which holds them together with the greatest firmness, every stone being concave on the other side, and fitting in the exactest manner the convexity of the upper part of that beneath it. The pillars are from one to two feet in diameter, and generally consist of about forty joints, most of which separate very easily, and one may walk along upon the tops of the pillars as far as to the edge of the water.

"But this is not the most singular part of this extraordinary curiosity, the cliffs themselves being still more surprizing. From the bottom, which is of black stone, to the height of about sixty feet, they are divided at equal distances by stripes of a reddish stone, that resembles a cement about four inches in thickness; upon this there is another stratum of the same black stone, with a stratum five inches thick of the red. Over this is another stratum ten feet thick divided in the same manner; then a stratum of the red stone twenty feet deep, and above that a stratum of upright pillars; above these pillars lies another stratum of black stone, twenty feet high; and, above this again, another stratum of upright pillars, rising in some places to the tops of the cliffs, in others not so high, and in others again above it, where they are called the chimneys. The face of these cliffs extends about three English miles."

The cavities, the romantic prospects, cataracts, and other pleasing and uncommon natural objects to be met with in Ireland, are too numerous to be called rarities, and several pamphlets have been employed in describing them. As to the artificial

artificial rarities in Ireland, the chief are the round Pharos, or stone towers, found upon the coasts, and supposed to be built by the Danes and Norwegians, who made use of them as spy-towers or barbicans, light-houses or beacons.

CITIES, TOWNS, FORTS, AND OTHER EDIFICES, PUBLIC AND PRIVATE. } Dublin, the capital of Ireland, is in magnitude and the number of inhabitants, the second city in the British dominions; much about the size of Stockholm, Copenhagen, Berlin, and Marseilles, and is supposed to contain near 200,000 inhabitants. It is situated 270 miles north-west of London, and sixty miles west from Holyhead, in North Wales, the usual station of the passage vessels between Great Britain and Ireland. Dublin stands about seven miles from the sea, at the bottom of a large and spacious bay, to which it gaves name, upon the river Liffey, which divides it almost into two equal parts, and is banked in through the whole length of the city, on both sides, which form spacious quays, where vessels below the first bridge load and unload before the merchants doors and warehouses. A stranger upon entering the bay of Dublin, which is about seven miles broad, and in stormy weather extremely dangerous, is agreeably surprized with the beautiful prospect on each side, and the distant view of Wicklow mountains; but Dublin, from its low situation, makes no great appearance. The increase of Dublin, within twenty years last past, is incredible, and it is generally supposed that 4000 houses have been added to the city and suburbs since the reign of queen Anne. This city in its appearance bears a near resemblance to London. The houses are of brick; the old streets are narrow and mean, but the new streets are more elegant and better planned than those of the metropolis of Great Britain. Sackville street, which is sometimes called the Mall, is particularly noble. The houses are elegant, lofty, and uniformly built, and a gravel walk runs through the whole at an equal distance from the sides.

The river Liffey, though navigable for sea vessels as far as the customhouse, or centre of the city, is but small, when compared to the Thames at London. Over it are two handsome bridges, lately built of stone, in imitation of that at Westminster, and three others that have little to recommend them. Hitherto the centre of Dublin towards the customhouse was crouded and inconvenient for commercial purposes; but of late a new street has been opened, leading from Essex bridge to the castle, where the lord lieutenant resides. A new exchange is building, the first stone of which was laid by lord Townshend, the then lord lieutenant, and several other useful undertakings and embellishments are in agitation.

IRELAND.

The barracks are pleasantly situated on an eminence near the river. They consist of four large courts, in which are generally quartered four battalions of foot, and one regiment of horse; from hence the castle and city guards are relieved daily. They are said to be the largest and compleatest building of the kind in Europe.

The linen hall was erected at the public expence, and opened in the year 1728, for the reception of such linen cloths as were brought to Dublin for sale, for which there are convenient apartments. It is entirely under the direction of the trustees for the encouragement of the linen manufactory of Ireland, who are composed of the lord chancellor, the primate, the archbishop of Dublin, and the principal part of the nobility and gentry. This national institution is productive of great advantages, by preventing many frauds which otherwise would be committed in a capital branch of trade, by which many thousands are employed, and the kingdom greatly enriched.

Stevens Green is a most extensive square, being one mile in circumference. It is partly laid out in gravel walks, like St. James's park, with trees on each side, in which may be seen, in fine weather, a resort of as much beauty, gaiety, and finery, as at any of the public places in England. Many of the houses round the green are very stately, but a want of uniformity is observable throughout the whole. Ample amends will be made for this defect by another spacious square near Stevens Green, now laid out and partly built. The houses being lofty, uniform, and carried on with stone as far as the first floor, will give the whole an air of magnificence, not exceeded by any thing of the kind in Britain, if we except Bath.

The front of Trinity college, extending above 300 feet, is built of Portland stone in the finest taste.

The parliament house was begun in 1729, and finished in 1739, at the expence of 40,000l. This superb pile is in general of the Ionic order, and is at this day justly accounted one of the foremost architectural beauties. The portico in particular is, perhaps, without parallel; the internal parts have also many beauties, and the manner in which the building is lighted, has been much admired. But one of the greatest and most laudable undertakings that this age can boast of, is the building a stone wall about the breadth of a moderate street, a proportionable height, and three miles in length, to confine the channel of the bay, and to shelter vessels in stormy weather.

The civil government of Dublin is by a lord mayor, &c. the same as in London. Every third year, the lord mayor, and the 24 companies, by virtue of an old charter, are obliged to perambulate the city, and it's liberties, which they call riding the Franchifes. Upon this occafion the citizens vie with each other, in fhow and oftentation, which is fometimes productive of difagreeable confequences to many of their families. In Dublin are two large theatres, that are generally well filled, and which ferve as a kind of nurfery to thofe in London. In this city are 18 parifh churches, 8 chapels, 3 churches for French, and 1 for Dutch proteftants, 7 prefbyterian meeting-houfes, 1 for methodifts, 2 for quakers, and 16 Roman catholic chapels. A royal hofpital, like that at Chelfea, for invalids; a lying-in hofpital, with gardens, built and laid out in the fineft tafte; an hofpital for lunaticks, built by the famous dean Swift, who himfelf died a lunatic; and fundry other hofpitals for patients of every kind. Some of the churches have been lately rebuilt, and others are rebuilding in a more elegant manner. And indeed whatever way a ftranger turns himfelf in this city, he will perceive a fpirit of elegance and magnificence; and if he extends his view over the whole kingdom, he will conclude that works of ornament and public utility in Ireland, keep pace with thofe erecting, great as they are, over the different parts of Great Britain. For it muft be acknowledged that no nation in Europe, comparatively fpeaking, has expended fuch fums as the grants of the Irifh parliament, which has been, and continues to be, the life and foul of whatever is carried on; witnefs the many noble erections, churches, hofpitals, bridges; the forming of harbours, public roads, canals, and other public and private undertakings.

It has, however, been matter of furprize, that with all this fpirit of national improvement, few or no good inns are to be met with in Ireland. In the capital, which may be claffed among the fecond order of cities of Europe, there is not one inn that deferves that name. This may, in fome meafure, be accounted for by the long, and fometimes dangerous paffage from Chefter and Holyhead to Ireland, which prevents the gentry of England, with their families, from vifiting that ifland; but as it is now propofed to make turnpike roads to Portpatric in Scotland, from whence the paffage is fhort and fafe, the roads of Ireland may by this means become more frequented, efpecially when the rural beauties of that kingdom are more generally known. For though in England, France, and Italy, a traveller meets with views the moft luxuriant and rich, he is fometimes cloyed with a famenefs that runs through the whole: but in thofe countries of North Britain and Ireland, the rugged mountains, whofe tops look down upon the clouds, the extenfive lakes, enriched with bufhy iflands, the cavities, glens, cataracts, the numerous feathered creation, hopping

hopping from cliff to cliff, and other pleasing and uncommon natural objects, that frequently present themselves in various forms and shapes, have a wonderful effect upon the imagination, and are pleasing to the fancy of every admirer of nature, however rough or unadorned with artificial beauties.

Cork is deservedly reckoned the second city in Ireland, in magnitude, riches, and commerce. It lies 129 miles southwest of Dublin, and contains above 8100 houses, inhabited chiefly by protestants. Its haven is deep, and well sheltered from all winds; but small vessels only come up to its quay, and stand about seven miles up the river Lee. This is the chief port of merchants in the kingdom; and there is, perhaps, more beef, tallow, and butter shipped off here, than in all the other ports of Ireland put together. Hence there is a great resort of ships to this port, particularly of those bound from Great Britain to Jamaica, Barbadoes, and all the Caribbee islands, which put in here to victual and complete their lading. Kinsale is a populous and strong town, with an excellent harbour, and considerable commerce and shipping: and it is, moreover, occasionally a station for the navy royal; for which end this port is furnished with proper naval officers and storekeepers. Waterford is reckoned next to Cork for riches and shipping. It is commanded by Duncannon Fort, and on the west side of the town is a citadel. Limeric is a handsome, populous, commercial, strong city, and lies on both sides the Shannon.

Belfast, a large seaport and trading town at the mouth of the Lagen water, where it falls into Carrickfergus bay. Downpatrick has a flourishing linen manufacture. Carrickfergus (or Knockfergus) is by some deemed the capital town of the province, has a good harbour and castle, but little commerce. Derry (or Londonderry, as it is most usually called) stands on Lough-Foyl, is a strong little city, having some linen manufactures, with some commerce and shipping. All this extreme north part of Ireland is situated so near to Scotland, that they are in sight of each others coasts. Donegal, the county-town of the same name (otherwise called the county of Tyrconnel) is a place of some trade; as is likewise Enniskilling. All which last mentioned places, and many more (though less considerable ones) are chiefly, and most industriously, employed in the manufacturing of linen and linen thread, to the great benefit of the whole kingdom, which, by its vast annual exportations of linen into England, is enabled to pay for the great annual importations from England into Ireland; and likewise to render the money constantly drawn from Ireland into England by her absentees, less grievous to her.

Though Ireland contains no strong places, according to the modern improvements in fortification, yet it has several forts and garrisons, that serve as comfortable sinecures to military officers. The chief are Londonderry and Culmore fort, Cork, Limeric, Kinsale, Duncannon, Ross-Castle, Dublin, Charlemont, Galway, Carricfergus, Maryborough, and Athlone. Each of these forts is furnished with deputy governors, under various denominations, who have pecuniary provisions from the government.

It cannot be pretended that Ireland is as yet furnished with many public edifices, that can compare with those that are to be found in countries where sovereigns and their courts reside, but it has many elegant public buildings, which do honour to the taste and public spirit of the inhabitants. The parliament house, castle, Essex-bridge, and several edifices about Dublin, already mentioned, are magnificent, and elegant pieces of architecture, and many noble Gothic churches, and other buildings, are to be seen in Ireland. The Irish nobility, and gentry of fortune, now vie with those of England in the magnificent structure of their houses, and the elegance of their ornaments; but it would be unjust, where there are so many equal in taste and magnificence, to particularize any. In speaking of the public buildings of this kingdom, I must not forget the numerous barracks, where the soldiers are lodged, equally to the ease and conveniency of the inhabitants.

COMMERCE AND MANUFACTURES.] What I have said of England under this head, is in a great measure applicable to Ireland. Her chief exports consist of linen-cloth, yarn, lawns, and cambrics, which are encouraged by the English government. Wool and bay yarn are by law allowed to be exported to England only, but great quantities of both are smuggled into other countries. The other exports are horses and black cattle, beef, pork, green hides, some tanned leather, calf skins dried, tallow, butter, candles, cheese, ox and cow-horns, ox-hair, horse-hair, lead, in no great proportion, copper-ore, herrings, dried fish, rabbit-skins, and furr, otter-skins, goat-skins, salmon, and a few other particulars.

The Irish in general complain of the vast disadvantages under which their country lies, from that prohibition which does not suffer them to cultivate to the full their woollen and iron manufactures, or to make the best of their natural situation and harbours. They even complain that the benefits of their linen manufacture are now greatly abridged by the vast progress made in the same by the Scots, and repeated attempts have been made to prove that their commercial discouragements are detrimental to England herself, and beneficial to her

her natural enemies. Whatever truth may be in this complaint, it is certain that the Irish have carried their inland manufactures, even those of luxury, to an amazing height, and that their lords lieutenants, and their court, have of late encouraged them by their examples, and, while they are in that government, making use of no other.

PUBLIC TRADING COMPANIES.] Of these I know none in Ireland, as the bankers cannot be admitted as such; neither can the Dublin society for the encouragement of manufactures and commerce, which was incorporated in 1750. The linen hall, however, that is erected at Dublin, is under as just and nice regulations as any commercial house in Europe.

CONSTITUTION AND GOVERNMENT.] Ireland is still a distinct, though a dependent subordinate kingdom. It was only entitled the dominion or lordship of Ireland, and the king's stile was no other than Dominus Hiberniæ, Lord of Ireland, till the 33d year of king Henry VIII. when he assumed the title of king, which is recognized by act of parliament in the same reign. But, as England and Scotland are now one and the same kingdom, and yet differ in their municipal laws; so England and Ireland are, on the other hand, distinct kingdoms, and yet in general agree in their laws. For after the conquest of Ireland by king Henry II. the laws of England were received and sworn to by the Irish nation, assembled at the council of Lismore. And as Ireland, thus conquered, planted, and governed, still continues in a state of dependence, it must necessarily conform to, and be obliged by such laws as the superior state thinks proper to prescribe.

But this state of dependence being almost forgotten, and ready to be disputed by the Irish nation, it became necessary, some years ago, to declare how that matter really stood: and, therefore, by statute 6th of George 1. it is declared, that the kingdom of Ireland ought to be subordinate to, and dependent upon, the imperial crown of Great Britain, as being inseparably united thereto; and that the king's majesty, with the consent of the lords and commons of Great Britain, in parliament, hath power to make laws to bind the people of Ireland.

The constitution of the Irish government, as it stands at present, with regard to distributive justice, is nearly the same with that of England. A chief governor, who generally goes by the name of lord lieutenant, is sent over from England by the king, whom he represents, but his power is in some measure restrained, and in others enlarged, according to the king's pleasure, or the exigency of the times. On his entering upon this honourable office, his letters patent are publickly read in the council-chamber, and having taken the usual oaths before the lord chancellor, the sword, which is to be carried before him,

him, is delivered into his hands, and he is seated in the chair of state, attended by the lord chancellor, the members of the privy-council, the peers and nobles, the king at arms, a sergeant at mace, and other officers of state; and he never appears publickly without being attended by a body of horseguards. Hence, with respect to his authority, his train and splendor, there is no viceroy in christendom that comes nearer to the grandeur and majesty of a king. He has a council composed of the great officers of the crown; namely, the chancellor, treasurer, and such of the archbishops, earls, bishops, barons, judges, and gentlemen, as his majesty is pleased to appoint. The parliament here, as well as in England, is the supreme court, which is convened by the king's writ; and generally sits once every second year. It consists, as in England, of a house of lords and commons. Of the former, many are English or British peers or commons of Great Britain; a few are papists, who cannot sit without being properly qualified; and the number of commons amount to about three hundred. Since the accession of his present majesty, Irish parliaments have been rendered octennial. The laws are made by the house of lords and commons, after which they are sent to England for the royal approbation; when, if approved of by his majesty and council, they pass the great seal of England, and are returned.

For the regular distribution of justice, there are also in Ireland four terms held annually for the decision of causes; and four courts of justice, the chancery, king's-bench, common-pleas, and exchequer. The high-sheriffs of the several counties were formerly chosen by the people, but are now nominated by the lord lieutenant. From this general view it appears that the civil and ecclesiastical institutions are almost the same in Ireland as in England.

REVENUES.] In Ireland the public revenue arises from hereditary and temporary duties, of which the king is the trustee, for applying it to particular purposes; but there is besides this a private revenue arising from the ancient demesne lands, from forfeitures for treason and felony, prisage of wines, light-house duties, and a small part of the casual revenue, not granted by parliament; and in this the crown has the same unlimited property that a subject has in his own freehold. The extent of that revenue is perhaps a secret to the public.

The revenue of Ireland is supposed at present to exceed half a million sterling, of which the Irish complain greatly that about 70,000 l. is granted in pensions, and a great part to absentees. Very large sums are also granted by their own parliament for more valuable purposes, the improvement of their country and civilizing the people; such as the inland navigation, bridges, highways,

highways, churches, premiums, proteſtant ſchools, and other particulars, which do honour to the wiſdom and patriotiſm of that parliament.

And it is alſo a happy circumſtance for the Iriſh, that the revenues neceſſary for the ſupport of their government, and other purpoſes, are raiſed with ſo much eaſe as to be ſcarcely felt by the people. Their lands are not ſaddled with heavy taxes, nor their trade with foreign nations cramped by innumerable duties. Hence proceed the amazing low prices of almoſt every article of general conſumption. Good claret wine is ſold in the metropolis of the kingdom at two ſhillings a bottle, and other liquors proportionably cheap. · Butcher's meat, though now on the riſe, is ſold at two pence per pound; turkies at twenty pence, and other poultry at a trifling expence. Soap and candles ſo low as to tempt coaſting veſſels to ſmuggle them into Britain. In the interior parts, butchers meat is ſold at one penny farthing per pound; large fowls at three pence each. And that the taxation upon inland trade ſits eaſy, appears from the cheapneſs of almoſt every article fabricated there. Newſpapers of a large ſize are ſold at a halfpenny, and advertiſements of a moderate length are inſerted for ſixpence. Such was the happy ſituation of Great Britain before the commencement of that load of debt, contracted in conſequence of our foreign connections, and fruitleſs campaigns in Germany and Flanders.

COINS.] The coins of Ireland are at preſent of the ſame denominations and the like fabric with thoſe of England, only an Engliſh ſhilling paſſes in Ireland for thirteen pence. What the antient coins of the Iriſh were, is at preſent a matter of mere curioſity and great uncertainty.

MILITARY STRENGTH.] Ireland maintains and pays an army of 16,000 men, who have been often of ſingular ſervice to England. The reader, from the ſketch I have already given of the population of Ireland, may eaſily form an eſtimate of the number of fighting men in the kingdom. Thoſe parts of Ireland that are moſt uncultivated, contain numbers of inhabitants that have very little ſenſe either of divine or human laws, and regular forces are abſolutely neceſſary for keeping them in order, witneſs the late inſurrections of the Whiteboys, and other banditti, who were inſtigated by their prieſts. It does not, however, appear that the bulk of the Iriſh catholics are fond of a revolution in government, as few or none of them joined Thurot in his deſcent upon Carrickfergus, or took any part with the pretender in the laſt rebellion.

HISTORY.] The Iriſh monks have formed a more regular plan of antient hiſtory, for their own country, than is to be

met

met with in other countries, and with such plausibility, that it has been adopted by men of considerable learning. They have carried up a succession of great, wise, and learned kings, almost to the time of the flood, and they have made Ireland flourish in all the arts and sciences, especially those of government, long before they were known in Egypt, or Greece. Writers, however, after the Augustan age, have mentioned the Irish, as being no better than savages, and the most credible of the modern historians, speak of them as being, in the beginning of the fifteenth century, a nation of Barbarians, though it may be admitted that before this period, some of their monks and clergy, who had travelled into other parts of Europe, were holy and learned men.

That the northern parts of Ireland were peopled from the west of Scotland, as being a far more inviting soil, is more than probable, and it is likely that emigrations from other parts of Europe, might mingle with the aboriginal Irish; but history gives us no sure lights, as to those matters. Sir James Ware, the best of the Irish antiquaries, and a man of great learning and candour, speaks with high contempt of the Irish, before they were converted to Christianity, by St. Patric, a Scotchman, who died in 493. After this they were occasionally invaded by the Saxon kings of England, but in the year 795 and 798 the Danes and Normans, or as they were called, the Easterlings, invaded the coasts of Ireland, and were the first who erected stone edifices in that kingdom. The habitations of the Irish, till that time, were of hurdles covered with straw and rushes, and a very few of solid timber. The natives, however, defended themselves bravely against the Easterlings, who built Dublin, Waterford, Limerick, Wexford and Cork, but they resided chiefly at Dublin, or in its neighbourhood, which, by the old Irish, was called Fingal, or the Land of Strangers. The natives, about the year 962, seem to have called to their assistance the Anglo-Saxon king Edgar, who had then a considerable maritime power, and this might have given occasion for his clergy to call him King of great part of Ireland. It is certain, that Dublin was about that time a flourishing city, and that the native Irish gave the Easterlings several defeats, though supported by their countrymen from the continent, the Isle of Man, and the Hebrides.

Though the use of letters had been by this time introduced into Ireland, yet its history is still very confused. We know, however, that it was divided amongst several petty princes, and that Henry II. of England, provoked at their piracies, and their assisting his enemies, by the instigation of the Pope, had resolved to subdue them. A fair pretext offered about the year 1168. Dermot Mac Murrough, king of Leinster, and

an

an oppreſſive tyrant, quarrelled with all his neighbours, and carried off the wife of a petty prince, O Roirk. A confederacy being formed againſt him, under Roderic O'Connor, (who it ſeems was the paramount king of Ireland) he was driven from his country, and took refuge at the court of Henry II. who promiſed to reſtore him upon taking an oath of fealty to the crown of England for himſelf, and all the petty kings depending on him, who were very numerous. Henry, who was then in France, recommended Mac Dermot's cauſe to the Engliſh barons, and particularly to Strongbow, earl of Pembroke, Robert Fitz Stephen, and Maurice Fitz Gerald. Thoſe noblemen undertook the expedition upon much the ſame principles as the Norman and Breton lords did the conqueſt of England under William I. and Strongbow was to marry Mac Dermot's daughter Eva. In 1169, the adventurers reduced the towns of Wexford and Waterford; and the next year Strongbow arriving with a ſtrong reinforcement, his marriage was celebrated.

The deſcendants of the Danes continued ſtill poſſeſſed of Dublin, which, after ſome ineffectual oppoſition made by king O'Connor, was taken and plundered by the Engliſh ſoldiers, but Mac Turkil the Daniſh king eſcaped to his ſhipping. Upon the death of Dermot, Henry II. became jealous of earl Strongbow, ſeized upon his eſtates in England and Wales, and recalled his ſubjects from Ireland. The Iriſh, about the ſame time, to the amount of about 60,000, beſieged Dublin, under king O'Connor; but though all Strongbow's Iriſh friends and allies had now left him, and the city was reduced to great extremity, he forced the Iriſh to raiſe the ſiege with great loſs, and going over to England he appeaſed Henry by ſwearing fealty to him and his heirs, and reſigning into his hand all the Iriſh cities and forts he held. During Strongbow's abſence, Mac Turkil returning with a great fleet, attempted to retake the city of Dublin, but was killed at the ſiege; and in him ended the race of the Eaſterling princes in Ireland.

In 1172, Henry II. attended by 400 knights, 4000 veteran ſoldiers, and the flower of his Engliſh nobility, landed near Waterford; and not only all the petty princes of Ireland, excepting the king of Ulſter, but the great king Roderic O'Connor, ſubmitted to Henry, who pretended that O'Connor's ſubmiſſion included that of Ulſter, and that conſequently he was the paramount ſovereign of Ireland. Be that as it will, he affected to keep a magnificent court, and held a parliament at Dublin, where he parcelled out the eſtates of Ireland, as William the Conqueror had done in England, to his Engliſh nobility. He then ſettled a civil adminiſtration at Dublin,

Dublin, as near as possible to that of England, to which he returned in 1173, having first settled an English colony from Bristol in Dublin, with all the liberties and free customs, says their charters, which the citizens of Bristol enjoyed. From that time Dublin began to flourish. Thus the conquest of Ireland was effected by the English almost with as much ease as that of Mexico was by the Spaniards, and for much the same reasons, the rude, and unarmed state of the natives, and the differences that prevailed among their princes or leaders.

Henry gave the title of Lord of Ireland to his son John, who, in 1185, went over in person to Ireland; but John and his giddy Norman courtiers made a very ill use of their power, and rendered themselves hateful to the Irish, who were otherwise very well disposed towards the English. Richard I. was too much taken up with the crusades to pay much regard to the affairs of Ireland, but king John, after his accession, made amends for his former behaviour towards the Irish. He enlarged his father's plan, of introducing into Ireland English laws and officers, and he erected that part of the provinces of Leinster and Munster which was within the English pale, into twelve counties. I find, however, that the descendants of the antient princes in other places paid him no more than a nominal subjection. They governed by their old Brehon laws, and exercised all acts of sovereignty within their own states; and indeed this was pretty much the case so late as the reign of James I. The unsettled reign of Henry III. his wars, and captivity, gave the Irish a very mean opinion of the English government during his reign; but they seem to have continued quiet under his son Edward I. Gaveston, the famous favourite of Edward II. acquired great credit while he acted as lieutenant of Ireland, but the successes of the Scotch king, Robert Bruce, had almost proved fatal to the English interest in Ireland, and suggested to the Irish the idea of transferring their allegiance from the kings of England to Edward Bruce, king Robert's brother. That prince accordingly invaded Ireland, where he gave repeated defeats to the English governors and armies, and being supported by his brother in person, he was actually crowned king at Dundalk, and narrowly missed being master of Dublin. The younger Bruce seems to have been violent in the exercise of his sovereignty, and he was at last defeated and killed by Bermingham the English general. After this Edward II. ruled Ireland with great moderation, and passed several excellent acts with regard to that country.

But during the minority of Edward III. the commotions were again renewed in Ireland, and not suppressed without great loss and disgrace on the side of the English. In 1333 a rebellion broke out, in which the English inhabitants had no
incon-

inconsiderable share. A succession of vigorous, brave governors, however, at last quieted the insurgents; and about the year 1361, prince Lionel, son to Edward III. having married the heiress of Ulster, was sent over to govern Ireland, and, if possible, to reduce its inhabitants to an entire conformity with the laws of England. In this he made a great progress, but did not entirely accomplish it. It appears, at this time, that the Irish were in a very flourishing condition, and that one of the greatest grievances they complained of was, that the English sent over men of mean birth to govern them. In 1394, Richard II. finding that the execution of his despotic schemes in England must be abortive without farther support, passed over to Ireland with an army of 34,000 men well armed and appointed. As he made no use of force, the Irish looked upon his presence to be a high compliment to their nation, and admired the magnificence of his court. Richard, on the other hand, courted them by all the arts he could employ, and bestowed the honour of knighthood on their chiefs. In short, he behaved so as to entirely win their affections. In 1399, Richard being then despotic in England, undertook a fresh expedition into Ireland to revenge the death of his lord lieutenant, the earl of March, who had been killed by the wild Irish. His army again struck the natives with consternation, and they threw themselves upon his mercy. It was during this expedition that the duke of Lancaster landed in England, and Richard, upon his return, finding himself deserted, and that he could not depend upon the Irish, surrendered his crown to his rival.

The Irish, after Richard's death, still retained a warm affection for the house of York, and upon the revival of that family's claim to the crown, embraced its cause. Even the accession of Henry VII. to the crown of England did not reconcile them to his title, as duke of Lancaster, and the Irish readily joined Lambert Simnel, who pretended to be the eldest son of Edward IV. but for this they paid dear, being defeated in their attempt to invade England. This made them somewhat cautious at first of joining Perkin Warbeck, notwithstanding his plausible pretences to be the duke of York, second son of Edward IV. He was, however, at last recognized as king by the Irish, and in the preceding pages the reader may learn the event of his history. Henry behaved with moderation towards his favourers, and was contented with requiring the Irish nobility to take a fresh oath of allegiance to his government. This lenity had the desired effect, during the administration of the two earls of Kildare, the earl of Surry, and the earl of Ormond. Henry VIII. governed Ireland by supporting its chiefs against each other, but they were tampered

tampered with by the emperor Charles V. upon which Henry made his natural son, the duke of Richmond, his lord lieutenant. This did not prevent the Irish from breaking out into rebellion in the year 1540, under Fitz Gerald, who had been lord deputy, and who was won over by the emperor, but was at last hanged at Tyburn. After this, the house of Austria found their account, in their quarrels with England, to form a strong party among the Irish.

About the year 1542 James V. king of Scotland, formed some pretensions on the crown of Ireland, and was favoured by a strong party among the Irish themselves. It is hard to say, had he lived, what the consequence of his claim might have been. Henry understood that the Irish had a mean opinion of his dignity, as the kings of England had hitherto assumed no higher title than that of lords of Ireland. He therefore took that of king of Ireland, which had a great effect with the native Irish, who thought that allegiance was not due to a lord; and, to speak the truth, it was somewhat surprizing that this expedient was not thought of before. It produced a more perfect submission of the native Irish to Henry's government than ever had been known, and even O Neil, who pretended to be successor to the last paramount king of Ireland, swore allegiance to Henry, who created him earl of Tyrone.

The Pope, however, and the princes of the house of Austria, by remitting money, and sometimes sending over troops to the Irish, still kept up their interest in that kingdom, and drew from them vast numbers of men to their armies, where they proved as good soldiers as any in Europe. This created inexpressible difficulties to the English government, even in the reign of Edward VI. but it is remarkable that the reformation took place in the English part of Ireland with little or no opposition. The Irish seem to have been very quiet during the reign of queen Mary, but they proved thorns in the side of queen Elizabeth. The perpetual disputes she had with the Roman Catholics, both at home and abroad, gave her great uneasiness, and the Pope, and the house of Austria always found new resources against her in Ireland. The Spaniards possessed themselves of Kinsale; and the rebellions of Tyrone, who baffled and outwitted her favourite general the earl of Essex, are well known in the English history.

The lord-deputy Mountjoy, who succeeded Essex, was the first Englishman who gave a mortal blow to the practices of the Spaniards in Ireland, by defeating them and the Irish before Kinsale, and bringing Tyrone prisoner to England; where he was pardoned by queen Elizabeth in 1602. This lenity, shewn to such an offender, is a proof of the dreadful apprehenfions Elizabeth had from the popifh intereft in Ireland. James I. confirmed the poffeffions of the Irifh; but fuch was the influence of the pope and the Spaniards, that the earls of Tyrone and Tyrconnel, and their party, planned a new rebellion, and attempted to feize the caftle of Dublin; but their plot being difcovered, their chiefs fled beyond feas. They were not idle abroad; for in 1608, they inftigated Sir Calim O'Dogharty to a frefh rebellion, by promifing him fpeedy fupplies of men and money from Spain. Sir Calim was killed in the difpute, and his adherents were taken and executed. The attainders of the Irifh rebels which paffed in the reigns of James and Elizabeth, vefted in the crown 511,465 acres, in the feveral counties of Donnegal, Tyrone, Colerain, Fermanagh, Cavan, and Armagh; and enabled the king to make that proteftant plantation in the north of Ireland, which now, from the moft rebellious province of the kingdom, is the moft quiet and reformed.

Thofe prodigious attainders, however juft and neceffary they might be, operated fatally for the Englifh in the reign of Charles I. The Irifh Roman-catholics in general, were influenced by their priefts to hope not only to repoffefs the lands of their forefathers, but to reftore the popifh religion in Ireland. They therefore entered into a deep and deteftable confpiracy for maffacring all the Englifh proteftants in that kingdom. In this they were encouraged by the unhappy diffentions that broke out between the king and his parliaments in England and Scotland. Their bloody plan being difcovered by the Englifh government at Dublin, prevented that city from falling into their hands. They however partly executed, in 1641, their horrid fcheme of maffacre: but authors have not agreed as to the numbers who were murdered; perhaps they have been exaggerated by warm proteftant writers, fome of whom have mounted the number of the fufferers to 40,000; other accounts fpeak of 10,000 or 12,000, and fome have even diminifhed that number. What followed in confequence of this rebellion, and the reduction of Ireland by Cromwell, who retaliated the cruelties of the Irifh papifts upon themfelves, belongs to the hiftory of England. It is certain that they fmarted fo feverely, that they were quiet during the reign of Charles II. His popifh fucceffor and brother, even after the Revolution took place, found an afylum in Ireland; and was encouraged to hope, that by the affiftance of the natives there, he might remount his throne: but he was deceived, and his own pufillanimity co-operated with his difappointment. He was driven out of Ireland by his fon-in-law, after the battle of the Boyne, the only victory that William ever gained in perfon. James, it is true, fought at the head of an undifciplined

plined rabble, but his French auxiliaries were far from behaving as heroes. It must be acknowledged, however, that he left both the field and the kingdom too soon for a brave man. The forfeitures that fell to the crown on account of the Irish rebellions and the Revolution, are almost incredible; and had the acts of parliament which gave them away been strictly enforced, Ireland must have been peopled with British inhabitants. But many political reasons occurred for not driving the Irish to despair. The friends of the Revolution and the protestant religion were sufficiently gratified out of the forfeited estates. Too many of the Roman-catholics might have been forced abroad; and it was proper that a due balance should be preserved between the Roman-catholic and the protestant interest.

It was therefore thought prudent to relax the reins of government, and not to put the forfeitures too rigorously into execution. The experience of half a century has confirmed the wisdom of the above considerations. The lenity of the measures pursued in regard to the Irish Roman-catholics, and the great pains taken for the instruction of their children, with the progress which knowledge and the arts have made in that country, have diminished the popish interest so much, that the Irish protestants have of late disputed many points of their dependency. The spirit of industry has enabled the Irish to know their own strength and importance, to which some accidental circumstances have concurred. All her ports are now opened for the exportation of wool and woollen yarn to any part of Great-Britain. And of late years acts of parliament have been made occasionally for permitting the importation of salt beef, pork, butter, cattle and tallow, from Ireland to Great-Britain.

How far the late act for rendering parliaments in Ireland octennial * may operate to its benefit, is as yet impossible to be determined: in all appearance, it will create a very material alteration in the civil policy of that kingdom, and will prove to be by no means for the benefit of that independency upon England which is so much the idol of the Irish patriots. It is likewise to be apprehended, that the octennial returns of general elections, may have a fatal effect upon the morals of the labouring people, as is too often seen in England, where industry flourishes most in those places (witness Manchester, Birmingham, and Sheffield) which send no member to the British parliament.

---

* Before this act took place, members, once chosen, sat in the house of commons during life; so that there were no new parliaments, except upon the accession of the prince to the throne.

I might here conclude the geography and history of Great-Britain and Ireland; were it not that several smaller islands are under the allegiance of the crown of England, and having local privileges and distinctions, could not be comprehended under a more general head. In treating of them therefore I shall deviate from my common method, but observe brevity as much as the subject will permit.

ISLE OF MAN.

THIS is not the Mona mentioned by Tacitus. Some think that it takes its name from the Saxon word *Mang* (or among) because lying in St. George's Channel, it is at an equal distance from the kingdoms of England, Scotland, and Ireland; but Mona seems to have been a generical name with the ancients for any detached island. Its length from north to south is about thirty miles, its breadth from eight to fifteen; and the latitude of the middle of the island is fifty-four degrees, sixteen minutes, north. It is said, that on a clear day, the three Britannic kingdoms may be seen from this island. The air here is wholesome, and the climate, only making allowance for the situation, pretty much the same as that in the north of England, from which it does not differ much in other respects. The hilly parts are barren, and the champain fruitful in wheat, barley, oats, rye, flax, hemp, roots, and pulse. The ridge of mountains which as it were divides the island, both protects and fertilizes the vallies, where there is good pasturage. The better sort of inhabitants have good sizeable horses, and a small kind, which is swift and hardy; nor are they troubled with any noxious animals. The coasts abound with sea-fowl; and the puffins, which breed in rabbit-holes, are almost a lump of fat, and esteemed very delicious. It is said that this island abounds with iron, lead, and copper mines, though unwrought, as are the quarries of marble, slate, and stone.

The Isle of Man contains seventeen parishes and four towns on the sea coasts. Castle-town is the metropolis of the island, and the seat of its government; Peele, which, of late years, begins to flourish; Douglas, which has the best market and best trade in the island, as well as the richest and most populous town, on account of its excellent harbour, and its fine mole, extending into the sea; Ramsey has likewise a considerable commerce, on account of its spacious bay, in which ships may ride safe from all winds excepting the north-east. The reader, by throwing his eyes on the map, may see how conveniently this island is situated for being the storehouse of smugglers, which it was till within these few years, to the inexpressible prejudice of his majesty's revenue; and this necessarily leads me to touch upon the history of the island.

During the time of the Scandinavian rovers on the seas which I have before mentioned, this island was their rendezvous, and their chief force was here collected, from whence they annoyed the Hebrides, Great-Britain and Ireland. The kings of Man are often mentioned in history; and though we have no regular account of their succession, and know but a few of their names, yet they undoubtedly were for some ages masters of those seas. About the year 1263, Alexander II. king of Scotland, a spirited prince, having defeated the Danes, laid claim to the superiority of Man, and obliged Owen, or John, its king, to acknowledge him as lord paramount. It seems to have continued, either tributary or in propeity of the kings of Scotland, till it was reduced by Edward I. and the kings of England, from that time, exercised the superiority over the island; though we find it still possessed by the posterity of its Danish princes, in the reign of Edward III. who dispossessed the last queen of the island, and bestowed it on his favourite, Montague, earl of Salisbury. His family being forfeited, Henry IV. bestowed Man, and the patronage of the bishopric, first upon the Northumberland family, and that being forfeited, upon Sir John Stanley, whose posterity, the earls of Derby, enjoyed it, till, by failure of heirs male, it devolved upon the duke of Athol, who married the sister of the last lord Derby. Reasons of state rendered it necessary for the crown of Great-Britain to purchase the customs and the island from the Athol family, and the bargain was completed by 70,000 l. being paid to the duke in 1765. The duke, however, retains his territorial property in the island, though the form of its government is altered, and the king has now the same rights, powers, and prerogatives, as the dukes formerly enjoyed. The inhabitants, also, retain many of their antient constitutions and customs.

The established religion in Man is that of the church of England. The king has now the nomination of the bishop, who is called bishop of Sodor and Man; and he enjoys all the spiritual rights and pre-eminences of other bishops, but does not sit in the British house of peers, his see never having been erected into an English barony. The ecclesiastical government is well kept up in this island, and the livings are comfortable. The language, which is called the Manks, and is spoken by the common people, is radically Erse, or Irish, but with a mixture of other languages. The New Testament and Common Prayer Book have been translated into the Manks language. The natives, who are said to amount to above 20,000, are inoffensive, charitable, and hospitable. The better sort
live

live in stone houses, and the poorer in thatched; and their ordinary bread is made of oatmeal. Their products for exportation consist of wool, hides, and tallow; which they exchange with foreign shipping for commodities they may have occasion for from other parts. Before the south promontory of Man, is a little island called the Calf of Man: it is about three miles in circuit, and separated from Man by a channel about two furlongs broad.

This island affords some curiosities which may amuse an antiquary. They consist chiefly of Runic sepulchral inscriptions and monuments of antient brass daggers, and other weapons of that metal, and partly of pure gold, which are sometimes dug up, and seem to indicate the splendor of its antient possessors.

I forbear to mention in this place the isles of ANGLESEY and WIGHT, the first being annexed to Wales, and the other to Hampshire. Also the SCILLY ISLES, or rather a cluster of dangerous rocks, to the number of 140, lying about 30 miles from the Land's End in Cornwall, of which county they are reckoned a part.

In the English channel are four islands subject to England; these are Jersey, Guernsey, Alderney, and Sark; which, though they lie much nearer to the coast of Normandy than to that of England, are within the diocese of Winchester. They lie in a cluster in Mount St. Michael's bay, between Cape la Hogue in Normandy, and Cape Frebelle in Brittany. The computed distance between Jersey and Sark is four leagues; between that and Guernsey, seven leagues; and between the same and Alderney, nine leagues.

JERSEY was known to the Romans; and lies farthest within the bay, in forty-nine degrees seven minutes north lat. and in the second degree twenty-six minutes west longitude, eighteen miles west of Normandy. The north side is inaccessible through lofty cliffs, the south is almost level with the water; the higher land in its midland part is well planted, and abounds with orchards, from which is made an incredible quantity of excellent cyder. The vallies are fruitful and well cultivated, and contain plenty of cattle and sheep. The inhabitants neglect tillage too much, being intent upon the culture of cyder, the improvement of commerce, and particularly the manufacture of stockings. The honey in Jersey is remarkably fine; and the island is well supplied with fish and wild-fowl almost of every kind, some of both being peculiar to the island, and very delicious.

The island is not above twelve miles in length, but the air is so salubrious, that in Camden's time, it was said there was

here

here no bufinefs for a phyfician. The inhabitants in number are about 20,000, and are divided into twelve parifhes. The capital town is St. Helier, which contains above 400 houfes, and makes a handfome appearance. The property of this ifland belonged formerly to the Carterets, a Norman family, who have been always attached to the royal intereft, and gave protection to Charles II. both when king and prince of Wales, at a time when no part of the Britifh dominions durft recognize him. The language of the inhabitants is French, with which moft of them intermingle Englifh words. Knit ftockings and caps form their ftaple commodity, but they carry on a confiderable trade in fifh with Newfoundland, and difpofe of their cargoes in the Mediterranean. The governor is appointed by the crown of England, but the civil adminiftration refts with a bailiff, affifted by twelve jurats. As this ifland is the principal remain of the duchy of Normandy depending on the kings of England, it preferves the old feudal forms, and particularly the affembly of ftates, which is as it were a miniature of the Britifh parliament, as fettled in the time of Edward I.

GUERNSEY is thirteen miles and a half from fouth-weft to north-eaft, and twelve and a half, where broadeft, eaft and weft ; but has only ten parifhes, to which there are but eight minifters, four of the parifhes being united, and Alderney and Sark, which are appendages of Guernfey, having one a-piece. Though this is a much finer ifland than that of Jerfey, yet it is far lefs valuable, becaufe it is not fo well cultivated, nor is it fo populous. It abounds in cyder ; and the inhabitants fpeak French : but want of firing is the greateft inconveniency that both iflands labour under. The only harbour here is at St. Peter le Port, which is guarded by two forts, one called the Old-Caftle, the other Caftle-Cornet. Guernfey is likewife part of the antient Norman patrimony.

ALDERNEY is about eight miles in compafs, and is by much the neareft of all thefe iflands to Normandy, from which it is feparated by a narrow ftrait, called the Race of Alderney, which is a dangerous paffage in ftormy weather, when the two currents meet, otherwife it is fafe, and has depth of water for the largeft fhips. This ifland is healthy, and the foil is remarkable for a fine breed of cows.

SARK is a fmall ifland depending upon Guernfey; the inhabitants are long-lived, and enjoy from nature all the conveniencies of life. The inhabitants of the three laft mentioned iflands are thought to be about 20,000. The religion of all the four iflands is that of the church of England, though formerly the inhabitants were Calvinifts.

www.ingramcontent.com/pod-product-compliance
Lightning Source LLC
Chambersburg PA
CBHW020834020526
44114CB00040B/713